The Mainstream of

CIVILIZATION
TO 1715

SIXTH EDITION

The Mainstream of
CIVILIZATION
TO 1715

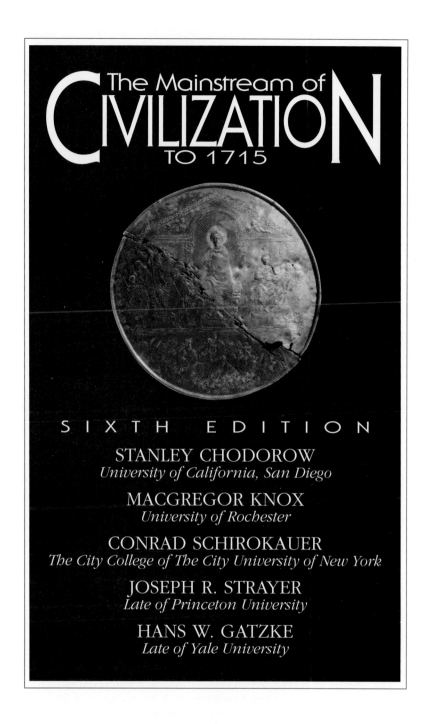

SIXTH EDITION

STANLEY CHODOROW
University of California, San Diego

MACGREGOR KNOX
University of Rochester

CONRAD SCHIROKAUER
The City College of The City University of New York

JOSEPH R. STRAYER
Late of Princeton University

HANS W. GATZKE
Late of Yale University

THE
HARCOURT
PRESS

Harcourt Brace College Publishers

Fort Worth Philadelphia San Diego New York Orlando Austin San Antonio
Toronto Montreal London Sydney Tokyo

Publisher	Ted Buchholz
Acquisitions Editor	Drake Bush
Senior Project Editor	Kay Kaylor
Associate Project Editor	Sandy Walton
Senior Production Manager	Kathleen Ferguson
Art Director	Burl Sloan
Picture Editor	Lili Weiner

Cover: Scala / Art Resource, New York. Background: © Masao Mukai / Photonica

Address for Editorial Correspondence: Harcourt Brace College Publishers, 301 Commerce Street, Suite 3700, Fort Worth, TX 76102

Address for Orders: Harcourt Brace & Company, 6277 Sea Harbor Drive, Orlando, FL 32887; 1-800-782-4479 or 1-800-433-0001 (in Florida)

ISBN: 0-15-501201-0
Library of Congress Catalog Card Number: 93-78966
Printed in the United States of America
3 4 5 6 7 8 9 0 1 2   048   9 8 7 6 5 4 3 2 1

PREFACE

Writing a history of civilization is an almost foolhardy enterprise. But it is easier to do if you have done it before, as the authors of the first four editions of this history, Joseph R. Strayer and Hans W. Gatzke, noted dryly in their preface to the Fourth Edition. We, their successors, had not done it before the mid-1980s. But we did have the robust framework the original authors left to us. In this Sixth Edition of *The Mainstream of Civilization,* we have built on that framework and on the major recasting of the work carried out in the Fifth Edition.

That edition integrated into the text new themes—such as social history and the history of women—that had figured less in earlier editions. Especially in the modern period, it emphasized the great driving forces—technology, demography, economics, and nationalism—that have made the twentieth century immensely different from any earlier age. It sought to explain the origins of key events, such as the Industrial Revolution, the Great Depression, and the World Wars. And unlike its predecessors, it used charts and graphs to present chronological and other quantitative data vividly, new picture captions to integrate the illustrations into the text, new boxed quotations from primary

sources (some of them translated for the purpose), and frequent primary-source quotations in the text to convey the flavor of the past.

Yet the Fifth Edition also drew on the greatest strength of earlier editions—their global perspective. Like its predecessors, it sought to follow the "mainstream of civilization" by gradually shifting its geographic focus from the Mediterranean to Europe, and ultimately to the wider world. It offered detailed treatment of the major civilizations east and south of Europe, from Byzantium and Islam to India, China, and Japan. And as that "mainstream" flowed toward the present, the text provided increasingly detailed analysis and narrative in order to make that present understandable. That narrative attempted to convey to readers the texture and flavor of past civilizations and the astonishing variety of human possibilities and accomplishments. It sought to emphasize the interrelationships of all spheres of life, from politics and warfare to economics, art, scholarship, and religion. It sought to suggest at least some of the differing ways in which contemporaries and historians have understood the past. But above all, the text attempted to explain that past, to explain historical change and the recurring patterns visible in the past. Why and how have states, institutions, and ideas risen, flourished, and crumbled into dust? Why did events happen as they did and not otherwise?

This new Sixth Edition, we are confident, has kept the strengths of its predecessors. But it also contains much that is new both in presentation and substance. We have reviewed and rewritten the entire text sentence by sentence for clarity and readability; the result is slightly shorter than the Fifth Edition. We have reorganized Chapters 9, 10, and 11 to group related topics more effectively and to strengthen the narrative line. We have sometimes written new chapter introductions to make clearer how the material presented in topical chapters, such as 24, 25, and 27, fits into our overall chronological and thematic framework. We have rewritten or added subheadings where necessary to group the text into more easily understood segments. And we have revised and updated the bibliographical suggestions at the end of each chapter.

The Sixth Edition also incorporates recent research and new material on topics that range from humanity's origins to the end of the Cold War. We have added material on Hebrew culture to provide a better understanding of the background of European religion. We have reorganized and strengthened the sections on Hellenistic civilization to better explain the transition from Greece to Rome. We have radically rewritten and shortened our chapter on the post-1945 non-Western world to simplify the presentation and bring it up to 1992. Finally, we have rewritten the final chapter almost completely to offer both narrative and interpretation of recent momentous events. We are confident that Chapters 34–36 of the new *The Mainstream of Civilization* offer the best short analysis of the world since the Second World War available in any similar textbook.

The Sixth Edition also comes with a totally recast package of ancillary materials: a testbook (also available in software form) and film guide with learning objectives, 50 map transparencies, and 25 color transparencies of major works of art and architecture. Above all, the Sixth Edition study guide is completely new; it contains new chapter summaries, chapter objectives, time-lines, maps and map questions, identifications, and numerous probing essay questions also designed to serve as topics for class discussion.

This edition, like its predecessors, inevitably draws heavily upon the publications, contributions, and advice of other scholars. We have sought wherever possible to hint at our major debts in the Suggestions for Further Reading that follow each chapter. We owe special thanks to Conrad Schirokauer, City College of the City University of New York, for his contribution of Chapters 6 and 15. We thank Carl Abrams, Bob Jones University; Ron Brown, Charles County Community College; Ann Sumner Holmes, Louisiana State University; Gilberto Ramirez, Auburn University; Randall Rogers, Louisiana State University; Alan Schaffer, Clemson University; and Marian E. Strobel, Furman University, for their perceptive comments and criticisms. And we are profoundly grateful to Everett M. Sims, who edited the final manuscript with tact, decisiveness, and a brilliant choice of synonyms. All have helped to make this book better, but they bear no responsibility for sins of omission or commission and errors of fact or judgment, which belong to the authors alone.

Finally, we remain deeply indebted to the late Hans W. Gatzke. Despite the debilitating effects of a tragic illness, he oversaw with tact and consideration the transition from one "team" of authors to the next. He set ambitious goals for the new team: a major revision and recasting of the book. He shaped the plan for that revision and suggested a number of the new themes that we have attempted to emphasize. To his memory, and to that of the late Joseph R. Strayer, we thankfully dedicate this Sixth Edition.

Stanley Chodorow   MacGregor Knox

A Note on the Paperbound Editions

This volume is one of a number of variant paintings of the Sixth Edition of *The Mainstream of Civilization*. It is not a revised or condensed text. Many users of the Fourth Edition found the various paperbound versions of that edition useful because the variant printings made it possible for them to fit the text into their own patterns of teaching and scheduling. In the Sixth Edition, the publishers have continued the practice of preparing separate paperbound volumes. Users may choose the volume that best corresponds to the chronological period covered by their courses. The variants are:

1. A two-volume edition

The first volume, To 1715 (Chapters 1 through 21), starts with the beginnings of Western civilization in the ancient Middle East and continues to the end of the Middle Ages. The second volume, Since 1660 (Chapters 20 through 36), begins with the seventeenth century and carries the account forward to the present day.

2. A two-volume edition

The first volume, To 1500 (Chapters 1 through 15), starts with the beginnings of Western civilization in the ancient Middle East and continues to the end of the Middle Ages. The second volume, Since 1500 (Chapters 16 through 36), after a Prologue that summarizes events to the year 1500, begins with the Renaissance and carries the account forward to the present day.

In all the variant printings, the pagination, index (except for *To 1500,* which has its own index), illustrations, maps, and other related materials from the one-volume version are retained. The difference between the one-volume and the other versions of this book is a difference only in form.

CONTENTS

ix

LIST OF MAPS

Introduction

History as Foresight and Memory

History is the story of the human past. It is also the only available introduction to the human future. That was how the first critically thinking historian, Thucydides the Athenian, justified his history of the great war between the rival Greek city-states of Athens and Sparta in the fifth century B.C. Thucydides addressed his work to those "who want to understand clearly the events which happened in the past and which (human nature being what it is) will, at some time or other and in much the same ways, be repeated in the future." He added that his book was "not a piece of writing designed to meet the taste of an immediate public, but was done to last for ever."

No modern historian would dare make that claim. Forever is a length of time beyond human grasp, and the tastes of the immediate public now have a weight that Thucydides the aristocrat would have roundly condemned. But Thucydides' book, the most penetrating historical work of the ancient world, has nevertheless survived for 2400 years, and has probably enjoyed more readers in the last three centuries than in its entire previous existence. Thucydides' claim that human affairs follow patterns meaningful to the trained eye has remained the fundamental argument for studying history.

The future is by definition unknowable and unpredictable; events are unique, and never repeat themselves precisely. But they often follow patterns. Individuals are unique, and are free to make their own history. That freedom gives the unfolding of history its element of suspense. But individuals also band together to create societies. Those societies have structures—languages, religions, intellectual traditions, artistic styles, and political, social, economic, and military institutions—that limit how individuals can make history, and that restrict the range of thoughts and actions open to them. Those historical structures operate in consistent and often predictable ways. Historical situations separated by centuries and continents have similarities, and sometimes develop according to a similar logic. Historical analogies—comparisons between one set of historical structures or events and another—are powerful if treacherous tools for probing future possibilities.

Historical analysis inevitably has limits. Evidence about the past is always incomplete. Politics, warfare, religion, philosophy, and art have left more traces than everyday life. The few with power and leisure loom far larger in the surviving sources than the peasants and workers on whose drudgery that power and leisure rested. Men appear in the sources more frequently than women. Societies with writing have left far more behind them than those without. Twentieth-century technology—aerial photography, radiocarbon dating, precise chemical analysis,

xvii

meticulous archaeological technique—has told us much about voiceless societies and groups, and has broadened our knowledge even of societies that left extensive literatures. Source criticism—close scrutiny of the style, content, context, purposes, and reliability of surviving texts—has deepened our understanding of the written sources and of the societies that created them. The fragmentary nature of the evidence transmitted from the past nevertheless limits the historian's ability to see clearly and to draw valid conclusions. And in the nineteenth and twentieth centuries, the written record has swollen geometrically with the coming of mass literacy and the creation of immense bureaucracies. Too much evidence rather than too little is the burden of the historian of the recent past.

The historian's own values also color and sometimes drastically distort both the selection of evidence and the analysis of ideas and events. The past is the key to the present, but the present can also crush the past. Crusading religions and combative secular ideologies such as nationalism or Marxism-Leninism alter history to fit dogma. Traumatic experiences such as wars, revolutions, or economic catastrophes sometimes lead the historian to seek escape in a largely imaginary and far more pleasant distant past, or to rewrite recent events as a one-way street leading inevitably to the unhappy present. And historians, although their craft should lead them to take the long view, sometimes fall victim to passing fads. The historian's only defenses against ideological distortion and trendiness are the search for detachment and the passionate commitment to the verifiable evidence that has distinguished the best historical writing from Thucydides onward. For history, if painstakingly and honestly written, gives to those who pursue it a sense of the probabilities, of the range of outcomes inherent in a given historical situation. Historical knowledge can teach us how the world works.

That knowledge is also indispensable in a second way. History is memory. Historical knowledge is self-knowledge. It tells us how our world, our own society, and we as individuals got to where we are. Memory can give pleasure, but is also decisive in our lives. For the individual, memory is identity. For society, the "collective memory" or knowledge of the society's past and shared values is equally central. It is part of the glue that binds society together. When a society suffers collective amnesia, when it loses its historical consciousness, the values formed through that society's history erode. That decay undermines the society's political, social, and intellectual cohesion, and may threaten its survival.

In the empires, city-states, monarchies, and tribal polities of the past and in the single-party dictatorships of the present, religion, custom, political indoctrination, and force have usually maintained cohesion. But our own civilization has over the last three centuries evolved a historically unique concept: laws that guarantee the rights of the ruled against the rulers, the rights of individuals against the state. Those laws have given individuals a measure of freedom unprecedented in history: freedom to worship as they please, to follow their economic interests, to pursue private happiness. The victories of rights against the state in the seventeenth and eighteenth centuries and of representative democratic government in the nineteenth and twentieth centuries marked an immense leap forward in human freedom and economic dynamism. But that freedom also carried with it the possibility that its heirs might one day lose it, through forgetfulness of the sacrifices and struggles that has secured it and through ignorance of its historical uniqueness and potential fragility. Historical knowledge can guard against that danger as no other knowledge can.

History as the History of Civilization

Our present comes from our past, but what is the shape of that past? All readers of this book, by the fact that they read the English language, are heirs to a tradition that stretches back to the first millennium B.C., to the Greeks on the one hand and to the Hebrew authors of the Old Testament on the other. That *civilization*—a term coined in the eighteenth century and derived from the Roman word for city, *civitas*—is the civilization of the West, the civilization of Europe.

Civilization above all means cities, a human institution less than 10,000 years old. Cities demand a highly developed peasant agriculture to feed them, architects and laborers to erect them, artisans to people them, bureaucrats to organize and tax them, soldiers to defend them, rulers to rule them, and religious or communal myths and customs to foster loyalty to the existing order. Cities mean a degree of social stratification, of differences between the high and the low, unknown in the hunter-gatherer or cattle-herding nomad societies that preceded them. Cities mean *literacy, organization,* and *specialization* of work. And the degree of literacy, organization, and specialization affects the density of population that a given civilization can support and the character and attainments of that civilization. The Greek city-states were capable of efforts and achievements far surpassing those of the Scythian nomads to their north and of the ramshackle Persian empire to their east.

Cities have meant the intensified development of religion, philosophy, technology, art, and literature. The great religions, from those of ancient Egypt and Mesopotamia through Hinduism and Buddhism to Christianity and Islam, were or became urban civilizations. Philosophy, the quest for the principles and realities underlying human knowledge and existence, was an offshoot of religion that first arose in the Greek cities and in the urban civilizations of China and India. Technological advance—from improvements in tools and weapons to the building of fortifications, roads, and aqueducts—made cities possible, and cities in turn accelerated technological advance. Highly developed art, from architecture and sculpture to ceramics and painting, has been the mark of urban civilizations. And writing, invented for the tax accounting of the bureaucrats and the records of the city priesthoods, eventually made possible the flowering of poetry, drama, history, and science.

Cities have meant common values that bind the inhabitants together, that inspire them to accept the sacrifices—often without immediate or apparent compensating benefits—that specialization and organization impose. Those values can derive from a variety of sources. The great religions, the cult of the nation-state, the modern ideologies that claim to grasp the meaning and destination of history, and the sense of duty toward the community that is the "civic religion" of democracies have all provided the myths and values needed to sustain urban civilization. Those myths and values have been closely related to the type of civilization they spring from and support.

Finally, cities have meant conflict as well as achievement. Hunter-gatherers and nomads raid their neighbors for booty, women, slaves, and cattle. All adult males are by definition warriors. But in urban civilizations, specialization of work extends to warfare: hereditary warrior castes or standing armies and navies that may command the entire resources of the state. Urban civilizations, by virtue of literacy, organization, and specialization, can wield violence far longer and more systematically than their predecessors. That violence led to the formation of *state systems,* of highly competitive groups of rival states. In such systems, as the greatest of Greek philosophers, Plato, bitingly remarked, "What most people call peace . . . is just a name; in fact there is by nature an everlasting undeclared war of all against all." And even within the city walls, fierce conflicts between rival groups among the ruling few or between the few and the downtrodden many have frequently broken the peace.

A history of civilization must therefore try to explain the gradual increase of literacy, organization, and specialization over the last three millennia. Such a history must be a political history, for politics is the key to understanding the nature, growth, and collapse of *states*—the large-scale political units whose character, success, or failure has been a matter of life or death for the inhabitants of all known civilizations. A history of civilization must be an economic and social history, for economic and social relationships shape politics and are in turn shaped by politics. A history of civilization must be a history of art, literature, and ideas—for art, literature, and ideas define and reflect the systems of shared beliefs without which no civilization is possible. Above all, a history of civilization has to explore the interconnections of politics, economics, and ideas that determine the character, development, and fate of civilizations.

And as seen from the late twentieth century, the history of human civilization as a whole centers around the history of the West, the history of Europe. For Europe's civilization, although at first merely one of the world's major traditions, spread outward after 1492 to dominate the entire globe. That outcome was not foreordained, for Europe started late. The earliest civilizations arose as early as 3000 B.C. in the great river valleys of Egypt, Mesopotamia, India, and China. The first recognizably Western civilization only appeared after 1000 B.C. in the Greek city-states of Greece, Asia Minor, southern Italy, and Sicily. The Greeks borrowed much from their predecessors to the east and south, including the alphabet they took from their Phoenician rivals. But the Greeks were unique. In the space of little more than three centuries—the sixth through fourth centuries B.C.—they invented the Western traditions of philosophical, historical, and scientific inquiry. They created the concept of individual freedom. They laid the foundations of Western literature. They made Western civilization self-conscious, inquiring, and *historical*. And in the fourth century B.C., the immense conquests of Alexander of Macedon, heir to a half-barbarian kingdom on Greece's northern border, spread Greek civilization—and Greek-ruled cities named Alexandria—from Egypt to the borders of India.

The successors of Alexander, the Romans, dominated the entire Mediterranean basin for five centuries. In art and literature they borrowed much from the Greeks. In law, statecraft, and military organization they were bold and ruthless innovators who solved brilliantly the problem that had perplexed the Greeks: how to create large-scale and long-lasting political units ruling over citizens and non-citizens alike. The only contemporary civilization that rivaled the brillance of Rome and the extent of Rome's power was China, which experienced a merciless unification in the same centuries as the Roman conquest of the Mediterranean.

Roman legions, Roman roads, Roman cities, and Roman laws civilized Europe as far east as the great river barriers of the Rhine and the Danube and as far north as the wild borders of Scotland. Rome provided the political order within which a new religion, which blended the Hebrew traditions of the Old Testament with the philosophical conceptions of the Greeks, could spread and prosper. In the fourth century A.D., that new religion, Christianity, became the official religion of the empire. By that point Rome was near collapse. Interrelated and mutually reinforcing pressures from within and without brought the empire down: bloody civil wars, brigandage and piracy, economic decay, plague epidemics, loss of intellectual self-confidence and social cohesion, and vastly increased barbarian pressure on the Rhine-Danube frontier.

In the fifth century A.D., Rome fell to waves of invaders, as the pitiless Huns on their shaggy steppe ponies drove the warlike Germanic tribes across Rome's crumbling frontiers. The western half of the empire collapsed. The unity of the Mediterranean basin was gone. A Greek-speaking remnant of the Empire centered on Byzantium survived in the East for another thousand years, but had small influence on developments in the West. In the seventh and eighth centuries A.D., the Arabian tribes, under the green banner of their new religion, Islam, conquered the eastern Mediterranean and swept across northern Africa to Spain. Those conquests further divided Rome's inland sea—between the heirs of Greece, Rome, and Jerusalem and the heirs of the prophet Mohammed. The *ancient world*, the Greco-Roman civilization of the Mediterranean basin, had ceased to exist.

The new *medieval* civilization that eventually arose in western Europe after the eighth century was thus thrown back on its own resources. It saved only a fragment of its Roman inheritance, as Rome itself had been only a part of the ancient world. And the new rulers of western Europe, the Germanic peoples, had never been part of that world. They only gradually absorbed the fragments of Latin literature and Roman law that Rome had left behind. They were slow to blend with the Latin peoples they had conquered. They and their subjects were equally slow to absorb Christianity. But the fusion over some six centuries of those diverse ethnic and cultural elements ultimately produced a distinctive European civilization.

Once its character was set, medieval Europe developed rapidly. It eagerly received lost Greek texts, decimal numbers, and algebra from its neighbors, the more highly developed Byzantines and Arabs. Many of its basic institutions and ideas, such as universities and representative assemblies, originated in the twelfth and thirteenth centuries. Its centers were in the north, in the triangle bounded by the formerly Roman cities of Paris (*Lutetia Parisiorum*), Cologne (*Colonia*), and London (*Londinium*) and in north Italian cities such as Florence, Bologna, and Padua. Its periphery, from Sicily, Spain, and Ireland to Scandinavia, Poland, and Bohemia, developed more slowly. And beyond that periphery Western influence almost ceased. Byzantium remained apart: Greek in language, despotic in politics, and Orthodox rather than Catholic in religion. Byzantium's influence dominated the southern and eastern Slavic peoples who had moved into eastern Europe as the Germanic tribes had moved west. Byzantium likewise inspired the early Russian state, until Mongol conquerors subjugated Moscow and Kiev in the thirteenth century and forced them to face eastward for more than 200 years.

South and east of Byzantium lay the civilizations of Islam, which began to close themselves off from new ideas just as Europe was beginning its ascent. Still further east lay the great civilizations of India, China, and Japan. Each had characteristic values—religious in India, scholarly and bureaucratic in China, military and bureaucratic in Japan. All three had on occasion borrowed from their neighbors, but

they nevertheless tended toward self-absorption and the perfection of existing modes of thought rather than the acquisition of new knowledge. India suffered Moslem conquest, constant wars, and crushing taxation. China after the fifteenth century showed little interest in exploration or seaborne trade. Japan, which had borrowed much from China, fiercely walled itself off after 1600. And after pioneering efforts—gunpowder, rockets, firearms, crucible steel, iron smelting with coke—none of the Eastern civilizations developed a tradition of scientific inquiry and technological innovation rivaling that of the West.

By the fifteenth century, medieval Europe had begun to break out of its original social and religious mold and out of its narrow and rain-sodden peninsula off the Eurasian landmass. Since the twelfth century, Europeans had shown an insatiable scholarly curiosity about distant lands and a thirst for trade and booty. They had shown a fascination with machinery—from clocks and windmills to ships and cannon—rarely seen to the south and east. European scholars had begun to lay the groundwork for the seventeenth-century scientific revolution that immeasurably increased humanity's mastery over nature and transformed its view of its place in the universe.

In the last decade of the fifteenth century, Europeans leapt across the globe—the Spaniards to the Americas in 1492 and the Portuguese around Africa to India in 1498. Europe's new seaborne empires—the empires of the *early modern* age of Western expansion—soon dominated the fringes of Africa and Asia and conquered three newly discovered continents: North America, South America, and Australia.

Then came two further revolutions within Europe itself. The collapse of the French monarchy in 1788–89 opened 25 years of revolution and war that spread the democratic ideas of the French revolutionaries and the notion of nationalism—the political religion of the nation-state—eastward across Europe. Simultaneously, an industrial revolution that transformed humanity's power over nature and over its own existence began in Britain. Those twin revolutions—of mass politics and nationalism, and of engine-powered machines and economic freedoms—have been the driving forces of the *modern* era in which we still live. They transformed Europe and the world. For the first time in history, one civilization brought all others into increasingly direct contact with it, and forced its rivals to adopt its techniques and ideas or go under.

Those rivals ultimately maintained or reasserted their independence—within the framework of the worldwide international system that Europe established—by adopting Western ideas and techniques. The world has not become one; mortal rivalries between states, religions, ideologies, and cultures continue to rend it. But for good or ill a recognizably Western global civilization has taken shape, bound together by an accelerating revolution of science and technology, an ever-expanding world market, and a thickening web of mass communications. That is the present that any history of civilization must seek to explain.

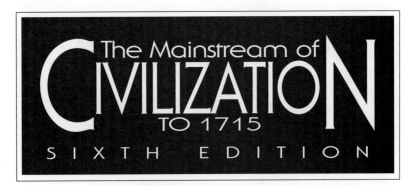

1

The Origins of Civilization: the Ancient Middle East To ca. 500 b.c.

We live in a complex environment. We are now conscious of being part of a world economy and of being affected by geological, climatic, and human events that occur around the globe. At the same time, we have developed a strong sense of ethnic and racial identity that makes us feel different from one another and even glorifies that difference. Human history has produced this uncertainty about whether we are part of a small group—such as an ethnic community within American society—or of a large one—such as Christianity or Islam—or of the global human community. When we read history, we learn of mass migrations, of the mixture of populations and cultures, of constant change in societies, economies, polities, ideologies. Change has produced our uncertainties. Change is the dominant fact of human life.

Recent findings in archaeology show that the human animal itself is the product of change. The primary force of human evolution has been climatic change, the same force that led to the extinction of the dinosaurs. Hominids, the family of animals that includes human beings, evolved in Africa, probably on the eastern side of the continent: The earliest hominid fossils were found in southern Africa, and the most important were found in the region east of Lake Victoria where the Serengeti Plain runs into the great Rift Valley. The oldest hominid fossil dates to about 3.25 million years ago, but archaeologists have found fossilized footprints made by a two-legged hominid ancestor about 3.75 million years ago.

Bipedalism (walking on two feet) was the first stage in human evolution, and recent studies show that it emerged about the same time the footprints were made,

Average Temperature: 55° F	Average Temperature: 59° F	Average Temperature: 50° F	Average Temperature: 59° F
2.5 Million Years Ago	125,000 Years Ago	18,000 Years Ago	11,000 Years Ago

a period when a major shift in climate took place. At that time, the earth's temperature fell dramatically, and the vast forests in which the ancestors of the hominids lived began to thin out. These animals had developed grasping hands and long arms to facilitate movement through the forest canopy, but they now had to travel from patch to patch of forest. Walking or running on two legs was much more efficient than gamboling along on feet and knuckles. Bipedalism was an adaptation to climatic change.

The next great leap in evolution took place about 2.5 million years ago, when the hominid began to develop a large brain and to make primitive tools. This period too was a time of climatic change, probably caused by the rise of the Himalaya Mountains, which altered wind patterns around the world. That change caused a cooling that produced the first polar ice caps and a drying of the African continent, which further reduced the extent of the forests. About this time, new species of antelopes adapted to the large grass plains emerged, and the vegetarian

hominid of the forests became omnivorous, eating grains, fruits, and meat, whatever was available.

The climatic change that took place 2.5 million years ago triggered a cycle of temperature fluctuations that, in turn, produced a series of ice ages. The ice would cover large parts of the earth for 50,000 to 80,000 years, and then about 10,000 years of relative warmth would cause the ice to retreat to the Arctic. The last ice age ended about 13,000 years ago. Scientists believe that plentiful food resources during the warm periods caused a rise in the hominid population and that when the ice returned only those with the best mental capacities survived. Repeated over 2 million years, this climatic pattern fostered the evolution of a large-brained animal that survived by its mental capacity, rather than its climbing ability, speed, teeth, claws, or physical size.

From about 700,000 years ago, we have evidence that *Homo habilis* (able or competent hominid) was making good tools of flint by striking flakes off a large "core" with a second rock. The flakes could then be shaped into hand-held blades. The tools, found in camps, were used to butcher animals, as the patterns of tooth and blade cuts on the bones show. The animal bones found in these camps show that *H. habilis* was sometimes a scavenger, fighting other carrion-eaters such as hyenas for carcasses, and sometimes a hunter who made the kills, took the meat, and left the remains for scavengers. The tools also reveal a great deal about the evolutionary progress the creature had made since it began to run across fields between clumps of trees. Scholars have learned to make the flint blades and have shown that *H. habilis* was right-handed. This means that the animal had developed a brain divided into two lobes, with the left side usually dominant. (Because of a twist in the brain stem, the left lobe of the brain controls the right side of the body.) Moreover, the skull structure

The Rise of the Himalayas and World Climate

The earth's crust is composed of huge plates—such as the North American plate, the Pacific plate, and the Asian plate. These are in constant movement caused by the continuous creation of new crust in deep ravines on the sea floor, principally in the Pacific and Atlantic oceans. Earthquake and volcanic zones are areas where two plates grind against one another. Millions of years ago, the plate on which India sits collided with the Asian plate causing the edge of the Asian plate to crumple as the Indian plate drove in under it. The crumpled region is the Himalayas, which are still being pushed upward. Geologists estimate that about 2.5 million years ago the range reached a height sufficient to alter worldwide wind patterns. The effect of this change was a cooling trend as cold air circulated to the south around the globe.

suggests that the voice box had moved down into the throat, a change required to produce the wide range of sounds needed for speech.

Homo habilis had many of the characteristics associated with modern human beings. It was bipedal, had a bicameral brain, made tools, and ate meat. Most important, it had a sense of time. It could plan its activities—for example, it could go to outcrops in the hills, gather flint, and take it back to camp for use in butchering. It was willing to spend energy on activities that only indirectly produced food. Yet the most recent finds show that *H. habilis* was more ape-like than human in appearance and lived in family groupings similar to those of modern apes, with several females and their young under the domination of a single male. Also, its young matured at about the same rate as those of apes. *Homo habilis* was definitely a transitional animal.

The great evolutionary changes experienced by *H. habilis* led to the next stage of human development, *Homo erectus*. This creature improved his mobility and posture and not only used tools, but also created a toolkit. *H. erectus* also began to migrate out of Africa. Remains of this hominid have been found from western Europe to China (Peking Man) and Indonesia (Java Man). The major finds date from 350,000 years ago and are associated with tools that are crude but of standard form. The common tools suggest that *H. erectus* took his kit with him from Africa; they also demonstrate the stability of human culture at this stage.

The last warm period before our own, about 125,000 years ago, seems to have produced two species of hominids. One of these, perhaps the older one, is called Neanderthal Man *(Homo sapiens neanderthalensis),* because the remains were first found in the valley *(thal* in German) of the Neander River in northwestern Germany. *Sapiens* means "wise," for Neanderthal had a very large brain and survived by its wits. Neanderthal hunted big game and appears to have practiced a primitive animism—a belief that spiritual beings inhabit inanimate objects and affect human life. The appearance of religion was a ma-

jor development in human evolution. It may have been related to the willingness, which first appeared among the Neanderthal, to care for members of the family or clan who through illness or injury were unable to gather food and protect themselves from predators. Among the Neanderthal skeletons studied by anthropologists are those of cripples who clearly lived long after they had become incapacitated.

The direct ancestor of the today's human beings, the fully modern hominid *(Homo sapiens sapiens),* emerged about 100,000 years ago, during the last ice age. The first find of this creature was discovered in Cro-Magnon, France, and it is commonly called Cro-Magnon Man. Neanderthal died out about 35,000 years ago, leaving Cro-Magnon in possession of the earth. There may have been interbreeding between the two species while they coexisted, though the evidence is inconclusive. In any case, the two were associated with different climatic conditions. In the Middle East, Neanderthal remains are associated with animals and plants adapted to a cooler climate than those associated with

Homo habilis made tools by striking flakes off of a core.

This bone shows the cut marks of the butchering process.

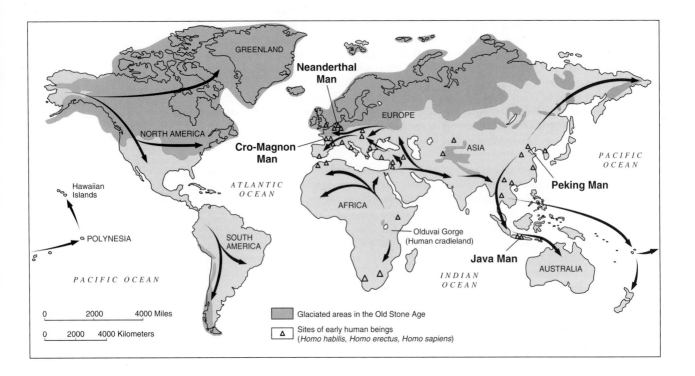

Cro-Magnon remains. This suggests that Cro-Magnon originated in Africa and migrated north during warming trends and retreated to the south when the climate cooled in the mini–ice ages that have occurred repeatedly during the interglacial periods.

The Culture of Early Hominids

Just before the end of Neanderthal Man, about 40,000 years ago, both species of

Climate and Neanderthal Man

Archaeologists discovered the connection between Neanderthal and particular climatic conditions by studying the remains of plants and animals found in their campsites. Many plants are sensitive to temperature and moisture and can be associated with a type of climate. Rodents are even more sensitive to climate than plants, and those that lived with the Neanderthals were cold-weather animals, while those whose remains are found in connection with Cro-Magnon bones and tools were adapted to warm climates.

hominid went through a cultural revolution stimulated, probably, by a rapid warming trend that forced the hominid communities to adapt to new plants and animals. Once started, the process of change gained momentum, so that in a few thousand years it resulted in greater technological advances than had been achieved during the previous 2.5 million years of toolmaking. Both Neanderthal and Cro-Magnon created sophisticated implements of stone, bone, and wood. Among these new tools were blades and spear points of better quality than those of their ancestors, fish hooks, and sewing needles for making clothing—and, perhaps, shelters—from animal skins and sinews. Ultimately, Neanderthal seems to have been unable to adapt to the warming climate, and Cro-Magnon carried on the cultural development, introducing the use of handles for tools and creating ornaments for personal adornment. Cro-Magnon communities also showed an interest in religion. About 30,000 years ago, they began painting elaborate scenes on the walls of caves and making sculptures, probably meant to increase fertility and ensure success in the hunt.

Archaeologists have not found any of the earliest Cro-Magnon dwellings, which must have been lightweight shelters that could be easily carried as the hunting society followed game, such as mammoth (ancestor of the modern elephant) and bison. The earliest known houses, dating from the end of the last ice age about 13,000–15,000 years ago, were found in southern Russia. These were substantial structures built on frames of mammoth bones and associated with storage pits for food, suggesting the existence of large, permanent communities. Why did such communities come into being?

Again, the evidence points to climatic change. According to one hypothesis, the end of the ice age produced a population explosion that forced people to curtail their migrations and to settle down in "home" territories. At the same time, the vast herds of ice-age animals died out as the warming trend reforested a world that for thousands of years had been covered with prairies. In the south—for example, in the Middle East—the warming trend led to the spread of the desert. In the region north of the Dead Sea, people reacted to

the encroachment of the desert by settling near the few remaining lakes. As we shall see, that decision led to the most momentous revolution in human history, the invention of agriculture.

Before turning to that story, we must ask one other question: What does the evidence reveal about the social life of the early hominids? So long as the animal relied on the gathering of fruits and other vegetable food for sustenance, there was no differentiation of sex roles, but biology did produce a size difference between males and females. Evolution favored large males, who had an advantage in creating and maintaining a clan—the grouping of a dominant male with several females and their young. Because size had little to do with female ability to reproduce, care for young, or gather food, their genes did not evolve toward largeness.

The shift from a gathering economy to a hunting economy, which *H. habilis* brought about, may have contributed to the role differentiation between males and females in hominid society. Once the species began to hunt large animals, the basic economy was divided into male and female realms. Hunting was a male activity because it required strength and speed,

In an effort to understand the ways of ancient people, archaeologists butcher a "mammoth" using primitive tools.

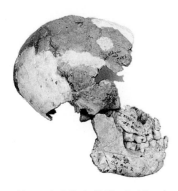

Homo habilis skull: The inside of the skull preserves an impression of the brain that scientists can analyze.

and it was a cooperative activity because a lone hunter could not kill big game. To succeed, the clans had to join together in larger bands, and the men had to learn to cooperate. This development must have produced a social system that permitted families to live together more or less in harmony. Studies of the cranial fossils of *H. habilis* seem to show that their brain, which left its imprint on the bones, had developed the regions that permit human beings to use speech, and this too would be consistent with an economic revolution that demanded cooperation and communal living.

The culture of early hominids from *Homo erectus* to *Homo sapiens sapiens* is called the Paleolithic Culture, or Old Stone Age Culture (400,000–10,000 years ago). Although the economy of Paleolithic peoples was limited to what nature provided, nature was relatively generous. Evidence from hunting camps of the late Paleolithic period suggests that the inhabitants may have "managed" herds of wild animals. The refuse found at some of the camps consists mainly of the bones of young animals, from which archaeologists conclude

that the inhabitants practiced some form of herding and culling. This impression is strengthened by the presence of dog skeletons in the camps. About 20,000 years ago, the hunters either domesticated dogs and used them in controlling the wild herds or, less likely, had already formed a symbiotic relationship—a relationship mutually advantageous to two independent species.

Still, it is clear that the Paleolithic hunter-gatherers did little to manipulate nature. Human beings did not truly domesticate nature until they invented agriculture about 10,000 years ago.

Agriculture and the New Stone Age

Recent finds suggest that agriculture was first practiced in Palestine just north of the Dead Sea. There, about 10,000–11,000 years ago, the Natufians (named for Wadi-al-Natuf, a site in the hills of the region), the people who had reacted to the drying trend by settling down near the remaining lakes, began to sow the grains they had been gathering in the wild for thousands of years.

About 11,000 years ago, the earth went through a mini–ice age that lasted 1,000 years, creating an environment that obliged the Natufians to take nature into their own hands. The cooling trend forced them to choose between moving away or finding a way to produce food where they were. They chose to cultivate wild grains and stayed where they were.

The first farmers cultivated wheat, barley, and other grains, and about 1,000 years later they began to domesticate sheep, goats, and cattle. They used dogs to guard their flocks and kept cats to protect their stored grain from rodents. The communities were larger than those of the hunter-gatherer societies and might contain as many as several hundred people.

In contrast to hunter-gatherer communities, agricultural communities did not require that everybody spend all their time producing food. At the peak periods of sowing and harvesting, everyone in the village would join in the farm work. In between, however, many of the people could engage in other activities. Some be-

Disease and the Agricultural Revolution

The principal result of the agricultural revolution was an enormous growth of the human population. Within a few hundred years, the number of people in agricultural regions had grown to be ten or twenty times larger than the hunter-gatherer economy supported. One result of this population growth and of the new contact with domesticated animals, was the spread of new diseases. The dense populations of the agricultural towns provided pools of hosts that permitted viruses and bacteria to sustain themselves as they could not in the small communities of hunter-gatherers. Even though people developed antibodies against the invaders, large populations always provided unprotected hosts. In addition, constant contact with domesticated animals introduced new diseases. Measles appears to be related to rinderpest, a cattle disease, and to distemper, common among canines; influenza probably came from hogs; smallpox from cowpox. The list of diseases shared by human beings and their domesticated animals is very large.

See William H. McNeil, Plagues and Peoples *(New York, 1976) esp. pp. 31–68.*

came specialists in weaving, making pots or tools, and house building, in what was essentially a revolution of technology and the arts. The villagers produced a wide variety of buildings, implements, and goods, and they engaged in trade. They exchanged stone to be used in the making of tools, and materials such as amber for art or personal ornamentation. The toolkit of these communities was extremely large and beautifully crafted of polished stone. Archaeologists have recognized the epochal change represented by such implements by giving this period a new name, the Neolithic Age, or New Stone Age, to distinguish it from the cruder culture of the Paleolithic hunter-gatherers.

From its beginnings in Palestine, agriculture spread north, east, and, perhaps, south. Some of the earliest agricultural sites are in the hills of northern Mesopotamia (the region between the Tigris and Euphrates rivers in modern Turkey and Iraq). Agriculture also spread east toward the Indus Valley, where the new technology provided a basis for the first Indian civilization. Whether the agricultural revolution to the south along the Nile stemmed from Palestine or arose independently is not clear, although archaeologists have found ancient evidence that grains figured in the diet of the people of that region. They used metates—a grinding stone—to prepare grains that grew in pools produced by annual floods, so they might have learned to sow their plants independently of the Natufians.

Certainly the Chinese and the Native Americans invented agriculture on their own. About 4000 B.C., the Chinese of the Yellow River Valley developed an agriculture based on millet. The farmers of that region practiced slash-and-burn agriculture, cutting and burning off the forest,

Origins of Agriculture　6000 B.C.

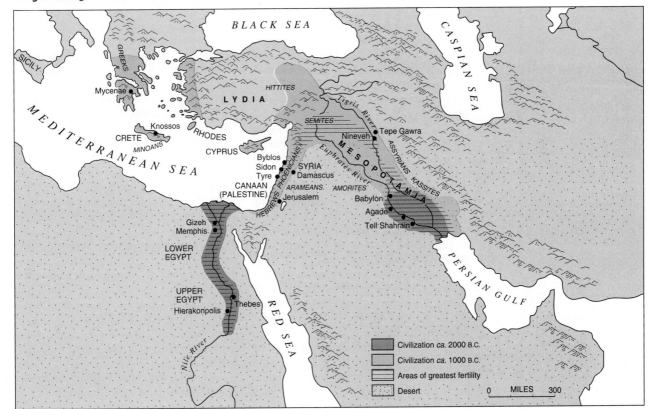

using the fields until the soil became infertile, and then moving on. Around 5000 B.C., the American peoples of central Mexico were growing peppers, squash, pumpkins, and avocados. It is not known when they succeeded in creating hybrid maize (corn), which became their staple crop.

Language and Language Groups

In 1786, Sir William Jones, an orientalist serving with the British government in India, published a work in which he claimed that Sanskrit, the language of the ancient Hindu classics, was related to Greek and Latin. The three languages must, Jones argued, have originated from a common linguistic source, which became known as Indo-European. Jones's study laid the foundation for historical linguistics, which has produced a historical map of language families and their relationships. In the last forty years, Soviet linguists have shown that modern languages preserve the remnants of the prehistoric languages from which they arose and that the great language families—Indo-European, Semitic, Altic (East Asian languages), and Amerind—arose from even earlier languages, leading back to the very first human language. That aboriginal language may have been spoken by *Homo erectus,* the hominid that first moved out of Africa to populate the world.

The reconstruction of the history of language has produced some interesting results. Proto-Indo-European ("proto" means the one before, in this case the language from which Indo-European evolved) and the ancestor languages of the Semitic and Altic families contain words associated with agriculture—for example, the names of domesticated plants. The even more ancient language from which these groups derived, called Nostratic (Our Language), lacks any such words, an indication that it was in use before the agricultural revolution. But Nostratic contains an ambiguous word, *kuyna,* that could mean either wolf or dog. (It evolved into the English word *hound.*) The ambiguity may reveal a stage in the relationship between human beings and canines during which canines first be-

came domesticated and the distinction between the wild and friendly breeds had not yet been established. Clearly, linguistic reconstructions provide a good deal of information about ancient cultures.

The Indo-European family, to which nearly all of the European languages belong, seems to have arisen in Anatolia, a region of modern Turkey. Because surviving traces of Proto-Indo-European contain words that were apparently borrowed from Mesopotamia, the language must have been spoken by people who were in contact with that region. Moreover, the language contains words for mountains and swift rivers as well as for domesticated plants and animals. Anatolia fits this linguistic environment perfectly, and scholars now think that the Indo-European language was carried into Europe by farmers from that region.

When and at what rate the language spread are difficult to determine. The migration may have begun in the third millennium B.C. and progressed at an average pace of one mile per year. At that rate, the speakers of Indo-European would have reached the western limits of Europe in 1,500 years. As they moved west, they broke into subgroups, each speaking a language, or a closely related group of languages—Greek, Italic, Gaelic, German, or Slavic—derived from Indo-European. Shortly after 2000 B.C., the Italic tribes moved into Italy, and the Greeks colonized the Balkans and the region around the Aegean Sea. By 1000 B.C., the Celts (Gaelic speakers) controlled most of Europe. Not long afterward, the Germanic and Slavic peoples migrated into central and eastern Europe and into Scandinavia.

During this same period, Indo-European speakers were migrating into southwest Asia and India. Among these peoples were the Kassites, who invaded Mesopotamia in the early 1500s B.C., and the Sanskrit-speaking peoples, the Aryans, who conquered parts of India about a century later. The Persians also were part of this eastward migration of Indo-European speakers.

During the second millennium B.C., (1800–1200 B.C.), as Indo-European culture and language spread across Europe

Family Tree of Indo-European Languages

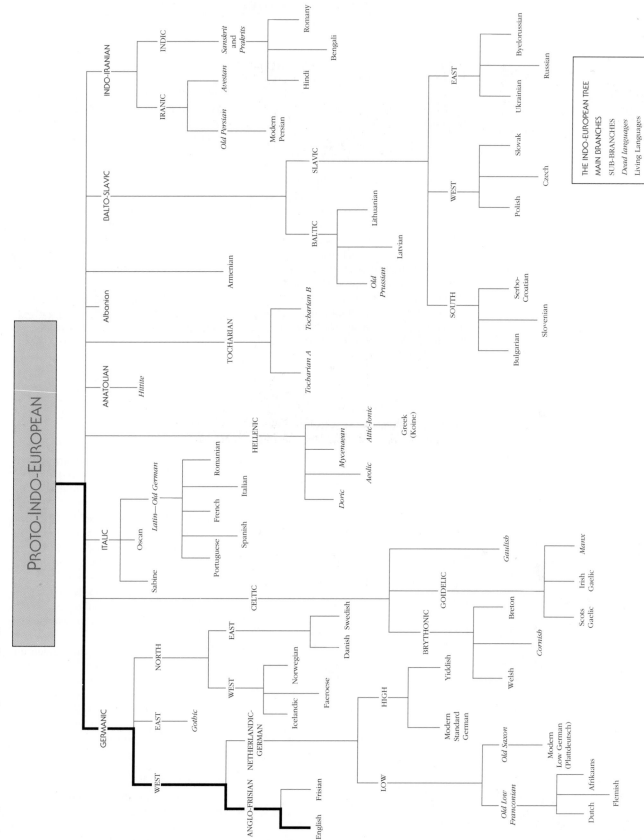

PROTO-INDO-EUROPEAN

THE INDO-EUROPEAN TREE
MAIN BRANCHES
SUB-BRANCHES
Dead languages
Living Languages

INDO-IRANIAN

INDIC — *Sanskrit and Prakrits* — Romany, Bengali, Hindi

IRANIC — *Avestan*, *Old Persian* — Modern Persian

BALTO-SLAVIC

SLAVIC

EAST — Byelorussian, Russian, Ukrainian

WEST — Slovak, Czech, Polish

SOUTH — Serbo-Croatian, Slovenian, Bulgarian

BALTIC — Lithuanian, Latvian, *Old Prussian*

Armenian

Albanian

TOCHARIAN — *Tocharian B*, *Tocharian A*

ANATOLIAN — *Hittite*

HELLENIC — *Mycenaean*, *Attic-Ionic*, Greek (Koine), *Aeolic*, *Doric*

ITALIC

Latin—Old German — Romanian, Italian, French, Spanish, Portuguese

Oscan

Sabine

CELTIC

GOIDELIC — *Gaulish*, Irish Gaelic, *Manx*, Scots Gaelic

BRYTHONIC — Breton, *Cornish*, Welsh

GERMANIC

NORTH

EAST — Danish, Swedish

WEST — Norwegian, Icelandic, Faeroese

EAST — *Gothic*

WEST

NETHERLANDIC-GERMAN

HIGH — Yiddish, Modern Standard German

LOW — *Old Saxon* — Modern Low German (Plattdeutsch)

Old Low Franconian — Dutch, Afrikaans, Flemish

ANGLO-FRISIAN — Frisian, English

9

and southern Asia, in the ancient heartland in Anatolia, the Hittites were creating a great empire that came to dominate the Middle East.

THE ORIGIN OF CIVILIZATION

In the culture of the Neolithic farmers, as in that of the hunter-gatherers, the skills and knowledge that governed a community's way of life were passed down by word of mouth from one generation to another. Because what was transmitted depended on the capacity of human memory, the sum of cultural knowledge remained relatively constant. Moreover, because the small communities survived by keeping rigorously to their ancient ways, cultural practices changed only slightly through the generations.

Civilization is culture that extends beyond the limits of human memory and the limits of the local community. A civilization—from the Latin adjective for city life (*civilis*)—requires great resources of food and large-scale social and political organization that permits many people to practice arts unconnected with food production. The growth of a civilization results from elaboration of every aspect of village culture. Agricultural production reaches new heights through political organization of the workforce. Trade becomes big business and connects the town to distant places. Religion acquires an elaborate ritual and body of beliefs. The large body of skills and knowledge required for such activities cannot exist without writing. Written records are necessary to maintain control over complex commercial, political, and social activities. They are both the repository and the source of intellectual invention.

The Early Civilization of Old Europe

A transitional phase from the farming culture of the Neolithic Age to an early stage of civilization has been identified in the Balkans and Central Europe. This advanced culture, called Old Europe, was based on large, stable, agricultural villages, and it can be traced back to about 5000 B.C. The people of the region did not, as far as we know, use writing, but they did use pictographic symbols, such as the bird, the bull, and the snake.

The soil of the region was fertile, though the climate was uncertain, and the villages were relatively wealthy. Even the oldest villages had granaries and produced well-crafted pottery for food storage. This economy permitted the Old Europeans to develop a large commercial trade. Their basic toolkit was made of stone, some transported from distant quarries, though they began to use copper very early. Some stone and metal came from the eastern Mediterranean.

These people depended on the regular cycle of the seasons and the fecundity of their animals. Their villages contained shrines and clay models of shrines, and

Old Europe   6000–3500 B.C.

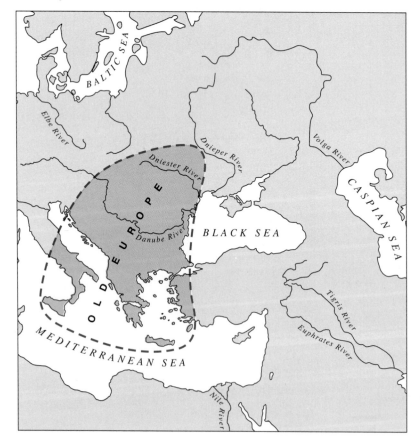

their pottery bore pictures and symbols that served as charms against the fury of nature. The bird goddess, who laid the universal egg, was painted on pottery and represented in figurines, sometimes realistically, but usually abstractly. The snake, which periodically sheds its skin and moves mysteriously, represented the world's turning and the cycle of the seasons. Often depicted abstractly as a spiral, the snake was a common motif in Old European art, as were the bull, the toad, the cross (which in Old Europe and in the hieroglyphs of Egypt represented life), and representations of water as rain, river, and ocean. All these symbols reflected the beliefs of people dependent on nature. Some motifs of Minoan and Greek mythology—such as the bull born of a woman and the bird-goddess aspects of Hera, queen of the gods in the Greek pantheon—have been linked with motifs found in the culture of Old Europe. Old Europe was apparently one of the sources of the civilizations that arose in the eastern Mediterranean.

THE CIVILIZATION OF MESOPOTAMIA, *ca.* 3500–1500 B.C.

The first true civilization arose in lower Mesopotamia, where farming depended on the flooding of rivers rather than on rain. Once agricultural communities learned to use dikes and canals to control and channel the floods, they greatly expanded their food production and, consequently, their populations. The first cities were not, however, merely enlarged agricultural villages; they were a new type of community. They were centers of political order and power and religious worship, and their population was both larger and more specialized than that of agricultural villages. The large urban market created a demand for the best products of the human imagination and fostered new levels of invention and specialization.

The development of cities required a more abundant agriculture than that of the ancient agricultural regions, where the climate and soil were marginal, and a more

certain agriculture than that of Old Europe, where the climate produced cycles of good and bad harvests. When the idea of farming spread into the rich countryside of the lower Tigris and Euphrates valleys during the fourth millennium B.C., the people there had to devise new methods of using the annual floodwaters of the rivers. To construct and maintain irrigation systems required larger and better organized communities than those of the rain-watered uplands. An intricate system of reservoirs was needed to catch the floodwater and a system of canals to distribute it. Failure to perform these operations meant widespread famine, but success in managing the floods produced a stable and prosperous economy that could support a large population. Within such a population, many were free to practice arts not directly connected with the production of food.

Around 4000 B.C., at places like Ur, Tell Shahrain, and Tepe Gawra, the people of Mesopotamia built large, mud-brick towns, each centered on a temple, which was furnished with equipment that took skill and time to make. The centrality of the temple reflected the importance of the priests who served in it. Next to farming, propitiation of the divine powers that controlled the environment was the most important activity of the community.

The sites of settlement in Mesopotamia were in continuous use for hundreds of years—some reveal twelve or more layers of settlement—so we can follow the course of their development closely. The temples were built on large rectangular platforms that rose above the town. About 3100 B.C., the towns began to erect ziggurats—stepped platforms—in place of the older temples. These immense stone works became the dominant features of the first cities. At about the same time, the Sumerians began using copper and silver vessels and producing larger-than-life sculptures, both signs of wealth.

It used to be thought that the Sumerians, who were among the earliest city-builders of Mesopotamia, invented writing in about 3500 B.C. Recent archaeological finds indicate, however, that writing arose more or less simultaneously throughout

Ziggurat at Ur (*ca.* 2250 B.C.).

the region. If any area had a claim on priority, it would be Elam, the hilly area to the north and east of Sumeria, though the evidence is inconclusive.

The First Writing Systems

The earliest form of writing was pictograms, in which concepts and things were represented by drawings. Over time, these pictograms became increasingly abstract, more signs than pictures.

The next stage was syllabic writing, in which signs represented syllables of words. This form of writing has the advantage of representing the spoken language, rather than the physical world, but it has the disadvantage of being tied to language. Thus, one cannot read syllabic script unless one knows the language it represents. Cuneiform was a syllabic script.

Finally, alphabetic writing is based on signs that represent individual sounds, or phonemes, of a language. This script is highly adaptable because, although syllables differ markedly from one language to another, elemental sounds are relatively common among languages, and an alphabet can be easily adapted to fit a large variety of languages (see p. 24).

For an excellent source of illustrations, see Reading the Past: Ancient Writing from Cuneiform to the Alphabet, *intro. J. T. Hooker (Berkeley: UC Press, 1990).*

Everywhere it is found, the earliest writing related to keeping accounts of storing and trading agricultural goods. The temple buildings included the city's storage facilities, and the priests played a central role in the economic life of the communities and in the economic relations among the cities of the region. Writing was the special skill of temple priests. In fact, for hundreds of years writing was used only for purposes of commerce.

About 3000 B.C., Mesopotamian society began to change rapidly. Apparently the cities had succeeded in exploiting their environment and had begun to achieve substantial wealth, indicated by discovery of an increasing number of metal tools and personal ornaments in the excavation layers of this period. Engraved cylindrical seals—used to mark trade goods—bear pictures of chariots and boats, indicating the importance of war and transport, and evidence exists that the Sumerian cities were now being ruled by kings.

Kingship was new at that time. It was the product of wealth, which attracted attacks by the poor tribes of the hills and deserts, and required military protection. But at the same time, the growth of wealth created a market for a wide variety of goods, which in turn created the need for raw materials. To avoid becoming dependent on the regions that could supply the raw materials, the cities often tried to bring them under their control, by war if necessary.

During the third millennium, the cities of Mesopotamia were fortified and kings became prominent. War became a constant in the river valleys. In the royal tombs at Ur, mosaic representations of troops led by a king provide striking evidence of the importance of war in the lives of the people and of the power of the kings.

Scholars are not sure how kingship arose. Some believe that the institution originated in the position of chief priest. Others think it came into being as a result of the rise of warfare. It is clear that the earliest kings served as war leaders, but they also performed religious functions. They were viewed as guarantors of the welfare of the city and its population, which led to the view that they had a special relationship with the gods.

The rise of kings created new uses of writing. To maintain their authority, the kings had inscriptions prepared that memorialized royal deeds. Lists of earlier kings provided proof that the current king derived his authority from an ancient line and that he was the successor of a continuous series that had guaranteed good luck in the harvests and victory in war for longer than any living person could remember. During the later third millennium B.C., scribes recorded the ancient traditions of the people, including the story of a great flood. The Israelites, who traced their history back to the Mesopotamian city of Ur, incorporated that story and others into their own historical tradition.

During the Early Dynastic Period in Sumeria, between about 3000 B.C. and 2370 B.C., each of the small city-states that dotted Mesopotamia was ruled by a king. These communities managed to organize the floodplain agriculture, develop bronze and other metallurgy, and build impressive temples. Eleven of them have been discovered—each the seat of a royal dynasty, and each with a history of alliances and wars.

About 2370 B.C., Sargon of Akkad, the king of the Akkadians—speakers of a Se-

mitic language—united the whole region of south Mesopotamia in the world's first imperial state. It appears that over time Sargon and his successors extended their control to Elam in the north and all the way to eastern Asia Minor in the northwest. The Akkadians were the first to use writing, which they inherited from the Sumerians, for purposes other than commerce and temple accounts. In the remains of their cities, archaeologists have found a treasure of literary works that represent the first written record of an ancient people's religious beliefs and historical consciousness.

The power of the Akkadians was broken about 2200 B.C. by raiders from the Zagros Mountains to the east. These newcomers founded a new dynasty, the Third Dynasty, at Ur, which had been one of

Minister or ambassador makes presentation to the king.

The Akkadian Empire   *ca.* 2370 B.C.

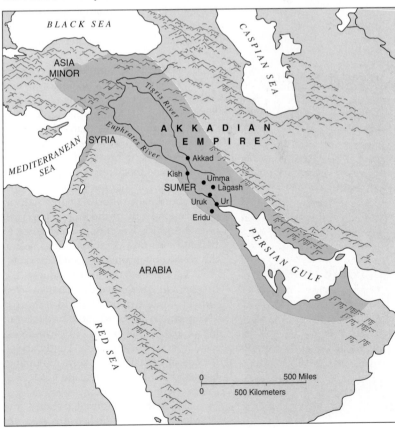

Tablet containing the code of
Hammurabi, *ca.* 1750 B.C.

the principal cities of the Akkadian empire. For the next century and a half, the kings of Ur dominated lower Mesopotamia, while the other sections of Sargon's former domain went their own ways. During this period, the Mesopotamians developed the pictographic writing they had inherited from the Sumerians and the Akkadians into an abstract form called cuneiform ("wedge-shaped": from the Latin word for wedge, *cuneus*), which was more compact and versatile than the earlier script. The technology, art, and architecture of the Third Dynasty make it the classical period of Mesopotamian civilization.

Just before 2000 B.C., the influence of Ur was broken by new raids of Elamites and Amorites, mountain peoples from the north and east of Mesopotamia. The Amorites were Northwest Semitic people, related to the Canaanites and Israelites. About 1990 B.C. they founded the first dynasty of Babylon, just up the river from Akkad, the old center of Sargon's power. Under their king Hammurabi (r. *ca.* 1792–1750 B.C.), the Amorites, also called the Babylonians, re-created the empire of the Akkadians.

Hammurabi is famous for having issued a great code of law that incorporated earlier codifications by Sumerian and Akkadian kings. Hammurabi's code was more comprehensive than the earlier ones, however, and served as a model for later codes. It provided the basis for economic and social relations. Knowledge of the law made it possible for merchants and subordinate officials of the state to act independently of the king and to plan ahead, and it gave people confidence to try out new ways of doing things within the well-known rules of social tradition.

The Babylonians also produced the first-known mathematics. They solved rather complicated problems in arithmetic and geometry and had some understanding of algebra. Their system of numbers used both base 10 (decimal) and base 60 (sexagesimal). The modern 60-minute hour and 360-degree circle are vestiges of their system of measurement.

Like older agricultural peoples, the Babylonians studied the heavens, because agriculture depended on a knowledge of the seasons. The movements of the sun and moon had long been followed—there is evidence of this in the art of Old Europe—but the Babylonians succeeded in tracking the regular movements of the visible planets as well. They also engaged in astrology, which predicts events on the basis of planetary movements.

Babylonian civilization was not limited to a tiny elite. The very publication of Hammurabi's law code indicates that literacy was widespread. During Hammurabi's reign, Akkadian language, with cuneiform writing, became the medium of commerce and culture throughout the empire. A common Mesopotamian culture and numerous economic ties enabled Babylonian civilization to survive the political collapse caused by the invasion of the Indo-European Kassites from the east about 1595 B.C. This invasion destroyed the First Babylonian Dynasty and gave the Kassites control of southern Mesopotamia for 400 years. Babylon did not again become an important political center until the seventh century B.C.

EGYPTIAN CIVILIZATION, THE PRE-DYNASTIC PERIOD, *ca.* 3800–3100 B.C.

Nine hundred miles to the southwest of Mesopotamia, another river, the Nile, provided a setting for irrigated agriculture. The Nile flows south to north for more than 600 miles, and each year it deposits fertile soil over its floodplains. In the south (Upper Egypt), the band of fertility is rarely more than ten miles wide, but in the north (Lower Egypt), the river forms a large, swampy, fertile delta.

The first agricultural villages in Egypt date from the early fifth millennium B.C., and the implements used by the first farmers show the influence of northern cultures such as Jericho in Palestine, where agriculture had begun at least a thousand years earlier. Though the northerners' influence was significant, the Egyptians preserved much of their own pre-agricultural culture. In fact, one of the characteristics of Egyptian culture was its ability to absorb external influences without losing its essential nature. At various points in their history, the Egyptians received new technologies from abroad, but absorbed them into a culture that diverged little from its ancient course.

The history of Pre-Dynastic Egypt—which might also be called pre-civilized Egypt—has been divided into several broad periods, representing the development of pottery and other implements. During the last of these periods, from about 3800 B.C. to 3100 B.C., the pace of change quickened, especially in Hierakonpolis (Greek for "City of the Falcon"; the Egyptians called it Nehken), a large community along the Nile in Upper Egypt supported by floodplain agriculture but dominated by the manufacture of pottery and other fine goods.

During the first centuries of the fourth millennium B.C., the population of Hierakonpolis grew to between 2,500 and 10,000. Throughout the settlement, archaeologists have found kilns and pottery "factories," some of them covering more than a quarter of an acre. The factories produced two types of pottery—a coarse ware made of clay mixed with straw and a fine ware called Plum Red Ware that was fired at high temperatures. Natural wind tunnels in cliffs near the town were used as kilns for the fine ware. The town also produced mace heads made of stone, which were used by the rulers of the Nile Valley as symbols of authority.

Most of the dwellings in Hierakonpolis were rectangular and built of mud brick. They were crowded close together, though some seem to have had gardens around them. This suggests that the town was large and wealthy enough to support an elite class. Moreover, in the town cemetery excavators have found large tombs, along with normal-sized ones similar to those found elsewhere in the valley. The elite, probably a merchant elite, dominated this society in death as in life.

The power of Hierakonpolis rested on its pottery works, but its survival depended on agriculture. After about 3500 B.C., the original agricultural economy began to decline as the climate became drier and the savannah (grassland

A Babylonian boundary stone (*ca.* thirteenth to tenth century B.C.), showing an example of cuneiform writing.

Pre-Dynastic Egyptian pottery jar decorated with gazelles and ostriches.

Ancient Egypt

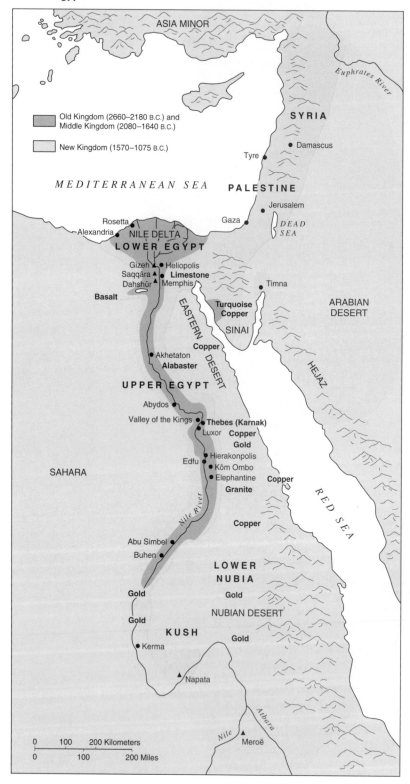

and sparse woods) turned into desert. The population was forced to move closer to the Nile, and the kilns and cemetery were abandoned.

In the ensuing decades, the old elite appears to have used its wealth to establish control over the new villages founded along the river. The villages were likely governed by individual merchant families, but any tendency toward independence was countered by the need for cooperation to control the floodwaters. During this period the ruling elites began large irrigation projects and built palaces, temples, and walled towns. They began to use the symbols of royal authority—particularly the crown and the mace—and conflict among the fortified villages became common. The history of Egypt between 3500 and 3100 B.C. was marked by both war and cooperation among the petty kings. There is also evidence of active trade with the Mesopotamian centers of civilization.

About 3200 B.C., the local kingdoms had grown powerful enough to check each others' ambitions, and constant war became a feature of life in the Nile Valley. During this period, the rulers of Hierakonpolis, which had become one of the royal centers, began again to use the old cemetery, continuing the ancient tradition of worship of the dead. The cemetery was built in the form of a necropolis, a city of the dead, to symbolize the society of the living. It was laid out along a dry stream (a *wadi*), which represented the Nile.

About a hundred years later, Narmer of Hierakonpolis (his name means Catfish) succeeded in unifying the valley. Narmer may have built on the success of his predecessor Scorpion, but the Egyptians regarded him as the first pharaoh, the founder of the First Dynasty.

The cemetery of Hierakonpolis is divided into sections representing the two halves of Narmer's united Egypt. The tombs of the southern section are built of mud brick in the manner of Upper Egypt, and those of the northern section are built of stone in the style of Lower Egypt. A particularly large tomb, on the border between the two sections, may be that of Scorpion. Its position symbolizes the unification achieved by the dynasty of Hiera-konpolis.

Dynastic Egypt, ca. 3100–333 B.C.

What we know about the history of unified Egypt comes from the work of a third century B.C. priest named Manetho, who wrote a history of his country in Greek. He grouped the kings into 30 dynasties, from the legendary Narmer (Menes in Greek) to the last native Egyptian pharaoh, Necta-nebo II, who died in 343 B.C. With the discovery of the Rosetta Stone in 1799 by Napoleon's conquering army, much older Egyptian historical sources became available. The stone, which is a tablet with parallel texts in Greek and in Egyptian hieroglyphics, provides the key to deciphering the ancient script. Modern his-torians count 31 dynasties and usually use Egyptian instead of Greek names for the pharaohs, but they follow Manetho's practice of dividing Egyptian history into dynasties. They also divide Egyptian history into long historical periods—the Early Dynastic Period (*ca.* 3100–2700), the Old Kingdom (*ca.* 2700–2150), the Mid-dle Kingdom (*ca.* 2050–1650), and the New Kingdom (*ca.* 1550–1100). Between these kingdoms were periods of political disorder, and after the New Kingdom a series of Middle Eastern empires domi-nated Egypt for a time.

The full unification of the northern and southern kingdoms took about 400 years (3100–2700 B.C.), during which the foundations of Egyptian civilization were laid. This is the period of the first two dynasties, the Early Dynastic Period. The

The Rosetta Stone, found by Napoleon's troops in 1799, provided the key to deciphering the hierogliphs. It has the text in Greek and Egyptian.

success of these dynasties provided both the resources and the peace necessary for rapid cultural development.

The cemetery at Hierakonpolis, which dates back to about 3800 B.C., already contained artifacts that archaeologists consider characteristic of Egyptian civilization. For example, the arrangement of the cemetery as a necropolis, with

wooden or reed houses built over many of the tombs, represented an early stage of the cult of the dead that later came to dominate Egyptian religion. In addition, some Hierakonpolis tombs from this early period contained pots bearing writing-like symbols that may actually be primitive writing, though archaeologists have not yet deciphered them. Painted scraps of a

Wall painting from grave at Hierakonpolis shows men and cattle.

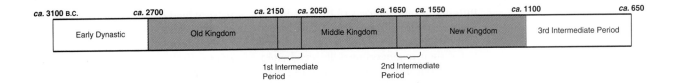

ca. 3100 B.C.	*ca.* 2700	*ca.* 2150	*ca.* 2050	*ca.* 1650	*ca.* 1550	*ca.* 1100	*ca.* 650
Early Dynastic	Old Kingdom		Middle Kingdom		New Kingdom	3rd Intermediate Period	

1st Intermediate Period

2nd Intermediate Period

papyrus-like plant have also been found in the tombs. The use of papyrus for written records, instead of the stone or clay tablets used in Mesopotamia, provided the Egyptians with a cheap, easy-to-use writing material and greatly expanded their ability to create and circulate lengthy works.

Under the first dynasties, the pace of cultural advance quickened. Early attempts to manage the Nile floods had shown that the river could be a source of great agricultural wealth but that its potential could not be realized until all the projects along its course were managed by a single authority. The unification of Egypt provided that authority, and the wealth of Egypt grew as large-scale irrigation and flood-control projects were organized. To ensure that those activities were set in motion at the proper time, the priests, in close association with the pharaoh, created a precise calendar around the time of unification.

The Egyptians believed that the Nile Valley belonged to the gods. The pharaoh, under whose authority the river was harnessed, was the divine representative of the gods on earth, and it was he who drew wealth from the land. This belief contributed to the power of the priesthood in the society.

The idea that the gods controlled the environment, common to all agricultural societies, had long ago led the Egyptians to contemplate the boundary between the visible world of humans and the invisible world of the gods. The interaction between these two worlds was represented in the belief that, like the cycle of the seasons, the life of a person cycled through life and death—from birth to death to rebirth.

The formal activities at the junctures between these states of existence were analogous to the activities in agriculture. Just as the most important act of the agricultural cycle was collecting and preserving seed for the next year's planting, so the most important moment of a person's life was the preparation for life after death, through which one would pass to rebirth. The Egyptians believed that for this cycle to be completed, the body of the dead person had to be preserved, and evidence of primitive mummifying has been found in the ancient cemetery at Hierakonpolis. One of the most striking aspects of Egyptian culture was the cult of the dead, with its holy book, the Book of the Dead. The Egyptians were especially concerned to ensure that the pharaoh, the embodiment of authority and divinity, would have safe passage from life to death.

The contrast between Egyptian and Mesopotamian civilization is illuminating. While the Mesopotamians first used writing to keep temple accounts and records of commerce, the Egyptians appear to have first used writing in connection with the cult of the dead. If the mysterious symbols on the pots found at Hierakonpolis

Egyptian Hieroglyphs

Hieroglyphs were used longer than any other script. The earliest date from about 3100 B.C., and they were used until the eleventh century after Christ. It was a pictorial script, with most signs representing whole words. Later versions of the script also contained signs signifying single sounds—phonemes—of the language and determinatives, symbols that indicated the precise meaning of a word.

See Reading the Past: Ancient Writing from Cuneiform to the Alphabet, *intro.* J. T. Hooker (Berkeley: UC Press, 1990).

turn out to be examples of the first Egyptian script, this will seem even more likely. Likewise, the Mesopotamians concentrated their engineering skills, celebrated in the biblical story of the tower of Babel (a ziggurat), on building temples, while the Egyptians concentrated on building tombs. Their tombs were far more impressive and technically advanced than the "palaces" built by the great men. For the Egyptians, the transient world of the living was of slight significance compared with the eternal world of the dead.

The principal architectural achievements of the Egyptians were in fact the great pyramid tombs. The first one was built at Saqqara by Djoser (Zoser in Greek), the first or second pharaoh of the Third Dynasty (r. *ca.* 2600 b.c.). This tomb was a stepped pyramid surrounded by an enclosure and outbuildings—a suitable dwelling for the pharaoh after death. Later, the style shifted to smooth-sided pyramids. About a century after Djoser, Khufu (Cheops in Greek) had the Great Pyramid of Giza built as a tomb for himself and his queen. This tomb covered 13 acres and was 482 feet high. It was constructed of more than 2,300,000 $2\frac{1}{2}$-ton blocks of

stone, which had been transported to the site from a great distance.

According to the Greek historian Herodotus (fifth century b.c.), it took 20 years to build the Great Pyramid. Archaeologists estimate that 4,000 stone masons worked steadily through those years and that crews of up to 100,000 men hauled the stone and lifted the blocks into place. The Great Pyramid stands as the most impressive memorial of the Egyptians' view of the passage from life to death.

Controlling the whole lower course of the Nile (about 500 miles long) was a difficult task even for a highly centralized government. After unification, the pharaohs of the Third Dynasty created a large bureaucracy to help with the job and divided the kingdom into districts, called *nomes,* each governed by a royal vizier (nomarch).

This system worked well as long as the central government was strong. But weakness at the center presented an opportunity, and sometimes a necessity, for the local nomarchs to act independently. Although the reasons for one dynasty replacing another are not usually clear, evidence suggests that weakness in the

The great pyramid of Khufu with the Sphinx in the foreground.

central government often gave rise to political turmoil, out of which a strong nomarch or a royal bureaucrat emerged to found a new dynasty.

After the Old Kingdom the pharaohs stopped building pyramidal tombs, not because the Egyptians no longer believed in the cult of the dead, but because power had become too widely distributed throughout the kingdom. The nomarchic system had contributed to the governance of the country, but it had also provided local governors with their own power bases. This duality helps explain why the history of Egypt was both tumultuous and remarkably stable. There was always a class of able men ready to make a bid for control of the central authority, and those who won out were well schooled in the techniques of governing.

Between the great periods of Egyptian history—the Old, Middle, and New Kingdoms—were periods of weakness and, on occasion, subjugation. The Old Kingdom collapsed with the end of the Sixth Dynasty. The following century, from *ca.* 2150 to 2050 B.C., was a period of internal strife. The country was finally reunited by the pharaohs of the Eleventh Dynasty, who founded the Middle Kingdom. The Middle Kingdom may have ended shortly after the explosion of Thera, a volcanic island in the Aegean Sea. The explosion, the largest in recorded history, spewed more than 50 cubic miles of rock and lava into the atmosphere, created a tsunami, or tidal wave, that rose to 800 feet in some places, and produced an artificial winter whose traces are still discernible in the rings of the bristlecone pine of California's Sierra Nevada. Tons of hot ash fell on Egypt, and the tidal wave flooded the Nile delta. These events may have been the basis of the biblical stories of the plagues associated with the rise of Moses among the Hebrews living in Egypt. For nearly a century after this disaster, from about 1630 to 1550 B.C., Egypt was under the domination of the Hyksos, a people of unknown origin who gained control of the Nile delta and eventually formed a new dynasty themselves. But the Hyksos kings—called the Shepherd Kings, an indication that they were a nomadic peo-

ple—were never absorbed into Egyptian society, and Ahmose (r. 1570–1546 B.C.), the ruler of Thebes in Upper Egypt, finally expelled them. Ahmose became the first pharaoh of the Eighteenth Dynasty and founded the New Kingdom.

During the Eighteenth Dynasty Egypt expanded its contacts with the world around it. With the south it carried on a rich trade in gold and ivory; several times the pharaohs campaigned in the Sudan, perhaps to protect that trade. The Egyptians also conquered parts of southwest Asia, and cuneiform documents have been found at Egyptian sites dating from this period. Egyptian influence in Asia lasted until the middle of the twelfth century B.C. and coincided with the great Anatolian empire of the Hittites, against which Egypt fought several wars.

This extended contact with foreigners may have led to the religious experiment conducted by Pharaoh Akhenaton (r. 1379–1362 B.C.), who abandoned the old gods in favor of Aton. This god was represented by a sun-disk and was considered by Akhenaton to be his father. Akhenaton built a new capital city at Amarna and devised a new theology to support his religion. The experiment ended shortly after Akhenaton's death, and his successor Tutankhaton (r. 1361–1352 B.C.) abandoned the cult four years into his reign. Tutankh*aton* then changed his name to Tutankh*amen* and returned to the old capital at Thebes, the center of the cult of Amon. Under this young pharaoh, royal officials undertook major building projects in the capital. The furnishings of Tutankhamen's tomb, which was discovered intact in 1922, seem to reflect his return to the old religion.

In the eleventh century B.C., powerful families from the delta region overthrew the Theban dynasty, and the New Kingdom collapsed. This shift of power to the north shows the effects of Egypt's involvement in the affairs of Asia. The delta region had become the area of contact between old Egypt and its subject territories, and the new dynasties themselves were headed by foreigners. From the tenth to the eighth century B.C., Libyans who had been settled in military camps in the

Chair and mummy case from Tutankhamen's tomb.

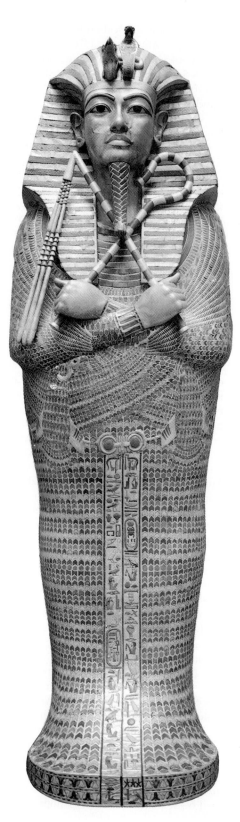

western delta formed new dynasties and dominated the country. Then power shifted to the south. From the late eighth to the middle of the seventh century, Kushites from Nubia in the Sudan held sway. Finally, from the seventh to the fourth century, Persians ruled the country.

After enduring centuries of conquest, probably few Egyptians recognized the finality of the Macedonian conquest led by Alexander the Great in 333 B.C. But from that time on, no Egyptian was able to revive the kingdom of Egypt even for a short time. After Alexander's death in 326 B.C., the Ptolemies, a Greek dynasty, ruled Egypt until the Roman conquest in 30 B.C.

Egyptian Civilization

By the time of the Middle Kingdom (*ca.* 2050–1750 B.C.), the scribes who ran the governmental bureaucracy had established an educational system that permitted talented men of humble origins to rise in the state service. The scribes also created a literary culture, which provided a basis for education in language and rhetoric, and which expressed the values and ideology of the educated elite.

Though the pharaoh was the head of all the cults, the priests of the various gods actually conducted the activities of the cults. Apparently, scribes enjoyed higher status than priests, because the scribes were exempt from the levy of troops and of labor, while the priests, at least those of the lower ranks, were not.

During the New Kingdom, the growth of the Egyptian empire in Asia and the conquest of the Sudan increased the importance of the military elite. The pharaohs received a military education and were supported by a professional officer class, which represented a new, third element in the upper classes of society. It seems that many pharaohs of the New Kingdom chose their wives from leading military families.

Although the early pharaohs appear to have been members of the merchant elite, merchants had little status in the mature civilization of Egypt. Their activities were limited to local markets and low-cost wares. Long-distance and large-scale trade was a state activity controlled by the priests, perhaps because the temples were so richly endowed with land that they were the largest suppliers of the market. The three segments of the upper class—the scribes, the priests, and the military—controlled the wealth of the society.

The upper classes provided a market for a substantial artisan class—woodworkers, metalworkers, artists, and others—in their households. Though the artisans constituted a "middle" class, they were not independent entrepreneurs, and they could not sell their goods in the open market.

Below these classes was the great mass of peasants, whose labor supported the rest of society. The peasants lived in villages and had their own farm plots, but the agricultural wealth of the society rested on the great state projects that controlled and distributed the floodwaters of the Nile. At each of the crucial times in the agricultural cycle, the pharaohs and nomarchs organized a labor draft, or corvée. The peasants formed the core of these great labor forces, but members of the artisan and priestly classes also were enlisted. When the agricultural chores were light, many peasants probably supplemented their income by working on the pyramids or other great building projects. The peasants also provided the manpower for the armies.

Slaves constituted only a small segment of the population. Most were foreign prisoners of war. Upper-class families generally had one or two household slaves, and the pharaohs maintained slave labor forces in the state mines and on some construction projects. Slaves were not commonly used in agriculture, however.

Egyptian society was tightly regulated and highly traditional, anchored in the ideas and artistic styles of the past. Although men dominated society, women were not altogether subordinate. Marriage, as in other ancient societies, was arranged by contract between the husband—or the husband's family—and the father of the bride, but women seem to have had the right to divorce and to make commercial contracts. There was a female

priesthood as well as a male priesthood, and men and women were accorded equal treatment in the cult of the dead.

Egyptian civilization, though often subjected to foreign influence, preserved its distinctive, indigenous character to a great degree. Moreover, it had an enormous influence on the civilizations of other Mediterranean peoples.

Small Kingdoms in the Near East

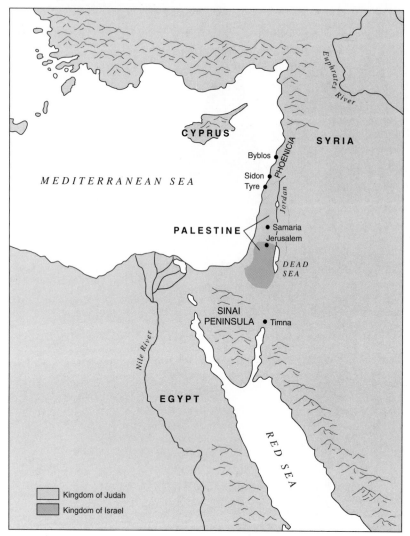

Kingdom of Judah

Kingdom of Israel

THE ERA OF SMALL KINGDOMS, *ca.* 1250–750 B.C.

Between about 1150 and 750 B.C., the absence of any great imperial power in the Middle East enabled several small kingdoms to flourish. Among them were the Phoenician city-states along the eastern coast of the Mediterranean, in present-day Lebanon, and the Canaanite and Hebrew kingdoms of Palestine.

The Phoenicians

The Phoenicians were a people of mixed background who lived in cities along the eastern Mediterranean coast. By about 1100 B.C., Phoenician ships were plying the Mediterranean trade routes, and for the next three centuries Phoenicians controlled commerce in the Mediterranean.

The Phoenicians built a great commercial empire by trading with the established cities of the Mediterranean world and by founding colonies in the western regions. Those colonies, most notably Carthage, near modern Tunis in North Africa, exploited the surrounding regions and helped supply Phoenician industry with raw materials. Phoenician ships regularly voyaged to Cornwall, Brittany, and Ireland for tin to be used in bronze manufacture. Egyptian writings suggest that the Phoenicians may have sailed all of the way around Africa, and some scholars believe that they may even have reached the Americas.

The oldest Phoenician city was Byblos, located on the coast north of Tyre (the largest of the cities), famous for the manufacture of writing materials. The Greek word for book, *biblion,* stems from its name. The Phoenicians helped to refine and spread the Northwest Semitic alphabetical system of writing. This was a great advance over Egyptian hieroglyphics and Sumerian-Akkadian cuneiform because it used simple-to-draw and easily recognizable symbols (letters) to represent sounds. The Phoenician alphabet consisted of 22 letters and was the basis of the three major alphabets now used in the Western world: Hebrew, Greek, and Latin. The Greek alphabet, in turn, was the basis of the Cyrillic alphabet used in Russia and parts of eastern Europe, and an Aramaic version of the West Semitic script formed the basis for the writing systems of India.

About 750 B.C., the Phoenician cities came under the domination of the Assyrian Empire and fell into rapid decline. Many of the leading merchant families migrated to the western colonies, especially to Carthage, which became the center of the Phoenician world until it was destroyed by the Romans in 146 B.C.

The Israelites

Between about 1250 and 400 B.C., the Israelites, or the Hebrews, as they were sometimes called, founded a state in Palestine.
If not for their innovations in religion and
for their use of the Northwest Semitic alphabet to record them, these people
would be only a vague presence in the
history of the region, almost indistinguish-
able from the Canaanites, to whom they
were closely related. (Hebrew is a dialect
of Canaanite.) In their written record, a
collection of books composed between
about 1000 and 150 B.C., they chronicled
their historical relationship with their God,
Yahweh, and that account subsequently
influenced Christianity and Islam, the
other two great religions of the Mediterra-
nean-European world.

The Israelites traced their origin to
Mesopotamia, from which, they believed,
their patriarch Abraham had migrated. In
fact, they preserved many of the historical
and legal traditions of Mesopotamia. The
story of the great flood, for example, was
known in Mesopotamia, and a fragment
of the Babylonian version of the story,
dating to the fourteenth century B.C., has
been found at Megiddo, a city in Palestine.
The legal code of the Israelites was derived in part from the Mesopotamian
tradition represented by the laws of Hammurabi.

Yet while the Israelites preserved the
memory of a migration out of Mesopotamia, they were really formed as a people
in the delta region of Egypt around the
town of Avaris, the old capital of the
Hyksos, who may have settled them
there. During the Hyksos period (1630–
1550 B.C.), many Semitic words had entered the Egyptian language. Long after
the Egyptians expelled the Hyksos, the
Egyptian pharaoh Ramses II (r. 1290–
ca. 1224 B.C.) rebuilt Avaris as Raamses,
the "house of Ramses," and the Hebrew
Bible (Exodus 1.11) tells us that the ancestors of the Israelites were pressed into
service building that city.

Not long after Ramses' death (date
uncertain), Moses emerged as leader of
the enslaved peoples living in the area of
Raamses (Goshen, Genesis 47.27), and led

Phoenician	Greek	Roman
𐤀	A	A
𐤁	B	B
𐤂	Γ	G
𐤃	Δ	D
𐤄	E	E
𐤅	[Y]	F
𐤆	Z	Z
𐤇		H
𐤈	I	I
𐤉	K	[K]
𐤊	Λ	L
𐤌	M	M
𐤍	N	N
𐤏	O	O
𐤐	Π	P
𐤒		Q
𐤓	P	R
𐤔	Σ	S
𐤕	T	T
	Υ	U,V
	X	X
	Ω	

Typical letters of the alphabet in
Phoenician, Greek, and Roman
forms. The final Greek letter,
omega, is pronounced like the
Roman long o.

Israelite or Hebrew?

We use the names Israelite and Hebrew interchangeably, but the
ancient sources indicate that the two are not synonymous. "Hebrew"
is used in the Mesopotamian, Hittite, and Egyptian sources to refer to
people who came from outside the established community, and the
term is associated with personal names belonging to many linguistic
groups. In the Bible, the term is used infrequently and then only in
the early texts. When the term is used in the Bible, it is nearly always
in the mouths of foreigners speaking of the Israelites (Gen. 39.14, 17;
Exod. 2.6), or the Israelites themselves are identifying themselves to
foreigners (Gen. 40.15; Exod. 3.18).

It appears, then, that "Hebrew" was a name used to describe those
elements of the middle eastern population who lived on the fringes
of civilized society. The Israelites arose from this nomadic element,
but they did not incorporate all who would have been identified as
Hebrews in the second millennium B.C.

them out of Egypt. They crossed over the Sea of Reeds, probably an arm of Lake Menzaleh, near what is now El-Qantara along the Suez Canal, into the Sinai Peninsula. There they lived a nomadic life for a generation—40 years, according to tradition—during which Moses created their religion, perhaps borrowing elements from Midianite quarrymen and metalworkers at Egyptian copper mines in the region. According to the Bible, Moses was related to the Midianites on his mother's side (Exodus 18.10–27).

A little before Moses led his people out of Egypt, the Midianites living near Timna in the region of Horeb (one of the names of Mount Sinai) destroyed the Egyptian temple there and replaced it with a tent shrine. This place has recently been excavated and may have been the site of the wilderness tabernacle of Moses mentioned in Exodus 26. Found at the site was a gilded snake image, like the one Moses raised up in Numbers 21.4–9. Moses adopted the local god of Mount Sinai, Yahweh, as the god of his people, Israel (the people of God).

After trying and failing to invade Palestine from the south, the Israelites wandered east through the southern Transjordan and, according to the Bible, made a successful attempt north of the Dead Sea. Archaeological evidence suggests that their settlement of Palestine was much slower and, perhaps, more peaceful than the Bible reports. In any case, during the late twelfth century, Palestine was settled by a group of related tribes—twelve, according to the biblical account—who later identified themselves as Israelites.

The tribes were united under Saul, the first Israelite king (r. *ca.* 1000 B.C.). The biblical text hints at a conflict between religious and secular authority in its account of the warning issued by Samuel, the religious leader who anointed Saul, that the Israelites would regret the act. Not long after this, Samuel named David (r. *ca.* 1000–960 B.C.) as Saul's successor. King David completed the conquest of the Philistines, who lived along the southern coast near Gaza, and the Canaanites, and built his capital at Jerusalem, already an ancient town site. David's son and successor, Solomon (r. *ca.* 960–930 B.C.), established lucrative trading and diplomatic relations with his neighbors and built a great royal palace and a temple to Yahweh in Jerusalem. But Solomon's strong style of governing created opposition among the tribes, and after his death the ten northern tribes seceded to form the Kingdom of Israel under another dynasty. The two southern tribes remained loyal to the house of David in the Kingdom of Judah. These two kingdoms experienced repeated conquests by three successive empires that dominated Mesopotamia and the eastern seaboard of the Mediterranean between about 750 and 333 B.C.

THE NEW AGE OF EMPIRES, *ca.* 750–333 B.C.

The Assyrian Empire, ca. 750–612 B.C.

The Assyrians, a Semitic people, lived in the highlands of the upper Tigris Valley. By the end of the eleventh century B.C., they had built a powerful army, with which, after 900 B.C., they terrorized and conquered their neighbors. By about 750 B.C., they had won control of all of Mesopotamia. They then moved swiftly to overwhelm Syria, the Phoenician cities, the kingdoms of Israel and Judah, and, finally, Egypt.

From their capital city of Nineveh, the Assyrians ruled by terror, killing and enslaving large portions of their subject populations. They destroyed the ten northern Israelite tribes and made the Kingdom of Judah into an Assyrian dependency.

Although the Assyrians managed to preserve their empire for more than a hundred years, they were not numerous enough to garrison their vast territories, and their systematic cruelty made it impossible for them to control their subject peoples except by force of arms. About 613 B.C., the Babylonians, joined by other conquered peoples, rebelled, and Nineveh fell in 612 B.C. The Assyrian empire collapsed almost overnight.

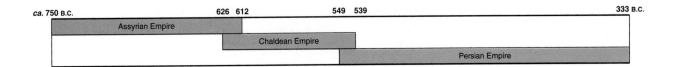

| ca. 750 B.C. | 626 | 612 | 549 | 539 | 333 B.C. |

Assyrian Empire

Chaldean Empire

Persian Empire

The Chaldean Empire, ca. 626–539 B.C.

The leaders of the rebellious Babylonians were the Chaldeans, a people from the southern part of Mesopotamia, the region bordering the Persian Gulf. After the fall of Nineveh, the Chaldeans built an empire of their own, centered on the ancient city of Babylon. In 587 B.C., the Chaldean king Nebuchadnezzar overran Judah, which had joined an anti-Chaldean coalition led by Egypt, and destroyed Solomon's temple in Jerusalem. To control the population of the conquered kingdom, Nebuchadnezzar carried off the leading citizens to Babylon. The so-called Babylonian Captivity lasted until the fall of Babylon in 539 B.C. Although the Hebrew prophets saw that event as divine punishment for the Chaldeans' treatment of the people of God, the proximate cause of the fall of Babylon was the rise of the Persians.

The Assyrian Empire   *ca.* 700 B.C.

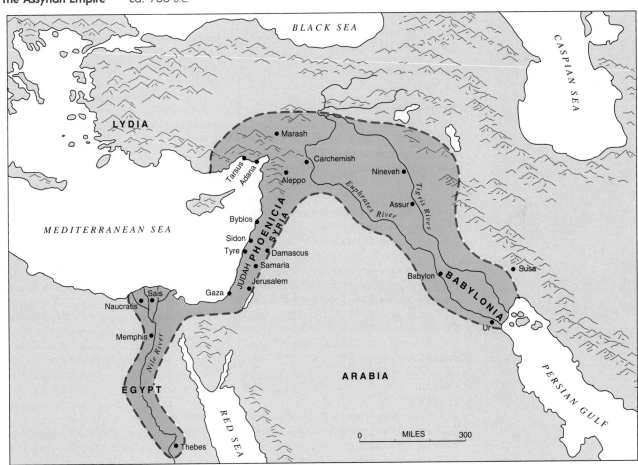

An alabaster relief showing an Assyrian king on a hunt.

The Persian Empire, ca. *549–333* B.C.

The Persians, an Indo-European people, lived on a high plain east of Mesopotamia, where they herded sheep and raised horses. They lived in a loose tribal federation with the Medes and other neighbors. In 549 B.C., Cyrus, an able military leader, set himself up as king (r. 549–529 B.C.) and brought the various tribes together under his leadership. From his headquarters at Ecbatana north of Mesopotamia, he led his forces first against Anatolia (modern Turkey), which he conquered in 543 B.C., thereby gaining access through the Greek cities of the western coast (Ionia) to the rich trade and advanced civilization of the Aegean. In 539 B.C., Cyrus overcame the Chaldean Empire and brought Mesopotamia, Syria, Palestine, and the Phoenician cities under Persian control. His son Darius (r. 529–486 B.C.) conquered Egypt in 525 B.C.

Cyrus created a new type of empire. Under the close supervision of his government, he permitted the conquered peoples to retain their own customs and religions and their own forms of govern-

ment. For example, he permitted the Israelites to return to Judah, reestablish their kingdom, and rebuild their temple. In each territory, a Persian governor and garrison kept the peace and supervised tax collection.

The Persians left a strong mark on the religions of the Mediterranean. The upper classes followed the teachings of the sixth-century prophet Zoroaster, who taught that the world was under the control of two divine powers, one good and one evil. The two were engaged in a battle that would last 6,000 years, and human beings were free to join one side or the other. Those who allied themselves with the god of good would go to paradise (a Persian word), and the others would be consumed by eternal fire. Although Zoroastrianism did not spread beyond Persia, it influenced the religions of the Middle East through the Persian imperial system and had immense historical importance. For example, it was from Zoroastrianism that the Israelites took the concepts of the devil, hell, paradise, and the last judgment.

Persian power was first checked by the Greeks in 490 B.C., at the Battle of Marathon. After a serious defeat by the Greeks in 479 B.C., at the Battle of Salamis, Persia ceased to be the dominant power in the Mediterranean. Nonetheless, the Persian Empire survived in the Middle East until Alexander the Great conquered it in 333 B.C., after which Persia became part of the Hellenistic world (see pp. 49–50). In A.D. 224, a native Persian dynasty deeply devoted to Zoroastrianism overthrew the Hellenistic successors of Alexander and recreated the empire in the Middle East. This empire became a formidable opponent of Rome, which by then had extended its power throughout the Mediterranean (see pp. 76–79). At the beginning of the seventh century, after the Roman Empire had collapsed in the West and become weak in the East, the shah of Persia made a new attempt to establish himself as the greatest power in the eastern Mediterranean. He conquered Anatolia, forced its population to convert to Zoroastrianism, and threatened Constantinople, the capital of the Eastern Roman

The Persian Empire   *ca.* 500 B.C.

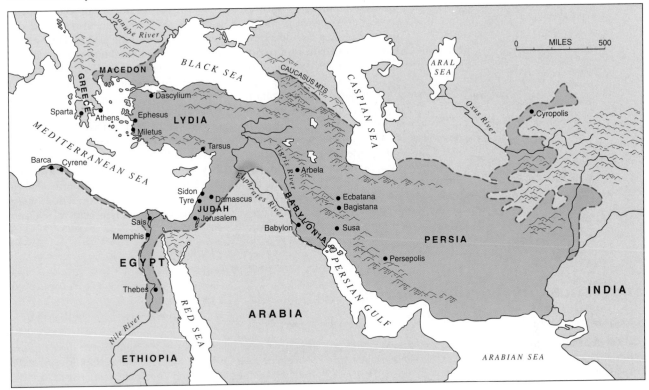

Lydians paying tribute to the Persian emperor Darius I.

Empire. The emperor Heraclius was able to push the Persians out of his territories and to weaken his enemy (see pp. 173–74). The Arabs, galvanized by their new religion of Islam, destroyed the remnant of the Persian empire in A.D. 637 (see p. 199).

Western civilization, the civilization of the Mediterranean Basin and Europe, is the heir of the civilizations studied in this chapter. The inheritance was transmitted to the Mediterraneans and Europeans in many ways, but principally through trade and the Israelites. The Phoenician traders of the Middle East were well known to the people of Crete and Greece, who got their alphabets as well as many other artifacts of middle-eastern civilization from them. Phoenician colonies in the western Mediterranean also spread culture along with trade goods. The Israelite religious and cultural tradition, preserved in the collection of books called the Hebrew Bible, transmitted an amalgam of middle-eastern thought, a selected part of what might be called the cultural point of view of the Middle East. For two thousand years before Europeans discovered early civilization through archaeology, they knew and had absorbed the basic characteristics of middle-eastern civilization through the Hebrew tradition, which was one of the cornerstones of western civilization.

Suggestions for Further Reading

General

On the geography of human habitation, see L. Febvre, *A Geographical Introduction to History* (1924). Excellent maps, with explanatory notes, for this and other chapters, are in *The Times Atlas of World History,* ed. G. Barraclough (1978).

For an overview of prehistory, see G. Clark, *World Prehistory in New Perspective,* 3rd ed. (1977). W. Howells reviews our understanding of human evolution in *The Evolution of the Genus Homo* (1973). No synthetic work has yet incorporated all of the newest discoveries about human evolution, but on the role of climatic change, see Elizabeth Vrba, ed., *Species and Speciation* (1985), and William Calvin, *The Ascent of Mind: Ice Age Climates and the Evolution of Intelligence* (1991). On the Old Stone Age, see K. P. Oakley, *Man the Tool-maker,* 4th ed. (1958), and F. Bordes, *The Old Stone Age* (1968). On climate and the origins of agriculture, see Ofer Bar-Yosef and F. R. Valla, eds., *The Natufian Culture in the Levant* (1991), and Ofer Bar-Yosef and A. Khazanov, eds., *Pastoralism in the Levant*

(1992). On Neolithic culture, see P. Singh, *The Neolithic Cultures of Western Asia* (1974); J. Mellaart, *Catal Huyuk. A Neolithic Town in Anatolia* (1967); and *The Domestication and Exploitation of Plants and Animals,* eds. by P. J. Ucko and G. W. Dimbleby (1969). On the spread of the agricultural revolution, see J. G. D. Clark, *Prehistoric Europe: the Economic Basis* (1971).

On the origins and differentiation of languages, see the provocative work of Joseph Greenberg, *The Languages of Africa* (1966) and *Language in the Americas* (1987).

On the dating of ancient civilizations, see C. Renfrew, *Before Civilization* (1979). For surveys of Old Europe, see S. Piggott, *Ancient Europe, from the Beginnings of Agriculture to Classical Antiquity* (1965), and C. Renfrew, *The Emergence of Civilization: The Cyclades and the Aegean in the Third Millennium* B.C. (1972). On the culture of Old Europe, see M. Gimbutas, *The Goddesses and Gods of Old Europe,* 2nd ed. (1982).

Mesopotamia

A. L. Oppenheim, *Ancient Mesopotamia* (1964), and H. W. F. Saggs, *The Greatness That Was Babylon* (1962), are detailed surveys of Mesopotamian history. For an appreciation of life in the valleys, see J. Hawkes, *Life in Mesopotamia, the Indus Valley and Egypt* (1973), and G. Contenau, *Everyday Life in*

Babylon and Assyria (1954). S. N. Kramer has translated original Sumerian documents in *History Begins at Sumer* (1959) and *The Sumerians* (1963). For the history of Dilmun, see Geoffrey Bibby, *Looking for Dilmun* (1969).

Egypt

On early Egyptian civilization, see W. B. Emery, *Archaic Egypt* (1961). There are two good surveys of dynastic Egypt. Of them, A. H. Gardner, *Egypt of the Pharaohs* (1961), is the more factual,

and J. A. Wilson, *The Culture of Ancient Egypt* (1956), the more interpretative. For a study of Egyptian monuments, see I. E. S. Edwards, *The Pyramids of Egypt* (1975). H. Frankfort, *Ancient*

Egyptian Religion (1958), largely replaces older standard works on this subject, and P. Montet, *Everyday Life in Egypt in the* *Days of Ramses II* (1958), is the counterpart of Contenau's book on Babylon.

Syria and Palestine

Informative studies on the non-Hebrew peoples of Syria-Palestine can be found in E. Anati, *Palestine before the Hebrews* (1963); J. Gray, *The Canaanites* (1964); D. B. Harden, *The Phoenicians* (1962); and R. A. H. Macalister, *The Philistines* (1913). Among the best of the many books on the Hebrews, see J. Bright, *A. History of Israel* (1959); W. F. Albright, *The Biblical Period from Abraham to Ezra* (1963); and A. Lods, *Israel* (1932).

Assyrians, Chaldeans, and Persians

The general histories of Mesopotamia mentioned above discuss the Assyrians and Chaldeans. For studies of the Persians and their subjects, see R. N. Frye, *The Heritage of Persia* (1963), and A. T. Olmstead, *A History of the Persian Empire* (1959).

GREEK CIVILIZATION

During the second millennium B.C., the civilizations of the Middle East became aware of new peoples in the "far west." This region was the Aegean, where an advanced civilization based on trade had grown up on the island of Crete and surrounding islands. As we saw in the last chapter, this civilization borrowed some of its motifs from Old Europe, the Neolithic culture of the Balkans and central Europe. It contributed a great deal, in turn, to Greek civilization, which succeeded it in the Aegean, and the Greeks established the basic characteristics of European civilization.

CRETE AND MYCENAEAN GREECE

Minoan Civilization

The first great civilization of the Aegean—the Minoan civilization—arose on the island of Crete. Minos was the dynastic name of the Minoan kings, and stories of a fabulously rich King Minos and of Perseus's defeat of the bull-man Minotaur found their way into Greek mythology.

By 2000 B.C., the Minoans had achieved a high level of civilization. Their central city, Knossos, on the northern coast of Crete, had a large population and was the site of a magnificent palace. Their commercial economy was so extensive and so complex they were obliged to keep written records of their transactions. Borrowing from the middle easterners, they devised a distinctive syllabic script to serve the purpose. Using clay tablets, they recorded contracts, sales, and bills of lading in a script that archaeologists call Linear A to indicate that it was the first of two scripts used by the Minoans and that it was written in lines. Linear A has not been fully deciphered, but the symbols clearly represent syllables rather than whole

The reconstructed throne room of the palace at Knossos.

words as in pictographic writing. We can often guess at the contents of the tablets by looking at pictographs in the margins that the Minoans used for handy reference.

The Minoans lived in comfortable apartment buildings with indoor showers and flush toilets. The pipes, made of clay rather than metal, were enclosed in the walls and emptied into elaborate sewer systems. The streets were lined with bakeries, smithies, and pottery shops. The partially excavated remains of a few Minoan cities reveal a middle-class society in which, despite the extraordinary wealth of the kings, prosperity was widely shared by the population. People decorated their well-furnished houses with frescoes of human figures and landscapes. Some of the wall paintings depict animals and plants native to the Middle East and the Nile Valley, an indication that this commercial so-

ciety had frequent contacts with those regions. The frescoes also show that women played important roles in Minoan society.

About 1630 B.C., Minoan civilization came to a catastrophic end. The agent of destruction was the explosion of a volcano on the island of Thera, about 150 miles north of Crete. The largest volcanic explosion known in recorded history, it was a hundred times more powerful than the explosion that blew off half of Mount St. Helens in Washington State in 1980. Before the explosion, the island of Thera had risen more than a mile out of the sea; after it, all that was left was a hole more than one-half mile deep surrounded by a remnant of land. The explosion instantly vaporized 50 cubic miles of rock and created a tidal wave that reached 800 feet high along the coasts of Ionia, Greece, and Crete and flooded large areas of the Nile

Delta. Oceanographers have found a layer of ash in the strata of the sea floor. The hot cloud traveled out at hundreds of miles an hour, burned the cities of Crete, and moved eastward. It was still hot when it fell on Egypt, perhaps giving rise to the story of the plague later associated with the escape of the Hebrews (Exodus 9.8).

Survivors of the disaster fled across the sea. The Phoenicians welcomed many of them to their coastal cities, where they entered into commerce. Meanwhile, Greeks from the mainland moved in and resettled some of the old Minoan sites. About this time, Linear B, also a syllabic script, replaced Linear A. An early form of the Greek language has been identified in Linear B inscriptions.

The Minoans devised a distinctive syllabic script: Linear A *(left)* that was later replaced by Linear B *(right)*.

Mycenaean Greece

The Greek homeland embraced the Peloponnesian peninsula, the islands of the Aegean, and the western coast of Asia Minor (modern Turkey), called Ionia. The rocky mountains of the peninsula made communication difficult and favored the settlement of small, independent communities. Across the Aegean Sea, dotted with scores of volcanic islands, the craggy promontories and jagged coast of Asia Minor again favored small, isolated settlements. This was an environment dominated by the sea, and from the earliest days the Greeks were people of the sea.

For more than a thousand years, the small city-states of Greece pursued their independent ways. The communities along the coasts emerged as cosmopolitan societies that absorbed and then surpassed the accomplishments of the Middle East in art and science. Western science, ethics, political thought, aesthetics, and literary criticism all arose from Greek foundations.

Recent excavations on the Greek mainland show that by the sixteenth century B.C., shortly after the destruction of the Minoan cities, the Greeks had developed a sophisticated Bronze Age civilization. Historians call the civilization Mycenaean, from Mycenae, the home city of the Homeric hero Agamemnon (see p. 38).

Deciphering Linear B

Linear B, the script of the Mycenaeans, is found on clay tablets small enough to be held in one hand. The tablets were held in one hand while being written on with the other, and many have finger marks impressed on the back side. The script mixes pictograms, each of which stands for a word, and phonetic signs, each representing a sound.

The scholars who undertook to decipher the script began with a serious handicap—they thought they were dealing with Minoan texts. They could "read" some of the pictograms, such as man, woman, and horse, but they could not tell what language was represented. Then in 1951, amateur scholar Michael Ventris made a breakthrough. He found pairs of words in the texts that he believed represented masculine and feminine forms, and he arranged these in a grid that aligned the words with similar consonants and vowels with one another. If he could find the sound values for some of the signs in some of these words, the grid would help him apply the values to other words. He began to find the sound values when he noticed a group of paired words that seemed to be the names of cities on Crete. He discovered that the names were close to those used by Greeks and he made an analysis of his grid using the sound values that would be true if the language of the tablets was Greek. With this approach, he was able to show that Linear B recorded a form of Greek. Next came the work of understanding the deciphered texts, which required establishing the characteristics of the Mycenaean Greek in which they were written.

The Bronze and Iron Ages

The first metal used was copper, which could be beaten into blades, bowls, and other implements. But copper could not be used for tools used in daily life because it is soft and difficult to melt and cast. The invention of bronze, an alloy of copper and tin, overcame these problems. The hardness of bronze makes it excellent for the manufacture of all sorts of implements, and it can be cast in a multitude of shapes.

The bronze revolution occurred about 3000 B.C. in the Caucasus (the mountainous region between the Black and the Caspian Seas) and in Asia Minor. The emerging civilizations of Mesopotamia and Egypt soon began to adopt bronze, and they completed the transition from stone to bronze by 2000 B.C.

Soon after that, however, bronze became obsolete, as the peoples of Asia Minor learned to use iron. The Hittites were the first Iron Age people, and the rapid expansion of their empire after 1800 B.C. was based on the superiority of iron to bronze. The Indo-European-speaking Celts brought Iron Age culture to Europe (see pp. 8–10).

Mycenaean society was dominated by the petty kings of the towns that had grown up in the fertile valleys of the peninsula. The survival of these communities depended on the strength of their kings, who engaged in constant warfare with one another, and for whom "commerce" included everything from peaceful trade to piracy and looting. Their goals were to accumulate wealth with which to dazzle their followers, to fortify their city against attack, and to demonstrate their greatness by erecting impressive buildings and supporting the arts. The myths dating from these times reflect the feats of these leg-endary figures, who led their people out of barbarism and helped fashion a civilization strongly influenced by the Minoan.

Mycenaean Greek civilization, like the Minoan, was based on cities, each controlled by a princely family. The cities were typically built around an imposing palace positioned on high ground, and the city held sway over a territory with a radius of six to nine miles. The topography of Greece, with its small fertile valleys cut off from one another by rugged mountains, encouraged this pattern of small, independent, princely states.

The palaces were built around the megaron, a spacious room with a large central hearth. The center of the room was two stories high, and an interior balcony around the walls provided space for living quarters. A covered porch led into the megaron, which was surrounded by corridors that opened off the porch. Beyond the corridors were workshops and storerooms. In addition to serving as a residence for the ruling family, the palace housed government offices and industrial and commercial facilities. The palace compound was surrounded by a wall, and the entry porch itself was fortified. The presence of workshops and storage areas in the palaces suggests that the commercial activities of the Mycenaean city-states came under direct control by the kings. Although information about the commercial economy is scanty, we know that Greek traders brought raw materials, particularly metals, from distant places to be processed in the workshops of the palace compounds.

This was a male-dominated society that drew its wealth from trading and raiding. Yet the tablets, on which commercial transactions were recorded, list forty female occupations, mostly connected with the manufacture and sale of textiles. Names of the craftswomen mentioned on the tablets indicate that some were refugees from other societies. Certain crafts were associated with specific towns, and the women who specialized in a particular craft were referred to by such names as "Tinwasian weavers," "Aswian flaxworkers," and "Milesian spinners." Women of the aristocratic class, however, generally

Six royal graves in Mycenae, the city of Agamemnon, leader of the Greeks at Troy.
Photo courtesy of The Granger Collection

The Aegean World   *ca.* 1500–146 B.C.

stayed at home in closely protected quarters.

The Mycenaeans did not build religious shrines, and we have little knowledge of their religion. Nonetheless, the tablets reveal that there were female priesthoods, whose aristocratic members occupied prominent places in the community and who, with their female helpers and servants, exercised control over considerable wealth.

THE SEA PEOPLES, THE TROJAN WAR, AND THE DORIANS

The heroic Mycenaean civilization survived for about 400 years, during which the Greeks became known as traders and mercenaries throughout the eastern Mediterranean. The petty kings of Greece

fought one another and made short-lived alliances, like those that figure in the mythological story of the Seven Against Thebes and the epics of the Trojan War. At one time historians thought that the Trojan War was purely legendary, the invention of the eighth-century B.C. poet Homer, whose epics *The Iliad* and *The Odyssey* recount the story of the war and its aftermath. Scholars now think the war actually occurred some time between 1200 and 1180 B.C.

Nineteenth-century scholars saw little historical value in the Homeric stories, beyond the information they provided about Greek society and religion during Homer's lifetime. Then, in 1870, Heinrich Schliemann, a successful German businessman who was convinced that the Greeks had actually laid siege to Troy, began excavations near the Dardanelles in Asia Minor on a mound traditionally thought to be the site of Troy. To the astonishment of the scholarly world, he discovered layer after layer of ancient cities, one of them a large fortified city that had been destroyed around 1200 B.C. and another older and very rich city that had been destroyed around 1800 B.C. Schliemann thought the older city was the Homer's Troy, but it is likely that the more recent city was the city of Priam and Hector.

Next, Schliemann conducted excavation at Mycenae in southern Greece, the legendary home of the Greek leader Agamemnon. There he found a royal palace

and evidence of a surprisingly advanced Bronze Age civilization dating back to at least 1800 B.C. Most of what we know of Mycenaean civilization is derived from the work of Schliemann and his successors.

At the time of the Trojan War, the eastern Mediterranean was dominated by the so-called Sea Peoples, who subjected the established societies of the region to constant raids and who, according to contemporary records, even engaged in several great sea battles. Presumably the Sea Peoples were residents of the area who took to piracy when the power of the great states—the Egyptians, the Hittites, and the Minoans—began to decline. Many of them were Mycenaean Greeks, and during the thirteenth century B.C. they helped to spread Mycenaean influence throughout the eastern Mediterranean.

Normally, these Mycenaean adventurers operated in small bands led by the petty kings of their city-states, but occasionally they took part in great expeditions led by the major powers. For example, around 1286 B.C., Mycenaean Greeks fought on both sides of a critical battle between the Hittites and the Egyptians.

The Greek bands also formed federations of their own. In 1233 B.C., they entered into a grand alliance with Sicilians, Sardinians, Lycians, and others against the Egyptian pharaoh Merneptah. Such ventures ended with two great naval battles—one between the Greeks and the Egyptians around 1187 B.C. and the other between the Greeks and the Hittites five to ten years later. The Greeks lost both engagements, and their opponents congratulated themselves on their victory over such formidable adversaries.

Greek mythology memorializes many of the events of the last years of the Sea Peoples, particularly the Trojan War, a conflict with a relatively insignificant enemy. Stories of the war were passed down from generation to generation, and in the eighth century B.C., Homer incorporated many of them into his two great epic poems, *The Iliad* and *The Odyssey*. *The Iliad* tells the story of the war itself, of the heroic deeds and clever stratagems that brought down the city of King Priam after a ten-year siege. *The Odyssey* tells of the

Oral Tradition in the Homeric Epics

In an oral tradition of poetry, the poets recite the works from memory. This does not mean that they have memorized poems hundreds of lines long, but that they know the stories and have a collection of memorized poetic elements to use to tell them. The storytelling process is one of relating the action by stringing together the phrases and descriptions from the stock of poetic elements in the poet's repertoire, and repetition of these elements is therefore a basic characteristic of oral poetry.

In the Homeric poems, the remnants of the oral tradition are found in such phrases as "the wine-dark sea" or "the sons of Atreus," which describes the leaders of the Greeks. The poet has whole lines to use for the introduction of characters, such as:

Son of Laertes and seed of Zeus, resourceful Odysseus

which occurs many times in the *Iliad* when Odysseus enters the action. Other traditional elements include the catalog of attributes of the hero, who can run, jump, swim, and fight with magnificent strength, speed, and agility.

Homer constructed from the inherited stock of poetic elements a powerful and wholly new work that expressed the basic moral and social values of the Greeks. The use of writing to record the epics gave the poet the opportunity to fashion the elements of his story more carefully than an oral poet could and gave the poems themselves a permanent existence, which no oral poem could have. These advantages made it possible for the Homeric epics to become classics—that is, works universally recognized as representing in a particularly powerful and complete form the moral, social, and artistic ideas and standards of society.

adventures of Odysseus, one of the Greek leaders, on his long journey home to Ithaca.

An international team of archaeologists is excavating Troy once again, hoping to discover what prompted the Greeks to attack the city in the first place and why many of the twelve cities built one on top another at the site were destroyed. The city lies inland from a natural harbor along the route to the Black Sea through the Dardanelles, the strait between Asia Minor and Europe. The passage is exceedingly difficult; the current runs south at three miles per hour, and a strong north wind blows almost every day of the year. Sailors often took refuge in the harbor, where they might wait for weeks or even months before getting a chance to run the strait. It seems likely that the Trojans exacted a price for allowing them to wait there unmolested. If so, it would not be surprising if from time to time the cities that depended on the Black Sea trade made common cause to destroy what they must have viewed as the pirate kingdom of Troy.

In the historical memory of the Greeks, the Trojan War marked the end of an epoch. The fifth-century B.C. historian Thucydides (p. 56) wrote, "After the Trojan War Greece was in a state of constant movement and was being settled in a way that left her no peace to grow strong again." The returning soldiers had learned new ways during the long years of siege, and while they were away, many of the kings had been displaced at home by usurpers. Thucydides notes that, following civil wars in many of the cities, the losers had left to found new cities elsewhere. He suggests that these troubles were connected with the arrival of a new people who had taken control of the Peloponnesus about eighty years after the war.

The newcomers were Dorians, Greeks from somewhere north of the Greek peninsula. The Dorian migration coincided with the end of the era of the Sea Peoples. The destruction of some cities, like Pylos in Messenia, may have taken place during this incursion, but on the whole the Dorians seem to have settled down peacefully. In fact, the only evidence of their arrival is the presence of writings in the Dorian dialect from a later period.

THE DARK AGE AND ARCHAIC GREECE, *ca.* 1150–500 B.C.

After the decline of the Mycenaean world, the cities of Greece declined both in number and size, and the Mycenaean ruling class gave way to local aristocracies little given to adventure or innovation. During the period from the late twelfth to the eighth century B.C., the Greeks produced no written records and little art or architecture of any significance. Historians call the period the Dark Age and usually blame the decline on the Dorian invasions, though archeological evidence does not support this conclusion.

Actually, Greek society during the Dark Age (roughly 1150–800 B.C.) was quite stable. For hundreds of years, the ruling families patronized minstrels and poets who preserved traditions reaching back to the heroic era of the Sea Peoples, gradually infusing them with universal themes. The minstrels and poets sang of the relationship between the human and divine worlds and between men and women, of admirable humans and despicable humans, of the limits of human wisdom and knowledge, and of the nature of moral and social life. Whatever troubles disturbed society during the Dark Age were not severe enough to cause a break in the cultural tradition.

Around 800 B.C., a revival of trade signaled that the Dark Age was coming to an end. Several cities on the mainland and in Ionia, the western coast of Asia Minor, emerged as commercial centers. Miletus and eleven other Greek cities set up a trading port in the Nile delta, and Miletus itself operated a string of trading posts along the shores of the Black Sea.

The rise of commerce created a sharp increase in population that upset the social balance of many cities. The cities became crowded, and few of them possessed enough farmland to support a large population. Together, the population pressure and the search for new markets encouraged people to move out and settle

A four-drachma coin from Athens showing Athena and her owl (*ca.* sixth century B.C.).

Scene from a Greek vase (*ca.* 550 B.C.) showing merchants weighing produce. As trade routes multiplied, Greek merchants and producers of wine and oil prospered.

Greek Colonies in Mediterranean and Black Seas

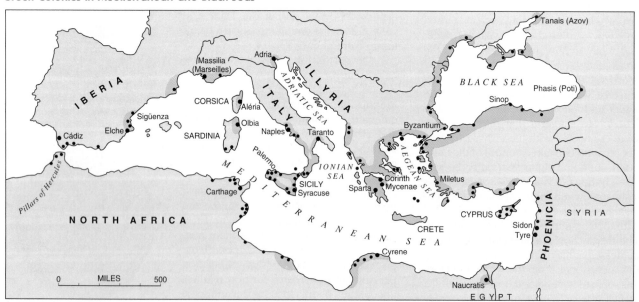

new areas. Greek pioneers ventured into the Black Sea region and into the countries bordering the western Mediterranean. Wherever they went, they founded cities modeled on those they had left behind and also retained their cultural and religious ties with the mother cities. At such places as Byzantium on the Bosporus, Phasis on the eastern shore of the Black Sea, Syracuse and Palermo in Sicily, Taranto and Naples in southern Italy, and along the eastern coast of Spain, the colonists extended the reach of Greek civilization.

The new era, known as the archaic period (800–500 B.C.), began at a time of rising prosperity. In the late seventh century B.C., the invention of coined money, probably in the kingdom of Lydia in Asia Minor, stimulated growth of commerce. Before this, the value of goods had been measured in terms of specific weights of gold and silver, but most of the actual trading had been conducted through barter. Coins were small, standardized pieces of gold or silver stamped to show who had struck them and who guaranteed their weight and content.

Because coins could be used over and over again, they allowed a new kind of trade. Formerly, traders had to trade one product for another and had to transport their trading stocks from market to market. For example, it was common for a merchant who set out to buy luxury goods in a distant port to engage in a series of barters all along the route. First, he would barter in a nearby city whatever goods he had started out with, then he would transport the goods he got in that trade to another city along the route, barter again, and so on all along the way. The successive trades were necessary to pay for his travel expenses and to enable him to make a rapid turnover of his goods, which were often bulky or perishable and could be transported only short distances. But a merchant with a pocketful of coins could travel directly from home to where he could buy the goods he wanted.

But coinage had a cultural significance as well. From early times, the Greeks had sought to possess objects of value that would reflect their personal worth. The prize awarded to the winner of an athletic, poetic, or dramatic contest signified his achievement and therefore his own value. In the story of the Argonauts, associated with Greek expansion into the Black Sea region, Jason had to win possession of the golden fleece, a symbol of royalty, before he could sit on the throne he claimed as his own. Coined money, too, was a sign of value, and "Money makes the man" was an old Greek expression. Even the inscription that identified the person who had issued a coin symbolized his value in society, and eventually emperors and kings claimed the exclusive right to coin money. Even today, the federal government of the United States retains that right as a symbol of its authority.

The Rebirth of Civilization

The economic revival of the eighth century B.C. brought the Greeks, particularly those of Ionia, into renewed contact with the old civilizations of the eastern Mediterranean, and the influence of those civilizations produced profound changes in Greek society. During this period, the Greeks of Ionia adapted the Phoenician alphabet so that it could be used for writing Greek, thereby creating a kind of renaissance of civilized life in the Greek world.

The growth of international trade brought enclaves of foreign merchants to many cities, causing the urban population to become increasingly cosmopolitan. The commercial classes sensed their growing power and began to challenge the authority of the ruling families, and the merchants who came to the cities to buy and sell brought new ideas and new attitudes with them. In a sense, even Homer's great epics of the Trojan War were the results of the new commercial ferment, for in them Homer brought together oral traditions formerly known only in isolated communities.

After Homer, the next Greek poet whose work we have retained was Hesiod, a small landowner who lived in Boeotia in the second half of the seventh century B.C. and who wrote long didactic poems explaining the origins of the gods and describing the life of the farmer-merchant. Life was hard, and Hesiod was cranky. He described his village as "awful in winter, miserable in summer, and no good at any time." And yet he preserved much of what we know of Greek religion and economic life during the archaic period.

Early in the next century, on the Aegean island of Lesbos, Sappho wrote lyric poems that became well known throughout the Greek world and influenced later Roman poets. Her poems, which survive only in fragments, seem to have been written for school girls, and some think Sappho was the mistress of a school for daughters of Ionian aristocrats. A few years later, in the Peloponnesus, where the old, aristocratic-military society remained strong, a Spartan commander named Tyrtaeus (fl. *ca.* 650 B.C.) composed martial songs to inspire his men. Communities throughout the Greek world, from Sicily to the Black Sea, but particularly in Ionia, held poetry contests at regular intervals.

Architecture, too, underwent a revival as many Greek cities rebuilt and enlarged their public buildings. It was during this period that the Greek temple acquired its characteristic design as an oblong building framed by pillars with sculptured figures on the doorposts and along the upper walls. Although early Greek sculpture owed much to Egyptian styles, by the sixth century B.C. the Greeks had created new ways to represent the human figure. They came to depict figures in frontal view, which the Egyptians did not do, and they highlighted the natural form of the human body. At the same time, realistic scenes showing men and women replaced the traditional geometric designs painted on pottery.

THE GROWTH OF THE *POLIS*

Origins

Both the Mycenaeans and the Dorians lived in communities that were utterly under the control of the kings, around whom all political, social, and economic life revolved. As the king fared, so did the community. After the fall of the Mycenaean world, Greek society underwent a gradual change.

During the course of the so-called Dark Age, small, independent communities began to coalesce into city-states, which were more complex and more powerful entities than the old Mycenaean towns. Each city-state (in Greek, *polis;* plural *poleis*) controlled the country around it, including, in many cases, subordinate towns. But what distinguished the *polis* was the idea that it was the common possession of its members, who at the same time were subject to its authority. Even those who controlled the *polis* were subject to its authority, because their power derived from the city-state's constitution.

For a time the *poleis* were governed by aristocratic clans formed during the Dark Age. As a result, the local kings lost much of their authority and became first among equals within the aristocratic class. Although each clan included the extended noble family and its household servants, it enjoyed the support of citizens from all classes. The clan protected lesser families in disputes, lent them money, and helped them arrange marriages, and in return the client families gave the clan their political allegiance.

Each clan (*genos* in Greek) claimed to have descended from heroes or gods, a claim that entitled it to perform religious

Model of the acropolis in Athens with the Parthenon, the temple to Athena, at the center.

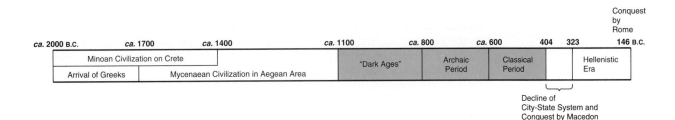

										Conquest by Rome
ca. 2000 B.C.	*ca.* 1700	*ca.* 1400		*ca.* 1100	*ca.* 800	*ca.* 600	404	323		146 B.C.

Minoan Civilization on Crete		"Dark Ages"	Archaic Period	Classical Period		Hellenistic Era
Arrival of Greeks	Mycenaean Civilization in Aegean Area					

Decline of
City-State System and
Conquest by Macedon

functions within the *polis*. The religious life of the clan centered on an ancestor cult, devotion to the gods of the *polis*, and participation in religious ceremonies. Social relations were viewed as part of the religious life of the *polis*, and justice—the regulation of what each person could expect from others and what each owed to others—was negotiated between the clans, with the priesthoods of the *polis's* cults playing the role of mediators.

The clans were keenly interested in matters of family and of succession and of who had the right to participate in religious ceremonies. Each clan, led by the head of its noble family, demonstrated through public expenditures that it deserved its place in society. Thus wealth came to be seen as a requisite for playing the aristocratic role. Public buildings, the equipping of the military, and the sponsorship of festivals and games all depended on the generosity of the aristocrats.

As we have seen, the Mycenaeans had accorded women some measure of independence in society. During the Dark Age, however, the clans relegated women to a subordinate position. The reason, presumably, was to ensure legitimate succession to the positions of leadership. The claim to royal authority in Mycenaean times rested on the certainty that the claimant was the son of the king, and the aristocratic clans adopted that practice to their own society. Women of the lower classes were probably freer than women of the aristocracy, because they had to contribute to family earnings.

This is not to say that all aristocratic women were ignorant and uncultured. Sappho's poetry suggests that girls of the upper classes attended schools to learn literature and music. Moreover, young women were probably expected to contribute to the cultivated society of the aristocratic household and to help with the management of the household as well.

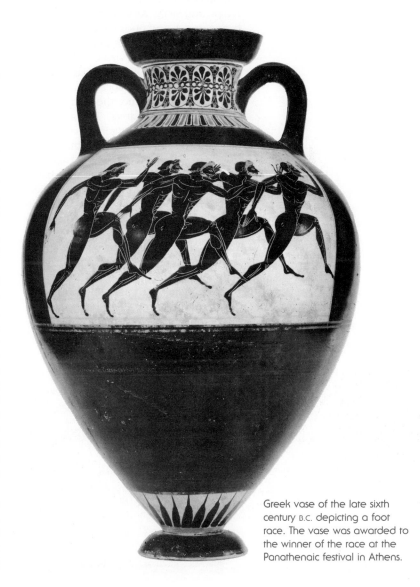

Greek vase of the late sixth century B.C. depicting a foot race. The vase was awarded to the winner of the race at the Panathenaic festival in Athens.

During the seventh century B.C., changes in the social life of the *poleis* affected political organization. Throughout Greece, vast tracts of land were given over to the production of olive oil and wine. Only the landlords with large holdings had the economic wherewithal to produce these commercial crops, because it takes years to bring vineyards and olive orchards to maturity, and the crops must be processed before they can be marketed. The peasants continued to grow grain, but their prosperity was undermined by the import of cheap grain from the Black Sea, Egypt, and Sicily. As time passed, the gulf between rich and poor widened, and traditional values began to erode. The yeoman farmer had been viewed as the ideal citizen of the *polis,* but the decline of that class inevitably led to social conflict.

At the same time, the military was also undergoing change. The armies of the Mycenaeans and their successors in the Dark Age had been little more than disorganized crowds in which each soldier acted pretty much on his own. A battle was a melée in which individual soldiers on one side fought individual soldiers on the other side, and victory was the sum of individual victories. Because speed and agility were all-important, the warriors wore light armor and carried spears and short swords.

Beginning near the middle of the eighth century B.C., soldiers began to wear heavy armor to protect themselves. They added greaves to protect their shins, plate corselets to protect their upper bodies, a closed helmet, and a large round shield (*hoplon*). The complete array had come into use by about 675 B.C., but not until about 650 B.C. were the heavily armed men (called hoplites, from the name of the shield) organized into a new battle formation, the phalanx. In the phalanx, the soldiers were positioned in tightly structured units several rows deep and fought as a coordinated, disciplined troop. The strategy was for each phalanx to attack the opposing phalanx and to force it from the field. In the line, each man held his shield on his left arm to protect his own left side and the right side of his neighbor. Because the man on the right end of the line was vulnerable, the line tended to swing around toward the right as the end man sidestepped to protect his right flank.

The new arrangements had important social effects. The armies of the past had consisted of small bands of lightly armed peasant-warriors led by aristocratic commanders. Once the armies were organized into hoplite phalanxes, the role of the individual soldier was sharply diminished. All citizens who owned a certain amount of land (five acres in the fifth century B.C.) were obliged to serve, and everyone in the phalanx had the same basic role. Order and discipline had replaced heroism and self-assertion.

The Tyrants

All these changes coincided, roughly, with the rise of tyranny, a new type of political leadership that spread from city-state to

Frieze depicting the hoplite phalanx, each man protecting the man on his left.

city-state during the seventh century B.C. Tyranny—the word was probably borrowed from the kingdom of Lydia in Asia Minor, where the king was called "tyrant"—meant the rule of a single man, as opposed to the rule of hereditary kings or an aristocratic oligarchy (the collective rule of the best men). The Greeks seem to have used the term to describe any leader who ruled without regard for the traditional political system of the *polis*. By the archaic period, the king had become the first among equals in the aristocratic oligarchy. He had some limited functions in the cults of the *polis*. By contrast, the tyrant stood outside the traditional power structure.

Some historians believe that tyranny emerged from the hoplite system, but the earliest tyrants rose to power before the phalanx became the basis of the army. Others argue that the tyrants came to power as representatives of the lower class. The fifth-century B.C. historian Thucydides, who was keenly interested in the causes of historical events, thought that tyranny had grown out of the widening disparity between the economic power of the upper and lower classes. Many modern historians agree.

The notion that the tyrants may have represented the lower class is supported by the actions of some tyrants. In many *poleis,* they altered the political structure to give more power to lower-class citizens. Some of the tyrants themselves seem to have come from the lower class.

In any case, the economic changes of the period clearly favored the ascendancy of the tyrants. In many *poleis,* friction had arisen between those aristocrats who had joined the commercial revolution and those who had continued as landed gentry. The economic interests of the two groups were in conflict, and soon a contest broke out for control of the *polis*. In the ensuing turmoil, a tyrant often seized power, sometimes with the support of the citizens, whose livelihood depended on social order.

Many of the tyrants were experienced politicians, some of them capable rulers, and they wooed the lower classes for support. Typically, they sought to weaken the landowning aristocracy and to bring about reforms that favored the urban commercial classes. Still they failed to cope with the social problems caused by economic change, and few of them remained in power for long. The Greeks were suspicious of tyranny, and in the long run the ancient idea that the community is the source of authority reasserted itself.

The Lawgivers

The social and political troubles of the seventh and sixth centuries B.C. also gave rise to the codification of laws in many *poleis*. In the early *poleis,* which were small and stable, everyone was familiar with the customs and laws transmitted through oral tradition. The heroes of the epic poems were exemplars of social values and lived in accordance with the laws.

The archaic period, however, created situations and relationships that were unknown in traditional law, which, having emerged from agricultural society, did not suit the commercial economy. On occasion, even the conservative aristocratic clans supported men who undertook to reform the laws.

The early law codes were rigid and severe; the word *draconian* testifies to the harsh laws imposed by the Athenian Draco, elected chief magistrate in 621 B.C. Later lawgivers were less severe and were more concerned with the welfare of the poor. For example, about 590 B.C. Solon of Athens established laws that eased the burden of debt on small farmers and prohibited enslavement for debt. Solon's code survived a period of tyranny and formed the basis of a new Athenian constitution at the end of the sixth century, and Solon became a heroic figure in Athenian history. Other cities had similar experiences.

The codes of the lawgivers strengthened social order in the *poleis* and altered the course of society and politics. Formerly, changes in the law had occurred through a subtle and hidden process as the law was passed down in oral tradition from generation to generation. Now, changes in the law resulted from conscious decisions of the citizenry, because written law could be altered only by a formal, public act.

The codification of the laws gave law-abiding citizens a sense that they were part of a community, and loyalty to the *polis* became a paramount commitment. The community was now embodied in its law code, its marketplace, and its public buildings. In short, the *polis* became a republic, and *res publicae* (public affairs) became the dominant concern of the citizens. The words "politics" and "political" both derive from the communal life of the *polis*.

The center of the *polis* was its marketplace, the *agora*. There, the citizens carried on their daily business and kept abreast of everything that affected the life of the city. Young men followed their teachers. Politicians argued about public issues. Artisans and artists sought their clients. The *agora* was the heart of the Greek *polis*.

The Social Life of the Polis

Athens is a convenient example of the society and social life of the *polis* at the end of the sixth century B.C.

From the age of seven to fourteen, the Athenian male was educated with his peers in the *palaestra*, where he learned wrestling and other physical arts, and in the *gymnasium*, where he practiced those arts with older boys and men. He would also learn to read and write, study the Homeric poems, and acquire the rudiments of arithmetic. When he reached age seventeen, so long as his father was a citizen and his mother the daughter of a citizen, he would be enrolled in a *deme*, one of the districts of the city. If his family was rich enough to support him, he might continue his education by following one of the teachers who set themselves up in the *agora*. These studies gave him a detailed knowledge of the laws and honed his skills as an orator, which was good preparation for political leadership.

As a citizen, he had the right and the obligation to serve on the jury, in the assembly, and in a hoplite phalanx or on a ship. He could hold public office, own land, and receive free distributions of grain. If he was wealthy, he was privileged to perform "liturgies," public functions of the greatest importance. They required him to organize and pay for festivals; sponsor poetic, musical, and dramatic performances; and command and pay for a *trireme*, the principal warship of the Athenian navy. As in ancient times, a man's social position depended on his generosity in supporting the *polis*, and wealthy citizens took pride in performing such time-consuming and costly services.

By the fifth century B.C., about half of the Athenian population consisted of citizens, their wives, and daughters. The other half was made up of metics and slaves, mostly metics. Metics were foreigners who lived more or less permanently in Athens and controlled manufacturing, banking, and commerce. They were subject to a head tax, could not own a house or land, and had only restricted access to the courts. All metics had citizen patrons who provided them with legal protection and often participated in their economic activities. Metics could serve as oarsmen in the fleet, where they shared the benches with poor citizens, and in times of trouble they could join the forces defending the city. One measure of the status of metics is that the premeditated murder of a metic was equivalent to the unpremeditated murder of a citizen. Both crimes led to exile.

Slaves were common in Greek society, and even families of modest means owned one or two slaves to help with farming or craft work, such as potterymaking or metalworking, necessary for daily life. Wealthy families might have many slaves, some serving in the household, some serving as pedagogues (guardians of the young boys of the family), and some acting as craftsmen. Some slaves took care of the family's business affairs. Slaves at that level might live independently and even put aside enough money to buy their freedom. Freedmen achieved the status of metics.

A few wealthy men kept crews of slaves that they rented out to individuals or to the state. For example, some of the slaves who worked the state's silver mines at Laurium were leased from private citizens. All in all, slaves made possible the life-style of the upper and middle classes of Athens. Although the slaves of Athens ran away fairly frequently, they never revolted, as did the slaves in Sparta and, later, in Rome.

Social life remained the province of the family, specifically the male head of the household. The Greeks of the fifth century B.C. had inherited the idea that the integrity of the family required that the female members be protected and controlled. Moreover, because men viewed females as wanton and more given to sexual desire than males, they saw to it that women stayed at home most of the time. When the women went out, they were accompanied by escorts, usually trusted male slaves.

Virtually all women in Athens were married, and in the marriage ceremony the father of the bride said, "I give you this, my daughter, for the procreation of legitimate children." This meant, apparently, the correct number and gender of children as well as children proven to be of the husband's begetting. Most men wanted two sons, in case one died, and a daughter. They could order any unwanted infants exposed to the elements and left to die.

Most girls were married between the ages of fourteen and eighteen—typically to men twice their age. The bride brought to the marriage as dowry a portion of her father's estate, which the husband managed but was obligated to return in case of divorce. Under Athenian law, women could get a divorce, but men could get one far more easily.

Greek Religion

Religion, like other aspects of Greek civilization, underwent profound changes through the centuries. The religion of Mycenaean Greece appears to have been based on family cults, perhaps related to ancient fertility rites. Through contact with the Minoans and with other civilized peoples of the eastern Mediterranean, the Mycenaeans became familiar with the idea of universal gods and over time created

their own pantheon (group of gods). Later they introduced legendary heroes to the unseen world of the gods. Mythological figures like Heracles, Theseus, and Medea were never regarded as fully divine, but they constituted a link between the human and divine worlds. The shrine of Apollo at Delphi continued to elevate men to the status of heroes, in a kind of sanctification, down to the fifth century B.C.

By the time of Homer, the pantheon consisted of a family of twelve major divinities living on Mount Olympus. As time passed, these gods absorbed many of the place-gods, the local gods revered by agricultural societies since prehistoric times. As a result, each local version of a god in the pantheon was somewhat different from other local versions. For example, the Apollo of Delphi was different from the Apollo of Delos.

Zeus was the ruler of the gods and the wielder of thunderbolts; his sister and wife, Hera, was goddess of women and marriage. Each god held sway over one or two human activities: Ares was god of war; Athena, goddess of wisdom; Demeter, goddess of the harvest; Apollo, god of music and poetry; Artemis, Apollo's twin sister, goddess of the hunt; and Hephaestos, god of fire and metallurgy. Each city had its own divine patron: Athena was revered in Athens. Artemis was the protectress of Sparta. At shrines dedicated to Apollo at Delphi and on the island of Delos, the god communicated with pilgrims through priestesses who went into a trance while the god spoke in their voice. Greeks consulted these oracles (divine prophecies) to learn about the future.

With the emergence of the *polis,* the community took over the practice of religion and transformed it into a civic function. Communal life centered on religious festivals, and people reaffirmed their sense of community by participating in the cult of the *polis*'s divine patron. This centralization of religion, however, revealed that many of the mythological stories of the gods were inconsistent and even contradictory. Those inconsistencies led many educated Greeks to become skeptical in their attitude toward religion

Marble grave relief of a girl with pigeons (*ca.* 450 B.C.).

Athena, goddess of wisdom, protector of the home and the citadel, is shown in this bronze statue in military dress (*ca.* seventh century B.C.).

and toward the community itself. Moreover, once the sacrifices and other religious rites became a function of the community, they lost much of their emotional power. The early family cults had played a direct role in people's lives; they had guaranteed the success of the family and had preserved the cohesiveness of the clan. The civic religion and formal rituals of the *polis* no longer gave people a sense of belonging at a time when the society of the burgeoning cities was itself growing more and more impersonal. The failure of the civic religion to provide a sense of identity was one of the reasons for the rising popularity of foreign mystery cults in Greece during the fifth century B.C. Those initiated into the cults became members of a select group, with secret knowledge and beliefs unknown to the rest of society.

A procession recorded in marble on the Parthenon (fifth century B.C.). The paraders on their way to the Acropolis carry jars containing sacrificial gifts.

THE RISE OF ATHENS AND SPARTA

During the sixth century B.C., Athens was ruled by a succession of tyrants who destroyed the power of the aristocracy. After the last tyrant was overthrown in 510 B.C., the popular leader Cleisthenes put through a program of far-reaching constitutional reforms. He divided the citizens into ten tribes, with each tribe constituting a cross section of the population, rich and poor, rural and urban. From each tribe, 50 citizens were chosen annually by lot to serve on the Council of Five Hundred. The Council prepared proposals that were submitted to the assembly of all the citizens, which had held legislative power in the *polis* from ancient times. The chief civilian and military officers were elected by the assembly; those offices carried no salary and were open only to the wealthy. Thus, Cleisthenes' new constitution created a mixed government with a balance of power between ordinary and aristocratic citizens. As a result, political life in Athens became more vigorous, and virtually every citizen began to take a deep interest in political issues. In the *agora,* argumentation became an art, and education a means of preparing young men for leadership. Every citizen was expected to participate in government and to contribute the best products of his intellect and judgment to the state.

The new constitution was well suited to the commercial society of Athens. The city had a large fleet of ships that plied the Mediterranean trade routes, and its military power rested on its navy, which relied for manpower on poor and rich citizens alike. Although the hoplite phalanx was an aristocratic force, manned by those citizens who could afford the required armor, the navy gave all citizens, and even metics, a role in the military. Participation in the defense of the state strengthened the claim of poor citizens to political participation, which Cleisthenes' reforms recognized.

Founded on the vigorous commerce of the Aegean and beyond and supported by a good agricultural base in its home territory of Attica, Athens became the dominant commercial power of Greece. By the beginning of the fifth century B.C.,

Athens had emerged as the capital city of a maritime empire and the commercial center of a mainland economy.

The history of Sparta was quite different. Originally, Sparta was an agricultural society located on the fertile plain of Laconia, in the southern Peloponnesus. By the early seventh century B.C., under the leadership of an aristocratic oligarchy, it had achieved dominance over its neighbors. About 650 B.C., one of its subject communities rebelled and launched a ferocious war that raged for 50 years. During this struggle, Sparta evolved into a tightly controlled military state. The entire male population of the *polis* became a standing army, and both the society and the economy of the state were organized to support this military force.

Sparta and the communities under its control constituted the state of Lacedaemon. Society consisted of three classes. The men of Sparta, who numbered fewer than 10,000, possessed full political rights and enjoyed full equality among themselves. The citizens of the subject communities managed their own affairs, but they had no say in the affairs of Sparta itself. The serfs, or *helots,* who may have descended from the pre-Dorian population, worked the farmland that supported the citizen-army.

Life in Sparta was rigidly regulated. Boys left home at the age of seven to begin their military training. They entered the army at age twenty and were then allowed to marry. They could not live with their wife until they were thirty, however, and during those ten years, they lived in barracks. They remained liable for military service until they were sixty years old.

By 500 B.C., Sparta controlled most of the Peloponnesus, either directly or through a system of alliances called the Peloponnesian League. The commercial competitors of the Athenians, such as the Corinthians, found natural allies in the Spartan sphere.

THE PERSIAN WARS, 499–479 B.C.

By the middle of the sixth century B.C., the powers of the eastern Mediterranean had decided that the thriving cities of Greece were ripe for conquest. Soon after Cyrus the Great consolidated his Persian Empire, he moved against the wealthy Greek cities of Ionia, and by about 540 B.C. had brought them under control. Now Persia stood as a formidable threat to the Greeks of the Aegean and the mainland. To withstand that threat Sparta and Athens must band together.

The first encounter of the war involved only Athens. In 499 B.C., the Ionian cities rebelled against the Persians, and Athens sent a fleet to assist them. When the rebellion failed, Shah Darius of Persia, son and successor of Cyrus, dispatched an army to punish the Athenians. In 490, a large Persian army sailed across the Aegean and landed north of Marathon, a narrow passage between the sea and the hills. An Athenian army of 11,000 took its stand at Marathon and in one of the great victories of military history defeated the much larger Persian force.

Humiliated by this defeat, Darius decided to stage a full-scale invasion of Greece. He died before he could do so, but in 480 B.C. his successor Xerxes crossed the Dardanelles with over 100,000 men and marched down the Greek peninsula. The small cities in his path quickly declared their neutrality and left the task of defending Greece to Athens and the Peloponnesian League under Spartan leadership.

This time, the Spartans and their allies formed the backbone of the resistance. A small, Spartan-led force of about 6,000 men took its stand at Thermopylae, a narrow pass. Meanwhile, the Athenians led a fleet against the Persian fleet that was supplying the land force. The sea battle was indecisive, however, and the entire force of heroic men at Thermopylae was killed. The Greeks withdrew to the Isthmus of Corinth and the Bay of Salamis, and the Athenians abandoned their city to the Persians, who looted and burned it.

Soon, under the leadership of a farsighted politician named Themistocles, the Athenians had rebuilt their fleet, using income from their silver mines at Laurium. Themistocles saw that the Persians would need their navy to control the hundreds of islands and inlets along the Greek coast and to supply their occupying forces. His

Head of a Spartan warrior believed to be King Leonidas, who commanded the Greek force at Thermoplyae (early fifth century B.C.).

The Persian Wars   499–479 B.C.

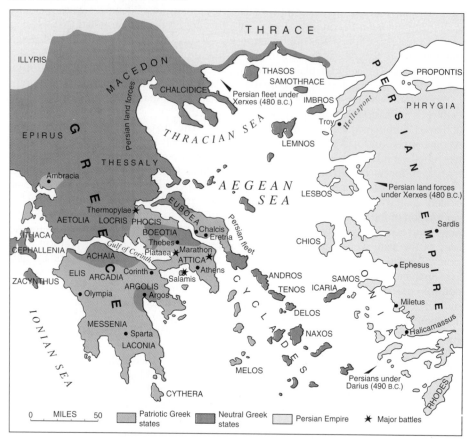

strategy was to destroy the Persian navy. The Greek fleet, which was two-thirds Athenian, defeated the Persians in the Bay of Salamis, and a short time later the Greek army, led by Sparta, defeated the Persians at Plataea (479 B.C.). Later in the year, the Greek fleet utterly destroyed the Persian navy off Ionia.

The Athenians recovered rapidly from the Persian occupation. During the two or three generations before the Persian War, Athens had already succeeded Miletus and the Ionian cities—then under Persian domination—as the principal commercial power of Greece. Its naval successes against the Persians gave Athens control of the Aegean and enabled it to bring the newly independent cities of Ionia into its orbit. The stage was now set for Athens

Phidippides and the Marathon

The Greek armies used runners to carry messages, and Phidippides was the runner at Marathon. After the victory, he was sent to Athens, a distance of 26 miles, with the news. He delivered the message and dropped dead. Phidippides' feat is commemorated in the marathon race, the longest of the Olympic games. To be fair to Phidippides, he had run from Athens to Sparta a few days earlier to inform the Spartans of the Persian landing. Herodotus says that he covered the 150 miles between the cities in two days.

to launch the brief but brilliant classical age of Greek civilization.

THE AGE OF ATHENIAN DOMINATION AND THE PELOPONNESIAN WAR, 478–404 B.C.

The Athenian Empire

During the struggle against the Persians, the Greek cities of the Aegean formed the Delian League, of which Athens assumed leadership. In 478 B.C., the members of the League met on Delos, its headquarters, to plan for defense against any attack by the Persians. They adopted a plan that called for each member to contribute an annual quota of ships or money. Athens dominated the meeting and won the right to name the admiral of the League and to control the League's treasury, which was kept on Delos.

In time, the navy of the Delian League became almost exclusively Athenian—the great majority of the other members chose to contribute money—and the League itself became an instrument of Athenian power. Gradually, most of the member cities became mere dependencies of Athens, and the League's treasury was moved to Athens in 454 B.C. In short, the Delian League had been transformed into a maritime empire under the control of Athens.

Because Athens had been dependent on foreign grain since the time of Solon (early sixth century) and grew only about a third of its own food supply, its survival depended on control of the seas and its sources of supply. Furthermore, its imperial role lent stability to its commercial economy. Finally, empire brought honor to the city.

After the Persian War, Sparta sought to consolidate its leadership of the Peloponnesian League. Although the Peloponnesian League never competed directly with the Delian League for control of the Aegean, it emerged as a countervailing force to the Athenians. Between 454 and 431 B.C., most of the cities that had not yet joined one of the leagues had to decide which one to join, and the Greek world was divided into two great empires.

A tablet, discovered in 1960 (it was being used as part of a doorway in a house), containing Themistocles' decree outlining the evacuation and defense of Athens in 480 B.C.

Athenian Politics

By the middle of the fifth century B.C., the population of Athens had grown to about 100,000, of whom only 20,000 men were citizens with full political rights. The city's new role as an imperial capital put a strain on the old constitution of Cleisthenes, which had been designed for a small city-state.

One example of the constitution's inadequacy was the growing abuse of ostracism, whose original purpose was to guard against the revival of tyranny. If any Athenian seemed to be gathering too much power, he could be exiled for ten years by a majority vote of the citizens. When someone proposed that a citizen be ostracized, those in favor voted by writing the name of the man on a pottery shard *(ostraka)* and depositing it on a pile in the *agora*. If the shards added up to a majority of the citizens, the man was sent into exile.

After a time, demagogues began to bribe the poorer citizens to vote for the ostracism of their political rivals, thus tilting the balance of power between the

Ostraka, or broken pieces of pottery, on which citizens wrote the names of those they wished to ostracize from Athens (*ca.* 470 B.C.). The names on these pieces are Themistocles, who was later recalled, and Cimon.

classes in favor of the lower economic class. In short, demagogic politicians sought to ostracize one another. Archaeologists have discovered "factories" that produced shards, already inscribed with names of competing politicians. In such a political climate, the calm deliberations envisioned by Cleisthenes degenerated into self-serving plots to drive one's opponents out of the city. By the middle of the fifth century, a long political career had become a rarity.

Given this state of affairs, the career of one political leader, Pericles, is remarkable. Pericles (b. *ca.* 495) came from the family of Cleisthenes and rose to prominence as one of the leaders of a campaign to ostracize Cimon, a popular leader in the 460s. From 463 to 429 B.C., he dominated Athenian politics, and for the last fifteen years of his career won annual election to the position of commander in chief as well. It was Pericles who led Athens during its period of high imperialism.

The Peloponnesian War, 431–404 B.C.

The uneasy coexistence of the two great confederations, the Delian League and the Peloponnesian League, was endangered by their economic relationship and by differences of constitution. The cities of the Peloponnesus provided agricultural surplus and a market for the commercial economy of the Delian League, and thus the two leagues had different interests while being dependent on one another. In addition, Sparta and its allies were conservative aristocratic states with oligarchic constitutions while Athens and its dependent city-states were democracies. Conservative *poleis* tended to ally themselves with Sparta, while democracies sided with Athens. Both leagues worked to intervene in the politics of uncommitted cities to bring aristocratic or democratic elements to power.

War between the two leagues broke out in 431 B.C. over a quarrel between Athens and Corinth, a Spartan ally. The issues were control of the colonies of Corcyra (an island off the coast of Epirus in western Greece) and Potidaea (a coastal city on Macedonia's Chalcidice peninsula) and Athens's decision to exclude merchants of Megara, also a Spartan ally, from the markets of the Delian League. In themselves, these issues were of little concern to both Corinth and Megara, but they loomed large because they followed a series of similar imperialistic actions by Athens.

Pericles' strategy was to abandon the rural areas around Athens, bring the farmers and their families inside the city walls, and rely on the navy to keep the sea lanes open for supplies. The Peloponnesian League had only small naval forces—mostly Corinthian. But in the second year of the war (429 B.C.), a plague broke out in Athens, perhaps as a result of the crowded conditions, and many Athenians died, including Pericles. No subsequent leader achieved Pericles' political power, and the city had no consistent policy or plan of action. Nonetheless, Athens forced Sparta to make peace in 421 B.C.

The peace was soon undermined by the unstable state of politics in Athens. Promises by politicians seeking popular support to open a new war with Sparta led to renewed hostilities. This time, the Athenians took greater and greater risks as competing politicians tried to curry favor by taking bold military action. Finally, they staged a disastrous attack on Syracuse, a great city on Sicily and an ally of Sparta, between 415 and 413 B.C. This failed adventure nearly destroyed Ath-

ens's naval power and brought the temporary collapse of the Athenian democracy. In 411, an aristocratic oligarchy seized power in Athens and opened peace negotiations with Sparta. The oligarchs also hoped to get military support from Persia, which was still the principal force in the eastern Mediterranean and which had maintained its keen interest in Greek affairs. Within the year, however, a popular revolution restored democratic government in Athens, and the war was renewed. A string of losses, culminating in a naval defeat in 405, forced Athens to surrender to Sparta in 404. But by 370 B.C. Athens and other cities had thrown off Sparta's control, and Sparta was too weak to resist.

The Peloponnesian War   431–404 B.C.

Delian League

Peloponnesian League

Neutral Greek States

THE CLASSICAL CIVILIZATION OF GREECE

The classical age of Greek civilization lasted little more than a century. It began in the early 470s and ended by the middle of the fourth century. Centered in Athens, its first manifestations were in architecture, sculpture, and drama; its last were in philosophy.

Architecture and Art

When the Athenians returned to their ruined city after the Persian War, they undertook a massive rebuilding program. The multitude of construction projects attracted architects, artists, and craftsmen from all over the Greek world. The Athenian festivals became showcases of dramatic poetry and music, and teachers of all sorts appeared regularly in the *agora*.

After coming to power, Pericles took control of urban renewal. He put his friend, the sculptor Phidias, in charge of the building program to ensure that the new public edifices and temples would be adorned with art of the highest order. The centerpiece of the plan was the Acropolis, the citadel of Athens, on which the major religious shrines and public buildings were erected. Dominating the Acropolis was the Parthenon, an enormous temple dedicated to Athena, and one of the most impressive structures of Western civilization.

Back in the sixth century B.C., as we have seen, Greek sculptors had discarded the ancient Egyptian style of sculpture and had begun to represent living forms in great detail. Led by Phidias, the sculptors of fifth-century Athens sought to represent the human body in ideal form. They saw no conflict between the real and the ideal. For them, art represented the perfection of the world as it is and provided an edifying picture of the ideals of form and action.

The Parthenon, covering an area nearly as large as a modern football field, was the crowning achievement of classical Greek architecture. The structure was a model of proportion and grace, and Phidias himself executed the sculptures. The reliefs that formed a frieze along the sides of the temple represented processions, athletic contests, and military exercises, incorporating both secular and religious themes.

Drama and Music

Greek drama grew out of religious festivals in which choruses sang poetic chants and danced as they sang. From at least the archaic period, festivals had served as occasions for poetry contests; the winners became famous men whose names are still known, though their poetry has been lost. By the late sixth century B.C., the festivals, particularly the festival of Dionysus, god of wine and revelry, had taken on a dramatic aspect with the introduction of a lead singer, who sang a story, accompanied by the chorus of singers and dancers. Poets composed dramatic works for the festivals, with a prize going to the best one. Each poet wrote three plays—a trilogy—all performed, sometimes with the poet playing the lead, in a single day.

At first, all the plays were tragedies in which poetry, music, and dance combined to tell the mythical stories from the heroic age of Greece. They explored the limits of human knowledge and power and the tragic conflict of fate with human aspirations. They dealt with the flaws inherent in human beings, the impossibility of living the perfect life, and the unpredictable consequences of one's actions. Beginning in the early 480s, a comedy, an old folk form of theater, was sometimes performed after the tragedies. Eventually, comedy developed into a genre of its own, with its own festival and competition.

The earliest festival dramas were performed in the *agora* with a wagon serving as the stage and with the audience sitting on wooden bleachers. Then, some time in the 460s, after the bleachers collapsed during a performance, the festival was moved to the shrine of Dionysus on the lower reaches of the Acropolis. An area at the foot of the hill was cleared and leveled to serve as a stage, and wooden seats were built in a hollow on the hillside. Finally, about 440, Pericles had the original structure replaced with a stone structure that contained a stage house for the

The Parthenon at Athens.

The theater at the foot of the
Athenian acropolis (restored).

actors that could also provide a support for the painted scenery.

Three of the tragedians famous in the Athenian theater—Aeschylus (525–456 B.C.), Sophocles (*ca.* 496–406 B.C.), and Euripides (*ca.* 480–406 B.C.)—created the foundations of Western drama. Aeschylus introduced a second lead actor in his tragedies to augment their dramatic possibilities. His *Oresteia,* the only trilogy to survive intact, tells the story of what happened to the family of Agamemnon, leader of the Greeks at Troy, after he returned home. His wife, who had taken a lover, murdered Agamemnon in his bath, and his son, Orestes, avenged his father by killing his mother. In the last play of the trilogy, the gods argue over whether Orestes' action was justified and at last agree to rehabilitate him at Athens. As a whole, the trilogy demonstrates that human beings are sometimes trapped in paradoxes, in which actions are neither altogether right nor altogether wrong. It also reveals the tendency of tragedians to link the ancient traditions to Athens, the center of Greek culture.

We have only a tiny fragment of the work of these dramatists. Sophocles wrote 123 plays during his long career, of which only seven survive. We have six by Aeschylus and only 17 by Euripides. We know the names of a few other dramatic poets, but we have nothing at all of their work. Aristophanes (*ca.* 448–*ca.* 380 B.C.), the leading writer of comedies, often lampooned contemporary politicians and their politics.

Greek Historians

Herodotus of Halicarnassus in Ionia (*ca.* 484–420 B.C.), who spent a good deal of time in Athens and was a friend of Sophocles, wrote a history of the Persian War, including the events at Marathon and Thermopylae. Herodotus saw the Persian War as the culmination of a struggle between the Greeks and the peoples of the Middle East for domination of the Mediterranean. He had traveled widely in the Middle East as a merchant and everywhere had picked up local lore. He wrote a history of the Persian War, and in an effort

to explain the background of the enemy he wrote a series of historical works in which he set down what he had learned about the peoples of the eastern Mediterranean. Later librarians organized these writings into a single work of nine books.

Thucydides (*ca.* 460–400 B.C.), an Athenian, wrote the history of the Peloponnesian War. Thucydides had served as a general in 424, but because he failed to protect an important city on the border of Macedonia and Thrace, he was exiled from Athens for twenty years. Before this setback, Thucydides had been preparing to write a history of the war, "believing," as he said, "that it would be a great war, and more worthy of relation than any that had preceded it." The enforced leisure of the exile gave him time to write that history and an opportunity to stand back and view the war objectively.

Thucydides thought that the Athenians's relentless pursuit of power had threatened the Spartans and their allies and that, so long as Athens pressed its imperialist aims, the Spartans would have to react. The specific causes of the conflict, the disputes over Corcyra and Potidaea, were not significant; they were only the sparks that ignited the tinder.

Thucydides wrote a history of very recent times, which made it unlike previous histories, including that of Herodotus. Moreover, he told the story through historical personages, creating a drama—what we might call a docudrama—in which the characters themselves explain their policies and the decisions they made. This was his way of conveying what he believed was the objective truth about the war and its causes. In his commitment to the truth he followed the method historians still respect:

With reference to the narrative of events, far from permitting myself to derive it from the first source that came to hand, I did not even trust my own impressions, but it rests partly on what I saw myself, partly on what others saw for me, the accuracy of the report being always tried by the most severe and detailed tests possible. My conclusions have cost me some labour from the

Sophocles, popular fifth-century playwright.

want of coincidence between accounts of the same occurrences by different eyewitnesses, arising sometimes from imperfect memory, sometimes from undue partiality for one side or the other. The absence of romance in my history will, I fear, detract somewhat from its interest; but if it be judged useful by those inquirers who desire an exact knowledge of the past as an aid to the interpretation of the future, which in the course of human things must resemble if it does not reflect it, I shall be content. In fine, I have written my work, not as an essay which is to win the applause of the moment, but as a possession for all time. *

For obvious reasons, Thucydides is considered the father of history. His reference to the lack of romance in his history may be a swipe at Herodotus, who provided romance aplenty and who was quick to believe whatever his informants told him.

Thucydides observed the rule of chronography, the precise determination of the dates of past events, a discipline first practiced in the sixth century B.C. Chronography was based on the regular four-year cycle of the Olympiad, the athletic contest in honor of Zeus, held for the first time in 776 B.C. Fragments of the works of the chronographers preserved in later writings have enabled modern historians to establish the chronology of many ancient events.

Philosophy

From the Egyptians and Babylonians, the Greeks learned the rudiments of astronomy and mathematics. Originally, these subjects had been valued for their usefulness in practical matters, but the Greeks turned them to intellectual ends. For the Greeks, astronomy and the science of numbers raised questions about the nature of the world, and by the early sixth century B.C. they had begun to propound theories to explain such phenomena as matter, time, and the changes observed in

* *The Complete Writings of Thucydides,* ed. by J. H. Finley, Jr., New York: Modern Library, 1951, pp. 14–15.

physical existence. In 585 B.C., Thales of Miletus had accurately predicted a solar eclipse, demonstrating that mathematics was more reliable than myth in explaining the mysteries of the cosmos. Speculation about the history and structure of the earth was a favorite pastime among the educated classes, and by the fifth century there were many competing theories.

As the cultural center of greater Greece, fifth-century Athens attracted a great many intellectuals, and it became fashionable among the upper classes to patronize teachers and thinkers as well as artists and architects. The teachers in particular were interested in politics and instructed their pupils in rhetoric, the art of argumentation, along with other subjects.

Among the teachers of rhetoric were the so-called sophists, who concentrated exclusively on technique and concerned themselves not at all with content. Some citizens regarded the teachings of the sophists as irrelevant and downright dangerous. The real questions, they insisted, were: What policies should guide the state? What were the duties of a citizen? Out of such criticism arose a new concept of intellectual life: philosophy—the love of wisdom, the pursuit of truth.

The first philosopher of note was Socrates (469–399 B.C.), a harsh critic of the sophists who sought to define the duties of the citizen and who devised a method for searching out the truth. He spent his days in conversation with anyone who would talk to him, asking simple questions about what they knew of such matters as love, justice, and the good. Aristophanes, a good friend of Socrates, ridiculed him in *Clouds* (423 B.C.), in which Socrates describes himself as walking "on air considering the sun." "I never understand things in mid-air, except by mingling my intellect and subtle thought with air, which is the same," he says. To some, Socrates must have appeared a charming crank; others saw him as a threat, for he exposed shoddy thought and argument even when it was cleverly presented.

Socrates left no written works. Yet he made a powerful impression on the youth of Athens, who delighted in his challenge to conventional wisdom and pomposity

Socrates, statuette from the Hellenistic period.

Plato (426–347 B.C.), Socrates'
pupil.

as they followed him about the *agora*. The more serious of the young aristocrats recognized him as the personification of philosophy, the search for truth.

Unfortunately, some of those young aristocrats took part in the oligarchic revolution of 411 B.C., and Socrates was suspected of having encouraged them. He seems to have escaped prosecution at the time, but in 401 another faction tried once more to replace the democracy with an oligarchy. This time Socrates was accused of corrupting the young of the city, and in 399 a citizen-jury condemned him to death.

The trial and death of Socrates were described in reports by two of his young followers, Xenophon (*ca.* 430–*ca.* 355 B.C.) and Plato (426–347 B.C.). Plato's account is presented in a series of dramatic dialogues in which Socrates defends himself before the jury and then, while awaiting death in prison, discusses with his friends the question of whether he has an obligation to obey the sentence or would be justified in escaping with their help. He argues that he must obey because he owes his identity as a civilized man to the *polis.* The dialogue form, which Plato used throughout his long career, and which he probably invented, wedded drama with philosophy. In all his works, Plato used the voice of Socrates to develop his arguments, and only in the early dialogues does he portray Socrates as a real-life person.

Plato was related to the man who had led the aristocratic rebellion of 411, and after Socrates' death he went into exile. We know he was in Syracuse in 387, after which he returned to Athens to set up a teaching institution near the ancient shrine of Akademos, just outside the city's walls. The school came to be called the Academy, and it was there that Plato spent forty years writing a series of philosophical works that he published as dialogues. In the course of this work, he explored the notion that the moral, political, or physical aspects of the world are only manifestations of ideas that exist eternally in the unseen world of the gods. In this view, called idealism, such objects as tables and chairs are the particular, temporal mani-

festations of the idea or form of table and chair. What we see in the world, Plato said, is but a dim reflection of true, unchanging reality, which is the reality of ideas. The philosopher studies mutable, visible things to learn the nature of immutable, invisible reality. Plato's greatest work was the *Republic,* a long dialogue in which he explores the ideal *polis,* which is ruled by a philosopher-king.

Among Plato's students during the last twenty years of his life was Aristotle, a brilliant young man who eventually succeeded him as head of the Academy. In the age-old pattern of students, Aristotle (384–322 B.C.) came to view his master's work as essentially wrong. Aristotle viewed the objects of this world as real, not as manifestations of unseen forms, and therefore as worthy of careful study for their own sake. For Aristotle, the aim of philosophy was to discover general principles or modes of behavior or patterns of organization. He took an interest in zoology and botany, trying to categorize and order the natural world. He wrote a work on physics in which he sought to describe the universe and how it originated. He sent students all over the Greek world to do descriptive studies of political constitutions—158 in all—and used the data to write a general work on politics that has influenced political theorists from his day to ours. He set the foundations of literary criticism in his *Poetics,* in which he analyzed the great tragedies of the preceding century. Finally, he worked out a method of rational inquiry in a series of treatises on logic that has dominated Western intellectual practice ever since.

In his own time, Aristotle's influence was not limited to the students of the Academy or the readers of his works. He also played a role in the upbringing of the most important ruler of his age. Born in Macedonia, Aristotle had a connection to the royal family of the kingdom, and in about 340 B.C. King Philip appointed him to tutor his son Alexander. Following on his father's success in dominating the mainland Greek city-states, Alexander would soon bring the whole Greek world into his power and spread the influence of Greek culture through the most spectacular series of conquests the ancient world ever saw. To understand Alexander's achievement, we need to follow the history of fourth-century Greece.

THE GREEK WORLD IN THE FOURTH CENTURY B.C.

In 404–403 B.C., Sparta, after its victory over Athens, had placed its representatives in cities throughout Greece, but almost immediately many of the cities had asserted their independence and thrown the representatives out. The Persians, still the dominant power in the eastern Mediterranean and still keenly interested in Greek affairs, encouraged the Greek cities in their struggle against Spartan control. With a provincial capital at Sardis, less than 100 kilometers from the Ionian coast, the Persians remained a factor in Greek politics throughout the fourth century B.C.

While Sparta tried to maintain its hegemony in Greece, new leagues of cities arose in Boeotia, Ionia, and elsewhere to challenge Sparta's power. In 395, Thebes (the leading city of the Boeotian League), along with Athens, Argos, and Corinth, joined in a war against Sparta. Both sides appealed for help to the Persians, who finally threw their support to the Spartans. In 388 B.C., King Artaxerxes II of Persia (404–359/58 B.C.) brought about peace through a treaty that preserved the Peloponnesian League and Sparta's area of control while guaranteeing autonomy to all the other Greek cities. The treaty therefore limited both Sparta's power and that of its major enemies, because it guaranteed the autonomy of the cities on which they had relied for support. Most important, the treaty imposed a common peace on all regions and cities of Greece. Until that time, treaties had settled conflicts only between certain states or leagues.

Between 385 and 378 B.C., however, Sparta violated the treaty by intervening forcefully in the affairs of several cities. In 378, Athens reacted by organizing the Second Sea League (the Athenian-led league, disbanded in 388, had been the First Sea League) in which the member

Aristotle (384–322 B.C.), pupil of Plato and organizer of Greek thought.

cities stood on an equal footing consistent with the treaty of 388 B.C. By the middle of the century, however, Athens had subordinated some of its allies. Finally, Greece was split up into several leagues, of which the most important were the Peloponnesian League, the Second Sea League, and the Boeotian League. Greek politics became a welter of alliances, wars, and peace conferences, usually influenced by the meddling Persians.

Philip II of Macedon (359–336 B.C.), the king who had appointed Aristotle tutor to his son, took advantage of this situation to expand his power to Greece. Like the Persians, he interfered in Greek politics—countering the ambitions of some cities while protecting other cities. By 354 B.C.,

Greek coin bearing the likeness of King Philip, conqueror of Athens.

he had gained access to the Aegean, and in the next decade he pushed east into Thrace and west into Epirus. By the late 340s, he had won control of Thessaly.

Philip's aggressive behavior posed a severe threat to the major Greek cities. Once established in central Greece, he insinuated himself into the affairs of the great shrine of Delphi, which was administered by an ancient league of Greek cities. In Thessaly, he challenged the power of the Boeotians. In Thrace, he threatened to cut off Athens's vital supply of grain from the Black Sea. Thrace controlled the Bosporus and the Propontis, the sea passage to the ports from which, once a year, a great Athenian fleet of some 200 ships fetched supplies of grain. In Thrace, Philip also challenged the Persians, who were now in alliance with Athens. In 340 B.C., when Philip at last gained control of the Propontis, he seized the Athenian grain fleet, precipitating war with Athens. For the next two years, he campaigned against the Athenians and their allies and in 338 defeated them decisively.

Philip dictated the treaty that ended the war. But the Athenians retained their fleet—the largest in the Aegean—and, though the Second Sea League was disbanded under the treaty, Athens held on to some of its overseas possessions. The treaty gave Philip great advantages elsewhere, enabling him, for example, to install garrisons in many cities to preserve the peace. From this time on, although the Greek cities remained independent and continued their habit of shifting from one alliance to another, the Macedonians dominated Greece. They kept a close watch on events in Greece and intervened when it suited their interests, but otherwise they left the Greeks to their political games.

Alexander the Great, 336–323 B.C.

Philip was assassinated in 336 B.C. and was succeeded by his 20-year-old son, Alexander. The young king was conceited, overbearing, undisciplined, temperamental, charming, and brilliant. His soldiers idolized him. He typified the heroic commander, always out in front,

exposing himself to danger, and stirring his men to victory. Philip had been a patient schemer, but Alexander was brash and mercurial and carried all before him.

Alexander embraced his father's plan to unify Greece and to lead a Greek-Macedonian army against the Persians. In 334 B.C., he led an army across the Hellespont to Asia Minor, launching a career in which he proved himself to be one of the great military geniuses of history. After defeating one Persian force, he proceeded to Syria and defeated a second one, led by the king himself (333 B.C.). Next year, he conquered Egypt. There, he founded the city of Alexandria, which was destined to become one of the great cities of the Mediterranean world. Following ancient tradition, the Egyptian priests declared Alexander the son of the god Amon, and Alexander incorporated a claim to divinity into his political propaganda.

After winning control of the eastern Mediterranean, Alexander defeated the remnants of the Persian army and declared himself king of Persia. The East was now open to him, and he marched north through the Transoxiana into Turkestan, on the eastern boundary of the Persian Empire. From this crossroads of the Eurasian continent, he led his army into the Indus Valley in the northwest corner of India, campaigning there in 327–326 B.C. and forcing the local rulers into an alliance with him. We know of two Greek cities he built there, but before he could continue his conquest of the East his army mutinied and he had to turn back.

Alexander's military conquests were motivated by a grand plan for creating a great Greek empire. Throughout the territories he conquered, he planted Greek colonies and encouraged the colonists to marry into the local population. Alexandria in Egypt was the most successful of these new centers. Throughout the growing empire, the Greek language and Greek culture were the rule. Alexander hellenized the upper classes of Egypt, Mesopotamia, Persia, and northwest India by encouraging them to accept Greek language and culture, and for 800 years Greek civilization prevailed among the

Idealized statue of Alexander, probably the work of an artist of Pergamum in Asia Minor.

Alexander's Empire   336–323 B.C.

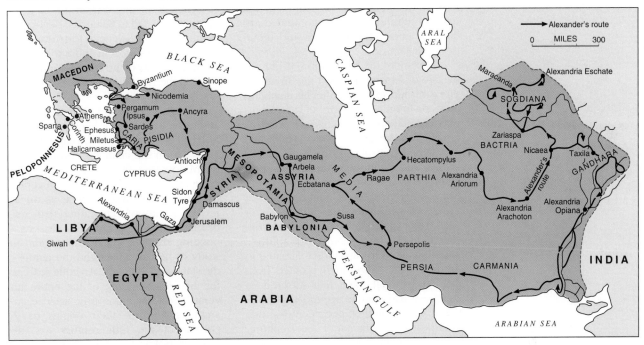

The Partitioning of Alexander's Empire   ca. 300 B.C.

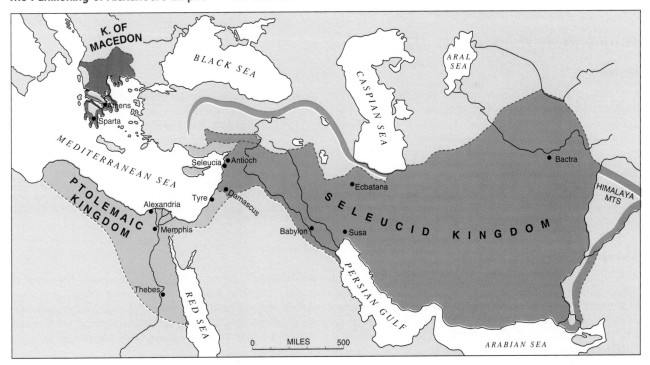

political and cultural elites of the Middle East. It did not, however, supplant the native cultures, which continued to flourish among the peasants and urban lower classes.

Alexander died of fever in 323 B.C., at the age of 33, and his great dream of empire vanished with him. After his death, his generals fought for control of the various regions and soon were calling themselves kings. The kingdoms they established maintained control over the native populations and continued Alexander's program of hellenization. Macedon, under Antigonus, retained its domination over the Greek peninsula, but its power over Asia Minor and the Balkans steadily declined. In Egypt, Ptolemeus established himself as king in Alexandria. Situated in the Nile delta, Alexandria profited from the international trade that Alexander's conquests had opened up, and its population reached a million people. Alexandria became a leading center of Greek culture, and its library became famous throughout the Mediterranean world.

The old Persian territories, which stretched from the Mediterranean to the Indus Valley, fell to Seleucus. Beyond the Hindu Kush, the Seleucids lost the territory Alexander had won in India to the new Maurya dynasty of the Ganges Valley, who created the first Indian empire.

The Greeks of the classical age created a new version of human society, of political entities, and of the natural world. Drawing on the centers of civilization in the Middle East, they transformed the ancient world view. From the sixth century B.C. on, they viewed science as an approach to knowledge rather than as a practical aid in tracking the seasons or building shrines. Socrates pioneered the study of human affairs and the nature of the state, and Plato and Aristotle searched for an understanding of the entire universe. Western philosophy, science, and architecture trace their origins to the Greece of the fifth century B.C., and modern political systems are based on Greek models.

Suggestions for Further Reading

General

J. B. Bury, *A History of Greece,* rev. ed. by R. Meiggs (1975), is the most comprehensive history of the ancient Greeks. A. A. Andrewes, *The Greeks* (1967), and F. J. Frost, *Greek Society* (1972), are interpretive works. Complete texts of all the Greek writers are available in the *Loeb Classical Library.* For Herodotus and Thucydides, see Herodotus, *The Persian Wars,* trans. G. Rawlinson (1942), and *The Histories,* trans. A. de Sélincourt (1954); Thucydides, *The Peloponnesian War* (1951).

The Mycenaean Era and Dark Age

On Bronze Age and Minoan civilization, see E. Vermeule, *Greece in the Bronze Age* (1964), and L. R. Palmer, *Mycenaeans and Minoans* (1965). See also A. E. Samuel, *The Mycenaeans in History* (1966). For the period of the Trojan War, see D. L. Page, *History and the Homeric Iliad* (1959).

The Greek World from 800 to 500 B.C.

A. R. Burn, *The Lyric Age of Greece* (1960), presents a detailed history of the politics and literature of Archaic Greece. See also M. I. Finley, *The World of Odysseus* (1954). On the Greek cities of Ionia and of Sicily and Italy, see J. M. Cook, *Greeks in Ionia and the East* (1962), and A. G. Woodhead, *Greeks in the West* (1962). On the political development of Greece in this period, see H. Michell, *Sparta* (1952); A. A. Andrewes, *The Greek Tyrants* (1965); W. G. Forrest, *The Emergence of Greek Democracy* (1966); and A. Lintott, *Violence, Civil Strife and Revolution in the Classical City: 750–330 B.C.* (1982). In general, see R. Sealey, *A History of the Greek City States, 700–338 B.C.* (1976).

The Fifth Century B.C.

Recent studies of the Persian Wars include A. R. Burn, *Persia and the Greeks* (1962), and C. Hignett, *Xerxes' Invasion of Greece* (1963). On Athens in the Golden Age, see C. A. Robinson, *Athens in the Age of Pericles* (1959); V. Ehrenberg, *From Solon to Socrates* (1968); and W. R. Connor, *The New Politicians of Athens* (1971). On the economic life of the period, see M. I. Finley, *The Ancient Economy* (1973), and K. D. White, *Greek and Roman Technology* (1984). For a comprehensive history of the Peloponnesian War, see B. W. Henderson, *The Great War Between Athens and Sparta* (1927), and D. Kagan, *The Origins of the Peloponnesian War* (1969), *The Archidamian War* (1974), and *The Peace of Nicias and the Sicilian Expedition* (1981).

Social History

For the social history of Greece, see the studies in M. I. Finley, *Studies in Ancient Society* (1974); S. B. Pomeroy, *Goddesses, Whores, Wives and Slaves: Women in Classical Antiquity* (1975); M. Balme, "Attitudes to Work and Leisure in Ancient Greece," *Greece and Rome* 31 (1984) 140–52; J. C. Billigmeier and J. A. Turner, "The Socio-economic Roles of Women in Mycenaean Greece," *Women's Studies* 8 (1981) 3–20; E. S. Stigers, "Sappho's Private World," *Women's Studies* 8 (1981) 47–63; and S. G. Cole, "Could Greek Women Read and Write?," *Women's Studies* 8 (1981) 129–55. For a general study of Athenian society in the classical age, see J. W. Roberts, *City of Sokrates* (1984).

Art, Literature, and Drama

For a thorough history of Greek literature, see G. Murray, *The Literature of Ancient Greece* (1956); A. Lesky, *A History of Greek Literature* (1966); and P. E. Easterling and B. M. W. Knox, eds., *The Cambridge History of Classical Literature,* Vol. 1, *Greek Literature* (1985). For a brief account, see P. Levi, *The Pelican History of Greek Literature* (1985). For an introduction to Greek art, see J. Boardman, *Greek Art* (1964), and G. M. A. Richter, *A Handbook of Greek Art* (1974). For an exhaustive history of Greek philosophy, see W. K. C. Guthrie, *A History of Greek Philosophy* (6 vols., 1962–81); more briefly, see H. D. Rankin, *Sophists, Socrates and Cynics* (1983). On science, see B. Farrington, *Greek Science* (rev. ed. 1961); G. E. R. Lloyd, *Early Greek Science: Thales to Aristotle* (1970); E. D. Phillips, *Greek Medicine* (1973). For an interpretation of Greek religion, see E. R. Dodds, *The Greeks and the Irrational* (1951).

Alexander the Great

The principal ancient sources on Alexander the Great are the *Anabasis* by Flavius Arrian and a much later biography by Plutarch, of which there are many editions. The standard biography of Alexander is U. Wilcken, *Alexander the Great* (1932), but see P. Green, *Alexander of Macedon: A Historical Biography* (1974), and E. Badian, "Alexander the Great and the Greeks of Asia," in *Ancient Society and Institutions* (1966), and R. M. Errington, "Alexander in the Hellenistic World," in *Alexandre le Grand: Image et Réalité,* ed. E. Badian (1976).

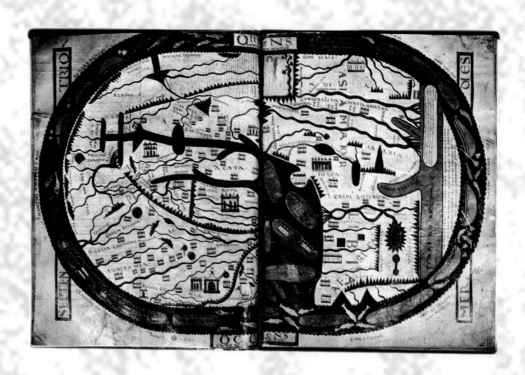

HELLENISTIC CIVILIZATION, ROME, AND THE MEDITERRANEAN WORLD

With the death of Alexander the Great in 323 B.C., the vast empire he had created began to fall apart, and for a time the eastern Mediterranean was a scene of political fragmentation. By 200 B.C., however, the Persian Empire, Egypt, Asia Minor, and the combination of Macedonia and Greece had come to dominate the region. The Macedonian rulers of these successor states, aware that their survival depended on continuing the program of hellenization that Alexander had begun, had, within a relatively short time, hellenized the upper and middle classes.

And yet, despite the ambitions of those rulers and the pervasiveness of Hellenistic civilization, the next great imperial power arose, not in the eastern Mediterranean, but in the West. A little more than half a century after Alexander's death, Rome, a small city-state in south-central Italy, had won control over most of the Italian peninsula, including the Greek colonies in the south. Within two hundred years, through a haphazard process of conquest, Rome emerged as master of the entire Mediterranean Basin. Ironically, as Rome imposed its imperial power on the states of the eastern Mediterranean, its culture was eclipsed by that of the hellenized East.

THE MEDITERRANEAN WORLD AFTER ALEXANDER THE GREAT

The Political and Commercial Powers

Throughout the third century B.C., the Hellenistic states that succeeded Alexander's empire continued to dominate the Mediterranean world. The three most powerful

(*OPPOSITE*) ROMAN MAP OF THE WORLD, SURROUNDED BY THE WORLD OCEAN.

The Mediterranean World during the Hellenistic Era

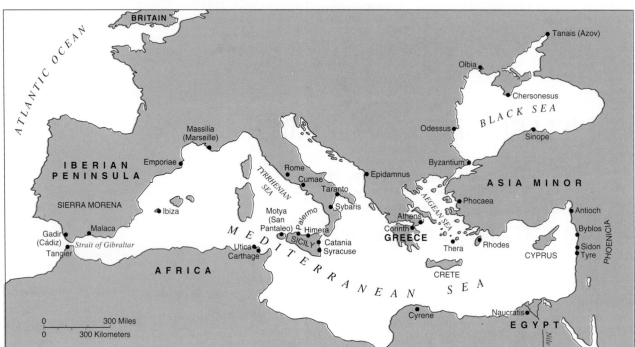

states in the eastern Mediterranean were Asia Minor, unified under the Macedonian regime centered in Pergamum; Seleucid Persia, which controlled both Mesopotamia and the eastern seaboard of the Mediterranean; and Ptolemaic Egypt, which stretched west from the Nile Delta into Libya. The Greek states remained nominally independent under the control of Macedonia, much as they had been under Alexander's father, Philip II.

In the western Mediterranean, Greek colonies dotted the coastline, their influence extending only a little way into the interior. The colonies of Sicily and southern Italy had pretty much gone their own way after the Peloponnesian War, when the mother cities in Greece were no longer able to keep up the old relationships. These colonies continued to trade with the East, but only Syracuse in Sicily emerged as a significant center of power and culture.

The greatest power in the western Mediterranean was the city of Carthage,

founded by the ancient Phoenicians of Tyre on the north African coast, near present-day Tunis. Carthage traced its origins to the arrival of Queen Dido, sister of Pygmalion, king of Tyre, at the end of the ninth century B.C. Strategically located as a trading center, the city dominated the commercial life of the western reaches of the Mediterranean.

While Tyre and other Phoenician cities were being absorbed by successive middle eastern empires, Carthage expanded its own sphere of commercial influence. It established colonies in southern Spain and drew wealth from the silver mines of the region. It controlled the trade of the north African coast, out to the Strait of Gibraltar, known then as the Pillars of Hercules. It produced rich grain harvests in the surrounding territory, where rainfall was more abundant than it is today. Carthaginian ships sailed to Cornwall and Ireland to trade for metals and may have made their way down the western coast of Africa. Despite its wealth and influence, however, Carthage never became a noteworthy center of civilization.

Massalia (Marseilles), one of the few Greek colonies west of the Italian peninsula, grew to be a serious rival of Carthage. Located on the Mediterranean coast of Gaul (present-day France), east of the Rhone River delta, Massalia was a major center of commerce. It exploited both the coastal and inland regions of southern Gaul and reached out along the coast to found subordinate trading towns at Antibes, Nice, and Monaco to the east, and Agde to the west. It established an inland center at Arles, where the Rhone begins to form its delta, from which it could trade with the tribes of the interior. Traders from Massalia sailed along the Atlantic and North Sea seaboards and probably reached Britain. Like the Carthaginians, they may have sailed down the west coast of Africa, perhaps as far as Senegal.

Hellenistic Civilization

After 200 B.C., an educated merchant could travel from the eastern margin of the old Persian Empire to Massalia and feel more or less at home throughout the entire trip. Artists and teachers found patrons in congenial surroundings throughout this vast region. Everywhere in Alexander's former empire—except in India, where an indigenous empire arose and wiped out Greek influence, aristocrats and merchants shared a uniform, cosmopolitan culture derived from that of classical Greece but influenced by local traditions. Hellenistic culture, like a thin veneer, extended over the myriad cultures of the eastern Mediterranean and the Middle East.

Beneath this veneer, the lower orders of society preserved their ancient ways— their languages, religions, and social habits. The hellenized upper classes modified those traditions to some extent, but the Persian and Egyptian societies, and the native populations of Asia Minor and the Balkans were little deflected from their traditional modes of living.

Hellenistic culture flourished especially in Egypt. In the third and second centuries B.C., Alexandria, the emporium of the eastern Mediterranean and the center for trade with India, was the wealthiest city in the world. Its ruling family, the Macedonian Ptolemies, encouraged artists and scholars and, next to the palace, built a magnificent temple to the Muses (called the Museum) for the study of the arts and sciences. Next to the Museum stood the famous library of Alexandria. Scholars from all parts of the Hellenistic world came to Alexandria, which rivaled Athens as a center of Greek culture. Egyptians made up most of the population, of course, but in the streets one could hear all the languages of the Mediterranean world. More Jews lived in Alexandria than in Jerusalem, and the city became the center of Hellenistic Judaism. Here, the Hebrew Bible was translated into Greek; this version later became the Old Testament of the Christians.

Antioch in Syria, the capital of the Seleucus, who succeeded Alexander in the Persian Empire, was also a great city and trading center. The island of Rhodes prospered as transshipment point for goods headed for the Aegean and goods destined for Black Sea ports passed through Pergamum (near the site of ancient Troy), the home of a group of talented artists. Dozens of other Hellenistic cities were centers of lively commercial, intellectual, and artistic activity.

A sixteenth-century vision of Alexandria at its height.

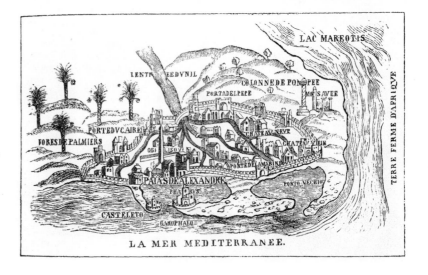

LA MER MEDITERRANEE.

Art and Literature

Although Hellenistic art lacked the serenity and self-confidence of the sculpture and architecture of fifth-century Greece, it displayed intense emotive power. Occasionally, it sought to impress by mere size, as did the gigantic colossus that stood astride the harbor of Rhodes and the Mausoleum at Halicarnassus in Ionia. Hellenistic sculptors created works that continue today to impress the viewer with their

The Winged Victory of Samothrace.

beauty and power—works such as the Winged Victory of Samothrace, the Venus of Milo, and the Dying Gaul of Pergamum. Hellenistic artists, in their paintings, mosaics, and statues, strove to depict everyday life realistically, showing men and women as they actually lived.

Among the Hellenistic poets, Theocritus (fl. *ca.* 270 B.C.) wrote lyric poetry on pastoral subjects in the *Idylls*, and Apollonius (*ca.* 295–215 B.C.), who may have served as head librarian at Alexandria, wrote an epic in the tradition of Homer, the *Argonautica*. The comedies of the dramatist Menander (*ca.* 342–292 B.C.) have amused audiences for 2000 years and, through their influence on Roman comedy, have influenced Shakespeare and other playwrights up to the present.

Alexandria was the birthplace of literary scholarship. Aristarchus of Samothrace (head of the Alexandria library *ca.* 180–*ca.* 145 B.C.) produced editions of Homer, Hesiod, Pindar, and other poets of the archaic and classical ages and wrote commentaries on many ancient texts. The study of literature was the principal activity of educated Alexandrians, who typically knew the works of Homer by heart. In a popular parlor game, the guests took turns telling a story using only lines and half-lines from the Homeric epics.

Science

Perhaps the most striking achievements of the Hellenistic age were in science. Scientists performed some remarkable experiments—such as Archimedes's studies of propulsion—and developed theories on such questions as the motion of bodies of different size that foreshadowed discoveries during the 1600s. In medicine, geometry, astronomy, botany, and zoology, they brought together the knowledge of the past and supplemented it with observations and findings of their own. Their work preserved for later generations Babylonian, Egyptian, and classical Greek knowledge that would otherwise have been lost.

The Alexandrian anatomist Herophilus (fourth–third century B.C.) identified the nervous system in human beings and came close to proposing a theory of circulation of blood. The astronomer Aristarchus of Samos (b. *ca.* 320 B.C.) was the first to propose that the planets revolve around the sun. Because he believed that the planets follow circular orbits, however, his theory failed to explain the observable pathway of their movements and his successors rejected his theory. And yet his ideas would influence Copernicus in the 1500s. The Alexandrian Eratosthenes (second half of the third century B.C.) wrote poetry, history, and literary commentaries, but he is best known as the mathematician who accurately calculated the circumference of the earth.

Most of the work of these gifted scientists sank into oblivion and the views of Aristotle continued to be regarded as the correct explanations of natural phenomena well into the Middle Ages. Finally, Moslem scholars in the 700s took up Hellenistic science, and through them it reached the West five centuries later.

Interest in mathematics remained strong, however, probably because mathematics could be put to practical use. Euclid (fl. *ca.* 300 B.C. in Alexandria) brought scattered theorems and proofs together into a coherent system of geometry that remains valid to this day. Archimedes of Syracuse (*ca.* 278–212 B.C.) worked out the basic problems of mass and motion and perfected a theory of machines, including the compound pulley and the type of pump called Archimedes' screw. His ideas had many everyday applications, particularly in the construction of war machines. His theoretical treatises, however, were forgotten until they were rediscovered by Europeans in the thirteenth century. They contributed to the scientific revolution centuries later.

Philosophy and Religion

Hellenistic philosophy and religion reflected what was to the educated classes a worldwide society. No longer was life circumscribed within the tiny city-states of the classical period. Now, life could be affected by unforeseen, mysterious events in distant places. In such a world, the efforts of individuals seemed futile, and edu-

cated people turned to philosophy and religion in their search for meaning in their lives.

The three most popular schools of philosophy emphasized private virtue and self-discipline rather than participation in public life.

Stoicism, which drew on the ideas of Zeno of Citium on Cyprus (fl. *ca.* 300 B.C.), spoke of a universal law that binds all men together as brothers. Everyone, from slave to king, must do his duty in the station in which he finds himself. Power and wealth, human desires and affections, are dangerous distractions. Public office is not to be sought, though it might be one's duty to accept it. The ideal existence is to live as a private citizen unaffected by political or other external influences.

Epicureanism, based on the philosophy of Epicurus (341–270 B.C.), holds that the wise man should seek the pleasure that arises from right conduct, serenity of mind, and moderation in all things. Ambition and the pursuit of wealth cause more pain than they are worth, and the wise man should avoid forming strong attachments to family, friends, or state.

Cynicism stemmed from the thought of Antisthenes (b. *ca.* 440 B.C.), who taught in the gymnasium called the Cynosarges in Athens. The Cynics doubted the possibility of achieving true knowledge and saw no sense in trying to save a world trapped in ignorance. They believed the wise man should pursue peace of mind and withdraw from worldly concerns.

Ordinary people sought solace in the so-called mystery cults rather than in the formal schools of philosophy that attracted the educated upper classes. The origins of these cults lay deep in the cultures of the societies Alexander had incorporated into his empire. The cults achieved wider visibility through his efforts to integrate Greek and indigenous cultures and by the late fourth century B.C. they were attracting followers throughout the Hellenistic world.

The cults borrowed freely from one another and from older religions of the Mediterranean world and the Middle East. Each cult engaged in elaborate secret ceremonies and claimed that initiates, after

In the sixteenth century, Archimedes was considered the greatest of the ancient scientists. Here is a sixteenth-century imagination of him.

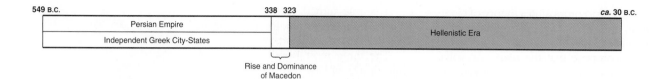

549 B.C.   338 323   *ca.* 30 B.C.

Persian Empire

Independent Greek City-States

Hellenistic Era

Rise and Dominance
of Macedon

performing a ritual purification of their sins, would be admitted to the mystery that opened the way to communion with the god of the cult. Especially popular were the Dionysian rituals from the Greek cities, Isis worship from Egypt, and the cult of the Great Mother from Asia Minor. The communities of believers were small, mystic cells that provided a sense of security and personal worth and a promise of eternal life as antidotes to the helplessness and harshness they experienced in their daily life. Like the formal schools of philosophy, they turned inward and offered an escape from reality.

The Fate of Hellenistic Civilization

The Hellenistic states never achieved military strength, and most of them were weakened by internal dissension and cultural conflict. The Seleucid Empire, for example, soon lost Bactria and Persia, and in 167 B.C. the Jews regained their independence under the leadership of the Maccabees. When Rome became the dominant power in the Mediterranean about 200 B.C.,

it annexed the Hellenistic states one by one, and with the seizure of Egypt in 30 B.C. it acquired all of Alexander's empire except Persia.

Despite its political collapse, the influence of the Hellenistic world persisted for centuries. The Romans admired Hellenistic culture and borrowed heavily from it. Greek continued as the language of the upper classes in the Middle East, and Athens and Alexandria were the cultural centers of the Roman Empire. When the Arabs built a great empire around the Mediterranean and in the Middle East during the seventh century, the Hellenistic populations exerted a profound influence on Moslem culture. Hellenism's sphere of influence began to shrink by about A.D. 500, however. In Greece, Asia Minor, and the Levant, it gradually gave way to Byzantine culture (see Chapter 7), which survived until the fall of Constantinople in A.D. 1453.

THE FOUNDATIONS OF ROME AND ITS POWER

Origins

By 1000 B.C., the Italic tribes, including the Latins, had settled most of the Italian peninsula and had begun to clear the forests for agriculture. Soon after 800 B.C., new civilizations arose in the north and the south. In the north, the Etruscans built fortified hill towns on the Lombard plain, in the Apennines, and along the western coast down to Campania. In the south and in Sicily, as we have seen, the Greek colonists founded cities and soon brought the Italic tribes of the area under control.

The Etruscans appear to have been a non-Indo-European people native to the Italian peninsula. Their ultimate origins are obscure, and scholars have been unable to decipher their writing. We do know that the Etruscans achieved a highly

Ancient Rome

Etruscan sarcophagus (third century B.C.) showing the deceased couple reclining on a couch and pouring libations as if at their own funeral banquet.

Etruscan kitchen utensils: a water bottle and a spoon.

developed civilization and employed sophisticated techniques in painting, terracotta, bronze, and precious metals. Their political organization was, like that of Mycenaean and classical Greece, based on independent city-states. Through trade they came into contact with the Greeks and the Phoenicians, whose culture influenced their own.

Etruscan funerary art—which is mostly what survives—shows men and women as equals; the Greeks regarded the Etruscans as decadent because of the prominence and freedom their women enjoyed. Etruscan society was an aristocratic society based on the family, and the union of men and women brought honor to both partners.

Rome originated as an Etruscan-type city during the late seventh or early sixth century B.C. It is not clear whether the coalescing of the villages into a city was accomplished by the Etruscans or by the villagers themselves as they tried to resist Etruscan encroachment. In any case, the Etruscans eventually gained control of the region, and throughout the sixth century B.C., an Etruscan dynasty, the Tarquins, ruled the small city-state of Rome. About 510 B.C. (Romans later fixed the date at 509), local aristocrats (the *patricians*)

ousted the Tarquins and established a republic.

The Republican Constitution

The patricians devised for the new republic a constitution carefully wrought to prevent another king or tyrant from seizing power. Two elected magistrates, the *consuls*, held executive power, and other officials, also elected in twos or threes, managed the treasury and presided over the legal system. All chief magistrates held office for only one year at a time. In times of emergency, the constitution allowed for the appointment of a dictator who could hold authority only until the crisis had passed and in no case for more than six months.

During the fifth century B.C., the various governmental offices became fixed. From the beginning, the consuls had had assistants called *quaestors*, who were generally up-and-coming young patricians. By the middle of the fifth century, the quaestors had become independent magistrates elected by the assembly. Eventually, there were four quaestors; two managed the public treasury, and two assisted the consuls in handling military finances. By about 435 B.C., two *praetors* had been added to the roster of magistrates. They were responsible for the administration of justice. One of them handled the cases of citizens and governed the city when the consuls were away. The other handled the cases of foreigners.

The electorate of citizens—as in Greece, only males were citizens—constituted an assembly that elected the magistrates, passed laws, declared war, and sat as the final court of appeal in capital cases. Voting in the assembly followed a form of military organization called the centuriate, which probably dated back to Etruscan days. Originally, the centuriate consisted of units of 100 men each, called centuries. Under the Republic, the centuries were of various sizes, and each century had one vote.

The assembly was divided into five classes according to wealth, each class having a prescribed number of centuries. The patricians had 80 centuries; the four lower classes—the *plebeians*—had, collectively, 90 centuries. So it would seem that the plebeians could outvote the patricians. Actually, though, the assembly included groups that did not belong to the five classes. The equestrians (wealthy plebeians who served in the cavalry) had 18 centuries; the artisans (part of the middle class) had 2; and the proletarians (landless men who belonged to no class) had 1. In practice, the equestrians voted with the patricians, and together they held the majority—98 centuries out of 193.

In normal times, the patricians governed the Republic. Only patricians could be elected as magistrates. In addition, the patricians formed a powerful council of former magistrates, called the Senate (from *senex* meaning elder). All those who had served as quaestor, praetor, or consul, became senators as soon as their terms expired. Until the late fourth century B.C., it seems no act passed in the assembly was executed by the magistrates until the Senate had approved it.

The Senate's influence over elected officials rested on class and family ties, as well as on the senators' political experience. The quaestors, holding their first major offices, were the sons, nephews, and cousins of senators. The praetors and con-

suls were already senators themselves. Consequently, the Senate usually determined policy, and Senate debates attracted more attention than the activities of the magistrates or the assembly. In fact, the senators also controlled the assembly through a client system. They gave economic and other support—such as legal assistance—to small farmers and city dwellers in return for political support in the assembly, so they rarely had to rely on their control of a majority of the centuries.

The Romans assigned military and civilian powers to the same officials but at the same time differentiated military and civilian functions. Although the consuls were both civilian magistrates and commanders in chief of the army, they could exercise their military authority only outside the city limits. Within the city, civilian government held sway. In the field, the citizen-soldier was subject to strict military discipline, but in the city he was a citizen free to voice his opinion on political matters and to vote as he wished. Moreover, because the consuls held office for only one year, no one could create a political following based on the army.

An able young aristocrat could be elected quaestor at the age of 25 and praetor at the age of 30. At the age of 35, he could stand for the consulship. A man could serve in these offices more than once, but in 342 B.C., the assembly passed a law prohibiting anyone from repeating a term of office, particularly the consulship, within ten years. This law soon proved impractical, however, because Rome became engaged in lengthy military campaigns that required continuous leadership. In 325 B.C., to get around the law, the Senate permitted a consul to continue as a military leader after his term expired by making him *pro consule*—that is, an officer who acted *for* or *as* the consul. In time, the proconsulate became embedded in the power structure of the state.

The patricians led the rebellion against the Tarquins, and they were firmly in control of the Republic. As time passed, however, the plebeians came to resent the patrician monopoly of power. Under the Etruscan king, ordinary citizens could seek royal protection from aristrocratic abuse, and the competition between the king and the aristocracy often made the king sympathetic to their complaints. But under the Republic, the power of the aristocrats went unchecked, and social relations, always rough, grew rougher still. The aristocrats often subjected small farmers to economic pressure or physical violence to force them to become clients or surrender their land. In neither the city nor the countryside were life and property safe any longer.

Patrician control over the workings of government made life nearly intolerable for the lower orders of society. The plebeian was obliged to stand before a patrician judge who was probably related to his opponent by blood, marriage, clientage, or politics. Moreover, at least during the first decades of the Republic, laws were neither written nor published. Consequently, the laws were whatever the aristocratic magistrates said they were. As grievances mounted, with no remedy in prospect, a prolonged struggle set in between the patricians and the plebeians.

The Struggle between the Patricians and Plebeians

Around 470 B.C. the plebeians forced the patricians to consent to election, by an assembly of plebeians, of two independent plebeian magistrates, called *tribunes*. One of these tribunes, in the late 450s B.C., proposed the Twelve Tables, the first written code of Roman law. This transition from unwritten law administered by the patrician magistrates to written law binding on all citizens brought increased security to the populace. Then, in 446 B.C., the old ban on intermarriage between patricians and plebeians was abolished. Even though patrician families were slow to enter into marriages with plebeians, the new openness had a significant effect on the social order in the long run.

For some time, the plebeians had sought access to offices, especially those that carried some measure of military authority, but the patricians had resisted their efforts. About 444 B.C., a compromise was achieved under which the plebeian assembly elected three military tribunes in addition to the two civilian tribunes. Yet this new arrangement continued to favor the patricians: Each year, the Senate decided whether military authority should be granted to the military tribunes or to the consuls; with the senators making the decision, the choice was rarely in doubt. Moreover, because patricians controlled the assembly, and the assembly elected the military tribunes, no plebeian reached that office until 400 B.C., when a difficult campaign made it necessary to choose the

Plebeian Reforms

Enslavement for debt was a constant threat to the poorer peasants of the ancient world. In this passage, the Roman historian Livy (59 B.C.–A.D. 17) shows how the plebeians gained constitutional safeguards against enslavement for debt by refusing to fight in a time of emergency.

An old man suddenly presented himself in the Forum. . . . Though cruelly changed from what he had once been, he was recognized, and people began to tell each other, compassionately, that he was an old soldier who had once commanded a company and served with distinction. . . . "While I was on service," he said, "during the Sabine War, my crops were ruined by enemy raids, and my cottage was burnt. Everything I had was taken, including my cattle. Then, when I was least able to do so, I was expected to pay taxes, and fell, consequently, into debt. Interest on the borrowed money increased my burden; I lost the land which my father and my grandfather had owned before me, and . . . I was finally seized by my creditor and reduced to slavery. . . ."

The man's story . . . caused a tremendous uproar, which spread swiftly from the Forum through every part of the city. . . .

On top of this highly critical situation, came the alarming news . . . that a Volscian army was marching on Rome. . . . For [the plebeians] it seemed like an intervention of providence to crush the pride of the Senate; they went about urging their friends to refuse military service. . . . [One of the consuls then issued] an edict, to the effect that it should be illegal . . . [to] imprison a Roman citizen. . . . As a result of the edict, all "bound" debtors who were present gave their names on the spot, . . . and in the ensuing fight with the Volscians no troops did more distinguished service.

From Livy, The Early History of Rome, *trans. by Aubrey de Sélincourt (Baltimore: Penguin Books, 1960), pp. 113–16.*

This head of a statue of Hermes (*ca.* 500 B.C.) was part of a group of terra-cotta figures that adorned the roof of a temple of Apollo in Veii. It became a spoil of war when Veii fell to besieging Romans in 396 B.C.

best-qualified men, regardless of social class.

By then, plebeians had finally begun to break down the barrier to election to the regular magistracies—the quaestorship, praetorship, and consulship. In 421 B.C., they became eligible for election to the quaestorship, although the patricians still controlled the assembly, which elected quaestors. Finally, in 367 B.C., plebeians became eligible for the consulate, the highest office in the Republic, and the military tribunate was abolished. Under the law of 367 B.C., one consul was to be patrician and one plebeian, though no plebeian was elected to the office until 340 B.C.

The struggle persisted for generations, with the patricians resisting every effort by the plebeians to win a share of power. When the patricians did make a concession, it was invariably occasioned by the exigencies of war—first, wars fought to defend the new republic and, later, wars of expansion. The tradition of aristocratic authority was embedded in the history of early Rome. This was a community created and governed by a small class of men who considered themselves the best among the citizenry. They felt they had an obligation to govern and a right to preserve their power. As they saw it, the prosperity of the Roman state and the

welfare of all citizens depended on their leadership.

THE GROWTH OF ROMAN ITALY, *ca.* 500–265 B.C.

The Expansion of Roman Power

In the early days, Rome's prosperity rested on agriculture, and for centuries Romans continued to revere the rural way of life. Like Sparta, Rome trusted its defense to an army of citizen-farmers.

When the Republic was founded, Rome controlled a territory of about 300 square miles, with a diameter of less than 20 miles. The Republic inherited the powerful position of the Etruscan kings among the towns of Latium. With the expulsion of those kings, the towns asserted their independence and, about 496 B.C., formed the so-called Latin League and rebelled against the Republic. Still threatened by the Etruscans to the north, the Romans entered into treaties with the League instead of trying to suppress it. Latins and Romans received rights in each other's courts and pledged to assist each other in times of emergency. Together they created a powerful army and achieved domination over central Italy. Wherever the combined forces won a battle over local tribes, they established a colony of veterans to consolidate their power.

Rome's settlement with the Latin League influenced Roman policy toward other peoples as well. By entering into

Cities of the Latin League　　*ca.* 400 B.C.

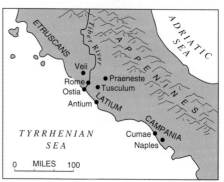

that settlement, Rome took a step toward opening its citizenship to outsiders. Having created a category of citizenship for conquered peoples, Rome ultimately became a city-state with the citizenry and power of an empire.

Not long after Rome's accommodation with the Latin League, the Etruscans in the north were weakened by the invasion of a new people, the Celts. The Celts were iron-using Indo-Europeans who, starting in the sixth century B.C., had spread out from the area just north of the Alps. In successive waves of migration and conquest, they had gained control of most of the continent from Spain to western Russia. The Galatians in central Asia Minor were Celts, as were the Gauls who moved into Italy beginning about 450 B.C.. After conquering the Etruscan cities in the Lombard plain, the Gauls pressed south into the peninsula. The Romans seized the opportunity to challenge Etruscan power in central Italy, and, between about 405 and 396 B.C., Rome and its Latin allies besieged the Etruscan city of Veii. With the fall of the city the balance of power shifted permanently from the Etruscans to the Romans.

The Gauls pushed on to the south, however. Around 390 B.C., they defeated a Roman army and seized the city of Rome; only the citadel held out. But the Gauls had reached the limit of their southern drive. After sacking the city, they returned north. Rome took a generation to recover from this disaster, and not until the 360s B.C. did Roman armies again go on the offensive. By about 350 B.C., Rome had completed its conquest of the Etruscans by annexing southern Etruria, their last stronghold.

After this success, the Romans consolidated their control over central Italy. Between about 340 and 338 B.C., they fought the Great Latin War, and defeated the Latin

League. The citizens of the Latin cities were then incorporated into the citizenry of Rome. From this time on, the Romans often granted citizenship to conquered peoples in Italy, a practice that added to their manpower and gave their former enemies a stake in Roman affairs.

Now the Romans turned their attention south to the Italic tribes. These tribes had occupied the Apennines and the plains of south-central Italy around 1000 B.C., and they had emerged as strong powers when the Greek cities of southern Italy declined during the fourth century B.C. They spoke Oscan, a language related to Latin much as French is related to Spanish or Italian. The most powerful of the Italic tribes were the Samnites, who controlled much of south-central Italy, including the plain of Campania.

About 325 B.C., the Romans turned on the Samnites and launched a long series of wars against them. The Samnites allied themselves with the remnants of Etruscan power and forced Rome into a two-front war. Although Rome lost most of the early battles, its superior military organization and firm control over its allies brought victory at last. During these difficult campaigns the Romans prolonged the military service of its consuls by creating the proconsulate. By 290 B.C., Samnite power was broken. After a little mopping up, Rome assumed control of all of Italy except for the Gallic cities in the Po Valley and the Greek city-states in the south.

After the Samnite Wars, some of the Greek city-states allied themselves with Rome, while others allied themselves with Epirus, a partially hellenized kingdom on the eastern shore of the Adriatic. Around 280 B.C., King Pyrrhus of Epirus sailed across to Italy to support his allies. Although he won numerous battles against the Romans, he lost the war. In winning one of his battles, he lost so many men that his victory was worse than defeat. Since then, a disastrous victory has come to be known as a pyrrhic victory. By 265, the Greek city-states had accepted Roman hegemony.

The Roman Military System

In the course of these long years of war the Romans created a first-rate military system and cultivated an ethos of perseverance. Their military system was based on the legion, an infantry unit of about 4,300 men, which was subdivided into smaller units for maneuverability. At first, the officer corps was made up of young patricians, but after the expansion of plebeian power wealthy plebeians came to serve as officers too. The officer corps was led by the consuls.

The legion was a highly flexible body manned by well-disciplined soldiers. When divided into its constituent units, it could be deployed in a wide variety of formations. The smaller units were under the close control of their officers, and the chain of command made it possible for the legionary commander to coordinate the performance of the whole. It was the best-organized and best-disciplined army of the ancient world.

Because Rome controlled rich farmlands capable of supporting a large population, it enjoyed a clear superiority in manpower over its enemies. Not even the

strongest states of the Mediterranean world could withstand the steady pressure that Rome could exert.

ROMAN EXPANSION OVERSEAS

The Punic Wars, 264–146 B.C.

When it subjugated the Greek city-states of southern Italy, Rome inherited their ancient struggle with Carthage for control of Sicily and the western Mediterranean. The war between Rome and Carthage was similar to the contest between Sparta and Athens: land power versus sea power. Carthage was the greatest naval power in the Mediterranean, whereas at the beginning of action Rome had no navy at all. The so-called Punic Wars (from *Poenicus*, Latin for Phoenician) between Rome and Carthage dragged on for more than eighty years.

The First Punic War broke out in 264 B.C., only a year after Rome had completed its conquest of southern Italy. This time, Rome was bent on winning control of Sicily, one of the great breadbaskets of the Mediterranean. To win this prize, Rome first had to build a fleet and learn the arts of naval warfare. It developed a ship that enabled its troops to board enemy ships and use the skills they had learned as infantrymen. After some early victories, Rome lost three fleets in storms. With a fourth fleet, the Romans defeated

A wall painting from Pompeii depicting the warships of the ancient Mediterranean.

Early Italy *ca.* 275 B.C.

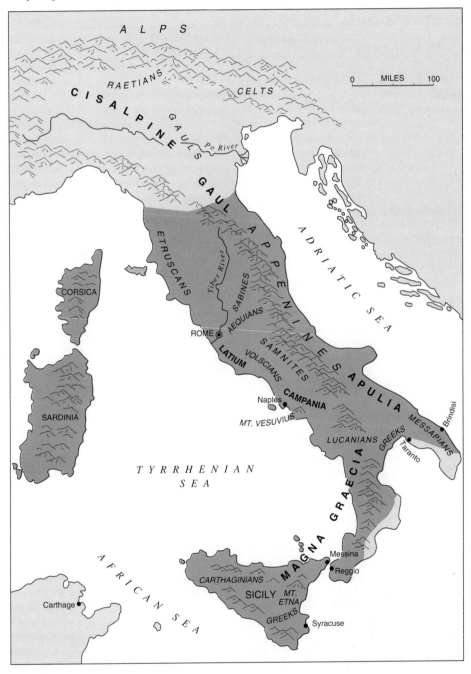

the Carthaginians off western Sicily in 241 B.C. and took control of the island.

After this defeat, Carthage turned its attention to Spain, and to the rich silver mines and farmlands it possessed there. Once again, Carthage and Rome fell into conflict. For more than a thousand years, southern Gaul (France) and Spain had

Founding of City of Rome ca. 750 B.C.		ca. 600		ca. 500			264		146		27 B.C.

Independent Roman Kingdom	Etruscan Dominance	Rome Conquers Italian Peninsula	Punic Wars	Rome Conquers Entire Mediterranean Area

played a prominent role in Mediterranean trade, and Rome had become well-established there, principally through an alliance with Massilia, Carthage's rival. A strengthening of Carthaginian power in Spain was a serious threat to Roman interests. The Second Punic War began in 218 B.C. with a Carthaginian attack on a northern Spanish city allied with Rome.

Had it not been for the brilliance and daring of Hannibal, the Carthaginian general, the war might well have been fought in Spain, or even in north Africa. As the war began, Hannibal marched through southern Gaul and crossed the Alps with a large army and fifty war elephants. For the first two years of the war, the Romans tried to pin down Hannibal's army without engaging in open battle. Then, in 216 B.C., two inexperienced Roman consuls decided to confront Hannibal. At Cannae, in eastern Italy, north of Bari, he inflicted one of the worst defeats Rome ever suffered. Nearly 70,000 Roman soldiers died in the battle, and 10,000 Roman prisoners of war were sold into slavery. After Cannae, Hannibal spent thirteen years ravaging the Italian countryside, defeating one Roman army after another. At one point he threatened Rome itself. But Rome's allies in central Italy forced him to spend most of his time in the south, where he found support among the Italic peoples. The Romans controlled the sea and denied Hannibal reinforcements from Africa. For thirteen years, the two sides were stalemated.

In 203 B.C., the Romans sent a gifted general, Scipio Africanus, into the field. Scipio first took the war to Spain and won the province for Rome. He then invaded North Africa itself, forcing Hannibal to rush to the defense of Carthage. After a difficult campaign, Scipio finally defeated Hannibal in 202 B.C. at Zama, a few miles from Carthage, and imposed surrender terms on the Carthaginians. Carthage ceded Spain to Rome, paid a heavy war

This third-century B.C. coin bears one of the few known contemporary portraits of Hannibal. The elephant appears on the reverse.

indemnity, and agreed to limit its fleet henceforth to ten ships.

Fifty years after the end of the Second Punic War, Carthage had recovered some of its wealth but was no longer a military threat to Rome. Nonetheless, the Romans had bitter memories of Hannibal's depredations, and for years the Roman Senate had debated whether Carthage should be destroyed. Finally, in 146 B.C., Rome moved against its old enemy. Carthage fell after a six-month siege, and every inhabitant was either killed or enslaved. The city was razed, its fields sown with salt, and the surrounding territory made into a Roman province. Rulers elsewhere in North Africa were forced to become clients of Rome.

Rome and the Hellenistic East

Although Roman expansion in the western Mediterranean was a matter of long-term strategy, it is difficult to find a compelling reason for the extension of Roman power to the eastern Mediterranean. Actually, Rome was drawn into eastern affairs by degrees, as one state after another asked for assistance against its rivals. The wealth of the East was attractive, of course, but Rome moved hesitantly and repeatedly refused to annex defeated states, making them independent client kingdoms instead.

Rome's first experience in the East had been its war with King Pyrrhus of Epirus during the 270s B.C. Later, during the Second Punic War, when the Macedonians lent support to Hannibal, Rome attacked and defeated them. Then, as time passed, the successor states to Alexander's empire—Ptolemaic Egypt, Seleucid Persia, Macedon, the leagues of Greek cities, and the small kingdoms in Asia Minor—repeatedly involved Rome in their affairs.

Exasperated, the Romans in 167 B.C. plundered Macedon and Epirus and sold thousands of their inhabitants into slavery.

They destroyed Corinth for its disobedience and sold much of its population into slavery. And they plundered Athens and brought thousands of its young men to Italy as slaves. By the late 140s B.C., Macedon had become a Roman province; the Greek cities were under Roman control; Asia Minor had become a Roman protectorate; and Egypt and Syria remained independent but were obliged to get Roman approval before acting in foreign affairs.

THE CONSEQUENCES OF EXPANSION

Governing the Provinces

The expansion of Roman power led to an expansion of Roman government. The constitution, which had been designed for a small city-state, now had to be altered to suit the governance of vast territories populated by foreign peoples. Previously, the consuls had served both as generals and as heads of the civilian government. But now the armies were often active in several theaters of war at once, and the state needed additional military leaders. As we have seen, Rome filled that need by creating the office of proconsul. Most of the provinces had military garrisons, and it became common to unite provincial administration with military command under the proconsuls. Separation of military and civilian power, one of the distinctive features of Roman government, was not exported to the provinces.

Military control enabled unscrupulous proconsuls to enrich themselves at the expense of the provincials, and in 149 B.C. Rome established a special court to try those who were suspected of corruption. The court soon fell under the influence of Roman politicians, however, not unlike what had happened to ostracism in Athens (see pp. 51–52). Once a proconsul returned to Rome, he could be sure that his political enemies would sue him for corruption.

Some of the older provinces had only token peace-keeping garrisons, and their governors concerned themselves mainly with civilian affairs. More recently acquired provinces and those threatened by enemies of Rome were under military government. Generally, however, the Roman governors kept small staffs and left local affairs to local leaders. Many of those leaders learned Latin, arranged for their sons to have a Roman education, and built Roman-style houses and public buildings. Thus they served as a link between the Romans and the native populations, which preserved many of their linguistic and cultural traditions.

Some provincial city-states enjoyed complete autonomy, though in close alliance with Rome. Elsewhere, Roman governors intervened only when necessary or profitable to do so. In North Africa and in some parts of the Middle East, the Romans permitted the old kingdoms to continue as client kingdoms. The rulers had control over internal affairs, but they had to act in accord with Rome's foreign policy and to seek Roman approval on succession to the throne. On the whole, Roman provincial government was less burdensome than that of earlier conquerors, and it succeeded in keeping the peace. Under Roman rule, the Mediterranean world enjoyed a period of extraordinary prosperity and peace, the *Pax Romana* (Roman Peace).

Economic, Social, and Political Change

By 146 B.C., Rome had become the capital of a great Mediterranean empire. Wealth poured into Rome, mainly to the benefit of the upper classes, and as time passed the difference between rich and poor grew wider and wider. In the old days of the city-state, the difference had been less noticeable, because the estates of the aristocrats were little larger than the farms of the yeomen, and all were prosperous. But the effects of empire transformed the Roman economy. The small farmers, unable to compete with the cheap grain brought in from Sicily and Spain, grew increasingly dependent on the noble families. Those families in turn bought out the ruined farmers and concentrated on producing

A stooped farmer takes his produce to the market.

wine and olive oil for export. Consequently, Roman Italy came to rely on the provinces for most of its food supply.

Economic change triggered social and political change. By the middle of the second century B.C., many of the farmers who had once formed the backbone of the Roman population had moved to the city. There they constituted a new element in Roman life—the urban mob. For a time, the noble families of their old districts continued to support them in the traditional manner and preserved the old client system in the assembly, but ambitious politicians soon wooed them away with offers of largess, including promises of land reform, which would provide the former farmers with acreage. But promises of reform were not kept, and the mob became a fickle electorate.

Imperialism advanced the fortunes of the traders and manufacturers who emerged from the equestrian class. With the movement toward empire, the equestrians derived new political and economic power from the growth of trade and from the imperial tax system. Instead of setting up a centralized tax bureau, the Roman government sold the right to collect taxes in the provinces. Companies of equestrians bid for the contracts that carried the right, and the winning bidders managed

to earn a handsome profit after covering the contract price. Tax collectors (called publicans) have never been popular, but those who collected taxes in the Roman provinces earned special hatred.

And yet, the Romans' readiness to grant citizenship and its attendant privileges won the loyalty of many provincials. Typically, the provinces were organized around cities that had emerged from small towns. The Roman governors usually permitted the local aristocracy to manage the political and economic affairs of the cities, and members of the city councils were awarded Roman citizenship. In this way, many provincial leaders became loyal Romans, legally equal to Romans by birth.

Finally, many of the prisoners taken in the Roman conquests were, according to the common practice, sold into slavery. As in classical Greece, most of the Roman slaves seem to have worked as household servants or as assistants to craftsmen. Others, especially those seized in the Hellenistic states of the eastern Mediterranean, were skilled artisans, and some were well educated. Many Roman families acquired Greek slaves as teachers for their children. Some slaves were put to work in distant mines, and a few were used in manufacturing, though there was little large-scale manufacturing at the time. It is not clear

Founding of City of Rome ca. 750 B.C.		ca. 600	ca. 500		264		146	27 B.C.
Independent Roman Kingdom		Etruscan Dominance	Rome Conquers Italian Peninsula		Punic Wars		Rome Conquers Entire Mediterranean Area	

whether the laborers on the great landed estates were slave or free, but the senatorial families are known to have had a great many slaves. Apparently all but the poorest families were slave owners.

Many slaves managed to win their freedom, either because their owners freed them voluntarily through the practice of manumission, or because they managed to buy their freedom. Freedmen continued to be obligated to the family of their former owner, and cadres of freedmen performed various services and contributed to the treasury of wealthy families.

Unlike the cities of Greece, Rome admitted freed slaves to citizenship. Although freedmen could not serve in the army, they could serve as oarsmen in the imperial fleet. Their children enjoyed full citizenship. The long process of creating the empire brought hundreds of the thousands of slaves to Italy, and by the end of the first century B.C., many Roman citizens were descendants of foreign slaves. Although Rome did not grant full citizenship to all the peoples it conquered, its liberal practices bound most of those defeated to its constitution and laws and reduced the incidence of rebellion.

Expansion of the Roman Republic beyond Italy   First Century B.C.

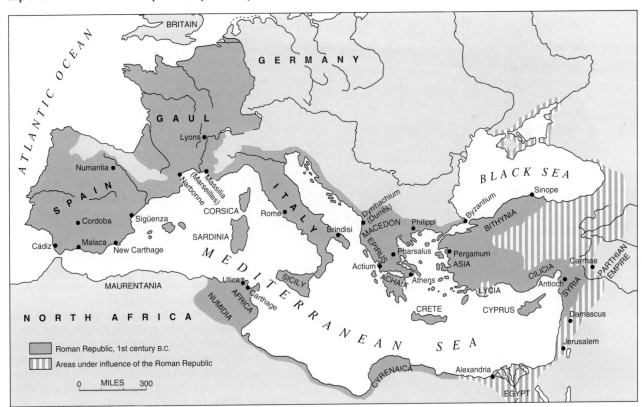

Roman Republic, 1st century B.C.

Areas under influence of the Roman Republic

0   MILES   300

Literary, Artistic, and Religious Change

Even before the eastern wars, educated Romans had been influenced by Greek culture. The subsequent influx of thousands of Greeks and others from the hellenized East literally transformed Roman civilization. Many artists, philosophers, and craftsmen arrived as slaves and worked their influence within and through the great families. Greek became the second language of educated people, and Greek poetry, literature, and art dominated Roman culture.

The more conservative Romans warned that these alien influences would undermine traditional Roman values. In their view, Rome had achieved its greatness as a result of its unique virtues, and to imitate foreign styles was tantamount to admitting that Romans were culturally inferior. Other Romans, however, were enthusiastic hellenizers, and some even went so far as to denigrate the old Roman culture. The disagreement between the two camps ran deep and showed itself in politics as well as cultural matters. Conservatives insisted that it was hellenization that had brought about the rise of the urban mob and had fostered other undesirable changes in Roman politics.

The conservatives were waging a losing battle. Roman artists became slavish imitators of Greek models. In fact, much of our knowledge of Greek sculpture comes from Roman copies made during this period. In architecture, too, Greek styles had come to replace Roman styles by about 200 B.C.

Greek influence is apparent in Roman literature as well. In fact, one of the first long poems written in Latin was a translation of Homer's *Odyssey*. The Romans also admired Greek drama, and the first Roman plays were written in Greek. Later, when the leading playwrights chose to write in Latin, they still based their work on classical or Hellenistic models. The works of Menander, the Greek playwright who wrote comedies in late fourth century B.C., were particularly influential, and many early Roman comedies are essentially reworkings of his plays.

The first Roman historians were already writing in Greek around 200 B.C. About 168 B.C., Cato, a senator who strongly opposed the Greek influence, used Latin when he wrote the first major history of Rome. Ironically, Cato's aim was to elevate Latin prose to the level of Greek. Perhaps the best account of Rome's rise to power, however, was that of Polybius (*ca.* 202–120 B.C.), a Greek who spent considerable time as a hostage in Rome and saw himself as a latter-day Thucydides. The Romans themselves emphasized the parallels between Rome and Athens. They dated the expulsion of the Tarquins to coincide almost exactly with the Athenians' expulsion of the last tyrant and Cleisthenes' creation of the democratic constitution (see p. 48).

In religion, the Romans created a pantheon that accommodated many local gods of the peoples they conquered. After their conquest of Greece, they combined their own pantheon with the Greek pantheon, identifying as best they could the twelve gods of Olympus with their own

The Roman Gods

Although Roman religion derived from the religion of the Italic peoples and the Etruscans, it was common among the ancients to equate the gods of different peoples. At the beginning of the second century B.C., the poet Ennius listed the twelve main Roman gods as representations of the Greek gods of Olympus. They were:

Roman	Greek
Jove (Jupiter)	= Zeus (king of the gods)
Juno	= Hera (marriage, queen)
Minerva	= Athena (handicrafts, war)
Mars	= Ares (war)
Apollo	= Apollo (prophecy)
Venus	= Aphrodite (love)
Mercury	= Hermes (trade)
Diana	= Artemis (hunting, woods)
Vesta	= Hestia (hearth)
Ceres	= Demeter (grain)
Vulcan	= Hephaestus (fire, smithing)
Neptune	= Poseidon (sea)

gods. During the second century B.C., the eastern mystery cults began to attract a following in Rome and the western Mediterranean, though they did not influence Roman religious life significantly until after the end of the republican period (after 30 B.C.).

So long as the patricians dominated Roman society and politics, Rome's traditional civic religion, led by a patrician priesthood, remained the dominant religion. By the second century B.C., however, the old religion was losing its grip on the Romans, who were turning more and more to the eastern cults.

Roman jurisprudence showed only slight Greek influence. From the earliest times, the Romans took special pride in their law and government. After the codification of the law in the Twelve Tables, Roman law developed into an impressive body of legislation. Much of it had to do with such constitutional questions as whether plebeians would be eligible for

This fresco found in a villa on the outskirts of Pompeii depicts initiation rites of a Dionysian mystery cult, but they are rendered in such a way as to make precise interpretation difficult for the outsider.

election to the magistracies. The edicts issued by the praetors, however, defined the cases the judges would hear and dealt mainly with private law. Each new praetor reissued the edict pertaining to his court, altering and extending the legal remedies available to citizens and foreigners to reflect changes in the society and economy of the city and empire. The praetors were under constant pressure from litigants to accept new claims, new remedies, and new procedures. In a sense, the Roman legal system developed in response to the clamor of litigants and was consequently flexible in dealing with the myriad legal disputes of an imperial society. By the end of the republican period, the texts of the edicts had become pretty well fixed and were re-issued annually with only minor changes.

Unlike modern systems, the Roman legal system was neither centralized nor run by professional lawyers. When a complainant brought a case before the praetor, the praetor merely decided whether or not the complaint was actionable. If he decided it was, he appointed a private citizen, usually a patrician or at least a wealthy and educated man, to judge the case. The judge could proceed in almost any way he chose—there were no established rules of procedure or evidence—but he had to meet the high standards of the praetor in handling the case. A judge who mishandled a case, either through incompetence or prejudice, was subject to severe penalties.

Litigation was part of everyday life, and most patricians were well versed in legal matters. Some of them became known as legal experts and were called on to advise judges, litigants, and even the praetors themselves. Starting in the first century B.C., these experts produced commentaries on the praetorian edicts and wrote treatises on various aspects of the law. They did not work for pay, however, and in no sense constituted a legal profession. The practice of law was simply something a gentleman did.

THE COLLAPSE OF THE REPUBLIC, 146–59 B.C.

The Society of the Late Republic

The vast changes in Roman society that came in the wake of empire finally weakened the political framework of the Republic. Many Romans, like Cato, clung to the ancient values of the farmer-citizen, but by the middle of the second century B.C., Roman society was far different from what it had been in the early days. The influx of foreigners had transformed the society of the capital city, and the countryside had undergone a social and economic revolution. Agriculture had become specialized in the production of olive oil and wine, and only the great landowners had the capital and the commercial contacts needed to make these crops profitable.

The upper classes, who were the main beneficiaries of the imperial conquests, acquired immense wealth and sought to acquire whatever land they fancied by whatever means. They lent money to the small farmers to plant, not, as of old, in keeping with the patron-client relationship, but so they could seize the farmers' land in the event of a bad harvest, sickness, or other disaster. Often, they helped disaster along. Accounts from later times tell of large landowners who permitted their flocks to destroy the crops of lesser neighbors and sent their crews to destroy irrigation ditches at crucial times

A funerary relief showing a man and his wife, a portrait of an ancestor, and an attribute of the man's profession (first century B.C.).

of the year. During the late third and early second centuries B.C., small farmers found it almost impossible to survive.

As land and wealth became concentrated in the hands of the upper classes, thousands of small farmers deserted the countryside and made their way to Rome. Sometimes they sought redress, though often that meant appealing to the very people who had deprived them of their land. Sometimes they sought a new livelihood. The population of Rome swelled with displaced farmers and their families living in unwholesome tenements. Poor and wretched as they were, they were Roman citizens, and many conservative politicians equated their fate with the decline of Rome itself.

The Gracchi

The leaders of the conservative faction were Tiberius and Gaius Gracchus, grandsons of the great Scipio who had defeated Carthage. They believed that the yeoman farmer was the foundation of Rome's greatness, and that the only way to save the state was to institute land reform that would return the farmer to his farm. Realizing they could never win the Senate to their cause, Tiberius Gracchus decided to work through the plebeian magistracy. In 133 B.C., he won election as tribune of the people and immediately proposed legislation to redistribute public land. Although the law would not have deprived the senatorial families of their estates, it so happened that the public land itself was at the disposal of these same families under favorable long-term leases. Not surprisingly, the senators vigorously opposed the law. The conflict precipitated a constitutional crisis, because it raised questions about the respective powers of the Senate and the tribunes. Moreover, according to an ancient constitutional principle, no proposal opposed by the Senate could be enacted into law. When the Senate persuaded another tribune to veto the enacted law, Tiberius, in an unprecedented move, had him voted out of office. Tiberius then ran for a second term as tribune, another violation of custom and a direct threat to the Senate's power. If a man could hold office indefinitely, the state's ability to check popular power would be destroyed. At last, a group of senators prompted their clients to stage a riot, which ended in the lynching of Tiberius Gracchus.

Ten years later, Gaius Gracchus overcame senatorial opposition and won election as tribune. He revived his brother's proposal for land reform and actually managed to set up colonies of small farmers on public land. To win a wide political base, Gaius sought the support of the urban mob by enabling people to purchase grain from the state at half price. He sought the equestrians' support by giving them control over the juries that heard cases of corruption in tax collecting. Finally, he responded to the old complaint of Rome's Italian allies, particularly of the Samnites, that they, like the Latins, had contributed much to Rome's success, but had never received full rights as citizens. It was Gaius's proposal to grant them citizenship that brought him down. His own supporters were split on the issue, and during the conflict that erupted, Gaius, like his brother before him, was murdered.

Marius and Sulla

The animosities generated by the Gracchi disrupted relations among the Senate, the tribunes and assembly, and the equestrians, and henceforth every proposal met with strong opposition from one quarter or another. The Republic's stability was further imperiled by the rise of independent military power, a consequence of Rome's indulgence in imperialism.

In 107 B.C., Rome was embroiled in a difficult war with a former ally in North Africa, and in desperation the citizens elected as consul Marius, an ambitious equestrian from a rural area. Already famous as a general, Marius quickly brought the African war to a successful conclusion. In 104 B.C., he was called on to meet a new threat. Indo-European tribes, the Germans, had come out of the northern European forests to invade Gaul and now threatened northern Italy. After they defeated several Roman armies that defended the peninsula, Marius was re-elected consul five years in a row (104–100 B.C.) to meet their threat.

In order to build an army strong enough to deal with the Germans, Marius violated the ancient rule that only land-owners could serve in the military and recruited landless men. Formerly, soldiers supported themselves, at no expense to the state. Marius rewarded his men by dis-tributing to them the booty won in battle and by settling them on conquered land. In so doing, he created an army loyal to its general, the source of its reward. More-over, he transformed army service into an attractive career for the poor and dispos-sessed by giving them the prospect of a new start in life. In sum, Marius profes-sionalized the army and set it on the path to independence from the civilian govern-ment it was supposed to serve. The army also acquired an aggressive stance on Rome's dealings with foreign powers, be-cause the soldiers' rewards were won through conquest.

In 90 B.C., Rome's Italian allies, disap-pointed by the death of Gaius Gracchus in their quest for full citizenship, rose in rebellion against the Romans. Marius again assumed military command in this so-called Social War (war with allies—

socii in Latin). After two years of conflict, Sulla, one of Marius's former officers, emerged as the most prominent figure in Roman politics.

Sulla was serving as consul in 88 B.C. when the Romans ended the Social War by granting full citizenship to the Italians. While the war was going on, Mithradates, king of a small Hellenistic state, was trying to create a Hellenistic empire in Asia Mi-nor. In 88 B.C. he instigated the massacre of 80,000 Romans in Greek cities along the coast of ancient Ionia.

Although still consul, Sulla marched on Rome to prevent Marius from receiving the command against Mithradates. Suc-cessful, he moved against Mithradates the next year and, after three years of hard campaigning, succeeded in putting down the rebellion. His long absence from Rome gave his enemies opportunity to under-mine his authority, and in 83 B.C. he again marched on the city. By now, the army had become a force to reckon with in Roman politics. In 82 B.C., Sulla was named dicta-tor to resolve a crisis he himself had pre-cipitated. He proscribed thousands of his enemies—put a price on their heads and confiscated their property. He then distrib-uted the property among his veterans. He installed supporters in the Senate and tried to weaken the powers of the tribunes and the popular assembly. In 79 B.C., he retired from public life and died the follow-ing year.

New Leaders: Pompey, Crassus, and Cicero

After Sulla, the chief object of a political career in Rome was a provincial military command, which brought great wealth and control of a loyal army. Following Sulla's retirement, one of his officers, Pom-pey, emerged as the leading general and politician. His chief rival was Crassus, who had made a huge fortune in questionable real estate dealings in Rome. In 71 B.C., while Pompey was putting down a rebel-lion in Spain, Crassus, though not much of a general himself, snuffed out a dangerous slave rebellion led by a former gladiator named Spartacus. Conflict between the

Sulla, dictator of Rome from 82 to 79 B.C.

two generals was avoided when they were both elected consuls for the year 70 B.C.

In the next few years, a third political figure, Cicero, entered the scene. Cicero was a member of the equestrian class and came from the same town as Marius. None of his ancestors had ever served as a magistrate, so he was a "new man" in town, an unusual figure in Roman politics. But he parlayed his extraordinary skill as a lawyer and orator into a distinguished senatorial career. In fact, Cicero has served as the model for aspiring orators to the present day. He wrote treatises on rhetoric and philosophy that set out the basic rules of public speaking and also set a new standard of Latin prose. His works ultimately became part of the standard fare of every student of the Latin language.

Cicero rose to prominence after he successfully prosecuted a spectacularly corrupt provincial governor named Verres. Throughout his political career, he tried to maintain his political independence. Nonetheless, when obliged to choose between Pompey and Crassus, Cicero threw his support to Pompey. The alliance with Pompey led to Cicero's election as consul in 63 B.C., and during his year in office he put down a conspiracy led by Catiline to seize control of the state. As he had after his prosecution of Verres, he published his speeches made against Catiline and his supporters, thus keeping his name before the public.

In 74 B.C., Mithradates rebelled again. This time, the Romans provided for stable military command in the East by permitting Pompey to remain there for more than a decade and by commissioning him to reorganize imperial government throughout the eastern Mediterranean. By the time he returned to Rome in 62 B.C., he had created a new Roman province in western Asia Minor, had converted Syria into a province, and had put the rest of the Near East under new client kings, including the Jewish Herodians.

When he returned to the capital, Pompey discovered that the Senate was unwilling to ratify all the arrangements he had made or to honor the promises he had given. In the struggle that ensued, he al-lied himself to a powerful urban politician named Gaius Julius Caesar.

THE END OF THE REPUBLIC, 59–30 B.C.

The Rise of Caesar, 59–52 B.C.

Caesar, the scion of an ancient patrician family, had won huge popularity with the Roman mob and while doing so had piled up huge debts. This gave Crassus, whose political power had dwindled after his consulship, a chance to reassert himself. He paid the young man's debts and helped him win rapid political advancement. In 60 B.C., Caesar convinced Pompey and Crassus to join him in a triumvirate, the so-called First Triumvirate. This alliance helped Caesar to win election as consul for the year 59 B.C. Once in office, he saw to it that Pompey's arrangements in the East were ratified and that Pompey's veterans were properly rewarded with public land. He also distributed land to his own urban supporters.

For his own reward, Caesar received a military command, though a less promising one than the command that had made Pompey's reputation. Caesar took command of Gaul, the weak link in Rome's western provinces. The Romans controlled only a narrow strip of territory along the Mediterranean coast, Transalpine Gaul, which linked Cisalpine Gaul (Gaul on the Italian side of the Alps) with the province of Spain. North of Transalpine Gaul, Gallic and German tribes posed a constant threat. Stabilizing this region was essential, but it was an unrewarding assignment for Caesar. The Gallic tribes had none of the wealth of the kingdoms Pompey had conquered in the East.

In 58 B.C., Caesar received a five-year proconsular command, later doubled in length, that included both Cisalpine Gaul and Transalpine Gaul. He immediately launched a campaign to pacify the tribes north of Transalpine Gaul. As he marched north, he saw new enemies further north, and in the end he subdued the whole of Gaul, which he organized as a province.

Bust of Pompey showing him late in life.

Bust of Julius Caesar showing him at the time of his assassination.

Caesar in Gaul   58–49 B.C.

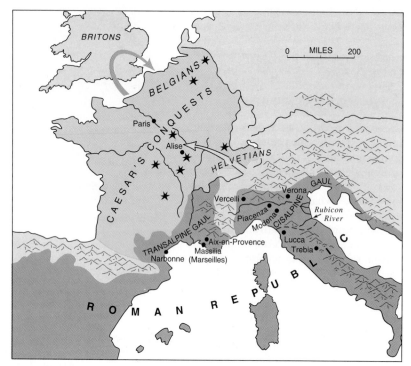

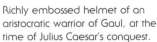

Richly embossed helmet of an aristocratic warrior of Gaul, at the time of Julius Caesar's conquest.

Moreover, he made two expeditions to Britain, where his Gallic foes often took refuge with their Celtic allies, and he crossed the Rhine several times to push the Germans back. He commemorated these campaigns in *Commentaries on the Gallic War*, a model of terse Latin prose that helped establish his fame.

Crassus also received a military command through the triumvirate and led an army against the Parthians, the Roman name for the Hellenistic successors of the Persian empire. In 53 B.C., the Parthians destroyed Crassus's army and killed Crassus himself, leaving Pompey and Caesar as Rome's political leaders. Pompey had returned to Rome by now, and Caesar was still trying to pacify the new province of Gaul.

Caesar and Pompey, 52–48 B.C.

In 52 B.C., Pompey was elected sole consul to put down mob violence in Rome. This extraordinary power gave him an advantage over Caesar, who depended on the Senate and assembly to legitimate his command. Pompey and Caesar had begun to drift apart even before Crassus's death. So long as Caesar remained in command of a fiercely loyal army, Pompey could not feel secure. So he tried to deprive Caesar of his command. Friends of Caesar in Rome blocked this attempt, but it was now clear that the two were enemies. The Senate tried to arrange a settlement by calling on both of them to give up their commands. When Caesar refused, the Senate ordered Pompey to march against him.

One of Caesar's assets as a general was his ability to act swiftly, and he did so now. On March 1, 49 B.C., he crossed the tiny Rubicon River, the border between Cisalpine Gaul and the territory of Rome itself, and began a civil war against Pompey. The Senate had assumed that Pompey would be able to raise an army quickly, but few of his veterans were settled in Italy, and he fled to Greece, accompanied by most of the senators. Rome was open to Caesar. After a year of indecisive fighting, which mostly went in Pompey's favor, Caesar defeated Pompey at Pharsalus in 48 B.C. Pompey escaped to Egypt, where the Ptolemaic king ordered him executed in a bid for Caesar's favor. For the next three years, Caesar and his lieutenants campaigned against Pompey's supporters in Spain, North Africa, and the East.

Caesar in Power, 48–44 B.C.

Caesar was named dictator in 48 B.C. Though this was a republican title, many Romans were aware that political reality had changed dramatically. Caesar held the *imperium*, the supreme military power, and was styled *imperator* (from which the word *emperor* derives), the supreme military commander. Thus he united military and civil authority not as the consuls had under the Republic, but as Sulla had 35 years before. His power derived from his military command rather than from election to civilian office.

Once in power, Caesar undertook reforms similar to those attempted by Sulla and Pompey. He settled his veterans on public land and tried to end corruption in the provincial administrations. He enlarged the Senate and even seated some provincial nobles there. The full incorporation of provincials into Roman government and society was still far in the future, however. He reformed the calendar, adopting the Egyptian year of 365 days with the addition of an extra day every four years to keep it synchronized with the solar year.

His reforms gained him support in Italy and in the provinces, where romanization proceeded rapidly. But the old senatorial class continued to oppose him. Caesar had tried to conciliate them by permitting many scions of the old families to retain their positions in the Senate, but that strategy had failed. The senators viewed the new government as a direct challenge to their ancient rights and an unconstitutional usurpation of power. At last they formed a conspiracy under the leadership of Brutus and Cassius, and Caesar was assassinated in the senate house on the Ides of March (March 15), 44 B.C.

Caesar was not in power long enough to reveal his intentions. It remains unclear whether he planned to set aside the ancient republican constitution or to try, like Sulla, to reform it. Whatever his intent, his death created a political crisis in which any hope that the Republic would be restored was lost.

Civil War and the Second Triumvirate, 44–30 B.C.

In the chaotic political situation that followed Caesar's death, Mark Antony, Caesar's chief lieutenant, won the support of Caesar's veterans and much of the Roman mob. Brutus had hoped to revive senatorial government, but the old system had broken down completely, and he and his co-conspirators found themselves with little support. Octavian, Caesar's grandnephew and adopted heir, a frail 18-year-old, received the support of Cicero and other senators who thought they could control him. But when Octavian had won sufficient support among the Roman mob, he suddenly joined Mark Antony and another of Caesar's former lieutenants, Lepidus, in the Second Triumvirate. Late in

44 B.C., the three led an army on Rome, where the assembly granted them full power for five years.

The new triumvirs began by ordering a bloody proscription against those who had opposed them. Like Sulla, they confiscated the property of those they proscribed and distributed it among their soldiers. Cicero, a personal enemy of Antony, was forced to commit suicide. Brutus and Cassius, who had escaped to Macedonia, were hunted down and were defeated and killed at the Battle of Philippi (in Thrace) in 42 B.C.. The triumvirs then offered favorable terms to the conspirators' army and quickly put an end to the civil war, at least temporarily.

Now the triumvirs had to deal with one another. Antony came out on top. He had the largest army and held command of the wealthy East. Octavian got Italy,

The Murder of Caesar   44 B.C.

The Lives, *written by the Greek historian Plutarch around* A.D. *100, supplies valuable information on Greek and Roman history, particularly on the confusing years of the late Republic. As may be seen from this passage, Plutarch's* Lives *served as a source of Shakespeare's play* Julius Caesar.

When Caesar entered, the senate stood up to show their respect to him, and of Brutus's confederates, some came about his chair and stood behind it. . . . Tillius, laying hold of his robe with both his hands, pulled it down from his neck, which was the signal for the assault. Casca gave him the first cut in the neck. . . . Those who were not privy to the design were astonished, and their horror and amazement at what they saw were so great that they durst not fly nor assist Caesar, nor so much as speak a word. But those who came prepared for the business enclosed him on every side. For it had been agreed that they should each of them make a thrust at him, and flesh themselves with his blood; for which reason Brutus also gave him one stab in the groin. Some say that he fought and resisted all the rest, shifting his body to avoid the blows, and calling out for help, but that when he saw Brutus's sword drawn, he covered his face with his robe and submitted, letting himself fall . . . at the foot of the pedestal on which Pompey's statue stood. . . .

From Plutarch, The Lives of Noble Grecians and Romans, *trans. by John Dryden, rev. by Arthur Hugh Clough (New York: Modern Library, n.d.), pp. 892–93.*

A coin commemorating the death of Caesar. One side bears the portrait of Brutus; the other side shows the assassins' daggers flanking the cap of liberty.

and Lepidus got Gaul and Spain. In time, Octavian forced Lepidus into retirement and won control of all the western provinces. Meanwhile, Antony entered into a love affair with Cleopatra, the Egyptian queen, and granted her large portions of the eastern provinces. Cleopatra was unpopular in Rome, and Antony's relationship with her cost him a great deal of support. Antony also opened a war with the Parthians and weakened his forces while gaining nothing.

By 32 B.C., Octavian had consolidated his hold over Italy and the West and was ready to move against Antony. He secured a decree from the assembly relieving Antony of his command. In 31, after a year of skirmishing, the two met in a great naval battle at Actium, on the Adriatic coast of Greece. There Octavian's fleet, commanded by the capable Agrippa, decisively defeated Antony and Cleopatra. The two fled to Egypt, where first Antony and then Cleopatra committed suicide.

Actium put an end to the civil wars that followed Caesar's death and left Oc-

tavian without rivals. On January 13, 27 B.C., he proclaimed the restoration of the Republic. The proclamation was a sham, but it enabled Octavian to establish a new state, republican in name, but a military dictatorship in fact.

The real genius of the Romans was not in conquest but in law and government. They anchored their society on a system of law, and from an early date dealt with the peoples they conquered according to law. They asked how the law should apply to the conquered. Over time, that emphasis led both their allies and their subjects to think of their position in the empire in legal terms. True, Rome planted garrisons in conquered territories and put down rebellions, but the real conflicts were over the legal rights of groups and individuals and the legal responsibilities of Roman officials. In short, the Romans created a new type of empire, a vast city-state in which ancient ideas of citizenship and government were played out on an international scale.

Suggestions For Further Reading

Hellenistic Period

There is an excellent new survey of Hellenistic history and civilization in P. Green, *Alexander to Actium: The Historical Evolution of the Hellenistic Age* (1990). On the hellenization of the East, see M. Avi-Yonah, *Hellenism and the East: Contacts and Interrelations from Alexander to the Roman Conquest* (1978). On Ptolemaic Egypt, see A. K. Bowman, *Egypt after the Pharaohs, 332 B.C.–A.D. 642* (1986), and P. M. Fraser, *Ptolemaic Alexandria* 3 vols. (1972). M. Hadas, *Hellenistic Culture: Fusion and Diffusion* (1959) is a general introduction. On the Hellenistic philosophical schools, see A. A. Long, *Hellenistic Philosophy:*

Stoics, Epicureans, and Sceptics (1974). For a general introduction to Hellenistic art, see C. Havelock, *Hellenistic Art: The Art of the Classical World from the Death of Alexander the Great to the Battle of Actium*, rev. ed. (1981); on sculpture, see M. Bieber, *The Sculpture of the Hellenistic Age* rev. ed. (1961). On Hellenistic science, see G. E. R. Lloyd, *Greek Science after Aristotle* (1973), and E. J. Dijksterhuis, *Archimedes*, trans. C. Dikshoorn (1987). On the classical scholarship of the Hellenistic period, see R. Pfeiffer, *History of Classical Scholarship from the Beginnings to the End of the Hellenistic Age* (1968).

Roman Political History

There are many reliable texts devoted to Roman history. Among the best are H. H. Scullard, *History of the Roman World from 753 to 146 B.C.*, 3rd ed. (1961); F. B. Marsh, *History of the Roman World from 146 to 30 B.C.*, 3rd ed. (1961); and H. H. Scullard, *From the Gracchi to Nero: A History of Rome from 133 B.C. to A.D. 68* (1975). For a shorter work, see A. E. R. Boak,

A History of Rome to A.D. 565, revised by W. G. Sinnigen (1977). On Pompey, see P. Greenhalgh, *Pompey: The Republican Prince* (1981). On Julius Caesar, see M. Gelzer, *Caesar: Politician and Statesman*, trans. J. Lloyd (1975). On Mark Antony, see E. G. Huzar, *Mark Antony: A Biography* (1978). The reign of Octavian will be treated in the next chapter.

Etruscans and the Roman Republic

On the Etruscans, see H. H. Scullard, *The Etruscan Cities and Rome* (1967), R. Bloch, *The Etruscans* (1958), and H. Hencken, *Tarquinia, Villanovans and Early Etruscans* (1968). O. J. Brendel, *Etruscan Art* (1978), is excellent. L. Bonfante uses Etruscan funerary art to reveal Etruscan society in "Etruscan Couples and their Aristocratic Society," *Women's Studies* 8 (1981) 157–87. R. Bloch, *The Origins of Rome* (1966), and H. H. Scullard, *The Etruscan Cities and Rome* (1967), treat the early history of Rome. On the early conquests, see E. T. Salmon, *Samnium and the Samnites* (1967), and *Roman Colonization under the Republic* (1969). Two works treat the development of Rome's overseas empire: R. M. Errington, *The Dawn of Empire* (1972),

and E. Badian, *Roman Imperialism in the Late Republic* (1968). On the social history of the period, see the studies by M. I. Finley, *Studies in Ancient Society* (1974), P. A. Brunt, *Social Conflicts in the Roman Republic* (1971), and K. R. Bradley, *Discovering the Roman Family: Studies in Roman Social History* (1991).

On aspects of Roman culture, see P. Grimal, *Hellenism and the Rise of Rome* (1968); W. G. Arnott, *Menander, Plautus and Terence* (1975). A rich sampling of selections from ancient Roman sources is collected in the first volume of N. Lewis and M. Reinhold, eds., *Roman Civilization* (1951).

4

THE ROMAN EMPIRE
27 B.C.–A.D. 476

Octavian's proclamation of the restoration of the Roman Republic in 27 B.C., actually marked the beginning of a new era. True, the Senate was restored, consuls and other magistrates were elected once again, and the assembly met from time to time. But these familiar forms of republican government cloaked a military dictatorship. Octavian still held the *imperium,* the supreme military command, and still had the backing of the army. After 14 years of civil war, he had swept the empire clean of challengers and could afford to give honor, if not substance, to the old institutions. He introduced his supporters into the Senate and accepted from them the position of *princeps* (first citizen)—that is, the man who spoke first on any issue before the Senate. When Octavian spoke, the senators listened. The period during which Octavian and his immediate successors controlled the government of Rome is called the Principate.

Shortly after the restoration, the Senate voted to bestow the title *Augustus* on Octavian. This was a title ordinarily used for gods, and a person called *augustus* was looked upon with awe and reverence. In this political usage, it emphasized Octavian's role as the beneficent protector of the state. In a masterstroke of propaganda, Octavian adopted the title as his name, thereby enhancing his authority while avoiding the charge that he was violating constitutional principles as Caesar had.

THE PRINCIPATE OF AUGUSTUS, 27 B.C.–A.D. 14

The Organization of Imperial Government

The backbone of Augustus's power was the army, which was made up of 25 legions of about 6,000 men each and an equal number of auxiliary units of provincial troops. Augustus kept the legions at

(*OPPOSITE*) MEDALLION DEPICTING EMPEROR THEODOSIUS I (R. 379–395).

27 B.C.	A.D. 14		68	96	A.D. 180
Principate of Augustus	Julio-Claudian Emperors		Flavian Emperors	The "Five Good Emperors"	

near full strength; he had about 250,000 men under arms at all times. Because the soldiers received large cash bonuses and an allotment of land when they retired after twenty years of service, they were completely loyal to their commander in chief.

Once he had consolidated his power in the government, Augustus turned his attention to the provinces. During the civil wars, the contenders for power had vied for control of the provinces and had pitted them against one another. Once the wars were over, Augustus assigned his military lieutenants to govern all the provinces in which military garrisons were stationed. The tax revenues collected in each province supported its garrison.

Yet, recognizing that the Senate had a right to participate in governing the provinces, Augustus appointed senators to govern those that were thoroughly pacified, which meant that the Senate controlled the richest, most romanized provinces. He also permitted the local elites to carry out most of the functions of government and continued the old practice of permitting semi-independent client kingdoms on the Empire's fringes to control their internal affairs.

In fact, Augustus encouraged local autonomy throughout the Empire. In Gaul, his governors helped transform the old tribal centers into romanized cities, from which they governed the surrounding region. The Romans devoted substantial sums of money to constructing public buildings in the provincial cities and made a great effort to romanize the tribal aristocracy. In Spain and North Africa, they planted cities in areas where they wanted to encourage agriculture; the North African province eventually had about 300 *municipia,* towns with the legal status of cities, though most of them were little more than agricultural villages. In the

The ruins of public structures at Djemila, Algeria.

East, the ancient city-states were permitted to govern themselves under Roman supervision. In short, the Empire was a collection of city-states under a centralized government in Rome.

Augustus's Social Program

The great theme of the Augustan program was "restoration." He restored peace in Rome and in the Empire, he restored the Republic and the provincial governments, and he sought to restore the fabric of traditional Roman society. He passed legislation to restore the family unit by encouraging marriage and childbearing. Moreover, he made a point of governing through the traditional magistracies and the Senate. All in all, he projected a thoroughly conservative image designed to link himself with the hallowed past of Cato, Cicero, and other heroes of the Republic.

In his efforts to restore traditional Roman religion, Augustus revitalized the old civic cults and reestablished the priesthoods, which had been decimated by the civil wars. After waiting for the old incumbent to die, he himself assumed the role of Pontifex Maximus (highest priest). Meanwhile, he prohibited practice of the mystery cults, which had gained strong followings in Rome during the preceding century (see p. 83).

Augustus's legislation relating to family life reveals a great deal about what had happened to Roman society during the last years of the Republic. Traditionally, Rome was a society of families, each dominated by a patriarch. The male head of the family, the *paterfamilias,* had supreme authority over all members of the household. He owned all the family's property and determined whom his sons and daughters could marry, where they would live, and what professional or economic goals they would pursue. A man who bought something from or lent money to another man whose father was alive was taking a big risk, for the son had no legal right to sell what belonged to his father, and the father was not responsible for his son's debts.

Daughters had even fewer rights than sons. Every woman had a male guard-

Wall painting from Pompeii depicting wealthy Roman women.

ian—usually her father, husband, or a male relative—and she could make decisions about such matters as marriage or buying and selling property only with the guardian's approval and assistance. Women were expected to spin and weave and perform all the household chores. In legend and funerary inscriptions, those who had produced many children were held in high honor.

By the time of Augustus, upper-class women may have been familiar with the domestic arts, but only slaves actually engaged in them. Upper-class Roman women often became patronesses of the arts and sometimes played a role in politics. Some were excellent businesswomen. In practice, most women seem to have had considerable freedom to manage their own affairs. A study of Cicero's wife, Terentia, reveals that she managed substantial property holdings by herself and even kept knowledge of her business dealings from her husband. When Augustus ruled that women who had borne three children would no longer need a guardian, he apparently repealed an old law that no longer had much force.

Augustus's view of the aristocracy emphasized duty to the state, hard work, avoidance of luxury, and traditional family values. He tried to bring the debauched, extravagant members of the upper classes to heel by passing sumptuary laws to control ostentatious expenditures and to encourage marriage and large families. During the last decades of the Republic, some upper-class Roman women practiced contraception and abortion, and many of them refused to marry. To ensure the succession of their property, some elderly women adopted adult men, often young lovers. Augustus's effort to change such behavior met little success.

The lower-class families of Rome needed no law to restrain them from ostentation or lascivious living. All members of the family shared the burdens of earning a living. Women tended shops, worked the fields, and ran the household. Augustus's program concerned itself only with the elite elements of society.

The Golden Age of Latin Literature

During the Augustan restoration, Latin literature achieved its highest level of excellence. Although Greek culture remained a powerful influence, Augustus and his associates patronized a group of writers and poets whose loyalties were rooted in the late republican period. As we have seen (p. 87), Cicero had achieved fame as an orator and essayist, and his prose had set a standard that was to stand for centuries. Caesar's history of the Gallic campaigns became a model for the sparse style of the man of action. Writers who grew up in the times of Cicero and Caesar did their mature work under Augustus.

The leading historian of the Augustan period was Livy (59 B.C.–A.D. 17), who wrote a monumental history of Rome from its origins to the age of Augustus. Though most of that history has been lost, enough remains to show that Livy celebrated the traditional virtues of Roman society that Augustus was trying to restore.

The poets of the late Republic set the basis for the achievements of their Augustan successors. Catullus (87–54 B.C.) wrote lyric poetry that was often of an intimate, sometimes sensuous, nature. Lucretius (99–55 B.C.), perhaps the greatest poet of the republican period, wrote *De rerum natura* (Concerning the nature of things),

a great work extolling the virtues of Epicurean philosophy. Lucretius was too speculative and abstract to appeal to the Romans, however, and had little influence on other poets.

The poets of the Augustan period sometimes chose to write on political themes, and when they did, they revealed some ambivalence toward the Augustan achievement. Horace (65–8 B.C.), Propertius (*ca.* 50–*ca.* 16 B.C.), and Vergil (70–19 B.C.) all wrote poems in which they dealt with the horrors of civil war and with the ethical problem of basing a new society on violence. But they and other poets, including Ovid (43 B.C.–A.D. 18), also wrote love poetry, pastoral idylls, and poems with mythological themes. Ovid was a friend of Horace and Propertius, but unlike them he never chose to extol the ancient Roman virtues so cherished by Augustus. In A.D. 8, after the publication of his *Ars Amatoria* (The Art of Love), Augustus banished him to a small town on the western shore of the Black Sea, where he died ten years later. Augustus considered this poem, and perhaps Ovid's behavior, lacking in the high moral character that he sought to restore to Roman life.

Of the poets of the early Empire, Vergil was surely the greatest. He was born near Mantua in the Lombard plain, and, after receiving his education in Cremona, Milan, and Rome, he returned to his ancestral farm. In 41 B.C., the government confiscated his property and gave it to the soldiers who had defeated Brutus and Cassius at Philippi. Vergil moved to the Campania, where his patron was Maecenas, one of Augustus's lieutenants, and also patron of Horace and Propertius. In the 30s B.C., after Vergil had published two poem cycles dealing with rural life, Augustus asked him to compose a work glorifying Rome and the achievements of the *imperator*.

For the last eleven years of his life, Vergil worked on the *Aeneid,* a great epic tale of the origins of Rome and made an analogy between Aeneas, legendary founder of the city, and Augustus. But Vergil rejected the Augustan propaganda that Rome's greatness rested on its moral superiority. In war, particularly in civil war,

Roman bust of Vergil.

basic moral principles were necessarily violated, and no state founded on war could claim the moral high ground. Aeneas's success in founding Rome rested on violation of the principle, "War down the proud, spare the weak." Augustus had violated this principle many times during the wars that brought him to supreme power.

THE SUCCESSORS OF AUGUSTUS, A.D. 14–68

Because Augustus had retained the republican constitution, there were no rules to determine who would succeed him. Nonetheless, Augustus made it clear that his successor must be from his own family, the Julians. Consequently, during the last two decades of his reign, members of the imperial family constantly jockeyed for position. An atmosphere of intrigue affected the reigns of virtually all of Augustus's successors, often paralyzing them with suspicion and fear. Yet, the imperial government would flourish for centuries.

When Augustus died in A.D. 14, he was succeeded by Tiberius, an able administrator and general who had grown embittered by Augustus's refusal, during his lifetime, to name him as successor. Although Tiberius, a Julian by marriage, came from a distinguished senatorial family, the Claudians, many senators resented his elevation and intrigued against him. It did not help that he set high standards for his administrative assistants and removed many incompetent or dishonest scions of senatorial families from the civil service. After a struggle broke out in his family over who would succeed him when the time came, several suspicious deaths occurred. Fearful for his own life, Tiberius eventually left Rome for the safety of Capri, an island in the Bay of Naples. With Tiberius off the scene, Rome seethed with intrigue. When he heard about it from his spies, he ordered his lieutenants to execute several officials and senators on charges of treason. Tiberius died in 37.

His successor, Caligula, won the hearts of Romans as a young boy, when he often appeared in the company of his elders at official events. People expected great things of him as emperor. But Caligula was insane, and his whimsical cruelty and incompetence in military affairs finally led the palace guard (the elite corps of the army) to put him to death. His reign lasted only four years (r. 37–41).

For a short time after the death of Caligula, the Senate tried to reassert its authority and to restore the Republic in fact as well as in name. But by now real power had resided in the army for a century, and soon the palace guard that had done away with Caligula found someone to take his place. This was Caligula's uncle Claudius (r. 41–54), a scholarly, sickly man of 51 who had survived intrigue by pretending to be a harmless fool. Claudius turned out to be a more capable ruler than anyone expected. He initiated the conquest of Britain and continued the ancient Roman practice of extending citizenship, by making all those who served on provincial city councils citizens of Rome. As an administrator, he established four permanent bureaus, each headed by a freedman of the imperial family (usually a Greek). Senators still commanded the armies and governed the provinces, and equestrians still handled most of the Empire's financial affairs, but Claudius had established the foundations of the imperial bureaucracy that would eventually control the government.

Claudius's good sense did not extend to family matters. He married his niece Agrippina, an evil woman who poisoned him in 54 so that Nero, her son from a previous marriage, could succeed him. For a time, Nero (r. 54–68) acted under the guidance of his tutor Seneca, a philosopher and writer of high standing, and Burrus, master of the palace guard. But in 62, after the death of Burrus, Seneca retired, and the young emperor fell under evil influences.

Nero was a megalomaniac who fancied himself a poet and artist. Rumor said he set a great fire that destroyed much of Rome in 64 to create a brilliant backdrop for a recitation of his poetry. This story is certainly false. Nero cast the blame on a tiny community of Christians in the city

A coin with the bust of Claudius (ca. A.D. 50).

and ordered them killed. According to tradition, St. Peter lost his life in this early persecution.

During his last years, Nero became increasingly fearful of intrigue. In 65, he forced Seneca to commit suicide on suspicion that he had participated in a plot.

Agrippina, Claudius's wife, with her child Nero.

Later, he condemned to death his mother, the poet Lucan, and the general Corbulo, who had defended the eastern frontier against the Parthians. He also executed many senators and confiscated their wealth. Obsessed by threat of intrigue, he paid no attention to the administration or to the army, and in 68 the legions rebelled. Nero was quickly overthrown and committed suicide, ending the Julian succession. A brief civil war followed among the main segments of the army, each comprising several legions. Each unit vied to raise its general to the imperial throne.

THE EMPIRE AT ITS HEIGHT, 69–180

The troubles of 68–69 revealed the weakness of the Augustan political system. The armed forces controlled all power, and each army was loyal to its own commander. So long as the emperor was popular and competent, he could command the loyalty of all the units and preserve order. But when the emperor was weak, as under the later Julians, each army looked to its local commander to provide the rewards of service. The various corps put forward their own candidates after the death of Nero, and there were four "emperors" in one year.

Vespasian, commander of the eastern legions, emerged victorious. He was a self-made man, with foresight and good judgment. Recognizing the need for competence at the top, he trained his sons to be worthy of the role of *imperator*. He wanted his successor to rise through the army ranks, to be experienced in the affairs of empire, and to know the provinces well. After Vespasian, for more than a hundred years, the emperors rose through service in the army.

Vespasian ruled for ten years and was succeeded by his able son Titus (r. 79–81), who had served as co-ruler since 71. Titus was succeeded by his brother Domitian (r. 81–96), who began well but grew increasingly suspicious and arbitrary as time went by. In 96, his wife had him poisoned and the line of Vespasian came to an end.

27 B.C.	A.D. 14		68	96		A.D. 180
Principate of Augustus		Julio-Claudian Emperors		Flavian Emperors	The "Five Good Emperors"	

Nero as emperor.

In this difficult situation, the Senate managed to elevate one of its own members, the elderly Nerva, to the imperial throne. Nerva, recognizing the danger that the state would face when he died, adopted an able legionary commander, Trajan, as his successor (r. 98–117). The practice of adopting an able man as heir and successor continued for four generations and produced the "five good emperors." These were wise and capable administrators, and under them the Empire prospered in peace.

Yet, these emperors instituted certain changes that served to weaken the Empire. The most important was in the military. Under Augustus and his immediate successors, the frontier armies had been mobile, able to make swift forays across the borders. The second-century emperors stationed the legions in permanent camps behind fixed, fortified frontiers. In northern Britain, for example, the emperor Hadrian (r. 117–138) built a wall across the island to keep out the northern tribes. Along the Rhine and Danube frontier, the Romans build a line of fortress camps and watchtowers. The armies that manned these fortifications had to be much larger than the mobile ones, and from the second century on they absorbed an increasing share of the Empire's wealth.

The years of unbroken peace during the second century encouraged farmers in various regions of the Empire to specialize in crops that could be sent to market. Earlier, the ready availability of grain from Sicily had motivated Italian farmers to turn to the production of olives and wine. Now, grain from Egypt and North Africa competed with grain from Sicily, and Gallic wine competed with Italian wine. In short, the regions of the Empire were becoming increasingly interdependent, making them more and more susceptible to any disturbance of the peace. No such disturbance occurred during the second cen-

tury, but in the next century a multitude of troubles erupted.

THE CRISIS OF THE THIRD CENTURY

Political and Military Weakness

The last of the "good emperors," Marcus Aurelius (r. 161–180), had to spend a great deal of time away from Rome dealing with renewed unrest among the Germanic tribes across the Rhine-Danube border. Trier, a city near the border, became his second capital. The trouble was partly the fault of the Romans themselves. By establishing a static defensive line along the border and ceasing to stage forays across the border to keep the Germanic tribes

Vespasian, founder of the Flavian dynasty.

Trajan (*ca.* A.D. 100).

off balance, they had permitted the tribes to gather strength. Moreover, they had contributed to that strength by trading with the tribes and by encouraging them to join together in confederations. The Romans found it easier to deal with large confederations than with a multitude of small tribes, and the Germans, even those far from the frontier, were gradually drawn into the Roman sphere of influence.

The Roman strategy worked for about a century, but starting at the end of the second century, the northern border defenses came under continual pressure. This put a strain on the military system and its supply system and strengthened the position of the local commanders. When under attack, the border armies looked to their commanders for leadership rather than to the emperor. So long as the emperors chose competent and experienced successors who could control their lieutenants in the field, the legionary commanders remained loyal and obedi-

ent. But when Marcus Aurelius passed the imperial power on to his incompetent son Commodus (r. 180–192), a rift opened between the central government and the border armies. When Commodus was assassinated, the events of 68–69 were repeated and legions put up their respective generals as candidates for the imperial seat. Out of the strife, Septimius Severus (r. 193–211) emerged to establish a new dynasty, which ruled from 193 to 235.

The brief civil war altered the balance of power in Roman government. Although the emperors had always risen to power through the army, the civilian government set policy and determined how the legions were to be used. From 193 on, the army determined policy. On his deathbed, Septimius is reported to have advised his son to ensure for himself the affection of the army and to ignore the civil government and the classes that supported it. Whether or not the story is true, under the Severan dynasty the army governed the Empire.

The Roman Empire at Its Height   A.D. 117

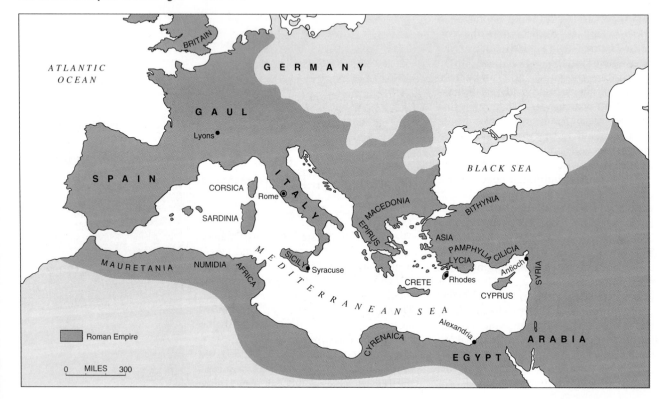

During the brief civil war that followed the death of Commodus, however, the legions had withdrawn from the frontiers, weakening the defenses, and the Severan emperors were unable to reestablish the defense line created by the second-century emperors. When Septimius Severus died in 211, he was in northern Britain pacifying the Caledonian tribes that had been raiding the British province from Scotland. His sons quickly ended the campaign because they had to return to Rome to take over the government. On the Danube, the Germanic tribes, repelled by Marcus Aurelius in the 170s, but now organized in large confederations, reasserted themselves soon after Septimius's death. To the north, in the lower Rhine Valley, a group of related tribes, called the Franks, formed a confederation of their own. To the south, along the upper Rhine, a confederation of Alemans emerged, and, to the east, along the lower Danube, the Goths formed from tribes that appear to have migrated from southern Scandinavia. The Goths even managed to put together a pirate fleet in the eastern Mediterranean. In the Middle East, the Parthians renewed their pressure on the Empire after 224, when the Sassanid dynasty overthrew the old hellenistic Seleucid state.

Under all these attacks, the imperial system, already weak, broke down. The number of demands made on the emperor, even if he was competent and energetic, could not be met. Again, the troops turned to their commanders for the rewards of service.

When the last of the Severi was assassinated in 235, the powerful border armies took over the Empire. Between 235 and 285, they created and killed 26 emperors and at least as many unsuccessful contenders. The troops concerned themselves only with their own interests and regarded the emperor simply as the guarantor of their well-being.

Economic and Political Problems

In fact, by the third century, maintaining the vast army had become a heavy burden on the government. In 212, the emperor Caracalla (r. 211–217) issued a law that

The emperor Marcus Aurelius (r. 160–180) entering Rome in triumph (detail from the column of Marcus Aurelius in Rome).

granted citizenship to all free men in the Empire and thus made them liable for military service and the payment of certain taxes. By this time, virtually all tax receipts were going to supply the vast border armies, and most taxes were being paid in

Third-century tomb relief showing an affluent banker and two struggling Roman laborers. The Roman economy was weakened by the gap between the wealthy few and the poor masses.

kind—that is, in grain or other produce rather than in coin—at stations along the military roads that ran throughout the Empire. The goods were then transported to the military installations at the border. But even this enormous supply could not support the hundreds of thousands of troops, and the state began to purchase great quantities of agricultural products in the market. The great landowners were the main beneficiaries of those purchases.

The government took over other sectors of the economy as well. Many goods were manufactured in state factories, including all weapons and most army clothing. Goods were sent to the troops through the government transport system, which virtually monopolized large-scale transportation. The government also organized and subsidized the provisioning of major cities, which meant that independent merchants were left to deal in a few widely available low-value raw materials such as timber, wool, and flax, and in ordinary tools and implements. They could also deal in luxury items such as spices, jewelry, and fine wines, but that trade was only a small part of the economy. Most of the traders in luxury goods were Orientals, including Syrians and Jews, who had connections in the eastern Mediterranean cities through which spices and the oils used in perfumes passed, some of them from as far away as India and China.

The civil wars of the third century put enormous stress on this government-dominated economy. Armies on the march repeatedly disrupted the operation of farms and the collection and transport of produce, and severe inflation set in. Now the armies began to compete for tax revenues as well as for the imperial throne and subjected the people in the provinces to repeated demands for taxes—demands backed by military force.

The main victims of this crisis were the provincial aristocrats who governed the towns; they were responsible for the

Roman Trade Routes at Height of Empire

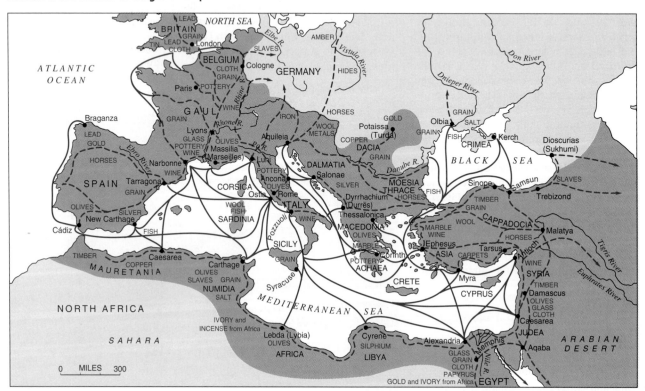

whole system of tax collection and government. Under the Roman system, the local government, run by a council (*curia,* pl. *curiae*) made up of the leading men of the town, collected taxes, maintained roads and bridges, and conducted all other government business in the district. Every man with property of a certain value was obliged to serve as a *curialis* (pl. *curiales*) of his *municipium* and, with his colleagues, was personally responsible for performing government functions. In practice, during normal times, the members of the *curia* had townspeople carry out most of their duties. During the civil wars, however, so many people were financially ruined that city councils had trouble finding anyone to perform public services or to pay taxes, and their personal liability became a very heavy burden.

Many of the *curiales,* who had once regarded their position as a sign of economic and social distinction, escaped their obligations by retiring to their country estates. As a result, the government of a great many provincial towns simply collapsed. From time to time, during periods of relative tranquillity, the imperial government tried to reestablish the municipal governments, but with little success.

Actually, the imperial government opened up another avenue of escape for the *curiales.* Civil servants were exempt from service in the *curiae,* and a great many local aristocrats won appointment to the imperial bureaucracy from emperors eager to please. As a result, the two governments dwindled as the bureaucratic class grew. Moreover, the civil wars and the swift comings and goings of emperors kept the bureaucracy in constant turmoil, torn by shifting loyalties and competing claims. With each new emperor, the civil servants appointed by the last one were purged, though some of them managed to survive.

IMPERIAL SOCIETY, FIRST TO THIRD CENTURIES

Rural Life

What was life like during these centuries? Even during times of tranquillity, the lives

Roman Military Weakness   Late Second Century

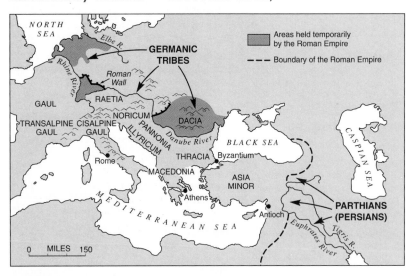

of ordinary men and women were not always peaceful. In the countryside, most people lived in small villages, many of them wholly owned by upper-class landlords. Outside the villages, thieves roamed

Municipal Services in the Greco-Roman Cities

What are today regarded as the municipal services *par excellence* are not very frequently mentioned in antiquity. . . . The first duty of the *astynomi* [controllers or *curiales* of the towns] was the care of roads and bridges, both in the city itself and in its territory. They had to prevent encroachments on the public highway; the . . . law laid down minimum widths for country roads, thirty feet for a main road, twelve feet for a byroad. They had to remove obstructions; shopkeepers were allowed to display their wares outside their shops, but not in such a manner as to block the traffic. They had to prevent rubbish being tipped into the streets. . . . Landowners and householders were responsible . . . for the paving of the roads on which their property fronted, and the *astynomi* had to enforce this obligation. . . . Another care of the *astynomi* was drainage. Progressive cities had a regular system of drains, running under the streets, which carried off both surface water and sewage. . . . For their water-supply all ancient cities relied to some extent on wells and rain-water cisterns, and it was the duty of the *astynomi* to see that the owners of these kept them in good order.

From A. H. M. Jones, The Greek City *(New York: Oxford University Press, 1940), pp. 212–13.*

A roman vegetable stall and its owner.

the land. Many villages had watchtowers, and almost all of them posted guards night and day. Farmsteads outside the village were situated well off the road and were fortified with walls and watchtowers. There was no police force, either in the cities or in the countryside, and the armed forces took action only during major insurrections.

At the bottom of the social hierarchy were the shepherds, who worked for either peasants or landowners and lacked even the protection afforded by the peasant villages. When the shepherd was out in the fields watching his sheep and goats and accompanied by his powerful mastiff, he had to be on constant guard against roving bands of rustlers. When he came to the village, he lived in a rundown section, referred to as the Shepherds' Quarter.

The peasants, by far the largest class in the Empire, were not much better off. Many of them, if not most, were tenant farmers working under the harsh supervision of the landowners' bailiffs and accountants. These men, unfettered by conscience and unrestrained by the landowner, could keep for themselves anything beyond what the landowner demanded from the tenants. The few records that survive, mostly from the province of Egypt, reveal the bitter conflict that raged between peasants and landlords. At times, desperate villagers, who were being ruined by the high rents and exactions, physically attacked the hated bailiffs.

There is some evidence of a small rural middle class of prosperous farmers and villagers, but farmers who owned their own plots were scarcely better off than the tenant farmers. Their holdings were likely to be small and poor (records remain of men who owned one-sixth of an olive tree and one-tenth of a small house), and their powerful, upper-class neighbors were a constant threat. Many of the landowners held an assortment of small parcels of land rather than a large, coherent estate, and they did whatever they could to force the farmers off the land to enlarge and consolidate their enormous holdings. The records show farmers complaining that powerful neighbors had turned animals loose in the fields to ruin their crops, or had sent work crews in to harvest their crops before they themselves could harvest them. Many of the farmers simply gave up and sold or abandoned their land to the great landowners.

If a powerful neighbor did not ruin a farmer, the state itself might do so. The government taxed districts on the basis of their total production, without taking into account the exemptions granted to many upper-class holders. Most of the tax burden fell on the small farmers. With the enormous growth of the armies, taxes grew heavier and heavier, and from time to time the government had to lighten the load to keep whole districts from being deserted as the farmers gave up and migrated to the cities.

To add to their hardships, rural families were constantly threatened by famine. The military roads ran straight to the borders, rarely providing connections between regions along the way. Consequently, a poor harvest in one region might mean starvation, even though a nearby region was enjoying a good harvest.

Although the evidence is spotty, it shows that overcrowding was the norm even in the countryside. In Egypt, records show that 25 people, more or less closely related, lived in one house. Unwanted infants were often abandoned, commonly left on the village dungheap where well-to-do families might pick them up to be raised as slaves. Such people were known as people "of the dungheap" throughout their life.

Urban Life

In such conditions, it is not surprising that wealth and talent were concentrated in the cities. The rents, taxes, and food produced in the countryside flowed to the cities, and often the countryfolk starved while the townspeople lived comfortably. Because the best craftsmen left the villages for the city, only simple implements were produced in the country. Rural folk relied on peddlers for things that required skill and good materials to make. With few exceptions, the great landowners lived in magnificent houses in the city and left their country holdings in the hands of bailiffs.

During the imperial period, great urban estates covered one-third of the city of Rome, and public buildings occupied another quarter of it. Ordinary folk lived in densely populated neighborhoods, usually arranged in blocks. The density of the larger Roman cities has been calculated at about 200 people per acre. Today in Europe, 150 people per acre is considered dense, and 250 per acre a slum. People spent as much time as possible in the streets, and only the existence of public areas made city life bearable. Every incident on the crowded streets instantly drew a crowd, and a person was never far from violence.

Property ownership in the cities was much like that in the countryside. The multistory tenements in which most city-dwellers lived were owned by large landowners who often let the buildings run down. Indeed the buildings were so badly built that they often collapsed. Cicero wrote to a friend about the collapse of two buildings he owned; he decided to rebuild them in the hope of getting a good return on his investment. Crassus (p. 86) made a fortune in Roman real estate. He created a private fire brigade, and when a building caught fire, his men would arrive,

This marble relief pictures a small Italian city as it looked in the days of the early Caesars. Blocks of two- and three-story tenements are enclosed by the ancient town wall. At the right, the country villas of the wealthy, with their gardens and colonnades, sprawl across the nearby hillsides.

strike a deal for the property, and then put out the flames.

Block associations organized by the city residents served as the basis of the census and of the government's tax system. These associations, which met at the corner cafe, took care of all sorts of business: They helped families in trouble, functioned as burial societies, and organized youth athletic clubs. Tradespeople and artisans formed associations of their own. People who worked in the same craft or trade—butchers, booksellers, cobblers, and so forth—usually lived in the same part of town, and buyers knew where to go to find what they wanted. The trade associations lobbied government officials on measures that affected their business. In fact, clubs and associations of one kind or another were ubiquitous in city life. Organizations supported shrines, promoted athletics, and served dozens of other purposes. A foreigner entering the city always headed for the shrine his countrymen had set up, confident that he would find someone there to help him.

The greatest cities of the Empire were Rome and Alexandria, each with nearly a million inhabitants. Antioch and Carthage (Carthage was recovering from its destruction by Rome) were next, with populations of several hundred thousand. About six other cities had populations of 75,000, and a great many had populations of about 20,000. Many cities, such as most of those in North Africa, were cities in name only. They had the status of *municipium* but were in reality simply agricultural villages.

In both country and city, the gulf between rich and poor was extreme, with only a small middle class at the economic center. Virtually all wealth was in land and loans. Senatorial families rarely participated in commercial activities, because they could make 6 percent annually on their loans, doubling their money every twelve years. Along with their vast holdings in land, rich men could afford to sit back and let their fortunes grow.

The turmoil of the third century made life more difficult for everyone, but Roman society remained remarkably stable. Although the great estates continued to grow larger, peasant agriculture remained the backbone of the economy. And although the cities had their troubles, the urban elite remained strong.

Culture and Society

The local aristocracies constituted the largest class of educated people in the Empire, and their education was remarkably similar from one end of the Roman world to the other. That similarity served to narrow the linguistic and cultural differences between the Latin West and the Greek East. Although Greeks did not study Latin unless they aimed to pursue a military or legal career—all official documents sent to the East were accompanied by a Greek translation—all educated westerners during the first and second centuries were fluent in Greek. The disruptions of the third century, which concentrated everyone's attention on local affairs, seem to have weakened the status of Greek as a universal language, however. By the fourth century, the corpus of Greek philosophy, science, and theology was being translated into Latin for the benefit of educated westerners who had not learned Greek.

Much like the upper classes of Hellenistic society, the aristocracy of the Roman Empire was a thin veneer over a great

A model of the Roman Forum, the heart of the imperial capital. The Forum, originally a market area, contained the main temples of the city, the Senate House, and other government buildings.

range of peoples with vastly different cultures. In fact, the Empire was a patchwork of ethnic societies. Because Latin and Greek were virtually the only written languages (Syriac and Hebrew were rare exceptions) and the only ones taught in schools, it is difficult to identify the linguistic patterns prevailing across the Empire. It seems likely, however, that the indigenous populations continued to speak their own languages. Several dialects of Celtic (from which modern Gaelic and Breton derive) were spoken in Gaul and Britain, and several native languages continued to be used in Asia Minor. Syriac and Coptic (the Egyptian language) also continued in common use. Thracian, the language spoken by tribes living in the southern Balkans, was still spoken in the fourth century, and modern Albanian is probably a survival of the language spoken by the ancient Illyrians.

Thus, the Empire accommodated two more or less distinct levels of culture. At one level were the leaders of the imperial government and the classes that served it, controlling a vast realm united by the Mediterranean and by a network of roads that carried communications, goods, and armies. The education, institutions, and tastes of this class were remarkably homogeneous; theirs was the culture known as Greco-Roman. At the second level were the myriad populations that maintained their pre-Roman customs and languages, even while living under the imperial government.

Although the upper classes were culturally unified, they were highly stratified. Under the Empire, with its vast imperial bureaucracy and many subject peoples, Romans and provincials alike developed a fondness for honorific titles to demonstrate their position in society and in government. In the late third century, the highest class, the senators, bore the title *clarissimi* (most distinguished), while the high judges of imperial courts were called *eminentissimi* (most eminent) and their immediate subordinates, *perfectissimi* (most excellent). The prestige that went with these titles declined as the emperors bestowed them on more and more public servants in return for faithful ser-

vice. In the late third century, approximately 500 senators were *clarissimi*; but by the middle of the sixth century, several thousand could claim that title. The same happened with other titles. Moreover, there was a proliferation of new titles— for example, *spectabiles* (nobles) and *viri illustri* (illustrious men). Such titles also defined the privileges accorded to their holders.

There were middle-class titles also, but these defined obligations rather than privileges. At the top were the *curiales,* the members of the municipal councils (see p. 103). The superintendents of state factories, which dominated the industrial economy of the Empire, were substantial men with appropriate titles of their own. They ranked above the merchants, who, even when they were successful, rarely rose into the class of *curiales*. On the whole, merchants were on the same social level as the craftsmen who worked in the state factories.

A Roman girl with a writing tablet is depicted in this fresco from Pompeii (*ca.* A.D. 70).

THE RISE OF CHRISTIANITY

During the last century of the Republic, Rome was flooded with mystery cults from the eastern provinces. Augustus tried to stamp them out, but they continued to grow in number and influence under the Empire. Yet, their influence was slight compared to that of Christianity. Originating in Palestine and other regions of the eastern Mediterranean as a religion antagonistic to Rome, Christianity had become by the late fourth century the predominant religion of the Empire.

Christianity emerged from Judaism at a time of ferment in that ancient religion. A split in the Jewish community had opened up between those who had assimilated into Hellenistic society and those who had preserved their Semitic identity. Symbolic of that split was the translation of the Hebrew Bible into Greek in Alexandria in the second century B.C., evidence that many Jews no longer knew Hebrew and were practicing their religion in Greek. Moreover, several conflicting sects emerged within Judaism itself.

After Pompey organized the eastern provinces (74–62 B.C.), the Jews lived in a semiautonomous client kingdom until the death of the last king, Herod the Great (r. 37–4 B.C.). The Romans then took over direct administration of the kingdom and made it part of the province of Syria. As long as the Jews had their own king, they had debated how their kingdom would achieve its historical destiny as defined by the Hebrew Bible. Now, the argument shifted to how to deal with the Romans, who the Jews believed stood in the way of that destiny. While the majority of the Jewish population accommodated itself to Roman rule, some of the religious sects were fanatically anti-Roman and agitated ceaselessly for rebellion. The Romans' insensitivity to Jewish sentiments sometimes provoked violent demonstrations and occasional acts of rebellion.

The first significant rebellion occurred at the beginning of Roman rule. In 4 B.C., the Romans announced that a census would be taken, following a practice initiated by Augustus as a basis for taxation. The Hebrew Bible prohibits the numbering of the people of God, and the Jews rebelled. The Romans put the rebellion down, and the Jews had to limit their activity to guerrilla warfare until A.D. 66. At that point, a great rebellion erupted that took the Romans four years of hard fighting to subdue. They then tried, unsuccessfully, to destroy the Jews' sense of identity by destroying the city of Jerusalem and its temple. The last great Jewish rebellion took place in 135. Thereafter, the Romans tried to cope with the Jewish problem by forcing many Jews to emigrate to other parts of the Empire. During this time of troubles, the Romans crucified thousands of Jews as subversives and conceived a strong dislike for the Jews and their troublesome religion.

Between about A.D. 26 and 29, Jesus of Nazareth attracted a small following among the Semitic Jews of Galilee, a part of the ancient kingdom of Samaria (see p. 26). But, like all Jews, Jesus regarded Jerusalem as the center of Judaism, and in 29 he led his followers to the city. According to the Christian scriptures, his followers eventually came to regard him as the Messiah, the anointed of God (in Greek, the Christ), who would lead the Jews to glory and establish the kingdom of God on earth. They associated Jesus with the Savior prophesied in the Bible by Isaiah (7:14).

Religious figures such as Jesus were common in Judea at that time—John the Baptist had built a following shortly before Jesus did. Such figures made both the Romans and the Jewish leaders nervous, because they often stirred up anti-Roman agitation or actual insurgency. When Jesus arrived in the environs of Jerusalem, he fell under suspicion, and the Romans soon arrested and crucified him. Crucifixion was the Roman punishment for insurgents.

The death of Jesus caused most of his followers to lose their faith in him as the Messiah. The committed few, however, believed that he had been resurrected after three days, and it is that belief that lies at the heart of Christianity. The believers, under the guidance of Peter (one of the first members of the sect), worked out an interpretation of the ancient prophesies to account for the death and resurrection of Jesus.

A small community of Christians soon came together in Jerusalem, where they were persecuted by the Jews but pretty much ignored by the Romans. At first, the sect grew modestly and slowly, if at all, and attracted only other Semitic Jews. Then the conversion of a hellenized Jew named Saul radically changed its fate.

Saul, who changed his name to Paul after his conversion, preached the message of Jesus to great numbers of hellenized Jews who had migrated to the great cities of the eastern Mediterranean. There, they had attracted many Gentiles who came to their prayer services and became familiar with the Jewish religion without actually becoming Jews. In these mixed communities Paul and his assistants found many of their converts.

By the time Jerusalem was destroyed by the Romans in 70, Christianity had spread to Antioch, Alexandria, Rome, and many lesser cities. The Christians formed small communities—much like the familiar urban associations. They met for com-

Symbol of Christianity, incorporating the Greek letters *chi* and *rho* (the monogram for Christ that forms the shape of the cross) and *alpha* and *omega* (meaning *beginning* and *end*).

mon worship—focused on a ritual meal modeled on the last supper of Jesus—in the houses of their richest members, and they performed works of charity toward their poorest members. At first, these communities seem to have had little formal structure, except that elders (presbyters) organized their worship and social work.

The Semitic Christians believed that Jesus was the Messiah who had come to save the Jews. Paul, aware that converts in the Hellenistic population would not respond to such a nationalistic mission, preached that Jesus came not to lead Israel to victory over its enemies, but to save mankind. The Semitic Christians emphasized the human Jesus and the continuity of their religion from Judaism. Paul emphasized the divine Jesus, the Savior of all who had faith in him, and the break with the Jewish past. The Semitic Christians continued to follow the dietary and other religious laws of Judaism. The Greek Christians could see no reason to obey those laws, and Paul argued that belief in Jesus as the Messiah freed one from the law of the Hebrew Bible, which became for Christians the Old Testament. These differences between Paul and the Semitic Christians led to a conflict, recorded in the New Testament (Acts 15), that was settled in Paul's favor. Henceforth, the church preached to both Jews and non-Jews, and Christianity emerged as a universal religion based on faith in Jesus rather than obedience to Mosaic law.

For the first century and a half, the Romans regarded Christianity as just one of the multitude of eastern mystery cults. Like those cults, Christianity emphasized individual religious experience and a personal, emotional, and intimate contact with the deity. Like them, it offered communion with the deity in this life, and promised union with the deity after death. Like them, it used sacraments, ritual acts that prepared the initiated for communion with the deity, and it had a body of doctrine that explained the mystery by which the deity survived death. In fact, Christianity absorbed several ideas and practices from the mystery cults, probably at the suggestion of Christians who had previously belonged to one of them.

Christianity had several advantages over the cults, however. First, it drew on the ancient Judaic heritage, which gave it a strong sense of identity. Second, it had originated in part from an interpretation of the Hebrew Bible, and that experience enabled it to integrate new ideas into its body of beliefs.

Third, Christianity was not a secret society. The Christians had inherited from the Jews a sense of community as evidenced in their open refusal to honor the Roman gods and their consistent attitude toward the Roman government. Christians were adamant in their refusal to render unto Caesar what was God's. Finally, Christianity, despite its Judaic origins, was deeply influenced by Hellenistic beliefs and ideas. It was thus both ancient and modern, a Judeo-Greco-Roman religion.

These unique characteristics complicated the relationship between Christianity and the Roman state. Every good Roman believed in the existence of gods who lived in an invisible world and had power over human affairs. The welfare of the state depended on the favor of those gods, and to ensure that favor, sacrifices (the ritual slaughter of animals) must be performed in which every member of the community participated. The Jews had refused to take part in such sacrifices for centuries, but the Romans recognized the Jews as a separate people with a separate religion, and they had always been tolerant of such "native" traditions. Some Roman officials, including Pontius Pilate, the governor of Judea (26–36) who had ordered the execution of Jesus, liked to bait the Jews, but on the whole the Romans left the Jews in peace.

The Christians were a different matter. Although they had originated as a Jewish sect, they had disassociated themselves from the Jews, particularly after the great Jewish rebellion of 66–70, and by the second century most Christians were gentiles. Consequently, because the Christians were not a distinct ethnic minority following an ancient religious tradition, the Romans would not tolerate their refusal to participate in the sacrifices. Before the end of the first century, a law was passed making it a capital offense to be

The Formation of the New Testament

The New Testament consists of 27 parts written between the 50s and the early second century. These works were not the only ones written and circulated among the Christian communities during the century after Jesus's death. But they were the ones eventually recognized by the church as divine revelation. The formation of the canon, or list, of books with scriptural authority took place in the mid-third century. It occurred in response to several challenges within the Christian community. Some bishops, such as Papias of Hieropolis in Asia Minor (d. *ca.* 130) claimed that his memory of the sayings of the apostles was sufficient for knowledge of the new religion. Writers of the second and third centuries pointed out inconsistencies in Papias's recollections and their contradictions to written testimony such as Paul's letters and the gospels. Marcion (d. *ca.* 160) claimed that the god of the Old Testament was different from the god revealed by Jesus, and his followers renounced the Old Testament as irrelevant to Christians. The Gnostics, a heretical group that believed that Christianity consisted not in faith in Jesus alone but in knowledge of his message, claimed that writings containing the wisdom constituted the holy book.

In response to such challenges, and particularly to counter the Marcionites, orthodox Christians began to define their holy scriptures, choosing works that affirmed the continuity between the Old and the New Testaments and that were connected with the apostolic age. The slow process of distinguishing the true from the false testament finally ended with the definition of Athanasius, bishop of Alexandria (r. 328–373), who listed the 27 books still included in the New Testament. Jerome (see p. 120) accepted this list when he translated the Bible into Latin. Officially, however, the New Testament was not defined until the Council of Trent in 1546.

a Christian, and for generations people circulated rumors that Christians engaged in immoral rituals during their services.

Suspicion of the Christians intensified during the third century, when assaults on the Empire made Romans eager for some show of divine favor. In 250, the emperor Decius ordered all Romans to participate in sacrifices and to obtain certificates showing that they had done so. This order was tantamount to official persecution of the Christians. In most places, the authorities permitted Christians either to ignore the order or to get a certificate through official connivance. But a few Christians made a public show of their refusal to conform and were executed. The persecu-

tion came to an end when Decius was killed by the Germans in 251 but was revived in 257 when the emperor Valerian ordered new prayers for success against the Persians. When Valerian was captured by the Persians in 260, persecution virtually disappeared for forty years.

By this time, the Christian communities were growing rapidly and were becoming influential in many towns. As local government weakened during the civil wars, many social functions, particularly caring for the poor and settling disputes that did not lead to a law suit, were left to private groups. The Christian congregations were well suited to perform those functions, and in doing so they gained many new adherents. The heads of the congregations, the bishops, became increasingly visible and respected in the urban communities.

The optimism and complacency generated by two generations of steady growth made the next persecution particularly traumatic. Known as the Great Persecution, it lasted from 303 to 311. To understand its place in Roman history, we must turn to the reign of the emperor Diocletian.

THE RESTORATION OF ORDER: THE REIGN OF DIOCLETIAN, 284–305

The prolonged crisis of the third century disrupted, but did not destroy the Roman army or the Roman bureaucracy. The potential for recovery remained, and restoration of peace and order became the goal of those seeking the imperial throne. The first step was taken by the emperor Aurelian (r. 270–275), who put an end to civil war and started to shore up the border defenses. His successors carried on his work, though the armies continued to make and unmake emperors at a rapid pace. In 284, Diocletian, general of the Illyrian legions, came to power and brought the work of restoration to a successful conclusion.

Diocletian abandoned Rome as his official residence and moved his court to cities closer to the frontiers of the Empire,

A.D. 96	180	284	305
The "Five Good Emperors"	Century of Disorder	Diocletian	

eventually settling at Nicomedia in northwestern Asia Minor. From these provincial capitals, he rebuilt the frontier fortifications and enlarged the army. At the same time, he broke the army down into smaller units and relieved the commanders of responsibility for supplying and paying their troops, which made it more difficult for them to use army backing in a bid for power.

In addition, he decided to share his power with Maximian, whom he named coemperor. Both took the title Augustus. Later he created two assistant emperors and designated them as heirs to the imperial title; they were both called Caesar. Diocletian's powerful personality dispelled the potential for conflict in this new arrangement.

Further, Diocletian increased the number of provinces from 50 to 100 and organized them into 13 dioceses. Under this reorganization, the new administrations were more effective in governing the provinces than the old one had been, and they absorbed some of the functions formerly handled by the municipal councils. Still, the curial class retained its claim to office, and Diocletian and his successors tried to close off the avenues by which its members were escaping their obligations. When those efforts failed, the municipal councils began to be replaced by imperial officials—in the West in the early fifth century and in the East toward the end of the century.

In an effort to stabilize the society of the Empire, Diocletian issued a series of laws designed to create a rigid caste system. Sons were now required to follow the occupations of their father. And farmers, both tenant and free, were required to remain on the land they had been occupying when the 290 census was taken and were obliged to register sons with the census-takers. The caste system was imposed on other occupations as well, including bakers and sailors. These actions ensured that the census would be kept

current, making it more reliable as a basis for taxation. The civil wars had inflicted heavy damage on the state-run industries, and taxes were more important than ever as a source of funds. Diocletian had his financial staff adjust the tax levies every year on the basis of the census. The tax rate doubled between 324 and 364.

In economic affairs, Diocletian tried to check the inflationary spiral that had set in during the civil wars. He reformed the currency, and, when that effort failed, he issued a decree fixing the prices of many goods. That policy failed as well, even though the penalty for violating it was death.

The Great Persecution of the Christians was part of Diocletian's comprehensive program of restoration. His aim was to restore the pagan cults, particularly the imperial cult that had long served to unify the Empire. When the Christians refused to participate in the rituals of the cult, he turned against them in 303. Subsequent Christian accounts of the persecution exaggerated the number of believers who were martyred, but the experience must

Diocletian and his coemperor stand in front, embracing each other; the two Caesars stand behind them (St. Mark's Cathedral, Venice).

The Administrative Divisions of Diocletian   Third and Fourth Centuries

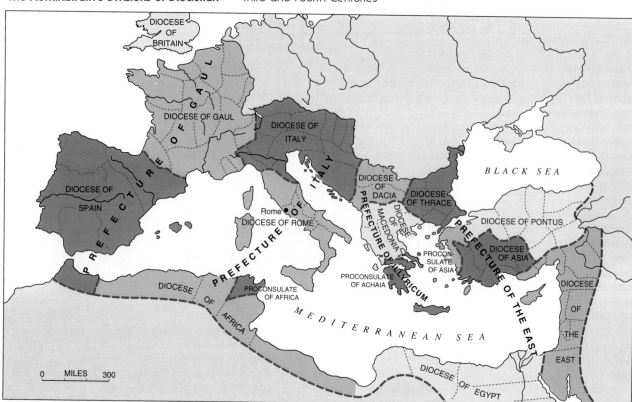

have been a profound shock to the Christian communities. For more than forty years, they had been left in peace, growing steadily under the able leadership of the bishops. They were gradually being assimilated into Roman society, and in many places they played an important role in their communities. Then, just as peace and order were returning to society at large, they were again subjected to persecution, which lasted until 312.

Diocletian retired in 305, apparently convinced that he had completed his ambitious program of restoration. He forced his coemperor Maximian to retire as well, and the two Caesars succeeded to the imperial throne. The dynastic ambitions of these men led to a new civil war eventually won by Constantine, son of one of the successors to Diocletian and Maximian. Constantine won control of the western provinces of the Empire in 312 and emerged as sole emperor in 324.

THE EMPIRE IN THE FOURTH AND FIFTH CENTURIES

The Fourth Century

Aside from rejecting Diocletian's commitment to divided authority, Constantine followed most of his policies. He ruled first from Milan and then from a new city built on the site of the ancient Athenian colony at Byzantium on the Bosporus, later renamed Constantinople. From Milan, he had ready access to the troubled western borders along the Danube and Rhine Rivers. And from Constantinople, he had ready access to the wealth of Asia Minor and could deal with the renewed threat of the Persians, who were once again pressing on the eastern borders.

He could also look back to Europe, where the Germans were on the attack again. Along the Rhine-Danube frontier, the Roman armies were seriously short of manpower, and the government had to rely more and more on the use of foreign troops. From ancient times, the Romans had supplemented the legions with auxiliary troops of provincials, but the distinction between Roman and provincial disappeared after the emperor Caracalla granted universal citizenship in 212 (see p. 101). Now the Romans began to make pacts with the German kings whereby German tribes could settle on Roman territory in return for serving as a military buffer against other Germans. The tribes enlisted in this way were called *foederati* (allied or confederated peoples), and by the later fourth century they constituted the bulk of the Roman army in the West. Consequently, German kings and military commanders became generals in the Roman armies, and large numbers of Germans became at least partially romanized.

In the long run, this process of federating and romanizing the Germans smoothed the transition to a new society following the collapse of imperial power in the West. But in the short run it made border conditions uncertain and unstable. The federated tribes did not break off relations completely with their fellow Germans on the other side of the border and, especially in times of peace, there was considerable commerce back and forth. Consequently the loyalties of the *foederati* could not always be relied on when tribes from across the board staged attacks against Roman positions.

The Romans coped as best they could by playing the tribes off against one another. But that was a chancy business, and in the second half of the fourth century frontier defenses broke down repeatedly. Franks, Alemans, Burgundians,

The Germanic Migrations   Fourth to Sixth Centuries

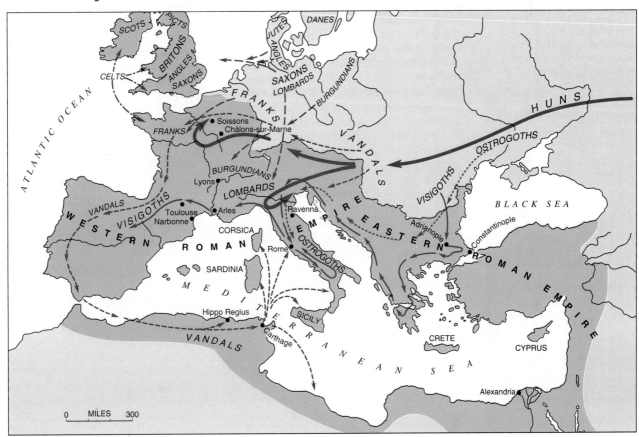

Lombards—all peoples whose names survive in modern Europe—fought their way into the Empire, were driven back, and came again. The greatest incursion of all was the massive influx of Visigoths toward the end of the fourth century.

Goths, a group of tribes that had migrated from Scandinavia to the plains of southwestern Russia (the Ukraine), had been troubling the Empire for a century and a half, but the imperial armies had fought them off. In the course of their migrations, they had divided into two large groups, the Ostrogoths and the Visigoths. In 375, both groups were suddenly overrun by the Asiatic Huns.

The Huns were a nomadic people from Central Asia who normally lived in small bands that ranged over a large territory in search of pasturage for their flocks. Over the centuries, they had become expert horsemen and had acquired most of the equipment needed for cavalry warfare, including horseshoes and stirrups. Occasionally, a strong leader would bring the bands together into a great horde that would force everyone in its path to join or be killed. Around the middle of the fourth century, the Huns attacked China and were driven back. They then turned west, meeting little resistance. In 375, they rode onto the plains of southern Russia and crushed the Ostrogoths.

The Visigoths immediately packed up and tried to escape. The Roman emperor Valens (r. 364–378) gave them permission to settle inside Roman territory, in present-day Bulgaria, on condition that they become *foederati* and defend the border. He promised to keep them supplied during the defense, but he broke his word. Soon the Visigoths renounced their allegiance, abandoned the border, and began to plunder the Roman provinces to the south, in the direction of Constantinople. Valens declared war and led an army against them. The war ended in 378 in a pitched battle at Adrianople, in which the Visigoths defeated the Romans and killed the emperor. For the next year, the victors wandered about pillaging towns in Greece and Macedonia. Finally the new emperor, Theodosius I (r. 379–395), managed to settle the Visigoths as *foederati*

Stilicho the Vandal general in the service of Rome. Although he is a barbarian, he wears Roman clothing (panel of an ivory diptych, *ca.* 410).

along the lower Danube. Meanwhile, the Huns had been moving west and soon settled in the Hungarian plain, the only extensive grasslands in Europe.

The Fifth Century: The End of Imperial Authority in the West

Soon after the death of Theodosius in 395, an ambitious king, Alaric, united the Visigoths and tried to gain control of the Balkans. Unable to take the fortified cities, he failed. Then, in 407, he led his people out of the Balkans toward Italy, which was defended by troops led by the romanized German, Stilicho, a former lieutenant of Theodosius. To meet the threat, Stilicho withdrew troops from the Rhine frontier and left its defense to Frankish *foederati,* who failed to hold the line. Moreover, he also paid no attention to the Roman commander in Britain, who, apparently seeking his own advancement, led his army across the English Channel and left Britain to defend itself against Caledonian and German marauders.

For a time, Stilicho kept Alaric from breaking into Italy. But in 408, he fell victim to an intrigue in the imperial court, and the defenses collapsed. The Visigoths now moved onto the Lombard plain and marched on Rome, which they took in 410. Though they did little damage, the event made a fearful impression on their contemporaries, not only in Italy but throughout the western provinces.

Alaric had no intention of staying in Rome. He needed land for his people, which Rome, surrounded by marshes and dependent on grain supplies from Egypt, North Africa, and Sicily, could not provide. So the Visigoths moved south, put together a fleet, and prepared to sail across the sea to the rich territory of North Africa. But Alaric died before they could get under way, and the fleet was destroyed by a storm. So the Goths turned about and headed for southern Gaul. There they settled down and established a kingdom that eventually extended into Spain.

Meanwhile, Stilicho's tribe, the Vandals, left the northern frontier and set off for Spain, cutting a marauding swath through Gaul. Then, in 428, under a young king, Gaiseric (r. 428–477), they crossed into North Africa and began a conquest of the Roman provinces there. Once settled, they built a fleet and disrupted the shipping on which Italy relied for grain. They even attacked Italy itself many times, and "vandalism" became a byword for wanton destruction.

At about the same time, the Franks, a large confederation of tribes living along the lower Rhine, moved westward. The Romans resisted for a time, but in time the Franks were able to establish themselves in northern Gaul. The Burgundians, a confederation from southern Germany, moved through the Jura Mountains and the Alps into the east-central part of Gaul.

Then the Huns came on stage again. After overcoming the Ostrogoths in southern Russia, they had formed a loose confederation with tribes of Slavs and Germans. In 433, this confederation was consolidated by a charismatic king, Attila. In the early years of his reign, his troops served the Romans as mercenaries against the Germans—in one battle they nearly obliterated the Burgundians—but in the 440s, he turned to plundering the Empire. He pillaged the Balkans and reached the walls of Constantinople. Then he turned west to Gaul. Along the way, his troops earned a reputation for slaughter and rapine, and he himself became known as "the scourge of God." In 451, Attila was finally turned back from western Gaul, and he retreated into northern Italy. There, in 452, he sacked the great city of Aquileia, whose refugees fled to the swamps and islands at the head of the Adriatic Sea and founded villages that eventually became the city of Venice. At this point, Leo I (440–461), the bishop of Rome, led an embassy to Attila's camp and persuaded him to withdraw from Italy. When Attila retreated, Leo got the credit. But because the Huns were already exhausted and sick with malaria, it seems likely that Attila's decision had little to do with Leo's intervention. Attila died in 453.

By the 470s, Italy was the only western territory of the Empire that remained under direct imperial governance, and the imperial government at Milan was decrepit. Throughout the fourth century, the Empire had usually been ruled by two emperors—one in the West and one in the East—Theodosius I was the last emperor to rule both parts. The emperors in the East had maintained their authority in Constantinople; but the emperors in the West had fallen under the influence of their German generals. In the early 470s, the western emperor was a puppet of Orestes, the German commander in chief. And in 476, Odoacar, another German commander, led a rebellion that overthrew both Orestes and his puppet emperor. Breaking with precedent, however, Odoacar did not enthrone a new emperor of his own. Instead, he had himself elected king by the German troops and turned Italy into a Germanic kingdom. In Gaul and Spain, the Franks, Visigoths, and Burgundians also were establishing independent kingdoms.

The emperor in Constantinople had no choice but to recognize these kingdoms. By doing so, he made them agents of Roman authority and kept alive the idea of an Empire unified under imperial authority, even though much of it was governed by autonomous rulers. Henceforth, the eastern emperors were determined to regain authority over the West, and in the late 480s the emperor Zeno (r. 474–491) commissioned the Ostrogothic king Theodoric, who had been raised in Constantinople, to reconquer Italy on his behalf. After the death of Attila, the remnants of the Ostrogoths had settled along the Danube as *foederati* and had thrived there. Theodoric entered Italy in 489 and within four years had conquered the peninsula and had killed Odoacar. But instead of restoring the imperial government in Milan, he did what other German kings had done; he established an Ostrogothic kingdom in Italy (see Chapter 5).

THE CHRISTIANIZATION OF THE EMPIRE

The Conversion of Constantine

Constantine, during his struggle for control of the West following Diocletian's death (see p. 112), fought a crucial battle for control of Rome at the Mulvian Bridge, just north of the city. After winning the battle, he became convinced that Jesus had helped him to victory. A year later, in 313, he issued an edict of toleration of Christianity and forced his colleague in the East, Diocletian's successor Licinius, to confirm the decree. Issued at Milan, it is known as the Edict of Milan.

Although Constantine was not actually baptized until 337, on his deathbed, his behavior indicates that he considered himself a member of the church from the time of his conversion. From 313 on, he surrounded himself with church leaders and was soon taking an active part in church affairs. Christians still constituted only a small minority of the Empire's pop-

Colossal head of Constantine, from his basilica in Rome (*ca.* 320).

ulation—about 10 percent in the East, and about 5 percent in the West. So it seems that Constantine embraced Christianity because he truly believed in Jesus, not because it was the politically astute thing to do.

Christianity was no longer an obscure cult, however. During the late third century, it had gained considerable strength in the cities, the centers of imperial society and government. When civic government collapsed during the civil wars, the Christian churches had taken on the government's social functions, thereby attracting several leading families who added to their prestige. So Constantine cast his support to a movement that could support him in turn: a church that linked the aristocracy with the lower classes in a cohesive organization.

Constantine permitted the churches to become corporations, entitled under Roman law to own property. Soon many of the private houses in which the Christians met were incorporated as churches. Moreover, Constantine authorized bishops to act as judges in disputes brought to them by their parishioners. As the church gained social and legal status, Christianity moved rapidly toward becoming the predominant religion of the Empire.

Constantine and the Unity of the Christian Movement

Constantine concerned himself with many of the thorny problems that arose during the early years of the Christian movement. Some of those problems stemmed from consequences of the persecutions, others from theological disputes over the nature of Jesus.

The first major controversy was over the priesthood of the western, particularly the North African, church. On one side, the Donatists, followers of the North African priest Donatus, claimed that the only true Christians were those who had resolutely resisted the imperial government during the persecutions. The Donatists held that priests and bishops who had hidden or had connived with imperial officials to avoid persecution were not legitimate officers of the church and that

Christians should avoid their masses and refuse to obey them. On the other side, the majority of bishops and church members argued that accommodation had been the only reasonable course under the circumstances. The dispute disrupted the African churches and affected many of the churches in Europe.

How was such a controversy to be settled? One means of settlement could be found in the church's doctrine of episcopal authority. In the second century, Irenaeus (*ca.* 120–*ca.* 200), bishop of Lyon, had propounded the theory that bishops derived their authority from their succession from the apostles. According to Irenaeus, the apostles had transmitted their personal knowledge of Jesus and his message to their successors in the churches they had founded and that each bishop had handed down the tradition to his successor. As the number of churches grew, the apostolic tradition passed from community to community, so that, in theory, the totality of the churches, represented by their bishops, possessed the totality of the Christian tradition.

Acting on this theory, in 314, Constantine summoned the bishops of Africa and the West to a council at Arles to deal with the dispute. The council decided against the Donatists, establishing the doctrine that the efficacy of the sacraments was independent of the personal character of the priest. Thus, even if the offending bishops and priests had been stained by their actions during the persecutions, Christians were justified in treating them as priests until and unless the church itself judged them unworthy. This decree established the principle that a priest's legitimacy was legal rather than spiritual in nature and that obedience to the church was a legal obligation.

Most theological conflicts arose in the East, where Christians from different ethnic and social backgrounds understood the Christian message in different ways, and where the educated classes introduced troublesome philosophical considerations into the new religion. Steeped in Hellenistic philosophy and accustomed to reading texts critically, educated easterners struggled to synthesize their own

Constantine's Religious Beliefs

The official policy of the Empire after 312 was toleration, as shown in a letter sent in the name of both Constantine and his coemperor to the governor of Bithynia in 313.

. . . we resolved to make such decrees as should secure respect and reverence for the Deity; namely, to grant both to the Christians and to all the free choice of following whatever form of worship they pleased, to the intent that all the divine and heavenly powers that be might be favorable to us and all those living under our authority.

But Constantine showed stronger personal convictions in a letter written only a year later to the governor of Africa, dealing with the problem of schism in that province.

Since I am assured that you are also a worshipper of the supreme God, I confess to your Excellency that I consider it absolutely wrong that we should pass over in insincerity quarrels and altercations of this kind, whereby perhaps the supreme divinity may be moved not only against the human race, but even against me myself, to whose care He has entrusted rule over all earthly affairs. . . . For then, and only then, shall I be able truly and most fully to feel secure . . . when I shall see all men, in the proper cult of the Catholic religion, venerate the most holy God with hearts joined together like brothers in their worship.

From Great Problems in European Civilization, *ed. by K. M. Setton and H. R. Winkler (Englewood Cliffs, N.J.: Prentice-Hall, 1954), pp. 75, 79.*

philosophical leanings with writings circulated among the churches and expounded in the preaching of the bishops. Theology—the representation of revealed truth in a systematic manner—originated among Hellenistic Christians and Jews. Notable among them was Philo the Jew (born *ca.* 10 B.C.), an Alexandrian who tried to reconcile Jewish doctrine and law with Greek philosophy. Later Christians followed his lead.

Origen (*ca.* 185–*ca.* 254), for example, also an Alexandrian, produced the *Hexapla,* in which he compared six versions of the Hebrew scriptures in parallel columns. He then used the comparisons as a basis for biblical commentaries. Origen sought to synthesize Neoplatonism, one of the main strands of Hellenistic philosophy, with Christianity. Although his contemporaries challenged some of his views, later Christians recognized him as one of the fathers of the church, a man who was inspired by God and whose writings were therefore authoritative in doctrinal matters.

Another controversy among the early theologians was over the nature of Jesus: Was Jesus man, God, or both? The Alexandrian priest, Arius (*ca.* 256–336), proposed the theory that, although Jesus was both human and divine, he was not wholly human or wholly divine, but rather a unique individual created by God. This theory violated the Christian view that Jesus was both God incarnate and fully human (that is, subject to all the conditions of human life, including death). Arius's view, called Arianism, set off a heated debate in the eastern part of the Empire.

Constantine chose not to intervene in this controversy until after he had consolidated his power in 324. Then he acted quickly. The unity of the church depended on agreement about what to believe; the peace and stability of the Empire depended on the unity of the church, which strongly supported Constantine's political program.

In 325, Constantine summoned a new council of more than 300 bishops to Nicaea in northwestern Asia Minor and presided over the council's sessions himself. Because of its size and the critical questions of faith it addressed, Christians consider the Council of Nicaea to be the first ecumenical—that is, universal—council of the church. The council, by confirming that Jesus was both fully man and fully God, made a start toward formulating the Christian creed. The creed was not fully enunciated until the Council of Chalcedon in 451, but it is called the Nicene Creed.

The council also established two important principles of ecclesiastical organization—first, that a council of bishops held the supreme authority in deciding matters of Christian doctrine and church law, and, second, that the emperor, as the supreme secular ruler, played an important role in church affairs. The first of these principles gave the church a means of settling disputes and contributed to its survival as a universal institution. The sec-

ond undermined the New Testament position that the Christians' obligation to Caesar was distinct from and often in conflict with their obligation to God.

The Progress of Christianity after Constantine

With the exception of Julian (r. 361–363), the fourth-century emperors adhered to the Christian religion and remained involved in its affairs. Nonetheless, strong opposition to the religion existed among members of the conservative senatorial class who linked the ancient rights of the Senate to the old pagan cults. As the church grew stronger, its opposition to the pagan cults became a serious threat, and the conflict came to a head in the 370s and 380s. Educated men on both sides wrote tracts defending their own positions and arguing strongly against that of their opponents. The emperors, meanwhile, refused to ban the pagan practices, because the senatorial class was an important component of the Empire and a bulwark of political stability. At last, however, in 390, the emperor Theodosius I declared Christianity the official religion of the Empire and ordered the destruction of the pagan altars.

Some of the responses to the pagan opposition to Christianity turned out to be significant documents in the subsequent life of the church. For example, the North African bishop Augustine (354–430) formulated what became the accepted view of what it means to be a Christian and the role of Christianity in human history. Augustine had been attracted to many philosophies before he converted to Christianity in his early thirties, while teaching rhetoric in Rome. After his conversion, he returned to North Africa, where he eventually become bishop of the little town of Hippo. About ten years after his conversion, he wrote his *Confessions,* in which he explored the meaning of that experience. How had he, a man who had entertained false philosophies and had engaged in sinful ways, been able to recognize the truth of Christianity? What had happened to his former self after the conversion? In answering these questions, he

A late Roman wall painting of St. Augustine in a church in Rome.

explained how God saves human souls and how Christians atone for the sin that weighs down all human beings since Adam sinned against God and was expelled from the Garden of Eden.

Augustine wrote many works in addition to his *Confessions.* Together, they constitute the basis of much of Christian theology. Perhaps his greatest work is *The City of God,* which he wrote over a period of twenty years in response to pagan attacks on Christianity. In it, he proposed a Christian theory of history and a Christian approach to understanding human society. Augustine died while leading the defense of his city against a Vandal attack.

The Growth of the Church as an Institution

During the fourth and fifth centuries, bishops appointed priests, deacons, and many lesser officials to help in governing their churches. Each bishop had complete authority over his subordinates and over the property owned by his church. Yet, no effective agency existed to bring the individual churches into a coherent organization. The emperor could call a council to deliberate questions of doctrine, but the church itself had no way to resolve disputes. In theory, all bishops, as successors of the apostles, were equal. But whose opinion would prevail when they disagreed?

The apostolic churches—churches actually founded by the apostles— claimed precedence in disputes over doctrine, but those churches often disagreed among themselves. To support their positions, the leading apostolic churches cited the status of their founders. Alexandria, for example, claimed to have been founded by Paul; Antioch and Rome claimed to have been cofounded by Peter and Paul. Rome won the contest when it came up with the so-called Petrine Doctrine, based on passages in the New Testament (principally Matthew 16:18–19) indicating that Jesus had chosen Peter as the leader of the apostles. Moreover, according to tradition, Peter had been head of the Roman church and had died in Rome. So the bishops of Rome claimed to have inherited his primacy and appropriated for themselves the title of pope (*papa,* meaning father), which had been widely used by bishops throughout the church. Pope Leo I, who led the delegation to Attila the Hun in 452 (see p. 115), was the first to enunciate the doctrine in its entirety. In the West, where Rome was the only apostolic see (seat of a bishop, diocese), the Petrine Doctrine was gradually accepted. But in the East, the great episcopal powers—particularly Antioch, Alexandria, and Constantinople—never accepted it.

Throughout the late imperial period, Christianity remained primarily a religion of the cities. As a religion created by educated Greeks, it had little appeal for the peasants of the countryside, and it took a long time for the church to proselytize the vast agricultural population of the Empire.

ROMAN CULTURE DURING THE MIGRATIONS

The eastern provinces of the Empire survived the invasions of the Germans and the Huns virtually unscathed, and the Persian threat that had troubled the eastern border in the third century did not again arise until the early seventh century. Consequently, during the fifth century, the East with its Hellenistic culture remained the most stable region of the Empire (see Chapter 7).

In the West, even as barbarian kings took over the old Roman provinces during the late fourth and early fifth centuries, the sophisticated Latin culture managed to survive. Though aware of the danger, people went on writing books of philosophy, theology, and history and kept up an active correspondence with one another. This was the time when Augustine wrote his *Confessions* and *City of God.* It was the time when Ambrose, a well-educated man high in the imperial service, became bishop of Milan, the principal western capital, and exerted a wide influence in Christian circles. Ambrose also led the final assault on the paganism of the upper classes.

This was also an important time in the history of the papacy. Pope Damasus

St. Augustine on the City of God

Accordingly, two cities have been formed by two loves: the earthly by the love of self, even to the contempt of God; the heavenly by the love of God, even to contempt of self. The former glories in itself, the latter in the Lord. For the one seeks glory from men, but the greatest glory of the other is God, the witness of conscience. . . . In the one, the princes and the nations it subdues are ruled by the love of ruling; in the other, the princes and the subjects serve one another in love, the latter obeying, while the former take thought for all. The one delights in its own strength, represented in the persons of its rulers; the other says to its God: "I will love Thee, O Lord, my strength." And therefore the wise men of the one city, living according to man, have sought for profit to their own bodies or souls, or both, and those who have known God "glorified him not as God, neither were thankful, but became vain in their imaginations, and their foolish heart was darkened. . . ." For they were either leaders or followers of the people in adoring images, "and worshipped and served the creature more than the Creator." But in the other city there is no human wisdom, but only godliness, which offers due worship to the true God, and looks for its reward in the society of the saints, of holy angels as well as holy men, that God may be all in all.

From St. Augustine, City of God, *in* Basic Writings of St. Augustine, *ed. by Whitney J. Oates, Vol. II, p. 274. Copyright 1948 by Random House, Inc. Reprinted by permission.*

(r. 366–384), who laid the groundwork for the Petrine Doctrine that Pope Leo I was to enunciate seventy years later, commissioned Jerome, one of Augustine's learned contemporaries and correspondents, to translate the Bible into Latin. A partial translation, made in North Africa, was already available, but it was faulty. Jerome's translation later become the standard, or vulgate (common), version.

At various times and places, the invasions and migrations of the Germans had a disruptive effect on the community of educated men, which was at most a small coterie. The Vandals virtually destroyed Latin culture in North Africa. But in most regions it declined only gradually. In Spain, for example, the Visigoths, who had been converted to Arian Christianity while still in Russia, persecuted orthodox Christians but did nothing to suppress cultural activities. In Gaul, the literary culture dwindled during the later fifth century as the migrations of the Franks and Burgundians forced the old provincial aristocracy to retire to the isolation of their estates. In Italy, neither Odoacar nor Theodoric had much effect on the life of the educated elite; in fact, Theodoric appointed many educated Romans to government posts.

The Romans created an empire that endured for seven centuries during which they imposed political, economic, and cultural unity on the entire Mediterranean world. Reminders of their extraordinary achievement survive in the ruins of their monuments and in the cultural and political entities that emerged in the centuries following the eclipse of the Empire.

The Romans created a literary tradition, governmental forms, and a jurisprudence that continue to influence Western societies. By dividing the Empire into eastern and western halves, Diocletian and his successors created the basis for the two regions to develop separately. The remainder of this book deals primarily with the history of the western half, but it is well to remember that Islamic culture also owes much to Greco-Roman culture. We will look at what happened in the eastern Mediterranean and the Middle East in Chapters 8 and 13.

Suggestions for Further Reading

General

On the transition from the Republic to the Empire, R. Syme, *The Roman Revolution* (1939), a classic, offers an exciting account of the social as well as the political changes wrought by Augustus. On the early Empire, see F. B. Marsh, *Founding of the Roman Empire* (1927), and M. Hammond, *The Augustan Principate in Theory and Practice* (1933). For the second century, see M. Hammond, *The Antonine Monarchy* (1959). For comprehensive histories of Roman literature, see J. W. Duff, *A Literary*

History of Rome to the Close of the Golden Age, 3rd ed. (1963); and *A Literary History of Rome in the Silver Age,* 3rd ed. (1964). See also E. J. Kenney, ed., *The Cambridge History of Classical Literature, II: Latin Literature* (1982). For a general intellectual history of late antiquity, see H. Marrou, *History of Education in Antiquity* (1948).

For a general history of the later Roman Empire, see H. M. D. Parker, *History of the Roman World from A.D. 138 to 337* (1935); A. H. M. Jones, *The Later Roman Empire* (1964); and M. Grant, *The Climax of Rome* (1968). F. Millar, *The Emperor in the Roman Empire 31 B.C.–A.D. 337* (1977), is a massive study of the role of the emperor in Roman government and life. The classic social and economic history of the Empire is M. Rostovtzef, *The Social and Economic History of the Roman Empire,* rev. ed. (1957). See also, R. MacMullen, *Roman Social Relations* (1974). M. I. Finley, *The Ancient Economy* (1973), and *Studies in Ancient Society* (1974), are also excellent. On social stratification and the legal system in the imperial period,

see P. Garnsey, *Social Status and Legal Privilege in the Roman Empire* (1970). On women in Roman society, see S. B. Pomeroy, *Goddesses, Whores, Wives, and Slaves* (1975), and J. P. Hallet, *Fathers and Daughters in Roman Society: Women and the Elite Family* (1984).

For the frontier provinces, see F. Millar, *The Roman Empire and its Neighbors* (1968), and, on provincial administration, see G. H. Stevenson, *Roman Provincial Administration* (1939). On the army, see J. B. Campbell, *The Emperor and the Roman Army 31 B.C.–A.D. 235* (1984). E. N. Luttwak, *The Grand Strategy of the Roman Empire* (1976), analyzes the military approaches the emperors took to defending the Empire's borders. On the cities, see F. F. Abbott and A. C. Johnson, *Municipal Administration in the Roman Empire* (1926), and A. H. M. Jones, *The Cities of the Eastern Roman Provinces* 2nd ed. (1971). For an interesting attempt to reconstruct late Roman tax policy and its social and economic consequences, see W. Goffart, *Caput and Colonate: Towards a History of Late Roman Taxation* (1974).

Christianity

On the rise of Christianity, see J. Lebreton and J. Zeiller, *The Emergence of the Church in the Roman Empire* (1962), and R. L. Fox, *Pagans and Christians* (1986), which puts Christianity in the context of Roman religion. On this subject, see also T. R. Glover, *The Conflict of Religions in the Early Roman Empire* (1960); R. MacMullen, *Paganism in the Roman Empire* (1981), and *Christianizing the Roman Empire (A.D. 100–400)* (1984); J. Ferguson, *The Religions of the Roman Empire* (1970); and T. D. Barnes, "Legislation against the Christians," *Journal of Roman Studies* 58 (1968) 32–50. On the persecutions, see

W. H. C. Frend, *Martyrdom and Persecution in the Early Church* (1967). The world of late Roman religion is illumined by Peter Brown, *Religion and Society in the Age of Saint Augustine* (1969), and *Society and the Holy in Late Antiquity* (1982). On Constantine, see R. MacMullen, *Constantine* (1969), and J. Eadie, ed., *The Conversion of Constantine* (1971), which surveys opinion about the emperor's motivation. The best biography of St. Augustine is Peter Brown, *Augustine of Hippo* (1967). Augustine's *Confessions* and *City of God* have been published in many editions.

The Fall of the Empire in the West

E. Gibbon's monumental, *The Decline and Fall of the Roman Empire,* ed. by J. B. Bury (1886–1900), has been the classic treatment of the subject since 1776. As a general history, it should now be supplemented with A. H. M. Jones, *The Later Roman Empire, 284–602,* 3 vols. (1964). For a history of the third century crisis and Diocletian's reestablishment of stability, see R. MacMullen, *Roman Government's Response to Crisis A.D. 235–337* (1976), and S. Williams, *Diocletian and the Roman Recovery* (1985). In *End of the Ancient World* (1931)

F. Lot attributed the fall to economic causes. For a recent survey of the invasions, see L. Musset, *The Germanic Invasions* (1975). Most recent studies have focused on specific aspects of the German migrations. See M. Todd, *The Northern Barbarians, 100 B.C.–A.D. 300* (1976); E. A. Thompson, *The Early Germans* (1965), *The Visigoths in the Time of Ulfilas* (1969), and *Romans and Barbarians: The Decline of the Western Empire* (1982). For contrast, see R. Van Dam, *Leadership and Community in Late Antique Gaul* (1985).

THE TRANSFORMATION OF THE WESTERN ROMAN EMPIRE

In 476, when the Roman emperor Romulus was supplanted by Odoacar, his German commander in chief, probably no one was aware that an epochal event had taken place; surely no one would have spoken of the "fall of the Roman Empire." To contemporary Romans, probably the only significance of the event was that the Empire now would once again have a unified government.

For a long time, German leaders had exercised governmental authority in the western provinces under imperial authority. So Odoacar, though a usurper, could be considered a romanized German king who would soon be recognized by the imperial court in Constantinople. Instead, the emperor Zeno sent another German, Theodoric the Ostrogoth, to oust Odoacar, but that action seemed to reaffirm the authority of the emperor. In fact, after Theodoric had taken control, Zeno's successor,

Anastasius (r. 491–518), recognized him as the provincial governor of the Italian provinces.

Even the disappearance of the imperial court in the West seems to have made little impression on the Romans. They had become used to German domination of the army and of the court. Moreover, the German kings in the provinces still relied on the old elite to run the government. For their part, the Germans viewed themselves as the perpetuators, not the destroyers, of the Empire in the West.

Yet, the cultural unity of the Empire soon began to erode under the new order. The members of the Roman aristocracy had already begun to lose touch with their counterparts in the East, and the old homogeneity of upper-class culture was fast disappearing by the end of the fifth century. By the late sixth century, it had become clear that no reunification with the East would occur, and cultural transition began. New vernacular languages and new forms of culture—the beginnings of medieval civilization—began to evolve. Ironically, the Christian church, a quintessentially Roman institution, was a principal agent of that change.

THE GERMAN "SUCCESSOR STATES" IN EUROPE

By the sixth century, Germanic kingdoms governed the western territories of the Roman Empire. The oldest was the Visigothic kingdom, which had arisen in southern Gaul and Spain during the 420s and 430s. Not long afterward, the Burgundians had created a kingdom in the western Alps, down toward the Rhone River. In the early 490s, Theodoric (r. 493–526) had founded an Ostrogothic kingdom in Italy. And about the same time, Clovis (r. 481–511) had set up a Frankish kingdom in Gaul after establishing his authority over the

Franks along the lower Rhine. By the time of his death in 511, Clovis had driven the Visigoths out of Gaul, confining them to the Iberian peninsula. In the 440s, small bands of Angles and Saxons, Germanic peoples from southern Scandinavia, had begun settling in Britain and by the sixth century had established several Anglo-Saxon kingdoms on the island. The indigenous population, descendants of the Celtic tribes conquered by the emperor Claudius during the first century (see p. 97), fled to Cornwall, Wales, and Ireland rather than accept life under the Germans.

Among these peoples, the Visigoths and the Burgundians were already Christians when they invaded the imperial territories. The Visigoths had been converted to Arianism during the fourth century, while still living in southern Russia. The conversion of the Burgundians to Arianism cannot be traced to a specific time and place. Neither of these peoples had given up their Arianism when the Council of Nicaea declared it heretical (see p. 118),

The Germanic Kingdoms   *ca.* 500

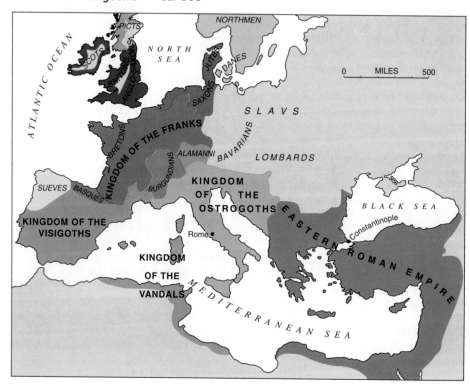

and once they had settled down in the Empire they and the leaders of the official church treated one another as heretics.

The Franks and the Anglo-Saxons, by contrast, came to the imperial lands as pagans, and their conversion to official Roman Christianity facilitated their integration into the old Roman society. It also set them at odds with the Arian Visigoths and Burgundians.

Nonetheless, the Visigoths and Burgundians readily absorbed Roman culture and preserved much of the Roman way of life. In the process, however, they began to lose their identity. During the sixth century, the Eastern Empire destroyed the Ostrogothic kingdom of Italy and the Vandal kingdom of North Africa, and the Franks conquered the Visigoths and the Burgundians in southern Gaul. But the Franks and the Anglo-Saxons, who had remained relatively unaffected by Roman culture, created kingdoms that developed into the strongest states of medieval Europe. Italy and Spain retained their old Roman names; they did not become "East Gothia" and "West Gothia." But the Franks imposed their name on Gaul, which became France, and the Angles imposed theirs on part of Britain, which became England.

The Settling of the Germans

Just how the Germanic tribes managed to settle down and acquire land in the Roman provinces is not altogether clear. Contemporary sources, mainly law codes issued by German kings, seem to indicate that the German soldiers received a portion— half or two-thirds—of the lands owned by the provincials, and historians have generally assumed that the land must have been expropriated by the Germans. If that is what happened, the Germans would have become farmers. In fact, much of the population of the new Germanic kingdoms seems to have consisted of yeoman farmers.

But such wholesale expropriation would have raised stronger protest than is evident in the Roman sources of the period. Recently, historians have suggested that the apportionment reported in

the Germanic law codes refer not to land but to tax revenues. The Germanic tribes, as *foederati,* appear to have been treated in accordance with the ancient rules governing the settlement of Roman armies. Those rules specified that the provincial landlords owed the armies hospitality, including quarters and tax revenues. In the case of the Germans, landlords provided troops with houses and plots, but the army, under its tribal king, took over revenues that had once been due to the Roman state. Moreover, it appears that the apportionment mentioned in the Germanic

Relations between Romans and Germans

The Burgundian Lex Gundobada *(ca. 484) deals mostly with crimes committed by Germans, specifying the penalties to be imposed in each type of case. But the code was written for a mixed Roman-Burgundian society and must occasionally treat cases involving members of both populations. These are typical of the passages historians use to study the process of Germanic settlement in the old Roman provinces.*

LEX GUNDOBADA

54.1: It was commanded at the time the order was issued whereby our people should receive one-third of the slaves, and two-thirds of the land, that whoever had received land together with slaves by the gift of our predecessors or ourselves should not require a third of the slaves nor two parts of the land from that place in which hospitality had been assigned him. . . .

[Hospitality was the system by which, in return for their service, foederati *were assigned portions of land and slaves or tenant farmers. It was based on the old Roman law pertaining to the settlement of soldiers.]*

55.1: As often as cases arise between two Romans concerning the boundaries of fields which are possessed by barbarians through the law of hospitality, let the guests of the contestants not be involved in the quarrel. . . .

55.5: But if a contention has been raised concerning the boundaries of a field which a barbarian has received intact with slaves by public gift, it is permitted him to settle the case by Roman law. . . .

From K. F. Drew, The Burgundian Code *(Philadelphia: U. of Pennsylvania Press, 1972) 62–63.*

A German king (*above*) and his bishop. From an early manuscript copy of Alaric's code of law.

codes was not between Germans and Romans, but between the German king and his troops. In most places, the king received one-third of the tax revenues, and his men received two-thirds. For the provincials, it appears, the settlement of the Germans only changed the recipients of the taxes they paid.

Apparently the Germans became landowners only gradually, through intermarriage or through victory in war. Roman landlords found it impossible to remain neutral in the incessant civil wars that plagued the Germanic kingdoms during the sixth century, and the victorious kings seized the land and wealth of their enemies and parceled it out to their supporters. Gradually, the rulers and their armies were integrated into the rural society of the European provinces.

The Burgundians and the Visigothic Kingdom of Spain

By the early sixth century, the Burgundians occupied a small kingdom on the western slopes of the Alps stretching down to the Rhone River, and the Visigoths controlled Spain and Septimania along the southwestern Mediterranean coast of Gaul. But these two kingdoms played an important role in the creation of medieval culture because they provided a bridge between the Roman and the German cultures.

The Burgundians and the Visigoths were the most romanized of the Germanic tribes because they had been christianized before entering the Empire, and they settled in the most thoroughly romanized of the western provinces. Their kings preserved much of the old Roman system of government and seem to have thought of themselves as rulers within the Empire, rather than as kings of independent kingdoms. Consequently, they tried to reconcile the social and legal differences between the two populations—Roman and German. The Burgundian king Gundobada (r. 474–516) published parallel codes of Germanic law (*Lex Gundobada,* The Law of Gundobad, *ca.* 484) and Roman law (the *Lex Romana Burgundionum,* The Roman Law of the Burgundians, after 484). In the Visigothic kingdom, Eu-

ric (r. 466–484) issued a code for his German subjects (*Lex Visigothorum, ca.* 483), and his successor Alaric II (r. 484–507) issued one for the Roman population (*Lex Romana Visigothorum,* 506). The Roman law in these codes was a vulgarized version of the system that Justinian's lawyers would later include in the *Corpus Iuris Civilis* (see p. 170). The Germanic codes consist of ancient customary law with traces of Roman influence. Together, these codes comprise the source of most of what we know about the settlement of the Germans in the Roman provinces.

Although the Burgundian and Visigothic kings tried to provide good government to the Roman population, their Arianism caused constant trouble between the Germans and Romans in their kingdoms. The orthodox Franks found support among the Roman population when they conquered the Gallic territories of the Visigoths and destroyed the Burgundian kingdom.

In Spain, the Visigoths also faced religious opposition from the Roman population, and by the 580s acceptance of the official doctrine became a means for members of the royal family and their aristocratic supporters to justify a claim to the throne. To remove this ground for rebellion, Recared I (r. 586–601) converted to official Christianity immediately after his succession. Thereafter, the king and bishops of the official church joined in a program of legislation and reorganization that aimed to incorporate the Visigoths into the church. Recared held a series of church councils that issued laws of lasting influence in the European church. The program to create a unified church in Spain also stimulated educated Romans to write comprehensive summaries of church doctrine and lore. The most important of the writers was Isidore of Seville (*ca.* 560–636) whose *Etymologies* was an encyclopedia of knowledge inherited from classical civilization. It became a basic medieval reference work.

Throughout that century, disputed successions to the throne and aristocratic rebellions weakened the Visigothic kingdom. The end came abruptly in 711, when Moorish armies crossed over from North Africa. After this disaster, Christians in the northern hills of Asturias and Galicia managed to establish small kingdoms, but the rest of the Christian population fell under the governance of the vast Arab Empire that had begun to emerge during the 620s (see Chapter 8).

The Ostrogothic Kingdom of Italy: The Continuation of Roman Culture

The Ostrogothic kingdom of Theodoric was in many ways the most successful of all the barbarian kingdoms. Theodoric, who had been raised in Constantinople, was a Roman citizen and had held the office of consul before Zeno sent him to conquer Italy. Finding Italy ruined by decades of war and misgovernment, Theodoric launched a public works program and took measures to revive agriculture and trade. He also tried to stabilize relations among the new Germanic kingdoms by arranging a series of marriage alliances. He himself married a Frankish princess; he married his sister to the king of the Vandals, his two daughters to the Visigothic and Burgundian kings, and a niece to a Thuringian king.

In his own kingdom, he tried to preserve whatever he could salvage of Roman civilization and Roman government by engaging members of the leading Roman families as advisers and ministers. At the same time, however, he sought to preserve the distinction between his Ostrogothic army and the Italo-Roman population by prohibiting the Italo-Romans from joining the army and by forbidding Ostrogoths to attend schools where they might be romanized. He also preserved the Arianism of the Ostrogoths, which helped to maintain the distinction between the two groups. His reliance on the senatorial families obliged him to tolerate their religion and their church, but he sensed that they were intolerant of his Arianism.

Two of Theodoric's Roman administrators, Cassiodorus (*ca.* 490–*ca.* 585) and Boethius (*ca.* 480–524), are commanding figures in the intellectual history of Europe. Cassiodorus, renowned for his learning, served Theodoric and his successor as quaestor, consul, and head of the civil service. A little after 540, he retired to his estate near Bari in southern Italy and founded a monastery, called the Vivarium, where he and his monks sought to preserve Roman civilization by creating a library and copying ancient works. He had already won recognition as a historian and a grammarian by publishing a world history and a guide to writing official documents. At the Vivarium, he turned to theological works, including a dissertation on the soul. His most important work was *An Introduction to Divine and Human Readings,* a compendium of classical learning, intended for the education of his monks. He also wrote a history of the Ostrogoths, which has been lost.

Boethius came from a senatorial family of high standing in Rome. His father and his sons—and he himself—all served as consuls. After his father's death, he was reared in the household of Symmachus, a leading Christian senator and a descendant of the leader of the pagans back in the 370s (see p. 118). Boethius married Symmachus's daughter.

Boethius published books on arithmetic and music in his early twenties, at an age when, as a contemporary said, most people were students, not teachers. Theodoric, in a letter drafted by Cassiodorus, asked the young Boethius to design a sundial and a waterclock for the palace. Theodoric also asked him to recommend a harpist to be sent to Clovis the Frank. In 510, the king named Boethius consul, a largely ceremonial post that left plenty of time for other pursuits. During his year in office, he worked on a translation of Aristotle's treatises on logic. (Another consul, who published an edition of Vergil during his year in office, had complained about the distractions caused by his official duties.) In 522, Theodoric appointed Boethius's sons consuls, though they were only boys, and appointed Boethius as head of the civil service, an office that carried real authority.

Boethius's grand project was to translate all the works of Plato and Aristotle into Latin. In the translations he completed he introduced illustrative examples to make the texts more palatable to Roman readers, who were not passionate readers of philosophy. In many of these examples

Gold coin of Theodoric, Ostrogothic king of Italy in the early sixth century.

he showed how logic could be applied to questions of Christian theology, thereby helping to ensure the survival of logic as a branch of medieval learning.

Boethius never completed his great project because he fell victim to suspicions that obsessed Theodoric in his old age. Theodoric had become convinced that the Romans were plotting with Constantinople to invade Italy, using his Arianism as a pretext. In 524, he accused Boethius of treason and condemned him to death. While in prison awaiting death, Boethius wrote his most famous work, *The Consolation of Philosophy,* in which he engages in a dialogue with Lady Philosophy, who leads him from despair to "that true contentment which reason allied with virtue alone can give." In this little book he makes an eloquent argument for the superiority of spiritual over material values.

Theodoric's kingdom did not long survive his own death in 526. The invasion he had feared came in 536, and Theodoric's successor was unable to organize any effective resistance. After suffering a series of defeats, the Ostrogoths established a new dynasty that struggled for twenty years against the army from the East.

The war devastated the peninsula. Cities were taken and retaken, and the countryside was ravaged. The population of Rome declined by perhaps 90 percent. To make matters worse, a plague struck the Mediterranean region in the 540s and persisted into the 570s. When the Eastern Empire finally won control of Italy in the 550s, it took over a ruined land that was easy prey for new invaders.

In 568, the Lombards, a northern Germanic people who were among the least romanized of all the Germans, invaded Italy and by 572 had won control of most of the peninsula. They had been mercenaries in Italy some twenty years before and now had come back to serve their own purposes. As invaders, they were only loosely united, and after winning control they founded several states. The Lombard king established his capital in Pavia, while his leading aristocrats settled in central and southern Italy. The government in Constantinople managed to retain

Childeric, father of Clovis and an early king of the Franks, from a signet ring found in his tomb. His long hair and his spear are signs of royal authority.

a few enclaves, notably Ravenna and its environs. Rome, though surrounded, also held out, loyal to Constantinople but hardly subject to it.

The Rise of the Franks

The Franks first appear in history during the third century, when they were raiding deep into Gaul, even into Spain. At the beginning of the fifth century, when Stilicho withdrew his legions from the Rhine to defend Italy against the Visigoths (see p. 114), he organized the Franks into *foederati.* But instead of defending the frontier, the Frankish kings occupied northern Gaul and permitted the Vandals, Suevi, and Alans to sweep through the province on their way to Spain. The Vandals eventually crossed over to North Africa, the Suevi settled in present-day Portugal, and the Alans settled in Spain, though some of them joined the Vandals in the crossing to Africa. During the fifth century, the Franks, now divided into two tribal confederations, controlled both sides of the Rhine: the Ripuarian Franks on the east bank of the Rhine and the Salian Franks on the west bank.

Within the confederations, constant warfare erupted among the petty kings who led the tribes. The competition was finally ended by Clovis, a Salian Frank who succeeded to a tribal kingship in 481. Only fifteen years old at the time, he was a scion of a royal family that claimed descent from the legendary king Merovech; the line is called the Merovingian line. The family's capital was at Tournai in present-day Belgium. Clovis (r. 481–511) soon started to consolidate the Salian tribes and then unified all the Franks under his kingship, expanding Frankish territory. In 486, he destroyed a Roman principality, the "kingdom of Soissons." In 496, his army annihilated the Alemanni in southwestern Germany. In 507, he defeated the Visigoths in a great battle and took control of most of southern Gaul. Theodoric, by occupying Provence and helping the Visigoths hold on to Septimania, prevented Clovis from reaching the Mediterranean.

The center of Frankish power was in northern Gaul, where the Roman popula-

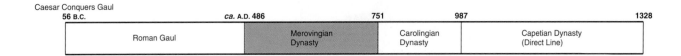

Caesar Conquers Gaul				
56 B.C.	*ca.* A.D. 486	751	987	1328
Roman Gaul	Merovingian Dynasty	Carolingian Dynasty	Capetian Dynasty (Direct Line)	

tion favored the heathen Franks over the Arian Visigoths and Burgundians who had settled in the central and southern part of the province. To keep the bishops of Gaul from stirring up rebellion, Clovis encouraged them to think that he might convert to Roman Christianity. Around 498, he finally did convert, along with about 3,000 of his men, thereby gaining a decisive advantage for himself. He was the only ruler among the Germanic kings who belonged to the official church, and the bishops and their flocks gave him their support. To amalgamate his Frankish and Roman subjects, he issued a great law code, the *Lex Salica* (usually dated 507–511), which reconciled their legal systems.

Clovis died in 511, the most powerful of all the Germanic kings. His four sons divided up the kingdom and proceeded to add to its territories. They conquered the Burgundians in 534. Two years later, they took Provence and reached the Mediterranean, thereby opening their kingdom to trade with the eastern Roman Empire, with which they became allied against the Ostrogoths. They also extended Frankish power in Germany, conquering Thuringia in 531.

The brothers fought incessantly, however, until by 558 only Chlotar I (r. 511–561) was still alive. He spent his last three years ruling a united kingdom, but when he died, his four sons divided it up again. Most of them died young, leaving their wives as regents for their infant sons. Continual internecine warfare in the kingdom lasted until 613, when Chlotar II (r. 584–629), a grandson of Chlotar I, emerged as sole ruler. But the long struggle had taken its toll on royal power. To win the support of the noble families, the kings had given them large tracts of land and many royal rights. By 613 the kingdom was no longer controlled by the monarchy but by the leading noble families. Under Chlotar's only son Dagobert

(r. 629–639), the royal family made a modest recovery, but the future belonged to the great noble families.

The first century of Merovingian rule was chronicled by Bishop Gregory of Tours (538–594) in his famous *Ten Books of Histories*. Clovis's conversion to Christianity had won him and his heirs the support of the bishops, most of whom, as members of the old provincial aristocracy, enjoyed great prestige among both the Franks and the Gallo-Roman landowners. Gregory was a member of that class. Portraying Clovis as a treacherous man, he told of one occasion on which Clovis bewailed his lack of relatives "not because he grieved at their death but with the cunning thought that he might perhaps find one still alive whom he could kill." Yet in summing up Clovis's career Gregory declared: "God was laying low his enemies every day under his hand, and was increasing his kingdom, because he walked with an upright heart before Him, and did what was pleasing to His eyes." Gregory was equally complimentary of Clovis's grandson Guntram (r. 561–593), of whom the best that could be said was that he murdered somewhat fewer people than his brothers did. "One would have taken him," Gregory says, "not only for a king, but for a priest of the Lord."

The decline of royal power left the way open for the aristocratic families to take control. The greatest prize was the position of mayor of the royal palace; originally, the mayor was the official who managed the king's private affairs. The Franks did not distinguish between private affairs and public affairs, however, so the mayor came to control government as well. After Dagobert, the mayor was the real king.

By 700 the kingdom of Clovis had been split into an eastern, largely Germanic kingdom called Austrasia, a western, more romanized kingdom called

The helmet (reconstructed from fragments) of a seventh-century Anglian king. From the Sutton Hoo treasure, one of the great archaeological discoveries of this century, found under the untouched funeral mound in East Anglia.

Neustria, and a weak southern kingdom called Burgundy, which was the most romanized of all. Southwest Gaul (Aquitaine) and southeast Germany (Bavaria) were virtually autonomous. In each of the major parts of the kingdom was a mayor of the palace who was constantly threatened with rebellion among his own supporters and with competition from rival mayors. The wars fought among the sons and grandsons of Clovis were now carried on by the mayors.

Out of these struggles one family emerged to reunite the Frankish kingdom and to transform it into the cradle of a new western European civilization. This family—the Carolingians, named for its most famous member, Charles the Great, or Charlemagne (from Latin, Carolus Magnus)—gained control of the Austrasian mayoralty in the early seventh century. Under Pepin of Heristal, Austrasia defeated an alliance of the Neustrians and Burgundians at the Battle of Tertry in 687. Pippin then became sole mayor of the whole kingdom. By the time he died in 714, the Frankish kingdom was again, as it had been under Clovis, the most powerful of the successor states in the West.

The Anglo-Saxons in Britain

As we have seen (p. 114), the Romans had pulled their troops out of Britain in 405, when Stilicho was consolidating his armies to protect Italy from the Visigoths. The romanized Celts then slowly reasserted their native culture, while at the same time preserving many elements of Roman culture. In the middle of the fifth century, Angles and Saxons began to arrive in Britain from the North Sea region. These Germanic peoples were hardly distinguishable from one another linguistically or culturally. They were pagans, almost untouched by Roman civilization.

The Celtic population, which had gained a sense of cultural identity during the fifty years following the withdrawal of the Romans, resisted the Anglo-Saxon incursions, but, for the most part, the resistance failed. As the newcomers settled in, much of the Celtic population retreated to the west. Finally, early in the sixth century, a military leader whose name has come down to us as Arthur organized a last heroic counterattack. Arthur was not a king—though legend has made him one—but a captain whose authority rested on what remained of the old Roman military system. He managed to stem the Anglo-Saxon advance for about a generation, but he lost his life in the struggle. After his death, no Celtic leader emerged to take his place.

Bust of a young German warrior of the type the Romans fought. The soldier wears a necklace believed to have magic power.

The Celts settled down in Cornwall, Wales, and Ireland, and a small group crossed to Brittany, where a form of the ancient Celtic language is still spoken. They took with them the remnants of Roman civilization, leaving to the Anglo-Saxons only the remains of the abandoned Roman cities. In their new homes, the Celts lost much of their romanized way of life, but preserved certain remnants of Roman civilization, including the study of Greek. Celtic society was based on extensive kindreds and retainers under the authority of a clan head. In Scotland, where some of the Celts settled, many of the clans survive to this day.

Meanwhile, the tribes of the Angles and Saxons each founded their own kingdom. In the Midlands, groups of Angles founded the kingdoms of Mercia, Norfolk, and Suffolk. North of the Humber River, they founded the kingdom of Deira, centered on York, and the kingdom of Bernicia further north. In the south, Saxon tribes established several small kingdoms—Sussex, Essex, and Wessex. Tradition associates the kingdom of Kent, across from the northern coast of Gaul, with the Jutes, but this people has not been identified, and historians now believe the distinctive society of Kent may have resulted from its close links with the Continent.

As time passed, several of the smaller kingdoms were absorbed by their neighbors, and by the middle of the seventh century there were seven Anglo-Saxon kingdoms. In the south were Kent, Wessex, Sussex, and Essex; in the Midlands were Mercia and East Anglia (the combination of Norfolk and Suffolk); and in the north was Northumbria (the unified kingdoms of Deira and Bernicia). A kind of weak union of the kingdoms existed by virtue of their recognition of a senior king called the *bretwalda,* whose function is hard to determine from the surviving records but who probably mediated disputes and organized common defense. Britain was not fully unified until the tenth century.

Still, the Anglo-Saxons shared a language, a religious tradition, and a culture. And when they were converted to Christi-

The Anglo-Saxon Kingdoms of England
Seventh Century

anity, the influence of the church extended across the boundaries of the kingdoms, though local bishops were appointed by their kings and were loyal to them.

GERMANIC SOCIETY

The Germans, who had originated in Scandinavia and northern continental Europe, were a group of related peoples who spoke similar, though not identical, languages. The Romans first encountered the Germanic tribes in the forests of northern Gaul and Germany, and the earliest references to them are in Julius Caesar's *Gallic Wars* (52–51 B.C.) and Tacitus's *Germania* (A.D. 98). Caesar's account deals with his campaigns against the tribes that had settled in northwestern Gaul, a region Caesar had conquered during his proconsular

The Pagan Gods of the Germans

Most of what we know of the Germanic pagan gods comes from Old Norse sources dating from the twelfth century. Those stories tell of two tribes of gods, the Vanir and the Aesir, and of a war between them. After the war, the tribes made peace and exchanged hostages. In that way, some of the gods of the Vanir joined the Aesir, which became the main tribe. The major gods were:

Odin (Aesir): poetry, wisdom, chief of the gods = Roman Mercury
Thor (Aesir): order = Roman Jupiter
Loki (Aesir): deception, evil
Frigg (Vanir): wife of Odin = Roman Venus
Freyr (Vanir): fertility of the fields
Freyja (Vanir): sister of Freyr, love, fertility, magic

An artifact of the migration period. Ostrogothic gilt bronze buckle with jewels (sixth century). The style is Germanic.

tenure (58–49 B.C.). In *Germania,* Tacitus drew on reports he had received from his father-in-law, Agricola, who had served in Germany. Of the two, Tacitus's is the more reliable work, but both were influenced by the view that the Germans represented an early stage in an evolutionary process that led to Roman society and culture.

Historians have tried to build a picture of the earliest Germanic culture by drawing on Germanic law codes and literature. But that effort is bound to fail, because from early times the peoples who came to be called Germans were influenced by the Celts and, probably, by the Greeks. By the time we hear of them, they had a pantheon strikingly similar to, though more primitive than, the pantheons of some Mediterranean societies. Certainly the origins of the Germanic pantheon are rooted in the same Indo-European sources as those of the Greeks and the Italic tribes. There is no way to tell what stems from the common sources, what is original, and what was borrowed from other cultures.

The same is true of the social and economic systems of the Germanic tribes. To archaeologists, Germanic villages of the first century look virtually identical to villages of the Gauls and the Slavs. They all had similar toolkits and agricultural practices, and they all had absorbed some measure of Roman culture through trade.

After the Romans had conquered some of the tribes, Roman cultural influence spread rapidly into the northern European forests, diminishing to the north and the east. Because Roman records and accounts deal only with the southern Germans, it is nearly impossible to identify the characteristics of the original Germanic society.

It appears that a significant difference existed between the eastern Germans and the western Germans. The easterners, mainly Visigoths and Ostrogoths who had settled on the plains of southern Russia, converted to Christianity in the later fourth century. The biography of an early Gothic saint describes a society of small agricultural villages dominated by elders. Villagers resisted outside influence. Everyone knew everyone else in the community. Foreigners were suspect and were usually driven off, and social relations were regulated by a sense of community and by personal relationships rather than by law.

By the time the Romans came into contact with the western Germans, who lived closer to the Roman Empire along the Rhine and upper Danube, the Germans had evolved a tribal society dominated by kings. Tribal members appeased the gods through the kings, whose authority rested on a claim that they were descended from the gods. For example, the Anglo-Saxon kings claimed descent from Woden (or Odin), the god of war and poetry. That association gave them great authority, but it also gave them fearful responsibility. They were the guarantors of the tribe's good fortune. When tribal luck went bad, the king was blamed, and a run of bad luck could result in his deposition or even sacrifice. His successor had to be a member of the royal family (the *kingling* or kin) who also could claim descent from Woden.

When they created *foederati,* the Romans relied on tribal kings to lead the federated troops. Consequently, the Romans did all they could to strengthen the power of the kings, though by so doing they weakened the idea that the kings' power depended on divine favor. By the time the Germans began to establish kingdoms in the western provinces, their kings had benefited from generations of Roman support and influence.

Germanic communities both beyond and within the imperial borders ascribed great importance to status. Every man's worth was determined by birth, wealth, and personal behavior. A man could improve his status by achieving economic success, by creating a family, and by acting honorably. The status he enjoyed affected a man's immediate family, and their behavior in turn affected his own status. Worthy service in time of war, success in trading, and a good marriage all affected the status of the man and his kin. Sons and daughters married whomever their parents chose for them, so it is not surprising that conflict between parents and children over marriages was a common theme in Germanic myth and literature.

When a man was insulted or injured in some way, he was obliged to recover his honor. One way to do so was by blood feud—inflicting an injury to match the one suffered—but the law provided a more peaceful means. It defined each man's rights and specified the penalties for common injuries. The community had a great stake in making the law work, because in a small society blood feuds would inevitably spread from family to family. In early medieval literature, the community often encourages—even forces—disputants to settle their differences according to the law. The kings stood behind the system of compensation and codified it in their legal codes.

At the center of Germanic society was the family or kin group. The kin group supported its members, shared their status, and guaranteed that they would live up to their obligations. If a man was unable to pay compensation for some wrong he had done, the law specified that his family was obliged to pay. The obligation fell first on his father and brothers. If they could not come up with the full amount, the obligation fell on his paternal and maternal relatives to the third degree—that is, all those descended from his grandparents. As a last resort, the man could seek support from his neighbors. If all failed, the man's life was forfeit, which usually

The crown of King Recceswin of the Visigoths (*ca.* 660).

meant that the offended party or his family could seize him and either enslave him or kill him. Enslavement seems to have been the more common course, and the enslaved criminal (called a *thrall* in Old German) is a common character in early Germanic literature.

Another important unit in Germanic society was the neighborhood. According to the Frankish *Lex Salica,* published in the early sixth century, no one could take over a vacant farm unless all the neighbors consented; the objection of even one neighbor was enough to keep the newcomer out. However, this rule did not apply to the son, daughter, or other heir of the former owner.

The law governing occupancy of a vacant property stemmed from the late

Two Ostrogothic brooches. The one below is made of gold inlaid with emerald and garnet and marks the zenith of the Ostrogothic style; the one at right, made after the defeats of 552–553, is poor in quality and crudely decorated.

could do no business, and no one would accept his suit for marriage.

To a large extent, the social life of the Germans reflected their military organization. The men of the villages were members of the army, and their relationship with the king was that of soldier to general as well as subject to ruler. The military relationship was not a formal relationship, however. Rather, a man's loyalty to his king was a personal matter. At the highest level, the king's associates formed a coterie, called the *comitatus.* They fought at his side, counseled him, and drank with him. His mead hall was the center of their world. (Mead is a strong wine made from honey.) Moreover, each nobleman had his own coterie of soldiers drawn from the neighborhood of his estate, who related to him as he did to the king. The army of the tribe was composed of these units.

Women in Germanic Society

Germanic society was dominated by men, in large part because status was a function of one's forcefulness, which depended on physical strength. Men controlled property, trade, and the arrangement of marriages.

Nonetheless, the Germans recognized that women played an important role in society not only as mothers, sisters, and wives, but also as actors in social relations. Women controlled the household and often stirred the men to action. In Germanic literature they upheld the family's interests. In the *Nibelungenlied* (Song of the Nibelungs), for example, the queens goaded the men into acts of treachery that led to the destruction of the Burgundian royal house. In the Icelandic saga, *Njal's Saga,* women stir the family conflicts that lead to the collapse of society. These works were written down in the twelfth and thirteenth centuries respectively, but they related stories that had been passed down from the early Middle Ages.

Marriage customs in early Germanic society differed little from those of the Greeks and Romans. Literary evidence suggests that the man usually took an active role in searching for a bride, whereas the woman was obliged to follow the will

Roman tax system, which treated estates and villages as fiscal units. When a piece of land fell vacant, the members of the community would search about to find someone to take over the previous owner's share of the tax burden. Otherwise, it would fall on them. The provision that a man could turn to his neighbors for help in paying a penalty rested on the same idea. His failure to pay might mean that he would be no longer able to meet his share of the communal tax burden. The idea of neighborhood was an ancient element of Indo-European society. Hesiod, a Greek poet of the seventh century B.C., once wrote, "If any trouble arises in your place, neighbors come as they are, but relatives dress for the journey."

A man's promise to honor a settlement or to come to court and obey its ruling was guaranteed first by his family and then by his neighbors. Those were the people, particularly the kin, who would have to stand in his place should he default. Consequently, no one would trust a man who was without kin or without a following among his neighbors; he of her father or male relatives. In most marriages, it seems that the man was a good bit older than the woman.

Nonetheless, women had certain rights under Germanic law. In legal actions, the relatives of the mother counted as much as the relatives of the father, and females inherited almost equally with their male siblings. Under the *Lex Salica,* property that a woman brought to a marriage went back to her family if she died without heirs. And if a couple had no heirs, the property they acquired during their marriage was divided equally between the wife's family and the husband's family.

The church, reflecting Greek and Roman attitudes, viewed women as weak and dangerous—weak, because they were considered likely to surrender to sexual desire; dangerous, because they could lead men into licentious behavior. The Germans had a more pragmatic view. Tacitus reports that the Germans expected women to share the burdens of earning a living and wanted them to take an active role in society and in the family. Further, he says that the Germans looked on women as having a special holiness, a quality that led people to seek their advice. Among some Germanic peoples, it seems to have been common for a king to marry the wife of his predecessor. In Sweden, charismatic power was thought to flow from the goddess Freyja through the queen to the king.

THE GROWTH OF CHURCH INSTITUTIONS

The Bishops and Clergy

By the second century, Christian communities had evolved a hierarchical organization that survives in developed form to this day. The church based its organization on the Roman administrative system, which centered on the city. Under Diocletian (r. 284–305), the municipal districts were reorganized as dioceses (see p. 111), and the church's organization changed to reflect the new arrangement. The territorial units of the church are still called dioceses (or sees).

The highest official of each church was the bishop (Latin, *episcopus*). From an early date, the bishop was assisted by various officials. Priests (Greek, *presbyters,* meaning elders) ministered to the spiritual needs of the community. Deacons took care of nonspiritual chores, such as maintaining church buildings and looking after any other property the church acquired. The deacons also distributed alms to the poor. Lesser officials—exorcists, cantors, readers, and others—performed a host of special functions. Together, these officials constituted the bishop's *familia,* his family or household.

Outside this official church organization, monasticism, a wholly different kind of Christian life, developed. At first, monasticism was a more or less independent phenomenon, but eventually it was integrated into the church and became an important influence on its development.

The Beginnings of Monasticism

Christian monasticism originated among simple laymen in Egypt during the latter part of the third century. For several decades, the stresses of village life during a time of civil strife in Roman society had driven many Egyptian villagers into the desert wilderness. (It is important to understand that in the ancient and medieval worlds, a desert was not a hot, barren waste, but rather a place where men did not live, a wilderness.)

Religion played a role in these withdrawals. Several Middle Eastern religions encouraged withdrawal from society, and the New Testament contains passages that encourage it (Mark 10:21–25; Romans 13:14; 1 Corinthians 6:13–20). But the Christians among the hermits of the desert got no encouragement from the church hierarchy.

The earliest Christian monks engaged in such practices as fasting, vigils, wearing rough clothing (such as hairshirts), avoiding baths (which they associated with the immoralities of the Roman public baths), and celibacy. Their asceticism represented rejection of the material, sinful life of contemporary society. Rejecting affluence and comfort, they practiced

A Northumbrian cross (*ca.* 700).

poverty and self-deprivation. Rejecting family life, they practiced celibacy.

The leading figure among these "desert fathers" was Anthony (251–356), a man of great sanctity and austerity and exceptional longevity. He and his fellow monks lived in scattered huts and caves. They might look in on one another from time to time and might even come together for worship on major church holidays, but most of the time they lived alone.

To live as Anthony did required an iron constitution and immense determination, and he must sometimes have felt the urge to leave the straight and narrow path. Many of the men who went to the desert faltered and returned to the comforts of home. Early in the fourth century, a disciple of Anthony named Pachomius created a monastic community in which men could live together and practice an ascetic life of prayer. Within a few generations, cenobitic monasticism (life in a *cenobium,* or community) became the dominant form of monasticism.

Pachomius drew up a rule, a set of regulations, for his monastic community that emphasized moderation. The community was to be led by an abbot (father). Pachomius also provided for common worship by the monks, thus combining asceticism with observance of the sacraments. Because only bishops could ordain the priests who administered the sacraments, the monasteries came under episcopal control at the outset.

The Origins of Western Monasticism

The idea of monasticism reached the West around 340, when Athanasius, patriarch of Alexandria and Anthony's first biographer, was living in exile in Italy. One of the earliest monasteries in the West was founded on the island of Lérins, near Marseilles, toward the end of the fourth century. Under one of its first abbots, John Cassian (d. 429), who had spent time in Pachomius's monastery, Lérins became the model monasticism for the West. John wrote two important books—the *Institutes,* which explained the rule of Pachomius's monastery, and the *Collations,*

which contained sayings of the desert fathers that John thought would inspire and instruct his monks.

Around 360, Bishop Martin founded a Pachomian type monastery at his episcopal church in Tours. He served both as abbot of the monastery and as bishop of the diocese, and the monks functioned as his episcopal *familia*. This union of monasticism with the regular hierarchy of the church became a model of ecclesiastical organization in the West. Augustine of Hippo founded a monastery in his episcopal church, and monk-bishops became common in European and North African churches.

Martin of Tours was also the first to send monks out into the world as missionaries. Christianity had made rapid progress in the cities, but not in rural areas, and the monks Martin deployed proved effective in bringing country people into the church. The most active missionaries, however, turned out to be Celtic monks from Ireland and northern Britain. To understand how this came to be, we must look briefly at the history of the Celtic church.

Celtic Monasticism

The Celtic population of Roman Britain had been partly Christianized during the third and fourth centuries. The Celtic church was already in place when the Anglo-Saxons invaded Britain in the late fifth century, and by that time the Celts had already begun their missionary work. The most famous missionary was the monk Ninian, who prepared in Rome and Tours for his mission (*ca.* 397) among the Picts of Galloway (southwestern Scotland). But the missionary movement was interrupted for a generation by the Anglo-Saxon invasions and was not revived until about 440, when Patrick (d. 461) began to preach among the Celts of Ireland. Patrick was a monk who was said to have spent time on the Continent, perhaps at Lérins, and he dedicated twenty years of missionary work toward the goal of establishing the Celtic church.

This new church united the Celtic clan organization with episcopal monasticism.

The chief administrative unit of the Celtic church was the monastery, and each monastery served the spiritual needs of a single clan under the leadership of the abbot. The bishop, whose duties were wholly sacramental, was subordinate to the abbot.

Although Celtic monasticism was based on the Pachomian model, the Celtic monks displayed a penchant for extreme asceticism and a zeal for missionary work, perhaps a legacy of Ninian and Patrick. Before 565, the Irish monk Columba had founded a monastery on the island of Iona in the Irish Sea, and from that monastery the conversion of the Picts continued and the conversion of the Angles of Northumbria began. In Britain, the monks from Iona founded the famous monastery of Lindisfarne, and Celtic monks were soon spreading Christianity among the rural population on the Continent. Between 585 and 615 Columbanus, a monk from Iona, founded a monastery at Luxeuil, which, with its 600 monks, was the monastic metropolis of the Frankish kingdom. He then traveled on to Italy, where he founded a monastery at Bobbio, between Genoa and Pavia. These houses and their daughter houses became major centers of education and culture.

Between 550 and 650 Celtic monasticism had a powerful effect on the western Christian world. But it clashed with the basic values of many westerners, to whom asceticism was irrational and suspect. Moreover, the monks rejected the conservatism and conformity valued in Rome and in the romanized provincial cities. As time passed, westerners who favored monasticism gradually introduced changes that made monasticism more acceptable to their society.

The Growth of the Monastic Rule

Monastic life was defined and governed by a set of regulations called a rule (from Latin, *regula,* meaning rules). Augustine wrote a rule for the monks of his monastery, and Bishop Caesarius of Arles (*ca.* 470–542) wrote one for nuns. These short, well-organized guides were written for communities living under the direction of a bishop. Yet, even in the West, most monastic communities were not governed by bishops. A need existed for a more comprehensive rule that would meet the requirements of independent communities. That need was filled by Benedict of Nursia (*ca.* 480–543), an Italian monk. After living among the unregulated hermits in the valley of Subiaco, east of Rome, Benedict founded a monastery at Montecassino between Naples and Rome. There he wrote a rule, influenced by John Cassian's works, that was a masterpiece of simplicity and comprehensiveness. Eventually virtually all monastic life in the West came to be regulated by Benedict's rule, and Benedict is considered the "father of western monasticism."

The main features of Pachomian monasticism were communal worship and the observance of poverty, chastity, and obedience. Communal worship, *opus Dei*

The Rule of St. Benedict

Chapter 3: Whenever an important matter is to be undertaken in the monastery, the abbot should call the entire community together and should set forth the agenda. After hearing the various opinions of the brothers, he should consider them all and then do what he thinks best.

Chapter 5: The first degree of humility is prompt obedience . . . These disciples [the monks] must obediently step lively to the commanding voice—giving up their possessions and their own will and even leaving their chores unfinished.

Chapter 33: The vice of private ownership must be uprooted from the monastery. No one, without the abbot's permission, shall dare give, receive, or keep anything. . . .

Chapter 48: Idleness is an enemy of the soul. Therefore, the brothers should be occupied according to schedule in either manual labor or holy reading.

Chapter 64: Always remember, concerning the election of an abbot, that he should be elected by the entire community, in fear of God, or, if that proves unsatisfactory, by part of the community, however small, who would choose more rationally.

From The Rule of St. Benedict, *trans. A. C. Meisel and M. L. del Mastro (New York: Image Books, 1975).*

(the work of God), was also the main feature of Benedictine monasticism, but Benedict introduced four new elements into his rule: First, it consisted of general regulations, rather than specific rules and examples. Consequently, it could be adapted to a wide variety of conditions. Second, it directed that the abbot be elected by the members of the monastic community but consecrated by the local bishop. Consequently, the abbot possessed divinely ordained power that put him above the monks, as an intermediary between them and God. Third, to the vows of poverty, chastity, and obedience, Benedict added the vow of stability. According to this vow, a monk could not leave the monastery without the abbot's permission, a prohibition that strengthened the abbot's power and the community's solidarity. Finally, the Benedictine rule required the monks to perform manual labor, so that the community would be self-sufficient.

Although Benedict did not mention intellectual labor in his rule, the life of the monastery demanded it. The work of God required that the monks know how to read, which meant that the monastery would have a library and a scriptorium for copying books. Although in Benedict's own time the monks would have learned to read and write in secular schools or at home, the later decline in literacy meant that the monasteries had to maintain their own schools for novices. Within a century after Benedict's death, the monasteries had become the principal intellectual centers of Europe.

From the beginning, monasticism attracted women as well as men. Many seventh-century biographies tell of holy women who withdrew from society to live as nuns, sometimes to escape the influence of their families or to avoid an unwanted marriage. For women as well as for men, monasticism offered an alternative to life in society. In most cases during this period, the communities of women were attached to and under the protection of monasteries, and some monastic houses had both men and women in them. According to the biographies, it often happened that a holy man who had helped a woman to escape secular life would enter into a spiritual relationship with her that paralleled the married state both had rejected.

In 580, after Benedict's monastery at Montecassino had been destroyed by the Lombards, the monks fled to Rome, where the new monasticism attracted many young men from the upper classes. One of them was the future Pope Gregory I (r. 590–604), who gave up a promising career in the imperial administration to found a Benedictine monastery on land owned by his family in the city. After he became pope, Gregory wrote a work called the *Dialogues,* in which he told the story of Benedict's life and accomplishments. With Gregory's support, Benedictine monasticism spread steadily and during the ninth century supplanted all other monastic rules in Europe.

Gregory I and the Papacy

After Leo I (r. 440–461) put the Petrine Doctrine in its final form (see p. 119), the bishops of Rome gradually established

St. Benedict giving his Rule to his monks. This eighth-century drawing is the oldest known representation of St. Benedict.

their primacy. Although the great apostolic sees in the East never accepted the claims, except when it suited their interests, the western churches eventually looked to Rome for direction in matters of doctrine and discipline. The western bishops often appealed to the pope for support in their disputes with one another, and in the course of resolving those disputes, the popes built up a body of precedent they used as proof of their primacy. Gregory I was crucial in this process.

Although Gregory had turned away from secular service to become a monk, he did not remain withdrawn from the world of affairs. For some twenty years he advocated a variety of reforms in the Roman church and then, in 590, was elected pope at the age of fifty. This was an unusual election, because Gregory had not risen through the papal bureaucracy and, by Roman standards, was very young. Those elected pope during the sixth century were commonly old men who had progressed slowly through the bureaucracy.

The election of Gregory was a response to the critical situation facing the church of Rome in the late sixth century. The Lombards had conquered most of the Italian peninsula and had surrounded Rome, which remained loyal to the eastern emperor. The Lombards held strongly to their pagan beliefs and were vehemently anti-Roman in their attitude. Moreover, the imperial government in the city was weak. The church was providing much of the government of the city, and it needed vigorous leadership.

As pope, Gregory set about converting the Lombards and restoring the finances of the papacy. With the work of conversion proceeding well, he turned his attention to the church, which had been severely weakened during the Gothic wars of the mid-sixth century. He brought poor bishoprics together to form strong ones, established new bishoprics where none had existed, and reorganized and restaffed the papal bureaucracy.

In his letters to subordinates, Gregory spelled out the principles of ecclesiastical organization, and in his commentary on the Book of Job he set the standard for

pastoral work. Priests, bishops, and popes still turn to his writings in their efforts to understand the nature of their duties.

Gregory also fostered the spread of Christianity throughout the Germanic world. When the Visigothic king Recared I converted to official Christianity (see p. 126), he turned to Gregory for help in rebuilding the Spanish church, which had been persecuted and weakened by Recared's predecessors. Around 595, the presence of Anglo-Saxon slaves in Rome apparently reminded Gregory that Britain had once been part of the Roman Empire, and he decided to send missionaries to the former province. In 597, the Roman monk Augustine (not the great Christian writer) arrived in Kent with a small entourage. Here again, Gregory provided advice to the missionaries and wrote many letters in which he instructed them on how

A self-sufficient monastery. Its produce included fish bred in the *vivarium* shown in the foreground. A *vivarium* was often taken as a symbol of a monastery. The fish represented the monks—note their faces.

Purse lid from the Sutton Hoo treasure. Note the depiction of Daniel and the Lions, revealing the influence of Christianity, *ca.* 675.

In Anglo-Saxon England, with no single king, the missionaries had to proceed kingdom by kingdom. This turned out to be a slow process, because it made religion a source of competition among the kings. Pagan kings defended their traditional religion against Christian kings, and Christian kings tried to step up the pace of conversion.

Irish monk-missionaries had been working north of the Humber River for about thirty years when Pope Gregory's emissary Augustine arrived in Kent. After proving his spiritual powers in a series of tests with pagan priests, Augustine converted King Ethelbert of Kent, who was married to a Christian princess from the Frankish royal family. Ethelbert's people followed their king into the new religion. But rival kings stubbornly resisted conversion, and it was more than fifty years before Christianity finally triumphed in Britain.

Even then, however, religious problems persisted. The tribes north of the Humber had converted to Celtic Christianity, which preserved liturgical practices given up on the Continent and followed a religious calendar that Gregory I had replaced. The tribes of the south and the midlands had converted to Roman Christianity. The matters at issue between them were settled in 664 by the Council of Whitby, which established the primacy of the Roman calendar and liturgy. After that, only scattered resistance came from Celtic monasteries in the north.

The centrality of the king in Germanic society and the view that the king served as an intermediary between man and God made the Old Testament of particular interest to German converts. The Christian communities of the Mediterranean region, on the other hand, had emphasized the New Testament, believing that Old Testament law had been superseded by faith in Jesus, as Paul had preached (see p. 109). With the conversion of the Germans, however, Christian intellectuals began to look more closely at the Old Testament, using it to demonstrate points of doctrine and to explain the sources of Christian ethics and political theory to the Germans. Moreover, they brought the Germans to an

to deal with the Germans. In reply to questions on what to do about pagan customs, for example, Gregory advised that they be incorporated into Christian practices whenever possible. Thus, certain pagan rituals, including the blessing of the fields during the planting season, found their way into the English church. Likewise, many of the pagan shrines were transformed into Christian churches, with the new religion supplanting the old in its most important venerated places. Gregory's letters on these matters became a kind of handbook for missionaries and enhanced the authority of the pope among the Germans.

The Conversion of the Germans and Its Effects

Following the lead of Martin of Tours, Gregory enlisted monks in his campaign to convert the Lombards and Anglo-Saxons and to spread Christianity to the isolated villages of the countryside. Yet the speed with which the Germans were converted was largely the result of their own religious tradition. The Germans regarded their kings as intermediaries between the divine world and human world. So when a king accepted a new god, his subjects followed suit. The conversion of Clovis, for example, brought virtually all the Franks into the church.

awareness of Greco-Roman civilization, which had a profound effect on Germanic society.

The idea of a corporation did not exist in Germanic law. But in Roman law, the church was a corporation with rights and privileges unfamiliar to the Germans. In Germanic law, only members of the community could own land, and the law specified who would inherit land when its owner died. Moreover, persons unattached to kin or community had no standing in law, for they had no one to guarantee their conduct or stand surety for them should the need arise. After conversion of the Germans, the church and its clergy had to be somehow integrated into this society of kin and community. On the Continent, the provincial populations had learned to live under Roman law, accepting the church as a landowner and its clerics as members of the community. When the Visigoths, Ostrogoths, Franks, and other Germanic peoples settled down in the provinces, they simply accepted the *status quo,* and their kings confirmed it in their law codes.

In Britain, integration of the church in Anglo-Saxon society was more difficult. Ethelbert of Kent had to find a way to enlarge the concept of community to include the clerics of his new religion. The people of his kingdom had had little contact with Latin culture, and when, at the urging of the missionary Augustine, Ethelbert issued a law code (*ca.* 606), it was written in Anglo-Saxon. Unlike the codes issued by the kings on the Continent, Ethelbert's contained no Roman law. Its purpose, however, was the same as that of the continental codes: to integrate the elements of the community into a cohesive whole under royal authority. In Kent, most in need of integration were the Christian clergy, who had no kin and, therefore, no value in society. Ethelbert's code assigned a value to the clergy for purposes of compensation. Moreover, by incorporating Kentish customary law, it provided a comprehensive legal framework for the new Christian community.

The problem of land ownership took longer to solve. Under normal circumstances, the opinion of neighbors and fam-

A writ from the first Anglo-Saxon King, Edward the Confessor, for Westminster Abbey (1065).

ily members decided a dispute over the ownership of land. But the church had no property rights under the law, because all such rights stemmed from the family through which the rights had passed. During the 630s, the Anglo-Saxon kings created a new form of land ownership based on a written charter rather than on the witness of family and neighbors. It was called *bookland,* because it rested on possession of a charter or book—that is, a written instrument—which conveyed rights in land. Only the king could issue a charter, because law flowed from God through the king. If a man wanted to give land to the church, he "booked" it by getting a charter from the king. He then handed the charter over to the church, which could produce the document if its rights were ever challenged. This was a major innovation in property law.

Thus, the Christian church brought Roman and Germanic ideas and ways of life together into what was to emerge as medieval civilization.

During the sixth century, western society and politics underwent a profound transformation. The Germanic kingdoms established themselves as successors to

Roman political power and began amalgamating their culture with that of the provincial populations. The Christian church, by converting the Germans, served as the principal agent of that amalgamation. At the end of the century, Pope Gregory I ensured the prestige and authority of the Roman church by leading the effort to convert the Germans. He also instituted reforms in the fiscal administration and liturgy that were accepted throughout the West. Henceforth, Rome was the undisputed source of guidance in doctrine, liturgy, and organization. The idea of imperial unity survived in the realm of religion.

By contrast, the civilizations of China, India, and the eastern Roman Empire remained largely intact. Religion, language, and political ideology continued along their ancient paths, and newcomers were absorbed into the dominant culture without deflecting it from its traditional course. Only in the Middle East, where a new religion, Islam, came into being, was there a cultural transformation similar to that of the West. Like the Europeans, the Arabs were deeply influenced by Greco-Roman civilization, which they reshaped to fit their new religion. The next chapters look at the civilizations of the East.

Suggestions for Further Reading

General

For general histories of the Germanic invasions and studies of early Germanic society, see the works cited at the end of the Chapter 4. On the relations between the old Roman population and the Germans, see S. Dill, *Roman Society in Gaul in the Merovingian Age* (1926); W. Goffart, *Barbarians and Romans, A.D. 418–584: The Techniques of Accommodation* (1980); and G. Ladner, "On Roman Attitudes towards Barbarians in Late Antiquity," *Viator* 7 (1976). J. M. Wallace-Hadrill, *The Barbarian West, 400–1000* (1952), is an excellent brief survey. A series of new studies gives a close look at several of the kingdoms: T. S. Burns, *A History of the Ostrogoths* (1984); C. Wickham, *Early Medieval Italy: Central Power and Local Society 400–1000* (1981); E. James, *The Origins of France: From Clovis to the Capetians 500–1000* (1982); and P. J. Geary, *Before France and Germany* (1987). The most important source for the history of the Franks is Gregory of Tours, whose work has been published as *The History of the Franks* (1974, and other editions). For the history of the Anglo-Saxons, see Bede, *The Ecclesiastical History of England* (many editions). F. M. Stenton, *The Anglo-Saxons,* 2nd ed. (1947), is an excellent general history. N. Howe, *Migration and Mythmaking in Anglo-Saxon England* (1989) studies the historical memory of the Anglo-Saxons. On the Goths, see H. Wolfram, *History of the Goths* (1988). On the Visigoths, see Thompson's *The Goths in Spain* (1969); P. D. King, *Law and Society in the Visigothic Kingdom* (1972); and R. Collins, *Early Medieval Spain: Unity in Diversity 400–1000* (1983).

Germanic Society

The picture of Germanic society has been altered by the study of A. C. Murray, *Germanic Kinship Structure* (1983). See also E. A. Thompson, *The Early Germans* (1965). The best modern studies of the early Germanic idea of kingship are J. M. Wallace-Hadrill, *Early Germanic Kingship in England and on the Continent* (1971); P. H. Sawyer and I. N. Wood, eds., *Early Medieval Kingship* (1977); and H. A. Myers (with H. Wolfram), *Medieval Kingship* (1977), which covers the whole subject up to the late Middle Ages. M. McCormick, *Eternal Victory: Triumphal Rulership in Late Antiquity, Byzantium, and the Early Medieval West* (1986) shows how Roman imperial ideas of rulership survived in early Germanic kingship. Much of what is known of early Germanic society derives from study of the law codes: See K. F. Drew, *The Burgundian Code* (1949), and *The Lombard Laws* (1973); and T. J. Rivers, *Laws of the Alamans and Bavarians* (1977). On the condition of women in the early period, see S. Wemple, *Women in Frankish Society: Marriage and Cloister 500–900* (1981) and S. M. Stuard, ed., *Women in Medieval Society* (1976). There is a chapter on the early medieval household in D. Herlihy, *Medieval Households* (1985). See also J. Chapelot and R. Fossier, *The Village and House in the Middle Ages* (1985).

The Early Church

For a comprehensive history of the early Church, see K. Baus and H. Jedin, *History of Church History,* Vol. 1 (1965), and J. Danielou and H. Marrou, *The Christian Centuries,* Vol. 1 (1964). Both of these works amply treat the growth of ecclesiastical institutions. On the development of Christian liturgy, see J. A. Jungmann, *The Early Liturgy to the Time of Gregory the Great* (1959), and G. Dix, *The Shape of the Liturgy* (1960). The standard study of Gregory the Great's pontificate is still F. H. Dudden, *Gregory the Great,* 2 vols. (1905). For his intellectual and spiritual program, see C. Straw, *Gregory the Great: Perfection in Imperfection* (1988). For an appreciation of Gregory's achievement against the background of the early medieval papacy, see J. Richards, *The Popes and the Papacy in the Early Middle Ages 476–752* (1979). On the formation of the Papal State, see T. F. X. Noble, *The Republic of St. Peter: The Birth of the Papal State 680–825* (1984). On early monasticism, see P. Rousseau, *Pachomius* (1985) and *Ascetics, Authority and the Church in the Age of Jerome and Cassian* (1978). For a provocative study of celibacy, see P. Brown, *The Body and Society: Men, Women, and Sexual Renunciation in Early Christianity* (1988). For translations of early saints' lives, see H. Delehaye, *The Legends of the Saints* (1962), and E. S. Duckett, *The Wandering Saints of the Early Middle Ages* (1958). For an interpretation of the monastic ideal, see P. Brown, *Society and the Holy in Late Antiquity* (1982). The Rule of St. Benedict has been published in many editions. C. H. Lawrence, *Medieval Monasticism: Forms of Religious Life in Western Europe in the Middle Ages* (1984) is a good general survey.

6

INDIA AND CHINA IN ANTIQUITY

Civilization in South and East Asia emerged later than in Mesopotamia and Egypt but well before it emerged in Greece and Rome. India and China resemble each other in their antiquity, their duration, and the vast extent of their cultural influence, but in many respects they represent a study in contrast. Furthermore, even though India, unlike China, shared in a broad and diffuse Indo-European heritage, it developed a civilization as distinct from those to the West as it was from that of China. Contact between civilizations is a fascinating theme, but the primary interest of Indian and Chinese civilizations lies in their own history, their cultural achievements, and in the wealth of material they offer for the study of the comparative history of civilization.

INDIA

The Indian subcontinent, stretching from the Himalayan Mountains to the tropical beaches of the south, is a vast area inhabited by peoples with strong regional and local traditions. In the course of time, sufficient unity developed so that we can speak of an Indian civilization, but within that civilization there has always been great diversity. The interplay of the factors making for and against unity is a major theme of Indian history.

Civilization in India dates to the third millenium B.C. when a sophisticated culture flourished, centered in the Indus River Valley. Over a territory of half a million square miles, some 300 sites have been investigated, most of them near rivers that sustained agriculture and provided trans-

(OPPOSITE) Bronze ceremonial vessel (early Zhou dynasty, 10th–7th century B.C.).

portation. The most impressive sites are those of Mohenjo-Daro and Harappa, the former a city of 25,000–30,000 inhabitants. Laid out on grids and capped by citadels, these two cities were complete with granaries and advanced drainage systems, and the presence of separate industrial areas points to class differentiation. Small square seals found as far away as Sumerian Mesopotamia attest to a flourishing commerce. These seals were probably used by merchants to mark their wares. Some are decorated with real or imaginary animals; others bear abstract symbols, including the Greek cross and the swastika. Written inscriptions on the seals have not been deciphered, although the script is generally considerd to be in a language belonging to the family of Dravidian languages still used in South India. The technological repertoire of the cities included wheel-made pottery, cotton spinning, and metallurgy. The impressive bath at Mohenjo-Daro, similar to water tanks in later Hindu temples, may attest to the importance of religion, but no temples have been uncovered from this period.

Environmental factors such as devastating floods, a shift in the course of the Indus River, and exhaustion of soil fertility may have accounted for the demise of this civilization. A decline in social organization followed, as mirrored in later city planning. By the time the crude Aryan tribal peoples entered the subcontinent, the old civilization was gone, leaving in its wake impoverished localized cultures.

Early Aryan–Indian Society

The Aryans began to enter India in substantial numbers through the Hindu Kush mountains around 1500 B.C. They were tribal peoples related to the inhabitants of Iran, and they spoke Sanskrit, an Indo-European language which became the classic language of India. They were a vigorous, indeed tumultuous and warlike people, not unlike the Greeks. Originally pastoral, as time passed they also turned to agriculture. They gradually achieved dominance, first in the Indus Plain, then in North India. After 1000 B.C. the Aryans

also raided in the region beyond the Vindhaya Mountain Range, which separates North from South India. Although ultimately the North Indian culture profoundly influenced that of the South, the various southern regions never lost their cultural or linguistic identity. Today, South India continues to be dominated by peoples speaking Dravidian languages unrelated to the Indo-European tongues of the North.

In the beginning the Aryans were divided into warriors, priests, and commoners, but as they settled down, their social organization became more complex. There developed what became India's classic division of society into four social orders (varnas). The varna system was classic in the sense that it became the model of how society was conceived, how it was supposed to be structured, even when actual social stratification was more complicated.

The warriors (kshatriyas) originally had pride of place, but the classic order ranks priests (brahmans) first with warriors second. Other Aryans were included in the third varna, that of the vaishyas, a term later used for merchants and cultivators. Members of these three orders were entitled to full membership in society as symbolized by the sacred thread granted to boys in an induction ceremony. This status was denied to the dark-skinned conquered people who formed the fourth order, the shudras, who were reduced to serfdom and forced to perform menial tasks. Still further down in social status were those whose work was considered polluting: attendants at cremation grounds, those who worked with animal carcasses, leather workers, and others. Later they became known as "untouchables," beyond the pale of Aryan society.

As political integration proceeded and Aryan influence spread, the interaction between India's various communities grew in complexity and extent. The process by which major components of North Indian culture were spread is frequently termed "Aryanization," but the influence was not all one way. The varna system did not operate everywhere in the same way. Another institution developed that

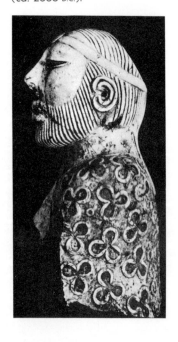

Statuette of a man, perhaps a priest, wearing an ornamental robe, from Mohenjo-Daro (ca. 2500 B.C.).

directly molded people's lives and made for a diversity of lifestyles and beliefs. This was *jati,* or caste.* *Jatis* were endogamous (intermarrying) groups that shared a common religious heritage, traditional values, dietary rules, and, characteristically, a common occupation. The *jati* to which people belonged gave them their sense of community and determined the pattern of their lives. Like membership in a family, membership in a *jati* was a matter of birth: *jati* means "birth." One could no more change one's *jati* than one's family. To be expelled from one's *jati,* to become an outcast, was the worst possible fate, for no other *jati* would accept such a person.

The origins of this institution are unclear. It is quite likely that some *jati* may have grown out of occupational groups. Others may have been tribal in origin. Fear of strangers, traditional marriage patterns, and dread of ritual pollution may all have contributed. Although the tendency was for the individual *jati* to be grouped under the five major social orders (the four *varna* and the Untouchables), the division was, as often as not, imperfect. There were regional differences in the dynamics of social relations and status as well as groups imperfectly assimilated into the *varna* system. And, like other institutions, *jati* experienced historical changes; there were splits, changes in mores and practices, and changes in the social status of individual *jati.*

Unfortunately, a good deal of the history of caste remains obscure. On the one hand, the *jati* system allowed aboriginal tribes and other groups to become part of Indian society while maintaining their own traditions and way of life. Not forcing people to assimilate made for tolerance and produced a notably pluralistic society in which people of diverse customs and beliefs could peacefully coexist. By the same token, however, the *jati* system also reinforced strict social differentiation between groups and inexorably bound the individual to the group. Although much has changed in the long course of history,

more than three thousand *jati* attest to the continuing importance of this institution in India today.

Religious Developments

The success of the brahmans (priests) in gaining first place in the social hierarchy suggests the importance of religion in early India. Like other Indo-European peoples, the Aryans worshiped a number of gods—some more important than others. As the civilization grew in complexity and sophistication, the old rituals and formulas no longer met everyone's religious needs, and there appeared a tendency toward abstract thought and a posing of such questions as those concerning the nature of being and nonbeing, questions which were to be central to India's loftiest religious and philosophical discourses.

These religious concerns were expressed in the *Upanishads,* a group of religious treatises of the eighth and seventh centuries B.C. The *Upanishads* contain the religious speculations of teachers working in the traditions of the *Rig Veda,* an ancient collection of hymns handed down orally from generation to generation and written down in its present form around 600 B.C. Because the *Upanishads* do not stem from a single source, they contain diverse ideas, but they do agree on one central theme: the invisible but essential "soul" within each of us *(Atman)* is identical with the world-soul *(Brahman),* the underlying reality of the world. Failure to realize this truth condemns people to be prisoners of their illusions and chains them to an unending cycle of birth and rebirth. Death provides no relief, for it is merely a stage, an interlude between lives. Release comes only when the individual Atman is rejoined with the Brahman, attainable only after comprehension is achieved through disciplined effort, meditation, and/or various spiritual exercises.

The individual fate of those who do not attain release is governed by the law of *karma,* according to which every action brings forth a reaction, not only in this life but in the next. Thus a person who has led a good life but still falls short of the perfection needed for release will at least

*Although *varna* is sometimes also translated as "caste," this is misleading because it confounds a social order and a kinship group.

enjoy a favorable rebirth. But a wicked person might come back as a pig, a goat, or even an insect. In later Indian thought, various theories were advanced to account for the operation of *karma*. Different behavioral conclusions were drawn (for instance, it reinforced a tendency toward vegetarianism), but the concept of

---

Vedic Hymns

Origins of the Four *Varna*

When they [the gods] divided the Man,
into how many parts did they divide him?
What were his mouth, what were his arms,
what were his thighs and feet called?

The brahman [priest] was his mouth,
of his arms were made the warrior.
His thighs became the vaisya [merchants and cultivators],
of his feet the sudra [servants] was born.

The moon arose from his mind,
from his eye was born the sun,
from his mouth Indra and Agni [the war god and the fire god],
from his breath the wind was born. . . .

♦ ♦ ♦

Hymn of Creation

Then even nothingness was not, nor existence,
There was no air then, nor the heavens beyond it.
What covered it? Where was it? In whose keeping?
Was there then cosmic water, in depths unfathomed?

Then there was neither death nor immortality,
nor was there then the torch of night and day.
The One breathed windlessly and self-sustaining.
There was that One then, and there was no other. . . .

But, after all, who knows and who can say
whence it all came, and how creation happened?
The gods themselves are later than creation,
so who knows truly whence it has arisen?

Quoted in A. L. Basham, The Wonder That Was India (London: Sidgwick and Jackson, 1954; New York: Macmillan, 1968), pp. 241, 247–248.

---

karma itself was accepted as a basic truth not only by ordinary folk but by all traditional Indian thinkers and holy men.

Most of the era's men of religion stayed within the Vedic tradition, but there were some important exceptions. One was Vardhamana Mahavira (*ca.* 540–468 B.C.), the founder of Jainism, a religion that teaches nonviolence and is centered on the belief that everything is animated. Even more influential was Gautama Siddhartha (*ca.* 563–483 B.C.), also known as Sakyamuni, who achieved religious illumination and became the Buddha, the "Enlightened One." He then spent the remainder of his life sharing his insights with others. His disciples renounced the world, took vows of chastity and poverty, and formed communities of monks and nuns. The idea of monasticism had such deep appeal to people of religious vocation that it spread not only to regions east of India but also west to the Middle East.

At the core of the Buddha's teachings were the Four Noble Truths: that life is suffering; that the cause of suffering is craving or desire; that to stop the suffering the desire must be stopped; that this is accomplished through the Eightfold Path (right views, right intention, right speech, right action, right livelihood, right effort, right mindfulness, and right concentration). Like his contemporaries, the Buddha taught that salvation lay in release from reincarnation, but he denied the existence of a soul and taught that what we think of as the self is merely a temporary aggregate of the material body, the sensations, perception, predisposition, and consciousness. It is a momentary cluster of qualities lacking any underlying unity. Transmigration, in this view, does not involve a substance but rather it is like the passing of a flame from one lamp to another until it is finally extinguished. The state of Nirvana, which literally means "extinguished," was the ultimate goal.

Another major difference between the orthodox Vedic traditions and Buddhism was that Buddhism rejected the hereditary claims of the Brahmans. For Buddhists, birth did not determine worth. This attitude naturally appealed to merchants, warriors, and others offended by the pretensions of the priesthood. As Buddhism developed, it acquired other features which enhanced its appeal and won it patronage. Its greatest Indian patron was the third emperor of the Mauryan Empire.

The Mauryan Empire, 321–181 B.C.

In a gradual process over many centuries, tribes and tribal confederations coalesced into more complex political organizations. By mid-sixth century B.C., there were sixteen kingdoms that we know by name. The largest of these was the Magadhan state, which from its base in the eastern Gangetic Plain (the plain formed by the Ganges River) expanded to become paramount in North India. In the meantime, India's northwest became part of the great Achaemeneid Empire of Persia, which was destroyed by Alexander the Great in the fourth century B.C. When the power of Alexander's empire receded, the Magadhan state, under the Mauryan dynasty, took its place. The Mauryans then expanded until they ruled over the entire Indian subcontinent, except for the extreme south.

The empire had a complex administrative structure. It built public works (es-

The Buddha was at first not pictured in human form; his presence here is indicated by the tree in the upper left corner (detail from a pillar at Sanchi, first century B.C.).

The Mauryan Empire   *ca.* 250 B.C.

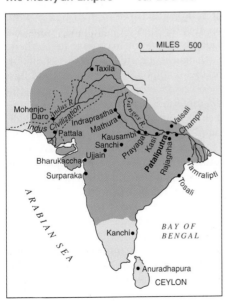

pecially roads and irrigation facilities), maintained an army, and collected taxes. Theoretically, all land belonged to the emperor. Cultivators paid about a third of their crop in taxes and were charged for the use of government water. There were also numerous levies on merchants and craftsmen, many of whom lived in Pataliputra (modern Patna), a cosmopolitan city whose bazaars offered goods from places as far away as China, Mesopotamia, and Asia Minor.

Much of the empire's success has traditionally been ascribed to Kautilya, the author of the *Arthashastra* (Treatise on Material Gain), India's prime text on practical politics and administration. It contains a good deal of sound, practical advice (for instance, officials should be selected on the basis of merit, and the king should devote himself to his tasks), but it also offers frank counsels of expediency. A notorious example is its advice to the ruler that he employ spies to inform him of what is happening in the state and also to spread propaganda for him.

Emperor Ashoka (r. 269–232 B.C.) is perhaps India's most famous ruler. Converted to Buddhism, Ashoka did much to advance the religion. He sponsored a great Buddhist council, sent out missionaries, and erected numerous stupas, Buddhist reliquary mounds. The largest of these, that at Sanchi, stands 56 feet tall and was later encased in sandstone and supplied with a beautifully carved railing and gateways. The lion column he erected to commemorate the Buddha's first sermon has become a symbol of India, adopted in the twentieth century to decorate the state seal of the Republic of India. In his patronage of Buddhism, Ashoka has been compared to Emperor Constantine and his support of Christianity in Rome, but the Indian monarch also maintained religious tolerance throughout his far-flung empire. In the edicts he had inscribed on rocks and special pillars, he displayed the imperial paternalism appropriate to a universal ruler. "I consider my work to be the welfare of the whole world," he proclaimed in one edict.

A half-century after Ashoka's death, the Mauryan Empire was in collapse. Its last ruler was assassinated by a general who had to content himself with ruling over a much-diminished state in central India. It would have taken an exceptionally strong ruler to organize a political machine and inspire the wide loyalty needed to maintain as huge and disparate a domain as that of the Mauryas, a domain with few economic or institutionalized political bonds that might have made for a more permanent union.

Political Division, 180 B.C.–A.D. 320

The next 500 years in India were complicated politically, but they were a time of cultural brilliance, economic growth, and increased contacts with other cultures.

The entrance of a succession of foreign peoples into India was a major source of the period's instability. We have already noted the invasion of Alexander the Great; the ultimate legacy of Greek interest in India was the formation of a number of Indo-Greek states, some of which issued bilingual coins. However, the most successful people to inhabit India during this period were the Kushans, who entered the subcontinent from Central Asia in the first century A.D. and created an empire that lasted until 240. The Kushan empire was the only one ever to straddle the Hindu Kush and Baluchi Hills and become a major power in both Central Asia and India. Most of the lucrative trade along the Silk Route from China to Europe passed through the Kushan empire in the north, while, at the same time, maritime trade flourished in the south. Hoards of Roman coins found in South India, beyond the borders of the Kushan empire, substantiate the complaint of Pliny the Elder that the trade was causing a gold drain in Rome.

The Kushans were converted to Buddhism and eventually spread their new faith to Central Asia and to China. Under the Kushans, the first statues of the Buddha appeared, executed in an Indo-Roman style that spread to the east. The growth of Buddhist art was only one of a number of ways in which Buddhism was gradually transformed and its appeal broadened. Another major development was the growth of worship of a number of Buddhas and *bodhisattvas,* beings who, on the threshold of Nirvana, postpone their own salvation in order to help others. Such figures attracted the pious veneration of the common folk even as Buddhist theorists developed subtle and profound doctrines that supplied spiritual and intellectual nourishment to those who dedicated their lives to the religious quest. These developments coalesced to constitute Mahayana Buddhism, and it was largely in this form that the religion spread from the Kushan empire to East Asia, while the older Theraveda (or Hinayana) form prevailed to the south.

Running parallel to the changes in Buddhism were changes that transformed the traditional Vedic religion into Hinduism. With Hinduism, as in Buddhism, worshipers felt the need for divine beings that

The Buddha (detail of a relief from Gandhara, second century A.D.).

were accessible to them, and there developed a rich pantheon of gods and deities even as Hindu saints and philosophers pointed to an ultimate unity underlying all diversity. Of the three main Hindu deities—Brahma (The Creator), Vishnu (The Preserver), and Siva (The Destroyer but also a Creator)—the latter two became the main wings of Hinduism, inspiring sects that gained a vast number of devoted adherents who regarded their gods as representative of the Absolute. Vishnu was believed to have appeared in nine incarnations. His ninth incarnation was as the Buddha, suggesting that Buddhism was simply part of a great Hindu whole. Vishnu also incarnated himself as Rama, hero of India's great epic, the *Ramayana*, and as Krishna, an important figure in the Hindu pantheon.

Vishnu appears as Krishna in the *Bhagavad Gita (The Song of the Lord),* which was inserted into the great and much older epic, *The Mahabharata.* In the *Gita,* Krishna appears as the charioteer and friend of a warrior named Arjuna, who, greatly distressed to see friends and relatives lined up in the enemy ranks as a

A stone relief of an amorous couple from a sculptured cave temple at Karli, A.D. 100.

The Ends of Man

Some say that dharma [virtue] and material gain are good, others that pleasure and material gain are good, and still others that dharma alone or pleasure alone is good, but the correct position is that the three should coexist without harming each other.

From Sources of Indian Tradition, *ed. by Wm. Theodore de Bary and others (New York: Columbia University Press, 1958), p. 213.*

battle is about to begin, lays down his bow. But Krishna urges him to perform his sacred duty *(dharma)* as a warrior, telling him that everyone has a social role that must be fulfilled. As long as one does so purely for the sake of duty and without attachment, he will not incur bad *karma*.

There are other subtle and profound concepts in the *Gita*, the most widely studied and revered Hindu text. One that fits in well with India's system of castes and social orders is the concept that people's *dharma* differs according to their social

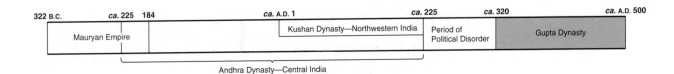

322 B.C.	ca. 225	184	ca. A.D. 1	ca. 225	ca. 320	ca. A.D. 500

Mauryan Empire

Kushan Dynasty—Northwestern India

Period of Political Disorder

Gupta Dynasty

Andhra Dynasty—Central India

group, and that salvation lies in everyone's following his *dharma* without regard for self-benefit. The basic idea that different duties and life-styles pertain to different groups of people was also involved in the theory of the four stages of life, which were prescribed as the ideal for members of the upper three *varnas*. First came the stage of the earnest student, diligently following the instructions of his teacher. Next came the phase of the householder, with all the joys and responsibilities of an active secular life. Love and pleasure *(kama),* as well as material gain *(artha),* were among the accepted goals of life. However, there came a time to retire from the active life of the householder and to partially withdraw into the forest to meditate. This was followed by the final stage, that of the ascetic wandering free from all human bonds, concerned only with the soul's liberation. Many, indeed most, householders did not actually end their lives in this manner, but it had its attractions in a land which honored ascetics and respected the religious quest.

The Guptas, ca. 325–550

Like the Mauryan Empire, that of the Guptas was based in the Gangetic Plain. From there they expanded west to the Punjab, northwest to Kashmir, east to Bengal, and established themselves as a presence in the south. However, the south was not fully incorporated into the empire; defeated rulers were largely reinstated in their lands as tributaries. There were also rulers in distant places such as Sri Lanka who, in theory, accepted Gupta overlordship and sent the emperor gifts, but who were well beyond the range of its authority.

The dynasty reached its greatest height of well-being under Chandra Gupta II *(ca.* 375–415), even though it had not attained its greatest geographical extent.

The account of Fa Xian (Fa Hsien), a Chinese monk who visited India at this time, testifies to the safety of travel and the general prosperity of the realm. He tells of cities with fine mansions, and that in Pataliputra (Patna) were "houses for dispensing charities and medicine." He also reports, optimistically, that no one in the kingdom killed animals, drank intoxicating liquor, or ate onion or garlic—no one except "wicked men" who had to warn others of their approach by striking a piece of wood so they could avoid contamination.

It was a time of prosperity and, at least at court, luxury, for there were great feasts with drink served in ruby cups or cups in the shape of dancing peacocks. The quantity and quality of Gupta coins attest to the importance of commerce. India's trade with China and Southeast Asia was on the increase, and trade with the West remained significant. Merchant and artisan guilds prospered. The fiscal basis

The Gupta Empire   *ca.* A.D. 400

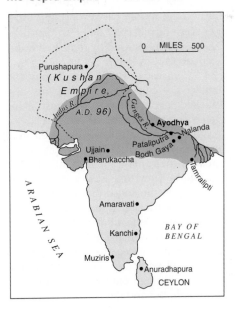

of the state included a land tax and various supplemental levies. There was also a government monopoly on salt and metal mines. Once again, as under the Mauryans, there was a complex administrative hierarchy and a strong network of government agents and spies.

The last great Gupta emperor was Skandagupta (455–67), who repelled the Hunas (Huns) who invaded India from Central Asia. After his reign, however, the dynasty went into decline. The throne was weakened by succession disputes, a recurrent problem in India where there were no clear rules of primogeniture (succession by the eldest son). In the end, the state was unable to withstand repeated attacks from the Huns.

The Gupta period is celebrated less for its political achievements than for its cultural brilliance. India's greatest playwright, Kalidasa, most probably served at the court of Chandra Gupta II. Notable advances occurred in mathematics and astronomy. The numerals later introduced into Europe by the Arabs and consequently known as Arabic numerals were actually Indian in origin, as was the decimal system. In 499 an Indian astronomer calculated the value of *pi,* determined that there are 365.3586805 days in a year, and argued that the earth is round, that it revolves around its own axis, and that lunar eclipses occur when the earth's shadow falls on the moon. However, these theories were disputed by other astronomers. As elsewhere, astronomy remained firmly wedded to astrology.

Along with a flourishing literary and intellectual culture, the visual arts also reached new excellence. The most lasting achievements were made under religious auspices. Although the Gupta rulers generally favored Hinduism, Gupta artists created their masterpieces in Buddhist sculpture. They achieved a classic style not only in the sense that it served as a touchstone for later artists, but also in that it achieved a perfect balance between the transcendental and the human in idealized figures representing the Buddha. India's finest wall paintings also date from this period, although they were produced in the south, beyond the bounds of the empire. These are the world-famous Buddhist caves at Ajanta, which are decorated with secular as well as religious scenes and constitute a narrative art of the highest quality.

South India

The fact that both of India's great empires were based in the north should not obscure the contributions of the south to the development of Indian civilization. Inscriptions began to appear in South India in the second century B.C. and a century earlier in Sri Lanka. During the first three centuries A.D., anthologies of poetry were compiled in Tamil, a major Dravidian language. The nucleus of the culture that produced this literature was a short distance south of modern Madras. The early Tamil poems describe a complex culture of farmers and townspeople—more than 100 towns are mentioned, as are numerous occupations. Politically the Tamil-speaking area was long divided between three competing states until the Pallavas (roughly 315–800, with their high point around 600) achieved dominance. Over the centuries the Tamil and other southern cultures were deeply influenced by Sanskrit culture without, however, losing their identities. The interaction between the southern cultures and those of the north forms a major theme in the study of South India.

The Spread of Indian Culture

By the middle of the sixth century, Indian influence had spread far beyond the subcontinent. It was a gradual and selective process of cultural diffusion. The peoples of Southeast Asia did not have Indian culture forced upon them. Local rulers, impressed by the achievements of Indian civilization and valuing the power of Indian knowledge and religion, selected and adapted certain Indian institutions to their own distinct cultural patterns.

The influence of India was deep and permanent in all regions of Southeast Asia, with the exception of the Philippines and North Vietnam. The figures of Borobudur, the great eighth-century Buddhist monument in Indonesia, clearly show the influence of Gupta sculpture, and elsewhere South Indian influences were also much in evidence. In later centuries, the temples at Pagan in Burma and the magnificent structures in the jungles of Cambodia were to attest to the appeal of Hinduism, as well as Buddhism. The largest religious building in the world is Angkor Wat in Cambodia. Dedicated to Vishnu, this Hindu temple was built in the first half of the twelfth century. It is a walled complex measuring approximately 4,900 × 4,200 feet and is surrounded by a moat 650 feet wide—just as the world, in Indian eyes, is surrounded by the ocean. The balustrades in the first interior section are in the shape of nine-headed snakes, referring both to an ancient snake cult and to Vishnu's rainbow, the magic bridge that leads to heaven. Relief carvings on the wall portray stories of Rama and Krishna, the two most prominent incarnations of Vishnu.

Although Angkor Wat was built much later than the period we are concerned with here, it symbolizes the enormous in-

fluence of Hinduism in the lands to India's east. Yet the influence of Buddhism was to be the more lasting; to this day it is the dominant religion of the Southeast Asian mainland and Sri Lanka. As a proselytizing religion of great force, Buddhism also spread from India through Central Asia to China, where it eventually had great impact.

CHINA

Archaeologists have uncovered a number of Neolithic cultures in China, but it was in the Shang period (*ca.* 1600–1027 B.C.) that the first real civilization emerged. As in India, the first substantial cities and states appeared in the north. A good indication of Shang organizational power was its ability to mobilize the manpower needed to build a wall estimated at 2,385 feet long, 60 feet wide, and 30 feet high surrounding an early capital city. It has been calculated that this wall took 10,000 laborers, working 330 days a year, 18 years to complete.

A ceremonial vessel in the form of an elephant (Shang dynasty).

A view of the temple of Angkor Wat, built in the twelfth century by the king of Cambodia.

The Spread of Buddhism   Sixth Century B.C. to Sixteenth Century A.D.

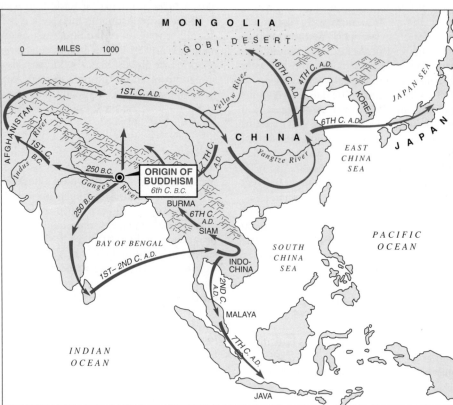

With the Shang, China entered the Bronze Age. The finest products of the period are bronze vessels unsurpassed in their artistry, as befitted their use in solemn sacred rites. Many such vessels have been found, along with jades and other precious objects, in Shang tombs of the rich and powerful. The remains of people buried alive also have been found in these tombs. In one case, a chariot was discovered, complete with horse and driver; in others, entire entourages accompanied the deceased in death. The victims were non-Shang barbarians, captured in war and reduced to slavery, who were believed to accompany the dead on a journey to the afterworld.

Of more permanent influence was the development of the Chinese system of writing during this period. The earliest Chinese characters were pictograms (stylized pictorial representations) and ideograms (visual representations of a thing or concept), but most characters were more complex, consisting of an element that indicated a category of meaning and another that functioned as a phonetic indicator. Unfortunately, the pronunciation of the language later changed so that today the phonetic element is not necessarily a reliable guide to pronunciation. The early characters were used to inscribe oracle bones and tortoise shells used for divination. Command of the written language was the prized possession of a privileged group, and full literacy, until modern times, remained the possession of an elite minority who prided themselves on working with their brains rather than with their hands.

Although the written language was associated with the perpetuation of social distinctions, it helped overcome geographical barriers. People who spoke mutually unintelligible languages could still communicate with each other in writing, particularly after the form of characters was standardized in 221 B.C. Thus today, even though Cantonese and Mandarin speakers cannot converse with each other, they can communicate in writing and they can read the same books and journals. Similarly, scholars in Korea, Japan, and Vietnam acquired a command over China's literary culture even though they were unable to speak Chinese.

When the Shang were overthrown by the Zhou (Chou)* around 1027 B.C., at first no break occurred in cultural continuity because the Zhou represented a variant of Shang culture. They even produced bronze vessels similar to those of their predecessors. However, the inscriptions on the vessels, as well as the decorations and artistic effects, gradually changed, indicating a process of secularization that transformed them into treasured family heirlooms. At the same time, burial practices changed, and the immolation of humans and animals in the tombs of the powerful became increasingly rare.

The Zhou did not attempt to govern directly the area they conquered. Instead, they invested members of the royal house, favored adherents and allies, with the authority to rule over more than a hundred separate territories without interference from the Zhou king. These subordinate rulers received ranks later systematized into a hierarchical order. They were obliged to render military service and tribute. In practice, these positions were hereditary under a system of primogeniture, but with each generation the succession to a local lordship had to be legitimized by formal royal investiture. Some of these Zhou arrangements resembled those of the feudal system that later developed in Europe and Japan.

We are inadequately informed about the political structure of local village life or the economic relations between those who cultivated the soil and their rulers. However, we can learn something from the folk poetry included in the *Book of Songs,* which was compiled around 600 B.C. and was later accepted as one of the classics of Confucianism. Some songs

*This text uses the *pinyin* system of romanization, followed in parentheses by Wade-Giles. An exception is that some common geographical names appear in their earlier customary forms.

show ordinary people at work: the men clearing weeds from the fields, plowing, planting, and harvesting; the girls and women gathering mulberry leaves to feed the silkworms, making thread, carrying food out to the fields for their men. There is much about the staple crop, millet—both the eating variety and that used for brewing. We hear about wheat, barley, and rice, and men building a house, stamping down the earth between planks to make the walls. There are joyful celebrations of granaries full of grain and references to men gathering thatch for their roofs. Mention is made of lords' fields and private fields, and a "bailiff" is referred to, but the details of the system remain hidden. There are also poems of complaint against the government. One compares tax collectors to big rats. Another tells of the hardships of military service, men constantly on the march, day and night without rest, living like rhinoceroses and tigers. Sometimes a soldier survives the dangers of war and returns home only to find that his wife has given him up for dead and married another. Among the most appealing in their freshness and the innocence of their language are the love poems, for this was a time when girls and

Chinese calligraphy. (*Left*) A rubbing from one of the ten "Stone Drums," an example of the Great Seal style of writing, which evolved in the latter part of the Zhou dynasty. (*Right*) A rubbing from a stone inscription of the Han dynasty, inscribed in the Official Style.

Bronze wrestlers (Zhou dynasty).

young women were not yet restricted by the rules of etiquette from free expression of their longing for their sweetheart or their wish to be married.

The Age of Philosophers

As the bonds that tied the lords to the Zhou king weakened, power eroded, and by the ninth century B.C. the Zhou kings were unable to prevent the local rulers from fighting each other. Nor could they check the incursions of non-Chinese barbarians. To evade the latter, in 771 B.C. the capital was moved from Shaanxi (Shensi) east to the Luoyang (Loyang) region. After this move the Zhou "king" nominally continued to reign for another 500 years, until 256 B.C., but actually he exercised no military, political, or economic power. China was now divided among competing states. During the aptly named "Warring States Period" (403–221 B.C.) the competition between the states became increasingly more desperate and ruthless. With strong states subduing and annexing the weaker, the number of states diminished. The successful states grew ever bigger and more formidable until the process reached its logical conclusion and only one huge state remained.

Confucius (*ca.* 551–*ca.* 479 B.C.), a contemporary of the Buddha, lived relatively early in this period of accelerating change. Distressed by the disintegration of the political and moral order, he sought to put the world back together again and hoped to find a ruler who would implement his ideas. When this failed, he turned to teaching. Confucius saw himself not as a creator but as one who merely transmitted the traditional wisdom and values of civilization. He was a creative transmitter who understood the tradition in terms suitable for his own age and thereby revitalized and transformed old values. A good example is his redefinition of nobility as a quality acquired through virtue and wisdom, not through birth. For Confucius, the ideal man is humane, wise, and courageous. He is motivated by virtue, and the ultimate virtue is *ren (jen),* a term sometimes translated as "benevolence" or "humaneness," but for which there is no exact English equivalent. *Ren* is the ground for all other virtues, the condition of being fully human in dealing with others. The written Chinese character for *ren* consists of the symbols for "man" and "two."

Morality and the achievement of social harmony were at the core of Confucius's concerns. He urged people to observe the *li,* a term meaning sacred ritual, ceremonial, and propriety, as well as good manners. The *li* were part of the precious heritage of antiquity, imbued with an aura of sacred reverence. When performed with true sincerity, life is truly human and civilized. When everyone follows the *li* and carries out his or her social role with genuine devotion, harmony will ensue. There will then be no need for coercion, no need for laws or punishments. Of crucial importance to achieve this was the initiative of the ruler who, by following the advice of a perfectly virtuous minister, could make government benevolent and win over the people.

Among the virtues and *li* emphasized by Confucius were those related to the family. He placed special importance on filial piety, the wholehearted obedience a

Ancient symbol *Yi,* which stands for "changes." One of the five Confucian classics is the *Classic of Changes.*

The Chinese States at the Time of Confucius   *ca.* 500 B.C.

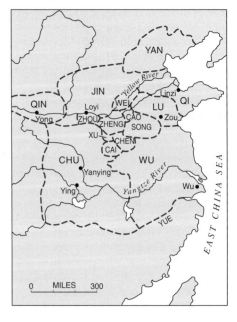

child owes a parent. The obligations toward a father have priority over those owed a state: a son should not turn in his father for stealing a sheep. The relationship between father and son formed one of the classic Five Relationships of Confucianism. The others were ruler/minister, husband/wife, elder/younger brother, friend/friend. They entail reciprocal obligations between people of superior and inferior status and illustrate the importance of the family. Even the two that are not familial were thought of in family terms: the ruler/minister relationship was compared to that between father and son, that between friends is analogous to that between elder and younger brother. The Confucian view of society was thus paternal and hierarchical.

Confucius and his followers also believed there was only one valid and true, eternal way. The Way was open to all, but only the morally and intellectually cultivated could understand it. The idea that there might be a number of legitimate ways to live one's life and conduct affairs was foreign to the Chinese, who at that time had no contact with other highly developed and literate civilizations radically different from their own.

Confucius's ideas were not widely accepted for many centuries, but ultimately he proved to be one of the world's truly seminal thinkers. His person became a model to be emulated by later Confucians. As he appears in the *Analects,* discourses written by his disciples, he was a man of moderation: gentle but firm, dignified but not harsh, respectful but at ease. One passage gives an account of his intellectual and spiritual progression, culminating at the age of seventy when he was able to follow his heart's desires without transgressing against morality. The Confucian sage personified these characteristics and perfected his moral wisdom to the point that he automatically did what was right.

Confucius was only the beginning of Confucianism. He left many issues unsettled, and his philosophy permitted various interpretations. His later followers, such as Mencius and Xunzi, further developed his teachings, partly in response to challenges from other schools, such as that

Confucius on Government

Zi-gong asked about government. Confucius said "Sufficient food, sufficient armament, and sufficient confidence of the people." Zi-gong said, "Forced to give up one of these, which would you abandon first?" Confucius said, "I would abandon the armament." Zi-gong said, "Forced to give up one of the remaining two, which would you abandon first?" Confucius said, "I would abandon food. There have been deaths from time immemorial, but no state can exist without the confidence of the people."

Analects *12:7. From* A Source Book in Chinese Philosophy *by Wing-tsit Chan (Princeton, N.J.: Princeton University Press, 1963), p. 39, with Wade-Giles transcription changed into* pinyin *here and in all boxes.*

founded by Mozi (Mo Tzu, *ca.* 470–391 B.C.), who taught the practicality of universal love. Mencius (371–289 B.C.) is famed for his view that human nature is fundamentally good but that this goodness has to be cultivated and nourished. Xunzi (Hsün Tzu, 298–238 B.C.) is associated with the opposite view, that people are naturally selfish but nevertheless have the potential to become good. Although for different reasons, education was of essential importance for both men. Consistent with these positions, Mencius stressed the need for benevolence in government, while Xunzi more readily accepted the need for laws and punishment. Mencius is also famous for developing the older idea of the mandate of Heaven, according to which a dynasty ruled only as long as it ruled properly. When a regime lost the mandate, rebellion was justified, and an evil ruler forfeited the right to rule.

Although Confucians put a premium on social harmony, the thinkers known as Daoists (Taoists) sought to understand the eternal order of the universe. Daoism deals with the unconditioned, unnameable source of all reality that transcends being and nonbeing by standing above and beyond all distinctions. The first great Daoist classic, the *Dao De Jing (Tao Te Ching)* or *Laozi (Lao Tzu),* is cryptic, paradoxical, and highly suggestive. Among its themes there is a preference for the nega-

Divine seal of Laozi used in Daoist magic.

Zhuangzi (also called Zhuang Zhou)

Once Zhuang Zhou dreamt he was a butterfly, a butterfly flitting and fluttering around, happy with himself and doing as he pleased. He didn't know he was Zhuang Zhou. Suddenly he woke up and there he was, solid and unmistakable Zhuang Zhou. But he didn't know if he was Zhuang Zhou who had dreamt he was a butterfly, or a butterfly dreaming he was Zhuang Zhou. Between Zhuang Zhou and a butterfly there must be *some* distinction! This is called the Transformation of Things.

The fish trap exists because of the fish; once you've gotten the fish, you can forget about the trap. The rabbit snare exists because of the rabbit; once you've gotten the rabbit, you can forget the snare. Words exist because of meaning; once you've gotten the meaning, you can forget the words. Where can I find a man who has forgotten words so I can have a word with him?

From Chuang Tzu: Basic Writings, *trans. by Burton Watson (New York: Columbia University Press, 1946), p. 45 and p. 140, respectively.*

tive over the positive, nothing over something, weak over strong, nonaction over action. It teaches silence is more meaningful than words and ignorance is superior to knowledge; in sum, "Those who know do not speak; those who speak do not know." This view of the limitation of language is shared by Zhuangzi (Chuang Tzu), author of the second great Daoist classic that bears his name. Zhuangzi had a keenly developed sense of paradox, as when he argues for the usefulness of the useless: when the able-bodied young men of the village are marched off to war, it is the hopelessly deformed hunchback who stands by the side of the road waving them off. Another theme he pursues is the relativity of everything.

The Unification of China

During the period from 771 B.C. to 221 B.C., momentous and rapid changes took place in all areas of human activity. Warfare is a good example. No longer were battles fought by gentlemen in chariots; now most of the fighting was done by foot sol-

diers, peasant conscripts commanded by professional officers. Armies grew enormously. Some are said to have numbered a million men, although that may be an exaggeration.

Armies had to be fed and supplied. To support the forces, an increase in agricultural production was achieved by reclamation projects, irrigation, and technological changes, including the introduction of iron. There were also changes in management and administration as states adopted systems of taxation and labor services. Land became a commodity to be bought and sold. Commerce increased along with the size of states and the development of roads. Metallic currencies appeared, replacing the cowrie shells used earlier. Among the items of trade were various kinds of textiles, metals, woods, bamboo, jade, and regional specialties. Urban centers grew and expanded until they required new city walls.

As ever, social change was inseparably linked to military, economic, and political change. Merchants and generals were not the only new professionals. It took a skilled diplomat to steer a state through the treacherous waters of international relations, someone with an eloquent voice to win a debate. Faced with internal and external challenges, rulers tended to pay more attention to a man's competence than to his pedigree. Old families declined, and new ones grew in importance.

Faced with a world of disturbing and baffling change, many Chinese turned for guidance to what they perceived as a much better past, but some, such as Han Feizi (Han Fei Tzu, d. 233 B.C.), held that new problems demanded new and drastic solutions. These so-called Legalists stressed the rationalization of administration, the improvement of managerial techniques, and the strict enforcement of punitive laws. Their theories, which were applied by the state of Qin (Ch'in), unified China in 221 B.C.

The Qin was located in the west of North China, the same region from which the Zhou had conquered North China. This area was economically able to support a strong military and political apparatus, and it was well situated strategically, protected by mountains whose passes were easy to defend and yet provided access to the east. It was something of a buffer region between the Chinese and various warlike tribal peoples. Making the best of this situation, the Qin toughened its armies by fighting the tribesmen. At the same time it drew on the administrative and technological expertise developed in the more sophisticated, centrally located states. Under Legalist influence the state was divided into districts governed by a centralized bureaucracy and financed by a direct tax on the peasantry. A system of mutual responsibility was introduced, with harsh penalties for criminals and those who failed to report a criminal. Everything was designed to make the state wealthy, strong, and disciplined.

The First Empire: Qin and Han

The unification of China by the Qin was the beginning of about four hundred years of imperial rule, even though the Qin Dynasty (221–207 B.C.) itself barely survived the first emperor, Qin Shihuangdi (Ch'in Shih Huang-ti). He and his Legalist adviser, Li Si (Li Ssu) applied to the whole domain the policies first enacted in the state of Qin, including the division of the state into administrative districts governed by a bureaucracy. The integration of the realm also was furthered by a program of road building, standardized official coinage, standardized weights and measurements and script, and suppression of scholars and writings critical of the new order. Qin hostility toward Confucianism was reciprocated in kind, so that once Confucianism prevailed, the Qin acquired the most negative reputation of any Chinese dynasty.

The traditional image of cruelty and oppression may well be exaggerated, but it seems clear that the regime tried to do too much too fast. Its ambitions found physical expression in vast building projects, including an enormous underground imperial mausoleum. The Qin also linked segments of earlier walls to protect its territories. Traditionally this has been considered the ancestor of China's famous Great Wall, but that famous and imposing struc-

A life-sized terra-cotta figure of an armored archer of the Qin dynasty. This is one of more than 7,000 such figures unearthed from the tomb of the first emperor of China.

ture, the remains of which are still extant, dates from the much later Ming Dynasty.

After the death of its founder, the Qin soon disintegrated, but it left foundations on which the Former Han (202 B.C.–A.D. 8) and the Later Han (A.D. 25–A.D. 220) erected more lasting edifices.

In many respects Han China was comparable to Imperial Rome. Both were great empires with powerful armies ranging far beyond the heartland: Han forces even crossed the Pamir Mountains. Both are celebrated for practical accomplishments, as in civil engineering: the Han maintained 20,000–25,000 miles of highway radiating out from the capital. They also made advances in shipbuilding (the axial rudder), medicine, astronomy, and agriculture. Intellectually, both empires built on the achievements of their predecessors and were noted more for the synthesis of old philosophies than for producing strikingly new ones. Both also excelled in writing

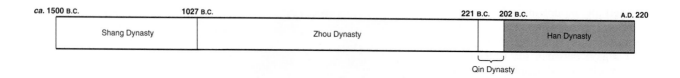

ca. 1500 B.C.   1027 B.C.   221 B.C.   202 B.C.   A.D. 220

| Shang Dynasty | Zhou Dynasty | | Han Dynasty |

Qin Dynasty

history. China's greatest historian was Sima Qian (Ssu-ma Ch'ien, *ca.* 145 B.C.– *ca.* 90 B.C.) whose *Records of the Grand Historian* is a literary masterpiece as well as a work of careful scholarship.

In China, as in Rome, it took great political ability to create and maintain a huge empire over a long period of time. But there was no counterpart in the Han to the Roman development of law. Instead, the Chinese relied on a bureaucracy staffed by men who shared a common education, a common fund of historical references, and a common set of largely Confucian values. To help mold these men there was an imperial university where, under the Later Han, 30,000 students were studying mostly Confucian texts. Imperial Confucianism did not preclude employment of pragmatic Legalist military and political policies, but it did provide the dynasty with legitimacy and could prompt ministers to faithful service. The Confucian ideal was one of unselfish public service, not unthinking compliance with the whims or policies of a ruler. Most officials came from families of notables who dominated the local power structure and who

The Han Empire   100 B.C.

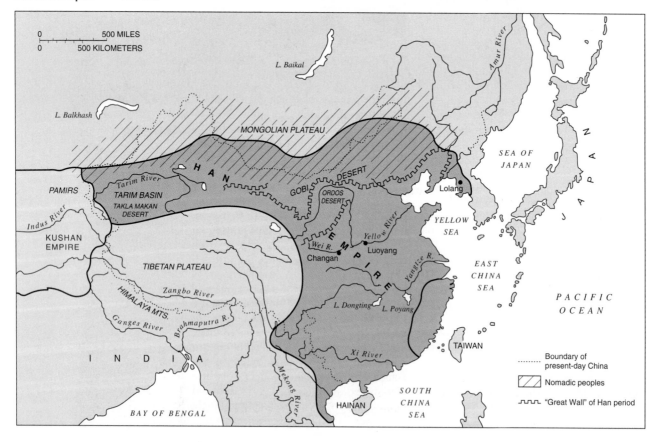

could thus afford a measure of political as well as intellectual independence.

The system operated best with a balance between central and local power. Because the wealthy and powerful were also the most apt to evade taxes, the state had a stake in preventing an undue concentration of landownership. But attempts to limit the size of landholdings failed, as did the attempt to stabilize grain prices through government purchases when grain was plentiful and cheap, for resale when it became scarce, causing prices to rise. For its own finances, the government drew heavily on agriculture but also collected commercial taxes and operated salt and iron monopolies.

As in Rome, in weak hands the throne itself became a source of political instability as various groups maneuvered for influence and control. In the Han, the families of imperial consorts became exceedingly powerful, and it was a member of one such family who, after serving as regent for a child emperor, overthrew the Former Han but did not succeed in establishing a lasting dynasty of his own. Instead, after a period of turmoil and fighting, a member of the imperial Han family established the Later Han in A.D. 25.

The Han established a Chinese presence in North Korea and North Vietnam, but the most challenging foreign policy problem was how to deal with the nomads who lived beyond the northern and northwestern frontiers. Nomadic peoples, like the Altaic-speaking Xiongnu (Hsiung-nu), were formidable opponents because of their skill in warfare. For them war was merely a special application of the horsemanship and archery skills they practiced every day in guarding their flocks. Their mobility was an asset in defense as well as attack, for, traveling light with their flocks and tents, they could elude Chinese military expeditions and avoid destruction or control. Chinese measures to deal with these troublesome neighbors ranged from military suppression to conciliation by means of gifts and marriage alliances, so that the nomads would accept tributary status. Tributaries had to acknowledge Han supremacy but profited by an exchange of presents and the opportunity

to trade. Much of this trade was conducted in markets along the borders. Chinese exports included lacquerware, ironware, bronze mirrors, and silk, which first reached Europe over the famous Silk Road. The Chinese also did whatever they could to foster disunity among the tribal people; "using barbarians against barbarians" became a permanent part of their foreign policy.

China in Disunity, 220–589

Disrupted by internal strife, in fiscal trouble because of a shrinking tax base, and beset by foreign challenges, the Han came to an end in 220. Beginning early in the next century, a succession of nomadic peoples carved out states in North China. Some of these, notably the Northern Wei (386–534), attained a good measure of success, but none matched the Han in du-

Han earthenware tile.

Pottery tile rubbing depicting hunters and peasants (Han dynasty).

ration or extent. To enjoy their Chinese conquests, the nomads required a more sophisticated political system than the tribal organization they brought from the steppes. They had to rely on Chinese administrators who knew how to operate a tax system, keep records, and run a government. There was also a tendency for the nomads themselves to become more like the Chinese. This not only jeopardized their cultural heritage but tended to alienate those nomads who had remained on the steppe.

Warfare and devastation in the north stimulated vast migrations to south China, especially into the Yangtze region, which underwent great economic development, foreshadowing the time when it would become China's rice bowl. Politically the south remained under Chinese control, but the southern states were unstable and weak. When reunification came, it was, as always, from the north.

When the Han fell, a whole civilization seemed to have collapsed. A spiritual and intellectual, as well as political vacuum was created. Some of China's most brilliant and talented men responded by turning to Daoism or to discovering new meaning in poetry, calligraphy, and painting. Others, both humble people and aristocrats, were attracted to Buddhism, which addressed itself more directly to human suffering than did any of the components of the native Chinese tradition. In the north, Buddhism also benefited from the patronage of rulers who, as foreigners themselves, could sympathize with a foreign religion.

Buddhism took many long years to overcome its foreignness in China, years during which Buddhist missionaries patiently labored to translate and explain the Buddhist teachings. It was a formidable task to render the highly inflected Indian languages and discursive Indian writings into uninflected and terse Chinese, to find Chinese equivalents for concepts such as *karma* or Nirvana, and to bridge the gulf that separated Indian and Chinese perceptions of the meaning of life and the nature of the universe.

The greatest of the translators was a Central Asian, Kumārajīva, who, early in the fifth century, directed a staff of about 1,000 monks. In a vivid comment on the translator's predicament, he once compared his work to that of a man who chews rice and then gives it to another to swallow. By the end of the period of disunity, the labors of such men had made Buddhism palatable to the Chinese, but not until after reunification in 591 did they feel sufficiently familiar with the faith to develop it in ways of their own.

For a time Buddhism provided a link between China and India, yet there remained distinct differences between the historical-minded Chinese tradition and the focus in India on the ultimate. The contrast between the two civilizations is also apparent in their different political histories. At the end of the sixth century, India was again politically fragmented, whereas China had entered one of its great ages of imperial unification.

Suggestions for Further Reading

India

A gold mine of authoritative information is *A Historical Atlas of South Asia* (1978), ed. J. E. Schwartzberg, which contains historical essays and bibliographies. A. L. Basham, *The Wonder that Was India,* 3rd ed. (1985), is a lucid and balanced account of Indian civilization. S. Wolpert, *A New History of India,* 3rd ed. (1989), is a good survey, although stronger on modern India. A good compendium for intellectual history is *Sources of Indian Tradition,* 2nd ed. (1988), edited and revised by Ainslee

T. Embree. Edward Said, *Orientalism* (1978), has stimulated rethinking of how Indian history is analyzed and perceived. A good but demanding recent example of post-Orientalist theory and practice is provided by Ronald Inden, *Imagining India* (1990). Diana L. Eck, *Banaras: City of Light* (1982), is a multifaceted account of India's most holy city. On India's greatest playwright, see Barbara S. Miller, *Theater of Memory: The Plays of Kalidasa* (1984). For readings on Southeast Asia, see Chapter 15.

China

C. Blunder and M. Elvin, *Cultural Atlas of China* (1983), provides an attractive and stimulating introduction to many aspects of Chinese civilization. *Heritage of China: Contemporary Perspectives on Chinese Civilization* (1990), edited by Paul S. Ropp, is a collection of interpretative essays by leading scholars. Kwang-chih Chang, *The Archaeology of Ancient China,* 4th ed. (1986), is authoritative, as is *The Cambridge History of China,* Vol 1, *The Ch'in and Han Empires 221 B.C.–A.D. 220* (1986). Also recommended on topics not represented in Ropp's anthology are Sarah Allen, *The Shape of the Turtle: Myth, Art, and*

Cosmos in Early China (1991), and B. Watson, *Ssu-ma Ch'ien: Grand Historian of China* (1958). Also recommended are three anthologies of translations: *Sources of Chinese Tradition* (1960), by W. T. de Bary et al.; Wing-tsit Chan, ed., *A Source Book in Chinese Philosophy* (1963); and P. B. Ebrey, *Chinese Civilization and Society: A Sourcebook* (1981). A general survey is provided by C. Schirokauer, *A Brief History of Chinese Civilization* (1991), and *A Brief History of Chinese and Japanese Civilizations,* 2nd ed. (1989), which include suggestions for further reading.

Buddhism

Heinz Bechert and Richard Gombrich, *The World of Buddhism* (1984), is a well-illustrated introduction. Another good place to begin reading about Buddhism and other religions is the *Encyclopedia of Religion* (1987), M. Eliade, general editor. Two well-regarded books on Buddhist thought are Paul Williams,

Mahayana Buddhism: The Doctrinal Foundations (1989), and Roger J. Corless, *The Vision of Buddhism: The Space Under the Tree* (1989). For China, see *Buddhism in Chinese History* (1959), by A. F. Wright. Buddhist materials are also included in the source books listed above.

Reference

Ainslie T. Embree et al., *Encyclopedia of Asian History* (1988), is a useful reference. For studies on specific topics see *Bibliog-*

raphy of Asian Studies, published annually by the Association for Asian Studies, Inc.

7

THE BYZANTINE EMPIRE

Following the loss of the western Roman Empire to the Germans, the Eastern Empire gradually evolved into a distinctive civilization, a successor to the Hellenistic civilization created by Alexander the Great. That civilization is called Byzantine and its political manifestation is called the Byzantine Empire. Both were centered in the city of Constantinople (present-day Istanbul), which Constantine the Great had built on the site of the ancient Athenian colony at Byzantium.

Though civilization proceeded along separate paths in the East and in the West, there was constant interaction between the Byzantines and the westerners during the period from the sixth century to the fifteenth. The idea of the Roman Empire never died, and both the Byzantines and the Europeans sought, from time to time, to reunite its two parts. Moreover, the Byz-

antine Empire served as both link and buffer between Europe and the Middle East, where momentous events in the seventh century changed the history of the Mediterranean Basin, indeed of the world. Finally, East and West were linked by Christianity. Over time, the eastern church and the western church deviated in liturgical practice, theology, and political status, but, like the idea of the Roman Empire, the notion of a single church of Christ never disappeared, and the two churches were often in close contact.

Throughout its history, the Byzantine Empire struggled with formidable political and cultural problems. Diocletian's decision to locate the imperial court in the East in the late third century was dictated by the need to protect the rich eastern provinces from the Persian threat, a threat that persisted until the start of the seventh century. It was then replaced by a greater threat—

(OPPOSITE) INTERIOR OF HAGIA SOPHIA, THE PRINCIPAL CHURCH IN CONSTANTINOPLE, BUILT BY EMPEROR JUSTINIAN I IN THE 530S AFTER RIOTS HAD DESTROYED THE CENTER OF THE CITY.

this time, from the new Arab-Islamic empire that destroyed Byzantine power in the Middle East and curtailed Byzantine movement in the eastern Mediterranean. While trying to cope with the Islamic threat, the Empire found itself challenged in its European provinces by the Bulgarians. And, to complicate matters even further, the ancient division between the Semitic culture and the Hellenistic culture in the eastern provinces gave rise to severe religious controversies.

Heresies of the Eastern Church

The emperors in Constantinople had to face a series of heresies that divided the church. Most of them were based on a view of Jesus that emphasized one of his natures, human or divine. The official church believed that Jesus was fully human and fully divine. The major heretical movements were:

Arianism: Followers of this heresy believed that Jesus was a created being and therefore not fully divine. Arians believed that God was unique, so that Jesus, the Son of God, could not be God. Arianism was condemned in 325 at the Council of Nicaea.

Nestorianism: The Nestorians admitted that Jesus had two natures, human and divine, but believed that the natures were separate. For them, the divine nature of Jesus could not be united to or mixed with his human nature, because the two were categorically different. Nestorianism was condemned in 451 at the Council of Chalcedon.

Monophysitism: The Monophysites (from the Greek, *monophysis* meaning "of one nature") believed that Jesus had only one nature in which the human and divine were inexplicably united. They were condemned at the Council of Chalcedon for failing to recognize that Jesus was both fully human and fully divine, one person with two natures.

Monotheletism: This heresy originated in the court of the emperor Heraclius, who wanted to win the support of the Monophysites while remaining true to the doctrine of the Council of Chalcedon. Monotheletism admitted the dual nature of Jesus, but said that he had one will (Greek, *monothelema* meaning "one will"). For the Monothelites, the unity of Jesus's will meant that he was one person, even if he had two natures. The official church held that the will was a function of the nature of a being, so if Jesus had two natures he also had two wills. Monotheletism was condemned in 680 at the Council of Constantinople.

Yet, as we shall see, Byzantine civilization achieved brilliant artistic, intellectual, and governmental successes. And it survived for a thousand years.

THE EASTERN ROMAN EMPIRE AFTER THE LOSS OF THE WEST

The changes that created the Byzantine Empire began in the fifth century. The principal change was from a Roman military government to a Greek civilian government. After centuries of Roman rule, the old Hellenistic culture of the East re-emerged.

During the fifth century, many hellenized Egyptians and Syrians—who had been excluded from service in the Roman government—made their way to Constantinople to take posts in the imperial administration. The influx of hellenized easterners accelerated under Emperor Anastasius (r. 491–518), the ruler who recognized Theodoric the Ostrogoth's authority in Italy (p. 127). The officials of Anastasius's government—financial wizards, advisers, and lesser administrators—were well-educated men who regarded civil service as a career. During this time Constantinople changed from being the capital city—the place where the emperor and his government were located—to being the "ruling city," the metropolis that dominated the cultural life of the Empire. Constantinople replaced Rome as the intellectual and cultural center of the world and was often referred to as the New Rome.

Meanwhile, trouble broke out again when Persia, under a revived Sassanid dynasty, began to stage successful attacks on the eastern borders. To meet the threat, Emperor Zeno I (r. 479–491), instead of putting together an army of mercenaries from among the Ostrogothic tribes to the north, marshalled his troops from the Isaurians of southern Asia Minor. Zeno's successor, Anastasius, also relied on armies recruited from the eastern regions.

The populations of the eastern provinces, though mostly Christianized, had kept their ancient religious traditions alive in a number of unorthodox theologies, of which Arianism was an example (p. 118). Because the trade of the East provided a ready medium for exchange of religious ideas, the eastern cities became hotbeds of religious disputes over the nature of Christ, the sacraments, and other issues. Anastasius, beset by the constant threat of invasion, tolerated the variety of religious ideas while seeking to reconcile them to the creeds enunciated by earlier ecumenical councils, such as the Council of Nicaea (325). Although the popes in Rome railed against such compromises, Anastasius refused to condemn and eradicate the heretical sects. He looked on religious differences as a political matter rather than a spiritual matter.

Anastasius left a full treasury and an efficient civil service. But the army reasserted itself after his death and installed as emperor a soldier from the Balkans, Justin I (r. 518–527). This shift back to a military government was short-lived, however. Justinian, Justin's nephew and successor, had been educated in Constantinople by Anastasius's court bureaucrats and had become thoroughly hellenized.

When he succeeded Justin in 527, he inaugurated a decade of exuberant cultural and political revival.

The Early Years of Justinian's Reign

Justinian (r. 527–565) was a reformer whose goal was to restore the Empire to its former glory. One of his first steps was to appoint a commission to revise and codify the Roman law. During the golden age of Roman law, from the reign of Augustus (r. 27 B.C.–A.D. 14) to A.D. 200, a succession of great jurists had shaped the system and had formulated its basic doctrines, in the centuries that followed a vast accumulation of laws, judgments, and learned commentaries had piled up. By Justinian's time, it would take a lifetime to read the law and another lifetime to master it. Judges were often stymied in trying to settle cases as the contending parties cited conflicting laws and opinions to support their cases.

Earlier emperors had tried to end the confusion by commissioning law codes.

Expansion of the Byzantine Empire under Justinian

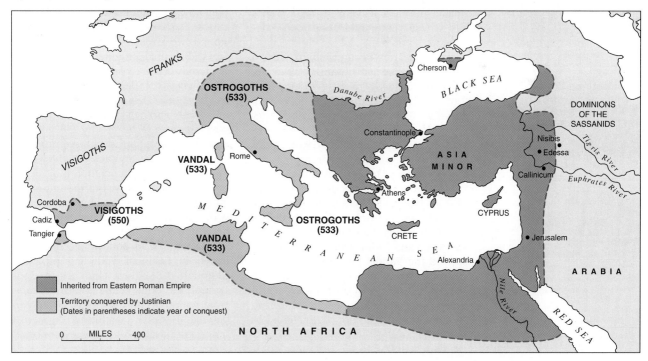

But none of the codes—such as that of Theodosius II, published about 480—dealt with the whole corpus of legislation and commentary. The members of Justinian's commission, led by law professors from Beirut, tried to weave a new fabric from the welter of tradition. In 534, they produced a comprehensive code called the *Corpus Iuris Civilis* (the Body of Civil Law), which contains one of the most sophisticated legal systems ever created. This code was symbolic of Justinian's goal of achieving a reunited, well-governed empire.

In 532, however, mob violence erupted in Constantinople in protest against high taxes and corruption in the government. Coping with the Persian threat, together with the growth of the bureaucracy, had led to a steady rise in the tax burden on ordinary citizens, and their growing frustration and anger finally exploded in riots. Back in the 480s, Emperor Zeno, fearing an Ostrogothic attack on the city, had armed the clubs that supported the teams that played in the games at the Hippodrome (the city stadium) to serve as a militia. Now these clubs, well organized and well armed, joined forces to loot and burn the city. The violence finally subsided, leaving Justinian with a city whose center had been totally destroyed.

Justinian now recognized that he had to find some alternative source of revenue. The simplest way to raise money was through conquest. In 533, Justinian sent an army to North Africa to begin the reconquest of the western provinces. Africa was an important grain producer, and it would provide an excellent base for a military operation. The general whom Justinian named to lead the troops was the brilliant Belisarius, who had helped suppress the riots in Constantinople. Belisarius took Carthage in the first year of the campaign and within a short time had destroyed the Vandal kingdom established in North Africa in 430. The collapse of Vandal power prompted the Moorish tribes to seek their independence, and the Byzantine forces did not pacify the province until 548.

Meanwhile, in 535, Belisarius took Sicily and reached Rome a year later. At this point, however, he fell from favor and was forced into retirement. The Ostrogoths now launched a determined war of resistance. Unable to hold Rome, the Byzantines set up their capital in Ravenna, a city on the Adriatic Sea well protected on the land side by extensive marshes and readily accessible by ships from Constantinople. By 556, after twenty years of war, most of Italy was under the control of the Byzantine governor in Ravenna. But, as we have seen (p. 128), in 568, three years after Justinian's death, new Germanic invaders, the Lombards, entered Italy and quickly overran most of the peninsula.

The Origins of Byzantine Art

Back in Constantinople, Justinian devoted himself to rebuilding the city on a magnificent scale befitting the city that ruled the world. He built public baths, new government buildings, and aqueducts and cisterns to supply the city with water. He dedicated 25 churches in the city and its suburbs. His crowning achievement was the church of Hagia Sophia. The church that originally stood on this site had been built by Constantine and had been reconstructed around 400. Justinian commissioned two Greeks, Anthemius of Tralles and Isidore of Miletus, to build a new kind of church centered on a great dome. The church was completed in just six years. Its dome rises 184 feet above the pavement and, with half-domes on either side, covers an area of 100 feet by 250 feet. The enormous lateral thrust of these domes is supported by great buttresses, which from the outside make the church look like a great pile of masonry. But the interior is light and airy, and the ceilings are covered with brilliant mosaics. Hagia Sophia was dedicated in 537.

Byzantine art and architecture originated in Justinian's building program. Although the earliest churches in Constantinople, built in the fourth century, were patterned on the elongated Roman basilica, Justinian's architects devised a new form based on the dome supported

Engraving showing Constantinople in the mid-fifteenth century, just before the Turks conquered it.

by half-domes. In time, the arrangement of the domes became fixed. The central dome covered the crossing point formed by four half-domes radiating symmetrically as a Greek cross—that is, a cross with arms of equal length. On the inner surfaces of the domes, artists executed frescoes or mosaics that also became standardized over time. The whole program of architecture and interior decoration solidified by the tenth century and remained virtually unchanged until the midfifteenth century when the Empire was conquered by the Turks.

The Byzantine church represented the cosmos. Inside, a representation of God the Father dominated the highest reaches of the central dome with the angels and archangels pictured below him. The walls of the church were covered with pictures of the saints arranged according to the importance of their feasts in the liturgical calendar. In the West, as we shall see, the decoration of churches was intended to provide instruction to the laity. In the Byzantine realms, it was intended to represent the universe under God's rulership.

The Byzantine style of representation suited the purpose of the art. It emphasized the spiritual presence of the figure rather than its physical portrayal. Unlike the naturalistic art of Greece and Rome, Byzantine art represented human figures in a flat, static pose that emphasized line and color. Frequently using a flat gold background, Byzantine artists gave the human figure a formal, somewhat abstract form with large, staring eyes that emphasized the spiritual aspect of the person represented. In the best work, the contrast between the flat monochrome background and the vigorously drawn and highly colored figure creates a three-dimensional illusion; the figure seems to be in front of the background.

Byzantine art exercised a powerful effect on Western art. The Byzantine churches built in Ravenna during the sixth century became models for later Western artists. The art in the churches of southern Italy also influenced westerners. During the twelfth century, when Europeans began to study Byzantine scientific works, Byzantine book illuminations began to influence Western artists. Art historians trace some aspects of early Renaissance painting to Byzantine influence.

The Last 25 Years of Justinian's Reign

The flamboyant spirit of the 530s ended with the revival of war with the Persians

Byzantine gold wedding ring (ca. fifth century).

Hagia Sophia, built *ca.* 535. The minarets were added after the Ottoman Turks captured Constantinople in 1453.

Procession of saints and martyrs, Sant'Apollinare Nuovo, Ravenna (*ca.* 574).

and with trouble in the Balkans. In 540, Shah Khusro I of Persia attacked the eastern provinces and, after taking the great city of Antioch in Syria, offered to sell it back to Justinian. The emperor rejected the offer. At about the same time, Slavic tribes moved into the Balkans and destroyed Byzantine authority there. These disasters deprived the Empire of two vital resources: from Syria it had drawn commercial wealth, and from the Balkan provinces it had drawn manpower. Then, in 542, an epidemic (of what sort is unknown) broke out in Constantinople and recurred over the next two years.

Faced with these misfortunes, Justinian was obliged to reduce the campaign in Italy to a holding action and to curtail his ambitious building programs. He experimented with a series of innovative tax measures and reorganized the military, which now had to make do with less money and manpower. The Byzantine commanders devised new mobile tactics for small forces, and in a major test the new model army executed a brilliant campaign in 552 that broke the last Ostrogothic resistance in Italy. In the East, Justinian compensated for the shortage of manpower by building a string of strategically placed fortifications, and used diplomacy instead of force whenever he could.

By the 560s, he had held off Khusro I, had defeated the Ostrogoths, had pacified and fortified North Africa, and had constructed an elaborate series of alliances along the Danube to limit the Slavic invasions. These accomplishments came, however, at significant expense. When Justinian dismantled the government's transport system to reduce expenditures, farmers in the interior of Asia Minor were forced into bankruptcy. The farmers had become economically dependent on the transport system.

The economic strain created by the wars and by Justinian's ambitious building program had depleted the imperial treasury, and it was empty when Justinian died in 565.

The crises also led to a concentration of power resting on the emperor. In reducing the size of the imperial bureaucracy, Justinian had taken onto himself much of the work of government. By the end of his reign, he simply had too much to do. To maintain his successes would have taken even more concentration and energy than he had spent in achieving them. Justinian's successor, Maurice (r. 582–602), was an able administrator, but he could not cope with simultaneous disasters in all quarters. The Lombards had invaded Italy; the Danubian alliances disintegrated as the Slavic Bulgars and the Altaic Avars (related to the Huns) began to put pressure on the border; and the Persians became aggressive once again.

FROM EASTERN ROMAN TO BYZANTINE EMPIRE

Under Maurice's successor Phocas (r. 602–610), the Byzantine world collapsed. The Bulgers and the Avars overran the Balkans and Greece. Asia Minor became a Persian province (a satrapy) in which the Persians carried out an anti-Christian campaign. When Phocas died, the Eastern Roman Empire consisted of the city of Constantinople, the marshlands around Ravenna and Rome, Sicily, Apulia and Calabria in southern Italy, and the North African provinces. Constantinople was virtually impregnable on its promontory, but it appeared incapable of reviving the Empire. Heraclius (r. 610–641), Phocas's successor, even thought of fleeing to North Africa but remained instead in Constantinople and began a campaign of reconquest in eastern Asia Minor.

The prospect was not promising. Heraclius spent more than a decade rebuilding the army and preparing for a long campaign. In 622, he sailed south to Ionia and began a war of attrition against the Persians. After four years of bitter fighting against superior forces, his troops broke the military strength of the Persians and reconquered Asia Minor. Thereupon, Heraclius forced the population to reconvert to Christianity. In 627, he led his army on a raid into the heart of Persia, prompting the Persian nobility to assassinate the shah, Khusro II, in 628. By that time, Heraclius had reestablished Byzantine control over Syria, Palestine, and Egypt.

This run of successes soon came to an end. Heraclius had managed to win back the eastern provinces with a small, well-trained army, but to defend them he would need a large, costly army. The Persian occupation and the long war had ruined the economy of the eastern provinces, and they could not support such a force. The provinces, once the richest in the Empire, were now a drain on the imperial treasury. At the end of his life, Heraclius had to watch a new eastern power, the Arabs, seize much of what he had won.

Nonetheless, Heraclius had reestablished the Hellenistic world and had preserved it as the heartland of Christendom. During the seventh century east–west trade had revived, and eastern churchmen—including the first great archbishop of Canterbury in England, Theodore of Tarsus (r. 669–690)—were playing an important role in the Roman church. Moreover, the eastern emperors continued to influence that church, in which many of the members of the clergy were actually Greek-speaking. And the Byzantine governor of Ravenna was still in control of Rome, even though the land between had fallen to the Lombards.

After Heraclius's death, his successors were unable to hold the borders of the Empire. The Arab expansion, the continuing settlement of the Slavs in the Balkans, and the establishment of a Bulgar kingdom north of the Danube made it impossible for them to continue the work Heraclius had begun. The Arabs built a fleet in the Mediterranean that challenged Byzantine naval supremacy, and they repeatedly attacked Constantinople itself between about 669 and 677. The Byzantines withstood these assaults and managed to hold Asia Minor, but they soon lost the provinces along the eastern seaboard of the Mediterranean. By the end of the seventh century, the Empire was nothing more than a late Hellenistic state with outlying provinces.

The Heraclian dynasty came to an end in 711, when its last emperor was murdered in a palace rebellion. After six years of anarchy, a provincial administrator and general, Leo the Isaurian, ascended the imperial throne as Leo III and founded a new dynasty. Leo (r. 717–741) came to power at a critical moment and was uniquely qualified to meet the threat of a great land and sea siege of Constantinople

The Byzantine Empire   SEVENTH AND ELEVENTH CENTURIES

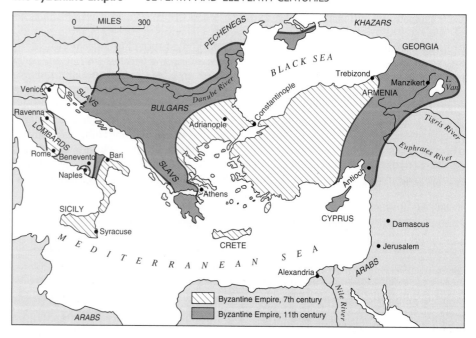

by the Arabs (717–718). The new emperor was born in northern Syria and knew Arabic. In his youth, his family had been forcibly removed to the Bulgarian border, and so he knew that troubled region as well.

Actually, the Arabs had helped Leo to the imperial throne. Early in 717, when they invaded the eastern province Leo was governing, he seems to have made a deal with them. If they promised to support him, he would seize the throne and as emperor would bow to their demands for territory or tribute. When the Arabs withdrew, Leo stormed the capital and became emperor.

But when the Arabs invaded Asia Minor again, Leo negotiated with them until he had gained the advantage and then he turned on them and defeated them. The crucial moment in the defense of the capital came when the Bulgars arrived and destroyed the Arab army. Shortly after this, Leo defeated the Arab fleet and began his reign as the savior of Constantinople. He followed this triumph with a series of campaigns against the Arabs in eastern Asia Minor that halted their hundred years of conquest. Syria and North Africa had been lost, but the Empire had consolidated its position in Asia Minor, the Balkans, and Greece.

Emperor Leo represented the landed aristocracy of Asia Minor against the court and the bureaucracy that had held sway since Anastasius. Once in power, he carried out the most important reforms since Justinian. He commissioned new law codes, including an abridged and modernized Greek version of the *Corpus Iuris Civilis*. He regularized the system of administrative districts, called *themes*, and by so doing significantly improved the quality of government. He also instigated a movement against the use of religious images (icons) called iconoclasm (hatred of icons).

The effect of these changes in the political, economic, and cultural orientation of the Empire—from a Mediterranean power to a state straddling Europe and Asia Minor, from a commercial economy to an agricultural economy, and from a bilingual society to a Greek society—constituted the final transition from Eastern Roman Empire to Byzantine Empire. The transformation had begun under Anastasius in the late fifth century and was completed under Leo III and his successors in the eighth century. Although the political and economic influence of the Byzantines in the West was diminished, the two halves of the old Roman Empire still carried on relations. The Byzantine government considered itself the only legitimate successor of the Roman imperial government, and religion continued to serve as a link and as a source of conflict between East and West.

THE CONTROVERSY OVER ICONOCLASM

Christianity had been established in Byzantium before Constantine I rebuilt the city, but once it had become the capital of the Empire its church also had become one of the leading sees. Constantine had regarded himself as the thirteenth apostle and the church in Constantinople had claimed the status of an apostolic church (p. 116) from the fourth century on. Its bishops took the title "patriarch," which was used by the bishops of the apostolic sees in the East—Jerusalem and Alexandria—and claimed authority over all the churches in the Empire. But the emperors regarded the church as a department of their government and controlled selection of patriarchs. Iconoclasm arose within the Byzantine church.

The Origins of Iconoclasm

In 726, nine years after he came to power, Leo the Isaurian stood in the porch of his palace and destroyed a famous picture of Christ. That act caused riots in Constantinople and in the western parts of the Empire, but the armies and the people of the eastern provinces accepted it without protest. The difference suggests that Leo was acting in accordance with his Syrian origins and that iconoclasm reflected a profound difference between Semitic religious views and Greco-Roman religious views.

The Hellenistic world had accepted the use of religious images in prayer and worship as part of Christian observance. The pagan Greeks had used idols in their religious rituals, and Hellenistic Christians had followed their lead. Plato had said in the *Symposium* that the contemplation of beautiful objects led one to the contemplation of beauty itself, and the assimilation of Platonic thought into Christianity suggested a similar role for icons in Christian worship. A beautiful image of Christ helped the worshiper rise from contemplation of the world to contemplation of the world's Maker.

The Semitic tradition ran counter to the Greek in this matter. In the Hebrew Bible, the second commandment states that men should make no images of the divine, and that prohibition survived in some Semitic Christian communities, as well as in Judaism and the new religion of Islam. The use of images in the Greek churches of the Middle East, which by the eighth century were under the protection—usually benevolent—of the Islamic ruler in Damascus. But from time to time the Arabs turned on the Christians, criticizing the use of icons, among other things. In 723, the caliph Yazid II—unhappy with the Christians after his failed siege of Constantinople in 717–718—ordered the destruction of representational art of whatever kind everywhere in his realm. In short, iconoclasm was a commonly held attitude throughout the eastern Mediterranean.

Monks, Icons, and the Theory of Imperial Government

In Constantinople, the Christian monks led the protest against Leo's destruction of the image of Christ. Monasticism had spread more swiftly in the East than in the West. In fact, by the eighth century people in the East were complaining that too many of their best young people, men and women, were being lost to monasteries.

Eastern monasticism was dominated by Basil (329–79), a monk who had risen to become bishop of Caesaria in Syria. About fifty years after the founding of Pachomius' community (p. 136), Basil created a carefully worded constitution of monasticism that set a balance between worship and work and identified the three basic values of monastic life: poverty, chastity, and obedience. By the time of Leo III, Basilian communities had been founded in many eastern cities and were playing an active role in the affairs of both church and state.

The influential role of monks was demonstrated during the conflict over the use of icons. Leo apparently viewed the opposition to iconoclasm as an attack on his authority, and in 730 he issued an edict prohibiting the use of icons. In this edict he asserted the idea of Caesaropapism, which held that as Christ's representative on earth, the emperor had authority over

This illumination of the crucifixion and resurrection in early Byzantine style comes from a Syriac translation of the Gospels.

religious affairs as well as secular affairs. This idea was rooted in Constantine's assumption of responsibility for church disciplinary and doctrinal unity in the councils of Arles (314) and Nicaea (325). It contradicted the theory of papal authority (the Petrine doctrine; p. 119), which held that the pope was the sole vicar of Christ on earth and that religious authority and secular authority were distinct and separate.

That Leo saw the controversy in this way is not surprising. In developing an argument against iconoclasm, the monks had emphasized the separation of church and state—a view at variance with the Byzantine position. Leo and his son Constantine V (r. 741–75) were therefore strongly antimonastic—Constantine fanatically so.

Under Constantine V, the controversy over icons entered a new phase. Constantine, an intellectual and a connoisseur of art, devised a theological rationale for the iconoclastic position. He cited early Christian writers, including Eusebius, the biographer of Emperor Constantine I, who had said that the divine is not describable. From this, Constantine V argued that when a painter paints a picture of Christ, either he paints only the human form of God or else he paints both the human form and the divine form. If the former, the painter commits heresy by depicting Christ as only a human being. If the latter, he commits heresy by giving the divine a human, and therefore limiting, form. In this argument, Constantine V assumed that the image and the object depicted were one and the same and argued that the God-man Christ could only be represented in the sacrament of the Eucharist, in which the bread and the wine became His body and blood.

In 754, Constantine V called a council to Constantinople, and under his forceful guidance the members of the council adopted his position on icons. Ironically, his opponents, the iconodules (lovers of images), claimed as their intellectual champion a Syrian Christian named Mansur, better known as John of Damascus (d. after 746), who wrote the classic defense of icons— namely that once God had become man in Christ, it became per-

An iconoclast whitewashing an image in a Byzantine church (from a ninth-century psalter). In 730 Leo III issued an edict forbidding the veneration of images. For a hundred years thereafter, icons, mosaics, and frescoes in churches were destroyed or whitewashed.

missible to represent Him in His incarnate form.

When the monks rejected the council's pronouncements, Constantine V responded by closing monasteries, drafting monks into the army, and forcing monks and nuns to marry and to take ordinary jobs. He recognized, however, that the controversy might precipitate a serious political division between the eastern and western parts of his Empire, and to prevent such a rift he married his son Leo to an Athenian, Irene, who supported the use of icons in worship. When Constantine died in 775, Leo IV moderated, but did not give up, the official position on iconoclasm. Leo died in 780, leaving a ten-year-old son as his heir, and the power of government passed to the empress Irene. Under her influence, the government began to move slowly toward restoration of icons, and in 787 she called a new council in Nicaea that reversed the iconoclastic decrees of 754.

From that time on, both the government and church favored the use of icons, though the old iconoclastic feelings remained strong in southern and eastern Asia Minor, from which the bulk of the

Roman Empire
Divided in Half
A.D. 395

Turks Take
Constantinople
1453

Byzantine Empire

Latin Empire

800
Charlemagne
Crowned Emperor
of the Romans

1204   1261

army was recruited. Consequently, the imperial court had to deal constantly with the politics of the controversy, and the court's position depended on the views of those in power. The final restoration of icons in Christian worship came in 843, but even then the government proceeded carefully. More than twenty years passed before the government moved in any overt fashion to restore images to the churches of Constantinople.

The decline of iconoclasm in the Empire was a result of both demographic and cultural changes. Demographically, expansion of the Arab Empire in Syria and in the eastern parts of Asia Minor diminished the role of Semitic Christian communities in Byzantine affairs. Culturally, a revival of secular Greek learning among the upper classes helped spread neo-Platonic ideas.

Although the struggle over iconoclasm had begun as a reflection of the ethnic diversity of the Byzantine Empire, it survived long after that diversity waned. Iconoclasm prompted a deep religious controversy between the monks, who rejected secular influence in religious affairs, and moderate churchmen, who accepted the union of ecclesiastical and secular authority in the emperor. This conflict between radicals and moderates became a perennial political problem in the Byzantine church and contributed to the later schism between the Greek and Latin churches.

THE BYZANTINE EMPIRE BETWEEN EAST AND WEST

When Leo III deflected the massive Arab invasion in 717, he did serious damage to the Arab fleet. The Arab army, however—after suffering heavy losses in engagements with Leo's Bulgarian allies—had made an easy retreat across Asia Minor. As a result, the Arabs continued their raids into Byzantine territory throughout Leo's reign, obliging him to spend much of his time leading armies to meet the threat. Meanwhile, the Slavs were migrating steadily across the Danube frontier and settling in Macedonia and Greece. The Slavs were pagans and were not converted to Christianity until late in the ninth century.

In eastern Asia Minor, where the Islamic and Byzantine worlds met, Leo's reign was an age of dashing military leaders whose feats were memorialized in heroic legends on both sides. The central government of neither the Byzantine Empire nor the Islamic Empire paid much attention to events in the border provinces.

Leo III's son Constantine V managed to consolidate the eastern frontier, but while he was doing so, the Lombards overthrew the Byzantine government in Ravenna (*ca.* 750). Constantine ignored the loss, for he recognized that maintaining Byzantine power in Italy was peripheral to the main interests of his government. This was a new attitude. Earlier, Leo III had punished Pope Gregory II (r. 715–31) for condemning iconoclasm by depriving him of jurisdiction over the churches of Dalmatia (the coastal area of modern Croatia) and southern Italy. This was a blow to the papal treasury. Moreover, it introduced jurisdictional and territorial elements into the conflict over iconoclasm.

Pope Zachary (r. 741–52) did not immediately recognize the significance of Constantine's new attitude toward Italy. When the Lombards, after taking Ravenna, turned on Rome, Zachary followed age-old custom by appealing to the emperor for help. When Constantine ignored his appeal, Zachary turned to the Franks, who had much to gain by undertaking the protection of the papal church (pp. 224–25). In fact, in 753, Zachary's successor entered into an alliance with the Frankish royal house that had momentous results for the history of western Europe.

In the second half of his reign Constantine V devoted virtually all his attention to the Bulgars, who had begun to carve a pagan empire out of the Empire's Balkan provinces. Constantine mounted nine campaigns against the Bulgars and was remembered, even by his enemies, as a successful general.

Constantine's successors were less successful. His son Leo IV survived him by only five years. After his death, the empress Irene, a cruel woman, controlled the government for her son, Constantine VI, who was ten years old when his father died (780). In 797, when Constantine VI finally tried to assert his independence, Irene had him blinded.

Irene retained power and signed her official acts "Irene Emperor." But people everywhere, except at court, felt that the Empire was without an emperor. The advisers of the Frankish king Charles the Great (Charlemagne), noting what they perceived as a vacant throne in Constantinople, urged him to resurrect the imperial title in the West. The Roman Empire had been ruled from Constantinople for centuries, and here was a chance to restore control to Rome. On Christmas day 800, Pope Leo III crowned Charles Emperor of the Romans. In 802, a rumor circulated that Charles might marry Irene, a union that would have reunited the Empire and consolidated Charles's position as emperor.

Although many people in Constantinople must have shared the westerners' view that Irene had usurped imperial authority, they regarded Charles's coronation as the presumptuous act of a barbarian who simply did not understand what it meant to be emperor. They believed that an emperor was elected by Christ, not by a pope. Though they viewed Irene as unacceptable, they thought the true emperor could only be elected in

Early map of Constantinople (fifth or sixth century).

Constantinople, not in Aix-la-Chapelle (Aachen), where Charles had his capital. Charles tried to pressure the Byzantines into recognizing him as emperor by seizing Venice, the Byzantine gateway to Europe. The Byzantines, who were engaged in more immediate dangers, responded by opening a long series of negotiations designed to get Venice back, to protect their western borders from attack by the Franks, and to resolve the legal and political dispute over the imperial title. In 813, the year before Charles died, a treaty was signed that recognized Charles as Emperor *of the Franks.*

In the meantime, the last years of Irene's rule were disastrous. The Arabs, taking advantage of the political disarray in Constantinople, invaded Asia Minor in 798 and reached the Aegean. The Byzantine government was paralyzed by competition among court officials, and Irene had drained the treasury by suspending taxes in an effort to win popularity. She was deposed in 802 by her minister of finance, Nicephorus, who declared himself emperor.

The Empires of Charlemagne and Byzantine   *ca.* A.D. 800

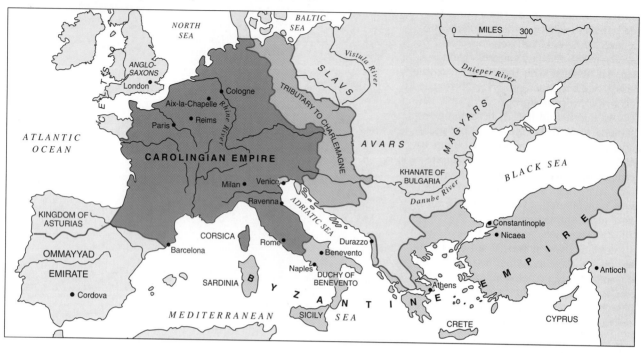

Irene and Nicephorus (r. 802–11) were both unfortunate to have ruled during the reign of the greatest king of the Franks, Charles (r. 768–814), and the greatest ruler of Islam, Harun al-Rashid (r. 786–809). Harun seized every opportunity to encroach on the Empire, and his great campaign of 798 was only the most spectacular of his many ventures. During Nicephorus's reign, Charles and Harun intensified the threat to Constantinople by exchanging embassies. After the death of Charles and Harun, their successors were occupied with internal political troubles, and the danger to the Empire faded. Leo V (r. 813–20) managed to restore a measure of stability to the frontiers, but during his reign the first signs of an important socioeconomic change in the Empire began to emerge.

Byzantine Society and Economy and the Founding of the Macedonian Dynasty

The Byzantine army and navy drew their manpower from the conscription of peasant-soldiers in the administrative districts (*themes*) of Asia Minor. The interior provinces provided infantry troops, while the maritime provinces supplied the fleet. Since the seventh century the Byzantine emperors had been careful to safeguard the prosperity of the yeoman class that provided their military manpower. When the provinces were devastated by war, famine, or disease, the emperors had repopulated them with contingents of small farmers drawn from tribes along the imperial borders. That practice had given the imperial forces remarkable stability.

In the early ninth century, however, the devastations of the Bulgars and Arabs ruined so many of the small farmers that the policy was no longer effective. The rural aristocracy, which had provided the military leadership of the provinces, created great estates by buying out the ruined farmers, who either became tenants or migrated to the cities. Though the process was slow, it did great damage to the Empire's economy and its military establishment. Moreover, it increased the power of the aristocratic generals, because their soldiers were now their tenants.

During this time, the Arabs made new incursions into the Byzantine territories. They took Crete and used it as a base for disrupting Byzantine shipping in the Aegean and the eastern Mediterranean. At the same time, North African Moors began a conquest of Sicily, which had been under Byzantine control since the time of Justinian. The Byzantines tried several times to enlist the Franks in an alliance against the Moors, but inevitably negotiations faltered over the question of the imperial title. By the early tenth century, the Moors controlled both Sicily and southern Italy.

The mid-ninth century was a period of weakness in Byzantine government. The government was conducted by a shaky regency for Michael III (r. 842–67), an alcoholic homosexual. After 852, the regents were Basil, formerly an Armenian stableboy, who may have been Michael's lover, and Bardas, Michael's uncle. Basil, an illiterate, was a man of towering stature and impressive strength in a court often dominated by eunuchs. Bardas was a man of great culture and a patron of the intellectual and artistic community in Constantinople. In 866, Basil murdered Bardas and took control of the government. A year later, when Michael went mad and threatened him, Basil had him killed and declared himself emperor.

An illiterate ruler in a highly literate society, Basil I founded a dynasty that brought the Byzantine Empire to its highest level of prosperity and culture. Though Armenian by ethnic origin, Basil had been born in Macedonia and was called "the Macedonian." The dynasty he founded is called the Macedonian dynasty.

Byzantine Culture and Relations with the West in the Mid-Ninth Century

During the ten years of his co-regency, before Basil had him murdered, Bardas sponsored a brilliant flowering of art, literature, and science. He brought about a renaissance of classical studies to which we owe the preservation of many ancient Greek literary and philosophical works. The center of this renaissance was Photius, a friend of Bardas who became patriarch—that is, head of the church of Constantinople. Bardas reestablished the secular university in Constantinople,

while Photius reformed the education of the clergy. Photius, the most learned man of his age, put together a monumental work called *Myriobiblion* (*The Library*), a compendium of history, philosophy, and theology. Among his associates in the court school were two world-renowned scholars, Leo the Mathematician and Constantine the Philosopher. The Islamic ruler in Baghdad invited Leo, whom Bardas named first rector of the university, to his court, which had an avid interest in mathematics and astronomy (p. 208). Constantine became a missionary to the Slavs and created a script for writing the Slavonic language (pp. 332–33). The university Bardas founded continued as a center of education, scholarship, and culture for two centuries.

In 858, Pope Nicholas I (r. 858–67), an intransigent, forceful man who was allied with the enemies of Photius, launched an investigation into how Photius had become patriarch of Constantinople. During

Interior view of St. Mark's cathedral, Venice. The mosaics were done by Byzantine artists (tenth century).

the inquiry, Nicholas suggested that it was time to restore to Rome the dioceses that the Byzantine emperor Leo III had removed from Roman jurisdiction in 731 (p. 178). Photius, who did not recognize the jurisdiction of the pope, replied that the emperor, Michael III, was not willing to do so.

What Nicholas had in mind was not just the recovery of long-lost territory and income but control of a whole new sector of Christendom. The Slavs and the Bulgars were ready to become Christians, and the Bulgarian Khan Boris was negotiating with both Frankish bishops and Constantinople about which church he should commit his people to. Nicholas wanted to recover Dalmatia to use as a base for missionary activity in eastern Europe. Photius sent his own missionaries to Boris and to Moravia, and in 865 Boris submitted to Constantinople. But the competition for the Slavs and the Bulgars, to which the

dispute over Photius's elevation was related, continued for the next six years, until at last the Bulgarians were committed to the Eastern church.

In the meantime, Nicholas found occasion to spell out for the Byzantine emperor and his patriarch the full theory of papal authority, relying on a document known as the *Donation of Constantine*. This document purported to record the donation of Rome and the western half of the Roman Empire that Constantine I (r. 312–37) made to Pope Sylvester I (r. 314–35) when Constantine moved his capital to Byzantium. Actually, the document had been written in the West some time during the first half of the ninth century, but it was not exposed as a forgery until 1440. Photius replied to Nicholas's argument in a learned, elegant document in which he refuted the *Donation* on every point. He argued that Constantine had retained both his spiritual authority and his secular authority when he moved to Byzantium and that the patriarch, as the emperor's principal ecclesiastical official, enjoyed status at least equal to that of the pope. This argument went back to Constantine I's claims to apostolic status made when he established his capital in Constantinople.

At this time, Basil I deposed Photius, thereby making rapprochement with the papacy possible. But Pope Nicholas had died, and his successor did not pursue the matter. Despite countless attempts to resolve it, the so-called Photian Schism between the Eastern and Western churches persists to this day.

THE MACEDONIAN PERIOD

Basil I

Basil I (r. 867–86) was determined to recover the West for the Empire. First he tried to engage the Frankish king of Italy, Louis II, who called himself emperor, in an alliance against the Moors, whose strongholds in southern Italy threatened Louis as well as the old Byzantine cities. But when Louis's claim to the imperial title proved an obstacle, Basil proceeded by himself. Under the great admiral Niceph-

---

The *Donation of Constantine*

Constantine tells how Pope Sylvester I cured him of leprosy. In gratitude Constantine accepts baptism and decrees

that the sacred see of blessed Peter shall be gloriously exalted above our empire and earthly throne. . . . And the pontiff who presides over the most holy Roman Church shall be the highest and chief of all priests . . . and according to his decision shall all matters be settled . . . for the worship of God or the confirmation of the faith.

We convey to the most blessed pontiff, our father Silvester, universal pope, both our palace [the Lateran] and likewise all provinces, places and districts of the City of Rome and Italy and of the regions of the West, . . . bequeathing them to the power and sway of him and his successors.

Wherefore we have perceived that our empire and the power of our government should be transferred to the regions of the East . . . for it is not right that an earthly emperor should have authority . . . where the head of the Christian religion has been established by the Emperor of heaven.

From the Donation of Constantine, *as quoted in* Select Documents of European History, *ed. by R. G. D. Laffan (London: Methuen, 1930), Vol. 1. pp. 4–5.*

orus Phocas, Byzantine forces made steady, though difficult, progress in southern Italy while the Moors consolidated their hold over Sicily. Following the example of Photius, Basil sent missionaries to the southern Slavs who had settled Dalmatia and Greece and established provincial administrations along the eastern coast of the Adriatic Sea, entering into close ties with Venice.

While pursuing his goal in the West, Basil also carried on a series of campaigns in the East. Here his armies regained strategically important territories and cities and kept the Arab armies at bay. By coordinating land and sea operations in the eastern Mediterranean he was able to maintain the upper hand against the Arab fleets. He defeated the pirates of Crete several times and may even have occupied the island for a while. In sum, Basil made an excellent start on reestablishing the Empire's territorial integrity and its military superiority against its traditional enemies.

Basil also undertook important governmental reforms. He commissioned the writing of a manual of administrative practice, which served as a guide to the bureaucracy until the publication of *On the Administration of the Empire*, written by Emperor Constantine VII, Basil's grandson. He also commissioned a new law code to clear away the clutter and confusion caused by the controversy over iconoclasm and the accumulation of cases and learned treatises.

In 879, Basil began to lose his sanity. Control of the government fell to the patriarch and other leading court figures. This was a time of intensive palace intrigue, which ended in 886 when the mad emperor was assassinated—probably by friends of his twenty-year-old son Leo. Unlike his father, Leo V (r. 886–912) was a highly educated, scholarly man.

Leo V

Like his predecessors, Leo V faced difficult military problems throughout his reign. In the eastern Mediterranean the Arab fleets had recovered and were once again doing great damage to coastal cities and shipping. Following Basil's example, Leo made the navy the Empire's principal military force. However, in 911 most of the Byzantine fleet was lost in a great battle with the Arabs.

Greek fire, a mixture of quicklime, petroleum, and sulfur that ignited when it came in contact with water, was introduced into the Byzantine navy after 675. It was a very effective weapon against the Arabs (detail from a fourteenth-century manuscript).

Meanwhile, the Bulgarian frontier was quiet. Though the Khan Boris (r. 852–89) had converted to Christianity in 865, many of his people remained pagans, and the last years of his reign were disturbed by religious conflict. In 889, Boris abdicated in favor of his eldest son Vladimir, a pagan. At this point, a civil war broke out that lasted until 893, when Vladimir was overthrown by his Christian, Byzantine-educated brother Symeon. These internal struggles kept the Bulgars occupied for a time. After consolidating his power, however, Symeon engaged in new attacks on the European provinces of the Empire.

Throughout these years of turmoil, Leo still managed to carry out important administrative reforms. He established new provinces in southern Italy and upper Mesopotamia, and he strengthened the *themes* to serve as the first line of defense against the Arabs' ceaseless raids. He completed the legal code begun by his father and issued 113 edicts designed to promote good government in church and state. He understood the importance of the church, and to ensure its loyalty to the crown he named his younger brother, Stephen, patriarch. From this point on, the Eastern church was not only a department of state but also an appendage of the imperial family. Finally, he regulated commerce through publication of the *Book of the Eparch*. The eparch was the leading official of Byzantine government, and the book spelled out his jurisdiction over guilds and corporations. Byzantine writers called the emperor "Leo the Wise."

The end of Leo's reign was troubled by a controversy over his fourth marriage. Both religious and civil law prohibited a man from marrying even a third time, unless it was absolutely necessary for continuation of his family; fourth marriages were out of the question. By 905 Leo had been married three times and was still without a male heir. When his mistress gave birth to a male in September of that year, he was determined to legitimize the child. He sought a dispensation from the legal prohibition and eventually forced the patriarch to permit him to marry the boy's mother. The patriarch's acquiescence set off a sharp debate within the church.

Romanus and Constantine VII

Leo V died in 912 and was succeeded by his seven-year-old son Constantine VII. Leo's dissolute brother Alexander now competed with Constantine's mother for control of the regency government. The competition encouraged the Bulgarian Symeon to claim the imperial title for himself, and when he was denied the title he launched a destructive war that raged for eleven years (913–24). In 919, a military commander named Romanus seized control of the government, married his daughter to the young emperor, and had himself crowned co-emperor with his son-in-law. Romanus (r. 920–44) entered into an alliance with the Slavs in the Balkans against Symeon of Bulgaria, and by the time the old khan died in 927 the Bulgarian threat had been contained.

Meanwhile, the eastern armies had been waging a brilliant campaign against the Arabs, putting the Byzantines on the offensive in the East. Moreover, the Empire established itself in Armenia and pushed into the Caucasus, the mountainous region between the Black Sea and the Caspian Sea. In the north, Romanus fought a war against the Russians, which ended in a lasting treaty (945).

When Romanus was overthrown by his own sons, the mob in Constantinople demanded that Constantine VII be named sole emperor. Then nearly forty years old, he had spent his life as a scholar while his father-in-law ruled as co-emperor. Still uneasy about his legitimacy, Constantine VII took the title Porphyrogenitus ("born in the purple"—that is, as the legitimate heir).

During Constantine VII's reign as sole emperor (944–59), literature, science, arts, and crafts flourished under his patronage. The period is considered the golden age of the renaissance that had begun nearly a century earlier under Bardas. Court scholars produced manuals of military strategy and books of law, philosophy, history, and theology. Many of these works were made up of snippets from the great works of the past, and, because many of the originals have been lost, we owe a debt to the mid-tenth-century compilers for preserving at least parts of them. Constantine himself compiled a great work on the ceremony of the Byzantine court, which is the principal source of our knowledge about those rituals. He also wrote a book on the history and practice of imperial administration and diplomacy, mentioned above, to guide his son Romanus II.

Following his grandfather Basil's example, Constantine VII carried on negotiations with the European kings, the successors of Charles the Great, and in 949 the German king Otto I (r. 936–73) sent an embassy to Constantinople. A proposed marriage was arranged between Romanus II and Otto's daughter, and tutors were sent to Otto's court to teach the young girl the Greek language and Byzantine manners. The marriage never took place, however, because Romanus rashly married another woman. The plan to link the German and the imperial houses was realized in the next generation, when Otto II (r. 973–83) married Theophano, daughter of Romanus II.

In the years from 959, when Constantine VII died, to 976, when his grandson Basil II succeeded to the throne, the military aristocracy was growing more and more powerful. Since the ninth century, when the strength of the yeoman class had declined (p. 180), the aristocracy had exercised economic and political control of the provinces. In 963, the naval commander Nicephorus Phocas, a descendant of the admiral who had served Basil I, seized power and in 969 was succeeded by the aristocratic general John (r. 969–76). Together these two men restored the Byzantine military system and recovered territory that had been lost by the Empire. But the idea that the emperor must be legitimate remained strong, and John's successor was Basil II, a peculiar man who is considered the greatest of the Byzantine emperors.

Basil II

Basil II (r. 976–1025) never married and seems to have avoided women. Although he grew up in a society that set a high value on the cultured life, Basil was totally uninterested in education, learning, and the arts. He was an ascetic, a man out of place; he was also a military genius.

Like Constantine V in the eighth century, Basil went out against the Bulgarians year after year. At one time he repatriated 14,000 Bulgarian prisoners of war, all of whom had been blinded. He was known as "the Bulgar Slayer." He also pacified the Russians, with the help of a force of Varangian (Scandinavian) troops. About 989 he entered into a treaty by which the Russian prince of Kiev would become a Christian and marry a member of the imperial family. Basil transformed the Varangians into an elite imperial guard. In the medieval Scandinavian sagas, service in the guard was considered a sign of high birth and great ability as a warrior, for the emperor was said to accept only men from the best families who had proven themselves in war.

At the turn of the eleventh century, Basil II campaigned successfully against the Arabs of Syria and moved forcefully into the provinces south of the Caucasus. In 1001, he entered into a ten-year truce with the Islamic ruler in Baghdad.

At home, Basil turned his attention to the military aristocracy, which, as we have seen, had become a dominant force in Byzantine society. The consolidation of small holdings into huge landed estates had ruined the small farmers, the ancient basis of Byzantine prosperity. Moreover, the landed aristocracy had a strong instinct toward independence and viewed the central government with suspicion and hostility. The reforms of the *themes* under Leo V at the beginning of the tenth century had further strengthened the provinces and their leading aristocratic families, and since that time most of the periodic rebellions against the central government had been fomented by the landed aristocracy. The destitution of the yeoman class, in addition to reducing the manpower available to the Empire, had widened the gap between rich and poor.

On January 1, 996, Basil issued a decree that required the great landholders to produce documentary proof that they had owned their land for at least 75 years.

If someone was occupying formerly government land, as shown by records in the imperial archives, he had to produce proof of ownership going back 1,000 years. That meant he would have to come up with an authentic document that had been preserved in the family since the reign of Augustus (r. 27 B.C.–A.D. 14)! With the support of the army and the populace, Basil managed to enforce this radical legislation and in doing so reduced many great families to poverty. A few years later, he added to the burden of rich landowners by requiring that they make up any deficit in the tax collections from the villages under their control. The law hit the churches hardest, but Basil ignored their protests and pleas for relief.

These measures halted the economic decline of the Empire for a generation and served to weaken the power of the aristocracy. After Basil's death in 1025, however, the great families recovered. Between 1025 and 1081, the civilian bureaucracy and the provincial military aristocracy competed fiercely for control of the Empire, each side setting up emperors who supported it. The bureaucracy found its emperors among members of the Macedonian dynasty, while the aristocrats put up men from their own ranks. Through most of this period, the bureaucracy held the upper hand. It tried to weaken the aristocracy by reducing the size of the army. When the Macedonian dynasty died out in the middle of the century, the Empire's military establishment was in ruins.

BYZANTIUM AND THE WEST

The Foundation of the Comnenian Dynasty

During this same period, while competition for power was weakening the Empire, its enemies were making inroads into the imperial territories. In the West, the Normans—from Normandy in northern France—conquered southern Italy (p. 274), driving out the Byzantines and the Arabs alike. In the North, the Patzinaks, an Asiatic people, threatened the Danubian border. Most serious, in the East, the Seljuk

Turks, who had come out of Central Asia, attacked the eastern provinces of the Empire (see pp. 211–12).

When the Turks devastated large areas of Asia Minor, an aristocrat named Romanus Diogenes seized the opportunity to mount the imperial throne. In 1071, he mustered what was left of the Byzantine army and met the Turks at Manzikert. There he suffered a disastrous defeat and was himself captured. After promising to pay a huge ransom, he discovered that the civilian bureaucracy had staged a coup d'état. Consequently, the promise he made to pay tribute to the Turks, which might have given the Empire some respite, went by the boards. That same year, the Normans captured Bari on the west coast of southern Italy and were in a position to invade Greece.

During the next decade, rival claimants to the Byzantine throne entered into alliances with the Turks and the Normans, hastening conquest from both the east and the west. In this time of crisis, the Ducas family, which had been supported by the bureaucracy, allied itself with the greatest of the aristocratic generals, Alexius Comnenus, who married a Ducas princess and became emperor in 1081.

By the time Alexius (r. 1081–1118) came to power, the Normans had crossed the Adriatic and were trying to conquer Epirus. Their leader, Robert Guiscard, wanted to become emperor himself. To deal with the Norman threat, Alexius made peace with the Turks and the Patzinaks, granting them, as vassals of the imperial throne, the territories they had already conquered. He then entered into an alliance with the Venetians, who since the tenth century had been building their commercial and maritime strength. The Venetians agreed to help the Byzantines in return for a monopoly of trade in the imperial territories. With this assistance, Alexius managed to drive the Normans out of Epirus.

Since the 1070s the Byzantine emperors had been appealing to the western powers for help against the infidel Turks. The Turkish conquest of Jerusalem in 1077 added urgency to the appeal, but not until 1095 was Pope Urban II (r. 1088–99)

able to organize a great crusade of Western knights to reconquer the Holy Land.

Although the fall of Jerusalem induced the westerners to join the battle against the Turks, Alexius's real purpose was to use the westerners to reconquer his lost territories in Asia Minor. He had little interest in the Holy Land. When the crusaders arrived at Constantinople, however, he found that their leaders were headstrong men determined to establish independent Latin principalities in the Holy Land. The crusaders passed through Asia Minor to engage the Turks in Palestine. When the westerners had won the major cities there, Alexius found that he had yet another enemy in the Middle East.

Like his diplomatic policies, Alexius's economic policies produced ambiguous results. He restored the value of the currency after decades of decline, but he also doubled taxes, which were already heavy. Moreover, the Venetian monopoly of trade kept prices artificially high. Late in his reign, Alexius tried to counter Venetian power by granting trading privileges to Venice's rival, Pisa, but this move merely intensified competition between the two cities.

Alexius also tried to strengthen the army by increasing the number of land grants made in return for military service. In the long run, this practice further increased the number of large estates and the power of the provincial military aristocracy. Those consequences did not surface until after Alexius's reign, however.

Finally, Alexius was a vigorous supporter of scholarship, at least of that aimed at the recovery of the past rather than at the discovery of new knowledge. Not surprisingly, the greatest works produced during his reign were histories. Michael Psellus wrote an exhaustive history of the Empire, the *Chronographia*, and Alexius's daughter Anna wrote a history of his reign. These works are valuable sources for modern historians.

The First Collapse of the Empire

The struggle to restore the Empire faltered during the last two decades of the twelfth century. After Alexius's death in 1118,

the Byzantines had failed to escape the Italians' commercial control, and rising power among the provincial aristocracy had led to creation of independent armies throughout the provinces. Between 1181 and 1204, the Serbians, one of the Slavic peoples that had settled in the Balkans, created an empire, and the Bulgarians reasserted their power. Meanwhile, the Norman rulers of southern Italy continued to covet the imperial crown, and in the late 1180s the German king Henry VI inherited the Normans' goals when he mounted their throne (p. 319).

In 1204 the pope assembled another great crusade—the fourth—and the Venetians were engaged to ferry the crusading army to the Holy Land. Over the years the

A Crusader's View of Byzantium

Odo of Deuil, the author of this piece, was a historian of the Second Crusade.

And then the Greeks degenerated entirely into women; putting aside all manly vigor, both of words and of spirit, they lightly swore whatever they thought would please us, but they neither kept faith with us nor maintained respect for themselves. In general they really have the opinion that anything which is done for the holy empire cannot be considered perjury. . . . When the Greeks are afraid they become despicable in their excessive abasement, and when they have the upper hand they are arrogant. . . .

Constantinople itself is squalid and fetid. . . . People live lawlessly in this city, which has as many lords as rich men and almost as many thieves as poor men. . . . In every respect she exceeds moderation, for just as she surpasses other cities in wealth, so too does she surpass them in vice. . . .

[The bishop of Langres] added that Constantinople is Christian only in name and not in fact . . . and that her emperor had ventured a few years ago to attack the [Crusader] prince of Antioch. . . . "Though it was his [the emperor's] duty to ward off the nearby infidels by uniting the Christian forces, with the aid of the infidels he strove to destroy the Christians."

From Odo of Deuil, De profectione Ludovici VII in orientem, *trans. by V. G. Berry (New York: Columbia University Press, 1948), pp. 57, 65, 69.*

A Byzantine View of the Crusaders

Anna Comnena, the author of this piece, was the daughter of the Emperor Alexius I.

Now he [the emperor] dreaded the arrival of the Crusaders, for he knew their irresistible manner of attack, their unstable and mobile character, and all the peculiar ... characteristics which the Frank retains throughout; and he also knew that they were always agape for money, and seemed to disregard their truces readily for any reason that cropped up.... The simpler-minded Franks were urged on by the real desire of worshiping at our Lord's Sepulchre, but the more astute, especially men like Bohemund ... had another secret reason, namely the hope that ... they might by some means be able to seize the capital itself.... For the Frankish race ... is always very hotheaded and eager, but when it has once espoused a cause, it is uncontrollable.

From Anna Comnena, The Alexiad, *trans. by E. A. S. Dawes (London: Kegan Paul, 1928), pp. 248, 250.*

Women of the Byzantine Imperial Family

Imperial women played an important role in Byzantine affairs. They were well educated and often exercised great political power. Here is a description by Anna Comnena, daughter of Emperor Alexius I (1081–1118), of her paternal grandmother Anna. The younger Anna wrote an excellent history of her father's reign.

[At the beginning of Alexius's reign] He [Alexius] really longed that his mother rather than himself should take the helm of the state.... Therefore in all daily business he did nothing, not even a trifling thing, without her advice.... When ... Robert's [the Norman ruler of Italy] crossing in Epirus forced Alexius to leave the capital [he entrusted] his mother single-handed with the imperial government.... For my grandmother was so clever in business and so skilful in guiding a State, and setting it in order, that she was capable of not only administering the Roman Empire, but any other of all the countries the sun shines upon. She was a woman of wide experience and knew the nature of things.... To put it concisely, the situation was as follows, he indeed had the semblance of reigning but she really reigned— moreover she drew up laws, administered and directed everything; all her orders, written or unwritten, he [Alexius] confirmed by his seal or by word...."

From Anna Comnena, The Alexiad, *trans. by Elizabeth A. S. Dawes (New York: Barnes & Noble, 1967), pp. 82, 83, 85–86.*

westerners had come to resent the Byzantines for a good many reasons: The Venetians resented Byzantine tampering with their trading privileges; church leaders resented Byzantine reluctance to reunite the two churches; and the military leaders of the crusade resented Byzantine attempts to take over the Latin principalities in the Middle East. Hence the Venetian Doge Dandolo found it easy to convince the crusaders that they should besiege Constantinople on behalf of the Venetians. He counted the attack on the city as partial payment for the cost of transportation, which the crusaders could not afford. Constantinople fell to the crusaders in July 1204.

Although the Westerners established an emperor of their own in Constantinople, the Empire had ceased to exist. In western Asia Minor, Byzantine émigrés set up the Empire of Nicaea. To the east was the Sultanate of Iconium, part of the old Seljuk Empire. In the northeast, survivors of the Comnenian dynasty established the Empire of Trebizond. On the Greek peninsula, the Despotate of Epirus became an independent Byzantine state, while Athens became the center of a Frankish duchy. Venice controlled most of the major coastal cities and their surrounding territory. In 1261 a Byzantine general, Michael VIII Paleologus (r. 1259–82), recaptured Constantinople and founded a new dynasty, which presided over the last two centuries of the Byzantine Empire.

THE AGE OF THE PALEOLOGI EMPERORS

That the Empire survived as long as it did under Michael Paleologus and his successors is evidence of the diplomatic skills of the Paleologi. The Empire was constantly threatened from all sides. In the West, the Normans in southern Italy were succeeded first by the Germans and then by the French, and these successors continued to seek the imperial crown, repeatedly plotting with Byzantine dissidents and the heirs of the Western emperors of Constantinople to retake the city.

The Westerners justified their designs on Constantinople by arguing that the

The Latin Empire of Constantinople   1204–61

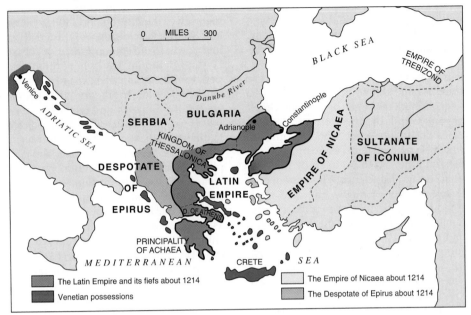

Map legend:
- The Latin Empire and its fiefs about 1214
- Venetian possessions
- The Empire of Nicaea about 1214
- The Despotate of Epirus about 1214

easterners were heretics and schismatics who did not recognize the primacy of the Roman church. So Michael VIII decided to negotiate with the pope over the unification of the Eastern and Western churches. The negotiations resulted in an agreement, embodied in an act of union, which was announced at a great church council held in the French city of Lyon in 1274. But the agreement raised a storm of protest in the East, and people of every class and condition ended up in imperial prisons. The act of union had failed.

Despite Michael's success in keeping his enemies at bay, his realm was only a minor state among all those that had been established by westerners and Turks on the old territories of the Empire. It was exhausted both militarily and economically. Michael's successors faced new enemies, the Serbs in the West and the Ottoman Turks in the East. During the fourteenth century the Serbs established a powerful state that included Bulgaria and most of the Empire's Balkan provinces, and the Ottoman Turks conquered all of Asia Minor. By 1329, the Empire controlled only a few cities along the western coast of Asia Minor, and the Turks sat

across the Bosporus in view of Constantinople.

The following decades were a time of civil war and palace intrigue in Constantinople, with the Ottomans extending their conquests into Thrace and Thessalonica. By the end of the fourteenth century, the Ottoman Turks had defeated the Serbs and their allies in several battles and had surrounded Constantinople. At this point, the Mongols, a people from eastern Asia led by Timur (called Tamerlane in the West), swept down on the Ottoman Turks and crushed them in 1401. But the Empire was too weak to take advantage of the situation. The Ottoman Turks eventually recovered from the disaster, and in 1453 Sultan Muhammed II brought a powerful army, supported by artillery he had acquired in the West, against Constantinople. After nearly two months of attacks and bombardment, he took the city on May 29. The last Byzantine emperor, Constantine XI, a capable man who had tried to cope with an impossible situation, died in the fighting. By 1461, the Turks had conquered all the remnants of Byzantine power, and the Empire was no more.

BYZANTINE GOVERNMENT

At the center of Byzantine government was an extensive, elaborate bureaucracy. Entry into the civil service rested on education, and the bureaucrats created a system of secular education focused on the study of Greek literature, philosophy, and science. Students began by learning Greek grammar and by memorizing Homer's epics and other great works. Normally, students completed this stage by age fourteen and then went on to study rhetoric, philosophy, and science. This system produced an elite of highly educated men. Although the small group of aristocratic families that dominated the bureaucracy had assurance that their sons would be properly educated for government service, any talented young man could gain access to the academic program and enter the power elite.

The bureaucracy was divided into departments. The chancellor ran the department responsible for all state correspondence. The postmaster general headed the department that operated the Empire's extensive communications system. And the *Sacellarius* (treasurer) headed the financial department. Lesser officers, too numerous to list, were supported by bureaucracies of their own. Most officers of the imperial household were eunuchs, who could be trusted because they could never usurp the imperial throne; both social custom and law determined that only men who could produce heirs could be legitimate emperors. Military officers had no place in the bureaucracy and were in constant competition with the civilian officeholders.

The military served as governors of the provinces, or *themes*. At the beginning of the ninth century, there were ten *themes*; by the end of the century, 26; and by the end of the twelfth century, 52. The emperors continually subdivided the *themes* to prevent the military aristocracy from using them as power bases and kept the governors under close surveillance. For example, a financial officer in each *theme* reported directly to the imperial government. In addition, the emperors maintained an effective intelligence network staffed by professional spies.

The center of government was the emperor. The Byzantines considered themselves the direct heirs of the Romans, and like the Romans they entrusted absolute power to the emperor. In both Roman law and Byzantine law, whenever the imperial throne was vacant, power resided in the people. In theory, the people elected the emperor and transferred their power to him. This fiction was symbolized in the rituals that accompanied the raising of a new emperor to the throne. The people in attendance at the ceremony yelled an acclamation that proclaimed the transfer of power from them to the emperor.

The Byzantine emperor was viewed as the vicar of Christ on earth, head of the church as well as of the state (Caesaropapism). He appointed the patriarchs of Constantinople and other bishops, and he promulgated both civil and ecclesiastical statutes. Although a divinely ordained emperor could not legally be removed, rebellion against him was justified. A successful rebellion was a sign from God that it was time to change emperors. An unsuccessful rebellion was viewed as treason against both God and emperor.

To symbolize this divine autocracy, the Byzantines developed an elaborate court ceremony patterned on the liturgy of the church. Every appearance and every act of the emperor was carried out according to a rigid ritual that dramatized the majesty of the imperial office. At the same time, the ceremonies prescribed the manner in which the emperor was to behave and reminded him of his responsibility to uphold justice and good government. Although Byzantine history is full of scoundrels, palace revolutions, and intrigue, Byzantine government was more stable and more consistent in both theory and practice than that of any other Mediterranean state.

BYZANTINE SOCIETY

The Empire embraced both the society of Constantinople and the society of the provinces. During its classical age, from the eighth to the twelfth centuries, the population of Constantinople ranged between 500,000 and 800,000. It was divided into three classes—the bureaucrats, the commercial class, and the poor. The commercial class, which included merchants, tradesmen, and small shopkeepers, was by far the largest. The bureaucratic class was smaller but still numbered in the thousands. The poor class may have numbered around 30,000.

Although the commercial class was huge, its upper crust of merchants never evolved into a powerful force in society or the state. Until the eleventh century, the government rigidly controlled all commerce by regulating the trade guilds. When government control broke down at the end of the eleventh century, the Venetians and other Italians took over Byzantine commerce.

The breakdown of government control extended to the countryside as well. Until the late eleventh century, the government had obliged the rural districts to supply specified quantities of foodstuffs to Constantinople. And it had kept food prices low, making it possible for people with low incomes to survive in the city. Moreover, the emperor, the church, and the leading citizens of the city carried on an extensive program of charities. Giving to the poor became a regular practice among upper-class families, and throughout the city were many hospitals and charitable institutions of various kinds. In a sense, the poor constituted a professional class, and companies of beggars carefully guarded the best places to beg.

Even so, life was hard for the lower classes. With the demise of government control over the countryside, food prices rose sharply. Clothing, which had always been expensive, became even more costly. Housing was grossly inadequate. Thousands of people slept in archways and in any sheltered spot they could find. Garbage and sewage fouled the streets, and disease was endemic. Not surprisingly, the sale of perfumes and aromatic herbs was brisk among the wealthy to mask the odors and to guard against disease.

Although the late Roman and Byzantine law gave women substantial rights, Byzantine women were constrained by elaborate rules of etiquette. Respectable women wore veils whenever they left

A Byzantine lady of rank (late fifth or early sixth century). Note her elegantly draped mantle and the snoodlike bonnet of the imperial type.

home, and they were expected to show diffidence toward guests in their homes. Constraints often led to secret liaisons and falls from respectability. Among lower-class women, prostitution was common. The owners of taverns and baths often maintained brothels, and pimps were easy to find. Historians estimate that at any given time there may have been thousands of prostitutes in the city.

Out in the provinces, life was hard but healthier than life in the cities. Until the middle of the ninth century, as we have seen, the central government repopulated devastated areas and curtailed the growth of the great estates. As a result, the rural population became multicultural, and the military officers who trained and led the peasant-soldiers were obliged to become familiar with at least one vernacular language.

The yeomen farmers lived in villages of from 50 to 500 people, depending on

Early Byzantine jewelry contained Hellenistic and Roman features. The clasp of this late-sixth-century necklace, for example, is of a Hellenistic type, while the cylindrical slides between the pendants are a late Roman feature.

the productivity of the land, and each family owned its own land. Some men escaped country life by entering the army or by seeking an education. Rural monasteries ran schools for talented young men, preparing them to enter the bureaucracy or the church.

Over the centuries from the sixth century to the fifteenth century, the eastern half of the old Roman Empire evolved into an imperial state that exercised a powerful influence on the political, economic, and cultural history of the Mediterranean Basin. From Scandinavia to Baghdad, the Byzantine Empire centered in Constantinople was regarded with awe and envy. For Europeans, it was a nostalgic reminder of the Roman Empire, the ideal state they still hoped to resurrect one day. For the rulers of Islam, the Empire was a formidable enemy that commanded their unwavering attention and absorbed immense resources. The Empire protected the Europeans from the Arabs until 1453, when it ceased to exist.

For a thousand years the Byzantine Empire withstood invasion and attack on all sides. And, during those centuries of turmoil, it produced a memorable civilization. Byzantine art and architecture influenced all the civilizations of the Mediterranean, and Byzantine scholars preserved Hellenistic learning for posterity. Byzantine government was a model of efficiency and its educated bureaucrats set forth the tasks and functions of government in classic works. In short, Byzantine civilization was an essential ingredient in the evolution of Western culture.

Suggestions for Further Reading

General

The leading general histories of the Byzantine Empire are G. Ostrogorsky, *History of the Byzantine State*, 2nd ed. (1968), which focuses on political history, and *Cambridge Medieval History*, Vol. 4 (2 parts), ed. J. M. Hussey (1966–67), which contains excellent articles on all aspects of Byzantine history and culture. On the early period, see A. H. M. Jones, *The Later Roman Empire*, 2 vols. (1964). On Constantine, see the works cited in Chapter 4. P. Charanis treats Anastasius I in *Church and State in the Later Roman Empire* (1974). On Justinian, see J. W. Barker, *Justinian and the Later Roman Empire* (1966), and R. Browning, *Justinian and Theodora* (1971). On the Heraclian dynasty, see R. Jenkins, *Byzantium: The Imperial Centuries, A.D. 610–1071* (1966).

On Iconoclasm, see E. J. Martin, *History of the Iconoclastic Controversy* (1930); S. Gero, *Byzantine Iconoclasm during the Reign of Leo III* (1973) and *Byzantine Iconoclasm during the Reign of Constantine V* (1977). On Irene, see C. Diehl, *Byzantine Empresses* (1963). For a history of the Byzantine church, see R. M. French, *The Eastern Orthodox Church* (1951); G. Every, *The Byzantine Patriarchate (451–1204)*, 2nd ed. (1962); and H. Margoulias, *Byzantine Christianity: Emperor, Church, and the West* (1970). On Caesaropapism, see E. Barker, *Social and Political Thought in Byzantium* (1957), and D. J. Geanakoplos, "'Caesaropapism' in Byzantium," in *Byzantine East & Latin West* (1966). On the relations between East and West, see F. Dvornik, *Byzantium and the Roman Primacy* (1966), and *The Photian Schism* (1950); H. Pirenne, *Mohammed and Charlemagne* (1939); and C. Brand, *Byzantium Confronts the West: 1180–1204* (1968). On the fourth crusade, see D. Queller, *The Fourth Crusade* (1977), and on the Byzantine recovery after 1261, see D. J. Geanakoplos, *Emperor Michael Paleologus and the West* (1959). For a history of the Bulgarians, see S. Runciman, *A History of the First Bulgarian Empire* (1930),

and on eastern Europe, see F. Dvornik, *The Making of Central and Eastern Europe* (1949), and M. Spinka, *A History of Christianity in the Balkans* (1933).

Byzantine Civilization

For a picture of classical Byzantine civilization, see A. Toynbee, *Constantine Porphyrogenitus and his World* (1973); J. M. Hussey, *Church and Learning in the Byzantine Empire 867–1185* (1937) and *The Byzantine World*, 2nd ed. (1961); and S. Runciman, *Byzantine Civilization* (1933). On Byzantine art, see D. Talbot Rice, *The Art of Byzantium* (1959). On the economic life of Byzantium, see the articles in the *Cambridge Economic History of Europe*, Vol. 1 (1942). A. P. Kazhdan and A. W. Epstein, *Change in Byzantine Culture in the Eleventh and*

Twelfth Centuries (1985), cover a wide range of topics, including society, daily life, education, art, and government. The classic study of Byzantine government is J. B. Bury, *The Imperial Administrative System in the Ninth Century* (1911). See Michael Psellus, *Fourteen Byzantine Rulers* (*Chronographia*), trans. E. R. A. Sewter (1966), and *The Alexiad of Anna Comnena*, trans. E. R. A. Sewter (1969). D. J. Geanakoplos, *Byzantium: Church, Society, and Civilization Seen Through Contemporary Eyes* (1986) contains a large collection of sources.

End of the Byzantine Empire

On the capture of Constantinople by the Franks, see K. M. Setton, *A History of the Crusades*, Vol. 2 (1962). On the Latin period, see M. Angold, *A Byzantine Government in Exile: Government and Society under the Laskarids of Nicaea, 1204–*

1261 (1975). On the fall of the Byzantine Empire, see D. M. Nicol, *The Last Centuries of Byzantium, 1261–1453* (1972), and P. Wittek, *The Rise of the Ottoman Empire* (1938).

8

ISLAM AND THE RISE OF THE ARAB EMPIRE

From the middle of the seventh century on, the Arab Empire, founded on the religion of Islam, served as a counterweight to the Byzantine Empire in the eastern Mediterranean. The Islamic religion drew heavily on the Judeo-Christian tradition and Islamic culture absorbed a great deal of Hellenistic philosophy and science.

The rise of Arab power wiped out the Persian Empire and negated the successes of the Byzantine emperor Heraclius. Before they appeared on the stage of history, the Arabs had lived in tribes on the fringes of the Byzantine and Persian worlds. Then, unified by their new religion, the tribes had become a formidible force that swept out of the Arabian Peninsula to conquer the whole Middle East, North Africa, and Spain.

THE EMERGENCE OF THE ISLAMIC WORLD

The Arabian Peninsula in Ancient Times

We know a great deal more about the origins of Christianity than we do about the origins of Islam, mainly because Christianity arose from a literate society whereas Islam emerged from a largely illiterate society. There is no body of Arabic literature that we can turn to in search of the seminal ideas of Islam.

The Arabian Peninsula had been known to the great civilizations of the ancient world for millennia. The Sumerians imported spices from Yemen and Oman in the south of the peninsula, and the Romans controlled the north and northwest

(OPPOSITE) POTTERY BOWL FROM IRAN, TENTH CENTURY.

and traded along the western coast. The Romans called the southern region Arabia Felix (Arabia the Fortunate), because it was the source of rare goods like myrrh (the basis of incense), perfumes, and medicines. The Persians held the northeast, with trade routes down the eastern coast and through the Persian Gulf, and they too traded for the spices of the south. Most important, the Arabian Peninsula lay athwart the trade routes between the Mediterranean world and the Far East.

The ancient kingdom of Yemen exercised direct control of trade at the midpoint of those routes and dominated the interior of the peninsula. During the third century, however, Yemen encountered strong competition from Abyssinia, on the African shore of the Red Sea. With Roman support, the Abyssinians had gained control of Yemen by the beginning of the fourth century.

During the fifth century, missionaries from Egypt converted Abyssinia to Christianity, and the Abyssinians in turn forced the Yemenites to accept Christianity. Seiz-

ing the opportunity, the Persians interfered in Yemen and fueled religious and political resistance to the Abyssinians. The Byzantines, who had inherited Roman interests in the region, supported the Abyssinians in this contest. Finally, in the 590s, when the Persian armies were beginning their final assault on the Byzantine Empire, the Yemenites reasserted their independence from the Abyssinians.

The Arabian kingdoms in the southern part of the peninsula, as well as the imperial powers of the Mediterranean had tried repeatedly to win control of the interior deserts so that they could control the trade routes, but none of their political arrangements had lasted for very long. The nomadic Bedouins had clung to their independence and to their ancient pagan culture and had ignored the meddling of outside powers. The Abyssinians had had some success, however, because their bishops had managed to establish bishoprics in some of the larger camps during the early seventh century. Perhaps as a result of that experience, several of the tribes came together in a confederation and defeated Persia in 604 or 611—the date is uncertain. The defeat meant little to the Persians, but it taught the Arabs that unity brought strength.

On the western coast of the peninsula, several towns served as way stations along the trade routes. Members of various tribes lived in each town, and the town itself was a kind of coalition of tribes. Medina and Mecca, two of the most important towns, were active in the international trade and cooperated in trying to keep the Bedouin tribes in the surrounding area under control. The role of these traders grew stronger as the imperial powers to the north weakened one another in constant war. At the beginning of the seventh century, the tribes' demonstration that they were capable of taking independent action, together with their victory over the Persians, gave rise to an Arab ethnic movement among the Arabs throughout the peninsula. The coastal cities led the movement, and Mohammed, who was born around 570 into one of the leading tribes of Mecca, became its principal figure.

Pre-Islamic Arabian Towns

Arabian towns originated in two ways, as settlements of an oasis and as religious precincts. Medina and Mecca illustrate the types perfectly.

Medina is located in an oasis, which gave it its wealth. The town's population was organized into tribal groups, each controlling a district of the town-oasis, with its housing, shops, and agricultural fields. The organization of the town differed greatly, therefore, from that of Hellenistic, Persian, and Roman towns. There was no central government, just a council of tribal elders that dealt only with matters that had to be faced in common, including defense, roads, and external affairs. All other matters were left to the tribes.

Mecca was founded on a holy shrine, the Ka'aba, a black rock cube. The shrine was tended by holy men, and because the men of the desert visited it regularly, the local tribes settled around it to profit off the pilgrims. Within the area immediately around the shrine, no one was permitted to bear weapons, so the holy precinct became a place where feuds could be settled. The holy men served as arbitrators and go-betweens. Thus, from ancient times Mecca was a holy place that played an important role in the politics of western Arabia.

Mohammed and the Creation of Islamic Religion

Around 610, Mohammed began to tell friends and relatives about his religious experiences. He felt that he was in direct communication with God and that God was revealing to him both God's nature and the obligations of men and women to God. Around 613, Mohammed began to speak of the revelations in public, and a small following formed around him. Most of the townspeople, however, were hostile to him, and eventually he was driven from Mecca.

The basic tenets of Mohammed's religion are that Allah, the name for God in Islam, is good and omnipotent; that Allah will judge all men on the last day and assign them either to heaven (the garden) or to hell (the fire); that men should be grateful to and should worship Allah for making the world as it is; that Allah expects men to be generous with their wealth, which comes from him; and that Mohammed, as the prophet of Allah, warns men that the last judgment is coming. These tenets, though clearly influenced by the Jewish and Christian religions, were not copied directly from them.

The leading merchants, offended by a teaching that urged all men to be generous with their wealth, tried to get the members of Mohammed's tribe to silence him. But the tribe protected him until about 619, when there was a change in its leadership. The new chief, himself a prosperous merchant, tried to force Mohammed to cease his preaching. Mohammed refused, and in 622, failing to find another protector, he left Mecca for Medina, where he found powerful supporters.

The journey to Medina, known as the *hegira* (journey), was later considered the founding event of Islam, as the crucifixion of Jesus was the beginning of Christianity. In fact, Moslems—those who follow the teachings of Mohammed—reckon their years from the *hegira*. (In English, the dates are followed by "A.H."—"After Hegira.") In Medina, Mohammed created an Islamic community and established the rules by which such a community should

Mecca and the Background of Islam

As a holy place, Mecca gave its inhabitants an opportunity to deal with the Bedouins on religious grounds. Mohammed's grandfather, Hashim, took advantage of this to create a large alliance based on the Ka'aba, the holy rock of Mecca. He persuaded the tribes along the trade route on the western coast of Arabia to honor special holy days of Mecca as days of truce, and, over time, he extended both the number of holidays and the number of tribes that honored them. In this way, he brought peace and prosperity to the trade route.

Hashim's religious and trade alliance depended on the willingness of the Meccans to keep their own greed in check, to maintain both their cooperation and the good will of the Bedouins. By Mohammed's time, that self-control had broken down, and many of the Bedouin tribes had left the alliance. One aim of Mohammed's preaching was to restore the restraint at the base of his grandfather's system.

live. He instituted dietary rules similar to those of the Jews and prohibited the drinking of wine, gambling, and usury. (In modern speech, "usury" refers to the charging of exorbitant interest, but in Islam and in medieval Christianity it referred to the charging of any interest.) He set up a legal system that substituted arbitration for blood feuds, prohibited infanticide, and regulated inheritance so that the rights of orphans and widows were secure. He put limits on polygamy and divorce: A man could not have more than four wives at one time, and a divorced wife was not to be sent away penniless.

Soon after his arrival in Medina, Mohammed and his followers began attacking caravans going to and coming from Mecca, and by 628 the attacks had evolved into a routine war of attrition. Then, with about 1,500 followers, Mohammed joined the annual pilgrimage to the holy shrine of the Ka'aba, a cube of black rock, in Mecca. When the Meccans refused to let him in, he negotiated with them and got them to agree that he could return the next year and that they would evacuate the town for three days during his stay.

During the following year, Mohammed proceeded to incorporate Bedouin tribes from the surrounding area into the

The holy Kaaba in modern Mecca is the most sacred Islamic shrine.

Islamic state of Medina. When he returned to Mecca in 629, its leaders recognized the futility of resistance and submitted to Islam and to his authority. The leaders of the Meccan tribes now began to serve as leaders of the Islamic state, though its administrative center remained in Medina.

The Founding of the Arabic Empire

War was endemic among the Bedouin tribes until Mohammed redirected their passion for war towards religious objectives. In time, Islamic leaders devised a rationale for wars fought for Allah. Such a war was called a *jihad* (holy war).

In 630, Mohammed himself led an army north against the Byzantine provinces. He also encouraged Bedouin attacks on the Persian Empire, already weakened by Heraclius and by the murder of Shah Khusro II (628). Before his death in June 632 Mohammed had extended Arabic influence into the kingdom of Yemen, which became part of the Islamic state when its population converted.

The death of Mohammed created a crisis, because he had made no provision for a successor. But the crisis was resolved when the leaders of the state, the men who had followed Mohammed to Medina in 622, elected one of his earliest followers, Abu Bakr, as caliph (representative or vicar of the prophet). Abu Bakr (r. 632–34) completed the work of bringing the Arabic tribes into the Islamic state and prepared the way for expansion of Arabic power beyond the peninsula.

His successor, Omar (r. 634–44), launched the conquests that helped create a new empire. Damascus fell in 635, Jerusalem in 638, and soon the Arabs were in control of all of Syria and Palestine. Jerusalem, along with Medina and Mecca, became a holy city of Islam. In 637, the Bedouin alliance that had earlier defeated the Persians seized the imperial Persian capital at Ctesiphon. Soon the Arabs were in control of the entire Persian Empire. Now they began to push east, and in 643 Arab raiders from Persia reached India. Meanwhile, between 640 and 642, Arab forces conquered Egypt—though the Byzantines held on to Alexandria until 646—and moved on along the North African coast as far as Tripoli. In the Mediterranean an Arab fleet defeated the Byzantines, and by the middle of the seventh

century the Arabs had occupied Cyprus. The Arab navy kept constant pressure on Constantinople until Leo the Isaurian destroyed it in 718 (p. 175).

This new empire was governed by a theocracy, and as Mohammed had done the caliphs exercised both spiritual and secular authority. The central government ruled the newly acquired provinces through colonies populated by Bedouin tribes. Mohammed had tried to suppress the tribes altogether to create a unified Islamic society, but his successors left the tribes intact, satisfied with their loyalty to the Islamic state. Under Omar and his successors, the tribes became agents of the government. They lived isolated from the conquered populations and carried out their military and administrative functions from a distance. Each colony had a governor appointed by the central government in Medina.

Though a theocracy, the Islamic government did not enforce conversion to Islam. Non-Moslems had to pay a heavy

The Growth of the Islamic Empire   632–750

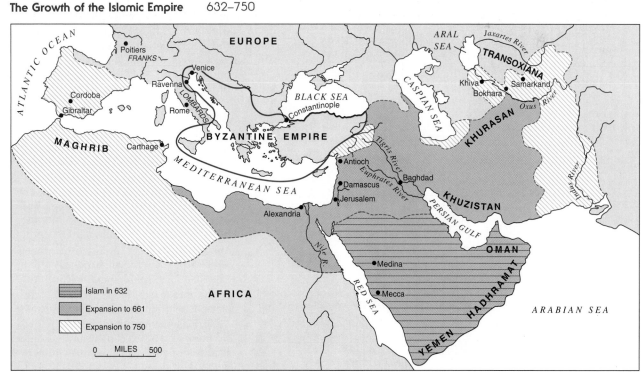

land tax and could not serve in the government, but they suffered no other disabilities. Aloof from their subjects, the Arabs came to view their empire as "a garden protected by our spears." Waging war by land was their special talent. When they needed a fleet, they ordered the subject populations to build and man the ships.

THE ISLAMIC COMMUNITY

Mohammed's mission lasted from about 610 until his death in 632. His followers memorized his revelations—called *koran*—but the uncertainties of oral transmission were recognized early, and the third caliph, Othman (r. 644–56), had them recorded in the *Koran,* the holy book of Islam.

Part of Mohammed's legacy was his ways (*sunna*) as head of the *umma,* the community of Islam. After his death, the inner circle of officials around the caliphs engaged in frequent discussions about what this or that action meant for the governance of the state. As a result, an extensive body of stories and commentaries relating to the *sunna* grew up. Unlike the revelations, these items could not be set

Mohammed choosing Ali as his heir.

down in simple form, and over time the *sunna* tradition became an elaborate body of lore relating to the nature of Islamic government and society.

As in any theocracy, religious disagreement in the Islamic state nearly always had political consequences, and vice versa. For example, the first civil war in the *umma* originated in a dispute over the succession to the caliphate. Omar, the second caliph, had confirmed that election by the inner circle of government officials should determine the succession. But when Omar was murdered by a Persian slave in 644, the electors faced a difficult choice. They all agreed that the succession must remain within the Hashimite clan, to which Mohammed had belonged (named for Mohammed's grandfather). But that clan included both direct descendants of Hashim and those who joined the clan through marriage. In 644, the leading members of the clan were Ali, Mohammed's cousin and son-in-law, and Othman, a member of the Ommayyad clan, who had married two of Mohammed's daughters.

The decision went to Othman, who, though a wealthy and urbane man, proved unable to deal with the growing financial problems of the Empire. Othman's enemies, encouraged by Ali, accused him of violating the *sunna.* In 656 Othman was murdered by a faction that included men of high standing in Ali's party.

The murder led to a civil war between Ali and Mu'awiya, a relative of Othman and governor of Syria. Mu'awiya demanded the blood revenge permitted by the *Koran.* After inconclusive skirmishing, the choice of a new caliph was handed over to two arbitrators, who disagreed. At this point, a group of fanatical supporters of Ali called Kharijites ("those who withdrew or rebelled") withdrew from his army, claiming that arbitration was contrary to the *Koran.* Ali had most of the Kharijites massacred, but in 658 one of them murdered him. Mu'awiya was then elected caliph and managed to persuade Ali's sons to acquiesce in the new regime. He then moved the capital of the Islamic state to Damascus and did away with the practice of electing the caliph.

The contest between Mu'awiya and Ali led to an enduring division within Islam between the Shiites (the party of Ali) and the Sunnis (the party of the Ommayyads). Ali's claim to the caliphate rested on his hereditary rights, but he also claimed to be a stricter follower of the *Koran* and the *sunna* than Mu'awiya was. The party of Mu'awiya responded that the Ommayyads preserved the truly orthodox *sunna* and that their victory made the Sunnis the orthodox party of Islam. The remnants of the Kharijites also developed distinctive religious views and remained a force in the Islamic world.

Even after the Ommayyads gained control of the caliphate, the Islamic state remained divided and difficult to govern. Arabic society was tribal at base, and even Mohammed had failed to suppress the ancient tribal authority. The first caliphs seem to have recognized the permanence of that authority, and, as we have seen, they used the tribes to help govern the newly conquered territories. Significantly, this practice seems to have arisen in Persia, which had been conquered by tribal armies. Those armies had been settled at Kufa and Basra in lower Mesopotamia in camps that soon became substantial tribal cities, like Mecca and Medina themselves.

Though we can speak of a *Pax Islamica* (Islamic Peace), the Arab Empire never achieved the administrative and political unity achieved by the Roman Empire and the Persian Empire, or by its contemporary, the Byzantine Empire. In the vast stretches of the Arab Empire, it seems that a tribal society simply worked best and that a formal imperial system conducted by a distant central government was an impossibility.

From the very beginning of the Islamic state, the Arabs regarded themselves as the people of Allah, and Islamic law granted them substantial privileges—including freedom from taxation and the right to serve in the army and in government. Those privileges were denied to other ethnic groups even after their conversion to Islam. Consequently, opponents of the caliph could always count on the support of the *mawali,* as the non-Arab converts were called.

THE OMMAYYADS

Further Conquests

The Ommayyad dynasty (661–750) signaled the ascendancy of the urban aristocracy over the Bedouins who had carried out the early conquests under the theocracy of Medina. Mu'awiya and his successors resumed the policy of conquest, though at a slower pace. They were interested in organizing and exploiting the territories they won, and that took time. They had only slight success in Asia Minor, where the Hellenistic population led by the Byzantine emperor put up stiff resistance. In the north, however, Arab armies reached the Caucasian Mountains between the Black Sea and the Caspian Sea and pushed into Samarkand, where they could control the trade route from central Asia to India and the Middle East. In India, around 710, they crossed the Indus River and established a loosely governed territory in the Sindh (modern Pakistan). Over the next generation the Arab governors suppressed the local rulers and organized the territory, including portions of the Punjab and Kashmᶦr, into a province of the Empire. The local populations managed to check further expansion, but contemporary sources indicate that they did not fully recognize the seriousness of the threat.

At the end of the seventh century, Arab armies moved westward from Tripoli. Here they met strong resistance from

Early Islamic calligraphy. Calligraphy was highly developed by Moslem artisans in part because of the religious proscription on representational art.

An Islamic coin (698–99), the first silver coinage struck of purely Islamic type. The inscription in the center of the coin reads: "There is no God but God alone; no one is associated with him." The insistence on God's oneness and the denial of an associate to him is directed against the Christians and their doctrine of the Trinity.

ca. 570	632	661	750		1258
Life of Mohammed	First Four Caliphs	Ommayyad Dynasty		Abbasid Dynasty	

the Byzantine garrisons supported by the Berber tribes of the North African desert. Carthage finally fell to the Arabs in 698 after they had defeated the Byzantine fleet that was bringing reinforcements. Following this success, the Berbers converted to Islam and joined the march westward. Morocco was occupied within the next ten years. In 711, the Berber leader Tarik led a force across the Straits of Gibraltar (gibal-Tarik, "the rock of Tarik") into Visigothic Spain.

Because the attack came at a time when the Visigothic kingdom was experiencing internecine war, victory was relatively easy. Within a few months, Toledo, the capital of the kingdom, fell to the invaders. With the help of Arab reinforcements from North Africa, the army occupied some of the fortified cities that had held out, including Seville. After pausing briefly to consolidate their conquests, the new Islamic rulers took control of the entire peninsula, except for a narrow strip along the southern foothills of the Pyre-

nees, where the Christian kingdom of Asturias clung to a precarious existence. In 720, the Moors (as the Spanish called the North Africans and their Arab allies) moved into Septimania and converted it into a base for raids to the north. Throughout the eighth century, the Franks struggled to push the Moors back into the Iberian Peninsula.

Ommayyad Society and Culture

Under the Ommayyad dynasty, the Arabs continued their lenient policy toward the conquered peoples. They taxed non-Moslems heavily but otherwise left them alone. Nonetheless, the pace of conversion to Islam accelerated during the seventh and eighth centuries, perhaps because the non-Arabs wanted to escape taxes.

The loss of taxes created a fiscal problem and caused many caliphs to insist that the new converts continue to pay them. Otherwise, the caliphs soon discovered,

The Great Mosque in Damascus, Syria, begun in the late seventh century.

they could not balance the budget. This policy annoyed the converts and made them a ready audience for opponents of the government. In fact, many of the converts turned to Arab noblemen for protection and support, creating a kind of client class dependent on Arab leaders.

Surprisingly, it was the language of the Arab nomads that won out over the languages of the subject peoples, many of whom were highly civilized. That was less surprising in Syria and Palestine, where the populations spoke related Semitic languages, than it was in Persia, Egypt, and North Africa. The Ommayyads contributed to the ascendancy of Arabic by making it the official language of government, but a more powerful influence was the emergence of an Arabic intellectual and literary culture during the Ommayyad period.

Poetry was the most popular literary genre, as it had been in pre-Islamic Arabia. Ommayyad poets wrote romantic and satirical poetry, as well as odes extolling the good life. There were Christian poets as well as Moslem poets, a reflection of the caliphs' policy of toleration.

The new imperial bureaucracy also adapted Arabic to the prosaic needs of government. To make Arabic, a language of the desert, function as an official language, the educated bureaucrats enlarged its vocabulary and gave it a formal grammatical structure. The new grammar made the language more precise and regular and enabled foreigners to learn it more quickly. The improved language also served as a good medium for theology, philosophy, and history. The earliest intellectual works in Arabic date from the end of the Ommayyad period. Though few of those works survive, quotations from them were often incorporated into later writings.

The Arabic tradition in architecture and in the decorative arts also emerged under the Ommayyads. In Damascus, they built a great mosque, a place of prayer, in a form influenced by the Roman basilica, with a long nave and side aisles. The design was copied in mosques elsewhere in the Empire. In Jerusalem, the Ommayyads built a huge mosque on the site sacred to the Jews, the Dome of the Rock, which enclosed a vast central space. This building too was imitated elsewhere.

A distinctive style of domestic architecture was favored for the desert palaces where the Ommayyads spent much of their time. Many of these palaces, of impressive size and richly decorated, contained apartments, private mosques, baths, and formal gardens. During this period, the contrast between town and desert became an established feature of the Islamic culture. Paradoxically, the city

The Dome of the Rock in Jerusalem. This mosque was built on the spot from which Mohammed was believed to have ascended to heaven.

Detail from a portal of an Ommayyad palace in Syria (*ca.* 720).

populations of Syria, Iraq, and Egypt embraced the Arabic language and Arabic culture, while the Arabs themselves kept to the desert and cherished their ancient Bedouin ways. The great palaces and hunting lodges of the Ommayyads symbolized the appeal of the desert but were in fact islands of urban comfort.

The Ommayyad caliphs maintained the distinction between Arabs and non-Arabs long after the actual power of government had passed into the hands of *mawali* officials and generals. By the eighth century, the *mawali* constituted a majority of the community of Islam, suggesting that a major change in the nature of the caliphate was imminent.

THE RISE OF THE ABBASIDS

The Collapse of the Ommayyad Caliphate

Although the Ommayyads made claims to orthodoxy, their court scandalized many Moslems. The palace at Damascus and the desert resorts of the caliphs were centers of luxury that offended hardy Arab tribes-

men and gave the *mawali* an opportunity for complaint. Moreover, the Ommayyads associated with non-Moslems and copied Byzantine governmental institutions that were unfamiliar and suspect to men of the desert. Their concern for the large Christian and Jewish communities of Syria, and the presence of educated Christians and Jews in the government, often in high positions, contributed further to the popular view that the Ommayyad government was verging toward the secular.

The Ommayyads were even accused of favoring the *mawali* community over the Arabs. Faced with almost constant financial crisis, the Ommayyad caliphs introduced new tax and financial schemes to bring the budget under control. These schemes proved particularly offensive to the subject populations, which had become progressively islamicized. Furthermore, the caliphs seemed unable to exercise regular administrative control over the provinces. Often the provincial governors, feeling their position threatened, rebelled against the central government with the support of their tribal contingents and the local *mawali*. Each time, the rebellious governor justified himself by charging the caliph with heterodoxy.

The endless war with the Byzantines also provoked opposition. During a century of conflict, the balance of victories had gone to Constantinople, with the caliphs investing enormous resources without winning either spoils or territory. The great naval and land defeats at Constantinople in 717–18, when Leo the Isaurian outsmarted and outfought the caliph's superior forces (pp. 174–75), were only the most spectacular examples of failure. Even though the caliphs' armies had some successes in the East—with the establishment of Moslem states in the Transoxiana and in the Indus Valley—few of the Ommayyads could claim to be noteworthy conquerors.

The main opposition to Damascus was centered in Iraq, the old heartland of the Persian Empire. It was in the Persian province of Khurasan, however, on the plains south of the Oxus River, that the last rebellion against the Ommayyads took

place, in the aftermath of a civil war among rivals within the Ommayyad clan. In 747, when the victor in this war, Marwan II (r. 749–50), tried to consolidate his power over the provincial governors, the governor of Khurasan Abu Muslim, of Persian descent, rebelled.

In this rebellion, tribal and religious rivalries joined with *mawali* anti-Arab sentiments. Khurasan had been converted by Shiite missionaries from Kufa in southern Iraq, the center of Shiism. Abu Muslim therefore declared that he was rebelling in the name of the Shiite *imam* (leader of prayers, religious leader) Ibrahim, a descendant of al-Abbas, an uncle of Mohammed (hence Abbasids). He thus brought the Shiites into his rebellion against the Sunni caliphs. Moreover, Kufa had been established by Yemenite tribesmen who favored the Shiites and the hereditary rights of the house of Mohammed had never been satisfied with the Ommayyads, whom they considered outsiders. Thus, by allying himself with the Shiites, Abu Muslim took advantage also of the ancient tribal rivalry between the Yemenites and Ommayyads.

The Ommayyads succeeded in imprisoning Ibrahim, who died in captivity, but they could not muster an army that could defeat Abu Muslim's forces. In November 749, Abu Muslim had Abu'l-Abbas, Ibrahim's brother, declared caliph in Kufa. Early in 750, Abu Muslim defeated and executed Marwan.

The first official act of the Abbasids was a systematic massacre of the Ommayyad clan, missing only one young boy. That boy, Abd al-Rahman, escaped with his supporters to Spain, where he established an independent Ommayyadc caliphate at Cordova. Thereafter, Spain remained outside the political power of Baghdad.

THE ABBASID CALIPHATE

The Abbasids represented the old Arab leadership and had in fact claimed the caliphate by virtue of their being members of Mohammed's tribe. And yet their accession accelerated the integration of the *mawali,* particularly the Persians, into the society and politics of the *umma.* The second Abbasid caliph, al-Mansur (r. 754–75), built a new capital a few miles from the old Persian capital at a place with the Persian name of Baghdad. Doing so, he completed the transition from an Arab Empire to an Islamic Empire.

Al-Mansur relied principally on Persian officials, and Abbasid government was soon run by a Persian bureaucracy under a new official, called the *wazir* or *vizier,* a kind of prime minister. The Persian *wazir* Khalid b. Barmak established his family as the leaders of the bureaucracy, and until 803 Barmakids were the most powerful members of the government. The court adopted many of the old Persian ways, and the caliphs, like the old Persian shahs, became inaccessible in a palace community of officials and eunuchs.

Soon after they came to power, the Abbasids turned away from their traditional support of Shiites and began to favor the Sunnis. By this time the Sunnis constituted the majority of Islam, and Shiism was deeply divided. As a result of this shift, however, the dynasty faced two Shiite rebellions early in its history.

Al-Mansur succeeded in restoring control over the provinces, except in Spain and the Maghrib (Tunisia, Algeria, and Morocco). In the Maghrib, the ancient Berber tribes asserted their independence once again, as they had under Roman domination. They defeated every force sent out by the central government, partly because the war between the Byzantine and Arab fleets made it impossible for the caliphs to secure supply lines to the distant province.

For a time after the move from Damascus to Baghdad the hostility between the caliphate and the Byzantines declined, but in the late eighth century it flared up once again. The Byzantine emperors were still trying to consolidate their eastern provinces and their eastern frontier, and warfare resumed in that region.

Although Al-Mansur's son, al-Mahdi (r. 775–85), fought the Byzantines with considerable success, he had to concentrate most of his attention on the internal affairs of the Islamic state. He was particularly challenged by a religious movement called Manichaeanism. The Manichaeans were followers of Mani, a third-century

Persian priest who had brought Zoroastrianism, the old Persian religion, together with Christianity in a kind of amalgam. The result was a belief in two world powers, one good and one evil, locked in a titanic struggle for supremacy. The sect had troubled both Islam and Christianity for centuries. Augustine, one of the fathers of Latin Christianity (pp. 118–19), went through a Manichaean phase in his youth, and the sect reappeared in Europe in the late eleventh century. Al-Mahdi carried out terrible purges ostensibly of Manichaeans, but most of the people he killed were not Manichaeans at all. He seems to have used the Manichaean threat as an excuse for ridding Islam of both its religious enemies and his own enemies.

Al-Mahdi was particularly taken with Persian customs and ceremonies. He

Hunting scene woven into a seventh-century fabric.

Islam *ca. 888*

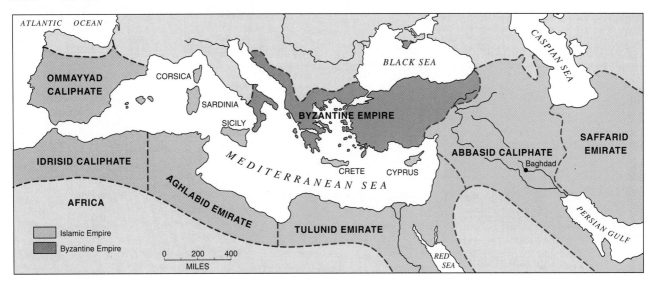

spent most of his time in leisure pursuits, leaving the government to be run, and run well, by his Barmakid *wazir* and Persian secretaries. Under al-Mahdi the Baghdad court became a famous center of art and entertainment.

Westerners became aware of the splendor of the Islamic court during the reign of Harun al-Rashid (r. 786–809), who received two embassies from the Frankish king Charles the Great. In turn, al-Rashid sent spectacular gifts (including an elephant) to Charles. The purpose of these exchanges seems to have been to plan a joint attack on Ommayyad Spain, though that attack never occurred. Al-Rashid carried out massive raids in Asia Minor and reached the Aegean Sea in 798 when the Byzantine government was in disarray under Irene (pp. 179–80).

Al-Rashid was obliged, however, to recognize the *de facto* independence of the Maghrib and to grant the governor of the province independent authority in return for a substantial annual tribute. He also agreed to let the governorship become a hereditary position. Thus was born the Aghlabid emirate of North Africa, which acted aggressively toward Christendom a couple of decades later. Aghlabid forces undertook the conquest of Sicily in 827, attacked Rome in 846, and menaced the coastal cities of Italy throughout the ninth century.

Under al-Rashid, the Barmakids continued to run the government and to dominate the cultural life of the Islamic Empire. The Barkamids tried to effect a settlement between the Abbasids and the Shiites, and they encouraged active discourse on law, philosophy, and theology in the hope of finding a common ground for reconciliation. As a result of these efforts, the Barmakids were suspected of favoring the Shiites during the Shiite rebellion, and the family fell from power in 803.

After al-Rashid's death in 809, the political cohesion of the Empire dissolved. Khurasan became independent under a Persian dynasty (820). A rebel leader set himself up in Azerbaijan (the region around the southern shore of the Caspian Sea) and could not be put down. Refugees from Spain, fleeing from internal conflict there, took Crete from the Byzantines and held it for 135 years. They also stirred up unrest in Egypt. The spiritual authority of the caliphs was still recognized, but their political power had diminished to the point where they were becoming just one of many dynasties in the Empire.

Early mosque and minaret,
Samara, Syria (ca. 850).

However, under al-Rashid's successors the court remained a center of intellectual activity. Al-Rashid's son, al-Ma'mun (r. 813–33), founded a university, the House of Wisdom, and built several observatories for the study of astronomy. He encouraged theologians to turn to Greek philosophy in their search for ways of reconciling the many strains of Islam.

The Appearance of the Turks

The Turks were a group of Asiatic tribes that had moved into Turkestan, the region north of the Transoxiana, and first appeared in Islamic history toward the middle of the ninth century. The caliphs, remembering all the undependable armies that had plagued their predecessors, created an army of Turkish slaves. During the 840s, that army grew to such an enormous size—some sources say 70,000 men—and so disrupted life in Baghdad that the caliph Mutawakkil (r. 846–61) built new quarters for the government and the army at Samara, some distance from the city.

The Turks were loyal to the caliph's family, though they sometimes became embroiled in family conflicts. In 861, Turkish officers killed Mutawakkil, who was then in conflict with one of his sons. The following decade was a time of anarchy. Eastern Persia broke away immediately upon Mutawakkil's death and retained its independence until about 910. Tulun, a Turk who was provincial governor in Egypt and had at his command a large slave army, seized control of the province in 871; his family retained control until 905. But trouble with the Turkish slaves paled beside that caused by black slaves in southern Mesopotamia. In 868, they started a dangerous revolt.

As in other ancient societies, slavery was common in the Islamic world. The *Koran* condoned slavery but also encouraged emancipation. Most slaves served either as soldiers or as personal secretaries and servants, and a good many of them gained their freedom. In the lower valleys of the Tigris and Euphrates, however, masses of black African slaves worked on sugar plantations under horrible conditions. When they rebelled in 868 the caliphs were powerless to put them down. A reign of terror raged over the region until 883, when the rebellion was crushed.

Following the end of the rebellion the Empire experienced a brief period of recovery under the Abbasid caliph al-Muktafi (r. 902–08). Under his successors, however, the provinces failed to satisfy the central government's demands for taxes and instability set in once again. In 924, the government put a military officer, the Turk Mu'nis, in control who transformed the government into a military dictatorship. He held the title *emir,* and from that point on the caliphs exercised only religious authority.

Throughout these troubled years, the power of the army, now led and manned primarily by Turks, grew steadily. What finally forced the government to surrender its authority to the army was the rise of the Isma'ili movement in North Africa.

THE ISMA'ILIS AND THE RISE OF THE FATIMID CALIPHS

The Isma'ili party was a splinter group of the Shiites. Al-Husain, the first martyr of Islam, was a son of Ali by Fatima, and the imams of his line succeeded one another without incident for six generations. Then, however, the imam Ja'far disinherited his eldest son and presumed heir, Isma'il, for not obeying the tenets of Islam. Ja'far named his younger son Musa as next in line for the imamate. Although Isma'il died before his father, a small party of Husainites insisted on Isma'il's right of succession and became "the Seveners"

(that is, seven generations), or Isma'ilis. Musa succeeded as imam in 765, and his line lasted until the twelfth imam disappeared in Baghdad in the 870s. The followers of that imam, who constituted the main body of Husainites, were known as "the Twelvers."

The Isma'ilis believed that Isma'il was the *mahdi,* the hidden imam who would return to lead Islam to the true religion. In 909, a group of Isma'ilis seized control of North Africa and, believing Ubaid Allah al-Mahdi to be the *mahdi,* proclaimed him caliph in opposition to the Abbasid caliph. Ubaid and his successors were known as Fatimids, because they were descendants of Fatima.

The Fatimid caliphs were determined to replace the Abbasids as the true leaders of Islam. Ubaid's son, al-Ka'im (r. 934–46), built a fleet that terrorized the central Mediterranean and attacked the coast of France and Italy. He also made a third attempt—the first two under Ubaid had failed—to conquer Egypt as a stepping stone to Baghdad. Egypt was finally conquered in 969 by al-Ka'im's grandson, al-Mu'izz (r. 953–75).

By 959, al-Mu'izz had won control of almost all of North Africa out to the Atlantic Ocean and had confined the Ommayyads of Spain to small enclaves near Gibraltar. During the first fifteen years of his reign, al-Mu'izz, with the help of two of his ministers, neither of them Arab, established the Fatimid military and administrative systems, which lasted into the fifteenth century. The architect of his military system was a general named Jawhar, an islamicized Greek slave who had led the conquest of North Africa and then of Egypt. Recognizing the strategic importance of the Nile Delta and the danger posed by the Byzantines, who had recaptured Crete (961), Jawhar and al-Mu'izz built a new capital at Cairo, which soon became known as one of the most beautiful cities in the Mediterranean world.

The architect of the administrative system was al-Mu'izz's *wazir* Ya'qub b. Killis, an islamicized Jew from Baghdad who served both al-Mu'izz and his successor al-'Aziz (r. 975–96). Through enlightened taxation and other well-conceived

The ibn-Tulun Mosque in Cairo, Egypt (eighth century).

measures, Ya'qub encouraged traders to travel through Egypt and the Red Sea on their way to the Far East and built a navy to protect Egyptian ports. Alexandria became once again, as it had been in Hellenistic and Roman times, one of the world's great emporia, and the new commercial powers of Italy—Amalfi, Venice, and Genoa—sent their merchants there to buy silk and spices for the expanding European market.

The Fatimids drew on the whole Mediterranean world in building their success and in bringing brilliance to their court. Al-'Aziz married a Christian, named Christians to high office, and permitted Jews and Christians to live in his realm without persecution or constraint. He also created a Turkish slave army to control the Berber troops that Jawhar had brought to Egypt. Al-'Aziz died in 996 at the age of 41, and under his son Al-Hakim (r. 996–1021),

who was then 13, the caliphate soon fell into decline.

Al-Hakim persecuted Jews and Christians and executed, one after another, the ministers and generals he appointed. He would slip out of the palace secretly at night, and during one of his excursions he disappeared. His body was never found.

The Fatimids' push to Baghdad had already lost momentum, for three reasons: First, the resurgence of the Byzantines under Basil II (r. 976–1025) kept the Fatimids pinned down in Egypt and North Africa (pp. 185–86). Second, the Fatimids had become more and more conservative and as a result had lost the support of the fanatical Isma'ilis who controlled the land between Egypt and Baghdad. Finally, the Abbasid caliphate of Baghdad, supported by the Turkish emirs, had grown strong enough to resist the Fatimid threat.

THE RISE OF THE TURKS

The Background

The Turkish slave armies had given evidence of their power on several occasions during the ninth century, particularly in the 860s when they made and unmade caliphs at will. By 924, as we have seen, a Turkish emirate controlled the central government in Baghdad. After 945, however, Turkish power was checked by the Buyids, a family from Azerbaijan that seized power in Baghdad and installed its own candidate as caliph.

The Buyids were Shiites aligned with the Twelvers against the Isma'ilis (the Seveners). When they took control of Baghdad, however, they accommodated themselves to Sunni orthodoxy, which still dominated the *umma*. The Buyid family itself was rarely united, and during its dominance the provinces of Iraq and Persia were often governed by contesting members.

Competition among the Buyid rulers meant peace for outsiders living in the caliphate. The Christians, for example, most of whom were members of sects considered heretical by both the eastern and western churches, played a role in the cultural life of the caliphate and reinforced the influence of Greek learning on Arabic intellectuals. And the Jews during the tenth and eleventh centuries were much better off in the Middle East and Spain than were their coreligionists in Europe. In fact, both Jews and Christians found employment as teachers and government functionaries during these years.

Buyid power was limited to Iraq and the region along the southern flank of the Caucasus. To the west, the Hamdanid dynasty controlled northern Syria and upper Mesopotamia from the old city of Aleppo. The Hamdanids patronized artists and scholars and helped keep the Buyids in check. To the east, the Samanids, the first native Persian dynasty since the Arab conquest, controlled Khurasan.

The Samanids encouraged revival of Persian as the language of science and poetry. And their court poets and writers created a language called "New Persian," or Farsi. Although it was written in the Arabic alphabet and contained many Arab words, Farsi was nonetheless truly Persian, and it remains the language of Iran to this day.

The Samanids sent out missionaries to the Turks living beyond the Transoxiana. Ironically, that good work prevented the Samanids from fighting off the Turks when they began to move into the Transoxiana, because it was impossible for them to conduct a holy war, a *jihad*, against fellow Moslems. Between 999 and 1004, the power of the Samanids collapsed under the Turkish attacks.

The Turkish Dynasty of Ghazna: Afghanistan and India

Still further east, in the region that is now Afghanistan, a Turkish military leader in service to the Samanids established a dynasty at Ghazna. The Ghaznavids, as they were called, rose to power on the ruins of Samanid authority and gained control of the southern and eastern regions of Persia under the great ruler Mahmud (r. 998–1030). Mahmud was the patron of Firdawsi, a Persian poet whose great epic poem, the *Shah-nama*, is considered one of the masterpieces of Islamic literature.

Mahmud took over the small Islamic principalities that had been established in the Indus Valley early in the eighth century and had remained in place for three centuries without expanding their influence. They continued to be important in the trade between India and the Middle East, although the bulk of that trade now went by sea to Fatimid Egypt. Mahmud used these states as a basis for annual campaigns to the east, beyond the Indus. These campaigns opened India to Moslem missionaries and opened the Islamic world to the cultural influence of India.

Another Islamic intellectual who attracted Mahmud's patronage was al-Biruni (973–*ca.* 1050), who ranks with Aristotle in the breadth of his interests and achievements. Al-Biruni fell under the influence of Indian culture, an influence that is apparent in his works on mathematics and astronomy. He also wrote a remarkable book (*ca.* 1030) on India that remains an

The Eastern Islamic World

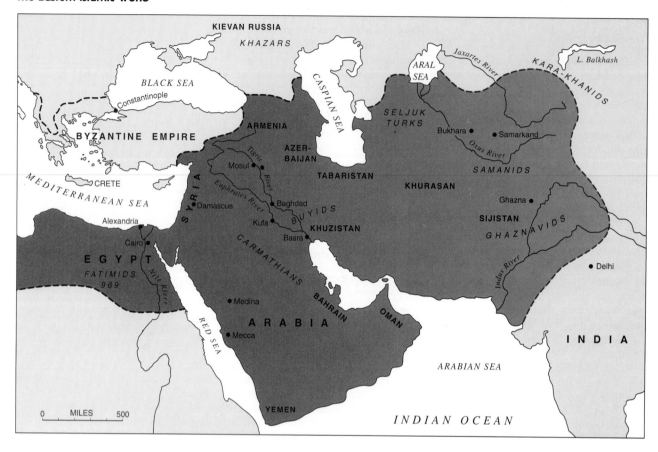

important source of our knowledge about medieval India.

The Coming of the Seljuk Turks

Mahmud pushed west as well as east. By the end of his reign, he had gained control of Khurasan and was ready to make an attempt on Iraq, where the Shiite Buyids still held sway. His plan was to reunify the caliphate under Sunni power, but that plan was spoiled by the irruption of the Seljuk Turks.

The Seljuks, named for an early chieftain, were nomadic people who had broken away from the main Turkish confederation that controlled the Transoxiana. In the 1020s, they moved into Khurasan and threatened Ghaznavid power. Mahmud's son and successor, Mas'ud I (r. 1030–40), tried to halt their advance, but in 1040 they defeated him in a decisive battle. Persia was open to the Seljuks, and Ghaznavid power shrank to the territories that are now Afghanistan and the Punjab in India, which Mahmud had organized as a Moslem state.

The Seljuks proceeded to implement Mahmud's plan themselves. In 1055, they invaded Iraq and occupied Baghdad. In the decades that followed, they established an empire within Islam, with a new form of political power. Instead of setting up an emirate, which was technically a governorship under the authority of the caliph, the Seljuks set up a sultanate, which was an independent political power loyal to the caliph.

Under Sultan Alp-Arslan (r. 1063–72), the Seljuks destroyed the Byzantine army at the battle of Manzikert (1071), in Armenia, and in 1077 his successor Malik-Shah (r. 1072–92) took Jerusalem. Their conquest of that holy city finally prompted a crusade that the Byzantines had tried to organize after their defeat at Manzikert (p. 186). Malik-Shah also took Damascus (1076) and established a powerful empire in the Middle East. Although the Seljuks managed to check the advance of the Fatimids, they were unable to conquer Egypt. Consequently the schism between the caliphs in Baghdad and those in Cairo continued until the rise of the Ottoman Turks in the fifteenth century.

Islamic Culture under the Seljuks

The Seljuks had been exposed to Persian culture by the Samanid missionaries, and once in power they encouraged Persian as the court language and were soon using it even in everyday life. Malik-Shah left the running of his empire to a brilliant Persian *wazir* named Nizam al-Mulk (1018–92). Nizam had served Malik-Shah's father, Alp-Arslan, and had acted as regent for Malik-Shah when he succeeded to the sultanate at the age of thirteen.

Nizam and Malik-Shah staged a Sunni renaissance after the long years of Shiite rule under the Buyids. In 1067, Nizam founded a school of law that became the intellectual center of Sunni Islam. One of the students, al-Ghazzali (1058–1111), became dissatisfied with the formalism of the law and went on to become the principal theologian of Islam. He wrote a massive work in which he stressed the importance of prayer and charity, and his ideas became the basis of the modern Sunni religion.

Al-Ghazzali turned away from philosophical and scientific speculation about the world and concentrated instead on the experience of the individual Moslem. In part as a result of his influence, the classical age of Islamic civilization is said to have ended around 1200.

During the reign of Malik-Shah a splinter group of Isma'ilis settled in the mountains of northern Persia around the fortress of Alamut, not far from modern Tehran. The leader of this group, Hasan-i Sabbah, hoped to find support for an anti-Seljuk (and anti-Sunni) rebellion. When he failed to do so, he organized a terrorist movement and sent agents to kill government officials and rulers throughout the sultanate. Orthodox Moslems, who believed that these agents chewed *hashish,* Indian hemp, before embarking on these suicide missions, called the terrorists "Assassins," from the name of the drug. Nizam al-Mulk died at the hands of an Assassin in 1092. Hasan-i died in 1124, but his movement lived on and for generations the Assassins were feared in the Islamic world.

After the death of Malik-Shah, the Seljuk empire broke into fragments under the control of individual leaders. There were Seljuk states in Asia Minor, Khurasan, Kirman (southwest of Khurasan), and Iraq. These states were so beset by internal problems that they were unable to resist the European invaders of Syria and Palestine, who arrived in the First Crusade in the late 1090s. As a result, the crusaders were able to establish the Latin kingdom of Jerusalem, which lasted for several generations.

Saladin and the Recovery of the Mediterranean Lands

Zengi, the Turkish governor of Mosul on the upper Tigris River, launched a counterattack against the Christians, and his recapture of Edessa in 1144 prompted a call for the Second Crusade. His son Nur al-Din (r. 1146–74) succeeded in confining the Europeans to small enclaves on the Mediterranean coast. A gifted ruler, Nur al-Din earned a reputation for good government and justice. Under his rule the Kurds, a people from northern Iraq, rose to prominence in the government and in the army, and one of their leaders, Saladin, emerged as a powerful military figure under Nur al-Din. Saladin led the defense of Egypt against attack by the Franks, who coveted Egypt's wealth and its control of trade with the East. By 1169, Saladin had taken over Egypt himself.

Saladin soon restored Egypt to peace and prosperity and expelled the Franks from Damietta, where they had established themselves during the Second Crusade (1147–49). After Nur al-Din's death in 1174, Saladin won out over rivals to succeed him in Mosul. Saladin (r. 1174–93) defeated the Byzantines in 1176, and after the emperor Manuel's death in 1180 the Byzantines became preoccupied by dynastic conflicts. This freed Saladin to concentrate on Palestine. In 1187 he invaded the Latin kingdom of Jerusalem and crushed its army, leaving the Christians with only the fortress city of Tyre and a strip of coast between Acre and Jaffa. In Europe, the call went out for a Third Crusade.

Saladin was known as a good ruler and a man of courtly manners. He put together a loosely united empire that included North Africa, Egypt, and the coastal regions of the Middle East up to Armenia. His family, the Ayyubids (named after Saladin's father, Ayyub), ruled this empire for sixty years after his death in 1193. Under the Ayyubids, Egypt remained prosperous, though not militarily strong. The commercial cities of Italy were permitted to trade there, ensuring Egypt's position in international trade.

THE MONGOL INVASION

In northern Persia and the Transoxiana, Khwarazm and its Seljuk government collapsed under assault by Oghuz tribesmen who appeared out of the central Asian steppes. At the same time, the Ghaznavids were overthrown by Ghurids, tribesmen from the foothills of the Hindu Kush who had recently converted to Islam. A new Persian dynasty, whose rulers used the old Persian title "shah," arose in Khwarazm and by the end of the twelfth century drove the Ghurids back beyond the Indus River.

In the first decades of the thirteenth century this dynasty, which was Shiite, tried to seize Baghdad, but in the midst of this effort the shah made a fatal error by ordering his men to massacre a caravan of merchants from central Asia. The merchants were Mongols, from an empire ruled by Chengis (Ghengis) Khan. To avenge the massacre, Chengis Khan attacked the Transoxiana in 1220 and overran it, using Chinese engineers to take the fortified towns by siege. In two years of campaigning, he totally destroyed the Kwarazmite state and then returned to Mongolia.

The next generation of Mongols launched a new phase of expansionism. They conquered Russia and pushed on into eastern Europe, reaching the Adriatic in 1241. Fourteen years later, the Mongol army, a composite of Mongol, Turkish, Armenian, and Georgian troops, moved into Persia and the Middle East. After destroying the Isma'ili Assassins, they marched on Baghdad. When the caliph failed to respond quickly enough to a demand that he open the gates, the Mongol army stormed the city and demolished it. According to the most conservative estimate, the Mongols slaughtered 800,000 people. Only Christians were spared, presumably because there were some Christians in the besieging army. The Abbasid caliphate, weakened by centuries of conflict, at last came to an end in 1258 when the last of the line surrendered to the Mongols.

By 1260, the Mongol army was in Syria, perhaps planning to set up a Mongol khanate in the Middle East. But when news arrived of the Great Khan's death in Mongolia, most of the army withdrew to the Caucasus to await the succession. The Mamluk Turks, who had won control of Egypt in 1250, now moved to halt the Mongol advance, and in late 1260 a Mamluk army routed the Mongol forces in Syria at Ain Jalut, near Nazareth, and broke the momentum of the Mongol conquest. Mamluk Egypt emerged as the most powerful state in Islam and remained so until the rise of the Ottoman Turks in the fifteenth century.

ISLAMIC SOCIETY AND ECONOMY

The Arabs came from a tribal society, and in the early years of the empire even their cities were controlled and organized by the tribes. But the towns had enough governmental organization to operate elaborate water systems and to maintain roads and fortifications. In time, the tribes lost some of their power and the towns became like those of other ancient cultures. The tradespeople lived in specific quarters, centered on the main mosque, and there is some evidence that they were organized into something like craft guilds. But we know almost nothing about those organizations.

The towns provided the major markets for wares and produced most of the manufactured goods. Long-distance traders brought in their goods by caravan and stored them in warehouses provided by the central government. After paying a duty on their cargoes, they sold their goods to the local townspeople. Wherever there was a caravansary (an inn for the caravans), the long-distance trade was kept separate from the local market, which was controlled by the town's own merchants.

Transactions were carried out by means of financial instruments that are still used in world trade. For example, Arab merchants used the letter of credit to transfer funds from one end of the Empire to the other. A merchant in one city would pay the bearer of a letter of credit a sum of money in full confidence that it would be paid over to his agent in another city. So long as there was a stable flow of goods in both directions, the principal merchants could assume that the accounts would balance. The Arabs also invented a kind of promissory note that evolved into the modern bank check. In fact, the word "check" probably derives from an Arabic word.

Islamic society was more tolerant of ethnic diversity than either Byzantine or European society. The Arabs intermarried with the local populations, and migrating peoples constantly added to the mix. Because most caliphs were the sons of slave women or of the lowborn wives of their royal sires, there was little room for the emphasis on racial purity that was so common in Constantinople and in the Germanic kingdoms.

The caliph's family served as a model for ordinary families in the society. The *Koran* permitted Moslems to have four wives and accepted the keeping of slave concubines. In practice, only wealthy men could afford to keep several wives and concubines, but most men above the lowest class had at least one wife and one concubine. So the typical Moslem household was large, with the wives and concubines, all their children, and the

The Moslem's Behavior around Women

Mohammed ordered women to cover their beauty, lest they become a cause of sin.

And let them [women] not display their beauty and ornaments except what [must ordinarily] appear thereof. And let them draw their garment over their bosoms and not display their beauty except in the presence of their husbands, or their own fathers, or their husbands' fathers, or their own sons, or their husbands' sons, or their own brothers, or their brothers' sons, or their sisters' sons. . . .

Koran 24:31

In his treatise (thirteenth century) about the duties of the muhtasib, *the law enforcement official of the medieval Islamic town, al-Ukhuwwa tells the muhtasib how to regulate the relations between men and women. The passage is headed "Reprehensible Conduct."*

The muhtasib must prevent people from placing themselves in dubious situations and from incurring suspicion. He must be timely in his warning and not hasten to punish. . . . The muhtasib may not interfere with a man and woman standing conversing in a frequented street and where their conduct shows no sign of offence. In an unfrequented street and in cases of doubt he must forbid them to continue yet must not be in haste to punish, for the woman may be closely related to the man. He must warn the man to keep the women of his family out of dubious situations. . . . The muhtasib must visit the places where women congregate, such as the thread and cotton markets, the riverbanks, and the doorways of the women's bath-houses. Any young men found there without lawful business must be punished by the muhtasib.

From The Ma'alim al-Qurba, *ed. and trans. by R. Levy (London: Luzac, 1938), pp. 9–10.*

household slaves. Most families had at least one or two slaves.

Moslem households were ruled by males, just as the desert tribes had been. Life in the desert depended on the cohesiveness of the group, and that in turn depended on the character of the leader. The quality of his leadership brought either honor or shame to the tribe and to himself and influenced the degree of respect the tribe commanded from other tribes. Islamic society continued to ascribe high value to the honor of men. Status, a measure of respect a man won from others, determined his every prospect—his

The caravansary at Siras-Kayser Road, Turkey. Merchants set up their booths under the arches. Centralization of foreign commerce made government control possible.

Moslem Values and the Behavior of a Prince

In the late eleventh century, Kai Ka'us Ibn Iskandar, ruler of a principality south of the Caspian Sea, wrote a treatise on how to be a prince for his son and heir. His advice gives a good picture of conventional Islamic social values, but it also contains advice to act expediently when necessary.

Much as you would not be parsimonious over kindly words, so also, if you have the means, do not begrudge your material largesse; men are more often beguiled by money than by words. Be on your guard against places of doubtful repute and flee from a companion who sets an evil example in conduct and thought. Do not of your own accord venture into dubious situations, and go only to places where, being sought, you may be discovered without shame. . . . The basis of all virtues consists of knowledge, discipline of the flesh, piety, truth, pure faith, innocuity, sympathy and modesty. As for modesty, although it is said "Modesty is part of faith," yet it may frequently happen that bashfulness is a misfortune to men. Do not therefore be so shamefaced as to cause failure or injury to your own interests. . . . Do not be over-hasty in shedding innocent blood, and regard no killing of Moslems to be lawful, unless they are brigands, thieves and grave-robbers or such whose execution is demanded by the law. . . . Yet do not neglect your duty where blood must rightfully be shed, for the general welfare demands it and out of remissness evil is born.

From A Mirror for Princes: the Oabus Nama, *trans. by R. Levy (New York: Dutton, 1951), pp. 23, 30, 88.*

success in trade and his chances of marrying well. Because every slight or injury was a challenge to a man's honor that had to be avenged, feud was endemic in Islamic society.

In Islamic law, women and men had virtually the same rights, but in everyday life men played the dominant role. Any improper approach to a man's wives or female servants was damaging to his status. It was injurious for someone even to mention the name of a man's wife in public. So women were closely protected and wore a veil whenever they left their home.

Within the household, all women and children lived in separate quarters called the harem. Several competing "families" lived in the harem, with each woman vying with the others to win favor with the head of the household for herself and her children. Mothers instructed their daughters in the household arts and in sex, to help them win favor with future husbands. Whatever influence the women had over the head of the household was exercised within the confines of the harem.

The inaccessibility of women may have contributed to the commonness of homosexual relations among Moslem men. Islamic society was tolerant of homosexuality, though foreigners found it scandalous. Although the percentage of men who were exclusively homosexual was probably no greater than in other societies, many Moslem men who ordinarily had relations with women also had occasional relations with men.

Perhaps the society's liberal attitudes toward racial and ethnic differences allowed men and women opportunities to rise from poverty and lowly status to wealth and, in the case of men, power. The Islamic aristocracy was less exclusive than its counterparts in the Byzantine Empire and Europe. Men often took wives and concubines from families less well placed than themselves, and their children enjoyed all the advantages of the household. Moreover, the educational system gave some talented young men an opportunity to enter the bureaucracy; others could grow rich through commerce. Islamic society was a society of self-made men.

ISLAMIC CIVILIZATION

Islamic civilization began in the attempt to turn the Arabic language into a medium of governmental and intellectual activity. Then it was transformed into a hybrid civilization by the revival of Persian literature and culture under the Saminids and the Seljuk Turks. Nonetheless, the acceptance of Arabic as the language of religion consolidated the Islamic world into a single intellectual community, and the availability of an inexpensive writing material—paper—sped the process along. The Chinese had used paper since about A.D. 100, but it did not become known to the Mediterranean world until 751, when Chinese prisoners of war were brought to Samarkand, north of the Transoxiana. From there, the use of paper spread to Baghdad, where a papermill was founded in 793, and then to Egypt (900) and Spain (950). The Europeans learned of paper from Spain, but as late as the thirteenth century paper was rare in Europe. By reducing the cost of written materials, the use of paper broadened the community of writers and readers.

Islamic civilization absorbed the philosophical and scientific traditions of Hellenistic culture, the astronomical and medical science of Persia and its predecessors in Mesopotamia, and the mathematics of India. ("Arabic" numerals came from India and were first used by Islamic writers in the late ninth century.) It also incorporated contributions from various ethnic groups in the population. The Syrian Christians were the heirs of the Hellenistic civilization and had translated many important Greek works into Syriac, including the works of Aristotle and other Greek authors. When those translations were subsequently translated into Arabic, they exerted a significant influence on Islamic philosophy and theology. Western Europeans rediscovered Aristotle through contact with Islamic and Jewish scholars in Spain, Sicily, and the Latin kingdom of Jerusalem and also received elaborate commentaries written by Moslem scholars. The most important of these commentaries were by the physician and scientist Ibn Sina (or Avicenna, 980–1037) and the philosophers al-Kindi and Ibn Rushd (or Averroes, 1126–98).

Ibn Sina was a Persian from Samarkand, al-Kindi was an Arab, and Ibn Rushd was a Moor from Spain. Although people from all over the Islamic world contributed to Islamic civilization, it was dominated by the Persians. The first great Islamic historian, Tabari (d. 923) was Persian, as were the mathematician and poet Omar Khayyam (d. 1123), the scientists al-Biruni (d. *ca.* 1050) and Ibn Sina, and the first scholar of comparative religion, Shaharastani (d. 1153). After the reemergence of Persian culture under the Samanids and Ghaznavids during the tenth century, Persian poetry and literature experienced a renaissance that continued under the Turks.

Advances in western Europe in the science of optics during the thirteenth century owed a great deal to discoveries made by Islamic scientists in their efforts to treat eye diseases, which were so prevalent in North Africa and the Middle East. Arabic medical works became available in Latin translations late in the twelfth century and served as the basis of medical study in Europe for centuries.

The study of medicine touched not just physiology and pharmacology, but all sciences: astronomy, physics, chemistry, botany, and optics. Arabic physicians dealt both with the bodily humors (fluids), which they believed caused disease when present in improper proportions, and with astronomical powers that they believed affected worldly events. Astrology, an ancient Babylonian science, had been kept alive by the successive civilizations of the Middle East and had spread throughout the Mediterranean Basin in Roman times. Christian writers of the late Roman period, notably Augustine (d. 430), condemned belief in astrology as a superstition, but the Arabs considered it a science. The influence of astrology grew in the West after Arabic medical texts became available to European physicians.

The Mongol invasion did serious damage to the Islamic civilization, as did the conquest of Spain by the Christians, who by the thirteenth century had pinned the Moslems down in the southern region of the peninsula. These events sharply reduced the intellectual activity in the two most vibrant centers of the Islamic world. Meanwhile, al-Ghazzali's theology (p. 213) had a deadening influence on philosophical and scientific pursuits. Ibn Rushd's work on Aristotle and on theology was meant as an answer to al-Ghazzali's school of thought, but it could not turn the tide. Because he argued that philosophy and religion were separable and contained different truths, he was condemned both in Islam and in Christendom, both of which insisted on the oneness of truth. For example, Ibn Khaldun (1337–1406), one of the most profound thinkers of Is-

lam, regarded all true knowledge as consistent with religious knowledge.

After about 1200, few creative minds were at work in Islam. Intellectual activity continued in places such as Egypt, which had escaped Mongol and Christian conquest, but the activity was repetitive and derivative at best, much like that of the later Byzantines. The true heirs of Arabic civilization were the Europeans, for whom the translations of Arabic works created an intellectual revolution during the twelfth and thirteenth centuries (see Chapter 11).

Today, most Westerners know little more about Islamic culture than what they perceive in the anti-Western fundamentalist movements of the contemporary Middle East. But we should be aware that Islam gave rise to a brilliant civilization that stretched from India to Spain and that influenced European civilization in countless ways. During the classical period, from the ninth to the twelfth century, Arabic poets, scientists, and philosophers were among the greatest in the world. They were making major advances in science and technology at a time when Europe was dominated by uneducated warlords and when no city in Europe could compare in size, intellectual activity, or commerce with even modest urban centers in the Islamic world. Arabic leaders who came into contact with Western crusaders found them unspeakably uncouth. By that time, Europe was approaching an intellectual renaissance of its own, but it would be a long time before Europe achieved the level of sophistication already achieved under Islam.

Suggestions for Further Reading

Islamic Religion

The basic source of Islamic religion is the *Koran* itself. A good translation is that of A. J. Arberry, *The Koran Interpreted* (1955). For a general history, see the *Cambridge History of the Islam,* 2 vols. (1970), a collection of excellent articles on all aspects of the civilization. M. G. Hodgson provides both a survey and an interpretation of Islamic history and civilization in *The Ven-*

ture of Islam, 3 Vols. (1974). J. J. Saunders, *A History of Medieval Islam* (1965); H. R. Gibb, *Mohammedanism: An Historical Survey* (1949); P. K. Hitti, *History of the Arabs,* 6th ed. (1958); B. Lewis, *The Arabs in History,* 4th ed. (1958); and F. Rahman, *Islam,* 2nd ed. (1979), are good brief surveys. B. Lewis published a large collection of sources in *Islam,* 2 vols. (1974).

The Arab Empire

On early Arabian history, see P. Crone, *Meccan Trade and the Rise of Islam* (1987). De Lacy O'Leary, *Arabia before Muhammad* (1927); M. Rostovtzeff, *Caravan Cities* (1932); and B. Thomas, *Arabia Felix* (1932), are still valuable. For a modern appreciation of Mohammed, see H. N. Kennedy, *The Prophet and the Age of Caliphates* (1986); T. Andrae, *Mohammed, the Man and his Faith* (1952); and W. M. Watt, *Muhammad at Mecca* (1953) and *Muhammad at Medina* (1956). On the early conquests, see F. M. Donner, *The Early Islamic Conquests* (1981), and, for an appreciation of the military achievement, see J. Glubb, *The Great Arab Conquests* (1961). On the historical role of the Prophet's sayings and practices, see A. Guillaume, *The Traditions of Islam* (1924), and P. Crone and M. Hinds, *God's Caliph: Religious Authority in the First Centuries of Islam* (1986).

The standard history of the Ommayyad dynasty is J. Wellhausen, *The Arab Kingdom and its Fall* (1927), which also gives a detailed account of the Abbasid revolution. See also the book by H. N. Kennedy cited earlier. On the problem of conversion to Islam and the economic aspects of relations between Moslems and non-Moslems, see D. C. Dennett, *Conversion and the Poll-Tax in Early Islam* (1950). For specific regions of the Arab Empire, see P. K. Hitti, *A History of Syria* (1951); S. Lane-Poole, *A History of Egypt in the Middle Ages,* 3rd ed. (1924); A. B. Chejne, *Muslim Spain, Its History and Culture* (1974); T. E. Glick, *Islamic and Christian Spain in the Early Middle Ages* (1979); L. P. Harvey, *Islamic Spain, 1250–1500* (1990); B. Lewis, *The Origins of Ismailism: A Study in the Historical Background of the Fatimid Caliphate* (1940) and *The Assassins: A Radical Sect in Islam* (1967); H. A. R. Gibb, *The Arab Conquests in Central Asia* (1923); and A. K. S. Lambton, *Islamic Society in Persia* (1954). D. S. Richards, *Islam and the Trade of Asia* (1971), shows the shift in interest toward the East under the Abbasids. On the Turks, see W. Barthold, *Turkestan down to the Mongol Invasion,* trans. of 2nd ed. (1958); D. Talbot Rice, *The Seljuks in Asia Minor* (1961); and C. E. Bosworth, *The Ghaznavids* (1963).

Islamic Society and Civilization

For studies of Islamic society, see the work of Hodgson, cited above and articles in the *Cambridge History of Islam.* The broadest treatments are R. Levy, *The Sociology of Islam* (1957), and I. M. Lapidus, *A History of Islamic Societies* (1988); see also, W. M. Watt, *Islam and the Integration of Society* (1961). N. Abbot, *Two Queens of Baghdad* (1937), focuses on life in the Abbasid court. S. Goitein, *A Mediterranean Society,* 4 Vols. (1967–80) is based on the discovery in Egypt of a treasure of Jewish documents, but, because the Jews were a well-assimilated minority, it reveals a great deal about the whole Islamic society and economy of the Near East. See also, A. Udalvitch, *Partnership and Profit in Medieval Islam* (1967); B. Lewis, *The Jews of Islam* (1984); and B. Ye'or, *The Dhimmi: Jews and Christians under Islam* (1985).

On Islamic civilization, see G. E. von Grunebaum, *Classical Islam, 600–1258* (1970) and *Medieval Islam: A Study in Cultural Orientation,* 2nd ed. (1953); see also, H. A. R. Gibb, *Arabic Literature,* 2nd ed. (1963); and the essays published in R. M. Savory, ed., *Islamic Civilization* (1976). On special topics, see R. Walzer, *Greek into Arabic, Essays on Islamic Philosophy* (1962); C. Elgood, *A Medical History of Persia* (1951); A. J. Arberry, *Revelation and Reason in Islam* (1957); and S. H. Nasr, *Science and Civilization in Islam* (1968). H. A. R. Gibb and H. Bowen, *Islamic Society and the West,* 2 vols. (1950 and 1957), explore the impact of the West on Islam. On the same general subject, see B. Lewis, *The Middle East and the West* (1964) and *The Muslim Discovery of Europe* (1982). For Western views of Islam, see N. Daniel, *Islam and the West: The Making of an Image* (1960), and R. W. Southern, *Western Views of Islam in the Middle Ages* (1962). In general, see T. Arnold and A. Guillaume, eds., *The Legacy of Islam* (1931).

THE EMERGENCE OF WESTERN EUROPEAN CIVILIZATION

As we saw in Chapter 5, the amalgamation of Germanic society and Christianity during the sixth and seventh centuries transformed the European provinces of the Roman Empire into a western Christendom unified in a church centered on the Roman pope. That amalgam became the basis of a new European civilization in the eighth and ninth centuries, when the Carolingians, the successors of the Merovingians, created new social and legal institutions and amassed wealth that enabled them to attract men and ideas from all over Europe. The Carolingian dynasty was named for its most famous member—in Latin, Carolus Magnus—in French, Charlemagne. We will call him by his English name, Charles the Great. By the time the dynasty collapsed in the mid-tenth century, the political and cultural foundations of modern Europe had been established.

The age in which these events took place is called the Middle Ages, the period between the collapse of the western Roman Empire in the fifth and sixth centuries and the beginning of the Italian Renaissance in the late fifteenth century. The term "Middle Ages" was coined by Renaissance thinkers who viewed themselves as heirs of Roman civilization and saw the age between the end of Roman civilization in the West and their own time as a benighted "dark age." As we shall see, they exaggerated the intellectual and artistic poverty of medieval Europe, which produced the foundations of their own "modern" civilization.

THE RISE OF THE CAROLINGIANS

The Mayors of the Palace under the Late Merovingians

By the early seventh century, the Merovingian dynasty founded by Clovis (r. 481–511) had declined, and its kings no longer exercised real authority. Dagobert (r. 629–39) was the last Merovingian who actually

The Frankish Kingdom   *ca.* 700

ruled his kingdom. After his death, though a succession of weak Merovingian kings still occupied the throne, the mayors of the palaces governed the various parts of the kingdom—Austrasia, Neustria, and Burgundy. That the Franks permitted weak kings to remain on the throne was an indication of how thoroughly they had absorbed Roman legal and political ideas. The old Germanic idea of kingship precluded a weak man from sitting on the throne; the king must lead his army to victory and protect the interests of his people. By contrast, the Romans had a legalistic view of authority that emphasized the legitimacy of the ruler rather than his competence.

The late Merovingians combined the Roman and Germanic views. They preserved the old Germanic notion that the king was a special person who stood between the community and God, but they accepted the Roman idea that power could be exercised by officials under royal authority, as well as by the king himself.

The idea that men other than the king could perform the functions of the king was the basis of the authority held by the mayors of the palace.

During the second half of the seventh century, the mayors of the various royal palaces contended for control of the Frankish kingdom. Although the Franks viewed the kingdom as if it were property to be distributed among the legitimate sons of the king when he died, they insisted that the kingdom itself remained a single entity, no matter how many kings ruled its various parts. In the civil wars of the sixth and early seventh century, it was the Merovingian kings themselves who sought to unify the kingdom under a single ruler. In the later seventh century, the struggle was carried on by the mayors of the palaces fighting on behalf of their titular kings. In 687, Pepin of Heristal, a forebear of the Carolingians who had been mayor of the palace in Austrasia since 680, ended the civil wars by defeating the mayors of Neustria and Burgundy at the battle of Tertry. By the time Pepin died in 714, he had unified the kingdom and restored the authority of the central government.

Pepin bequeathed the mayoralty to his two young grandsons. But a group of aristocrats, led by men from Neustria and Burgundy, rebelled, and the regents lacked the power to put them down. In the chaos that ensued, one of Pepin's illegitimate adult sons, Charles, defeated the aristocrats, did away with his nephews, and seized power. A hard man and seasoned warrior, Charles (r. 719–41) earned the nickname Martel, "the Hammer."

In addition to trying to keep the unruly aristocrats under control, Charles had to cope with efforts by the Moors in Spain to seize Frankish territory. The Moors had conquered the Iberian peninsula in 711, and in 720 they captured Narbonne, the capital of the ancient Roman province of Septimania. From that city as a base, they carried out raids against Aquitaine, a rich province in the southwest of Gaul. For decades, the dukes of Aquitaine had maintained their independence from the Merovingian government, but, faced with these devastating raids, Duke Eudes now turned to Charles for help. Around 732, Charles

Gold fibula decorated with paste and precious stones (seventh century).

THE CAROLINGIANS

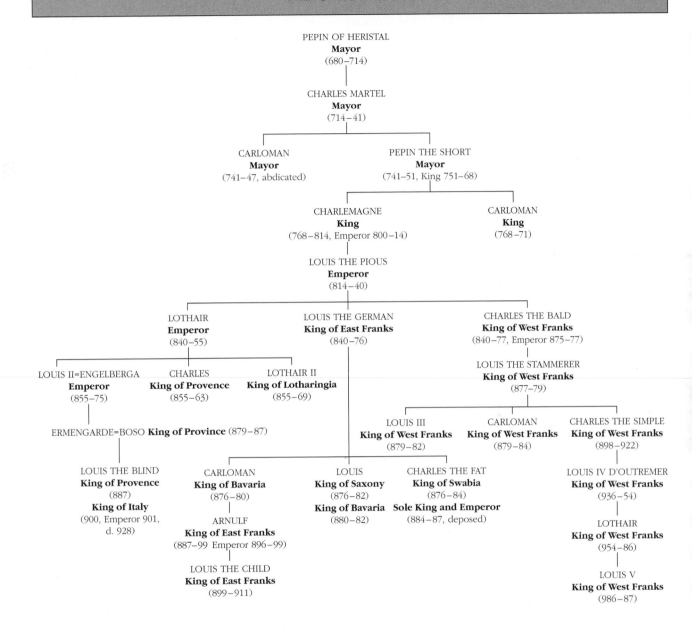

PEPIN OF HERISTAL
Mayor
(680–714)

CHARLES MARTEL
Mayor
(714–41)

CARLOMAN
Mayor
(741–47, abdicated)

PEPIN THE SHORT
Mayor
(741–51, King 751–68)

CHARLEMAGNE
King
(768–814, Emperor 800–14)

CARLOMAN
King
(768–71)

LOUIS THE PIOUS
Emperor
(814–40)

LOTHAIR
Emperor
(840–55)

LOUIS THE GERMAN
King of East Franks
(840–76)

CHARLES THE BALD
King of West Franks
(840–77, Emperor 875–77)

LOUIS II=ENGELBERGA
Emperor
(855–75)

CHARLES
King of Provence
(855–63)

LOTHAIR II
King of Lotharingia
(855–69)

LOUIS THE STAMMERER
King of West Franks
(877–79)

ERMENGARDE=BOSO **King of Province** (879–87)

LOUIS III
King of West Franks
(879–82)

CARLOMAN
King of West Franks
(879–84)

CHARLES THE SIMPLE
King of West Franks
(898–922)

LOUIS THE BLIND
King of Provence
(887)
King of Italy
(900, Emperor 901,
d. 928)

CARLOMAN
King of Bavaria
(876–80)

LOUIS
King of Saxony
(876–82)
King of Bavaria
(880–82)

CHARLES THE FAT
King of Swabia
(876–84)
Sole King and Emperor
(884–87, deposed)

LOUIS IV D'OUTREMER
King of West Franks
(936–54)

ARNULF
King of East Franks
(887–99 Emperor 896–99)

LOTHAIR
King of West Franks
(954–86)

LOUIS THE CHILD
King of East Franks
(899–911)

LOUIS V
King of West Franks
(986–87)

defeated a large Moorish army near Poitiers that had been on its way to plunder the rich church of Tours, which contained the shrine of St. Martin, the monk-bishop (p. 136). From this time on, the Moors remained on the defensive in southern Gaul and Aquitaine accepted the rule of the royal government.

Charles encouraged the Irish and Anglo-Saxon monks who were carrying on the missionary work of Columbanus and his confreres (pp. 136–37) and became closely associated with Wynfrith, the greatest among them. Wynfrith was a monk from Wessex who, after visiting Rome in 718 and winning papal approval of his work, had taken the Roman name Boniface. He founded the monastery of Fulda in central Germany as a missionary base and for two decades was the most prominent churchman in the Frankish kingdom. In 722 Pope Gregory II (r. 715–31) consecrated Boniface as a missionary bishop to Germany, where he worked under the protection of Charles Martel. And in 751 Pope Zacharias (r. 741–52) consecrated him as the first Archbishop of Mainz, which subsequently became the principal diocese in Germany.

It may have been through Boniface that Pope Gregory III (r. 731–41) approached Charles Martel in 739 for help against the Lombards, who were threatening Rome. The pope had asked Constantinople for help, but the emperor had ignored his plea. Relations between the papacy and Constantinople were severely strained at the time by the controversy over iconoclasm (pp. 175–78). Moreover, the Byzantine armies were busy fighting wars against the Ommayyad caliphate and the Bulgarians. Charles, too, turned down the pope's request for help against the Lombards. The Lombard king, Luitprand, had aided the Franks in their war against the Moors, and Charles had sent his son Pepin III to the Lombard court to cement relations between the two royal families. Charles had nothing to gain by helping the pope.

When Charles Martel died in 741, the mayoralty went to his sons, Pepin the Short (r. 741–68) and Carloman (r. 741–47). Like their father, they supported Boniface in his missionary and reform efforts, including his plan to establish Benedictine monasticism (pp. 137–38) as the principal form of monasticism in the Frankish kingdom. Frankish monasticism existed in a bewildering variety of forms at the time, and the disarray disturbed right-thinking churchmen like Boniface. Further, because people associated political unity with religious unity, the confusion threatened the unity of the kingdom. Shortly after they succeeded to the mayoralty,

Pepin and Carloman summoned councils in which Boniface tried to bring to the monasteries some degree of uniformity. Then, in 747, Carloman, who had become caught up in the reform movement himself, retired to a monastery, first in Rome and then at Montecassino, the mother house of Benedictine monasticism, leaving Pepin the Short in control of the kingdom.

The Making of a New Royal Family

Under Charles Martel, the king had been reduced to a nonentity, and during the last years of his life Charles had actually ruled without a king. When Pepin and Carloman succeeded to the mayoralty, however, they felt they needed a king to establish their legitimacy. A search throughout the kingdom produced a distant relative of the royal family, who in 743 was crowned as Childeric III. But after governing for a time, Pepin decided that he had no need for Childeric, who was living a dissolute life under virtual house arrest. So he took the revolutionary step of transferring royal power to himself, with the support of the aristocracy.

To replace the ancient dynasty was a tricky matter. Pepin lacked the divine character that the Germans attributed to their kings, and the right to be God's minister on earth rested not on the exercise of power, but on hereditary right. In his search for a way to overcome this defect in his legitimacy, Pepin turned to the pope, whose goodwill he had gained by his support of Boniface.

In 749 or 750, Pepin wrote to Pope Zachary and asked the question: "Was it right that the king of the Franks, though he had no power, nevertheless occupied the royal office?" Zachary answered that Pepin, who was in fact exercising royal authority, was indeed king, and in 751 the Frankish bishops anointed him in the manner in which the Old Testament kings had been anointed. This was a ceremony practiced in Spain, and the idea may have been brought to the Frankish kingdom by refugees from the fallen Visigothic kingdom. But it was unprecedented in the

Frankish kingdom. The anointment was a symbolic declaration that Pepin possessed the divine character of a king and was the true heir of the Merovingians.

The Franks and the Papacy

The warm relationship between Pepin and Pope Zachary led to a change in the Frankish attitude toward the war between the papacy and the Lombards. In the winter of 752–53, Zachary's successor, Stephen II (r. 752–57), asked Pepin for help against Aistulf, the Lombard king who had recently conquered Ravenna, the last Byzantine stronghold in Italy.

Pepin invited Stephen to his kingdom and in January 754 met with him at Ponthion, a royal residence east of Paris on the Marne River. At the meeting, Pepin promised to help Stephen, and in the spring he persuaded the Frankish aristocracy to support this new policy toward the papacy. At Easter, Pepin promised the pope, who had remained in the Frankish kingdom, that he would restore the territories of the papacy. In July, at Saint Denis, Stephen himself anointed Pepin and anointed his wife and sons as well, naming Pepin *patricius Romanorum* (patrician of the Romans) as special protector of the Roman see. The anointment of Pepin's sons confirmed the legitimacy of the new dynasty.

Over the next year or so, Pepin negotiated with Aistulf, but the talks failed to produce what Pepin had promised. In 755, Pepin invaded Italy and in 756 forced the Lombards to restore to the pope the territory centered on Ravenna. The restoration was recorded in a document, now lost, that was deposited in St. Peter's. Known as the "Donation of Pepin," it later served as the basis of papal claims to secular authority in central Italy.

CHARLES THE GREAT AND THE CAROLINGIAN RENAISSANCE

Charles the War Leader and King

Pepin died in 768, leaving the monarchy to his sons, Charles, who became known as "the Great," (Charlemagne, from the Latin, *Carolus Magnus*) and Carloman. These brothers did not get along well, and the Franks might have experienced another round of civil wars had Carloman not died suddenly in 771. His widow and children took refuge with the Lombard king, Desiderius, who renewed Lombard claims to the territory that Pepin had donated to the papacy. This gave Charles a double incentive to respond to Desiderius's challenge: By defeating the Lombard king, he would honor his father's alliance with the papacy and at the same time would eliminate competing claimants to the crown. He invaded Italy in 773. Within a year he had conquered the Lombard kingdom and in 774 he took the crown of the Lombards for himself. Carloman's widow and children disappeared.

Charles was a warrior king. For 32 years (772–804), he led a campaign almost every year against the pagan Saxons on

Charles the Great's Conquests and Empire 814

The Golden Psalter, presented to Charles the Great by Pope Hadrian I (*ca.* 780–95).

the northeastern border of his kingdom and finally brought them under control. He was helped by missionaries whom he supported and who cemented his alliance with the church. In the southwest, Charles continued his father's and grandfather's wars against the Moors. Between 778 and 801 he established a strong buffer territory along the southern flank of the Pyrenees—the Spanish March. During the campaign of 778, the Moors ambushed his rear guard as he was returning home. The story of that engagement was memorialized in the great medieval epic *The Song of Roland*. On the eastern frontier, Charles brought the Bavarians under his power in 787 and established another buffer, the Ostmark (East March), between his kingdom and the restless Slavic tribes of eastern Europe. The Ostmark formed the core of what later became Austria. About 796, Charles crossed the eastern frontier and crushed the Avars, seizing from them an immense treasure of gold. This campaign put Charles in touch with the western frontier of the Byzantine Empire.

Charles matched these military successes with successes in government. He followed his father and uncle in using councils, which he adapted to all sorts of purposes. While presiding over them, he issued legislation for the church, settled disputes, and reviewed his army. Because the councils were attended by the leading men of the kingdom, Charles's pronouncements were immediately conveyed to those who were affected by them or who had to carry out his orders. Charles also issued numerous capitularies (so called because they were divided into chapters, *capitula*), which regulated the administration of royal and ecclesiastical estates and dealt with other functions of government. To implement these regulations, he used the countship, a late Roman office that combined military and civilian authority, and appointed counts throughout the kingdom. Although the counts were royal officials, they were not entirely dependent on the central government for their power. Their standing derived as well from their own ancient families and landed estates, so that even under the powerful Charles they could not always be trusted to be loyal. Consequently, Charles appointed *missi dominici* (men sent by the king) as special agents of his government. These men traveled regular circuits to check up on the counts and the bailiffs who managed the royal estates.

The *missi* usually traveled in pairs, a layman and a cleric, a reflection of Charles's concern with ecclesiastical as well as with secular affairs. Here too, he was following in the footsteps of his father and grandfather. Under Charles Martel many bishoprics and abbeys were actually controlled by secular men who drew on the great wealth of the church to provide him with support. Despite their reliance on the church for political support, however, Pepin and Charles both claimed that, as king, they were God's vicar on earth.

The Carolingian Renaissance

As time passed, Charles grew concerned that the churches of the kingdom, which had developed independently, differed from one another in many significant ways. Boniface had failed in his attempt to consolidate the monasteries under the Benedictine rule, and the old variations in practice and tradition remained a source of disunity throughout the Frankish church. The liturgy and even the doctrine of the bishoprics often differed. So Charles decided to undertake a major church reform.

The reform movement was centered in the royal court at Aix-la-Chapelle (Aachen), the ancient Carolingian estate that Charles had made his capital. Charles had become interested in reform early in his reign, and almost from the beginning he had invited intellectuals to his court. In 774, while he was in Italy after defeating the Lombards, Pope Hadrian I (r. 772–95) had presented him with a copy of the papal collection of canon law. In the 780s a number of scholars took up residence at the court, and Charles himself studied with them. It was said that he had difficulty learning Latin, but he was interested in the scholars' learned discussions.

The influence of the Anglo-Saxon missionaries continued under Charles the Great. Their leader was a monk named Alcuin (*ca.* 735–804), who had come to Aix-la-Chapelle in 781 at Charles's invitation. Alcuin had been educated in York—a great intellectual center—and he stood in a line of scholars that reached back to the Northumbrian monk Bede (*ca.* 672–735), one of the most important scholars of the Middle Ages (pp. 242–43). Under Alcuin, Charles's court became a seedbed of ecclesiastical reform and an influential intellectual center.

The goal of the reform program was to train a new generation of clerics whom Charles would appoint to the principal bishoprics and abbeys of the realm. The

A small bronze statue of Charles the Great or his grandson Charles the Bald. He wears a crown and carries an orb, symbol of royal power (ninth century).

pope had sent Charles a sacramentary giving the order and content of the Mass along with a carefully prepared copy of the Benedictine Rule. In an effort to standardize liturgical practice, the court scholars used these works to produce model texts from which certified copies were made for churches throughout the realm.

in patria pax inuiolata in regno·
& dignitas gloriosa regalis palatii·maxi
mo splendore regiae potestatis· oculis
omnium luce clarissima coruscare
atque splendescere · qua splendidissi
mi fulgoris maximo pfusa lumine·

Lowercase letters and a bold, rounded design were characteristic of the elegant Carolingian handwriting, which is the basis of modern type (detail from a ninth-century manuscript).

That effort met with only moderate success, and in 816–17 Charles's son Louis tried again to impose the Benedictine Rule on all monasteries of the realm, again with moderate success.

Alcuin and his fellow scholars thought that the success of the reform movement depended on their attempt to reestablish the intellectual tradition of ancient Rome. What they accomplished was a true renaissance, the rebirth of a civilization of the past. Bits and pieces of Roman civilization had survived in isolated places in England and Spain during the centuries of barbarian rule, but the Roman tradition had been debased and had lost much of its cultural authority.

Alcuin, who was best known as a teacher, developed a curriculum based on that of Rome for the court school. He divided the seven liberal arts, as defined by the late Romans, into the *trivium* and the *quadrivium*. The *trivium* included grammar, dialectic (logic), and rhetoric. The *quadrivium* included arithmetic, geometry, astronomy, and music (which was thought to derive from the structure of the universe). Alcuin recruited a great Italian grammarian, Peter of Pisa, to come to Aix-la-Chapelle, and produce new editions of Roman works on grammar. Paul the Deacon, another Italian, came to the court to seek the release of his brother, whom Charles had imprisoned, and stayed on for a couple of years compiling a book of model sermons for pastors. Meanwhile, Alcuin undertook a new edition of Jerome's Latin translation of the Bible, which had become riddled with errors in the course of nearly four centuries of copying. The work was finished by his students after his death. Alcuin's edition established Jerome's translation, which had competed with an earlier North African version, as the vulgate (*vulgatus,* meaning common) Bible of Europe.

The reform effort inspired by Charles continued throughout his reign, spurred on by his legislation in the Capitularies of 789, 802, and 811–13. The first of these contained a summary of the most important sections of the papal law book Charles had received in 774 and a general statement of the aims of the reform. Its principal effect was to establish the idea that law was the basis of religious life—in other words, that religious life should be regulated by a coherent body of written rules. Previously, religious life had been based on local custom, which was the product of communal practices and the personal preferences of the bishops who had governed the dioceses over the centuries. The Capitulary of 802 reaffirmed the authority of the papal law book, and the Capitulary of 811–13 dealt with various aspects of the reform in detail.

The palace school produced numerous new editions of Roman works as well as new works patterned on them. During the 780s (the exact date is unknown), Charles issued instructions to monasteries and cathedrals to make copies of the old manuscripts in their possession. The scripts used in Merovingian and early Carolingian times were difficult to read and full of puzzling abbreviations and letter forms. This lack of uniformity in scribal practice had contributed to the corruption of the texts as they were copied again and again. At some of the monasteries, particularly the monastery of Corbie (north of Amiens), a clear, easy-to-read script had begun to emerge by the middle of the eighth century, and Charles's instructions to increase production brought it to perfection. For the first time, the monasteries developed distinctive house styles based on standardized ways of writing taught to the scribes. Modern scholars can often date ninth-century manuscripts on the basis of their script.

The new script, called Caroline Minuscule, used few ligatures (connected letters that could become mysterious in the hands of artful or minimally competent scribes) and few abbreviations. The monastic scribes used this script to produce a large library of beautifully written copies of ancient texts in their scriptoria (writing rooms). When the humanist scholars of fifteenth-century Italy were searching for works of classical literature, they mistook these Carolingian manuscripts for ancient copies, because of their clarity and beauty. In their zeal for ancient civilization, they revived the Caroline Minuscule and established it as the script of scholarship and culture. This script continues to be used today: The type you are reading is based on Caroline Minuscule.

The Coronation of Charles as Emperor

After Charles seized the Lombard crown in 774, Pope Hadrian I gave him the title earlier conferred on Pepin: *patricius Romanorum* (patrician of the Romans). But the time came when Charles made claims to spiritual authority that his father probably never entertained, such as sending out clerics as *missi dominici* and taking the lead in the reform of the Frankish church. Around 794 Charles declared himself "rector of the Christian people," a title that suggests Caesaropapism (pp. 176–77). Like Leo III and Constantine V in Constantinople, Charles, though not a cleric himself, thrust himself into the theological debates of his age.

With the golden treasure he had seized from the Avars in 796, Charles built a "second Rome" at Aix-la-Chapelle, using craftsmen and materials imported from Italy to create a palace and a church modeled on the Byzantine structures at Ravenna. The grand style of the Byzantines was also suggested by his entry into international politics when, in the 790s, he sent and received embassies from the caliph Harun al-Rashid (probably to discuss their common enemies, the Moors in Spain). By the mid-780s, intellectuals at the court had already begun to use the word *imperium* (imperial authority) to describe the authority Charles exercised.

After the empress Irene had her son Constantine VI blinded in 797, both easterners and westerners regarded the imperial throne as vacant. Why not, they asked, resurrect the Roman Empire with Charles as emperor? In 800 Pope Leo III (r. 795–816), threatened by political opponents in Rome, called on Charles, the *patricius Romanorum,* for help. Charles responded by setting off to Rome.

In December 800, Charles summoned a council of churchmen in Rome to deal with the dispute between Leo and his opponents. The assembled churchmen declared that they were unable to make a

The Coronation of Charles the Great 800

Now when the king upon the most holy day of the Lord's birth was rising to the mass after praying before the tomb of the blessed Peter the Apostle, Leo the Pope, with the consent of all the bishops and priests and of the senate of the Franks and likewise of the Romans, set a golden crown upon his head, the Roman people also shouting aloud. And when the people had made an end of chanting praises, he was adored by the pope after the manner of the emperors of old. For this was also done by the will of God. For while the said Emperor abode at Rome certain men were brought to him who said that the name of Emperor had ceased among the Greeks, and that there the Empire was held by a woman called Irene, who had by guile laid hold on her son the Emperor and put out his eyes and taken the Empire to herself. . . . Which when Leo the Pope and all the assembly of the bishops and priests and abbots heard, and the senate of the Franks and all the elders of the Romans, they took counsel with the rest of the Christian people, that they should name Charles king of the Franks to be Emperor, seeing that he held Rome the mother of empire where the Caesars and Emperors always used to sit.

From Chronicle of Moissac, *trans. by J. Bryce,* The Holy Roman Empire *(New York: Macmillan and St. Martin's Press, 1911), p. 54.*

judgment, because the pope, as successor to St. Peter, could be judged by no one. That opinion confirmed the hierarchical view expressed in the Petrine Doctrine, on which papal authority rested. To clear himself of the charges that his opponents had leveled against him, Leo merely took an oath declaring his innocence. With that, the case was closed.

A couple of days after these events, Charles and his entourage went to St. Peter's church, the basilica built by Constantine I just outside Rome, to celebrate Christmas Mass. When Charles rose from prayer at the altar, Pope Leo placed an imperial crown on his head and the congregation shouted the traditional acclamation to the emperor. So began the conflict between Charles and the Byzantines over the imperial title (pp. 179–80).

According to Charles's biographer Einhard, Charles said that he would not have gone to church that day if he had known what Pope Leo had in mind. It is hard to believe that Leo had tricked

Interior of the Palatine Chapel,
Aix-la-Chapelle (Aachen).

Gold coin bearing the likeness of
Irene, empress in Constantinople
from 797 to 802. She was the
first woman to assume sole rule
over the Byzantine Empire,
taking the title of emperor. Her
rule provided the pope with an
excuse to crown Charles the
Great emperor in 800 to fill the
allegedly vacant throne.

Charles, though he may have persuaded
him to go through with a scheme that
Charles later regretted. Charles did not use
the title until 801, and in 806 he divided
the empire among his three sons. This was
traditional for a Frankish king, but it was
inconceivable to the imperial court in Constantinople, which was now convinced
more than ever that Charles did not understand the nature of imperial authority.
Nonetheless, Nicephorus, who had seized
power from Irene in 802, was in a difficult
position. He engaged Charles in tortuous
negotiations that finally, after Nicephorus
had been overthrown, led to a treaty by

which the Byzantines agreed to address Charles as Emperor of the Franks and by which Charles agreed that the emperor in Constantinople was still the Emperor of the Romans. Neither Charles nor his successors ever used the title Emperor of the Franks, however.

Charles was survived by only one of his sons, Louis, who inherited both the kingdom and the title Emperor of the Franks. Louis's sons and grandsons competed for possession of that title, and it continued to be a source of friction with the Byzantine court.

THE DECLINE OF THE CAROLINGIANS AND NEW INVASIONS

The Disintegration of the Carolingian Kingdom

Louis (r. 814–40) was a merely capable man who succeeded a giant, and his reputation has suffered accordingly. His image was not helped by his nickname "the Pious," which he earned by associating with churchmen and monks. In fact, one of his first acts as king was to reform the morals of the royal court, which under his father Charles had become a rather licentious place.

While his father ruled, Louis had been King of Aquitaine, where he had come to know a monk named Benedict of Aniane, a monastic reformer. When Louis became emperor, he invited Benedict to Aix-la-Chapelle and carried on Charles's program of church reform, particularly as it related to the monasteries. Louis held a series of councils to work out the details of various reform measures, and in 816–17 he and Benedict tried to impose the Benedictine Rule on all the monasteries in the realm. The Rule was ultimately accepted, though many of the old monasteries held on to their ancient rules for many years. Louis was not a vigorous patron of learning, and the pace of the renaissance started by his father slowed during his reign.

Louis came to power at the age of 36, when his three sons were virtually adult. In 817, following Charles's precedent, he

Louis the Pious, son of Charles the Great. The words in the poem written across the portrait can also be read as a crossword puzzle, so that the letters in the cross and halo also form verses.

divided the kingdom among his sons, who became kings of various parts of the realm. This arrangement, though it guaranteed the succession, failed as a strategy for governing the vast domain. During the 820s, the sons began warring with one another and with their father, and in 833 they defeated him in battle. Lothair, Louis's oldest son, imprisoned him in the monastery of St. Medard of Soissons, and the leading churchmen of the realm, at Lothair's urging, declared Louis unfit to rule and deposed him. After several months, powerful nobles and churchmen returned to Louis's camp and helped him to regain the throne. But he had to do penance before the churchmen would recognize his legitimacy.

The Division of Charles the Great's Empire

The Treaty of Verdun 843

Aix-la-Chapelle
Paris
TO LOUIS
TO CHARLES
TO LOTHAIR
Pavia
Rome
MEDITERRANEAN SEA
0   MILES   200

The Treaty of Mersen 870

Aix-la-Chapelle
Paris
EAST FRANKISH KINGDOM
WEST FRANKISH KINGDOM
KINGDOM OF ITALY
Pavia
Rome
MEDITERRANEAN SEA

The events of these years did great damage to the prestige of the royal house as the various aristocratic families played Louis and his sons off against another and seized for themselves royal lands and royal privileges. Moreover, the church-men's humiliation of Louis reinforced the church's claim that it had the right to participate in crowning the emperor. Charles himself had crowned Louis as emperor in 813. But in 816 Louis was crowned again, this time by Pope Stephen IV (r. 816–17), who had journeyed to Reims to perform the ceremony. Then, in 824, Louis sent Lothair to Rome to be crowned as emperor by Paschal I (r. 817–24). These precedents served to support the church's claim.

After Louis's death in 840, his son Louis (r. 840–76) inherited Germany; he was called Louis the German. Charles (r. 840–77) inherited West Frankland; he became known as Charles the Bald. And Lothair (r. 840–55) inherited a middle kingdom that stretched from the Netherlands (Frisia) in the north through the region west of the Rhine (later called Lotharingia after Lothair's son Lothair II) and Provence to Italy. Lothair also inherited the title of emperor, which he had actually held since 824. In theory, the three held joint power, but immediately after their father's death they renewed their civil war. In 842, Louis and Charles formed an alliance against Lothair. To ensure that their armies would understand the terms of the alliance, Louis took his oath in the Romance language that was then spoken by the West Franks, while Charles took his oath in Old German. The written record of

Lothair I in Roman dress seated on his throne (ca. 817).

Louis's oath is the earliest evidence of the use of the Old French language.

The war that stemmed from this alliance ended in the Treaty of Verdun in 843, by which the Frankish kingdom was divided into three independent parts. Louis and Charles agreed to recognize the superior authority of Lothair, who retained the imperial title, though they usually treated him as an equal. Lothair in turn tried to force his brothers to respect his authority. When Lothair died in 855, his holdings were divided among his three sons. Lothair II (r. 855–69) received the northern portion; Charles (r. 855–63) received Provence; and Louis II (r. 855–75) became king of Italy and emperor. When Lothair II died without a legitimate heir, his uncles, Charles the Bald and Louis the German, fought over his part of the "middle kingdom." In 870 the two brothers made a treaty at Meersen that called for Lotharingia to be divided between them. The division was made according to the number of cities and bishoprics in each section, rather than along a natural boundary. Since then, West Frankland (France) and East Frankland (Germany) have continued to vie for control of the region.

The Viking and Magyar Invasions

These endless conflicts opened the way to new invaders. As far back as 793, a raiding party of Northmen from Norway or Denmark had attacked and destroyed the famous English monastery of Lindisfarne. When Alcuin, who was living at the Frankish court, heard about it, he was shocked by the destruction of this distinguished spiritual and intellectual center. As raids continued over the years, Charles the Great fortified the Frisian coast against the marauders. In 810 a large Danish force broke through these defenses; but for several years afterward, power struggles that followed the murder of the Danish king kept the Danes otherwise occupied.

The new invaders were Vikings— "those who go abroad." They usually were beyond the control of the Scandinavian kings. In Scandinavian society men were expected to spend some time at sea trading and raiding before settling down to life as a farmer. The raiding parties arrived along the coast in their swift longboats and descended on the populace without warning. After seizing whatever they could find of value, they fled.

Some of the Vikings traveled up the broad, slow-moving rivers of northern Europe and carried out raids deep in the interior. In 834, a large band sailed up the Seine and sacked Paris, and another sailed up the Elbe and destroyed Hamburg. In the succeeding decades, Viking bands established settlements in Brittany and raided up and down the Atlantic coast. They even made their way into the Mediterranean and sacked Seville, in the heart of the powerful caliphate of Cordova.

During the second half of the ninth century, the rise of a strong monarchy in Norway under Harald Finehair drove many aristocratic clans that opposed royal power to Iceland and England. In southern England they banded together in a force known as the Great Army, which by the 870s had taken over several of the

Prodõ amur & pxpian poblo & nr̄o cõmun saluament . dist di ẽn auant . inquantdi̇ saur & podir me dunat . si saluaraieo . cist meon fradre Karlo . & in ad iudha . & in cad huna cosa . sicũ om p dreit son fradra saluar dist . Jno quid il mi altre si fazet . Et ab ludher nul plaid nũqua prindrai qui meon uol cist . meon fradre Karle in damno fit | Quod cũ lodhuuic̃ expleffet . karolus teudisca lingua sic oc eadé uerba testatus est. 9,10 Jngo des mi̇nna in duurhes xpanes folches . in dunser bedhero gealnissi . font bese moda ge framm ordesso framso mirgot gewuzei in dimadh fur gibiz sohal dithres du mnan bruodher soso man mit rehtu sinan bruher scal inthi irtha zermig soso maduo . in dunit lub eren in nóhein iut hing nege ganga . zhemi nan uuillon imo ces cadhen uuerhen .

Section from the Strasbourg Oaths, earliest examples of the dialects that became French and German. The oath was taken by Louis the German and Charles the Bald in 842, when they agreed to oppose their brother Lothair. The first paragraph gives the oath in French, taken by Louis, the second the same oath in German, taken by Charles. *The oath of Louis:* "For the love of God and the salvation of the Christian people and our common salvation, from this day forward, in so far as God gives me knowledge and power, I will succour this my brother Charles in aid and in everything, as one ought by right to succour one's brother, provided that he does likewise by me, and I will never undertake any engagement with Lothair which, by my consent, may be of harm to this my brother Charles."

A rune stone (*ca.* ninth century) found in Scandinavia. The carving is distinctly Viking: Within an elaborate border are two panels, one showing a chieftain on a horse and the other a Viking ship on a voyage.

Remains of a Viking ship at Osberg, Norway.

Anglo-Saxon kingdoms and was threatening the others. Alfred (r. 871–99), king of Wessex, spent most of his reign fighting the Great Army and finally forced it to stop its expansion. Large contingents of the Northmen then settled in a band of territory in eastern England, called the Danelaw (the area subject to Danish law), which Alfred's successors brought under their control. Old Danish, a language closely related to Old Norse, had a strong influence on the development of English.

Some of the members of the Great Army crossed over to the continent where, using northwestern Gaul as their base, they raided deep into Frankish territory. After a generation of warfare, the West Frankish king Charles the Simple (r. 898–922), great-great-grandson of Charles the Great, made peace with Rollo, one of the Viking leaders. Under the terms of the peace, Rollo converted to Christianity, became a vassal of Charles with the title of count, and agreed to defend the kingdom against other Vikings. Charles granted Rollo the lands on which his men had already settled. (That territory became known as Normandy, because the Europeans called the Vikings "Normans" or "Northmen.") These events were among the last of the Viking invasions. Before the

end of the ninth century, however, a new wave of invasions had begun.

The new invaders were Magyars, ancestors of the Hungarians. Linguistically, the Hungarian language does not belong to any known language group; the Finnish language is its only linguistic relative. The Magyars seem to have originated in central Asia. They first appear in history in 895, when the Byzantines set them upon the Bulgarians, thus introducing them into eastern Europe. In a short time, the Magyars had conquered the Hungarian plain, once occupied by the Huns and Avars, and were raiding deep into Germany and Italy. During the first half of the tenth century, they were known as the scourge of Europe. In 955, Otto I of Germany defeated them at Augsburg, and they settled down in what is now Hungary.

THE ORIGINS OF FRANCE

When Charles the Great and then Louis the Pious divided the Frankish kingdom among their sons, they were following the precedent set more than a half-century earlier, when Pepin the Short had had his sons anointed as kings by Pope Stephen. The idea was to ensure the succession of

Invasion of the Northmen, the Moslems, and the Magyars   Eighth to Tenth Centuries

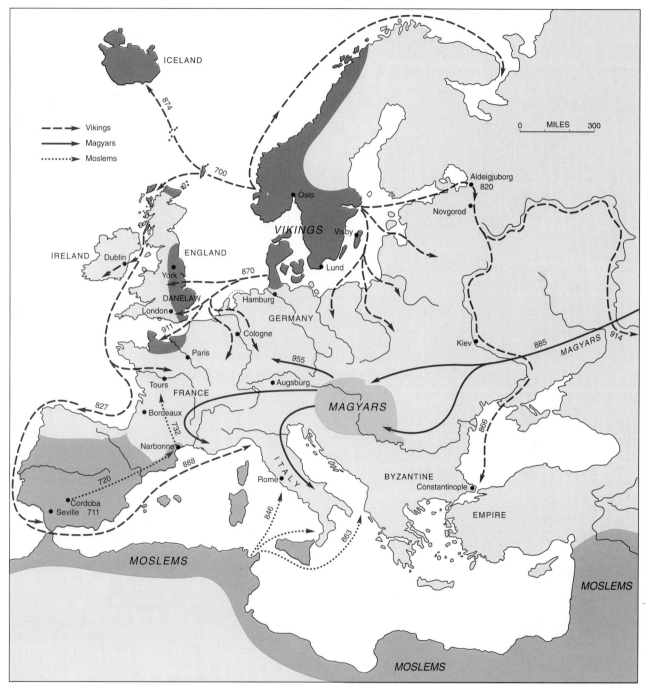

the Carolingian family and to keep the kingdom unified though under the rule of three kings. The Treaty of Meersen (870) in effect sanctioned the independence of the three parts of the kingdom—West Frankland (the future France), East Frankland (the future Germany), and Italy (to which the imperial title was attached).

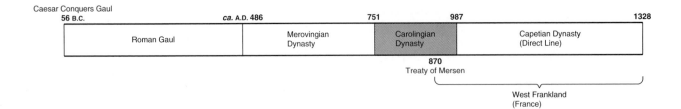

Caesar Conquers Gaul
56 B.C.   *ca.* A.D. 486   751   987   1328

Roman Gaul	Merovingian Dynasty	Carolingian Dynasty	Capetian Dynasty (Direct Line)

870
Treaty of Mersen

West Frankland
(France)

Those parts then began to follow separate courses.

Charles the Bald and his Descendants

As we have seen, when Louis the Pious died in 840, his son Charles the Bald (r. 840–77) was king of West Frankland. In the late 850s and early 860s, factions of the nobility rebelled against him, and his brother Louis the German invaded the kingdom at their invitation.

In an effort to strengthen his position, Charles granted lands, abbacies, and royal offices to the great men of his realm, including the bishops, who could offer him substantial support from their seats in the major cities of the kingdom. But this practice only strengthened the recipients of the grants. So long as they supported Charles, the monarchy was strong. But when some of them withdrew their support, Charles found himself in trouble. As a result, the power of the monarchy declined under Charles.

Charles did manage to achieve some notable successes, however. He defended his realm against the Vikings, sometimes by paying them enormous sums of silver. He also reformed the coinage and continued the Carolingian practice of issuing capitularies.

Most significant, Charles revived the Carolingian renaissance, which had slowed under his father. He was a great patron of artists and commissioned some of the masterpieces of the early Middle Ages. Archbishop Hincmar of Reims (r. 845–82), the leading churchman of the kingdom, once compared Charles with the kings of the Old Testament, and several of the illuminated Bibles commissioned by Charles contain portraits that associate him with those kings and with God.

Charles was succeeded by his son Louis II the Stammerer (r. 877–79), whose mind was not much quicker than his tongue. Louis tried to secure his grasp on the kingship by giving away still more royal honors and offices to powerful lay and ecclesiastical figures. He died only sixteen months after his coronation.

The aristocratic factions that had emerged under Charles the Bald now declared themselves in support of one or the other of Louis's teenaged sons, Louis III and Carloman. (Another son, Charles, was born after his father's death and did not figure in the contest for power for several years.) Hugh*, a Welf who had risen to power under Charles the Bald, wanted Louis III to succeed as sole ruler because he was sure that he could dominate the kingdom through Louis. The other main faction, led by Gauzlin, the royal chancellor (responsible for issuing documents and for royal correspondence), and Theudebert of Vermandois wanted to divide the kingdom between the two sons. Gauzlin and Theudebert won the contest by inviting Louis the Younger, son of Louis the German, to invade the kingdom. After defeating Hugh, they paid Louis the Younger to leave (see chart on p. 223).

In 882, Louis III won a major victory against the Vikings, but soon afterward he died in a fall from his horse while chasing a girl. Carloman died two years later in a hunting accident. Because Charles the Simple, Louis the Stammerer's last son, was only five years old at the time, the West Frankish nobles invited Charles the Fat, Louis the German's youngest son and

Charles the Bald enthroned from the St. Emmeram Gospels (Regensburg). The hand of God above his head instills him with divine authority.

---

* The Welfs were an ancient noble family that rose to prominence under Charles the Bald. In the eleventh century, they became dukes of Bavaria and remained active in German and Italian politics for centuries.

by then king of East Frankland, to become king of West Frankland as well. Charles accepted and for the next three years ruled the Frankish kingdom as sole king. Actually, both parts of the kingdom were governed by the nobles, and Charles the Fat was so ineffective that he was forced to abdicate in 887. In East Frankland, the nobles, exercising a right they did not have, elected as king Arnulf (r. 887–99), an illegitimate scion of a branch of the Carolingian line. In West Frankland, the nobles, also taking matters into their own hands, broke with precedent and chose a non-Carolingian ruler, Odo.

The Rise of the Capetians, Counts of Paris

The family of Odo (r. 887–98) had risen to prominence as a result of Charles the Bald's largesse. Odo's father, Robert the Strong (d. 866), had received many countships and abbacies from Charles and had been one of Charles's favorites. His power was centered in Paris. When Odo succeeded his father as count of Paris, he proved himself by defending the Paris region against the Vikings, and as king he continued to fight the Vikings. Odo relied heavily on his brother Robert throughout his reign. After Odo's death, and the death of Odo's infant son, Robert became Odo's heir.

By the early 890s, Robert of Paris had become a *marquis,* a royal officer superior to all the counts in the region. This title had once designated a royal officer responsible for a march (a border region). Thus Odo continued the Carolingian policy of relying on the aristocracy to conduct government. Over time, the kingdom became a collection of semiautonomous principalities ruled by aristocrats.

That the great men of the realm regarded Odo's kingship only as a brief interlude in the history of the Carolingian monarchy became apparent in 893. They rebelled against Odo and had Charles the Simple, now fourteen years old, crowned king. Odo quickly put down the rebellion, and Charles withdrew to Lotharingia. But when Odo died on January 1, 898, Charles was accepted as king. Odo's brother Robert was one of the young king's principal

supporters, and Charles rewarded him handsomely for his loyalty.

Although Charles the Simple (r. 898–922) was dependent on the aristocratic factions, he had some noteworthy successes of his own. His action against the Vikings was impressive, and he dealt from strength in making the treaty with the Viking leader Rollo in 911. In that same year, the nobles of Lotharingia chose him as king, rejecting the non-Carolingian East Frankish king, Conrad of Franconia. From that time on, Charles spent most of his time in Lotharingia, leaving the aristocrats in West Frankland, including Robert of Paris, to govern their territories with little interference.

By 920, Charles's neglect of West Frankland and his favoritism toward certain Lotharingian aristocrats led to a rebellion orchestrated by Robert, who was elected king of West Frankland in 922. Charles met Robert in battle in June 923, and, though Robert was killed, his forces won the battle. About a month later, Ralph, son of Richard the Justiciar of Burgundy, was elected king, and shortly afterward Herbert of Vermandois captured and imprisoned Charles the Simple, who died in prison in 929.

Ralph (r. 923–36) concentrated on strengthening his power in Burgundy and continued the practice of awarding lands and offices to noblemen elsewhere in the kingdom to ensure their loyalty. In fact, they accorded him little more than token recognition of his kingship. The most powerful nobleman in the kingdom was Hugh the Great, Robert's son, who ruled the Paris region as count. When Ralph died, Hugh supported Charles the Simple's son, Louis IV, and received the title "Duke of the Franks" as a sign of his power in the kingdom.

Louis IV (r. 936–54) grew up in England, where his mother, sister of the king of Wessex, had retreated after Charles's capture in 923. Louis soon fell out with Hugh and other powerful nobles and was especially determined to break the power of his former supporter Hugh the Great. He might have succeeded had he not died in a fall from his horse in 954.

When Louis's son, Lothair (r. 954–86) ascended the throne, Hugh the Great was the most powerful man in the kingdom, but Hugh's death in 956 left Lothair free to rule on his own. Actually, he spent his reign in constant struggle with the nobles, working tirelessly to set them against one another and to win over their subordinates.

Lothair was succeeded by his son, Louis V, the last Carolingian ruler of West Frankland. He began his reign under the guidance of his mother and of Hugh Capet, the oldest son of Hugh the Great. Once he was free of their guidance, Louis carried on his father's struggle with the nobles. He died without leaving an heir in an accident in 987.

Now the West Franks elected Hugh Capet as king. Like Ralph before him, Hugh (r. 987–96) concentrated on his own region, centered on Paris, and permitted the great men of the kingdom to rule their own principalities with little interference. He was content with their recognition of his kingship. It has been said that his greatest success was in passing the crown on

German Expansion to the East
800–1400

to his son, Robert. And it is true that the Capetian dynasty endured until 1789.

THE RISE OF THE GERMAN EMPIRE

Henry I

The East Frankish Carolingian line died out in 911, with the death of Louis the Child, who had succeeded his father Arnulf in 899 at the age of six. Instead of reuniting East and West Frankland by accepting the rule of Charles the Simple, the easterners elected Duke Conrad of Franconia as king (r. 911–18). Conrad spent the seven years of his reign vainly trying to assert his authority over the men who had elected him, and on his deathbed he named Duke Henry of Saxony as his successor. Assuming that Henry would be no more forceful than Conrad I, those same men elected him king.

The end of Carolingian rule in East Frankland led to a definitive split between the two main parts of the old Frankish empire, West Frankland and East Frankland. From 911 on, Germany as such became the successor of East Frankland. The last Carolingian rulers of West Frankland might have aspired to reunite the empire, but the loss of the eastern realm was permanent, and the two began to evolve separately.

In 918, the royal house of Germany was in dreadful financial trouble. Powerful nobles had gained control over hundreds of royal estates, which had provided the economic basis of Carolingian power, to such a degree that when Conrad died, only 180 royal estates remained. The dukes of Saxony had been among the most successful usurpers; only five royal estates were left in Saxony. When Henry ascended the throne and added his family holdings to those of the royal house, the number of royal estates held by the German king jumped to about 600.

Henry I (r. 918–36) has been criticized for ignoring the affairs of his kingdom while concentrating on adding to his ducal power. Actually, he devoted considerable attention to his royal obligations. He pushed back the northern Slavs and began

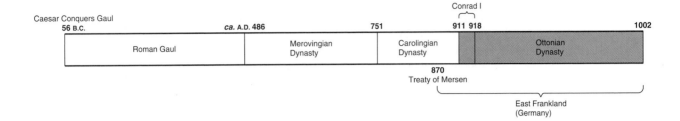

an eastward expansion based on missionary activity and colonization. Henry and his successors supported missionary activities in eastern Europe and established new colonies populated by Germans. Many of the major cities of Poland and Czechoslovakia began as German colonies in the tenth and eleventh centuries.

Henry also built up a cavalry force to deal with the swift-riding Magyars, who were raiding his kingdom almost every year. In 933, his cavalry inflicted the first defeat on the raiders. Meanwhile, Henry worked assiduously to force the dukes to recognize his authority. He forced the Swabians to accept his nominee as duke; he made a marriage alliance between his family and the family of the duke of Lotharingia; and he struggled to regain control of the old royal estates. He also initiated a policy of appointing supporters to bishoprics and major monasteries whenever he could. In this way, Henry tried to tie the wealthiest and most influential ecclesiastical institutions of the realm to the monarchy. He was the most effective German king since Louis the German.

Otto I

When Henry died, his son Otto I (r. 936–73) became king by hereditary right, though he was formally elected in accordance with the precedent of Conrad's election in 911. Building on his father's success, Otto strengthened the monarchy and continued Henry's effort to bring the Slavs into the church. As part of that program, he carried on the colonization of the eastern frontier and supported establishment of the bishoprics of Magdeburg and Prague. During the first five years of his reign, he put down several serious rebellions led by dukes and substantially reduced ducal power in Bavaria, Swabia, and Lotharingia. In 939, he annexed Franconia to Saxony. His strategy was to put members of his own family in control of the duchies, though he soon discovered that they too had a penchant for rebelling against the central government to advance local interests. So he adopted Henry's idea of using the churches as a basis of royal authority.

To gain control of the churches, Otto had to assert his authority over the appointment of bishops. This authority had once been held by the Carolingians, but it had long ago been usurped by the dukes and other nobles. After reclaiming it, Otto used the royal chapel as a training ground for clerics who later became bishops. Once they had taken up their position as

Ivory plaque showing Otto the Great offering a model of Magdeburg Cathedral to Christ (late tenth century).

heads of episcopal churches, he granted them land and privileges, which provided them with the wealth and power to help him. He also assumed control over the appointment of abbots in the richest monasteries, and they too became agents of royal authority.

Through these policies Otto ensured that the best-educated and most able men in the kingdom would be loyal supporters of his monarchy. Moreover, by seeing to it that the rule of celibacy was enforced among the higher clergy, he reduced the likelihood that bishops would try to launch dynasties of their own. All in all, Otto arranged matters so that the bishops would counterpoise the nobles in their districts and remain loyal supporters of royal authority. The success of these policies was demonstrated in 982, when Otto's successor Otto II campaigned in Italy with an army in which 76 percent of the soldiers had been provided from church-held lands.

Otto I was the most powerful king in Europe, and his court was a center of intellectual and artistic life. In 951, he married the heiress to the throne of Italy—partly to prevent the king of Burgundy from marrying her—and announced that he was assuming the title of emperor, which had been vacant since 924. But

when the pope expressed his hostility to the idea, and when a rebellion broke out in Germany, Otto was obliged to return home. Over the next decade he was occupied with the continuing threat of Magyar raids.

In 961, when the new pope, John XII (r. 955–64), appealed to Otto for help against an Italian usurper, Berengar of Friuli, who claimed to be king of Italy, Otto crossed the Alps for a second time. After dealing with Berengar, he again sought the imperial crown, and at last, in 962, Pope John crowned him Emperor of the Romans. But relations between Otto and the pope soon soured. As emperor, Otto felt that he could assert the same rights in the papal church as he had in the German bishoprics, and John objected. In 963, Otto drove John from Rome and presided over a council that deposed him and elected a pope more to Otto's liking. Otto rigged the election of two other popes during his reign, setting important precedents for later debates over the relationship between secular and ecclesiastical authority.

From 962, Otto spent most of his time in Italy trying to consolidate his position as emperor. He had better success in that effort at home than he did in Italy. The Byzantines did recognize his new title, however, and he achieved the long-sought alliance between the western and eastern imperial houses by arranging the marriage of his son Otto II to the Byzantine princess Theophano.

Germany and Italy at the Time of Otto the Great   962

Otto II, Otto III, and Archbishop Gerbert

Otto II (r. 973–83) spent most of his reign in Germany, trying to cope with widespread rebellions against the monarchy. Otto I had kept the great men in line, and they hoped to regain some of their power under the new king. When Otto II died, they made some progress in that direction. Otto left an infant heir, Otto III (r. 983–1002), in whose name the government was run by the queen mother Theophano and by Adelaide, Otto I's elderly widow.

Although Otto III's authority was recognized immediately in Italy, the regents had to give up a great deal to the German

Papal Coronation of
Otto the Great
962

Death of
Frederick II
1250

Napoleonic
Reorganization
of the Germanies
1806

H   O   L   Y   R   O   M   A   N   E   M   P   I   R   E

dukes and magnates to win their recognition. Young Otto III was raised in a court deeply influenced by his Byzantine mother, and when he became king, he dreamed of restoring the Christian empire of Constantine the Great. He was encouraged in this dream by a scholar named Gerbert, who had been Otto II's tutor and who was reputedly the most learned man in Europe.

Gerbert (*ca.* 945–1003) was born in Aurillac in Aquitaine. He studied in Spain, where he learned some mathematics and astronomy from the Moslems. He then traveled to Italy, where he met Otto I, who named him tutor to Otto II. From this time on, he had a close relation with the German royal family. About the time Otto II became king, Gerbert went to Reims in West Frankland to study logic with a famous teacher, and he was soon teaching philosophy at the cathedral school in Reims. About 980, he returned to Otto II's court, and Otto appointed him abbot of the great Italian abbey of Bobbio, near Piacenza. But Gerbert made the mistake of trying to revamp the monastery's financial system, which was controlled by the local nobility, and soon returned to Reims. There he became involved in West Frankish politics, eventually coming down in support of the house of Capet against Charles of Lotharingia, brother of Lothair, the last Carolingian king. With Hugh Capet's support, Gerbert became archbishop of Reims in 991. But some controversy arose over the appointment, and he eventually returned to Italy. There Otto III appointed him first as archbishop of Ravenna and then, in 999, as pope.

Gerbert took the name Sylvester II to signify that he and Otto III were renewing the cooperation between emperor and pope that had prevailed between Constantine I and Sylvester I. In 1000, Sylvester authorized the establishment of an independent archdiocese in Poland and crowned Stephen king of Hungary. He also brought King Olaf Tryggvason of Norway and his new church into the orbit of papal authority. The dream of rebuilding the empire faded when Otto III died childless in 1002. Sylvester died the next year.

Nonetheless, Gerbert's career was of enduring importance. By bringing teaching and scholarship to the service of the highest authority, he demonstrated that the acquisition of learning was a viable road to success. Moreover, his experience in Spain opened up a world of knowledge formerly unknown to the West. Gerbert was credited with introducing Arabic numerals to Europe; he also reorganized the study of logic. Sophisticated in both political and intellectual matters, Gerbert helped seed a cultural revival that would blossom eventually into the renaissance of the twelfth century.

Ivory plaque showing Otto II, his wife Theophano, and their son Otto III kneeling before Christ (*ca.* 980).

The four provinces of Slavinia, Germania, Gallia, and Roma *(left)* paying homage to Otto III *(right)*, from the Reichenau Gospels (tenth century). Note that Otto wears a Roman imperial costume, not a Germanic one.

Page from the earliest manuscript of *Beowulf* (eleventh century).

ANGLO-SAXON ENGLAND

Anglo-Saxon Culture

By the end of the seventh century the Anglo-Saxon kingdoms had been fully converted to Christianity and had achieved political stability. During the eighth century, they were carrying on an active trade with the Continent and enjoyed a period of prosperity and cultural activity under Offa of Mercia (r. 757–96), the *bretwalda* or chief king among the seven kingdoms.

Although Offa looked on Charles the Great as a leader and model, it was England, not the Frankish kingdom, that had emerged as the intellectual center of northern Europe during the eighth century. At the beginning of the century, the monk Bede from Jarrow in Northumbria rose to prominence and set a tradition that would eventually include Alcuin and other intellectual leaders of early medieval Europe.

Bede (*ca.* 672–735) wrote commentaries on both the Old Testament and the New Testament and helped establish the practice of biblical commentary. He also wrote works on astronomy and intro-

duced the dating system based on the birth of Christ, invented by a Greek writer of the sixth century, that we still use today. His most important work was the *Ecclesiastical History of the English People,* our principal source of information about early Anglo-Saxon history. Bede's greatest contribution was as a teacher, however. His pupil, Egbert (d. 766), became head of the cathedral school in York and then archbishop of the city, which under him became the intellectual capital of England. Egbert's student Aelbert succeeded him as archbishop and appointed his favorite student Alcuin (see p. 227–28) as head of the cathedral school.

As England changed from the pagan warrior society of the migrations to a settled Christian society, poets set down in writing some of the ancient stories that had been recited in the halls of kings for generations. One of those poems was *Beowulf,* an anonymous work that tells of a heroic king who lived in southern Scandinavia before the migrations. The version we have comes from a manuscript that dates from around A.D. 1000, but the earliest version was written about 725. The great battle poems *Maldon* and *Brunanburh* date from the ninth century, though

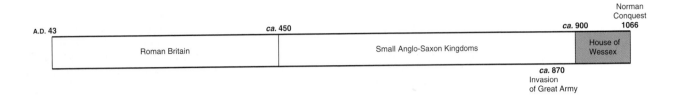

they achieved their final form in the tenth century. Toward the end of the ninth century, King Alfred the Great (r. 871–99) translated Bede's *Ecclesiastical History of the English People* from Latin into Anglo-Saxon and ordered Anglo-Saxon translations of works by Boethius and other Latin writers. Apparently he also commissioned the writing of the *Anglo-Saxon Chronicle,* a history that was continued into the twelfth century.

Anglo-Saxon Government

As we have seen (p. 234), King Alfred defeated the Great Army of the Vikings, and his successors brought the Danelaw, virtually the whole eastern half of England, under control early in the tenth century. Alfred's royal house of Wessex had brought the Anglo-Saxon kingdoms together into the united kingdom of England. To buttress their position, the kings instituted a program of church reform that brought Benedictine monasticism to England and bestowed monastic constitutions on the bishoprics. Henceforth, the clergy of the bishoprics were to be members of the monasteries located in the cathedral churches. The kings also set in place new institutions of local government so effective that they survived for centuries and still appear in modified form in county governments of the United States.

The tenth-century kings divided the country into shires, or counties, headed by shire reeves, or sheriffs, who were royal officials. The shires were subdivided into smaller units called hundreds. These units were judicial as well as administrative units: The sheriff raised soldiers for the army, managed the royal estates in the shire, made sure that the roads, bridges, and any fortifications were kept in good condition, and judged disputes between

the king's subjects. The sheriff presided over the shire court, which met twice a year, and oversaw the hundred courts, which met about once a month. Fortified towns were organized as boroughs, with courts of their own.

England from Alfred the Great to Edgar

Powerful as the sheriffs grew over time, they never became independent of the king. Though they came to rank as nobles, below the earls, who were the companions of the king and who were each responsible for several shires, the king could replace a sheriff who failed to do his job loyally and efficiently. By the end of the tenth century the English king had a representative in every part of the country, and during the next century England came to rival Germany as the most powerful kingdom in Europe.

MEDIEVAL SOCIETY: THE GROWTH OF FEUDAL INSTITUTIONS

Until recently, historians referred to medieval society as a "feudal society." The term "feudal" was coined in the eighteenth century to describe a society based on the fief (*feudum* in Latin), a property held by a man in return for services, primarily military service, rendered to its owner, a king or a lord. Although its holder did not own the fief, it was granted to him for life. The services due were personal in nature, including the obligation to attend the lord's court, to support him in arranging marriages for his children, to give him advice about the affairs of the region, and to join him in war. The relationship between lord and subordinate (eventually called a vassal), provided the subordinate with a means of support and thus enabled him to serve his lord.

Peasants held their land from the fiefholder in return for furnishing him with labor and part of their produce. The fiefholder could eject a peasant from his land whenever he felt like doing so. In short, medieval society was seen as a hierarchical structure based on a descending order of rights and obligations.

In recent years historians have revised this view of medieval society, pointing out that simple ownership of land existed side by side with fiefholding, and medieval society now appears to have had a more complex structure than was once believed. Still, feudal institutions did play a distinctive role in medieval society.

Twelfth-century seal depicting a vassal giving homage to his lord.

Those institutions were based on the notion of "tenure"—that is, one's right to occupy land. Tenure might consist of freehold (outright ownership), leasehold for a finite term, or a right subject to the will of the landlord (villeinage). In the Middle Ages, the right to use a farm or mill often entailed a chain of tenures: the possessor of the property held it by one kind of tenure from another person who held it by another kind from another, and so on. For example, a friend of the king might receive land as a fief and grant some parts of it as fiefs to his supporters, some parts of it under lease to clients, and other parts "in villeinage" to peasant farmers.

In a typical peasant village, some families had freeholds and others were leaseholders or villeins. There were also cottagers, families without land who lived in cottages that belonged to someone else. Cottagers usually kept a small vegetable garden and supplemented their meager living by working for others. A person's legal status depended on the nature of his tenure. Freeholders and leaseholders were freemen with full legal rights. Villeins were subject to the authority of those from whom they held their land. Cottagers were subject to the authority of the lord of the village.

Other aspects of medieval society had little or nothing to do with land tenure, including the personal relationship between lord and vassal, the fragmentation of political authority, and the devolution of royal authority into private hands.

Vassalage derived from an old Roman institution called commendation, by which one person would voluntarily commend himself to another. The act created a legal relationship between them that required the superior party to protect the inferior party and required the inferior to show loyalty and provide assistance to the superior. The man who commended himself became the *fidelis* (faithful man) of the other and took an oath of fealty to him. For example, a small farmer facing ruin might commend himself to a great landowner. That act would lead to a subject tenure, which would enable the farmer to go on using the land.

Obviously, commendation was not something that great men ordinarily entered into, and until the eighth century a stigma attached to the idea of a subject relationship, which was then called vassalage. To be sure, an aristocrat owed allegiance to his king, a relationship that derived from the ancient relationship between the Germanic war leader and his warriors, which Romans called the *comitatus*. But obedience and loyalty within the *comitatus* were honorable relationships between free men and their king.

During the eighth and ninth centuries, the idea of the *comitatus* gradually merged with vassalage. In 757, for example, Pepin the Short caught the Duke of Bavaria in a web of intrigue and treason and forced him to commend himself as a vassal. In 787, Charles the Great forced that same Duke of Bavaria to acknowledge his status as a royal vassal. As the device came into use as a means of disciplining presumptuous subjects, the stigma began to wear off.

The idea of feudal tenure derived directly from the Roman law of property. Under Roman law, a person could grant land as a *benefice,* under which the grantee held the land on favorable terms while the grantor retained ownership. In Roman times such grants were made for a definite term, but by the seventh century, under the Merovingian successors to Roman authority in Gaul, benefices were usually made for the life of the grantee. By the tenth century, the fief (as the benefice came to called) had become hereditary. The lord still granted the fief for life, but he always granted it to the eldest son of the previous holder.

The original purpose of the benefice was to cement relations between grantor and grantee. But under Charles Martel and Pepin the Short, it became common to combine the granting of a benefice with a commendation—in effect, creating a lord-vassal relationship. Because the benefice was a way of providing the vassal with a means of support, a man could actually increase his wealth by becoming a vassal. As a result, by the late ninth century a feudal hierarchy was beginning to

The Ceremony of Becoming a Vassal   1127

This description comes from the period when feudalism was fully developed. It is detailed because the leading men of Flanders had just accepted a new count after a disputed succession. Homage (the specific obligation of the vassal) is carefully distinguished from the more general obligation of fidelity. By the twelfth century it was assumed that most vassals had fiefs.

On Thursday, homages were done to the count. First, they did homage in this way. The count asked [the vassal] if he wished to become his man without reserve, and the latter answered: "I do." Then, joining his hands together, he placed them in the hands of the count, and they bound themselves to each other by a kiss. Then the man who had just done homage pledged fidelity . . . to the count in these words: "I promise on my faith to be faithful from now on to count William and to observe [the obligations of] my homage completely, in good faith, and without deceit." This he swore on the relics of the saints. . . . Finally, with a little stick that he held in his hand, the count gave investiture of fiefs to all those who had . . . promised security, done homage, and taken the oath.

From Galbert of Bruges, De Multro Karoli comitis Flandiriarum, *ed. by H. Pirenne (Paris, 1891), p. 89.*

emerge. Many members of the old aristocratic families who held large tracts of land by freehold chose to become vassals of the king to receive a benefice. About the same time, the word "benefice" was giving way to the term "feudum," or fief.

Under a fief, the service a vassal owed to the king was usually military service. He was bound to serve in the king's army for a certain period—eventually forty days per year. He had to serve at his own expense, which meant that the income from the fief was usually great enough to cover expenses. The smallest military fief was the knight's fief or, as it came to be called in English, the knight's fee. Fiefs were valued according to the number of knightly soldiers they could support, and many were much larger than the knight's fee.

The idea of the knight's fee was not so different from the old Roman idea that anyone who owned a piece of land had an obligation to serve in the army. And

Mailed knight with large shield and spear used by foot soldiers.

A feudal knight accompanying a traveling king (eleventh century).

remember that the Byzantines had tried to ensure the prosperity of yeoman farmers so that they would have an adequate supply of military manpower (see p. 180). Of course, the landholdings in the West were much larger than those in the East, and the fiefs had to support a new kind of soldier. Although the yeomen continued to serve as the backbone of the medieval army, heavily armed mounted knights—professional soldiers—emerged as its elite troops.

The Medieval Military System

The emergence of the new warriors rested on the introduction of a new technology, the use of horseshoes and stirrups. There is disagreement about when these implements came into use. The Huns had been using them in the fifth century, but in Europe their use probably coincided with the appearance of the mounted knights during the eighth century. Horseshoes made the horse a reliable military vehicle, and stirrups gave the rider the support and leverage he needed to fight on horseback.

In an expansion of the vassalage-benefice system, Charles Martel and Pepin the Short built up their new troops by forcing the churches and monasteries to grant benefices to royal vassals, thus bringing the ecclesiastical powers into the

military system. Henry I and Otto I were able to incorporate bishops and abbots into their government because for generations the officials of the church had been supplying knights to the royal armies and were already members of the feudal aristocracy.

Feudal Government

The distinction between military and governmental functions did not exist in early medieval society. It was assumed that the military elite, the king's companions, were also part of his government. In this way, the new feudal hierarchy functioned much like the ancient *comitatus,* which also combined military and governmental functions. The difference was that the *comitatus* was made up mostly of young men who lived with the king but ceased to play a role in royal government when they went home to their farms and estates, whereas the members of the feudal hierarchy held land from the king and were part of his government both at court and at home.

The governmental functions of the early medieval kings were conducted from royal estates spread around the kingdom. Under Charles the Great, the royal bailiffs and counts governed their districts from seats on the royal estates and supported themselves from the income of the estates. Consequently, the rights of government in each district were associated with specific properties, and when the late Carolingians gave away those properties during the civil wars, the powers of government went with them.

In France, where the royal government had been powerless to cope with the bands of Viking raiders that struck without warning, local men had organized the defense of their districts and in the process had arrogated governmental authority to themselves. Some of these men held fiefs, others did not, so the fragmentation of governmental authority into the hands of locals was not related to the emergence of the feudal system. On the eastern frontier, by contrast, the threat posed by the great Magyar armies required a centralized

defense that enhanced the power of the German kings and made it possible for Otto I to revive the *imperium* of Charles the Great.

Up to the end of the eleventh century, no region of Europe was totally dominated by feudal institutions. In most regions, some land was held by fiefholders and some by men who held their estates through ancient freehold tenure. Many great men held estates under both systems. The rise of truly feudal states in England and in the Latin kingdom of Jerusalem resulted from conquests that will be discussed later (see pp. 274–75).

LIFE IN EARLY MEDIEVAL SOCIETY

For most people, life was hard in the early Middle Ages. The peasants struggled to produce enough food to feed themselves and their lords, who sometimes had large households that ate a great deal but produced nothing. The lower classes suffered from malnutrition, which stunted their growth and intelligence. No system existed to move foodstuffs readily from one area to another when drought or flood wiped out the crops, so the peasants suffered frequent famines while the upper-class families moved from estate to estate living on the produce of their lands.

The military society of the early medieval kingdoms was dominated by men, and most feudal institutions rested on relationships between men. As hereditary tenure grew more common, however, it became possible for the daughters as well as the sons of a vassal to inherit his fief. Consequently the feudal relationship between lord and vassal was altered to give the lord the right to approve the marriage of the vassal's daughters. An orphaned heiress became the ward of the lord, who could marry her to whomever he wished. It was imperative that the lord choose as vassals only those who were likely to carry out their feudal duties loyally and properly. At the same time, marriage to the daughter of a vassal provided up and coming young men with an entry into the feudal hierarchy, and many men who had

achieved some standing during the Viking period followed this route. In fact, many of the aristocratic families of later times originated from such marriages.

Still, women remained subordinate to men under the law. A woman could not buy or sell property on her own. Whatever she brought to a marriage had to be given over to be managed by her husband. She could not appear in a court of law unless her husband or a male relative accompanied her and acted on her behalf. Although she might influence her family's decision about whom she was to marry, the power to decide resided with her father or with male relatives.

Reality did not usually conform to law, however. The mistress of a feudal household was often left to manage its affairs herself. The husband was often away at the royal court or visiting his other properties, and in his absence the bailiffs reported to her and took orders from her. Moreover, she supervised the education of the children and advised her husband on political matters.

If we turn our attention from the countryside to the cities, we would see that city life was not so different from rural life. Townspeople relied on the market rather than on farming for their livelihood, but they kept gardens and at harvest time many of them went out to the surrounding villages to help bring in the crops. Just as the villages were subject to their lords, so towns were under the control of lords, usually the bishops, who collected fees and taxes from the town market and town court as well as tolls from the local bridges. The lord of the town organized the townspeople for the defense and for the maintenance of the roads and bridges. Townspeople owed service to their lord much as the country villagers owed services to theirs. The early medieval kings came to recognize the commercial potential of the towns only after becoming aware of the prosperous Italian cities that were growing wealthy from the eastern Mediterranean trade. It would be a long time, however, before cities became a significant feature of the economy of northern Europe and before the ways of city life influenced the general society.

Infants were swaddled in the Middle Ages to protect their "loose" limbs and bodies. Here two thirteenth-century nurses hold swaddled infants.

Suggestions for Further Reading

General

On the rise of the Carolingians, see P. Geary, *Before France and Germany* (1988), and J. M. Wallace-Hadrill, *The Barbarian West, 400–1000* (1952). The best work on the Carolingian period is R. McKitterick, *The Frankish Kingdoms under the Carolingians* (1983). On the missionaries, see W. Levison, *England and the Continent in the Eighth Century* (1946), and C. H. Talbot, *Anglo-Saxon Missionaries in Germany* (1954), which treats the relationship between Pepin the Short and Boniface and provides a view of religious life in the eighth century. On Pepin's coronation, the most recent study is M. J. Enright, *Iona, Tara and Soissons: The Origins of the Royal Anointing Ritual* (1985).

Charles the Great

On Charles the Great, see the almost-contemporary life by Einhard, *Life of Charlemagne* (several editions, some with the later life by Notker). For a survey of the Frankish empire, see H. Fichtenau, *The Carolingian Empire* (1957), which emphasizes social conditions. D. Bullough, *The Age of Charlemagne*, 2nd ed. (1973), is a well-illustrated survey. For studies of Frankish institutions, see F. Ganshof, *Frankish Institutions under Charlemagne* (1968) and *The Carolingians and the Frankish Monarchy* (1971). On the economic history of the period, see R. Latouche, *The Birth of the Western Economy* (1961), and G. Duby, *The Early Growth of the Medieval Economy* (1974). For the different views of the coronation of Charles, see R. E. Sullivan, ed., *The Coronation of Charlemagne: What Did It Signify?* (1959). On the relations between the Franks and the papacy, see T. F. X. Noble, *The Republic of St. Peter: The Birth of the Papal State, 680–825* (1984). On the way people of the period lived, see P. Riché, *Daily Life in the Age of Charlemagne* (1978).

Later Carolingians

On Charles the Bald, see the studies in J. L. Nelson and M. T. Gibson, eds., *Charles the Bald: Court and Kingdom* (1981). On the ecclesiastical politics of the ninth century, see P. McKeon, *Hincmar of Laon and Carolingian Politics* (1978), and J. L. Nelson, "Charles the Bald and the Church in Town and Countryside," *Studies in Church History* 16 (1979): 103–18. On the Carolingian view of kingship, see W. Ullmann, *The Carolingian Renaissance and the Idea of Kingship* (1969), and J. M. Wallace-Hadrill, "The *Via Regia* of the Carolingian Age," *Trends in Medieval Political Thought,* ed. B. Smalley (1965). On the origins of the nobility, see the essays in T. Reuter, ed., *The Medieval Nobility* (1978), and D. H. Green, *The Carolingian Lord* (1965). P. Sawyer, *The Age of the Vikings,* 2nd ed. (1971), gives a good picture of the Viking invasions. See also, J. M. Wallace-Hadrill, *The Vikings in Francia* (1975). On Viking civilization, see J. Brønsted, *The Vikings* (1960). C. A. Macartney, *The Magyars in the Ninth Century* (1930), is a scholarly study of the origins and wanderings of the Magyars.

The Carolingian Renaissance

On the origins of the Carolingian Renaissance, see M. L. W. Laistner, *Thought and Letters in Western Europe, 500–900* (1966); P. Riché, *Education and Culture in the Barbarian West* (1976); and L. R. Reynolds and N. G. Wilson, *Scribes and Scholars,* 2nd ed. (1974). For a survey of the Renaissance, see J. Broussard, *The Civilization of Charlemagne* (1969). On Charles the Bald as a patron, see R. McKitterick, "Charles the Bald (823–877) and his Library: the Patronage of Learning," *English Historical Review* 95 (1980): 28–47 and *The Uses of Literacy in Early Mediaeval Europe* (1990). K. J. Conant, *Carolingian and Romanesque Architecture* (1959); A. Grabar and C. Nordenfalk, *Early Medieval Painting: From the Fourth to the Eleventh Century* (1957); and J. Hubert, *Carolingian Art* (1970), give surveys of Carolingian art.

West and East Frankland (France and Germany)

For an overview of the period in which the Carolingian dynasty ended, see R. S. Lopez, *The Tenth Century* (1959). On the history of West Frankland (France) in the period, see E. James, *The Origins of France: From Clovis to the Capetians, 500–1000* (1982). For a general introduction to the history of the Ottonian empire, see G. Barraclough, *The Origins of Modern Germany* (1947); J. Fleckenstein, *Early Medieval Germany* (1978); and B. H. Hill, *The Rise of the First Reich: Germany in the Tenth Century* (1969). K. J. Leyser, *Rule and Conflict in an Early Medieval Society: Ottonian Saxony* (1979), provides a view of politics and social relations in tenth-century Germany.

Feudalism

On the growth of feudal institutions, see F. L. Ganshof, *Feudalism,* 3rd ed. (1964), which gives a good account of "classical feudalism" from the Carolingian period on. J. R. Strayer, *Feudalism* (1965), emphasizes political factors. For the role of feudalism in medieval society, see G. Duby, *Rural Economy and Country Life in the Medieval West* (1968), and G. Fourquin, *Lordship and Feudalism in the Middle Ages* (1976).

Women and Society

For studies of women in early medieval society, see P. Stafford, *Queens, Concubines and Dowagers: The King's Wife in the Early Middle Ages* (1983); S. Wemple, *Women in Frankish Society,* (1981); and S. M. Stuard, ed., *Women in Medieval Society* (1976), which is a collection of articles on the various roles played by women. See also, A. M. Lucas, *Women in the Middle Ages* (1983); E. S. Duckett, *Women and their Letters in the Early Middle Ages* (1964). On childrearing, see L. deMause, ed., *The History of Childhood* (1974).

REVIVAL AND REFORM IN WESTERN EUROPE

By the end of the Carolingian period, what had once been the kingdom of Charles the Great consisted of three separate kingdoms—the realms that would become France, Germany, and Italy—ruled by monarchs with only a vestige of the power that Louis the Pious had left to his sons. Each kingdom was divided into powerful duchies whose rulers acted independently while pretending to support their king. When, in the tenth century, the Saxon dukes in Germany and the Capetian counts in France became kings, they were more assiduous in strengthening their own ancestral principalities than they were in trying to restore royal authority.

During the tenth century only a trickle of long-distance trade found its way to the towns, and urban populations were on the decline. Secular authorities controlled the churches, and the bishops and abbots were little more than feudal lords busily engaged in managing their estates and leading their troops rather than in ministering to the spiritual needs of their parishioners or following the Rule of St. Benedict. Even the papacy had lost much of its stature. After Otto I imposed his control on the church of Rome, the papacy had fallen into the hands of the Roman aristocracy, who used it as a pawn in advancing their dynastic and political strategies. For a moment, under Sylvester II (r. 999–1003), the papacy recovered its international standing, but after his death the Roman families began to buy and sell the throne of St. Peter once again. Finally, the cultural centers of the Carolingian age were without their former luster, and only a few scholars were left to keep Latin learning alive.

Yet, despite this depressing state of affairs, agriculture, the basis of the European economy, began to improve and population growth began to pick up, which fostered a revival of trade. A Burgundian monk launched a program monastic reform that would eventually rekindle intellectual life and reform the church as a whole. And the new kings would slowly turn to the business of ruling their kingdoms.

THE AGRICULTURAL ECONOMY AND SOCIETY

Village Agriculture

The agricultural economy of the Middle Ages was based on the villages, many of which had existed since Roman times. The land of western Europe, which had once been heavily forested, had deep, rocky soil capable of producing rich crops if properly cultivated.

From time immemorial, life in the villages had been controlled by the great landowners. Most of the villages had grown up on the sites of old Roman villas that had been taken over by the new Germanic aristocracy. The lord of the village held part of the fields, controlled the pasturage and woodland, and required the

villagers to work his domain. The villagers were under a variety of obligations to the lord, and sorting out who owed what kind of labor service was a matter of great interest.

The confusion arose from the different tenures by which the various families held their land. Many of the families owned their land outright, some held land by villeinage tenure, and some were cottagers with no land at all (see p. 244). The luckier families held strips of land distributed here and there in the common fields that were worked by all the villagers. At harvest time, each family claimed the produce of its own strips. The cottagers worked for others, often for the lord of the village.

Because some strips of land were more productive than others, most of the families held some good land and some poor land. Good luck, good husbandry, or a good marriage gave some families more than others, and every village had poor families and relatively well-to-do families. A run of bad luck, however, such as the death of the husband, or the failure to produce offspring, or a disastrous lawsuit, could alter a family's fortunes. All lived in fear of disaster.

The market square of a thirteenth-century town.

The lord's domain and the village together constituted a unit called a villa or manor. To develop the manor into an economically viable entity, the lords built mills, fish ponds, smithies, and other "industrial" works. Millers and smiths held their respective manufactories from the lord and paid a rent in kind. The rights of villagers to take fish from the ponds were similar to their rights to let their pigs forage and to collect firewood in the woodland or to graze their cattle in the common pasture. Patches of woodland were measured by the number of pigs they could support. Although the typical manor was not altogether self-sufficient, it was a stable, productive economic entity.

The diet of the villagers consisted mainly of bread and cereals, with little meat. The lord kept for himself the right to hunt in the woodland, and what meat the villagers had came from pigs and cattle. But the pasturage always seemed inadequate to provide enough hay to feed the animals through the long winters. Moreover, the fields yielded only about four grains for every seed planted. (Today's U.S. farms yield about 25 to 1.) Consequently, the entire grain crop had to be saved for human consumption and for the next year's planting. The villagers often indulged in great feasts in late winter or early spring—which in pagan times had been associated with fertility cults—in which they consumed animals that would probably have died anyway for lack of fodder.

The Agricultural Revolution

In ancient times, villagers had learned to leave half their fields fallow each year to given them a chance to recover needed nutrients. Cattle grazed on the unplanted fields and helped to replenish them with their manure. The two-field rotation system was used for centuries across northern Europe. At last, however, innovations arose that triggered an agricultural revolution.

One major innovation was the introduction of the heavy wheeled plow. This plow had been used in a few places in late Roman times and may have been invented by the Celts of northern Gaul, though it has been found in early Germanic settlements as well. The simple scratch plows the Romans brought north with them had worked well enough in the dry regions of the south, where deep plowing would have exposed too much soil and would have allowed the moisture to evaporate. But in the moist climate of northern Europe, the heavy wheeled plow fitted with a moldboard could cut deep into the soil and turn it over to bring the nutrients to the surface.

This new tool had a profound effect on village life as its use spread throughout northern Europe during the ninth and tenth centuries. It proved expensive to maintain, however, because the rocks dropped by the glaciers of the ice ages often damaged the plowshare. So the villagers began to band together to buy and maintain their village plow. They needed skilled smiths to keep it in good repair, and the smiths created other farm tools as well.

Pulling such a heavy plow took a great deal of animal power, and teams of six to eight oxen were not uncommon. To put such teams together, several families would pool their resources, another incentive toward cooperation. The more powerful plow increased the yield from old fields and made it possible to bring new fields under cultivation. Consequently, food production climbed steadily from the ninth through the twelfth centuries.

A second great innovation was the introduction of horses to replace oxen as the source of power. Though horses generate a bit less power than oxen, they pull at twice the speed. The use of horses not only increased the amount of plowing

Illustration from an eleventh-century manuscript depicting plowing and sowing.

done each season but permitted the farmers to go out much further from the village before beginning their day's work. The disadvantage of horse power is that horses are more susceptible to disease and injury than oxen.

The change from oxen to horses depended on two technological advances—the use of horseshoes and the development of an improved collar that would enable a horse to pull the heavy plow without injury. The Huns had used horseshoes, as had the Carolingian cavalry. The hooves of horses are quite fragile, and iron horseshoes protected them from the breakage and hoof rot caused by the rocky, moist soil of northern Europe. Horseshoes made it possible to use horses for transport as well as farm work. But until the invention of the new collar, horses could not pull wagons or plows of any great weight because the old harnesses cut across their windpipe. During the ninth century, a new collar, which rested on the horse's withers (the highest points of the shoulder blades), came into use, enabling horses to perform both farm and team work.

Although horses were expensive to maintain, their use gradually spread over Europe during the eleventh century. That development had several important effects. It increased the efficiency of land transport, both for commerce and for military campaigns, and encouraged the growth of an industry served by guilds of teamsters. Moreover, it led to road improvements that in turn opened up new commercial opportunities for crossroads communities. It also advanced the agricultural expansion that was steadily pushing back the medieval forest.

A third technological innovation was the introduction of the three-field rotation system. Although this change took place only slowly in the old villages, which were reluctant to abandon their traditional ways, it was favored by farmers in the new settlements. The shift to three-field farming was complete by the thirteenth century.

The new system expanded the amount of land in production while preserving the old principle that land should be left fallow to recover. This system kept two-thirds—instead of half—of the fields in production at any one time. It also encouraged the villagers to adopt a new scheme of crop rotation, because now they had two large fields to plant instead of just one. They usually planted one field in winter wheat, which they harvested in July, and then let that field rest until the following spring, when they sowed it with a summer crop. After harvesting that crop in the fall, they plowed and sowed the field again in winter wheat. They planted the other two fields according to the same pattern but on a different cycle, so that in any year, one-third of the land was in winter wheat, one-third was in summer grain, and one-third was lying fallow. Over every three-year period, each field lay fallow for a year and a half. In many regions, the summer crop was a legume, such as soybean, which restores nitrogen to the soil.

Horse in harness pulling a harrow (detail from a thirteenth-century manuscript illustration).

The Three-Field System

	Field A	Field B	Field C
First Year	FALLOW until the fall Sow wheat in the fall	Harvest wheat in July FALLOW from July until the spring	Sow oats in the spring Harvest oats in the fall FALLOW until the next fall
Second Year	Harvest wheat in July FALLOW from July until the spring	Sow oats in the spring Harvest oats in the fall FALLOW until the next fall	FALLOW until the fall Sow wheat in the fall
Third Year	Sow oats in the spring Harvest oats in the fall FALLOW until the next fall	FALLOW until the fall Sow wheat in the fall	Harvest wheat in July FALLOW from July until the spring

So the yield increased even more than would be expected from the extra land kept in production.

The three-field system succeeded only where an even distribution of rainfall throughout the year permitted a summer crop to grow and only where farming was done on a village basis. In the Mediterranean region the summers are too dry for growing crops, and in Scandinavia the rocky soil and the short growing season are not conducive to the existence of villages. So the Mediterranean villages stuck to the two-field system, while in Scandinavia most farming occurred on individual homesteads.

THE REVIVAL OF TRADE AND TOWNS

Commerce and the Settlement of Jews in Europe

The political and economic crises of the late Roman period, together with the Germanic invasions, had reduced the size and the economic importance of European towns. Because many of the Germanic kings chose to spend their time on royal estates scattered across the countryside, the towns ceased to enjoy the central role they had enjoyed under the Romans. This was particularly true in northern Europe.

In Italy, the Gothic wars of the sixth century devastated the cities, and it was more than two centuries before they again became major centers in the Mediterranean trade. In Spain, the Moslem conquest cut off the old cities of Valencia, Seville, and Granada from the former European provinces of the Roman Empire and brought them into the Mediterranean commercial system of the Arabic Empire. Not until the slow Christian reconquest of Spain during the eleventh and twelfth centuries did these cities renew contact with the West.

The collapse of Roman power had led to a decline in international trade, which contributed to economic depression in the cities. In ancient times, the long-distance trade had been mainly in grain, but through much of the Middle Ages it was mainly in luxury goods from the eastern Mediterranean. During the sixth through the eighth century, the towns had become local market centers and seats of episcopal administration, hardly conducive settings for population growth or cultural activity.

The later Carolingians tried to revive international trade. They encouraged Jewish merchants to emigrate from Italy to the northern cities by offering them special privileges and protection. The Jews maintained their connections with Jewish communities in commercial centers throughout Italy and the Mediterranean.

The Jews in Northern Europe

The Jews tended to settle into their own sections of town and formed a distinctive cultural community. Jewish religious practice required that they live near the synagogue—the place of worship and study—in buildings centered around a courtyard. On Saturdays, the sabbath, Jews are not permitted to work, cook, or handle money, but they can carry on ordinary activities within their own home. The rabbis defined the courtyard communities as "homes," so their inhabitants could get along on Saturdays. Because the Jewish community was under the protection of the king, it enjoyed a special legal status. All of these features of Jewish life contributed to the isolation of the Jews from the surrounding population.

During the late ninth and tenth centuries, they shipped to southern markets the agricultural surplus produced by the great northern estates. With local markets tied to international trade, the late Carolingian economy experienced a vigorous revival.

Merchants who engaged in long-distance trade had to have safe repositories for goods and funds in the towns they did business in and had to be familiar with the local markets and the men who ran them. Jewish merchants solved those problems by maintaining contact with Jewish communities in various towns and by sending their sons and nephews to be

A manuscript illustration of the barter economy.

their representatives in distant towns. Robbers knew that if they attacked a Jewish merchant, they would have to answer to the royal authorities. They also knew that they would have difficulty peddling the goods they stole. Once a theft was reported, everyone would be on the lookout for the rare goods—the spices, silks, and jewels—that could be easily identified as having come from the merchant's stocks.

The merchants needed substantial amounts of capital to purchase expensive goods in the eastern markets and to cover the cost of shipping them to the West. They borrowed most of their capital from the great landlords, who accumulated money by selling their agricultural surplus in the local markets. In fact, until the late eleventh century Jews were more likely to be borrowers than lenders. But when the crusaders, most of whom were knights with modest holdings, needed to finance their journey to the Holy Land, they turned to Jewish and other merchants for loans secured by the produce of their estates. From the middle of the twelfth century on, the great lords began to borrow money to cover the cost of building their grand fortified castles. And monasteries borrowed money to build their impressive new churches. Thirteenth-century bishops were often concerned about the indebtedness of the churches and monasteries in their dioceses, and many merchants evolved their businesses away from trade into banking.

The Recovery of the Italian Cities

The recovery of the Italian cities began around 800. Venice, on the Adriatic coast, had already been an active center in the trade between Europe and the Byzantine Empire. Founded in the fifth century by refugees fleeing the Huns, the city had come under Byzantine influence during the period in which Ravenna was the capital of Byzantine power in Italy. The city declined during the period of iconoclasm, because the controversy disrupted trade between the eastern and western parts of the Mediterranean (see pp. 175–78). The end of iconoclasm eased relations with the West, and during the ninth century

Medieval Trade Goods   Tenth to Twelfth Centuries

several northern Italian cities, including Venice, had grown slowly as trade with the recovering Byzantine Empire grew stronger.

After the Fatimid caliphs conquered Egypt in 969 and reformed the Egyptian fiscal system to encourage trade (see pp. 209–10), the recovery of the Italian cities gathered momentum. Amalfi (south of Naples), Venice, and Genoa were soon active trading partners of Egypt, and the new wealth spread to secondary markets in Italy and northern Europe. This was the time of the Viking raids, and Italian merchants benefited from the disruption of the trade routes from the eastern Mediterranean through the Baltic Sea and Russia to the Black Sea. The Vikings had moved down the Dnieper River from the Baltic and settled at Kiev. From the late tenth century on, Italian merchants be-

came numerous in Europe, forming the nucleus of a substantial Christian merchant class.

By the middle of the twelfth century, the Italians had come to dominate long-distance trade in Europe. The Italian cities were well positioned to take the lead in international commerce. The breakdown of Carolingian authority began much earlier in Italy than in the north. Even under Lothair, the son and successor of Louis the Pious, Italy found the yoke of royal authority relatively light. One of the reasons for the prosperity of the Italian cities was that they were relatively free of the onerous fiscal impositions of the great aristocratic landholders.

Given all these advantages, the Italian cities responded vigorously when trade began to pick up toward the end of the tenth century. Moreover, through their

An Early Medieval Merchant

When the boy had passed his childish years quietly at home [in Norfolk, England], he began to follow more prudent ways of life, and to learn carefully and persistently the teachings of worldly forethought. He chose not to follow the life of a husbandman but . . . aspiring to the merchant's trade, he began to follow the peddler's way of life, first learning how to gain in small bargains and things of insignificant price and thence . . . to buy and sell and gain from things of greater expense. For in his beginnings he was wont to wander with small wares around the villages and farmsteads of his own neighborhood, but in process of time he gradually associated himself by compact with city merchants. . . . At first he lived for four years as a peddler in Lincolnshire, going on foot and carrying the cheapest wares; then he traveled abroad, first to St. Andrews in Scotland and then to Rome. On his return . . . he began to launch on bolder courses and to coast frequently by sea to the foreign lands that lay about him. . . . At length his great labors and cares bore much fruit of worldly gain. For he labored not only as a merchant but also as a shipman . . . to Denmark and Flanders and Scotland; in all which lands he found certain rare wares, which he carried to other parts wherein he knew them to be less familiar and coveted by the inhabitants. . . . Hence he made great profit in all his bargains, and gathered much wealth in the sweat of his brow, for he sold dear in one place the wares which he had bought elsewhere at a small price.

From Life of St. Godric of Finchale, *trans. by G. G. Coulton,* Social Life in Britain from the Conquest to the Reformation *(Cambridge: Cambridge University Press, 1925), pp. 415–17.*

The Industrial Cities of Flanders

In Flanders, the cities of Bruges, Ghent, St. Omer, and Ypres also were emerging as centers of commerce and industry. Under its counts, Flanders achieved political stability quite early, and the combination of domestic security and rich farmland encouraged both trade and population growth. But the trade was smaller both in volume and in value than the Italian trade. It consisted mostly of raw materials, particularly wool and wood, brought in from England and Scandinavia.

Wool was the basic clothing material of western Europe. But to turn raw wool into cloth took a great deal of work by a variety of specialists. The wool had to be cleaned and carded, spun into thread, woven, smoothed by shearing off the knots and rough spots, and dyed. The production of high-quality cloth required the services of well-trained, experienced craftsmen. The market for good cloth grew stronger as wealth from agricultural production increased, and Flanders emerged as the center of textile production and the most thoroughly urbanized region of medieval Europe. Until the advent of the industrial revolution in the eighteenth century, textile manufacture continued as the most important industry in western Europe.

connections with the cities of the eastern Mediterranean they became familiar with several advanced business techniques. From the Arabs they learned how to form partnerships in which a group of men invested various sums for a period of years. The records of such companies specify the kind of business to be undertaken, the shares of the individual investors, and the partners responsible for conducting the business. Partnerships enabled the Italians to accumulate much more capital for their enterprises than the northern Europeans could put together with their borrowed funds. The Italian cities built huge fleets that made regular voyages to Constantinople, Alexandria, and Acre. As trade increased, the fleets grew larger and larger, and Italian merchants became the masters of the Mediterranean.

The Incorporation Movement

Except in Italy and Flanders, medieval towns were small and slow to grow. Nonetheless, starting in the tenth century the older towns showed some signs of growth and new towns were being founded in certain regions. Most of the new towns were located inland from the coastal ports by kings eager to expand the agricultural economy of their realms.

Although the new towns were under the direct control of the kings, the older towns were still subject to local feudal lords. Towns that had grown up around monasteries were subject to the jurisdiction of the abbot, and those around old villas were under the authority of the lord of the villa. The local lords imposed a variety of taxes, tolls, and market fees on the merchants who traveled from town to town and thereby hindered the growth of the commercial networks on which trade depended. At the end of the eleventh century, merchants and kings came together to devise a way of removing these obstacles to trade.

The device they came up with was the royal charter of incorporation, under which the king would grant the merchants of a town a charter that gave them the right to govern themselves as an independent corporation under royal law and protection. The town would pay for the privilege to incorporate and would agree to pay taxes into the royal treasury, but the town fathers, who were invariably the leading merchants, could arrange to have the taxes collected in a way that would not discourage commerce.

By the early twelfth century, as a result of trial and error, a model charter of incorporation had been perfected. The model was copied over and over again and the charter movement spread rapidly across Europe. By freeing towns from their feudal obligations, the charter created conditions conducive to the growth of commerce and industry. Any person under some feudal obligation to another was freed from his servile condition after living in an incorporated city for a year and a day. It was said that "city air makes one free."

The newly incorporated cities were run by the merchants, who formed guilds to organize and control commercial activities. Their guildhall commonly served as the city hall as well. But various craftsmen—butchers, weavers, smiths—formed guilds of their own and competed with the merchants for political power. In industrial cities—like those in Flanders—the craftsmen's guilds were especially powerful, and riots often broke out between guilds competing for political advantage.

The Fairs and the Ways of Trade

After unloading the goods they had imported from the East, the Italian merchants packed them up again and transported them north over the Alps by pack train. Commerce in Italy concentrated in the cities. But in the north it took place at great seasonal fairs held in towns that had grown up as transit points along the trade routes. The fairs may have come into being as a result of the foreign merchants' ignorance of local markets and their fear that they would be at a disadvantage trying to do business in them. The great fairs made it possible for sellers and buyers to come together on an equal footing. In any case, northern Europe was too vast for merchants to cover by traveling from town to town, and the fairs served as focal points throughout the vast economic network of the Continent.

The greatest of the fairs were held in Champagne, which lay across the river valleys leading south to the Mediterranean and north to Paris, the English Channel, and western Germany. Here, merchants bringing textiles and wool from Flanders and England met with Italian merchants bringing goods from the eastern Mediterranean. The French merchants brought wines; western Germans brought metal products; northern Germans brought furs. Over time, the merchants adopted the practice of settling their accounts when they met in Champagne, thus making the fairs the money market as well as the commodity market of the West.

To settle their accounts, they used the bill of exchange, a device that may have originated in Fatimid Egypt. The bill was a promise to pay. It was also negotiable, which meant that the recipient could use it to pay his own debts. Suppose merchant A owed merchant B 100 shillings, and merchant C owed merchant D 100 shillings. A gave B a bill of exchange promising to pay his debt, and B sold it to C for 100 shillings; C used it to pay his debt to D, who then went to A and collected 100 shillings, the amount he promised to pay, as evidenced by the bill. The convenience of using such a credit instrument is obvious if A and D were merchants of one town and B and C were merchants of another town. No money was shipped from one place to the other—along routes infested with highway robbers—but both A and C paid their debts. As gathering places for merchants from all over Europe, the

An illustration from a fifteenth-century book shows women engaged in the textile industry: carding, spinning, and weaving.

Money changers are portrayed in the stained-glass window at Le Mans Cathedral (thirteenth century).

Local and Regional Trade

By the twelfth and thirteenth centuries local and regional trade had grown more important than long-distance trade in the commerce of Europe. All over Europe towns supported local markets on which the surrounding villages relied for marketing their surplus produce. Gradually, the towns transformed their economic power into political power over the villages that supplied them with raw materials and bought their manufactured goods. As the towns—now cities—became territorial powers, they displaced the feudal lords in the surrounding region. By the thirteenth century, most of the lords were outside the orbit of the cities.

Urban Life

The growth of the towns during the twelfth century and afterward came mostly from migration from the surrounding region and from more distant regions. The villages had been gaining in population for centuries, and young people were attracted to the exciting life and economic opportunities they were sure they would find in a nearby city. Larger cities drew population from smaller cities, and a few cities, like Paris and Bologna, drew population from all over Europe.

Incorporated towns, which most towns were by the end of the twelfth century, were governed by a council and mayor elected by the merchants. Below the merchants was a substantial middle class of artisans—shoemakers, butchers, leather workers, textile makers, and the like—who tended to live in separate quarters of town. The more noxious trades, such as butchering and leather tanning, were located away from the main part of town. From the late eleventh century, earlier in some places, independent artisans organized into guilds, which were similar to the associations of craftsmen in Roman cities. Through their own elected officers and councils, the guilds set product quality standards and restrictions on competition. They also collected funds to assist the families of members who became disabled or died. Along the way, they set up

fairs provided a perfect opportunity for settling accounts with bills of exchange, which were always written on a specific currency, such as Venetian ducats or Flemish gilders, that was well known and widely trusted.

The growth of commerce created a special class of men. Among men who lived all the time in the same community and whose status depended on their obligations to others, the question was always, "Whose man are you?" With merchants, however, who traveled constantly, the answer to that question was of no consequence. Even if a merchant owed loyalty and service to someone in his hometown, that meant nothing to someone 500 miles away. So merchants became known as a special class—bürger in Germany, burgesses in England, bourgeois in France. All these names stemmed from *burg*, the old German name for a fortified town.

some simple financial institutions, much like banks, to serve their members.

Most guilds were local in nature, extending their power only to the city walls or into the adjacent countryside, but a few were international in scope. The teamsters, for example, who were engaged in both regional and distant activities, maintained a loose organization that extended over a large area. And the stonemasons, whose highly specialized craft could not be supported in any one market, even those of Paris or London, traveled from job to job and formed a loose guild-like organization. Unlike the local guilds, both of these international guilds were made up of men who worked for others.

In the early period of guild activity, entry into a guild was relatively easy. A young boy—twelve or thirteen years old—was taken on by a master craftsman as an apprentice. In effect, he then became a member of the master's family and was trained in the master's shop. After several years spent on the simple, repetitive tasks of the trade, the young man rose to the status of journeyman. He was still subject to the direction of the master, but now he performed as a craftsman in the shop. When he had reached full maturity, he could set up on his own as a member of the guild. This system worked well so long as journeymen could expect to become masters in due time. In the later Middle Ages, however, guild membership tended to become hereditary, and relations between journeymen and masters often turned sour. This development was probably caused by changes in manufacturing practices that threatened guild monopolies and by economic decline in the fourteenth century (more on this in Chapter 14).

Jurisdictional disputes often arose among the guilds, as they do among trade unions today. For example, a horse harness contains both metal and leather: should it be made by leather workers, metalworkers, or both? In addition, the guilds competed with one another for political influence and sometimes formed alliances to challenge the merchants' guild for control of the town's government.

As international trade grew, money changing became increasingly important.

If the merchants were the patricians of the towns—as they were often called—then the laborers were the proletariat. The laborers were at the bottom of the social order. In addition to apprentices and journeymen there were day laborers hired to work on the roads, bridges, and walls of the towns. The position of the day laborers was always precarious. They might be working on a construction project one day and helping out with the harvest the next. They lived poorly, but so long as the economy continued to expand, as it did from the late eleventh through the thirteenth century, they were relatively peaceful members of the town population.

Family Life in the Cities and Towns

The core of the urban family consisted of the father, mother, and children, along with the apprentices and journeymen. The family was a social unit, an economic unit, and an educational unit. Although families were usually headed by men, women too could be heads of household. Some women succeeded their deceased husband as "master" and took his place in his guild. The apprentices and journeymen were then subject to her. Others worked in the textile industry, mostly as spinners and weavers. Women of all classes were expected to run their households efficiently, and in upper-class families that function took on the character of a profession.

During the fourteenth century a wealthy merchant of Paris wrote a book to instruct his young bride on her duties. She was never to go out unaccompanied and was always to walk calmly and look straight ahead. She should focus her eyes on the ground in the middle distance. She should be patient and calm when her husband was silly or difficult and should counsel him when he was about to do something foolish. The husband also instructed his wife on how to manage the steward and the servants and how to see to the food and wine. The book included instructions on what to do when the wine was sour or bitter or muddy or when the white wine looked red. The helpful man also provided his wife with recipes for stews and spicy preserves of nuts, vegetables, and fruit.

The birthrate was probably higher among upper-class women than among lower-class women. Upper-class women did not nurse their own infants. Instead, the infants were usually "put out" to a wet nurse in the village. Middle-class infants were usually wet-nursed at home by a live-in nurse.

At all levels of society, babies were delivered by midwives. These women also took charge of the newborn infant, rubbing its body with salt, cleansing its mouth with honey, and swaddling it. A thirteenth-century writer explained that swaddling was necessary because an infant's limbs were so "fluid" that they might become deformed unless they were closely bound. Women were advised to put their babies in cradles, because the common practice of taking them to the parental bed often led to their being suffocated during the night. The mother rocked the cradle, prechewed the infant's food, played games with the children, and taught them to talk. She also instructed them in religion and morals. The father's job was to train his sons for work and to arrange good marriages for both his sons and his daughters. It appears that the father was often much older than the mother and must have appeared a rather distant figure to his children.

Impoverished single women and those widows who were unable to carry on their husbands' business and were unsupported by a guild, were at the bottom of the social scale and led a troubled life. The widow struggling to make ends meet was a common figure in folk tales.

Prostitution was common, and medieval governments frequently issued regulations concerning that behavior. The main subjects were sanitation, living conditions, and working hours. One theologian argued that prostitutes, like other workers, deserved what they earned, but he agreed with the common view that prostitution was evil and that prostitutes should give up such employment. Churchmen found in prostitution a symbol of the evils of worldly society.

Single women and widows of the upper classes could escape their predicament by entering convents, which did not accept women of the lower classes, and many widows did so after their children had grown up. They usually brought an endowment to help the convent meet expenses. There were frequent complaints that convents would not accept applicants unless they paid an entry fee, but the practice was never stopped.

THE RURAL NOBILITY

The nobility of the Middle Ages had been established in the eighth and ninth centuries, with the amalgamation of the old provincial aristocracy of the Roman Empire and the aristocracy of the new Germanic kingdoms. During the late ninth and the tenth centuries, many men who had risen to power as local leaders against the Vikings married into the older aristocratic families and produced the class of warriors who fought in southern Italy, Spain, and the Holy Land during the eleventh century.

Until the late eleventh century, many towns were under the control of local lords who dealt directly with the growing classes of merchants and craftsmen. These nobles never viewed the townspeople as quite honorable, because they did not perform military service or serve as companions to the king. Moreover, they did not fit into the "regular" social hierarchy, which stretched from the king through the great lords to the knights and peasants. Yet, the nobles and the townspeople were obliged to associate with each other so long as the nobles governed the towns. With the incorporation of towns under royal char-

A midwife helps deliver a baby in the Middle Ages.

ter, however, many local lords retreated to the adjacent countryside and the distance between the classes grew wider. They now led different ways of life—rural and urban—and had different economic interests.

From the late eleventh century on, Europe's unruly military aristocracy began to settle down and adapt to the political life of the medieval kingdoms. These were the years that produced the code of chivalry. This code embodied the virtues of knighthood as formulated by churchmen during the Peace of God movement of the previous century in which the church had tried to designate classes of the population—including women, children, and clergy—that the knights must protect from violence. According to that code, the knight was an honorable man loyal to his lord, courteous to women, gentle with the poor and the less fortunate, and generous. Though there were vast differences in wealth and station within the military aristocracy, from simple knight to king, all were seen as following a single calling under a single code.

Rearing a Knight

At the age of about seven, the sons of knights began their schooling in the arts of war and in the proper conduct for members of their class. They first learned to ride a horse and began playing games with toy weapons. When they reached the age of twelve or thirteen, they were trained to take part in exercises on horseback and were instructed in the use of weapons.

In his later teens, such a boy became a squire, the servant of a knight. Under the knight's tutelage, he continued his education and also took care of the knight's horses, armor, and weapons. Although no rule dictated when a squire became a knight, it usually happened when the squire was in his early twenties. The young man knelt before the lord of his knight in a pledge of fidelity, and the lord took the young man's sword and hit him on each shoulder. In the later Middle Ages, this ceremony might become quite elaborate, with the young man spending an all-night vigil in a chapel, wearing special robes and armor, and with the delivery of

ceremonial speeches. But in the twelfth and thirteenth centuries it was still a simple ceremony.

Few knights inherited land or title. Most of them were knights-errant who drifted about the kingdom, attaching themselves to landed men when they could. They participated in tournaments, fought wars, and went off on crusades. During the tournament season, from late spring to fall, tournaments occurred somewhere every few weeks, and the knights-errant traveled from one to another. The tournaments were mock battles in which many were seriously injured or killed. The object of the tournament was to capture one's opponents and hold them for ransom. Good fighters could make a decent living on the tournament circuit. Many lords formed teams to participate in the tournaments and provided their men with horses and arms. The participation of teams added verisimilitude to the tournaments. As in real cavalry battles, victory went to the men who fought most bravely and most skillfully. The church disapproved of tournaments and denied burial in consecrated ground to men who died fighting in them.

The goal of all landless knights was to receive a fief from a lord or to marry an heiress. The goal of the fathers of heiresses was to marry their daughters to men with large inheritances. Knights who failed to win an estate carried on as knights-errant for as long as they could and then retired to the countryside as bailiffs or estate managers for the great landholders. They became important figures in the rural hierarchy, and many of them probably married the daughters of prosperous peasants.

Home Life of the Nobility

Most of the landed nobles lived in a manor house or in a motte-and-bailey castle. The manor house was usually a large timber structure surrounded by vegetable gardens and village fields.

The motte-and-bailey castle was a more substantial establishment. The motte was a large mound of from one to six acres in area surrounded by a wooden palisade. The bailey was a courtyard or

A stone "shell keep" on a motte surrounded by a ditch or moat.

open space adjacent to the motte and usually much larger in area. The bailey too was enclosed by a palisade. Depending on the terrain, the motte or the bailey, or both, might be surrounded by a ditch or moat outside the palisade. In the center of the motte was the donjon or keep, a strong wooden tower with slits through which archers could shoot. The ground floor (and sometimes the cellars) were used for storage, and the living quarters were on the upper floors. The tower was entered by way of a stairway to the second floor that could be pushed away in times of danger. Except for the largest castles, the keep was the only building on the motte. All the other buildings—barracks for the garrison, storehouses, stables, workshops, and the chapel—were in the bailey.

Only the greatest lords could afford stone castles, which were built according to a plan much like that of the motte-and-bailey castles. The Tower of London was the keep of a stone castle that William the Conqueror built shortly after coming to England. From it, his garrison could survey the city of London and the surrounding countryside.

Life in the castle revolved around the affairs of its lord. Here he held court to decide disputes among his fiefholders and tenants and entertained the great men who passed by. When he was not away on a campaign with the king or attending the king's court, he spent his time hunting

and managing his estate. During the long winter evenings he listened to professional storytellers and singers or played chess and other games. The members of this class were rough men familiar with violence who lived in a society of professional soldiers. They were quick to defend their own rights and to seize those of weaker men. Many of them ate and drank too much and became quite fat, particularly after giving up wars and tournaments.

Knights-errant retired about the age of 35, and until then they were considered "youths." Because they did not marry until after retirement, they tended to marry women much younger than themselves, and an age difference of twenty years was not uncommon. At the highest levels of society, however, marriage between children as young as seven was legally permissible, and many young boys were married to older girls. Under church law, a marriage was not valid unless the parties to it consented and consummated it. Children could renounce a marriage when they reached fourteen, the age of consent, but if they waited any longer the courts generally ruled that their failure to protest sooner counted as tacit consent.

The wife of the lord usually ran the estate, and many wives were excellent managers. In the great families, the households were very large, with stewards, cooks, stablemen, servants, and family retainers. The women of such families often played a significant role in the politics of the realm and acted as important patrons of the arts. The women of the French royal family were the ones who encouraged the authors of the literary romances that appeared toward the end of the twelfth century (see pp. 297–98).

REFORM OF THE CHURCH

The Condition of the Church in the Eleventh Century

By the middle of the eleventh century many of the institutions of the church had been secularized and were in need of reform. For more than a hundred years, the

Twelfth-century ivory chessmen from the Island of Lewis: Queen, King, and Bishop.

German kings had been appointing bishops and abbots who, though usually men of character and ability, were loyal to the monarchy and often engaged in secular affairs. Moreover, the kings had often granted lands and rights to the bishops, making them part of the feudal structure and obliging them to do homage and take an oath of fealty to the monarch.

Even the parish churches and lesser monasteries had become secularized. Before the Germans converted to Christianity, many of them had maintained private temples and shrines on their properties. After conversion, the lords had renewed that practice by building private churches in the villages adjacent to their estates. Under Germanic law, those churches belonged to the lords, who were therefore entitled to appoint the priests and collect the church income, which consisted of first fruits (an offering from the harvest) and tithes, a tenth of the produce of the land. The lords often appointed parish priests who had not been educated for the priesthood and who might even be serfs of the lord. Consequently, the condition of many rural parishes was scandalous.

Before the Germans were converted to Christianity, the inheritance of an estate had been determined by Germanic folk laws according to rules that no one could alter. In effect, the estate was owned by the family rather than by the man who happen to be head of the family. With the advent of the Christian church a new element entered into this system of inheritance. As we have seen (p. 141), during the seventh century the kings created a new form of landholding called *bookland*, whereby the church could own land under a royal charter. This new form of tenure was available only to the church. By 700, however, large landholders had figured out that by establishing a monastery on their estate they could get a royal charter for the land that they granted as the monastery's endowment. But, because they had complete control over the monastery they had created, they could reclaim the chartered lands any time they wanted to. By this clever ruse, the large landholders evaded the Germanic folk law and assumed power to bequeath their land

Bronze figure of a monk writing on the tail of a monster, on which he is seated (from a cross or candlestick base, north German or English, *ca.* 1150).

to heirs of their own choosing. Soon, churchmen were complaining that the landholders were founding captive monasteries just so they could get a royal charter for their land. As might be expected, monasteries created in this fashion were rarely dedicated to contemplation, prayer, and poverty.

The Establishment of the Reform Movement

In 910, Duke William of Aquitaine asked the monk Berno to found a monastery on his estate at Cluny in Burgundy. Berno agreed to do so on condition that William not interfere with the life or property of the monastery. Racked by guilt for his many sins, William accepted this condition. In fact, he arranged to put the new monastery under the protection of the pope, so that his heirs would not interfere with it either. The new monastery soon became famous, and other nobles asked its leaders to set up similar houses on their lands. And already-established houses asked Cluny to send monks to help them institute reforms of their own. By the eleventh century, under a series of talented, long-lived abbots, Cluny had become the hub of hundreds of reformed monasteries and had inspired reform movements among monasteries in Germany and England.

When the Cluniacs turned to Rome for protection from the heirs of their founders and other aggressive nobles, they discovered that the papacy had become the target of the dynastic and political ambitions of the leading families of Rome. Further, they saw that the popes were men lacking in vision, without pastoral character or genuine religious interests. The Cluniacs soon raised a cry for reform that was echoed by the leading bishops of Europe and finally won the support of King Henry III of Germany (r. 1039–56).

In 1046 Henry marched to Rome to receive the imperial crown from the pope. There he found three self-styled popes contesting for the papal throne, each supported by one of the aristocratic factions. In an action that recalled Otto I, Henry summoned a council of churchmen, who deposed all three of them. He then installed a German as the legitimate successor of St. Peter, and that pope crowned Henry emperor. Soon after Henry returned to Germany, the new pope died mysteriously and Henry appointed Bruno, bishop of Toul, who took the name Leo IX (r. 1049–54). Under Leo, the Germans began the reform of the Roman church and reestablished its spiritual and disciplinary leadership of Christendom.

The church leaders responsible for that reform held councils to render their program into church law. They prohibited the buying and selling of ecclesiastical offices, clerical marriage, and lay interference in ecclesiastical affairs. They also sought to gain control over the city of Rome, from which the papacy drew most of its revenues. The architect of that effort was a Roman monk named Hildebrand, who for two decades, starting under Leo IX, served as the archdeacon, or principal administrative officer, of the Roman diocese. Through his influence with some of Rome's leading families, Hildebrand gained control of most of the ancient shrines in the city, which produced substantial revenue as pilgrimage sites.

The Investiture Controversy

The reformers' views of the church's role and structure were set down by the German monk Humbert, who had come to Rome with Leo IX. According to Humbert, the church was superior over secular authorities because it was responsible for the spiritual welfare of the people, while the emperor and kings were responsible for their material well-being. The church was to secular authorities as the sun is to the moon, he wrote, implying that they received their authority from the church as the moon receives its light from the sun. In support of this claim, the reformers cited the Donation of Constantine (see p. 182) and the bishops' deposition of Louis the Pious (see p. 231). Humbert further pointed out that Christ had established the church as a hierarchical

Cluniac Monasteries   Tenth and Eleventh Centuries

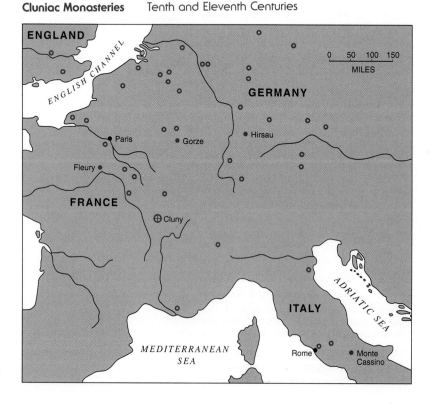

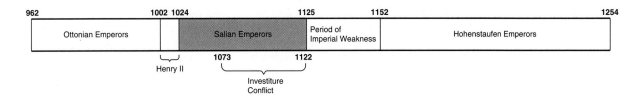

institution, with the pope, as successor of St. Peter, at the apex of the hierarchy.

Similar views were expressed by the north-Italian monastic reformer, Peter Damian, who justified Henry III's participation in the reform movement and his appointment of the reform popes. Damian argued that, because royal authority like papal authority derives from God (citing the example of the Old Testament kings and St. Paul's *Letter to the Romans* 13), kings have a role to play in spiritual as well as secular government. Though the king cannot perform the sacraments, he is responsible for the well-being of the church. Only when a king, or a lesser secular official, acts against the interests of the church by appointing evil or incompetent men or by seizing church property is the church justified in resisting secular participation in ecclesiastical affairs. By this argument, Henry III's actions were not only justified but deserving of applause.

Henry III died in 1056, and left his son Henry IV, a boy of six, as his heir, under a regency. Taking advantage of this situation, the great feudal lords rebelled, hoping to recover some of their autonomy; the regents had to rely on the bishops and monasteries for support. Consequently, they seized every opportunity to appoint loyal men to church posts, and these men were not always of the sort the reformers in Rome would have preferred. The papal court became increasingly estranged from the regents.

In 1059, Pope Nicholas II (r. 1059–61) issued new reform legislation aimed at the practices of the German kings and emperors. It prohibited the investiture (installation) of priests and bishops by laymen and declared that henceforth popes would be elected by the college of cardinals. This new electoral college represented the clergy of the diocese of Rome, because under ancient law those clerics who had the right to say Mass in the churches of the Roman diocese were called cardinals. Gradually during the tenth and eleventh centuries the number of cardinals had been fixed to those bishops, priests, and deacons who had been "incardinated" in the oldest churches of Rome. By 1059, all of these men were supporters of the reformers. With only slight modifications, the electoral system conducted by the college of cardinals is still in use today. After 1059, the cardinals became increasingly important as administrators in Rome and as ambassadors, or legates, to all the provinces of the church.*

During most of the 1060s, though the German government was in no position to challenge the new decrees, it effectively ignored them and continued to treat the German church as part of the royal government. When Henry IV (r. 1056–1106) came of age in 1066, he made the royal appointment and investiture of bishops a cornerstone of his political program. The act of investiture, during which the bishop swore an oath of fealty to the king and received from him the ring and shepherd's crook symbolic of episcopal authority, guaranteed the relationship on which the king relied for support against his enemies.

Meanwhile, the aristocratic opponents of the king sided with the reformers, who forced them to obey the papal decrees. In particular, they had to agree that the priests of their own private

---

The church was organized into provinces, each with an archbishop and bishops who were subordinate to him. Thus the province of Canterbury contained most of the bishoprics of southern England and the province of Reims contained many bishoprics of northern France. The bishops always tried to maintain their independence of the archbishop of their province. Papal legates were generally sent to represent papal authority in one or more provinces. They were superior to the archbishops and bishops of the province.

churches would be appointed and invested by the proper ecclesiastical authorities in accord with church law. This requirement prompted the lords to divest themselves of their private churches, sometimes turning them over to reformed monasteries, which they viewed as ecclesiastical institutions. But soon those monasteries were under attack for taking control of the churches. In other cases, the lords gave up the right to collect church income and to install priests but kept the right of patronage that permitted them to nominate priests. The bishop of the diocese almost always accepted their nominations, though disputes over the installation of priests were common. From 1060 to 1160, virtually all rural parish churches that had once belonged to the lords of the villages became church property under control of the local bishop.

Pope Gregory VII

Manuscript illustration of Gregory VII. Photo courtesy of The Granger Collection.

In 1073, when the archdeacon Hildebrand became pope as Gregory VII (r. 1073–85), the reform movement entered a new phase. While his predecessors had been engaged in diplomacy to get first the regency government and then Henry IV to obey the reform decrees, Hildebrand had been engaged in a struggle to establish papal power in the city of Rome. Though a master of city politics and a committed reformer, he was no diplomat.

At the beginning of his pontificate as Gregory VII, he reaffirmed the reform decrees, particularly the prohibition of lay investiture. Then, in June 1075, Henry IV reasserted the ancient rights of the monarchy in ecclesiastical affairs. For Henry, the church was the basis of royal power, and he was determined to control the appointments to its highest offices. At the end of 1075, Gregory threatened Henry with excommunication—which would prevent him from entering a church and would prohibit all Christians from dealing with him—if he did not obey the papal decrees.

Henry reacted by summoning his loyal German bishops to a council at which they prepared a letter attacking Gregory as a false pope and demanding that he give up his usurpation of the Roman see. Gregory responded by first excommunicating and then deposing Henry. That action triggered a new rebellion of the German magnates against Henry, and for a time it looked as if he might indeed lose his throne. In January, Gregory traveled to Germany to attend a great council that was scheduled to approve his action against Henry. Along the way, he stopped at the castle of Canossa in northern Tuscany, and Henry suddenly appeared to beg forgiveness and absolution from the sentence of excommunication. As a pastor, the pope had no choice but to absolve him. But by doing so, he destroyed the grounds on which he had deposed the king.

Officially, Henry was now an obedient son of the church, and the rebellion in Germany quickly disintegrated. Gregory turned back to Rome, having lost the trust of many of the magnates in Germany who had counted on him for support in their rebellion.

The absolution at Canossa merely demonstrated the limited usefulness of excommunication as an instrument of political policy without resolving the underlying issues between the pope and king. When the continuing dispute over investitures led Gregory to excommunicate Henry again in 1080, his action was largely ignored in Germany.

The Consequences of the Investiture Controversy

The controversy over investitures lasted for 47 years (1075–1122), changed the course of history in Italy and Germany, and revolutionized the relationship between the ecclesiastical and secular authorities in Europe. During the controversy the German kings invaded Italy several times and delayed the reestablishment of papal power. For their part, the popes fomented a series of rebellions in Germany that kept the kings off balance for much of the period and impeded progress toward a strong monarchy.

Both sides spun out theories about the nature of secular and ecclesiastical authority. The papacy, adopting Humbert's position, argued that the church led by the pope was the highest human authority because it was responsible for the highest human goal—salvation. Henry's supporters, following Peter Damian's theory of dual authority, maintained that both secular authority and ecclesiastical authority were divinely ordained. The compromise that ended the investiture controversy in 1122 was based on the theory of dual authority. Henceforth, disputes between the two centers of authority were resolved according to the peculiarly Western idea that both church and state have limited authority. No other civilization has recognized a spiritual authority independent of the secular power.

Religious Life:
New Monastic Orders

The resolution of the contest between church and state was not the only outcome of the reform movement. As a result of the reformers' efforts the pope became more and more powerful in church affairs, and by the twelfth century papal legates were active in many parts of Europe. The reformers also improved the education of priests and established the principle that priests could not marry. By the late twelfth century, married clerics had become rare, except in Scandinavia.

The reform movement also stimulated a religious fervor that affected all levels of society and led to a new expansion of monasticism. Cluniac monasticism, though it required that individual monks remain poor, permitted the monasteries themselves to accumulate wealth. Over the two centuries since they had been founded, the Cluniac monasteries had grown into wealthy institutions, with the monks living in sumptuous surroundings. Cluny itself had become the largest landowner in Burgundy.

Within the monasteries, as St. Benedict had ordained, the monks still came together seven times a day for communal prayer services, or offices. They were to spend the rest of the day working to support the community. In the Middle Ages, when people believed that God was more likely to listen to the prayers of holy men

---

Principles of Gregory VII   *ca.* 1075

This document was certainly drawn up in Gregory's circle, and probably by the pope himself. It expresses the views of those who were trying to increase papal power in both church and state.

1. That the Roman church was founded by the Lord alone.
2. That only the Roman pontiff is rightly called universal.
3. That he alone can depose or reestablish bishops.
4. That his legate, even if of inferior rank, is above all bishops in council; and he can give sentence of deposition against them. . . .
12. That it is permitted to him to depose emperors. . . .
18. That his decision ought to be reviewed by no one, and that he alone can review the decisions of everyone.
19. That he ought to be judged by no one.
20. That no one may dare condemn a man who is appealing to the apostolic see.
21. That the greater case of every church ought to be referred to him.
22. That the Roman church has never erred nor will ever err, as the Scripture bears witness.
23. That the Roman pontiff, if he has been canonically ordained, is indubitably made holy by the merits of the blessed Peter. . . .
24. That by his precept and license subjects are permitted to accuse their lords. . . .
27. That he can absolve the subjects of the unjust from their fealty.

From Dictatus Papae Gregorii VII, *trans. by E. Lewis,* Medieval Political Ideas *(New York: Knopf, 1954), Vol. II, pp. 380–81.*

---

than to the prayers of ordinary folk, the men who donated money and land to monasteries demanded that the monks pray for them in perpetuity. As time passed, the monks came to spend virtually all day in church praying for patrons. The Cluniac liturgy became extremely elaborate, and the monasteries built large, ornate churches in which the monks used richly decorated ritual implements and books.

Starting around the middle of the eleventh century, perhaps influenced by the papal reform movement, some monks withdrew from the monasteries to live as hermits. Ecclesiastical authorities, complaining that they had no way of knowing

Henry IV before journeying to Canossa. Miniature from an early twelfth-century manuscript of the life of Countess Matilda of Tuscany. Henry, kneeling, asks Abbot Hugh of Cluny and Countess Matilda to intercede for him with Pope Gregory VII.

An illuminated liturgical book from Spain (thirteenth century).

whether these men were really living a holy life, put pressure on them to come together in communities. In Italy, several communities were formed in which the monks lived solitary, ascetic lives of prayer except when they worked together to support themselves. Peter Damian entered one such community, Fonte Avellana, as a young man and became its prior in 1043. The most famous hermit communities were the Charterhouse (La Grand Chartreuse), from which the Carthusian order stems, and the Camaldoli, which gave rise to the Camaldolese order.

The largest and most influential of the new monastic orders was the Cistercian order, which followed the Benedictine Rule. About 1098, a group of monks withdrew to a desolate place in Burgundy called Cîteaux (Cisterciensis in Latin; the name means marshy place). Determined to live an austere life, they renounced the ownership of property both for themselves and for their community, and they stressed the role of manual labor in monastic life. The harsh region to which they withdrew demanded that they work hard just to survive, and after several years the number of monks at Cîteaux had dwindled. Then, in 1112, when it seemed that the community was about to fail, a young man named Bernard (*ca.* 1090–1153) arrived with relatives and friends to join the house. Bernard, a genius with extraordinary personal magnetism, soon attracted others to Cîteaux. In 1115, he led a group of monks to found a daughter house at Clairvaux, where he served as abbot for the rest of his life. In those four decades, the Cistercian order grew to more than 350 houses, and Bernard became a leading figure in Europe. He wrote hundreds of letters and many commentaries on books of the Bible. In 1145 a former member of his community at Clairvaux became pope as Eugene III.

Unlike the Cluniacs, the Cistercians founded a true order of formally related monasteries. Although many monasteries had copied Cluny's rule and practices, and many had asked Cluny to send monks to give them guidance, those houses were not subject to Cluny in any formal way. By contrast, all of the Cistercian houses were founded by one of the older houses: Clairvaux was a daughter house of Cîteaux; Clairvaux in turn had many daughter houses; and many of those had daughter houses of their own. All followed the same rule, and every year the abbot

Cistercian Monasteries   Twelfth Century

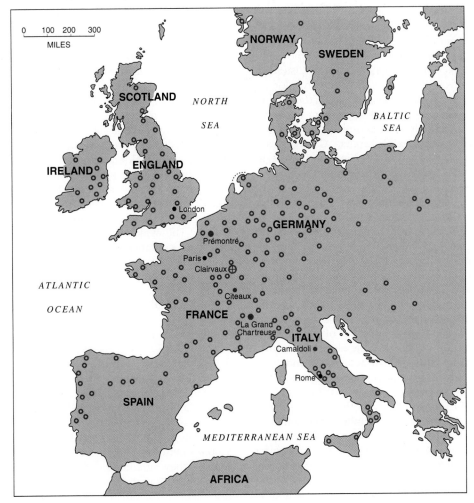

Cistercian monks shown living by their own labor. Illuminated capital letter from a manuscript of St. Gregory's *Moralia in Job*, written at the mother house of Cîteaux in the twelfth century.

of the mother house visited each of its daughter houses to make certain that it was following the rule in every particular. Also once a year, all the abbots of the order gathered at Cîteaux to review the rule and to hear the cases of abbots who had been found wanting.

But as the Cistercian order grew and as the fame of its monks' holiness spread, its monasteries, like the Cluniac monasteries, received valuable gifts from pious donors. Within a generation, the Cistercian houses had grown wealthy. No longer were they committed to life in the wilderness, for society followed them wherever they established themselves. By the middle of the twelfth century, Cistercian abbots were playing an influential role in ecclesiastical and secular politics throughout Europe.

About the time the Cistercians were building their order, other forms of religious life were emerging. Attached to cathedral churches were priests called canons who performed the divine offices—the daily series of prayers—in the church and assisted the bishop with the management and the pastoral work of the diocese; the canons were the descendants of the ancient *familia* of the bishop (see p. 135). By the late eleventh century, many of them had accepted a monastic rule and become regular clergy (from the Latin *regula*, meaning rule). Small groups of canons in many of the rural churches followed suit. The canons lived much as monks did, but they were priests who performed pastoral duties. In the early twelfth century, a German priest founded an order of canons regular at Prémontré (the Premonstratensians) and created a new

form of religious life, the order of priests destined to influence the organization of the church as a whole.

The new interest in monastic life affected women as well as men. For generations, convents had received widows and the unmarried daughters of noble families, but now they also began to receive women who chose to enter them instead of marrying. The Cistercians created an order of nuns who followed their rule, and there also developed various orders of canonesses who lived according to the same rule as the canons but did not perform priestly duties.

Although most of the men and women who lived in monasteries and convents were members of the noble classes, the movement also stimulated a religious enthusiasm among the lower classes. During the twelfth century a host of preachers wandered from town to town urging the townspeople to give up their worldly life and live like the apostles. A few of these preachers formed communities that lasted for years. The followers of a preacher named Waldo, for example, left everything behind to live a common life and to help convert others to holiness. The bishops became concerned about the orthodoxy of the Waldensians, as they were called, because they had had no formal training and had no authority from the church. Moreover, they were often critical of the wealth and worldliness of the church. The Waldensian movement endured for centuries and was never formally condemned by the church.

THE CRUSADERS

When Byzantine military power collapsed after the battle of Manzikert in 1071 (see p. 186), the imperial court in Constantinople appealed to the pope and the western kings for assistance. Although these leaders had little interest in recovering territory for the eastern emperor and hardly understood the role the Empire had played as a buffer between Europe and the Arabic Empire, they agreed that something had to be done about the Moslem conquest of Jerusalem (1077). Still, it took them nearly two decades to put together an army to advance that cause.

In 1095, Pope Urban II (1088–99), seizing the opportunity to assert papal leadership of all Christendom, proclaimed a crusade against the Turks. At a great council in Clermont, France, he preached a famous sermon in which he urged the assembled knights to raise an army to help Constantinople fight the infidel. The effect was startling. Thousands of knights took the cross, which became the symbol of the crusaders—the warriors who had dedicated themselves to fight for Christ.

There were several reasons for this surge of religious fervor among the usually hard-bitten, self-interested knights. First, since the late tenth century, bishops had tried to protect their parishioners from the horrors of war by inducing knights to observe a truce toward certain groups in the population. The movement, called the Peace of God, began in central France and was led by associations of knights who swore not to attack peasants, merchants, or churchmen. The bishops also tried to get the knights to forswear all fighting on feast days, but this so-called Truce of God was far less effective than the Peace of God. The great lords supported the movement because it helped keep the lesser lords and knights under control. The Peace of God may have served as the inspiration for the chivalric code that was featured in the vernacular literature of the twelfth century.

Moreover, Europeans had already moved against Moslem states closer to home in something like the *jihad*—the Moslem's holy war. For example, the Normans had led a kind of domestic crusade against the Moslems in southern Italy and Sicily and by the middle of the eleventh century had set up independent principalities there. In fact, Robert Guiscard (*ca.* 1015–85), the leader of the Normans

Crusade Routes   1096–1270

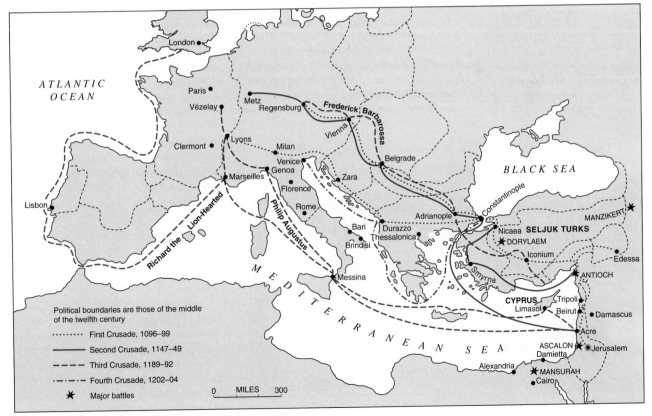

Urban's Speech at Clermont   1095

I exhort you . . . to strive to expel that wicked race [the Turks] from our Christian lands. . . . Christ commands it. Remission of sins will be granted for those going thither. . . . Let those who are accustomed to wage private war wastefully even against believers go forth against the infidels. . . . Let those who have lived by plundering be soldiers of Christ; let those who formerly contended against brothers and relations rightly fight barbarians; let those who were recently hired for a few pieces of silver win their eternal reward. . . . The sorrowful here will be glad there, the poor here will be rich there, and the enemies of the Lord here will be His friends there. Let no delay postpone the journey . . . when winter has ended and spring has come . . . enter the highways courageously with the Lord going on before.

Adapted from Fulcher of Chartres, History of Jerusalem, *trans. by M. E. McGinty (Philadelphia: University of Pennsylvania Press, 1941), p. 16. Fulcher was at Clermont and went on the First Crusade.*

Medieval knights besiege a city. The troops fight before the city gate, while the besieging army catapults missiles into the city.

in Calabria, had grown so strong that he was able to mount expeditions aimed at seizing the Byzantine throne (see p. 186). His successor, Roger I (r. 1085–1111), completed the conquest of Sicily in 1091.

In Spain, meanwhile, the collapse of the caliphate of Cordova in 1031 opened the way for the Christian states on the southern flank of the Pyrenees to move against the independent emirates on the peninsula. The Iberian Crusade attracted men from France and other regions who in 1080 took Toledo, the former capital of the Visigothic kingdom. By the thirteenth century the emirate of Granada was all that remained of Moorish Spain.

Finally, during the investiture controversy many members of the aristocracy had sided with the reformers against the kings. Particularly in Germany, they were aware that if the church achieved its independence of the king, the monarchy would be weakened and the aristocracy would grow stronger. Consequently the knights and the members of the lesser nobility gathered at Clermont responded with great enthusiasm to Urban II's appeal for a crusade. After about a year of organizing, thousands of knights gathered in eastern France to march to Jerusalem. Significantly, no kings joined them.

In the meantime, thousands of lesser folk set off for the East on their own. When they arrived at Constantinople, the emperor was horrified. He had expected a disciplined army, not a peasant mob, to help him reconquer Asia Minor and the Holy Land. To get rid of this scourge, he had the peasants ferried across the Bosporus, where they were massacred by the Turks. Few survived to join the march on Jerusalem.

The crusading army proper was led by several great lords from France, who spent much of their time feuding while on the march across the Balkans and Asia Minor. When the army arrived at Constantinople, the emperor discovered that it was almost as disorganized and unruly as the peasant mob, quite unlike the well-disciplined Byzantine army. He was also dismayed to find that the westerners had come, not to serve him, but to stage a raid across Turkish territory to Jerusalem. After he declined their services, they set off on their own.

In their trek eastward, the crusaders suffered disease, hunger, and, in two battles with the Turks, heavy casualties. The leaders continued to feud, and when the crusaders arrived at their destination they split up into separate forces and attacked different targets. One force succeeded in taking Jerusalem in 1099, and the rest took other major cities. By 1100, a string of crusader states stretched from Antioch in the north to the Dead Sea in the south.

The condition of these states was precarious, and from time to time the Moslems made serious inroads into them. At such times the westerners called out for reinforcements, and the churchmen back home set about raising new crusades. In the 1140s, Bernard of Clairvaux preached a crusade and even got the kings of France and Germany to promise that they would join it. Louis VII of France (r. 1137–80) actually went all the way to Palestine but accomplished little after arriving.

After Saladin retook Jerusalem in 1187, the church leaders preached a Third Crusade. This time the German and English kings led the crusaders, but it all ended badly. Frederick I of Germany (r. 1152–90) died along the way, and Richard the Lionhearted, the English king (r. 1189–99), set out for home after an inconclusive campaign. He was captured on the way, and the English had to raise a huge ransom to free him.

Though all these twelfth-century crusades were ostensibly aimed at Palestine, the crusaders occasionally staged attacks on the Nile delta of Egypt, which, under the Fatimid caliphs, had become the richest and most powerful Moslem state. Though the attacks were thrown back, they disrupted the lucrative trade that had grown up between Egypt and the cities of Italy. So, when a Fourth Crusade, aimed specifically at Egypt, was organized in 1202, the Venetians, who had been contracted to provide transport, diverted it to a Byzantine port that was competing with Venice for trade. Soon the crusaders were on their way to Constantinople itself. They took the city in 1204 and established a Latin empire there that lasted until 1261 (see pp. 187–88).

Suggestions for Further Reading

The Medieval Economy

For a good general survey, see R. H. Bautier, *The Economic Development of Medieval Europe* (1971). On the agricultural economy of medieval Europe, see N. Nielson, *Medieval Agrarian Economy* (1976); G. Duby, *Rural Economy and Country Life in the Medieval West* (1968) and *The Three Orders: Feudal Society Imagined* (1980); and M. Bloch, *French Rural Society* (1966). The first three volumes of the *Cambridge Economic History of Europe*, ed. by M. M. Postan (1952–66), contain excellent articles on agriculture, commerce, and industry. The second edition of Volume 1 is much improved over the first edition. See also R. Lennard, *Rural England* (1959). On the agricultural revolution, see L. White, Jr., *Medieval Technology and Social Change* (1962), and J. Gimpel, *The Medieval Machine* (1976).

On the revival of trade, see R. S. Lopez, *Medieval Trade in the Mediterranean World* (1961) and *The Commercial Revolution of the Middle Ages* (1976). C. Cipolla, *Before the Industrial Revolution*, 2nd ed. (1980), is a good one-volume survey based on recent scholarship. A. R. Bridbury, *Economic Growth. England in the Later Middle Ages* (1962), brings W. Cunningham, *The Growth of English Industry and Commerce* (1910), up to date, but the older work remains useful. P. Boissonade, *Life and Work in Medieval Europe* (1929), is also still valuable, but J. Le Goff, *Time, Work, and Culture in the Middle Ages* (1980), has given a modern perspective on many of the same issues. R. de Roover, *Money, Banking and Credit in Medieval Bruges* (1948), is a readable introduction to the operations of the Italian merchant-bankers in Flanders. A. Sapori, *The Italian Merchant in the Middle Ages* (1970), is an excellent general work; see also S. Thrupp, *The Merchant Class of Medieval London* (1948).

Urban Development

On the rise of the cities, see H. Pirenne, *Economic and Social History of Medieval Europe* (1937). F. Rörig, *The Medieval Town* (1967), and M. M. Postan, *The Medieval Economy* (1972), are very good on the towns. C. T. Smith, *An Historical Geography of Western Europe before 1800* (1978), is very good on the growth of the cities. F. Lane, *Venice: A Maritime Republic* (1973), is the best account of the rise of a major trading city. On England, see S. Reynolds, *An Introduction to the History of Medieval English Towns* (1977). There is also interesting material in I. Agus, *Urban Civilization in Pre-Crusade Europe,*

2 vols. (1965), which contains translations of rabbinical *responsa* (legal opinions). See also, J. W. Parkes, *The Jew in the Medieval Community: A Study of his Political and Economic Status* (1938). On life in the cities, see M. Girouard, *Cities and People: A Social and Architectural History* (1985), and J. and F. Gies, *Life in a Medieval City* (1969), which focuses on Troyes and the fairs of Champagne. For studies of individual cities, see C. N. L. Brooke, *London 800–1216: The Shaping of a City* (1975); G. Williams, *Medieval London* (1970); J. W. F. Hill, *Medieval Lincoln* (1948); P. Llewellyn, *Rome in the Dark Ages* (1971); R. Brentano, *Rome Before Avignon* (1974); D. Herlihy, *Medieval and Renaissance Pistoia* (1958); P. Strait, *Cologne in the Twelfth Century* (1974); and D. Nicholas, *The Domestic Life of a Medieval City: Women, Children, and the Family in Fourteenth-Century Ghent* (1985).

Medieval Society

For a general survey, see G. Duby and P. Aries, *A History of Private Life*, vol. 2 (1989). For the earlier period treated in this chapter, see H. Fichtenau, *Living in the Tenth Century* (1991). The manual written in the fourteenth century by a bourgeois man for his young wife has been newly translated in *A Medieval Home Companion: Housekeeping in the Fourteenth Century*, trans. by T. Bayard (1991). For studies on women of all classes and conditions, see M. W. Labarge, *A Small Sound of the Trumpet: Women in Medieval Life* (1986); M. C. Howell, *Women, Production, and Patriarchy in Late Medieval Cities* (1986); and *Sisters and Workers in the Middle Ages*, ed. by J. M. Bennett et al. (1989). See also D. Herlihy, *Women in the Middle Ages* (1971); J. Ferrante, *Women as Image in Medieval Literature* (1975); and V. L. Bullough, *The Subordinate Sex: A History of Attitudes toward Women* (1973). D. Herlihy, *Medieval Households* (1985), places women in the context of medieval domestic life. E. Power's *Medieval Women* (1975) contains imaginative recreations of women's lives. For essays on childrearing, see L. deMause, ed., *The History of Childhood* (1974).

The life of the nobility is recounted in S. Painter, *William Marshal* (1933), and G. Duby, *William Marshal* (1985). See also G. Duby, *The Chivalrous Society*, trans. by C. Postan (1977), and J. Burke, *Life in the Castle in Medieval England* (1978). On the origins of the code of chivalry, see C. S. Jaeger, *The Origins of Courtliness: Civilizing Trends and the Formation of Courtly Ideals, 923–1210* (1985). On women of the aristocratic class, see M. W. Labarge, *A Baronial Household of the Thirteenth Century* (1965).

Ecclesiastic Reform

On the monastic background of the eleventh-century reform movement, see H. E. J. Cowdrey, *The Cluniacs and the Gregorian Reform* (1970). On the ideologies of the reform movement and German kings, see G. Tellenbach, *Church, State, and Christian Society in the Time of the Investiture Controversy* (1940). For a general study of the investiture controversy, see U. R. Blumenthal, *The Investiture Controversy* (1988). On the polemics of the controversy, see I. S. Robinson, *Authority and Resistance in the Investiture Contest* (1978). For a survey of the reform, see R. W. Southern, *Western Society and the Church* (1976), and for the effect of the investiture controversy in Germany, see H. Fuhrmann, *Germany in the High Middle Ages* c. *1050–1200* (1986). On Cluniac monasticism, see B. Rosenwein, *Rhinoceros Bound: Cluny in the Tenth Century* (1982); N. Hunt, ed., *Cluniac Monasticism in the Central Middle Ages* (1971) and *Cluny under Saint Hugh (1049–1109)* (1967); and G. Constable, *Cluniac Studies* (1980). For the English background of the monastic reform, see D. Knowles, *The Monastic Order in England* (1951). For a survey of the whole period, see C. N. L. Brooke and W. Swaan, *The Monastic World 1100–1300* (1974). On the conflict of values between Cluniac and Cistercian monasticism, see D. Knowles, *The Conflict between St. Bernard and Peter the Venerable* (1955). On the spirit of the new monasticism of the twelfth century, see J. Leclercq, *The Love of Learning and the Desire for God* (1961).

The Crusades

On the idea of the Crusade, see C. Erdmann, *The Origins of the Idea of Crusade*, trans. by M. W. Baldwin and W. Goffart (1977), and J. Riley-Smith, *The First Crusade and the Idea of Crusading* (1970). For a study of the preaching of the Crusades in Europe, see P. J. Cole, *The Preaching of the Crusades to the Holy Land 1095–1270* (1991). A. C. Krey, *The First Crusade* (1921), gives a very good picture of the Crusade from the accounts of eyewitnesses and participants. For a readable account, see S. Runciman, *A History of the Crusades*, Vol. 1 (1951). M. L. W. Baldwin, ed., *The First Hundred Years* (1955), Vol. 1

of *A History of the Crusades*, ed. by K. M. Setton, is a collection of essays by leading historians of the crusades. On the Latin kingdom in the Levant, see J. L. La Monte, *Feudal Monarchy in the Latin Kingdom of Jerusalem* (1932), and J. Prawer, *The World of the Crusaders* (1972), which emphasizes the social and intellectual life of westerners in the Levant. On the conquest of Constantinople by the crusaders, see D. E. Queller, *The Fourth Crusade* (1977). The primary sources on the Crusades have been published in many collections. See especially, E. Peters, ed., *The First Crusade* (1971), and J. Muldoon, ed., *The Expansion of Europe: The First Phase* (1977). For an enlightening view of the Crusades, see F. Gabrieli, *Arab Historians of the Crusades* (1969). On the Crusade in Spain, see R. I. Burns, *The Crusader Kingdom of Valencia* (1967), and on the Crusades in the Baltic region, see E. Christiansen, *the Northern Crusades* (1980).

11

MEDIEVAL CIVILIZATION
AT ITS HEIGHT

After 1150 the results of the economic and political revival of the eleventh and early twelfth centuries began to become apparent in western Europe. As agricultural production expanded, the rate of population growth picked up. Farm produce and other goods moved along the rivers and over newly improved roads. The roads were busy with travelers: merchants with their goods; students on their way to Paris or Bologna; agents seeing to the business of their lords; peasants carrying their produce to market. The wealth accruing from the marketing of surplus farm goods encouraged the growth of cities and supported a large class of educated men who transformed the practice of government. It also triggered vast new architectural projects. Monasteries erected gigantic churches in the new Gothic style; merchant guilds built spacious guildhalls; and feudal lords built imposing stone castles. Most of the medieval buildings still standing were built or started in the second half of the twelfth century.

THE MEDIEVAL CHURCH AT ITS HEIGHT

The Growth of Papal Government

The eleventh-century reform movement produced an independent church government that came to resemble secular government in many ways. In the second half of the eleventh century, popes began to use cardinals as agents of papal authority, sending them as legates to churches throughout western Europe. At the beginning of the twelfth century, the cardinals began to take over the organs of papal

(OPPOSITE) THIRTEENTH-CENTURY RELIQUARY OF SILVER WITH GILT. THE RELIQUARY HELD RELICS OF A BISHOP-SAINT.

government, creating a bureaucracy to manage its political and economic concerns. By the middle of the century, the church had become a polity with its own legal system and government and was on its way to becoming a highly bureaucratic institution with vast wealth and power.

The first phase of this development was the growth of the ecclesiastical legal

Contemporary mosaic portrait of Pope Innocent III, from the old basilica of St. Peter in Rome.

system. The church had jurisdiction over a great many cases that are now handled by secular courts, including cases having to do with marriage, the legitimacy of children, and the validity of oaths and promises. Church courts also had jurisdiction over clergy and monks and handled any criminal cases involving them. The pope was the highest ranking judge in this legal system, and any litigant could appeal from his bishop to the papal court. By the end of the twelfth century, the papal court was hearing thousands of cases every year. The legal system of the medieval church had a profound effect on the secular legal system of the Middle Ages, which in turn served as the foundation of modern systems.

By calling councils to legislate and promulgate their programs the early reform popes had made the council one of the principal instruments of church government. After Pope Calixtus II (r. 1119–23) and Henry V of Germany (r. 1106–25) settled the investiture controversy in 1122 (see pp. 266–69), the pope had summoned a great council at the Lateran Palace, the papal residence in Rome, to celebrate the event and issue legislation related to the investiture of bishops and other favorite themes of the reformers. And when a schism caused by a divided vote in the college of cardinals was finally resolved in 1138, Pope Innocent II (r. 1130–43) held a second Lateran Council to decide what to do about the actions of his former opponents who had ordained priests and granted church offices. Again, in 1179, following an eighteen-year-long dispute between two claimants to the papal throne, Pope Alexander III (r. 1159–81) held a third Lateran Council. This council revised the law of papal elections (originally set by a church council in 1059; see p. 267) by introducing the idea of majority rule. Henceforth, the election of a pope required a two-thirds majority of the college of cardinals; this rule is still in effect.

Pope Innocent III

Pope Innocent III (r. 1198–1216) made frequent use of the legal and governmental powers of the papacy. A vigorous man who became pope when he was only 37 years old, Innocent often interfered in the politics of the European kingdoms and was never at a loss in justifying his interference. For example, he argued that because he was the one who crowned the emperor, he had the right to decide who was best qualified for the position. As the high priest of Christendom, responsible for the salvation of every man, he insisted that he had to act whenever he detected the presence of sin in any political dispute. Innocent always had a ready-made justification for acting as arbiter, and he acted as arbiter repeatedly.

When Emperor Henry VI of Germany and Italy died in 1196, he left a young child as his heir. Following the boy's succession as Frederick II, rival claimants made a bid for the throne and a civil war broke out. In a demonstration of his papal power, Innocent decided that both were dangerous to papal interests and threw his support to Frederick, whom he thought he could control (see pp. 320–21).

Again, when King John of England (r. 1199–1216) refused to accept Stephen Langton as archbishop of Canterbury, Innocent excommunicated him for interfering with ecclesiastical authority. After John submitted and became a vassal of the pope, Innocent sought to protect him from the barons who were trying to force him to accept the *Magna Carta* (see pp. 310–11). Innocent also found occasion to assert his authority in France, Spain, and eastern Europe.

From the mid-twelfth century on, the church had been beset by recurrent heresies—belief systems contrary to church doctrine—perhaps as a result of the reform movement of the eleventh century and the religious fervor it engendered (see pp. 265–66). By Innocent's time, heretical sects were common in Italy and southern France. Many of the sects were merely anticlerical, charging that priests were ignorant and immoral and that the church had been corrupted by wealth. Others were theologically heretical, claiming that baptism of children was invalid or challenging some other doctrine. The most important of the sects, that of the Cathars, was not Christian at all. The Cathars were

Clama ne ceffef quafi tuba exalta uocem tuam. ant 7 dotun Jacob peccata eo;. Unde apt's inquid epl mee a fanguine omium iurm. no eni fubtfug quom; confilium dei. Mundus ergo a fanguine ipo; no ei cum noluffer. q; cum increpare slinquntef noluerut; tor occidit. Cum itaq; in tremendi die iudicii de ur debeanf reddere rationem. qnenam 7 de omi uerbo ot

Detail from a page of Innocent's Register showing two wolves, one in friar's clothing, probably assisting in a heretical mass. The page deals with the church's power to punish sinners.

Manichaeans, followers of an ancient religion that combined Zoroastrianism with elements of Christianity and other religions (see pp. 205–06). After being purged by the caliphs of the tenth century, some of the surviving Manichaeans migrated from the Middle East to India (where there are still Manichaeans). Others moved west into the Byzantine Empire and began to migrate to Europe during the eleventh century, settling in northern Italy and southern France.

The Cathars believed that all material things had been created by the god of evil, and all spiritual things had been created by the god of good. They formed their own church, in which they followed a simple ritual and relied on leaders renowned for their learning and asceticism.

Innocent sent missionaries to convert the Cathars, but when peaceful means failed, he proclaimed a crusade in 1207. The crusaders were recruited in northern France and were led by Louis, the son of the French king. When it became clear that the crusaders were bent on conquering the south, which had never obeyed the French king, many of the Catholic lords of the region threw their support to the Cathars. The war was vicious. The northerners salted the fields of the countryside, rendering them unproductive for hundreds of years, and massacred thousands. By 1215, the northerners had incorporated the region into the French kingdom.

Many of the Cathars continued to practice their rites in secret, however. To search them out, Innocent established a new court, called the Inquisition, at the Fourth Lateran Council, held in 1215.

The Inquisition used an old procedure provided for in canon law whereby the judge both investigated the case and ruled on the innocence or guilt of the defendant. The judge could bring suspected criminals or heretics before his court on the mere rumor of guilt. But he had to observe stringent rules of evidence that in effect made it necessary to get a confession in order to convict. This requirement led to the use of torture as a legitimate means of extracting a confession from an alleged heretic. The Inquisition encouraged informers and false accusers, and in the hands of fanatical inquisitors it sometimes brought terror to an entire region. Generally, however, the church supervised the inquisitors carefully to ensure that they followed canonical procedure.

The popes of the thirteenth century built on the successes of Innocent III. For example, in 1234 Pope Gregory IX (r. 1227–41) published a great collection called the *Decretals* that incorporated many of Innocent's judicial decisions and many of the decrees passed by his councils, along with more than five hundred decisions and decrees from the second half of the twelfth century, that became one of the basic texts of canon law. And Gregory's successor, Innocent IV (r. 1243–54), one of Europe's greatest lawyers, held a great council in Lyons in 1245 that produced important legislation to supplement and advance the legislation passed under Innocent III. During the thirteenth century the papacy achieved the height of its political and religious authority.

The Franciscans and The Dominicans

At about the time Innocent III was preaching the crusade against the Cathars, two saintly men—the Italian Francis and the Spaniard Dominic—took a quite different approach to heresy. By simple preaching and by living exemplary Christian lives they and their followers sought to confirm people in their orthodox beliefs. Pope Innocent recognized the value of the preaching orders founded by Francis and Dominic and gave them his support.

Francis (*ca.* 1182–1226), the son of a wealthy merchant of Assisi, experienced a religious conversion as a young man and gave all he owned to the poor. He became a mendicant—a wandering beggar—preaching the Christian message as he imagined the apostles themselves had done.

Francis soon attracted others to his mission. These first Franciscans were simple men who were at ease with common people. But as time passed, scholars and professional men came to dominate the order, which had been approved by Innocent III in 1209. By the middle of the thirteenth century, Bonaventure, a leading theologian, was minister general of the Franciscans, and the order had become a powerful force throughout Christendom. Among its members were some of the leading intellectuals of the age, including the scientist Roger Bacon.

Dominic (*ca.* 1170–1221) was a trained theologian, who approached heresy as an intellectual problem. He set out to create an order of mendicant preachers trained to refute the arguments of the heretics. Innocent approved the order in 1215. From the first, many intellectuals were attracted to the Dominican Order, which developed a string of schools and became influential in the universities (p. 291). The great Aristotelian scholar, Albert the Great (see p. 296), became a Dominican in 1223, and his student Thomas Aquinas joined the order as a young man. The order also attracted Raymond of Peñafort, who compiled the *Decretals* of Gregory IX and wrote the constitution of the Dominican Order.

The Dominicans developed preaching into an art. They wrote manuals on preaching that outlined ways of approaching various audiences, and much of what we know about the popular beliefs of the late Middle Ages comes from

St. Francis strips off the garments he wore as a well-to-do young man and renounces all worldly goods. Painting by Giotto (1266?–1337) in the church of St. Francis of Assisi.

such books. But the training in Christian doctrine and argument that the Dominicans received made them excellent judges of heresy, and many of them became inquisitors.

Both mendicant orders became closely associated with the papacy, and soon Franciscans and Dominicans were being labeled as agents of papal authority. The popes used them as legates, agents, and judges and gave them freedom to preach wherever they wished. That grant of freedom conflicted with the right of bishops to control the priesthood in their dioceses, and many bishops began protesting to the pope that the mendicants were violating their rights. But the popes steadfastly supported the friars—as the mendicants were called (from Latin *fratres*, meaning brothers), who were indeed loyal supporters of papal authority.

THE RENAISSANCE OF THE TWELFTH CENTURY

The reform movement of the eleventh century (see pp. 265–66) had stimulated a cultural awakening that matured into the golden age of medieval civilization. Both the intellectual energies and the artistic impulses of the twelfth-century renaissance derived from a desire to recover the glories of ancient Roman culture.

The reformers, in an effort to improve the education of clerics, encouraged research and intellectual activity. Monasteries and cathedral libraries were searched for precious books, which were copied and distributed to rising academic centers. The conflict between the reformers and the German kings lent urgency to the research effort as both sides searched for historical precedents and the opinions of church fathers. The search for vestiges of ancient culture reached into Spain, southern Italy, and Syria, which had been intellectual centers under the Arabs. In all of these places, Jewish scholars were busy translating Arabic works of philosophy and science into Latin.

ROMANESQUE AND GOTHIC ART AND ARCHITECTURE

Romanesque

The economic revival of the eleventh and early twelfth centuries provided Europeans with the means to replace their modest churches with grand new churches built of stone and adorned with handsome sculptures. As one observer said, Europe was "clothed in new churches." At first, the builders and their master masons tried to recreate the style they associated with old Roman buildings. This style—called Romanesque—was based on the arch. They designed churches shaped like a cross, the so-called cruciform plan. The basic design called for a nave with aisles on either side crossed at a right angle by a transept. The cross was completed by a continuation of the nave beyond the transept that ended in a round or square apse. The ceiling was formed by an arched vault that tended to emphasize the vast internal space of the church and the sweep of the nave toward the alter just beyond the transept. The church was oriented so that the alter and apse were at the east end; the main entrance to the nave was at the west end.

Some of the Romanesque churches were immense. The monastic church at Cluny, with a vaulted ceiling about 160 feet high, was the largest church in Christendom until St. Peter's in Rome was rebuilt in the sixteenth century. They were also marvelously ornate, the exterior walls bright with whitewash and the interior walls covered with colorful murals depicting the life of Christ and other scenes from the Bible. The murals served as a Bible for the faithful, most of whom were illiterate. The capitals of the great pillars supporting the vault were richly decorated with naturalistic sculptures of everything from plants and animals to saints.

The building boom occasioned by these ambitious projects gave rise to a class of professional stonemasons who eventually organized themselves into a craft guild. The members of this cadre of craftsmen traveled from one building site to another, participating in the design and construction of the splendid new churches. Over time, they became sophisticated masters of technique and design and developed an artistic consciousness attuned to innovation and creativity. The churchmen who employed the masons also encouraged innovation, because it set their church apart from those being built elsewhere and satisfied their desire to create a unique monument to their piety.

Gothic

In 1150 a completely new style of architecture made its appearance in the monastic church of St. Denis near Paris, which for centuries had been the burial place of the

French kings. Abbot Suger (*ca.* 1091–1152), an educated man experienced in affairs of government, had served as regent while King Louis VII was away on the Second Crusade, and as abbot of St. Denis he was a distinguished figure in the kingdom.

Suger wanted to flood his new church with light, which emanated from God. But the round arch used in Romanesque churches produces great outward pressure that must be absorbed by exceptionally thick walls—twelve feet in some instances. And those walls could not be weakened by having large windows cut through them. Masons had already experimented with pointed arches, with more nearly vertical thrust, which therefore do not require massive walls. Suger's masons based the design of the church at St. Denis entirely on the pointed arch with great windows piercing the walls. The new architectural style was called Gothic, because Italian critics of the sixteenth century associated it with the "Gothic," or Germanic, Middle Ages.

The stained-glass windows of St. Denis were designed as illuminated murals and served the same function as the wall paintings of older churches. The designers of the church also introduced a new style of sculpture—carefully proportioned though somewhat abstract. Altogether, St. Denis revolutionized architectural and artistic taste of churchmen and patrons, although Romanesque churches continued to be built in some regions until the end of the century.

Gothic emerged as the dominant architectural style of the Middle Ages, eventually acquiring an angular, ornate character that emphasized height and complex vaulting. As time passed, the sculpture became increasingly realistic, and, curiously, the plants and animals depicted in stone "matured." In the sculpture of early Gothic churches, the plants and animals tend to be young, but as the tradition aged so did the flora and fauna.

More churches were built in these centuries than in any other period of European history. By the middle of the thirteenth century, the cities were competing to build the largest and most spectacular cathedrals—bishops' churches—ever built. For example, the city fathers of Beauvais decided to build the loftiest

Abbot Suger depicted in a stained-glass window at St. Denis (twelfth-century).

(Left) Barrel vault, church of St. Savin (eleventh century). Although no light could be admitted in the upper part of the nave, the vault could be covered with fine Romanesque painting. (Center) Groin vault formed by the intersection of two barrel vaults, Mont-Saint-Michel (twelfth century). The walls could now be pierced with windows. (Right) Rib vault, Mont-Saint-Michel (late Romanesque). Ribs made it easier to design and build a groin vault, but the effect is still heavy.

(Left) Early Gothic rib vault, Mont-Saint-Michel. Greater height and light are now being exploited. (Right) Rib vaulting on a grand scale, the nave of Chartres Cathedral (1194–1220). Great height and light have been achieved; the upper (clerestory) windows are larger and more useful than those at floor level.

Two representations of the Visitation. *(Left)* Romanesque façade of the abbey church of St. Pierre at Moissac (twelfth century). *(Right)* Gothic façade of Reims cathedral (late thirteenth century). The Romanesque work is linear and heavily stylized, like a manuscript illustration. The Gothic sculpture is more naturalistic.

church in Christendom, and for years their master masons struggled to overcome the technical difficulties of building an unprecedently tall structure in stone. They finished their work in the mid-1250s, but thirty years later the nave collapsed. Recent studies have shown that the collapse was caused by winds that weakened the mortar in the walls.

In effect, the architects of the era were trying to extend the principles of height and light embodied in the first Gothic church at St. Denis. They emphasized vertical lines and steadily increased the size of the windows. In the small royal chapel of Sainte-Chapelle in Paris the walls consist almost entirely of magnificent stained glass supported by a few slender mullions. Even in the larger churches, there was far more glass than stone at the upper (clerestory) level. To make the walls strong enough to bear the lateral thrust, arched buttresses were built along the exterior. These flying buttresses are a characteristic feature of Gothic churches.

The great portals of the cathedrals were covered with hundreds of statues of Christ, the Virgin, apostles, and saints. The windows told stories or interpreted a moral in brilliant colors that shifted as the day proceeded. At Chartres the cathedral windows depict the continuity between the Old and New Testaments by portraying a prophet carrying an evangelist on his shoulders. Typically, the capitals of the pillars inside the cathedrals, along with the walls and roof are adorned with sculptures of animals and plants so realistic that they have been used to study medieval flora and fauna.

Technically, Amiens is perhaps the most perfect Gothic cathedral of all though many prefer the massive solidity of Notre Dame of Paris or the less unified but more interesting style of Chartres, which was built in stages over a century. As the Gothic style spread to England, Germany, and other countries, it underwent modifications dictated by local taste. Only the Italians preferred to stay with the Romanesque style, modeling their churches on the basilica of Santa Maria Maggiore in Rome (fifth century) or Justinian's churches in Ravenna (sixth century).

THE INTELLECTUAL RENAISSANCE

Philosophy and Theology

The rediscovery of philosophy as a formal method of enquiry led to extraordinary advances in theology, law, and science. Dialectic, as logic was called, made it possible to order what was known and then to make new inferences from that knowledge.

Gerbert of Aurillac (Pope Sylvester II; see p. 241) had revived interest in the so-called Old Logic, an elementary system of logic based on Aristotle's treatises, the *Categories* and *On Interpretation*, which were known in the West in Boethius's translations (see pp. 127–28). By the end of the eleventh century, the study of dialectic had gained momentum and was being taught by famous teachers in schools at Laon, Tours, and Chartres. The Italian philosopher/theologian Anselm (1035–1109), who emigrated to Normandy and was appointed Archbishop of Canterbury in 1087, provided a striking example of the power of logic when he created the ontological argument for the existence of God. This proof rested on a definition of God as a being greater than any being that can be conceived, from which it followed by logical deduction that God must exist (because otherwise one could conceive of a greater being).

Among the students of the time was Peter Abelard (*ca.* 1070–1141), a prodigy who earned a reputation as a troublesome genius by challenging his teachers and pointing out how muddled their thinking was. By his early twenties, he was teaching himself, wandering from school to school lecturing on Aristotle's logic. Around 1113, he decided to study theology and went to Laon to study with a famous teacher there. Disappointed, he went on to Paris, set himself up as a teacher, and soon fell in love with one of his students, Heloise, the niece of a powerful Parisian cleric. They had a son and were secretly married, but on learning of the affair, Heloise's uncle had Abelard castrated. Abelard then entered the monastery of St. Denis, and Heloise became a nun at a convent near Paris.

At St. Denis, Abelard continued his studies. Although Anselm and a few others had used logic in their approach to theological problems, the prevailing method was to collect relevant passages from the church fathers and to present them as the answer to a particular theological question. Abelard discovered a great many contradictions in the patristic writings and worked out a new method for dealing with them. In the book *Sic et Non* ("Yes and No"), he set down a series of theological questions, arranged the patristic texts on both sides of each question, and used logical analysis to reconcile the differences. This new method was the foundation of scholasticism, an intellectual practice that eventually became the standard approach in medieval schools. But the immediate effect of Abelard's book was to call into question the opinions of the church fathers, who were considered to have been inspired by God. In 1120 Abelard's work was condemned, and he was expelled from St. Denis. After spending some time in a monastery in the wilds of Brittany, he returned to Paris and resumed his teaching. By the late 1130s, he again faced condemnation for his views.

The Problem of Universals: Reason versus Revelation

Abelard participated in the most important philosophical debate of his age, over the problem of universals. The Old Logic had raised a fundamental issue about the relationship between what is seen and what is unseen. Porphyry, a Greek philosopher who wrote an introduction to Aristotle's *Categories* in the late third century, had noted that it was not clear whether classes of things (universal terms) in the physical world were real in the same way as things themselves. It was possible that classes of things were only mental constructs that were useful in categorizing entities. For example, if we observe various individual dogs and treat them as the category *dog*, is the category a real thing, like the dogs themselves, or is it only an idea that permits us to accommodate the multiplicity of dogs found in the world? In time, philosophers who thought that universals were real came to be called realists, while those who thought that only concrete objects were real came to be called nominalists (because they considered nouns like *dog* to be only names, *nomina*).

The question about the nature of reality underlying the realist-nominalist debate had great significance for Christian thought. The problem was that human reason could not, it seemed, corroborate Christian revelation; indeed, it might even contradict revelation. If only those things that we can observe are real, then how can we understand the reality of God as revealed in the Bible? A form of this question arose in the late eleventh century, when Lanfranc (archbishop of Canterbury 1070–89 and teacher of St. Anselm) and Berengar of Tours (d. 1088) engaged in a controversy over whether Christ was really present in the bread and wine of the Eucharist. Berengar, a nominalist, held that only the bread and wine existed as real objects, while Lanfranc, a realist, argued that the body and blood of Christ were real in the bread and wine after the priest had consecrated them.

The realist-nominalist controversy reached a new stage with Peter Abelard, who tried to resolve it by concentrating on the distinction between a thing and the word that designates it. He suggested that nouns that designate universals, such as *dog*, are neither mere words, as the nominalists held, nor things-in-themselves, as the realists argued. Instead, they were concepts in the mind that had an objective reality derived from a process of mental abstraction. When one sees several dogs, one discovers the concept *dog* by a mental abstraction from the actual animals to the class of animals. This concept is real in a different way from the actual animals it designates.

The ecclesiastical authorities did not view Abelard's resolution as satisfactory because it did not explain the reality of God. According to that resolution, God was real neither as a particular being nor as a mental abstraction. How, then, was God real? The failure of Abelard's argument to answer this question led to its being condemned as heretical. The apparent conflict between reason, exemplified by logical thought, and revelation remained a problem for many philosophers.

Only the realists could get around the problem, essentially by ignoring it. By accepting the idea that concepts are real in the same way as things observed in the physical world are real, the realists ignored the difficulty that logic could not show this to be true. But at least they could remain orthodox in their Christian belief in revelation, and by the late twelfth century the philosopher/theologians had moved on to other metaphysical questions. These questions too centered on the nature of reason and revelation, but they arose, not from the realist-nominalist controversy, but from the study of Aristotle's metaphysical and scientific treatises, which came to the West accompanied by the commentaries of Arabic thinkers.

The Two Approaches to Intellectual Work

Scholasticism attracted many followers and became the basis of the mainstream of medieval philosophy and theology, but it did not go unchallenged. Among the leading opponents of Abelard and his school was the Cistercian monk Bernard of Clairvaux (see p. 271), who held that the purpose of intellectual work is to enhance spiritual experience. Further, he insisted, that purpose imposed both form and limitation on the work. Because the Bible is the basis of divine revelation, it must be the principal object of study. And that study must consist in a contemplation of

Abelard on Scholarship

. . . Investigation is the first key to wisdom: it is the kind of industrious and repeated inquiry which Aristotle, the wisest of all philosophers recommended to his students in saying: "It is difficult to solve problems with confidence unless they have been frequently discussed. It is not useless to express doubts about some matters." For through doubting we come to inquiry and through inquiry we discover the truth, as Truth Himself said: "Seek and you will find, knock and the door will be opened to you."

♦ ♦ ♦

St. Bernard on Abelard

We have in France an old teacher turned into a new theologian, who in his early days amused himself with logic and who now gives utterance to wild imaginations upon the Holy Scriptures. . . .

There is nothing in heaven above nor in the earth below which he deigns to confess ignorance of: he raises his eyes to heaven and searches the deep things of God and . . . brings back unspeakable words which it is not lawful for a man to utter. He is ready to give a reason for everything, even for those things that are above reason. Thus he presumes against reason and against faith. For what is more unreasonable than to attempt to go beyond the limits of reason? And what is more against faith than to be unwilling to believe what cannot be proved by reason? . . .

And so he promises understanding to his hearers, even on those most sublime and sacred truths that are hidden in the very bosom of our holy faith. He places degrees in the Trinity, modes in the Majesty, numbers in the Eternity. . . . Who can endure this? . . . Who does not shudder at such new-fangled profanities?

Translated from Sic et Non, *ed. by V. Cousin,* Ouvrages inédits d'Abélard *(Paris: Imprimerie royale, 1836), p. 104; translated from* Patrologia latina, *Vol. 182, cols. 1055–56.*

could produce a truth that was independent of revelation. He believed there were two sources of knowledge about God and the world—biblical and "scientific"—and the two were compatible and consistent with one another. Drawn by this heady stuff, young men flocked to Abelard's lectures. Bernard, who believed that the way to truth was through the monastic profession, viewed Abelard as a dangerous influence on the young.

These two approaches represented two intellectual milieus, both of them popular and powerful in the twelfth century. The monastic orders were growing rapidly and were attracting men of great ability and personal magnetism. The monks led a special way of life and had a special way of achieving knowledge, and they constituted a strong moral force in the political and social life of western Europe.

By contrast, Abelard and men like him occupied teaching positions in the cathedral schools, which educated future clerics. But their influence went beyond the confines of church schools. When Abelard sought a position in the cathedral school of Paris, the bishop refused to let him teach there. So Abelard taught under the aegis of a monastic house in the city, and hundreds came to hear his lectures. Other masters took advantage of the pool of students to set themselves up in Paris, which soon became the leading intellectual center in Europe. Not having the specific task of training clerics, these independent masters developed philosophical and scientific curricula that provided students with skills and knowledge useful to secular rulers, and many of them subsequently entered the service of kings and great lords.

The Origins of Universities

By the late twelfth century so many masters were teaching in Paris that they decided to form a separate guild, or *universitas* (the Latin word for guild). The exact date is unknown, but by 1200 the guild had existed for some time. Each master was an independent entrepreneur who offered his courses for pay just as a leather craftsman offered his goods for sale. Students who attended a master's lectures or

the meaning of the sacred text, which contains the whole truth about God and the created world. In short, Bernard was insisting on the use of reason to attain the mystical experience of oneness with God. Many Cistercians and other monastic thinkers followed Bernard's mode of theological discourse, which consisted mostly of sermons on biblical passages.

To Abelard, using logic to analyze sense perceptions of the created world took private instruction from him paid him directly. The guild regulated the fees charged, the rental rate of rooms, and, most important, the standards of entry to the guild. A person admitted as a teaching master had to pass an examination, a practice that eventually led to the definition of a curriculum that would prepare students for entry to the teaching profession.

The guild of masters was the beginning of the university, an institution of higher learning based on the cooperative activities of teachers. In its early days the guild was subject to episcopal control, but by the early thirteenth century the masters were seeking independence. The conflict between the guild and the bishop was primarily over the election of the rector, the chief official of the guild, and it was some time before the masters established the principle that they alone had the right to choose their leadership.

As they developed, universities came to offer instruction not only in the liberal arts, based on dialectic, but in theology, law, and medicine. Each of the professional faculties formed their own guild. The theology curriculum was centered on the work of Peter Lombard (*ca.* 1100– *ca.* 1160), the master of the cathedral school in Paris (later bishop of the see) and the author of a scholastic treatment of church doctrine called the *Four Books of Sentences*, which contained the opinions of the church fathers. Lectures consisted of reading the *Sentences* along with commentaries on the text.

Unlike the mystical theologians, who continued to flourish in the monasteries, the scholastic theologians took a speculative, systematic approach to the Bible. In the late twelfth century, the Englishman Stephen Langton, then a professor at Paris but later the archbishop of Canterbury (r. 1207–28), introduced the chapter and verse divisions into the text of the Bible. Once this was done, scholastic commentators could cite passages with precision, making it easier to carry on systematic study and to debate the meaning of particular passages.

The curriculum in law was based on Justinian's *Corpus Iuris Civilis* (Body of Civil Law; see p. 170) and on a parallel

Medieval Schools and Universities   1100–1250

compilation of church law, which came to be called the *Corpus Iuris Canonici* (Body of Canon Law). The discovery of the *Corpus Iuris Civilis* in Italy during the later eleventh century had revolutionized thinking about law. The coherent, sophisticated legal system embodied in Justinian's code soon prompted the setting up of a law school by legal scholars in Bologna who reintroduced the idea that law was not just a collection of old legislation but a logical system based on principles of justice. The discovery of Justinian's code also fostered the study of secular law, now firmly positioned in the grand tradition of Roman jurisprudence.

Church, or canon, law dated back to the fourth century, after the emperor Constantine recognized the church as a legal institution under Roman law (see pp. 116– 17). Canon law was based on Roman law, just as the administrative structure of the church was based on the Roman diocese. After the collapse of Roman authority in the West, canon law absorbed many of the elements of Germanic law. Then, in the eleventh century, the contestants in the investiture controversy turned to the sources of canon law in their search for proof of their arguments. Their efforts produced vast collections containing many contradictory provisions and ideas. By the end of the eleventh century, several experts in canon law, including Ivo, the bishop of Chartres (r. 1090–1116), declared that the conflicting doctrines and ideas found in the canons somehow had to be reconciled.

That goal was finally reached around 1140, when Gratian, who was teaching canon law at Bologna, published a great compilation of canon law, appropriately called *The Concordance of Discordant Canons*. In compiling this work, Gratian had followed Abelard's scholastic method. It soon gave rise to a school of canonical jurisprudence and formed the first part of the *Corpus Iuris Canonici*.

The excitement engendered by the rediscovery of Roman law and by the emergence of a new school of canonical jurisprudence made Bologna an important center of legal studies, and during the late twelfth century a university was founded in the city. The goal of a student of law was the doctorate, though most students studied only long enough to prove their worth to an employer, such as the church, a king, or a duke.

Unlike the guild in Paris, whose members were teaching masters, the members of the Bolognese guild were students. The student guild established the curriculum and regulated the activities of faculty and students alike. It required masters to proceed in an orderly fashion through all the material to be studied in a course and would not permit a master to leave the city during term without posting a bond to ensure that he would return. Although the guild of teaching masters eventually became the model for universities in the West, the student guild was favored for a long time by schools of professional studies such as law and medicine, in which the students were commonly in their thirties and already advanced in their education. The University of Montpellier in southern France, for example, was founded on the model of the student guild in the early thirteenth century.

Formal studies in medicine rested on Arabic science (see p. 217). The first center of medical study in the West arose in Salerno, a city south of Naples, where Europeans came into contact with Arab influences. By the twelfth century, Bologna had become a center of medical studies, and students eventually founded a university there. A medical university was founded in Montpellier in 1221. Through the faculties of these early schools of medicine the West became acquainted with Aristotle's scientific treatises.

The course to a doctorate was long. Few received their degree before they were forty. When a student had completed his course of study and his adviser deemed him ready, he stood for the doctorate. That meant going to a public place, usually the steps of the cathedral or, after the university acquired its own building, in front of the university hall, and standing there all day answering any question put to him by the people who happened by. A panel of faculty members observed and judged his performance and, if they were satisfied with it, awarded him the doctorate. The student was then admitted to the guild of his faculty and received a license to teach in the university.

Aristotle's Scientific Treatises and the Problem of Reason versus Revelation

The Arabs had begun to study Aristotle in the tenth century, and an active school of Aristotelian philosophers and scientists in Baghdad studied and annotated Aristotle's scientific treatises (see pp. 217–18). When the Latin translations of those treatises reached the West, they were accompanied by the commentaries of the Arab scholars.

Aristotle believed that the world had always existed, that it was without beginning or end. That view was in direct contradiction to the Judeo-Christian-Islamic notion of the Creator-God. Arabic and Jewish philosophers had already confronted this conflict between Aristotle and revealed truth and had responded to it in three ways. Some ignored the problem, much as the Christian realists did, and some tried to explain away Aristotle's assumptions about the eternality of the world. Others, led by the Arabic philosopher Ibn Rushd (Averroës in Latin; 1126–98; see p. 217), proposed that there were two truths, one accessible through observation and logical analysis and the other through divine revelation. So Averroës declared that the problem was a false one and that both truths were true. To reconcile them into one truth about the world was beyond the capacity of human beings.

The appearance in the West of Aristotle's *Metaphysics* accompanied by Averroës's commentary set off a storm in the church. In 1215 the ecclesiastical authorities banned their study. And in 1231 Pope Gregory IX appointed a commission of scholars to review all the works of Aristotle and all the commentaries on those works and to purge them of error. Despite the papal ban, university faculties in Paris, Bologna, and Naples (founded in 1224) continued to teach Aristotle—whom scholars called "The Philosopher"—and the controversy over the two truths carried on into the later thirteenth century. To reconcile Aristotle with Christian revelation was the great problem of the thirteenth-century philosophers.

The man who achieved that reconciliation was Thomas Aquinas (1225–74), who created a systematic explanation of the world that matched the structural perfection of a Gothic cathedral. Aquinas brought reason and revelation together in a grand synthesis of the Christian world view.

Saint Thomas Aquinas

Aquinas, the son of a southern Italian nobleman, entered the Dominican order as a young man. His intellectual ability was soon recognized, and he studied at various Dominican houses. At last he was sent to Paris, where the Dominicans had a study center and where Dominicans had begun to become professors in the university. In 1252, Aquinas received his doctorate in theology at the age of 27 and was elected to a professorship at the university. A university professorship lasted for three years, during which time the professor was to give a course based on Peter Lombard's *Sentences*. The best of the courses were published as theological commentaries or treatises. After completing their course, the professors left the university for other duties. Many of them became deans of cathedral chapters or bishops; some rose to become cardinals or popes—like Cardinal Robert of Courson (*ca.* 1160–1219) and Pope Innocent IV.

Aquinas, after completing his professorship, taught for a time at Dominican houses in Rome, Bologna, and Naples. Then, in 1268, he was recalled to Paris

St. Thomas Aquinas, detail from the Crucifixion, by Fra Angelico (1387–1455). Although this representation was made two centuries after Thomas lived, it seems to accurately depict his large head and bearlike appearance.

for a second professorship, an unheard-of honor. Throughout his lifetime, he was renowned for his extraordinary intellect.

Aquinas argued that through reason alone men can achieve only a partial understanding of the world. To achieve complete understanding, both reason and revelation are necessary. Using the scholastic method of argument, he set out to show that the two approaches, and the truths attainable through each, are consistent with one another. As he saw it, the role of reason is to make deductions from first principles, those being the truths about the world found in the Bible, and from the data of sensory experience. According to the medieval view, religion is not just a system of belief but a body of knowledge about the material and spiritual universes.

Aquinas's method of reasoning represents the ultimate refinement of the scholastic analysis that Abelard introduced in the early twelfth century. Aquinas built

a vast analytical structure concerning the nature of God, man, and the universe in which each topic is taken up in logical order. During his second professorship at Paris he produced the *Summa Theologica*, a large work divided into three parts, each subdivided into Questions dealing with general topics. There are more than six hundred such Questions. Each Question is broken down into Articles, or specific queries, beginning with "Whether. . . ." For example, Question 94 of the second part is titled "Concerning Natural Law," and the fifth Article of this Question is headed, "Whether natural law can be changed?" The specific queries are answered through a series of opposing arguments. In this example, Aquinas set down all the arguments and authorities (mostly patristic texts and Aristotle) to support an affirmative answer (natural law can be changed) and then listed the arguments and authorities in support of a negative answer. He then proceeded to reconcile the arguments and authorities by showing

A university lecture, as portrayed in a fourteenth-century Italian miniature. Attention to the lecturer is not undivided; several students are talking, and one is certainly asleep.

that the contradictions between them were only apparent.

Aquinas's vision of a unified understanding of God and the universe and his systematic presentation of that unity made his work exceptionally persuasive. It led to his early canonization as a saint and to his being regarded as the leading philosopher of Catholicism. Yet not all of his contemporaries shared his views. The most eminent Franciscan philosopher, Bonaventure, who received his doctorate in the same year as Aquinas, thought Aquinas put too much emphasis on reason and relied too heavily on Aristotle and other Greek (that is, non-Christian) philosophers. Bonaventure emphasized will, following Augustine, who believed that his will to salvation had brought about his own conversion. For Bonaventure and his followers, systematic knowledge of the world was less important than an understanding of the way man's will engenders God's act of salvation.

In any case, Aquinas's arguments were too technical to have much influence on laymen, and they led to a distancing between ordinary people and the doctrines of the church. That distancing strengthened the tendency toward the secularization of life that emerged in the late thirteenth and fourteenth centuries.

The Revival of Science

Scientific knowledge had declined to a low ebb in late antiquity and the early Middle Ages. As we have seen, the first stirring of revival occurred in eleventh-century Salerno, when scholars first became aware of Arabic treatises on medicine. Arabic works on medicine and other sciences had been translated in the kingdom of Sicily and in Spain by Jewish scholars who had mastered Arabic and Latin.

Through the influence of these translations, the first three sciences of the *quadrivium*—arithmetic, geometry, and astronomy—were transformed from elementary studies into the mathematical disciplines that are necessary for advanced scientific work. About 1126, for example, Adelard of Bath translated Euclid's *Geometry* into Latin and introduced the West to

> ## The Reconciliation of Christian and Classical Philosophy
>
> *This extract from the* Summa Contra Gentiles *by St. Thomas Aquinas shows how a thirteenth-century scholar was able to use the ideas of Aristotle.*
>
> We have now shown that the effort to demonstrate the existence of God is not a vain one. We shall therefore proceed to set forth the arguments by which both philosophers and Catholic teachers have proved that God exists.
>
> We shall first set forth the arguments by which Aristotle proceeds to prove that God exists. The aim of Aristotle is to do this in two ways, beginning with motion.
>
> Of these ways the first is as follows. Everything that is moved is moved by another. That some things are in motion—for example, the sun—is evident from sense. Therefore, it is moved by something else that moves it. This mover is itself either moved or not moved. If it is not, we have reached our conclusion—namely, that we must posit some unmoved mover. This we call God. If it is moved, it is moved by another mover. We must, consequently, either proceed to infinity, or we must arrive at some unmoved mover. Now, it is not possible to proceed to infinity. Hence we must posit some prime unmoved mover.
>
> *From* On the Truth of the Catholic Faith. Summa Contra Gentiles, *trans. by A. C. Pegis (New York: Doubleday, 1955), p. 85.*

trigonometry by translating the works of the Arabic mathematician al-Khwarizmi (*fl. ca.* 825). About twenty years later, another Englishman, Robert of Chester, translated al-Khwarizmi's *On the Restoration and Opposition of Numbers*, which Arab scholars called "The Book" (*Al Gebra*). The word algebra itself comes from that phrase.

In astronomy, Ptolemy's *Almagest* (second century) was translated around 1160 in Sicily from a Greek manuscript that the Byzantine emperor had given to the king of Sicily. A little later, Gerard of Cremona, working in Toledo, made a translation of the work from Arabic; this translation was preferred, because the Arabic scientists had corrected Ptolemy's original text with their own, more accurate observations. Gerard remained in Toledo for twelve years (*ca.* 1175–87), during which time the city became the chief center of translation. He himself translated more than seventy treatises into Latin and, with other translators, introduced the West to physics, optics, mechanics, biology, meteorology, and psychology. Together, they translated most of the scientific works of Aristotle, along with the Arabic commentaries.

By the early thirteenth century, Aristotle's works had become the textbooks of European science. Albert the Great (1193–1280) was the first to master the whole corpus of Aristotle. He wrote 21 large volumes, most of them devoted to commentaries on Aristotle's scientific treatises. He was particularly concerned with the reconciliation of Aristotle's philosophy with Christian theology, as was his more famous student, Thomas Aquinas.

Oxford was one of the most important centers of science in the thirteenth century. The first rector of the University of Oxford, Robert Grosseteste (1168–1253), did important work in optics. When Grosseteste became bishop of Lincoln in 1235,

he assembled a school of translators, Jews and Christians, to translate scientific works. He designed an optical illusion for the new cathedral he built in Lincoln that can still be seen, which makes it seem there is an aisle where there is only a wall. Grosseteste's successor as the leading scientist at Oxford was Roger Bacon (*ca.* 1220–92), who described eyeglasses, airplanes, self-propelled ships, and a process for making gunpowder. He also conducted experiments, though they were rather crude in design and produced inconclusive results.

It was the work of these and many other thirteenth-century scholars that made possible the scientific revolution of the sixteenth century. While remaining faithful to the work of Aristotle, medieval scientists reintroduced the idea of scientific discovery and experiment.

History and Vernacular Literature

The twelfth and thirteenth centuries were a time of intense literary activity, both in

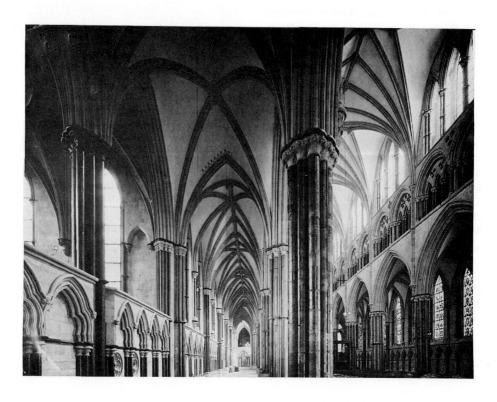

The side aisle of Lincoln Cathedral (thirteenth century). Bishop Robert Grosseteste designed the side wall, with its line of arches, as an optical illusion. In certain lights, created by the windows opposite, the wall gives the illusion of an additional aisle.

Latin and the vernacular languages. The great monastic writers of the twelfth century, such as Bernard of Clairvaux (see p. 271), were brilliant stylists whose Latin sparkled with rhetorical flourishes. About the middle of the twelfth century, it became common for writers to publish collections of their letters, which were consequently treated as a literary form. Others wrote Latin poetry in imitation of the ancient poets, and university students wrote satirical poetry celebrating youth and youthful pursuits, particularly drinking and womanizing, while attacking the church and the secular powers. The student poets were called Goliards, from Golias, their mythical king (in Old French, *goliarde* meant gluttony).

The principal form of medieval Latin literature was history. Ever since the time of Eusebius (early fourth century), Christians had seen in history the working out of God's plan for the world. In the early Middle Ages, Gregory of Tours and Paul the Deacon had written extensive histories of the Germanic peoples who had inherited Roman authority in the West, and during the Carolingian renaissance Einhard and Notker had written biographies of the Carolingian kings. During the eleventh century, when both sides in the investiture controversy (see pp. 266–69) were carrying on historical research to justify their positions, many monks and priests wrote histories of their churches. And in the twelfth century, kings began to patronize writers who would glorify their deeds and ensure their place in history. Otto of Freising (*ca.* 1114–58) in Germany, Geoffrey of Monmouth (*ca.* 1100–54) in England, and Guillaume le Breton (*ca.* 1159/69–after 1226) in France wrote histories that gave historical legitimacy to the royal dynasties of their kingdoms. Counts and bishops also sought to have their acts recorded in local histories.

Outside the circle of monks and scholars, there was a flowering of vernacular literature. The Germanic peoples had possessed an oral literary tradition made up of epic cycles centered on some heroic figure, like the Celtic hero Arthur or Charles the Great. Only a few of those stories, including the Anglo-Saxon poem

Beowulf (see p. 242), had been written down before the early twelfth century. But from that time on many of the epics were recorded. The first was *The Song of Roland,* an epic about an incident that took place in Charles's campaign against the Moors in Spain. About the middle of the century, a German poet wrote down the *Nibelungenlied* (Song of the Nibelungs), an epic based on the story of Attila the Hun's destruction of the Burgundians (see p. 115).

Soon, however, poets gave up epics for romances. Romances told of the quest of chivalric knights for a high position in feudal society, a good marriage, and a large estate. The new literary genre was created in France but soon spread throughout Europe. Its earliest patrons were the women of the family of King Louis VII of France (r. 1137–80), particularly his first wife Eleanor of Aquitaine and their daughter Marie of Champagne. Most of the early romances were based on the Arthurian cycle, a series of stories about the knights around the Celtic hero Arthur. Once the romance emerged as the most popular literary style, writers of every language and every country used it. About 1200, a German author (identity unknown) rewrote the *Nibelungenlied* as a romance, and that is the form in which we have the story. The greatest of the early writers of romance was Chrétien de Troyes (*fl.* 1160–90), who wrote romances based on the exploits of Perceval, Lancelot, Erec, and Cligès. By the end of the century, German writers such as Gottfried von Strassburg and Wolfram von Eschenbach were copying the style— Gottfried with *Tristan und Isolde* and Wolfram with *Parzival.* In England, the popularity of the romance endured for centuries, as represented by *Sir Gawain and the Green Knight* (fourteenth century) and Sir Thomas Malory's *Le Mort d'Arthur* (late fifteenth century).

The romance may have grown out of the tradition of the minstrels, or troubadours, professional singers who entertained the households of the great lords. Their songs began to be written down in the late eleventh century. It was around that time that the chivalric code took shape, and knights learned to sing the old songs as part of their education. Some of them, including Eleanor of Aquitaine's grandfather William of Poitou, were themselves accomplished poets. William was the first to write down his lyrics.

The troubadours promoted *courtoisie*—gallantry, gentility, and generosity—as part of knightly virtue and made romantic love—a nonphysical devotion that ennobled both the man and the woman, especially the man—a central virtue of the true knight.

In a typical romance, the heroic knight sets out to perform military feats that will make him worthy of a woman's love. Throughout his encounters he tries to reconcile the violence of his deeds with the gentleness of romantic love. Once romantic love had become intimately associated with the idea of knighthood, every knight felt obliged to fall in love. And, because love meant romantic love, the object of his affection might well be a married woman. Marriage was a dynastic or political affair that had nothing to do with romantic love.

In *The Art of Courtly Love*, a book written some time between 1174 and 1186, Andreas Capellanus systematized the romantic ideals in a set of rules, the first of which was "Marriage is no real excuse for not loving." He described a mythical "court of love" that decided cases involving lovers' rights against each other.

This literature of courtly love placed women on a pedestal and prescribed their behavior, especially toward men. More and more, the image of women conveyed by the romances diverged from their real life, in which their role as surrogates for their husbands in the management of the family estates continued to dominate.

In contrast to the literature of the nobility, the *fabliaux* that became popular with the bourgeoisie were brief tales told in a realistic vein. One purpose of the *fabliaux* was to amuse, and their humor was often crude and broad. Stock characters included hypocritical, unscrupulous monks and priests, the innkeeper with a beautiful daughter but no common sense, and the wealthy merchant who was sharp in trade and stupid in everything else. Whereas the women of the romances rarely took part in the action of the story, the women of the *fabliaux* played important roles and were often portrayed as clever, if not always ethical. The heroes were usually wandering scholars or poor but quick-witted commoners who outwitted aristocrats and merchants. Closely related to the *fabliaux* were the fables, in which a moral was added to the story. The characters of the fables were animals that represented stock human types. The most famous fables were known collectively as the *Romance of Reynard*, in which Reynard the Fox played approximately the same role as the protagonists of the *fabliaux*.

The Rules of Courtly Love

Writing in the third quarter of the twelfth century, the cleric Andreas Capellanus described the nature of courtly love, the new ethos of upper-class society and of the romance literature with which it was enamored. In his work, Andreas imagined a Court of Love that would decide cases brought by forlorn lovers, and for this court he prescribed rules that would help it discern true love, some of which follow.

I.   Marriage is no real excuse for not loving.

II. He who is not jealous cannot love.

IV. It is well to know that love is always increasing or decreasing.

VIII. No one should be deprived of love without the very best of reasons.

X.   Love is always a stranger in the home of avarice.

XI. It is not proper to love any woman whom one would be ashamed to seek to marry.

XIII. When made public love rarely endures.

XIV. The easy attainment of love makes it of little value; difficulty of attainment makes it prized.

XVI. When a lover suddenly catches sight of his beloved his heart palpitates.

XIX. If love diminishes, it quickly fails and rarely revives.

XXV. A true lover considers nothing good except what he thinks will please his beloved.

XXIX. A man who is vexed by too much passion usually does not love.

XXXI. Nothing forbids one woman being loved by two men or one man by two women.

From Andreas Capellanus, The Art of Courtly Love, *trans. by J. J. Parry (New York: Norton, 1969), pp. 184–86.*

Dante

The poet Dante Alighieri (1265–1321) was one of the first serious writers to use the Italian language, which up to then had been used only for *fabliaux* and other popular literature. He wrote in the Tuscan dialect, which he helped to establish as the standard form of Italian. As a student of philosophy, Dante had studied the works of Aristotle and Thomas Aquinas, and he was fully conversant with the Latin poetic tradition. He was born in Florence, and as a young man he earned a reputation as a lyric poet. His greatest work, however, was the *Divine Comedy*, an epic poem divided into three parts and one hundred sections or *canzone*. He also wrote two notable treatises in Latin, one defending his use of the vernacular, the other a strong plea for preserving the empire, which he considered the only viable form of government.

Dante had a troubled life. Having become deeply involved in Florentine politics, he was permanently exiled from the city in 1302 and wrote the *Divine Comedy* in exile. Like Aquinas, Dante was convinced of the unity and significance of all human experience. Thus, at least as a poet, he could view his own experience in the context of man's relationship with God.

In the *Divine Comedy*, Dante imagined a journey through Hell, Purgatory, and Heaven to the beatific vision of divinity. The journey is patterned on the descent of Vergil's hero Aeneas into the underworld, and Dante made Vergil his guide through Hell, the domain of the eternally damned, and through most of Purgatory, where souls purge themselves of sin before ascending to Heaven. In these sections of the poem Dante made frequent allusions to classical and contemporary poetry and history and placed himself alongside the greatest poets of western civilization. The events of the journey parallel the Christian liturgical calendar—specifically between Good Friday and Easter in the year 1300. Dante drew on the courtly romances of medieval literature by setting out on his quest with the help of Beatrice, a young girl he had fallen in love with but who died before any real

relationship could develop between them. It is Beatrice who sends Vergil to guide Dante in his journey. Thus Dante united all the main traditions of medieval literature, just as Aquinas had united Aristotelian and Christian philosophy. Dante's poem sums up the medieval idea of man's salvation, so we should look at its basic outline.

In the *Divine Comedy*, Dante, in the middle of his life—that is, about 35 years old—finds himself in a dark wood, sensing that he has swum across a swirling body of water. He is standing at the base of a mountain, but when he tries to climb it, seeking the sun, he is driven back by animals that symbolize his sins. He then meets Vergil, who leads him down into Hell, which is the way one must approach the light of truth. This is the route Augustine followed in his *Confessions* on his way through error and sin to conversion.

In Hell, Dante finds the sinners who did not ask forgiveness before they died. Near the entrance are the ancients, who, though not sinful, did not know the true God and are relegated to a sort of limbo until the Last Judgment. Lower down are those who sinned against themselves, such as gluttons and suicides. Then come those who sinned against others—thieves, murderers, and such—and finally, those who sinned against authority, Cassius and Brutus, who murdered Julius Caesar, and Judas, who betrayed Christ. Dante imagines these three figures in the mouth of the behemoth Satan, the ultimate symbol of sin as the one who sinned against God.

After this vision, Dante and Vergil climb down the body of Satan, through the ice in which it is embedded, and then turn to climb up the inverted leg of Satan to the base of the mountain of Purgatory. Thus the descent has actually been an ascent.

In Purgatory, souls who had confessed their sins and asked God for forgiveness but who had not completed a penance before dying now purge themselves through suffering. As Dante and Vergil climb up the mountain, they first meet sinners who are more heavily burdened than those higher up, and they find that the climb gets easier as they approach the top, shedding the weight of sin. At the top, Dante has a vision of the corrupt

Dante and his guide, Vergil, visiting the circle of Hell to which usurers have been relegated (illustrated from a fourteenth-century Italian manuscript).

church and of the Antichrist and his armies who will battle Christ and his forces at the end of time. He then sees the victorious Christ presiding over the Last Judgment. The pilgrim now enters the Garden of Eden, having cleansed himself in the river Lethe (which wipes out the memory of sin) and in the river Eunoë (which prepares him for entry into Heaven). He has left sinfulness behind and become perfect as Adam was before the fall. Vergil is left behind, beyond the river Lethe, unable to achieve perfection, because he did not have faith in Christ.

From the top of Purgatory, Dante enters Heaven, which is a spherical universe, with neither beginning nor end, symbolizing eternity. Here Dante is alluding to a medieval definition of God as a three-dimensional circle whose center is everywhere and whose circumference is nowhere. To Dante, it appears that the structure of Heaven is a series of concentric spheres that correspond to the Ptolem-

aic view of the universe, and as he proceeds through them he is guided by Bernard of Clairvaux (renowned as a mystic who had himself achieved the beatific vision). He meets the saints of Christian history (including Augustine and Aquinas) and learns that the division into spheres is only an illusion. Here, Dante draws on the ideas of contemporary physics. Finally, he achieves the beatific vision, the sight of "the love which moves the sun and all the stars." It is a vision of man, made in God's image, within a circle. The way to God is through human life, and the mystery of Augustine's conversion and of Dante's descent in order to ascend are explained. Human beings journey to God through the dark ways of human life, and the miracle of salvation is that such a route can lead to perfection.

The *Divine Comedy* was recognized as a classic almost immediately, and it has remained an important source for an understanding of the medieval world view.

The Significance of Vernacular Literature

Although the Anglo-Saxon poems of the early Middle Ages were in a sense the first examples of literature written in a vernacular language, they had little influence on medieval culture. The main tradition of vernacular literature was launched with the advent of twelfth-century masterpieces like the *Song of Roland.*

Vernacular literature introduced themes that are still common in western literature, such as romantic love and the effort to reconcile nature and civilization. And in dealing with those themes medieval poets created most of the poetic forms that have become traditional in the West. Moreover, vernacular literature helped to weaken Latin as the universal language. Portions of the Bible were translated into French during the twelfth century, and several histories had been written in French by the early thirteenth century. If French could be used for such purposes, it could also be used for official documents, and during the thirteenth century royal letters and government documents were often written in French. The same was true of the use of vernacular languages in other countries, a trend that gave each country a sense of its own identity and contributed to the rise of nationalism.

Finally, vernacular literature instructed people at all levels of society—from aristocrats to town dwellers—in the manners and mores of civilized life. True, many thirteenth-century knights were ignorant and brutal, but many people took the style of life depicted in the romances and poems as a model for their own behavior.

Dante's Divine Comedy

THE INSCRIPTION ON THE ENTRANCE TO HELL

Through me you pass into the woeful city
Through me you pass into eternal pain
Through me you go amid those lost forever.
Justice it was that moved my Great Creator;
Power divine and highest wisdom made me
Together with God's own primeval love.
Before me there was nothing save those things
Eternal, and eternal I endure.
All hope abandon, ye who enter here.

THE FINAL VISION

O grace abundant, through which I presumed
To fix my gaze on the eternal light
Which near consumes who dares to look thereon.
And in those depths I saw, bound up by love
Into one volume, all the universe. . . .
Here vigor failed the lofty vision, but
The will moved ever onward, like a wheel
In even motion, by the love impelled
Which moves the sun in heaven and all the stars.

From Dante, Inferno, *canto 3;* Paradise, *canto 33, trans. by H. F. Cary (London: Bell, 1877).*

Suggestions for Further Reading

The Church at its Height

On the later medieval Church, see S. R. Packard, *Europe and the Church under Innocent III* (1927), and C. Edwards, *Innocent III: Church Defender* (1951). The best biography is H. Tillman, *Pope Innocent III* (1980). For an excellent study of Innocent's relations with England, see C. R. Cheney, *Pope Innocent III and England* (1967).

On the origins of heresy, see J. B. Russell, *Dissent and Reform in the Early Middle Ages* (1965), and R. I. Moore, *The Origins of European Dissent* (1975). On particular heretical movements, see S. Runciman, *The Medieval Manichee* (1947), which traces the history of the dualist heresy, and E. W. McDonnell, *The Beguines and Beghards in Medieval Culture* (1954). On the crusade against the Cathars in southern France, see J. R. Strayer, *The Albigensian Crusades* (1971); W. L. Wakefield, *Heresy, Crusade and Inquisition in Southern France* (1974); and J. Sumption, *The Albigensian Crusade* (1978). On St. Francis, see P. Sabatier, *Life of Saint Francis of Assisi* (1894), and O. Engelbert, *Saint Francis of Assisi*, 2nd ed. (1966), which has a good bibliography. Two important works on the development of the Franciscan order are R. Brooke, *Early Franciscan Government* (1959), and M. D. Lambert, *Franciscan Poverty* (1961). The latter work traces the controversy over the Franciscans' claim that neither individual monks nor the order owned anything, even though they used property and goods. See in general, J. Moorman, *A History of the Franciscan Order* (1968). B. Jarrett's *Life of Saint Dominic* (1924) is rather adulatory. P. Mandonnet, *Saint Dominic and his Work* (1944), emphasizes the spirit and work of the Order. For a general history of the order in its early period, see W. A. Hinnebusch, *History of the Dominican Order* (1966).

Twelfth-Century Renaissance

On the renaissance of the twelfth century, see the classic work by C. H. Haskins, *The Renaissance of the Twelfth Century* (1927). This work has been brought up to date in R. Benson, G. Constable, and C. D. Lanham, eds., *Renaissance and Renewal in the Twelfth Century* (1982). For an interpretive study, see R. W. Southern, *The Making of the Middle Ages* (1953), and essays by the same author in *Medieval Humanism and Other Studies* (1976). On Abelard and Bernard, see E. Gilson's *The Mystical Theology of Saint Bernard* (1940) and *Heloise and Abelard* (1948). B. S. James, *Saint Bernard of Clairvaux* (1957), focuses on Bernard the man. For a general study of twelfth-century theology, see M. D. Chenu, *Nature, Man, and Society in the Twelfth Century*, trans. by J. Taylor and L. K. Little (1968).

Gothic Architecture

On the development of Gothic architecture, see E. Panofsky, trans., *Suger on the Abbey of Saint Denis* (1946). E. Male, *The Gothic Image* (1913), is a classic study of Gothic art. For interpretive essays, see E. Panofsky, *Gothic Architecture and Scholasticism* (1951), and O. von Simpson, *The Gothic Cathedral* (1956). On the social context, see G. Duby, *The Age of the Cathedrals: Art and Society, 980–1420*, trans. by E. Levieux and B. Thompson (1981). For a study of the stone masons, see J. Gimpel, *The Cathedral Builders* (1961). P. Frankl, *Gothic Architecture* (1963), is the best treatment of Gothic art in the High Middle Ages. He traces the development of the style in all areas of Europe. See also the studies of individual cathedrals: A. Temko, *Nôtre-Dame de Paris* (1955), and A. E. M. Katzenellenbogen, *The Sculptural Program of Chartres Cathedral* (1959).

Philosophy, Science, and Literature

On medieval philosophy, see D. Knowles, *The Evolution of Medieval Thought* (1962), and the articles in *Renaissance and Renewal in the Twelfth Century*, cited earlier. On later medieval philosophy, see N. Kretzmann, A. Kenny, and J. Pinborg, eds., *The Cambridge History of Later Medieval Philosophy: From the Rediscovery of Aristotle to the Disintegration of Scholasticism, 1100–1600* (1982). On medieval logic, see A. Broadie, *Introduction to Medieval Logic* (1987), and D. P. Henry, *Medieval Logic and Metaphysics: A Modern Introduction* (1972). On Abelard and his influence, see D. E. Luscombe, *The School of Peter Abelard* (1969). The introduction of Aristotle and his Arabic commentators is covered in F. Van Steenberghen, *Aristotle in the West* (1955); R. J. Lemay, *Abu Ma'shar and Latin Aristotelianism in the Twelfth Century* (1962); and F. E. Peters, *Aristoteles Latinus: The Oriental Translations and Commentaries in the Aristotelian Corpus* (1968). On Thomas Aquinas, see the biography by J. A. Weisheipl, *Friar Thomas d'Aquino: His Life, Thought, and Work* (1974). On Thomism, see M. De Wulf, *Philosophy and Civilization in the Middle Ages* (1922). The best scholarly treatment of Thomas and his influence is E. Gilson, *History of Christian Philosophy in the Middle Ages* (1954). For the universities and their intellectual life, see G. Leff, *Paris and Oxford Universities in the Thirteenth and Fourteenth Centuries* (1968).

There are two monumental histories of medieval science: L. Thorndyke, *A History of Magic and Experimental Science*, 8 vols. (1923–58), and G. Sarton, *Introduction to the History of Science*, 3 vols. (1927–48). But the best history of medieval science is A. C. Crombie, *Medieval and Early Modern Science*, 2 vols. (1959). On the introduction of Arabic science in the twelfth century, see C. H. Haskins, *Studies in the History of Medieval Science* (1924); B. Stock, *Myth and Science in the Twelfth Century* (1972); and the works on the introduction of Aristotle cited earlier. In *Robert Grosseteste and the Origins of Experimental Science 1100–1700* (1953), Crombie argued that the scientific method developed long before Galileo. This view is not universally accepted. For a history of mechanics in the Middle Ages, see M. Clagett, *Archimedes in the Middle Ages*, 4 vols. (1964–80). J. Gimpel, *The Medieval Machine* (1976), treats the history of medieval technology. R. P. Multhauf, *The Origins of Chemistry* (1967), replaces all earlier studies.

On the historical writing of the Middle Ages, see S. Vryonis, Jr., *Readings in Medieval Historiography* (1968), which treats Latin, Byzantine, and Moslem historians. W. T. H. Jackson, *Medieval Literature* (1966), is a general treatment of medieval literature. P. Dronke, *Medieval Latin and the Rise of the European Love-lyric* (1968), is very useful. See also F. J. E. Raby, *A History of Secular Latin Poetry in the Middle Ages*, 2 vols. (1957). R. S. Southern, "From Epic to Romance," *Medieval Humanism and Other Essays* (1976), provides an interpretation of the literary history of the twelfth century in a brief essay. R. S. Loomis, *The Development of Arthurian Romance* (1963), is a good general introduction to the origins of the romance. For French literature, see U. T. Holmes, *A History of Old French Literature*, rev. ed. (1962). See also Holmes's *Chretien de Troyes* (1970). For Germany, see J. G. Robertson, *A History of German Literature* (1947). The best critical study of the vernacular literature of the twelfth and thirteenth centuries is E. Curtius, *European Literature and the Latin Middle Ages* (1963), which has excellent bibliographic materials. Many of the romances have been translated. F. Goldin provides ample collections of medieval lyrics in *Lyrics of the Troubadours and Trouveres* (1973) and *German and Italian Lyrics of the Middle Ages* (1973). See

also Andreas Capellanus, *The Art of Courtly Love*, trans. by J. J. Parry (1941).

Many editions exist of Dante's *Divine Comedy* and other classics of medieval literature. See especially, C. Singleton, *The Divine Comedy*, 3 vols. (1970–75), which contains the original Italian, a facing-page translation, and commentary.

For a history of vernacular culture as a whole, see A. W. Ward and A. R. Waller, *The Cambridge History of English Literature*, Vol. 1 (1907), and E. Vossler, *Medieval Culture: An Introduction to Dante and His Times*, 2 vols. (1929).

12

THE RISE OF THE SECULAR STATE

Although the church was the dominant political power during the thirteenth century, the kings continued the consolidation of their power that had begun in the twelfth century. By 1300, the church found itself facing secular powers strong enough to resist its claims to interfere in their business. Throughout the thirteenth century, however, the idea of secular power was still inextricably intertwined with Christian doctrine. People still believed that the king's authority derived from Christ, and they could not conceive of legitimate royal power wholly divorced from the church. Yet by the end of the thirteenth century, the monarchies had achieved both ideological and actual independence from the church.

THE EFFECTS OF ECONOMIC CHANGE ON THE CHURCH

Even as the power of the church was at its peak, changes were taking place that would undermine its position and ultimately lead to its subordination to the secular state. The growth of trade and commerce was accompanied by a rise in prices that affected people living on fixed incomes more severely than it did those who were actually engaged in trade. The church and many aristocratic landowners were particularly hard hit by inflation. In the Middle Ages, because rents were fixed in perpetuity, landowners who rented their land to peasant farmers were badly squeezed by rising prices. During the thirteenth century, they took back their land whenever they could and farmed it themselves, leaving the farmers with plots too small for them to take advantage of the high prices in the market. Many of the farmers grew discouraged and moved to the cities.

As the church tried to cope with the rapidly increasing urban population, it encountered a shortage of parish priests to minister to the spiritual needs of the people. By the middle of the thirteenth century Franciscans and Dominicans were helping the priests and providing a good deal of the ministry in the cities. These mendicants won a reputation for holiness, and people flocked to their churches. Wealthy people gave them gifts, and soon the mendicant orders themselves were wealthy. The prominence of the mendicants in the cities angered the bishops, who claimed that only they could authorize priests to preach in their dioceses (see p. 283). In the end, the papacy and the mendicants prevailed because the papacy could claim universal authority in the church, but not before the prestige of the church had been seriously damaged.

Prosperity created another problem for the church. Wealth engendered pride and callousness among the newly rich members of society, and the church strove, with some success, to bring them a heightened sense of social responsibility. It condemned profiteering and neglect of the poor, and created many charitable institutions—such as hospitals for the homeless and destitute as well as for the sick.

The church accepted the idea that a man who invested in a commercial enterprise was entitled to a return on his money, but it denounced the practice of lending money for interest. As the medieval economy tended more and more to become a money economy, many moneylenders amassed huge fortunes. That some of them left substantial endowments to charitable institutions did not alter the fact that they were in violation of church doctrine. With money becoming more important to society than inherited status, men found it difficult to follow the teachings of the church and to put its interests ahead of their own.

Churchmen themselves were affected by these economic changes. To support themselves at the level to which they had grown accustomed, ecclesiastics sought and received multiple offices. When it became apparent that even members of the papal curia were having trouble living on their fixed incomes, the popes gave them offices in churches throughout Europe. A member of the curia might hold an office in one or more Italian bishoprics, one in England, and another in France. He would collect income from all of them, without performing any of the functions they entailed. He might appoint a substitute, to whom he would pay a low wage, but in most cases the far-flung offices went without a head. Bishops who faithfully carried out their duties complained about this papal practice, but in vain.

The church was criticized for its financial policies. As time passed, the income tax on the clergy, first imposed by Innocent III, was levied with increasing frequency and at rising rates. Fees were imposed or raised on papal letters, legal documents, court costs, and on confirmations of appointment to high church offices. Because a high percentage of church income derived from tithes (one-tenth of produce) and other payments by the laity, they felt much abused by the additional fees imposed by the ecclesiastical bureaucracy. The church was criticized for being too eager to raise money and too ready to grant spiritual benefits in return for cash payments. The more zealous wing of the Franciscans urged the clergy to give away all their property and to lead lives of poverty. Actually, the Franciscan order itself was acquiring large amounts of property while trying to disguise the fact by vesting title in trustees. Even popes and bishops with an appetite for reform found that they could do little to alter the church's financial system, and many people came to suspect that the church was no different from the rapacious secular governments of the period.

ENGLAND

The Creation of the Anglo-Norman State

During the eleventh century, the Normans had led the reconquest of southern Italy and Sicily and had participated in both the reconquest of Spain and the crusades to the Holy Land. But the Norman achievement that had the most far-reaching implications was the conquest of England in 1066.

England had been in the Scandinavian orbit since the late ninth century, when the Great Army of Vikings battled Alfred of Wessex for control of the island. Even after Alfred had defeated the Vikings, Scandinavians continued to view England as part of their world. In the early eleventh century, after driving out Edward, the son of the previous Anglo-Saxon king, Ethelred the Ill-Counseled (r. 978–1016), the Danish king Canute (r. 1016–35) incorporated England into a vast Scandinavian empire. Edward went into exile in Normandy, the country of his mother Emma, daughter of the duke of Normandy. When the Scandinavian empire collapsed in 1042, Edward ascended the English throne.

The Danish kings had mostly left the Anglo-Saxon aristocracy in place during their reign, and Edward (r. 1042–66) found himself surrounded by Anglo-Saxon earls eager to participate in the governance of the country. But Edward was more comfortable with the Norman friends he had brought with him to England, and his reign was troubled by competition between the two groups of aspirants. The leader of the earls was Godwin of Wessex, who persuaded Edward to marry his daughter.

When Edward died without an heir in 1066, Godwin's son Harold claimed the throne on the basis of a weak hereditary right—his sister was the widowed queen. His political claim was a good bit stronger—he had the support of the Anglo-Saxon aristocracy. Edward's cousin, Duke William of Normandy, claimed the throne for himself and prepared an invasion to pursue that claim. William landed on the English coast near Hastings in 1066 and overcame Harold and the Anglo-Saxon army in the battle of Hastings. In a remarkably short time, William had assumed control of the entire country.

William set about creating an almost entirely new political system in England. He dispossessed most of the old Anglo-Saxon nobility and granted their lands in fief to his own men. Henceforth, all land in England was held by feudal tenure from the king, and the fiefholders—the tenants-in-chief—granted some of the land in fief to their own supporters and companions. Within a few years, the Normans had transformed the country into a model feudal hierarchy.

Even though he replaced the Anglo-Saxon aristocracy, William the Conqueror (r. 1066–87) claimed to be the rightful heir of Edward and sought to preserve the old laws and governmental system of Anglo-Saxon England. In doing so, he and his two sons, William II (r. 1087–1100) and Henry I (r. 1100–35), used the institutions of local government (see p. 243) to force the population to accept and obey the royal government. They installed Norman

Silver penny bearing the likeness of William the Conqueror.

A section of the Bayeux Tapestry, which told the story of the Norman Conquest of England (1066) from the Norman point of view. Here, Harold, who claimed the English throne in 1065, takes an oath to William of Normandy promising that he would support William's claim to the throne.

Norman troops on horseback engaging Anglo-Saxon foot soldiers in battle (detail from the Bayeux Tapestry, late eleventh century).

England after the Norman Conquest   LATE ELEVENTH CENTURY

sheriffs in the shires and held the courts of the hundreds responsible for keeping the peace in their districts.

Henry II and the Origins of Common Law

Under the Norman kings, England was the best-governed and most politically unified kingdom in Europe. But England was only one part of the territory under their control. William I had remained duke of Normandy after becoming king of England, and his sons followed his example. Henry I died in 1135, leaving as heir his daughter Mathilda, who was married to Count Geoffrey Martel of Anjou, with whom she had a son, Henry. On her father's death, Mathilda claimed the English throne and the duchy of Normandy for Henry.

Both claims were challenged by Stephen of Blois—the grandson of William I through his daughter Adele. A faction of the Anglo-Norman nobility favored Stephen, in part because of their traditional enmity toward the men of Anjou, the Angevins. With the support of that faction, Stephen was able to take the English throne. But his reign (1135–54) was troubled by almost constant civil war over the succession. Then, toward the end of his reign, an agreement was worked out:

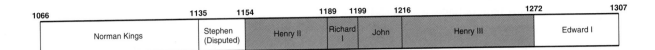

1066		1135	1154		1189	1199	1216		1272	1307
	Norman Kings	Stephen (Disputed)	Henry II		Richard I	John		Henry III		Edward I

Mathilda would permit Stephen to rule in peace, and Stephen, whose own son had just died, would declare Mathilda's son Henry to be his heir.

Meanwhile, young Henry had succeeded his father as count of Anjou and had married Eleanor of Aquitaine, the heiress of the duchy of Aquitaine, the largest and richest duchy in the French kingdom. Thus, when Henry succeeded Stephen as king of England and duke of Normandy in 1154, he was ruler of the largest kingdom in all of Europe. When he had added Brittany to his realm, the empire included England and more than half of the kingdom of France.

Henry II (r. 1154–89) traveled constantly around his vast realm keeping the barons in line and building royal power in England. He spent the first few years of his reign settling the affairs of the kingdom after the disruption caused by the twenty-year civil war over the succession. As he traveled about, he installed his own men as sheriffs and ordered the demolition of castles built by the barons without royal permission. In many places, finding that Stephen and Mathilda had granted the same fief to two different claimants, he issued a writ (a royal order) to the local sheriff instructing him to decide which had the best right to the fief.

These writs gave rise to complicated legal proceedings that sometimes went on for years. Under Anglo-Norman law, the question of right was decided in a trial by battle, but the courts were slow to authorize that procedure. In 1164, to speed things up, Henry decreed new remedies for settling disputes over property.

Those remedies contained three features that eventually transformed English law. First, they pertained only to the right of possession of disputed land, not to the right of ownership. They bypassed the question of who owned the land and the old procedure by which that question was decided. In practice, of course, as soon as the sheriff had decided the issue of possession, the loser gave up the case.

Second, the writs required an old but rarely used procedure—the jury trial. The practice of having a jury decide points of fact had arisen in the early Middle Ages as part of the inquest, the procedure by which a landowner checked on the rents due him. For example, when the king wanted to determine the ownership of various properties in a village and how much the villagers owed to the lord of the village, he would empanel a group of the leading men, make them take an oath to tell the truth, and have them answer questions about the issue. It was assumed that the information produced by the members of the jury (the word comes from the Latin *juratus,* which means sworn) would be accurate, for no one would let another understate his obligations or overstate his rights. Henry's writs put this procedure to a legal purpose by ordering the sheriff to empanel a jury of the disputants' neighbors to answer questions about who had the best right to possess the disputed property.

Third, the writs were "returnable." This meant that someone to whom a writ had been issued could "return" it to the king's sheriff, bringing about the case that

A writ from Henry II to the sheriff of Lincoln, instructing him to summon a jury to determine a land dispute between a layman and the canons of Lincoln. The sheriff is to restore the land to the canons pending the outcome of the trial.

England and France at the Time of Henry II   1154–89

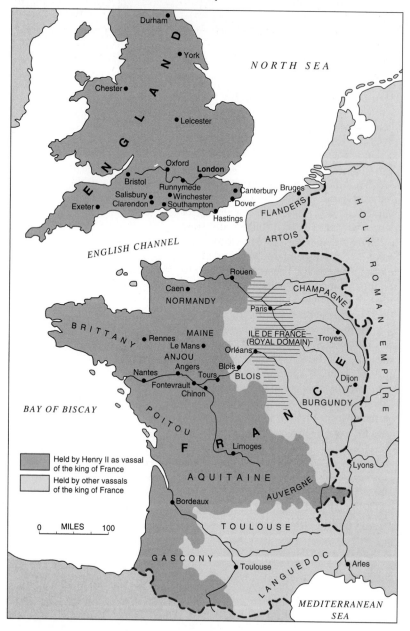

ferred to the king for decision. Over time, a "case law" developed in the king's court that was binding throughout the kingdom—as opposed to "customary law," which was valid only in a particular hundred or shire court. That case law became known as *common law*.

John and Magna Carta

Henry II's sons, Richard I, "the Lionhearted" (r. 1189–99), and John (r. 1199–1216), lacked their father's political skills. Richard was a warrior who spent his entire reign, except for ten months, either participating in the Third Crusade or fighting King Philip II of France (r. 1180–1223). Despite Richard's neglect of government, however, Henry's astute political arrangements continued to function smoothly.

John, by contrast, was a poor soldier but a shrewd administrator. Early in his reign he lost Normandy, Anjou, and most of Aquitaine to Philip II and spent the last twelve years of his reign trying to get them back. He was constantly in need of money to pay for his campaigns and squeezed revenue from every source he could. On occasion he would impose heavy fines on men he suspected of plotting against him and might even seize their property. His military failures and the repressive measures to which he resorted prompted the English barons to rebel against him in 1215. The rebellion succeeded, and John was obliged to sign the *Magna Carta* (Great Charter) at Runnymede just outside London on June 15, 1215.

The Charter contained 63 chapters covering a wide variety of topics. Among its main provisions was John's promise not to demand taxes without "taking counsel with the kingdom," which meant consulting with the barons. Further, he promised not to convict any freeman of a crime without a trial by his peers and not to charge litigants for bringing cases to his court. He also promised to consult with his vassals and bishops before undertaking campaigns. Although the purpose of the *Magna Carta* was to protect the barons and the ecclesiastical lords, it established the principle that the government of En-

would decide if the complainant had been unjustly dispossessed. Because this practice put the king's law at the disposal of anyone who had a complaint, it generated a huge number of cases, many of them having to do with problems that had never arisen before. When a case came up for which no precedent existed, it was regland was based on law and that the king as well as his subjects were bound by the law.

Henry III

The signing of the *Magna Carta* seemed to be a defeat for the monarchy in England, but John's son, Henry III (r. 1216–72), reissued it, and royal government grew stronger under him. Henry's financial ministers strengthened the administrative and judicial institutions of the country and created new types of taxation. His chancellor, who oversaw the royal courts, devised additional writs to bring more cases into the courts. Moreover, the church's condemnation of trial by ordeal (see the box) at the Fourth Lateran Council of 1215 (see p. 282) increased the number of cases that came to the royal courts because they had a procedure—the jury trial—that was acceptable to the church. The ordeal was the preferred procedure of the courts where customary law was enforced, and once they were deprived of their procedure they lost business because people conceived of a court and its procedure as one and the same.

All these developments were summed up in a remarkable treatise on English law based on the research that Henry de Bracton, a royal judge, did in the records of the royal courts. (The treatise was attributed to Bracton, but scholars are not convinced he wrote it.) Written in the 1250s, this treatise gave a clear, logical, and thorough explanation of the common law through use of precedents and general principles. The author's familiarity with Roman law helped him to bring together hundreds of individual cases into a comprehensive, coherent reference book. Partly as a result of that achievement, the common law has maintained its identity as a legal system up to the present time.

Despite these advances, there was constant conflict between Henry III and his barons. The barons were trying to gain control of the central government to protect their rights—particularly to limit taxes—and often declared that they were defending the realm against a foolish and spendthrift monarch.

Excerpts from Magna Carta   1215

We [John] have conceded to all free men of our kingdom, for us and our heirs forever, all the liberties written below, to be held by them and their heirs from us and our heirs: . . .

12. No scutage [redemption of military service] or aid [grant to the king] shall be taken in our kingdom except by the common counsel of our kingdom. . . .

14. And for obtaining the common counsel of the kingdom, for assessing an aid . . . or a scutage, we will cause to be summoned by our sealed letters the archbishops, bishops, abbots, earls and greater barons, moreover we will cause to be summoned generally by the sheriffs . . . all those who hold of us in chief [the other vassals] for a certain day . . . and place . . . and once the summons has been made the business shall proceed on the assigned day according to the advice of those who are present, even if all those summoned have not come. . . .

39. No free man may be seized, or imprisoned, or dispossessed, or outlawed, or exiled . . . nor will we go against him or send against him except by the legal judgment of his peers and by the law of the land.

40. To no one will we sell, to no one will we deny or delay right and justice.

Translated from W. Stubbs, Select Charters *(Oxford: Clarendon Press, 1921), pp. 294 ff.*

Henry had inherited the throne as a child, and the government had been run by regents until he came of age in 1225. At that time the barons persuaded him to reaffirm the *Magna Carta,* granting him a tax in return. The version of 1225 was little changed from that of 1215, but it was accepted by everyone as the law of the land and marked an auspicious beginning for the young king.

Harmony prevailed until the 1240s when the barons raised a protest against Henry's foreign policy. In addition to pouring money into vain attempts to reconquer the lost French territories, Henry was naming his French relatives and friends to bishoprics and to important secular offices. And he was permitting the pope to draw large sums of money out of

Judicial Ordeals

People in the Middle Ages believed that ordeals revealed God's judgment of the issue of a case. They were used in criminal cases to determine the guilt or innocence of the accused. After hearing testimony the court assigned the proof by ordeal to the accused or accuser, depending on which one seemed to have the best case. Usually, the accused had to undergo the ordeal.

There were three basic forms of ordeal—hot iron, water, and compurgation (the swearing of innocence with a number of "oath helpers").

Hot iron: A piece of iron was heated until it glowed. Then the person undergoing the ordeal picked it up in his bare hand and carried it a certain distance and dropped it. The hand was bandaged, and if the wound was clean after three days, then the person was innocent. If it was infected, he was guilty. (A similar ordeal used boiling water, from which the person had to lift an object.)

Water: The person was tied up with his knees against his chest and lowered into a tub of water. If he sank, the water was deemed to have "accepted" him, and he was declared innocent. If he floated, the water had rejected him, and he was found guilty.

Compurgation: The court ordered the person to swear an oath declaring his innocence. Depending on the status of the person and the nature of the case, the court assigned up to 72 others from the community to swear that the man's oath was true. To prove the principal oath-taker innocent, all of the swearers had to pronounce the oath without mistake. A verbal stumble by any of them proved him guilty.

An early copy of the Magna Carta with the royal seal.

England to fight a war against the German rulers of Italy. The barons had no interest in the French territories; they resented Henry's French friends; and they saw no reason why the donations of pious Englishmen should go to the pope. They were supported in their opposition to foreign intruders and foreign entanglements by many lesser landholders and by a surprising number of clergymen.

In his efforts to overcome his chronic shortage of money, Henry played into the hands of the barons. Ordinary income from the royal domain was barely enough to keep the royal government afloat even during peacetime, and the *Magna Carta* made it difficult to raise additional revenues without the consent of the barons. If Henry wanted to wage war, he had to

levy taxes. But after 1240 the barons refused to let him do so. Nevertheless, Henry went ahead with an ambitious project to help the pope conquer Sicily. The English clergy, under papal pressure, came up with some money to advance the cause, but not enough. By 1258 Henry was hopelessly in debt and his foreign policy was a complete failure. In desperation he appointed a committee of barons to help put matters right.

The barons promptly set about making policy and appointing officials to carry it out. The committee soon split into factions, however. The barons were united in their opposition to Henry, but found it hard to agree on a policy of their own and resented anyone who sought to assume leadership. When the ablest member of the committee, Simon de Montfort (Henry's brother-in-law), gained control of the government, he found that the barons had deserted the cause of reform. In 1265, Henry's eldest son, Edward, raised an army and killed Simon in battle, thereby restoring Henry's authority.

This episode was significant for two reasons. First, it set a pattern that was to be repeated in England many times in the next two centuries. Again and again, the barons would seize control of the government only to split into factions and lose control once again. Second, it speeded up the emergence of a representative assembly. Henry and the barons each summoned knights from the shires and representatives from the towns as well as great lords and high churchmen to give them support in assemblies.

The Origins of Constitutional Government

In the early thirteenth century, several elements began to coalesce into what was to emerge as constitutional government. In the realm of theory, church lawyers began to apply the Roman law of corporations to church organization. They used the principle that "what touches all, ought to be approved by all" to support the right of the clergy and the members of a monastery to participate in the affairs of the church. At about the same time they were discussing how to deal with a vacancy in

super interiul + comunitat e malte +
latate sunt o's aie q cunit iiseruo t
clamalunt note magna dicers un
dicimus te rxe cu di mu q dignat

es nob iesingeui taie sj dici t li uot
tis quam totum temp q uminus
et tua . vi ergo qui tusso duit die tua
qui npi lievint pte ni cas i tela telor

Manuscript illumination of the coronation ceremony from a Coronation Order (text of the ceremony) written between 1272 and 1325. The king may be Edward II.

the office of a bishop or an abbot. The old canon law said that the bishop was the ruler of his see and the abbot was the ruler of his monastery. But who was the ruler during a vacancy? The lawyers found the answer in the Roman law of corporations: the members of the church or monastery collectively exercised the power until a new leader was installed. That conclusion gave further impetus to the idea of representation. The officers of a corporation or those appointed by them could act on its behalf and could represent it before others.

The idea that the state itself was a legal community like a corporation spread to many areas of Europe during the early thirteenth century. In many places, rulers called on barons and representatives of the towns to lend their support to the government. Pope Innocent III called together the barons and representatives of the towns in the areas under papal control, the so-called Papal States of central Italy, and the kings of Spain and Hungary summoned meetings of their own. But adherence to the idea was strongest in England.

In England, a meeting called for such purposes came to be called a *parliament* (literally "talk-fest"). The parliament was an enlarged meeting of the king's council, which normally consisted of the king's tenants-in-chief—the great men, both lay and clerical, who held fiefs directly from the king. Under feudal law, these men owed the king advice and counsel, and

An illustration of a parliament under Edward I. Edward is flanked by King Alexander of Scotland and Prince Lewellyn of Wales, who were subordinate to him.

the king was bound to consult with them on business that concerned them—essentially the business of the realm. At a parliament, this inner group was joined by other barons and important men, to ensure that actions would receive support throughout the kingdom. The king also heard important appeals while sitting in parliament and would ask those in attendance to help him decide difficult cases and to support his decisions.

Knights of the shires—sheriffs, royal bailiffs, and tax collectors—were often invited to attend the parliaments. Awed by the occasion, they usually gave the king their support and went home to report what had taken place. Both Henry III and Simon de Montfort followed this practice. In 1265, Simon, to compensate for his loss of baronial support, went even further by inviting the towns to send representatives. These precedents were not forgotten. In 1268, after Simon's death, Henry III summoned both knights and townsmen to a parliament, hoping to win their political and financial support in return for being included in such an august assemblage of great men.

Edward and the Development of Parliament

Although the foundations were laid under John and Henry III, the principles of constitutional government were established under Henry III's son, Edward I (r. 1272–1307). Constantly in need of money to fight his wars with the Scots and the French, Edward summoned several parliaments to ask the barons and the towns for financial support. After calling both knights and townsmen to a parliament in 1275, for the next twenty years he summoned such representatives only rarely. The core of a parliament was still the king's council, made up of high officials, bishops, and barons. In 1295, however, Edward again summoned knights and representatives of the towns to a full meeting (the "Model Parliament"), and from that time on they were frequently present. Edward could probably have managed with the approval of the barons alone, but he found that the full parliament assured wider support for his actions.

Edward also found that working with a parliament was an efficient way of doing business. He and his officials could take care of all sorts of business at one time and in one place. However, it was advantageous to obtain parliamentary sanction whenever possible, for actions taken in parliament carried great prestige. Edward controlled parliament as effectively as he did every other branch of government, and he could not have foreseen that he was nurturing a powerful institution that might one day develop a will of its own.

The knights and townsmen Edward summoned to parliament seem to have viewed their role as largely passive: "to hear and to obey," as some of the early summonses put it. Any opposition came from the barons. In 1297, when Edward pushed through a new tax at a council meeting that did not include knights and townsmen, the barons protested and forced him to promise that in the future he would levy taxes only "with the common assent of the whole kingdom." This was not quite an admission that parliament had to grant permission to levy taxes, but it implied that the assent of a large number of people was needed; and clearly the easiest way to obtain such assent was in parliament.

The idea of constitutional government—that government has limited authority and is subject to law—originated

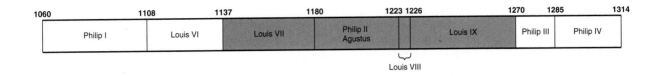

1060	1108	1137	1180	1223 1226	1270	1285	1314
Philip I	Louis VI	Louis VII	Philip II Agustus	Louis IX	Philip III	Philip IV	

Louis VIII

in the distinction between ecclesiastical power and secular power established in the course of the investiture controversy (see pp. 266–69). Europeans, having accepted that distinction, were prepared to set limits on the authority of both popes and kings. The question of when a king or pope controlled the law and when the law controlled him was basic to a constitutional system of government. In answering it, lawyers, both ecclesiastical and secular, helped to define a system of government that was unique in the world. The parliament of thirteenth-century England was the institutional realization of that system.

THE GROWTH OF ROYAL POWER IN FRANCE

Because of the strong opposition of the great lords, royal power emerged more slowly in France than in England. Until the twelfth century, the French kings could only rule the kingdom through the great lords who were virtually autonomous in their counties and duchies. Louis VI (r. 1108–37) was the first to make progress in making royal power felt outside the county of Paris—the so-called Ile de France.

Louis VI and Louis VII

Philip I (r. 1060–1108) had issued few grants to individuals or ecclesiastical institutions outside the Ile de France. Philip's son Louis VI increased the number of grants issued from an average of three or four each year to about twelve, an indication that he was taking a more active role in the affairs of bishoprics and monasteries throughout the realm. Moreover, he ruled that all bishops who were not already under the protection of some great lord were to accept the king's protection, an assertion that substantially augmented

royal power. Henceforth, bishops dissatisfied with the performance of local magnates could turn to the king for relief.

By taking advantage of his opportunities, Louis added substantially to the number of his *fideles*—that is, the men who took an oath of fealty to him. He recognized that he could not insist, as the Carolingians had, that everyone in the kingdom owed him allegiance, but he worked

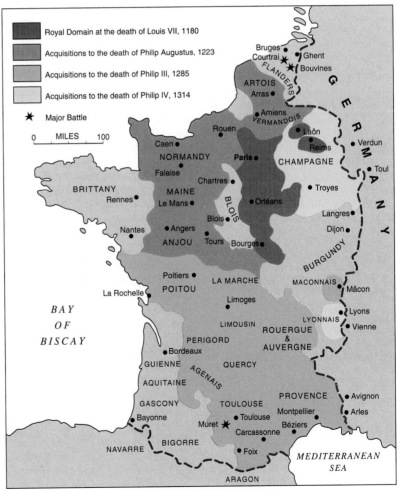

The Expansion of the Royal Domain in France   1180–1314

steadily to extend his circle of vassals. His chief adviser, Abbot Suger of St. Denis (abbot 1122–52), eventually fashioned a theory of royal authority that harked back to the Carolingian idea of kingship. In his biography of Louis, written shortly after the king's death, Suger asserted that all men in the kingdom were subject to the king, either directly or indirectly. Lesser men were subject to Louis through the greater men who were his *fideles*. The king himself, Suger said, was subject to no one; his only obligation was to St. Denis, the patron saint of the monarchy and the kingdom. Here Suger was making a subtle distinction between the French king and the English king. The English king at the time was also the duke of Normandy, and, as a duke, he was subject to the French king. Thus Louis had been superior to Henry I of England. Though Suger's theory was never accepted by the majority of the French nobility, it justified Louis's efforts to impose his authority on the dukes and counts of the kingdom.

Louis himself was at his best in managing practical affairs. Toward the end of his reign, he extended the reach of royal authority by arranging the marriage of his heir Louis VII (r. 1137–80) to Eleanor of Aquitaine, heiress to the richest duchy in the kingdom. After ascending the throne, young Louis staged a royal progress to Aquitaine to dramatize his role as monarch. He was the first king to visit Bordeaux in 300 years. But Eleanor was a strong, independent woman, and the marriage was not a success. In 1147, she accompanied Louis on the Second Crusade (see p. 275) and along the way engaged in a dalliance with her cousin the count of Toulouse. Louis decided to have the marriage annulled and succeeded in getting the church's judgment of annulment in 1152. A year later Eleanor married Louis's great rival, Henry of Anjou, soon to become Henry II of England.

Louis VII continued his father's policies and seized every opportunity to extend his authority. During Louis VI's reign, the abbot of Cluny had placed his abbey and its daughter houses under the protection of the French king, because the local counts were seizing the abbey's possessions. In 1166 and again in 1171, Louis VII responded to the abbot's complaints about the local nobility by marching into Burgundy, the first time a French king had visited the duchy since the middle of the tenth century. To give Cluny more permanent protection, Louis left a group of royal officers in the duchy to serve as the nucleus of royal authority. Whenever he was able to interfere in the affairs of bishoprics in other parts of the kingdom, he installed royal officials to ensure that his arrangements lasted. By the end of his reign, half the bishoprics of the kingdom were under royal protection.

Philip II Augustus

Yet the work of building royal authority in France progressed only slowly while Henry II and Richard I of England retained their holdings in France and continued to regard Louis VII and his son Philip II Augustus (r. 1180–1223) as no more than suzerains. After John succeeded Richard I as king of England, the picture changed.

In 1203, John made the mistake of violating feudal law by mistreating one of his vassals in France. The injured baron appealed to Philip, John's overlord, and Philip summoned John to his court. When John refused to appear, Philip declared that he was a contumacious vassal and deprived him of his fiefs—Normandy, Anjou, Brittany, and most of Aquitaine. In 1204, when Philip moved to take control of those areas, the barons gave him their support.

Philip II was an exceptionally able ruler, well deserving of the title "Augustus" bestowed on him by later historians. He had inherited a kingdom with an annual income equivalent to about £60,000 of silver and left it with an income of £438,000. He accomplished this feat through his wise management of the territory he had wrested from John. He permitted the duchies and counties to retain their own laws and institutions of government, but at the same time he divided them up into small districts governed by men from his own court. Thus Normandy kept its law and its court system but was divided into thirteen administrative districts, each governed by a royal bailiff. Philip treated the bailiffs well enough, and they in turn demanded less from the people than the barons had. Philip gleaned an additional measure of popularity from this policy and strengthened his hold on the kingdom. His practice of governing through royal officials served as the model for later governments on the Continent.

Philip was succeeded by his son Louis VIII (r. 1223–26), who had been an active participant in government before his father's death and had led the crusade against the heretics in southern France that resulted in the annexation of that region (see p. 281). But Louis's reign was cut short by his premature death, and it was left to Louis IX to continue his grandfather's work.

Louis IX (St. Louis)

Louis IX (r. 1226–70) managed to put down a few halfhearted rebellions early in his reign, and for the rest of his life no one dared challenge his authority. He was not an arrogant man, however. Rather, he was imbued with the ideals of the Christian ruler, which held that the king should be good, generous, and conscientious. He settled France's longstanding conflict with England by arranging a generous treaty that let the English king retain the coastal district in Aquitaine (around Bordeaux). He kept faith with all men, even with Moslems. In France, he submitted all disputed questions to his courts, and he discouraged his administrative agents from overstating the reach of royal power. He insisted that his subjects observe his prerogatives and rights, but he was scrupulous in observing the rights of others. Throughout his reign he was known for his honesty and fair dealing.

Louis was a pious man, but he held the church to his own high standards. He refused to join Pope Innocent IV (r. 1243–54) in the attack on Frederick II (see p. 321), and he rejected the demand of the French bishops that he punish men who refused to bow to their ecclesiastical

---

St. Louis as Described by Joinville

Jean de Joinville, a noble of Champagne, was a friend of St. Louis and went with him on his crusade of 1248.

This holy man loved God with all his heart, and imitated his works. For example, just as God died because he loved his people, so the king risked his life many times for the love of his people. . . . He said once to his eldest son: . . . "I beg you that you make yourself loved by the people of your realm, for truly, I would rather that a Scot came from Scotland and governed the people of the kingdom justly and well than that you should govern them badly. . . ." The holy king loved the truth so much that he kept his promises even to the Saracens.

A friar told the king . . . that he had never read that a kingdom was destroyed or changed rulers except through lack of justice. . . . The king did not forget this lesson but governed his land justly and well, according to the will of God. . . . Often in summer he went to sit down under an oak-tree in the wood of Vincennes, after hearing mass, and made us sit around him. And all those who had suits to bring him came up, without being hindered by ushers or other people. And he would ask them: "Does anyone here have a suit?" And those who had requests would get up. . . . And then he would call Lord Pierre de Fontaines and Lord Geoffroi de Villette [two of his legal experts] and say to one of them: "Settle this affair for me." And if he saw anything to correct in what they said on his behalf, he would do so.

From Jean de Joinville, Histoire de Saint Louis, *ed. by N. de Wailly (Paris: Firmin Didot, 1874), pp. 11, 34.*

---

punishments. He felt that, as a Christian king, he could himself provide for the spiritual and material welfare of his people.

Louis's concern for law and justice led to a strengthening of the royal judicial system. Since time immemorial, in France as in England, each community had lived under its own customary law, passed down from generation to generation. Louis did not interfere with customary law that dealt with strictly local matters—for example, rules governing the inheritance of property or the penalty for theft. Rather, his royal courts dealt only with matters that concerned the interests of the crown. These matters included litigation over royal lands and rights, disputes over who had the obligation to maintain bridges and roads, and the handling of disturbances of the king's peace.

As time passed, the jurisdiction of the royal courts extended further and further, and the theory of the Christian ruler seemed to give Louis almost universal authority. Nearly every crime came to be seen as a disturbance of the king's peace. Out of this extension of royal power rose one of the great institutions of the French monarchy, the Parlement of Paris—the king's own court, staffed by his closest advisers. It never became an assembly, as the parliament in England. Rather, the Parlement of Paris heard appeals from the decisions of the king's local bailiffs and from the feudal courts of the great lords. In feudal law, these courts were independent of the king's court, but the Parlement managed to establish its position as a court of appeal, which served as a legal basis for royal claims to supremacy over all subjects.

Statue of Louis IX, in the church of Mainville in Normandy.

The bailiffs' courts were even more zealous than the Parlement in upholding royal rights. No exact boundary between the privileges of local lords and the rights of the monarch had ever been drawn, and on issues for which no clear precedents existed, it was only natural that the bailiffs should rule in favor of the king. Although the Parlement often modified the more extreme claims of the bailiffs, the net result was a further increase in royal power. Still, most people felt that Louis had saved them from the demands of local lords and saw him as the one who had suppressed disorder and brought peace.

As a Christian ruler, Louis was a zealous crusader against the enemies of Christendom. The Moslems had taken Jerusalem in 1187, and all efforts to recover it had failed. Emperor Frederick II had arranged a treaty that restored the city to Christian control, but it had lasted only a short time. In 1248 and again in 1270 Louis led crusades to recover Jerusalem. The first expedition seemed to have some chance of success, but after an early victory Louis's army had been cut off from its supplies and forced to surrender. The second expedition was hopeless from the start, for Louis let himself be talked into attacking the outlying Moslem state of Tunis, which had been interfering with western shipping in the Mediterranean for centuries. Soon after landing, Louis and many of his men died of fever.

The church declared Louis IX a saint during the 1290s as part of a general settlement of disputes between the papacy and Philip IV (r. 1285–1314), Louis's grandson. Louis's commitment to justice and order had created a vast reservoir of support for his dynasty, and now his accomplishments had been officially recognized by the church. Some of those who succeeded him on the throne were evil, and some were weak, but for centuries loyalty to the king was the strongest political force in France. The king stood as the symbol of unity and good government; he alone could settle provincial differences and override local ambitions. Though France remained strongly Catholic, loyalty to the state began to overshadow loyalty to the church.

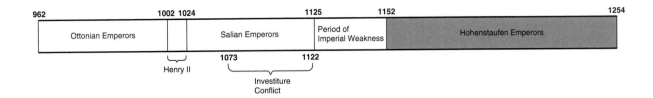

962	1002 1024	1125	1152	1254

Ottonian Emperors | Salian Emperors | Period of Imperial Weakness | Hohenstaufen Emperors

Henry II

1073 — 1122
Investiture Conflict

THE RISE AND FALL OF ROYAL POWER IN GERMANY

The Hohenstaufens

The building of royal power in Germany was beset with problems similar to those in France. When Henry I (r. 918–36) was elected to the throne, his power was based primarily on his own duchy of Saxony. To extend that base, the monarchy had to bring the other duchies under control. Henry and his son Otto I (r. 936–73) made substantial progress toward that goal (see pp. 238–40). But building a strong monarchy in Germany was difficult because in principle the king was chosen through an election by the dukes.

Henry I's predecessor Conrad I (r. 911–18) and Henry himself were elected by the dukes. And even though Otto I and his heirs inherited the crown, they still achieved their elevation through a formal election. Whenever the direct line of male heirs failed—as it did in 1002 when Otto III died without heirs—the electors exercised genuine power and a real election took place. Whenever that happened, the leading ducal families competed fiercely for the crown.

The Hohenstaufens* emerged victorious from such a competition in 1152, when Frederick I Barbarossa (r. 1152–90) became king. Frederick, who was Duke of Swabia, set out to restore royal power, which had been weakened by the competition. His first step was to marry the heiress of the kingdom of Burgundy. Then in 1154 he went to Rome to receive the imperial crown, to which he had a claim as the successor of Otto I. As emperor, he claimed authority over northern Italy, a

---

* The Hohenstaufen descended, in the female line, from Henry V (r. 1106–25). They took their name from their ancestral castle in Swabia.

source of tax revenues that would help him to overpower the German dukes. By firming up his control over a collection of territories stretching from Swabia to Rome, Frederick managed to acquire real authority in Germany as well. In 1180, he deprived his principal rival, Henry the Lion, Duke of Saxony and Bavaria, of all his fiefs. But Frederick could not wholly destroy Henry's power base, because Henry remained the richest duke in Germany on the basis of the lands he owned outright. Although the duke had to go into exile after he lost his fiefs, he eventually returned to his position of influence in Germany.

Frederick's strategy of basing his power as king of Germany on his role as emperor inevitably embroiled him in Italian affairs. Northern Italy was divided into city-states that were always ready to assert their independence and resented having to pay taxes to Frederick. And both the papacy and the kingdom of Sicily, which viewed Frederick as a threat, were eager to support any opposition to him. To secure his empire's southern flank, Frederick arranged the marriage of his son Henry VI (r. 1190–97) to the daughter of the king of Sicily. When the male line of the Sicilian kings failed, young Henry inherited that crown, and the Hohenstaufens found themselves split between their interests in the north and the south even more than before.

Frederick died in 1190 while traveling to the Holy Land on the Third Crusade, and Henry VI succeeded him. But Henry died young in 1197, leaving an infant heir, Frederick. Now it fell to the German electors to choose a king. The competition led to a civil war between Henry VI's brother, Philip of Swabia, and Henry the Lion's son, Otto of Brunswick. Pope Innocent III asserted his right to choose the one best

Late twelfth-century gilded reliquary bearing the features of Frederick I Barbarossa.

qualified to occupy the imperial throne (see p. 281). He threw his support to Otto IV (r. 1197–1215), who secured his hold on the throne when Philip was murdered in 1208. But when Otto broke his promises to the pope in 1209 by invading the kingdom of Sicily, which young Frederick was ruling as a vassal of the papacy, Innocent switched his support to Frederick. Determined to prevent the unification of Italy under a single king, Innocent stirred up a rebellion in Germany against Otto and in favor of Frederick.

Otto returned home in 1212, and in 1214, with the support of King John of England, he invaded France in retaliation for Philip II's support of Frederick. At the battle of Bouvines in Flanders, Philip defeated the combined forces of England and Germany. In England, the defeat precipitated the crisis that led to the signing of the *Magna Carta*. In Germany, it cost Otto his crown: he was deposed by an assembly of the dukes and other nobles in 1215. Frederick II (r. 1215–50; in Sicily, 1197–1250) was now king of Germany. But the long civil war had weakened the monarchy, and the dukes were able to force concessions from him.

Frederick II and the Papacy

By birth and upbringing, Frederick II was an Italian. Though he had spent a few years in Germany after becoming emperor, he never felt at home there and never exercised much power over the German dukes. Apparently deciding that he could do nothing with Germany until he had brought Italy fully under his control, he abandoned almost all authority to the dukes. All he expected from Germany was a steady supply of soldiers for his Italian wars.

In Italy, his first move was to eliminate all opposition in his hereditary kingdom of Sicily by transforming it into a nearly absolute monarchy. Then he began to revive the imperial claim to rule central and northern Italy. Thanks to factional quarrels within and among the Italian towns, he managed to acquire substantial territory in those regions. Some of the northern cities became so alarmed by his success that they revived the Lombard League, which had fought Frederick I in the twelfth century. Frederick crushed the League's forces at Cortenuova in 1237, and for the moment he appeared to be in control of the whole peninsula.

However, the papacy was still determined to preserve the independence of the Papal States, which stretched from Rome to Ravenna, by keeping Italy divided. No pope could believe that an emperor who ruled all Italy would respect the papacy's right to govern the Papal States,

Germany and Italy at the Time of the Hohenstaufens   1138–1250

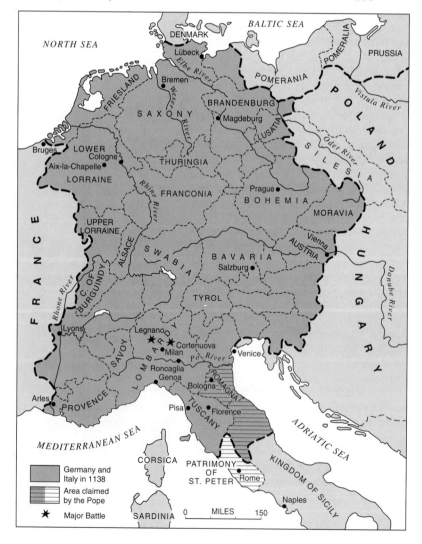

especially in view of the long history of imperial meddling in papal affairs. Pope Innocent III, who had crowned Frederick II emperor, kept the empire in turmoil rather than risk that danger, as did his successors.

Frederick was a brilliant, inquisitive man who exchanged friendly letters with Moslem rulers, dabbled in science and magic, and was suspected of having written a book called *The Three Impostors: Moses, Jesus and Mohammed.* To convince the world that he was an orthodox ruler, he took the cross and went on a crusade. Moreover, he was the first to condemn heretics to death by burning them at the stake. Yet his actions raised more doubts than they settled. After taking the cross, he waited for years before leaving on the crusade and the pope excommunicated him for violating his oath. When he finally arrived in the Holy Land, he chose to negotiate with the Moslems rather than fight them. He managed to arrange a treaty that gave the Christians control of Jerusalem for a few years, but the pope renewed his excommunication anyway.

When it became clear that Frederick intended to solidify his control of the Italian peninsula, Pope Gregory IX (r. 1227–41) took drastic measures and called a council in Rome to deal with the problem. But Frederick intercepted the fleet bearing the prelates and captured or drowned most of them, an act that did nothing to improve his reputation for piety. Gregory's successor, Innocent IV (r. 1243–54), a famous lawyer, succeeded in holding a council at Lyons in 1245, which declared that Frederick had forfeited all his possessions and that neither he nor any member of his family should ever again be permitted to rule in Germany or Italy. Innocent proclaimed a crusade against Frederick and imposed a tax on the clergy to pay for the armies to carry it out.

This papal attack on Frederick destroyed the last vestiges of central government in Germany. The dukes refused to obey either Frederick or an opposing ruler elected by a faction that favored the pope. Germany became a loose confederation of states under the control of the dukes, who could either accept or reject the poli-

Portrait of Emperor Frederick II, from a manuscript of his treatise, *The Art of Hunting with Falcons.*

cies made by the king. No German emperor after Frederick exercised any real authority, except over his family holdings.

Frederick held on to most of the territory he had acquired in Italy. After his death in 1250, however, the cities of northern and central Italy asserted their independence, though the kingdom of Sicily remained loyal to his sons. The papacy might have settled for this state of affairs, but it had been too badly frightened to take any chances. So the popes carried on a war against the "viper brood" of Hohenstaufens until the hated family had been ejected from Sicily and Naples. They preached crusades, levied taxes on the clergy to cover their expenses, and sent cardinals out with armies to battle Frederick's heirs. And when they found they could not do the job by themselves, they

In 1241 Frederick's fleet captured (or drowned) two cardinals and a hundred bishops who were on their way to a council summoned by Pope Gregory IX to depose the emperor. This manuscript illustration shows Frederick in the ship on the left, though actually he was not present. On the right, his soldiers attack the prelates in a ship bearing the papal ensign of the keys of St. Peter.

litical ends, and people found it difficult to distinguish the pope's actions from those of a secular prince. One could argue that if it was proper for the pope to tax the clergy to defend his territories, it was equally proper for a king to tax the clergy to defend his kingdom.

Moreover, the popes had won their victory over the Hohenstaufens by creating political instability in both Germany and Italy, and in the long run the church itself was weakened by that instability. With no one in Germany strong enough to protect them, the bishops had to fight and intrigue to protect themselves from the rapacious dukes and local lords. Nor was the German government strong enough to deal with the heresies that sprang up in the fourteenth century, which opened the way for Luther's revolt against the papacy in the sixteenth century.

In Italy, the absence of a strong central government enabled the powerful city-states to dominate the surrounding districts. Genoa and Venice, which controlled the lucrative eastern trade, remained fairly stable and even established colonies in the Aegean and on the northern shores of the Black Sea. But the inland cities, including wealthy trading centers such as Florence and Pisa, were plagued by factionalism and were constantly at war with one another.

turned to England and France for help. Their attempt to involve Henry III of England in the struggle failed and led to the baronial rebellion of 1258 (see p. 312). They were more successful in France. Louis IX reluctantly permitted his brother, Charles of Anjou, to attempt the conquest of the kingdom of Sicily. Charles, aided by crusade privileges for his troops and financed by crusade taxes, defeated the last Hohenstaufen ruler of Sicily in a swift campaign in 1266. A grandson of Frederick II made a desperate attempt to regain the kingdom, but his forces were crushed in 1268, and the young man was executed. The papacy had finally rid Italy of the Hohenstaufens.

The Consequences of the Struggle

In winning this political victory, the papacy had lost much of its moral prestige. Many people had questioned the decision to depose Frederick II—Louis IX himself had maintained a careful neutrality in the struggle—though the church clearly had a case against him. But Frederick's heirs posed no great threat, and it seemed vindictive of the papacy to harry them for two decades. Throughout that time, moreover, it was apparent that the church was using its spiritual authority to achieve po-

The situation was no better in the kingdom of Sicily. In 1282, Peter III of Aragon, who had married the daughter of the last Hohenstaufen king of Sicily, took advantage of a rebellion against the French ruler and seized the kingdom. Although Peter never acquired Naples or the mainland territories of Sicily, which remained in the hands of a younger branch of the French royal family, the kingdom of Naples was itself torn by quarrels over the succession.

In Rome, whether the popes recognized it or not, the destruction of imperial power left political chaos in its wake. The emperors had often helped the popes control the local nobility, for if the emperor wanted to have influence in Rome he was better off supporting the pope than trying to control the local lords. With imperial authority gone, the state of affairs in and around the city deteriorated for the papacy. Members of the Roman nobility were trying to strengthen their hold on the region around the city; small towns around Rome were struggling for independence and for more territory; and Rome itself was divided among the great families. As a result, the pope's position was desperate. He could either flee Italy and lose the prestige associated with the city of Rome or he could stay and participate in the petty politics as a minor prince. In fact, the church was feeling the effects of the rise of the secular states throughout Europe. None of the great thirteenth-century popes ever became a saint, though several kings were canonized. And one of those saintly kings, Louis IX of France, probably exercised greater moral influence over the Europe of his day than did any churchman.

ENGLAND, FRANCE, AND THE PAPACY IN THE LATE THIRTEENTH CENTURY

English Foreign Policy under Edward I

In England, the central government had grown strong by the end of the thirteenth century. After the baronial rebellion of 1258–65, Edward I had reestablished royal authority and was determined to increase it further. Edward was a hardworking, intelligent ruler who chose capable men to serve his government. He was also a man of terrifying rages—the dean of St. Paul's Cathedral in London dropped dead of fright during a dispute with him—and few men dared to contradict him openly. Yet he was careful to keep the support of the propertied classes, both the aristocracy and the townsmen, which he needed in his plan to become supreme ruler of the British Isles—England, Scotland, Wales, and Ireland. He avoided getting involved in affairs on the Continent, except when he went to war with the king of France over France's attempt to seize the duchy of Aquitaine, the last of the English holdings in France. Instead, Edward I concentrated on the conquest of Wales and

Scotland, a policy that pleased the aristocracy. He kept his administration under firm control and was never overpowered by a baronial council.

Edward completed the conquest of Wales that William the Conqueror's barons had begun long before. He replaced the last native prince of Wales with his own infant son, thereby creating a precedent that has endured to the present day—the heir to the English throne is the Prince of Wales. But Scotland proved more troublesome. Edward first installed a puppet king, but when he tried to act independently Edward deposed him and tried to rule the country himself. He was unable to maintain a large enough army in Scotland to suppress dissent, and the Scots rebelled, first under William Wallace and then under Robert Bruce. The rebellion was still raging when Edward died in 1307, and the Scots won their independence at Bannockburn in 1314.

France under Philip IV the Fair

In France, royal power followed a different course. At the end of the thirteenth century, the French barons were still struggling to preserve the right to govern their own holdings. Not particularly interested in what was going on in Paris, they just wanted to keep the central government from interfering with their affairs. The chief problem of the French king was not to keep the counts and dukes from trying to dominate his council but to see that they enforced his orders and his rights.

That problem came to a head during the reign of Philip IV, called Philip the Fair (r. 1285–1314), the grandson of Louis IX. Like his grandfather, Philip was a pious man, upright in his private life and imbued with a sense of divine mission. But he was narrow-minded where Louis had been magnanimous and grasping where Louis had been merely firm. He increased the number of bureaucrats enormously and encouraged them to expand royal authority whenever they could. He would condone any expedient to break the power of a local lord who tried to retain some measure of independence. Lesser vassals

Edward I of England (1272–1307) on this throne (illustration from a fourteenth-century manuscript).

were unable to resist, but the more powerful vassals responded with indignant refusal. Consequently, Philip spent a good part of his time warring with his greatest vassals, including the king of England (as duke of Aquitaine) and the count of Flanders. Though he won some land from both, he never took the rich textile cities of Bruges and Ghent from Flanders nor the flourishing port of Bordeaux from Aquitaine.

Edward I had been reasonably successful raising money for his wars from Parliament; Philip the Fair had a harder time. The French had never been subjected to a general tax, whereas the English had been paying national taxes since the end of the twelfth century. In any case, France had no central assembly like the English parliament to impose a uniform tax on the whole country. Instead, royal agents had to negotiate with each region, and often with each lord or each city within each region. Although France was at least four times larger than England in both area and population, it is doubtful that Philip's tax revenues ever matched those of Edward.

That shortage of funds helps explain France's military weakness during the next hundred years. It also explains why the French representative assembly, the Estates General, never became as powerful as the English parliament. Philip was the first king to call a meeting of the Estates General, but he never asked it for a grant of taxes. He knew that the country would pay little attention to a tax levy ordered by Paris. The lack of power over taxation remained one of the chief weaknesses of the Estates General. Philip had much better luck negotiating tax levies with local leaders. Though the negotiations were tedious, they made it possible to play one region off against another. The royal negotiators would win assent to a tax in an area by indicating that a neighboring area had agreed to pay it and that the royal government would favor the region that agreed to pay with trade monopolies and protection from bandits. The king's bureaucrats became extremely persistent and skillful in conducting these negotiations.

Thus England had emerged as a strongly united country in which the king and the propertied classes cooperated in carrying out policies that they both approved of. Though France was united more by the royal bureaucracy than by common interests, the propertied classes usually trusted the king on policy matters. And in both countries some of the ideas that distinguish the modern state were beginning to appear: The welfare of the state is the greatest good; the defense of the realm is the greatest necessity; opposition to duly constituted authority is the greatest evil. As one of Philip's lawyers remarked: "All men, clergy and laity alike, are bound to contribute to the defense of the realm." People who were beginning to think in these terms were not likely to be impressed by the appeals and exhortations of the papacy.

The Struggle with Pope Boniface VIII

After the death of Pope Nicholas IV (r. 1288–92), the cardinals had had great difficulty choosing a pope. Finally in 1294 they agreed on a most unlikely candidate, Peter Murrone, a hermit who lived on the slopes of Mount Vesuvius near Naples and who took the name Celestine V. Though he was a truly spiritual man, he could not manage the vast machinery of papal government or the complexities of international politics. As the church drifted, calls came for his abdication, and before the end of a year Celestine had indeed abdicated, the only pope ever to do so. The cardinals, chastened by the experience, then elected one of their leading members, who took the name Boniface VIII (r. 1294–1303).

Boniface was an able canon lawyer and a veteran of political conflict. Sensing that the rise of secular authority was posing a serious threat to the papacy, he set about restoring the independence and authority of the church. He made no claim that had not already been made by his predecessors, but the climate of opinion had changed. Many people now believed that their chief duty was to support their king rather than to obey the pope. As a

Pope Boniface VIII receives St. Louis of Toulouse, a grandnephew of St. Louis of France and son of Charles II of Naples. The representation of the pope corresponds to other pictures of him. Fresco by Ambrogio Lorenzetti, Siena (ca. 1330).

result Boniface was defeated in a head-on clash with the kings of England and France—a defeat from which the medieval church never recovered.

The issue was clear: Were members of the clergy to be treated as ordinary subjects of the king, or were they to be responsible only to the pope? Specifically, could they be taxed for the defense of the realm without the pope's consent? The kings of England and France were always short of funds, and they were strongly tempted to tap the resources of the church. The popes themselves had provided a precedent for taxing the clergy when they raised money for their political battles against the Hohenstaufens. When Edward I and Philip the Fair drifted into war over Aquitaine in 1294, they both asked their clergy for a grant of taxes. They were outraged when Boniface prohibited those grants in 1296, and they stirred up public opinion against the clergy as disloyal members of the community. Further, they both seized church property and forbade any transfer of money to Rome. Edward virtually outlawed the English clergy. In the end, the harassed churchmen begged the pope to reconsider and remove his ban. Grudgingly, Boniface did so in 1298.

The Issue between State and Church

1302

Boniface VIII says in the Bull Unam Sanctam:

Both the spiritual sword and the material sword are in the power of the Church. But the latter is to be used for the Church, the former by her; the former by the priest, the latter by kings and captains, but by the assent and permission of the priest. The one sword, then, should be under the other, and temporal authority subject to spiritual power. . . . If, therefore, the earthly power err, it shall be judged by the spiritual power. . . . Finally, we declare, state, define and pronounce that it is altogether necessary to salvation for every human creature to be subject to the Roman pontiff.

One of Philip's ministers, speaking for the king, says:

The pope pretends that we are subject to him in the temporal government of our states and that we hold the crown from the Apostolic See. Yes, this kingdom of France which, with the help of God, our ancestors . . . created—this kingdom which they have until now so wisely governed—it appears that it is not from God alone, as everyone had always believed, that we hold it, but from the pope!

From Select Documents of European History, *ed. by R. G. D. Laffan (London: Methuen, 1930), p. 117; from C. V. Langlois,* St. Louis, Philippe le Bel, et les derniers Capetiens directs *(Paris: Hachette, 1911), pp. 149–50.*

Worse was to follow. In 1301 Philip the Fair imprisoned a French bishop on a flimsy charge of treason and refused to obey a papal order to free him. Boniface cited the old principle of canon law that the clergy were not subject to secular courts and threatened to punish the king and his agents. It was at this time that Philip called the first Estates General to assemble at Paris (1302). The assembly gave him its full support and emphatically rejected papal authority over France. When the dispute continued, Philip, through his minister, Guillaume de Nogaret, accused Boniface of immorality and heresy and appealed to a general council to condemn him. Local assemblies throughout France endorsed Philip's plan—the nobility and the bourgeoisie enthusiastically, the clergy reluctantly but almost unanimously. Philip certainly had the support of the people. Though they may not have believed that the pope was guilty of treason, they believed that the church was corrupt and that the pope had no right to interfere in the internal affairs of France.

Assured of support at home, Philip now embarked on a high-risk venture. In 1303 he sent Nogaret to Italy with a small force to join Italian enemies of the pope. Together they staged a surprise attack on Boniface's summer home at Anagni and succeeded in capturing him. They probably hoped to take Boniface back to France to stand trial before a church council, but they were unable to carry out such a plan. The Italians had no great love for the pope, but they cared even less for the French. The people of Anagni and the neighboring areas freed Boniface after a few days, and the French retreated through hostile country. The shock of the experience was too much for Boniface— he was in his eighties—and he died soon after.

Force had been used against earlier popes, but after the assault at Anagni the church became cautious. No one in France—or anywhere else, for that matter—seemed disturbed by what had happened, and Nogaret remained Philip's favorite minister. Now that it was clear that the papal court would have to deal with

Philip, the college of cardinals elected a pope who was at least acceptable to him, though not his own candidate. Clement V (r. 1305–14) yielded to Philip on every matter and even allowed that Philip had acted out of good motives in seizing Boniface. The power that Innocent III had bequeathed to his successors was but a memory.

THE POPES AT AVIGNON

After being elected pope, Clement V set off for Rome from Bordeaux, where he had been archbishop. But after learning that the city-states of Italy were at war and that the Papal States were unsafe, he decided to stop off at Avignon, a small city in the Rhone Valley. Clement apparently planned to continue on to Rome as soon as order had been restored, but as things turned out, Avignon became his permanent residence. Philip and the French cardinals urged him to stay on, and conditions in Italy continued chaotic. So Avignon remained the seat of papal government for more than seventy years.

The long exile in France (1305–78) is known in church history as the Babylonian Captivity—an allusion to the Babylonian captivity of the Jews in the sixth century B.C. Avignon was situated in a small principality that was not subject to the French king, but it was certainly kept under his watchful eye. Surprisingly, however, the popes who succeeded Clement V at Avignon were less subservient to the French kings that he had been, and many of them were excellent administrators. During its time in Avignon, the papacy developed into the largest government in Europe, with an elaborate and powerful bureaucracy and a large income. But the pope was supposed to be the bishop of Rome, and some of Europe's leading intellectual and spiritual figures urged the popes to return to the Holy City. As successful as the papal government was in Avignon, the scandal of the Babylonian Exile damaged the prestige of the pope as the spiritual leader of Christendom.

Suggestions for Further Reading

Economy

On the economic changes that took place in the thirteenth and fourteenth centuries, see the works cited after Chapter 10. M. M. Postan, *Medieval Trade and Finance* (1973), is a general work. R. S. Lopez and I. W. Raymond, eds., *Medieval Trade in the Mediterranean World* (1955), contains much interesting source material. See also A. R. Lewis, *Naval Power and Trade in the Mediterranean* (1951) and *The Northern Seas* (1958). On the merchant class, see the works cited in Chapter 10 and E. M. Carus-Wilson, *The Medieval Merchant Adventurers,* 3rd ed. (1967).

England

W. L. Warren has written two excellent works on the Angevin kings in *Henry II* (1973) and *King John* (1961). See also J. Gillingham, *Richard the Lionheart* (1978). A. L. Poole, *From Domesday Book to Magna Carta,* 2nd ed. (1955), provides an excellent general history. The most thorough treatment of *Magna Carta* is W. S. McKechnie, *Magna Carta* (1914), which studies the document chapter by chapter. For a shorter treatment, see J. C. Holt, *Magna Carta,* 2nd ed. (1990). On English history in the thirteenth century, see F. M. Powicke, *King Henry III and the Lord Edward,* 2 vols. (1947), and *The Thirteenth Century* (1953). For the later period, see M. McKisack, *The Fourteenth Century* (1959). The classic history of medieval common law is F. W. Maitland and F. Pollock, *The History of English Law,* 2 vols., rev. ed. by S. G. F. Milsom (1968). This work is brought up to date in J. H. Baker, *An Introduction to English Legal History,* 2nd ed. (1979). See also D. M. Stenton, *English Justice from the Norman Conquest to the Great Charter* (1964). A large collection of sources for the history of common law was published in J. H. Baker and S. F. C. Milsom, *Sources of English Legal History* (1986).

Constitutional Government

All works on medieval England cited above contain much material on the growth of constitutional government. See also J. E. A. Joliffe, *Angevin Kingship* (1955), which traces the growth of royal power in England and the development of the institutions of government through the twelfth century. On the idea of kingship in relation to law and political thought, see the classic by E. H. Kantorowicz, *The King's Two Bodies* (1957). For a survey of the institutions of constitutional government, see G. L. Haskins, *The Growth of English Representative Government* (1948); A. Marongui, *Medieval Parliaments: A Comparative Study* (1968); T. N. Bisson, *Assemblies and Representation in Languedoc in the Thirteenth Century* (1964); and F. L. Carsten, *Princes and Parliaments in Germany* (1959).

France

On France, see the works cited in Chapter 10, particularly J. Dunbabin, *France in the Making, 843–1180.* (1985), and E. M. Hallam, *Capetian France, 987–1328* (1980). On Philip II Augustus, see A. Luchaire, *Social Life in France at the Time of Philip Augustus,* trans. E. B. Krehbiel (1912). On Louis IX, see J. R. Strayer, *The Administration of Normandy under St. Louis* (1932), and W. C. Jordan, *Louis IX and the Challenge of the Crusade* (1979). For a comprehensive history of Philip IV the Fair, see J. R. Strayer, *The Reign of Philip the Fair* (1980). On the conflict between Philip and Pope Boniface VIII, see C. T. Wood, ed., *Philip the Fair and Boniface VIII* (1967), which contains a selection of historians' work on the subject. On Boniface VIII, see T. S. R. Boase, *Boniface VIII* (1930).

Germany

On the rise and fall of the Hohenstaufens, see G. Barraclough, *The Origins of Modern Germany* (1947); H. Fuhrmann, *Germany in the High Middle Ages,* c. *1050–1200* (1985); J. B. Gillingham, *The Kingdom of Germany in the High Middle Ages* (1979); and J. Leuschner, *Germany in the Later Middle Ages* (1980). On Frederick Barbarossa, see M. Pacaut, *Frederick Barbarossa* (1969), and P. Munz, *Frederick Barbarossa: A Study of Medieval Politics* (1969), which takes the questionable view that Frederick was a "rational" politician whose every action was carefully calculated. The classic study of Frederick II is E. H. Kantorowicz, *Frederick II* (1931). T. C. Van Cleve, *The Emperor Frederick II* (1972), is also highly recommended. On the formation of the late medieval empire, see J. Bryce, *The Holy Roman Empire* (many editions), and C. Bayley, *The Formation of the German College of Electors* (1949).

The Avignon Papacy and the Late Medieval Church

The classic work on the late medieval church is A. C. Flick, *The Decline of the Medieval Church,* 2 vols. (1930). See now, F. Oakley, *The Western Church in the Later Middle Ages* (1979). On the Avignon period, see G. Mollat, *The Avignon Papacy* (1963), and Y. Renouard, *The Avignon Papacy* (1970).

13

EASTERN EUROPE IN THE MIDDLE AGES

Up to this point, eastern Europe has been mentioned only as a region through which various peoples moved from central Asia into western Europe. In the third century, the Huns created an empire based in Hungary. In the seventh century, the Avars followed suit. In the ninth century, the Magyars succeeded the Avars, establishing a kingdom that survives as a modern state. To the north, the Slavs followed the Germans into the forests of Poland and mountains of Bohemia and Slovakia. To the south, they moved into the Balkans.

Clearly, then, the peoples that migrated into eastern Europe formed kingdoms much as those in western Europe, though the eastern states rarely escaped the interference and influence of the western European rulers. The Franks and their successors in Germany took a keen interest in eastern Europe. The popes sought the conversion of the peoples there. The westerners found themselves in competition with the Byzantines, and both faced resistance from eastern European rulers who sought to create independent states that could take their place within the political system of the Continent.

THE SLAVS

The civilized peoples of the Mediterranean first came into contact with the Slavs at the end of the fifth century and the beginning of the sixth century. Slavs originated in the north between the Vistula and Dnieper rivers and had followed the Germans into southern Russia and eastern Europe during the third century (see pp. 113–15). They did not appear on the borders of the Roman Empire until later, after the Germanic tribes had moved on to the south and west. By the early sixth century, the Slavs were in control of Lithuania, the Ukraine, central Russia, Poland, Bohemia, and Slovakia and had moved south toward modern Yugoslavia. During these early migrations, they often fell into conflict with the Avars and Sarmatians who stormed out of the central Asia in successive waves and set up short-lived empires in southeastern Europe. Following the collapse of those empires, the Slavic tribes gradually absorbed their remnants.

By the sixth century the Romans were fighting the Slavs along the Danube frontier and settling some of them as *foederati* (see p. 113) to help repel further incursions from the northern forests. But like the Germanic *foederati* before them, the Slavic tribes sometimes broke their contract with the Roman government, and in the seventh century Constantinople was threatened by Slavic armies.

THE SOUTHERN SLAVS

When Heraclius (r. 610–41) mounted the throne in Constantinople, he needed allies against the Persians (see pp. 173–74) and enlisted the Slavic Serbs and the non-Slavic Croats, who were eager to escape the domination of the Avars. He persuaded the Croats to settle in the old Roman provinces of Illyricum along the Dalmatian coast and in Pannonia to the northeast. And he persuaded the Serbs to settle in eastern Illyricum. This whole region had been devastated by the Avars early in the seventh century, and Sirmium, the one-time capital of Pannonia, had ceased to exist. Though the Roman population had been Christian, hardly a church or a bishopric remained intact.

Heraclius now set about ensuring the loyalty of these pagan settlers by having them converted to Christianity. Because the ancient churches along the Dalmatian coast had been under the ecclesiastical jurisdiction of Rome, he asked the pope to send missionaries to the Croats. Pope Gregory I (r. 590–604; see pp. 138–40) had already been trying to reestablish the church in Illyricum, but no one made much progress until Honorius I (r. 625–38) sent out missionaries from Rome and Ravenna. Slowly, the missionaries rebuilt the ecclesiastical system, with Spalato (Split) as the center. It was this ecclesiastical province that the Byzantine emperor Leo III (r. 717–41) removed from papal jurisdiction when the popes opposed his iconoclasm (see p. 178).

Meanwhile, Heraclius arranged for missionaries to be sent to the Serbs. Although some of those missionaries came from Bari, the capital of Byzantine Apulia, it appears that survivors of the old Christian population of Pannonia took the lead. Recently discovered archaeological evidence reveals that the Serbs began building churches in significant numbers only in the early ninth century, by which time they must have been fully Christianized.

Behind the Croats and Serbs came the non-Slavic Bulgars from central Asia, who had, like the Croats, settled in southern Russia among the Slavs and had been absorbed into the Slavic culture. They may have arrived as part of the Hunnish horde that invaded the region in the 370s. In any case, they moved into the Danubian region of the Empire in the sixth and sev-

The Settlement of the Croats and Serbs   SEVENTH CENTURY

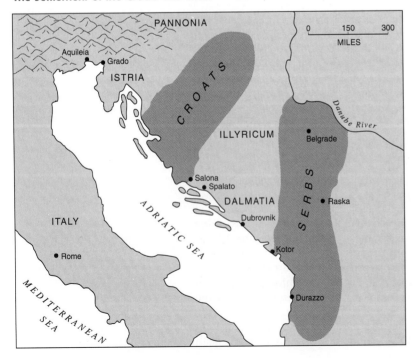

enth centuries and became particularly troublesome during the reign of Heraclius. Under the first known Bulgarian khan (king), Kurt, or Kuvrat (r. 605–65), the Bulgars created a state that the Byzantines called Great Bulgaria.

It was under the auspices of the Bulgarian khanate that Serbs moved south and established independent communities in the mountainous regions of central and northern Greece, particularly around Thessalonika. The Byzantines, under constant pressure from the Persians and the Arabs, made no effort to recover these regions, and for centuries the Christian population lived in isolated pockets surrounded by Slavic settlements. Not until late in the ninth century did the Byzantine government manage to bring the Slavic intruders under its power and begin to convert them to Christianity. In time, they became fully christianized and so completely assimilated that their language left few traces in Greek.

MORAVIA AND THE CENTRAL EUROPEAN SLAVS

Slavs between East and West

The Slavic settlements in Pannonia lay across the rich trade routes of central Europe, where they seem to have formed a loose confederation of principalities centered on the revived towns of Sirmium (now called by the Slavic name Morava; in Latin, its region was called Moravia) and Belgrade, among others. The picture that emerges, though the evidence is meager, is of a group of petty princes constantly jockeying for position, rather like the Franks before the rise of Clovis (see p. 128).

These central European Slavs were constantly threatened with invasion by their neighbors—the Germans to the west and north, the Avars to the east, and the Byzantines to the south. From early on, the Bavarians, a Germanic tribe settled in southern Germany and Austria, meddled in their affairs and sent missionaries to convert them to Christianity. Then, after Charles the Great (r. 768–814) assumed control of Bavaria (788), the Moravians

Greater Moravia   NINTH CENTURY

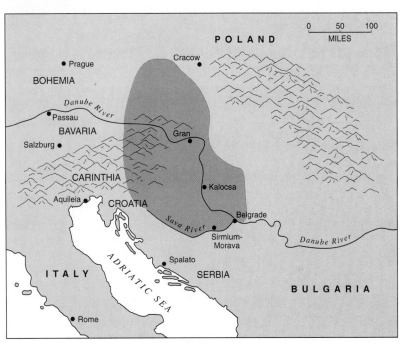

and their neighbors began to fall under Frankish influence. By playing the Franks off against the Avars, however, the Slavs managed to preserve some measure of independence and continued to resist conversion. But when Charles the Great crushed the Avars in 796, the Slavs fell entirely under Frankish influence.

To resist the pressures that were acting on them from every side, and to preserve what they could of their cultural identity, the small tribes of Moravians and their Slavic neighbors began to join together in loose political federations. They soon discovered that they could play the Byzantines off against the Franks as they had the Avars. In the early ninth century, the Moravians and their neighbors had achieved enough self-confidence to try to launch an independent Slavic state. But Charles the Great was determined to prevent them from doing so. In 803 he forced the capitulation of both the Moravians and the Bohemians, who lived in the Carpathian Mountains north of the Danube. He then set about consolidating his control by sending missionaries to convert the

Mounted warrior with a captive (detail from a gold vessel from the ninth century found in Sînnicolau Mare, Romania).

for a Slavic state. In fact, in 817 a Bavarian geographer reported that Moravia had eleven fortified "cities," a report that archaeologists have recently confirmed. Nonetheless, by the time of Mojimir's death, around 845, most of Moravia had become Christian, with a church organization subject to the Frankish bishops of Germany.

Following his death there was a brief pagan revival that aimed to recapture the cultural heritage of the Slavs and to renew the quest for independence. Many Slavic leaders thought Mojimir's strategy of accommodating the Frankish influence to achieve his ends had been a failure. Louis the German stepped in, however, and put Mojimir's nephew Rastislav (r. 846–70) in power. He proved the leaders wrong. Soon Louis became engrossed in the conflicts with his brothers (see pp. 232–33), and the Moravian prince was free to go his own way. By about 850, Rastislav was the ruler of a virtually independent state that included most of the old province of Pannonia, with influence as well over Bohemia and Hungary. To keep Louis off balance, Rastislav supported Louis's son Carloman in his rebellion in the early 860s.

Though Louis had installed Rastislav as a puppet king, he now found himself with a rival rather than a trusted ally on his southeastern frontier. To counter Rastislav, he suggested to the Bulgarian khan Boris that they form an alliance against him. In search of an ally of his own, Rastislav turned to Rome, apparently hoping that the pope would help him meet the threat and at the same time free the church of Moravia from Frankish control. Pope Nicholas I (r. 858–67) did not respond, however, because he was already having trouble with Louis and chose not to make matters worse.

In 862 Rastislav sent an embassy to Constantinople with a request for assistance from the emperor Michael III (r. 842–67):

Our people has renounced paganism and is observing the Christian law, but we do not have a teacher to explain to us the true Christian faith in our own language in order that other nations

defeated Slavs, just as he and his predecessors had done in northern and eastern Germany.

But the Moravians, under their leader Mojimir, seem soon to have slipped away from Frankish control, and in 820 Louis the Pious and his son Louis the German embarked on a new campaign that brought the Slavic princes back into the Frankish orbit in 822.

Still, Mojimir managed to stay in power and nurture the Slavic dream of creating an independent state. In 818 he had agreed to convert, though he may not have done so until 822 after convincing his tribal leaders to accept the religion of their conquerors. He may have accepted conversion merely as a way of mollifying the Franks while continuing with his plans *even, seeing this, may imitate us. Send us therefore, Master, such a bishop and teacher, because from you emanates always, to all sides, the good law.*

Behind this request was another message: Though there were many Frankish missionaries in Moravia, their purpose was to impose the authority of the pope on the Slavs instead of helping them to establish a church of their own. Actually, Rastislav's request was also a plea for a political and military alliance, for religion and politics were regarded as one. A Moravian church allied with Constantinople would mean a political alliance as well. Michael did send missionaries to create the alliance, but it produced little political result. It did, however, contribute significantly to the preservation of Slavic culture.

The Mission of Constantine (St. Cyril) and Methodius

Emperor Michael thought he had just the man for Rastislav. Constantine the Philosopher (*ca.* 826–69), as he was called, was then about 35 years old and was teaching in an ecclesiastical college in Constantinople. He had been born in Thessalonika in 826 or 827, the son of a Byzantine military officer on the staff of the provincial governor. After his father was killed fighting the Slavs, young Constantine had become the ward of Theoctistus, the *logothete* or prime minister of the Empire. Theoctistus took him to Constantinople and enrolled him in the court school, where he studied under Photius, the future patriarch and the most learned man in the Empire (see p. 181). Within a short time, Constantine earned a reputation for learning and linguistic ability. He had learned Slavic as a child in Thessalonika, and he may have learned Arabic as well. When he was about 28 years old, he succeeded Photius as the principal teacher of philosophy at the university. Some evidence indicates that the emperor sent him to Baghdad in 851 to debate religious questions with Moslem scholars.

In 856, the Khazars, a central Asian people who had carved out an empire in southern Russia, asked the emperor to send a theologian to participate in a debate among Christians, Moslems, and Jews. The emperor summoned Constantine from the monastery he had entered and sent him north, along with his brother Methodius, to participate in the debate. On the way, Constantine stopped in the Crimea to learn Hebrew and Samaritan from the Jews living there. While he was in Khazaria he translated most of a Hebrew grammar into Greek, and on his return to Constantinople he took a teaching post in one of the city's many ecclesiastical colleges. There he continued his study of Hebrew and Samaritan and was often called on to interpret inscriptions and texts written in unfamiliar languages and scripts.

Constantine's fame as a participant in ecumenical debates and his familiarity with both Greek and Slavic made him well qualified to carry out the mission to Rastislav. Methodius, who also had learned Slavic as a child, accompanied his brother to Moravia. The Byzantines were eager to establish a foothold in Moravia, but they had no interest in setting up a church in competition with the Franks. That might happen in time, but it would involve working through some complicated politics with the western powers,

Constantine's Embassy to the Khazars   856

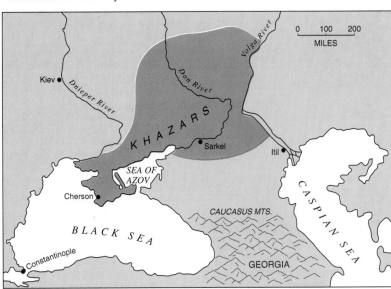

including the papacy, which claimed jurisdiction over the Slavs. So Constantine and Methodius busied themselves with their missionary work, and Rastislav's request for a bishop went unanswered.

Constantine left for Moravia in 863. But before setting out he invented an alphabet with which to write the translations of the scriptures and the missal, which gave instructions and the prayers for the Mass, into the Slavic language. That alphabet was well suited to Slavic phonology. The earliest works in Slavic were written in this alphabet, and only much later was it replaced in the eastern Slavic countries by an alphabet based on Greek characters, now called Cyrillic even though Constantine, who later took the name Cyril when he reentered a monastery, had nothing to do with it. In most western Slavic countries, the alphabet of Constantine was eventually replaced by the Latin alphabet, which is ill suited to Slavic. Constantine's alphabet is now used only in isolated Eastern Orthodox institutions in Dalmatia and Montenegro.

Using this new alphabet, Constantine and Methodius translated the missal, the psalter, and some other basic liturgical works into Slavic. This meant that Slavic Christians—unlike western Christians—would use their own language in the Mass and in other liturgical ceremonies, such as baptism and marriage. Conservative churchmen argued that only Hebrew, Greek, and Latin were acceptable languages for the liturgy, because those were the languages that Pilate had ordered used for the inscription on Christ's cross. Constantine referred to those churchmen as disciples of Pilate.

The Frankish missionaries in Moravia derided the books translated by Constantine and Methodius as foreign innovations. The brothers responded by translating a missal based on the Roman practice. This missal was essentially the same as the Latin missal used by the Franks, but because it was in Slavic the Moravians favored it over the Latin. Many of the Byzantine liturgical instructions and prayers translated by Constantine became part of the Slavic liturgy.

In making his translations from the Greek, Constantine sought to capture the literary quality and texture of the original. In so doing, he created a literary language for the Slavs and revealed himself as a gifted poet in his own right. His translations marked the beginnings of a literate culture among the Slavs and advanced their language as a vehicle for sophisticated thought.

Constantine and Methodius left Moravia in 867 and headed for Venice, where they expected to take a ship to Constantinople. But the political situation in the Empire had changed during their absence. Basil had murdered Bardas, the patron of their own patron Photius, and had deposed Photius as patriarch (see pp. 182–83). So they accepted an invitation to Rome from the pope. There they lived in a Byzantine monastery and waited for news from home. Constantine went on working, but his health, which had been poor for many years, grew worse. Concluding that he would never return to Constantinople, he joined the monastery and took the name Cyril. He died in Rome in 869 and is known in church history as St. Cyril.

Constantine designed the Glagolitic alphabet for the Slavic language. It is still used in a few isolated monastic communities in the Balkans. The Cyrillic alphabet, named after Constantine's religious name, was designed later. It is based on the Greek alphabet.

modern European	Latin	runes	Greek	Cyrillic	Glagolitic
A	A	ᛉ	A	Ⰰ	ⴀ
B	B	ᛒ	ᛒ	Ᏼ(v) Ᏼ(b)	ⴂ ⴔ
C	Ɔ	ᚲᚤᚴᚵ	ᚲᛆ	Г	ⴘ
D	D	ᛞᛈᛈ(th) ᛙᚺᚺ	DΔ⊖	Ⰴ	ⴁ
E	Ɛ	ᛖᚨᛮᛯ	Ᏼ	Є	Э
F	F	ᚠᚹᚿᛂ	φF	Ⰼ	ⴅ
G	G	ᚴ+			
H	日	ᚾᚺᚼᚺ	H	H(i)	Ⰸ Ⱅ
I	I	ᛁ	I	I(i)	ⴑ ⴜ(g)
J					
K	ᛉ	ᛢ	k	Ⰽ	Ⱇ
L	ᛄ	ᛜ	ᛜ	Ⰾ	Ⰰ
M	ᛰ	ᛗ	M	M	Ⱍ
N	N	ᚵᚴᚵ	ᛜ	Н	ⴘ
O	O	ᛤᚪᛤ	o o	Ⱁ	ⴐ
P	ᛉ	ᛜᛗ(e)	Г	п	ⴈ
Q	Ⱋ		Q		
R	ᚳ	ᚱ ᚱ	ᛕ	Ⱃ	ⴂ
S	ᛋ	ᛋ	ᛋ	Ⲥ	Ⰳ
T	T	ᛏ	T	Т	ⴔ
U	V	ᛚᚻ	V		
V					
W		ᚹ ᚹ			
X	X	X (g)	X	X (h)	Ⰱ
Y	Y	ᚤᛋᛚ		Ⲩ (u)	ⴀ
Z	Z	ᛉᚦ(ih,eo)	I	Ⲯ(ů)Ⲥⳡ3(z)	Ⱎ ⴅ θ
NG		ᚦ ᚷ(ng)	Ⲭ +		
value	o sħ ts ch sh ů	y	ï é yu ya ye	ę ję ya kh ps θ(th,f)	
Cyrillic	ⲯ ⳡ ⲩ ⲭ ⲩ ⳡ	ⲩ ⲭ ⲯ	ⲭ ⲯ ⲓ ⲯ ⲭ ⲉ ⲇ ⲇ	ⲭ ⲩ ⲭ ⳡ ⲭ ⲭ ⲩ ⲭ	
Glagolitic	Ⱁ Ⱎ Ⱁ Ⱁ Ⱎ θ	ⴅⲱ⸳ⴁⴅ⸳ⴁⴈ ⸳ⴁⴀⴘ	⸳	Є XXX	θ

The Results of the Mission

Although Constantine and Methodius did not bring the Moravians into the jurisdiction of the church of Constantinople, they had a profound influence on the country's religious practices. In 864 Khan Boris of Bulgaria accepted baptism under the auspices of the Byzantine emperor, and the Bulgarians became part of the Eastern Orthodox church. Soon the liturgical translations of Constantine and Methodius were being used in Bulgaria. At about the same time (864–66), Byzantine missionaries converted the Kievan Russians. Although that conversion did not last, for a while it looked as if all the Slavs would come under the Byzantine church.

But Moravia's political future was with the West. From early times the Franks had looked upon the central European lands as satellites, and the Carolingian kings had done their best to subjugate them. Try as he might, Rastislav was unable to maintain his independence from Louis the German, who constantly interfered in his realm. This failure led Rastislav's own nobility to abandon him. In 870, they captured him and turned him over to the Franks, who blinded him and locked him up in a monastery.

Immediately, another pagan revival was attempted in Moravia, but it was soon put down by Sventopolk, Rastislav's nephew, who had been among his uncle's most formidable enemies. Sventopolk had the support of the Franks, who put him in power in Rastislav's realm. In the first year of his rule in Moravia, Sventopolk asked Rome to send a bishop to establish an independent Slavic church subject to Rome. Pope Hadrian II (r. 867–72) sent Methodius, who had remained in Rome after Constantine's death, and Methodius became Archbishop in Moravia, with his seat in Morava.

Sventopolk then struck out in every direction, creating a state that later historians called Great Moravia. He won control of Croatia down to Istria and the Dalmatian coast and of Bohemia north of the Danube. He also conquered the remnants of the Avar principalities to the east. Meanwhile, Methodius established an independent Moravian church and did missionary work in Bohemia and Poland. Sventopolk was at last crowned king of Moravia some time between 880 and 885 and reigned until his death in 894.

Throughout his reign, Sventopolk maintained reasonably good relations with the Franks. He had been on friendly terms with Arnulf of Carinthia even before Arnulf became king of the East Franks in 887 (see p. 237), and events soon solidified their friendship. About 890, the Magyars, who had come out of central Asia to settle Hungary, arrived in Pannonia and initiated the raids that would make them the scourge of central Europe. At a meeting in 890, Arnulf gave Bohemia in fief to Sventopolk, probably in return for his help in defending East Frankland from the marauding Magyars. Sventopolk proceeded to extend his power over Slovakia in the northern Hungarian plain and entered into an alliance with the Magyars. The result of these actions was that Arnulf turned against him, and in 892 and 893 Arnulf led armies into Moravia and devastated everything in sight.

When Sventopolk died in 894, a civil war broke out between his young sons. The East Franks and the Magyars entered the fray, because Moravia formed an important buffer zone between them. Within a few years, the Magyars had overrun Moravia and made it the base for their raids on Bavaria and Italy. Great Moravia had died with Sventopolk.

BOHEMIA

Bohemia was a duchy settled by Slavs in late Roman times. It centered on the castles of Prague, which straddled the Moldau River. From as long ago as the paleolithic period, hunters had frequented the passes through the Carpathian Mountains and the river valleys below them, and each year they had returned to their camps along the migration routes of the great ice-age mammals—the mammoths, rhinoceros, and buffalo. Later, these routes had been incorporated into the Amber Road, the trade route along which precious amber (fossilized pine sap) was carried from the

Baltic to the Mediterranean. The Carpathian Mountains were rich in minerals. Salt had been mined there since the paleolithic period, and the Celts had extracted metal ore from the Carpathians and the northern Alps.

The Bavarians had exercised control over the pagan Slavs of Bohemia even before Charles the Great took over Bavaria in 788. For a long time, the Bohemians refused to be converted to Christianity, and not until the 820s did the Frankish missionaries begin to win converts in the border areas. In the late ninth century, the Bohemians were caught for a time between the Franks and the Moravians, but after the destruction of the Moravian state

The Tyn Church (center) and Astronomical clock (left) in Prague. The Tyn Church was founded in the fourteenth century by Germans living in Prague and became the main Hussite church (see p. 427).

Bohemia
ELEVENTH TO TWELFTH CENTURIES

by the Magyars they fell completely under Frankish domination. Both Henry I (r. 918–36) and his son Otto I (r. 936–73) encouraged Germans to set up colonies in Bohemia to strengthen German control and to advance the acceptance of Christianity, but not until 973 was Otto able to establish a bishopric in Prague.

For many years the German kings kept the duchy of Bohemia under subjugation by constantly interfering with the dynastic plans of the dukes. Though the agents of German meddling were usually the dukes of Bavaria, almost every German king during the eleventh and twelfth centuries was at one time or another personally involved in Bohemian affairs. The Bohemians, whenever they could, played Germany, Poland, and Hungary (the Magyar state) off against one another in an effort to win some measure of independence. In 1158, the duchy became the Kingdom of Bohemia when Emperor Frederick I Barbarossa rewarded Duke Vratislav II for his assistance in an Italian campaign. In the fourteenth century, after the collapse of the Hohenstaufen monarchy (see p. 322), the Kingdom of Bohemia fell to the Luxembourg family, which had succeeded to the imperial throne of Germany. From that point on, the fate of Bohemia was determined by the imperial family's dynastic strategy. Emperor Henry

Poland in the Middle Ages

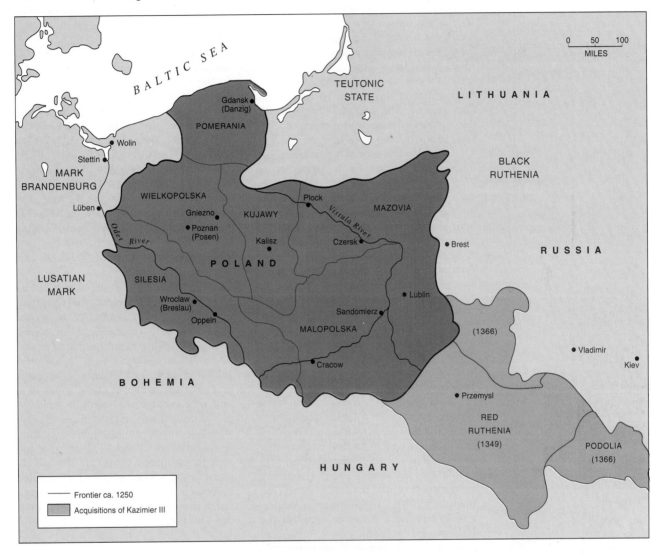

VII of Luxembourg (r. 1309–13) gave Bohemia to his son John (r. 1313–46), who passed it on to his son Charles IV (r. 1346–74), who was elected emperor in 1347. In the fifteenth century, Emperor Sigismund of Luxembourg (r. 1410–37) arranged the marriage of his daughter Elizabeth to the Habsburg Albert II of Austria (emperor 1438–39). When Sigismund died without a male heir, Bohemia passed through his daughter to the Habsburgs (see next section), who eventually created a central European empire that lasted until World War I (1914–19).

POLAND

Poland, the westernmost Slavic region, is situated on a vast plain that stretches from the Atlantic to the Ural Mountains of Russia. It has no natural barriers either to the east or to the west. On the south it is bounded by the Tatra Mountains, a branch of the Carpathians, and on the north by the Baltic Sea. In part as a result of its vulnerability, this vast area, larger than any other European country, has suffered frequent invasion and political instability through the centuries. The Kingdom of

Poland arose from the unification of several tribal domains, which survived as duchies in the kingdom. Throughout the country's history these regions have variously joined together in a federation, have been ruled by a single king, and have allied themselves with foreign and domestic powers in opposition to the central government. The political history of Poland is bewildering, and periods of unity and strength have been rare.

The first attempt to unify the tribes occurred in the early ninth century, when the ruler of the Polanians of Wielkopolska, centered on Poznan and Gniezno, established his hegemony over the regions of Kujawy, Malopolska, and Mazovia. That ruler, who was called Piast, is a semilegendary person, who seems to have succeeded in setting up a dynasty that maintained two seats of power—one in Gniezno and the other in Cracow, the city of the Vistulanians of Malopolska. This dynasty, which historians call the Piast, or Polanian, dynasty, dominated Poland from the time of Louis the Pious (r. 814– 40) until 1370, when Kazimierz III the Great died.

Otto I's efforts to convert the Slavs to Christianity and to colonize the eastern frontier of the German kingdom extended to Poland as well as to Bohemia. Shortly after subjugating the Bohemians in 950, Otto turned his attention to Brandenburg on the north-central border between Germany and Poland. In 961, he received permission from the pope to establish the bishopric of Magdeburg as a missionary outpost, and he began to encourage his subjects to migrate into the area. Duke Mieszko I (r. *ca.*963–92), having observed the forcible conversion of Bohemia and its incorporation into the German kingdom, sought baptism directly from the pope and by doing so was able to maintain some measure of independence. Still, hoping to stay on good terms with the German king, he may have acknowledged the superiority of Otto III in 984. Mieszko succeeded in gaining control of Pomerania, which gave Poland an outlet to the Baltic Sea.

Mieszko's son Boleslaw I the Brave (r. 992–1025) solidified the relationship with Otto III, who visited Gniezno in 1000 and established an independent bishopric there. With that act, Otto revealed that he expected the Poles to be substantial partners in his empire.

Boleslaw extended the boundaries of the Polish state to the east and to the west. In the west, he added Lusatia up to the Saal River (a tributary of the Elbe), and in the east he reached the Dnieper and incorporated Red Ruthenia and Kiev into his kingdom. The pope crowned Boleslaw king of Poland just before he died (1025), but the ability of Boleslaw's successors to claim that title depended on the strength of the German monarchy at the time. The next Polish king, Boleslaw II (r. 1058–79), took advantage of Henry IV's preoccupation with the investiture controversy (see pp. 266–68) and crowned himself king in 1076.

The presence of the independent bishopric at Gniezno meant that Christianity would spread from a Polish rather than from a German center. As time passed, Gniezno established subordinate bishoprics at Płock in Mazovia in 1076, Lubus in Lusatia in 1128, and Wolin in Pomerania in 1140. Meanwhile, political unification under the Piasts continued to proceed until the end of the reign of Boleslaw III, who failed to have himself crowned king (r. as Duke of Poland 1102–38). For the next two hundred years, the various regions of the former kingdom were ruled by branches of the Piast family that steadfastly asserted their independence from one another.

Polish Society and the German Colonization

Under the Piast princes Polish society was dominated by noblemen living on sizable estates associated with peasant villages. The villagers were freemen who paid rent and were obligated to serve in the duke's army. As in the West, the Polish army consisted of a troop of mounted knights and peasant foot soldiers. Apparently, the peasants had not been reduced to servile status.

The eastern half of the North German Plain, from the Elbe River to the Urals, was only sparsely populated, and it seems

The farmers of eastern Europe were still using primitive methods, such as this unwheeled plow, in the thirteenth century.

that the Germans' more advanced farming techniques—such as the heavy wheeled plow, the use of horse power, and three-field rotation—had not penetrated this far. Here the peasants were still using the hook plough, a simple wooden implement that worked only in sandy soils and produced little reward for great effort. When the Polish lords and princes became aware of the superior technology of the West, they encouraged German peasants to colonize their land. Typically, they would hire a so-called locator to round up hundreds of German peasants and transport them to the east. There the locator would find a suitable site and settle the peasants in a new village. Each peasant would receive a homestead, and the locator would receive an estate and would become the mayor of the village. He would also preside over the village court, which heard less-important cases. Important cases or charges of serious crime were heard by a district court presided over by a representative of the prince.

To attract settlers, the princes offered low rents, light labor obligations—typically two to four days a year—and exemption from military service except in defense of the district. Often rent payments were suspended for the first ten or fifteen years to give the villagers a chance to make a good start in their new environment. The locator held a hereditary title to his estate and to his office as mayor and could pass them on to his heirs.

The extent of colonization varied from region to region. In the early thirteenth century, the Piast prince Henry I of Silesia (r. 1231–38) brought more than 10,000 German peasants to his province and settled them in 400 villages. His province became a patchwork of village communities, some under Polish law, some under German law. The settlers and their descendants held tenaciously to their native ways, and the Germans of Silesia are still a distinct ethnic community.

The Poles also encouraged the founding of new cities. Following the practice of the Germans, they gave their cities legal codes based on the law of Magdeburg, which assured them of substantial autonomy and freedom from feudal obligations.

During the thirteenth century even older Polish cities like Poznan and Cracow were brought under German law. To encourage the growth of the new cities, the Piast princes encouraged the settlement of merchants from Germany and the Baltic, and several Polish cities, including Gdansk (Danzig), Cracow, and Wroclaw, became members of the Hanseatic League, a confederation of Baltic cities that controlled northern trade during the thirteenth and fourteenth centuries.

The Polish princes also encouraged Jews to immigrate from Germany and Austria. In 1264, Prince Boleslaw V of Cracow (r. 1243–79) issued a General Charter of Jewish Liberties, which ensured the legal rights of Jews and permitted them to travel without restriction and to practice their religion without interference. Although some cities refused to abide by the charter, its issuance led to the emergence of a wealthy and powerful Jewish community in Poland. In the late Middle Ages, the Jews acted as a separate community with their own rabbis and secular leaders who dealt directly with the princes and lesser authorities.

The Reunification of Poland

Despite the years of political disunity, agriculture and trade flourished and by the late thirteenth century Poland had become relatively strong. Wladislaw I of Mazovia (r. 1306–33), sensing that the time had come to reunify the country, slowly began the process. Led by the archbishop of Gniezno, the Poles set about ridding themselves of the Germans. In 1320, in Cracow, Wladislaw was crowned King of Poland, the first Polish king since Boleslaw II in the eleventh century. He then tried to reclaim Kujawy and Pomerania from the Teutonic Knights (see pp. 341–42). Though he failed in that attempt, he left a strong kingdom to his son Kazimierz III (r. 1333–70).

Kazimierz began his reign by entering into a truce with the Teutonic Knights and arranging a treaty with the kings of Bohemia and Hungary. He paid the Bohemian king John of Luxembourg to give up his claim to Poland and agreed to arbitrate the status of Silesia. The arbitration went

Kazimierz III (from a seventeenth-century engraving).

in favor of Bohemia, and Kazimierz renounced the province in 1339. When he finally made a formal peace with the Teutonic Knights in 1343, he acquired Kujawy but gave up Pomerania. With the security he had gained through these settlements, he turned to other fronts. He successfully challenged the Bohemians for Swidnica, west of Silesia, gained control of Mazovia, Red Ruthenia, and the dukedom of Russia. In Red Ruthenia, he was challenging Lithuania and Hungary. By the end of his reign, Kazimierz had enlarged and unified the Polish state and had earned the sobriquet "the Great."

Yet Kazimierz was much more than a warrior king. In 1347, he issued a great codification of Polish law that served as the basis for legal reforms until the eighteenth century. He also created a royal bureaucracy to ensure the proper administration of the law, encouraged trade, and had fifty fortresses built across the country. As the condition of the country improved, many Polish cities undertook the construction of new buildings. Cracow, for example, tore down its old wooden buildings and replaced them with stone and brick buildings around a market square 200 yards on each side. By 1363, a new cathedral had been completed and a new royal castle was under construction. The renovation of the ancient St. Mary's

church on the market square was begun; it took fifty years to complete.

In 1364, Kazimierz founded the University of Cracow, the first non-German university in eastern Europe. There he established chairs in the arts, medicine, and law; he named eight professors of law, reflecting his own deep interest in the subject.

During that same year Kazimierz hosted a meeting of five kings and five dukes in Cracow to discuss a new crusade against the Saracens. The meeting was prompted by the visit of Peter of Lusignan, king of Cyprus. Though the meeting produced no crusade, it furnished evidence of Kazimierz's prestige in the international community.

Kazimierz had many children, including several sons, but only his daughters were legitimate. Early in his reign, he arranged for King Louis of Hungary to succeed him if he died without a male heir, and immediately after his death Louis seized the kingship despite the opposition of the Polish churchmen and nobles. The Piast dynasty was at an end.

Under Louis (r. 1370–82) Poland entered into a long-lasting alliance with Hungary. He had no interest in preserving the strength of the Polish monarchy and consequently granted the nobles royal rights and land to keep them happy. By the end of his reign he had severely weakened the monarchy. He left no heir. With the concurrence of the Polish nobility, he was succeeded by his daughter Jadwiga, who was only eleven years old in 1382. (An older daughter was married to the emperor Sigismund of Luxembourg, who thereby added Hungary to his home kingdom of Bohemia.) Jadwiga was supposed to have married William of Habsburg, prince of Austria, but the Poles refused to accept a German king. Instead, she was married to Jagiello of Lithuania, creating a union of the two states and establishing a new dynasty in the process.

LITHUANIA-POLAND

The Lithuanians were an ancient Baltic people related to the Latvians and the Prussians. The Balts, as the members of this

The square of a late medieval city.

ethnic group have been called since the nineteenth century, were Indo-European peoples distinct from the Germans and Slavs. Latvian and Lithuanian are their only surviving languages. The Baltic tribes settled in northwestern Russia and along the eastern shore of the Baltic Sea, perhaps as early as the third millennium B.C. We know almost nothing about their history until the thirteenth century, however, when the Teutonic Knights began to subjugate them and forcibly convert them to Christianity.

The Teutonic Knights

The Order of St. Mary's Hospital in Jerusalem was one of several knightly orders founded in the Holy Land in the twelfth century to defend the new Latin states and to protect Christian pilgrims. The Order of

St. Mary's was made up of German knights who eventually became known as the Teutonic Knights. When Saladin took Jerusalem in 1187 (see p. 214), the Knights left the Levant and returned to Europe, looking for a crusade nearer home. After a short sojourn in Transylvania in Hungary, they were invited by the north German lords to help subjugate and convert the Pomeranians and Prussians, who lived along the Baltic coast. They arrived in Prussia in 1226 and began conquering the local tribes two years later.

The Knights, a highly organized group, had created an advanced administrative system while in the Levant. They now set about erecting a string of impregnable fortresses and, through the use of calculated cruelty, systematically reduced the pagan Prussians. By the early fourteenth century, the Teutonic Knights had

The Teutonic State and Lithuanian Empire   FOURTEENTH CENTURY

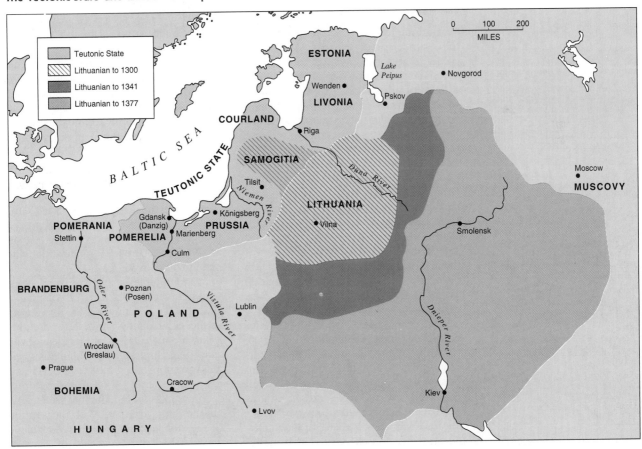

created a powerful, well-run state in Prussia centered on the fortress of Marienburg.

Like the Poles, the Knights encouraged German immigration to their realm with offers of low rents and special concessions. They too used locators to settle new villages in their thinly populated region, and large parts of their state became Germanized. But unlike the Poles, the Knights encouraged the Prussian and Slavic peasants already in their realm to adopt the advanced agricultural methods of the Germans and to become Germanized. Gradually, the Prussian language and culture disappeared.

Beyond Prussia, the Knights conquered Samogitia, Courland, Livonia, and Estonia and forced the inhabitants to convert to Christianity. Though they still professed to be crusaders leading a monastic life, the Knights earned a reputation for viciousness and rapaciousness.

The Lithuanians

Toward the middle of the thirteenth century, under their leader Mindaugas (d. 1263), various Lithuanian tribes joined together to resist pressure of the Teutonic Knights. Under Mindaugas's successors, the Lithuanians extended their frontiers south and east into Russia, and in the first half of the fourteenth century Gedymin (r. 1316–41) created a powerful grand duchy centered on Vilna. He conquered all the land between the Baltic and the Black Sea, incorporating the Russian principalities of Smolensk and Kiev into his state. Lithuania now stood as the greatest state of eastern Europe. The Lithuanians saw themselves as the last practitioners of the ancient religion based on a pantheon headed by Perkun, the god of thunder. To them, the Christian god was a German god.

In 1377, Jagiello (r. 1377–1434) inherited the grand duchy at the age of 26. Notwithstanding his youth, Jagiello perceived that he was in great danger. The powerful state of Poland was now allied with Hungary, and the Teutonic Knights were at the height of their power. Searching for a way of safeguarding his duchy, he agreed to accept Christianity from the

Poles and to marry their queen Jadwiga. The Poles welcomed this arrangement, because it eliminated a dangerous enemy and countered the power of the Habsburgs to the south and the Teutonic Knights to the north. In 1386, Jagiello was baptized, married to Jadwiga, and crowned King of Poland.

Under Jagiello, the Poles and Lithuanians were united in a single state, by far the largest and most powerful in eastern Europe. In 1413, the Polish and the Lithuanian nobles agreed to settle all matters of dispute in a joint assembly, and the Poles won the right to vote in the election of the Grand Duke of Lithuania.

Throughout the fifteenth century the neighbors of Poland-Lithuania were in a state of disarray. The Luxembourgs of Bohemia were preoccupied with disputes with their cousins in Hungary and with the Habsburgs of Austria. The Ottoman Turks, who had moved into southeastern Europe after taking Constantinople in 1453 (see p. 189), were trying to put down the resistance of the survivors of the Byzantine Empire and of the southern Slavs. To the east, the Mongol horde had split up into several unpredictable tribal states, and the Russian principalities were small and weak (see the next section). The Teutonic Knights were the only formidable enemy, and the Poles and Lithuanians fought them from 1409 to 1422, from 1454 to 1466, and from 1519 to 1521. Then suddenly, with the arrival of Luther's Reformation in Prussia, many of the Teutonic Knights switched to the new religion. In 1525, the Knights ceased to be a secular power, though to this day they continue to exist as a Catholic service organization with headquarters in Vienna.

Under Jagiello and his successors, who held the titles of King of Poland and Grand Duke of Lithuania, the Poles converted Lithuania to Christianity, bringing it into the mainstream of European civilization. Beginning with Zbigniew Olesnicki, bishop of Cracow (r. 1423–55), a remarkable series of Polish bishops pursued the mission in Lithuania while serving the kings at home. With the support of the nobility and the church, Jagiello reestablished the University of Cracow, which had ceased to exist after the death of Kazimierz, and encouraged cultural and economic activity. Salt production, metal production, and trade all increased, and Poland became a major supplier of raw materials. With the collapse of the Teutonic Knights, the Poles finally gained control of Gdansk and acquired a direct outlet to the Baltic through which they could ship goods to western Europe. The Polish kings were major patrons of the arts and sciences; Copernicus (1473–1543) was trained at the University of Cracow and conducted his revolutionary work in astronomy in East Prussia, which had become a fief of the Polish crown.

The fortunes of the Polish-Lithuanian state began to wane in the late sixteenth century. Moscow had succeeded in uniting the Russian principalities and had begun to behave aggressively toward its western neighbors. The last of Jagiello's successors, Sigismund II (r. 1548–72), was defeated by the Russians in the east, the Bohemians and Austrians in the south, and the Germans in the west. After his death the crown went first to the prince of Transylvania, a mountainous region in southeastern Hungary, and then to the king of Sweden. Poland-Lithuania was ruled by Swedish kings until the late seventeenth century.

RUSSIA

Throughout the Middle Ages, Russia was a sparsely populated region traversed by waves of migrating peoples. In the ninth century, Vikings traveled down the Dnieper River under their leader Ruric and settled at Kiev, which may already have been a trading center under the Khazars or even earlier. The Vikings made Kiev an important station on the trade route over which goods from the eastern Mediterranean traveled to northern Europe and Scandinavia. This trade brought the Kievan Rus, as the Vikings of the area were called, into contact with the Byzantine Empire, and in the spring of 860 the Kievans led a coalition of Slavic tribes in a surprise attack on Constantinople. In typical Viking

---

The Rus

In 860 the Rus led a large coalition of Slavic tribes in an attack on Constantinople. Not only were the Byzantines surprised by the attack, but they also had no knowledge of the Rus and their allies. The earliest description of the Rus comes from Ahmed ibn-Fadhlan, an Arab traveler of the first half of the tenth century.

I saw the Rus, when they arrived to trade and camped at the River [Volga]. I have never seen [people] with more perfect bodies than they had. They were like palm trees, blonde, with ruddy cheeks, and white skin. They wore neither jacket nor caftan; but the man wore a *kisa* [a kind of robe], which he wrapped around one shoulder off to one side so that one of his arms protruded from it. And each of them had an axe, sword, and knife, from which he was inseparable. . . . And from his nails to his neck he had green trees, figures, and other things painted on his body.

As regards their women, each wears on her breast a little box, either of iron or silver, copper, gold, or wood, corresponding to the wealth and position of her husband. . . . And around their necks were chains of gold and silver. . . .

The *Rus dirhem* [monetary unit] is a grey squirrel [pelt] without fur, brush, front and back paws and head; and the same goes for sables. If something was missing, the monetary value of the skin was less. They also use them for trade transactions and they cannot be exported because they exchange them for wares. They do not have scales, only standard metal bars. They use a measuring cup for buying and selling.

From I. Spector and M. Spector, eds. Readings in Russian History and Culture *(Palo Alto, CA: Pacific Books, 1965), pp. 14–15.*

---

fashion, the attackers appeared along the sea walls of the city in 200 small ships.

The Byzantines, shocked into awareness of the danger to their north, sent an embassy to the Khazars of the Crimea with whom the emperor hoped to form an alliance against Kiev; this was the embassy in which Constantine and his brother Methodius participated before being sent to Moravia (see p. 333). In the late 860s, the Byzantines also sent missionaries to Kiev. The mission succeeded at first, but it triggered a pagan reaction, which also succeeded. When Christian missionaries reappeared in Kiev in the 980s, they had to start from scratch. The Grand Prince of Kiev, Vladimir I (r. 980–1015), converted

The Church of the Savior at Novgorod (twelfth century). This is an early example of what became a typical style of ecclesiastical architecture in Russia.

During the twelfth century, after the Italians opened up new trade routes between Europe and the eastern Mediterranean (see p. 257), nomadic Pechenegs had arrived in the Ukraine from central Asia and raided the cities and countryside around Kiev. As a result, the center of power shifted to the north, and by the late twelfth century the principality of Suzdal had emerged as the strongest of the many small Russian principalities. During this time the town of Moscow was founded.

Early in the thirteenth century, Chengis (Genghis) Khan (*ca.* 1167–1227) had unified the Mongol tribes on the borders of China and had begun a western push across the steppes of central Asia. When Chengis Khan died, his khanate was divided among his sons, who continued his conquests. By 1234, one Mongol contingent had conquered Korea, and others had moved west into Russia. Another Mongol army crossed the Transoxiana into the Middle East, taking Baghdad in 1258 and Damascus in 1260. Later in 1260, the Mamluk Turks of Egypt defeated the Mongol invaders (see p. 214). The western contingent took Kiev in 1240 and reached the Adriatic Sea in 1242. At that point the Mongol leaders turned back and settled their army in the lower Volga Valley. They permitted the Russian principalities there to govern themselves but demanded heavy annual tribute and insisted on controlling the succession to the princely thrones.

The Mongol conquest cut the Russians off from the West but opened up contact with the advanced societies of the East. Then, in the fourteenth century, the Mongol empire broke up and Russia became isolated from both East and West. From then on, Russia's relations were mostly with the so-called Golden Horde—the Mongols living in the Volga region. Those Mongols dealt with any threat to their authority and failure to pay the tribute by destroying towns and massacring entire populations. To avoid such reprisals, the Russian princes asserted absolute control over their populations. They won the loyalty of the lesser nobles by permitting them to subjugate their peasants. Just when peasants in the West were beginning to achieve freedom from the obliga-

in 988, and the permanent Christianization of Russia proceeded from that date.

Russian society was transformed by conversion to Christianity. The church brought a literate culture to the Russians, but, as an alien institution it created a problem for Kievans, who were governed by customary law that did not cover the church. To fit the church into the community's life, the prince issued a statute that recorded and codified the customary law, with modifications introduced for the benefit of the churchmen.

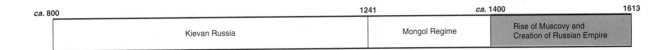

ca. 800		1241	*ca.* 1400	1613
Kievan Russia		Mongol Regime	Rise of Muscovy and Creation of Russian Empire	

tions of villeinage, the Russian peasants were being bound in serfdom.

During the fourteenth century, the principality of Moscow, which had become the center of the old principality of Suzdal, developed into the strongest state in Russia. For several generations, only one surviving heir to the Muscovite throne remained when the reigning prince died. So the successions were orderly, and Moscow avoided the strife that weakened many other states. Moreover, the bishop of Russia—the so-called metropolitan bishop—had moved his seat from Kiev to Moscow, suggesting that the Muscovite princes were the protectors of the church.

The Golden Horde soon came to work through the prince of Moscow in its dealings with Russians everywhere and accorded him the title Grand Prince to symbolize his role. Unwittingly, by so doing, they gave the various principalities a sense of unity and created a potential threat to their own power. They probably little suspected that the subject states might ever challenge the power they had endured so long, but late in the fourteenth century the Grand Prince of Moscow himself led a rebellion to throw off the Mongol yoke. A Russian army defeated the Mongols in 1378, but the Golden Horde struck back and destroyed the city of Moscow a few years later. During the next century, the Muscovite state began to absorb the neighboring principalities one by one, and at last, under Ivan III the Great (r. 1462–1505), it annexed the Republic of Novgorod, which controlled all of northern Russia. Now the Grand Prince was in a position to challenge the Golden Horde once again, and during the sixteenth century the Russians gradually took over the Mongol territories in the lower Volga region. Meanwhile, they were moving against Poland-Lithuania and claiming Kiev and its region as their patrimony. By the end of the century, Russia—once a tiny state of about 500 square miles—had become the largest empire in Europe.

With the rush of conquest and consolidation, the power of the Grand Prince of Moscow had risen steadily. The peasants had already lost their rights, and now most of the nobles lost their independence and

Alexander Nevsky

Throughout the first half of the thirteenth century the Russian city-states were threatened by Lithuanians, Swedes, and Prussians. After the arrival of the Teutonic Knights in Prussia, they became a great threat. One of the early heroes of the struggle against the Germans was Prince Alexander Nevsky of Novgorod. The Chronicle of Novgorod reports his great battle of 1242 on the frozen Lake Peipus (here called Chud) against the Knights and Prussians (men of Chud).

A.D. 1242. *Knyaz* [Prince] Alexander with the men of Novgorod and with his brother Andrei and the men of the lower country went in the winter in great strength against the land of the Chud people, against the *Nemsty* [German foreigners, the Teutonic Knights], that they might not boast, saying: "We will humble the Sloven race under us," for Pskov was already taken. . . . And when they came to their land, he [Alexander] let loose his whole force to provide for themselves. And Domash Tverdislavich and Kerbet were scouring [the country] and the *Nemsty* and Chud men met them by a bridge; and they fought there, and there they killed Domash . . . and others with him, and others again they took with their hands, and others escaped to the troops of the *Knyaz*. And the *Knyaz* turned back to the lake and the *Nemsty* and Chud men went after them. Seeing this, *Knyaz* Alexander and all the men of Novgorod drew up their forces by Lake Chud [Peipus] at Uzmen by the Raven's Rock; and the *Nemsty* and Chud men rode at them driving themselves like a wedge through their army; and there was a great slaughter of *Nemsty* and Chud men. And . . . God helped *Knyaz* Alexander. And the *Nemsty* fell there and the Chud men gave shoulder, and pursuing them fought with them on the ice, seven *versts* [about four and a half miles] short of the Subol shore. And there fell of the Chud men a countless number; and of the *Nemsty* 400, and fifty they took with their hands and brought to Novgorod.

From B. Dmytryshyn, ed., Medieval Russia: A Source Book, 900–1700 *(New York: Holt, Rinehart and Winston, 1967), pp. 123–24.*

The Growth of the Grand Principality of Moscow   1300–1584

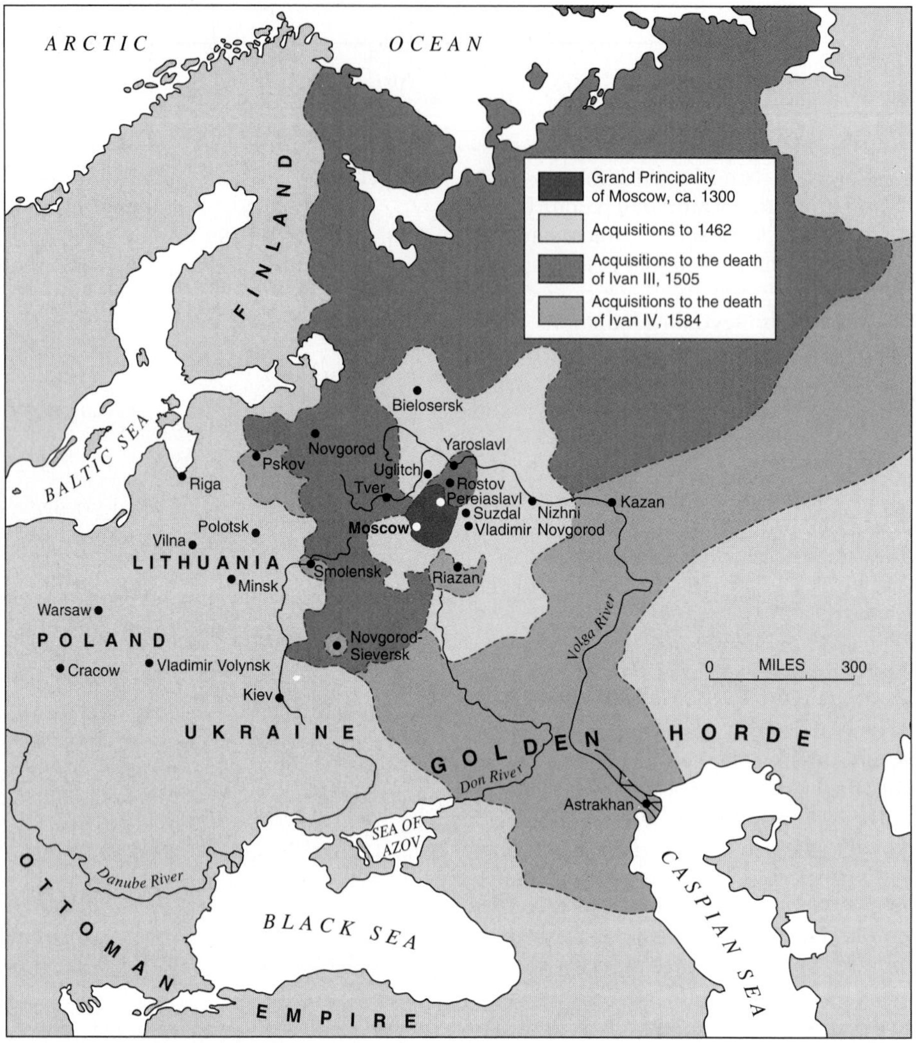

Map showing Eastern Europe with labeled regions and cities.

Legend:
- Grand Principality of Moscow, ca. 1300
- Acquisitions to 1462
- Acquisitions to the death of Ivan III, 1505
- Acquisitions to the death of Ivan IV, 1584

Map labels: ARCTIC OCEAN, FINLAND, Bielosersk, Novgorod, Yaroslavl, Pskov, Uglitch, Riga, Rostov, Tver, Pereiaslavl, Kazan, Polotsk, Suzdal, Nizhni Novgorod, Vilna, Moscow, Vladimir, BALTIC SEA, LITHUANIA, Smolensk, Riazan, Minsk, Volga River, Warsaw, POLAND, Novgorod-Sieversk, Cracow, Vladimir Volynsk, Kiev, UKRAINE, GOLDEN HORDE, Don River, Astrakhan, OTTOMAN, SEA OF AZOV, CASPIAN SEA, Danube River, BLACK SEA, EMPIRE

0   MILES   300

Ivan the Terrible (from a seventeenth-century engraving).

became servants of the crown. The greatest men in the land could be put to death on the mere suspicion of disloyalty, and bishops who offended the sovereign were sent into exile. When Ivan the Great married Zoe, the niece of the last Byzantine emperor, he began to think of himself as successor to the Caesars and styled himself Autocrat and Sovereign of All Russia. Sometimes he called himself "tsar" (a Russian form of Caesar). That title did not become official, however, until the reign of Ivan IV the Terrible (r. 1533–84), one of the bloodiest tyrants in history, who massacred nobles and ordinary people on

the smallest pretext and killed his own son in a fit of rage.

Russia was still a backward country, with none of the technology and commerce that had long fueled the economic development of western Europe. Russian peasants were still farming the poor soils of the north with their primitive tools and had not yet opened up the rich black earth of the Ukraine. Russia was also far behind the West in science and technology, and in scholarship and literature. Only after 1600 did the Russians embark on the economic and cultural advancement of their country.

HUNGARY

Hungary is situated on a true prairie, a flat grassland bordered by mountains on the north, south, and west. The region was ideally suited to the horsemen who rode west from the Asian steppes. The Huns, Avars, and Magyars all made it the center of short-lived empires. As we have seen, the Magyars, the last of these invaders, arrived late in the ninth century and for sixty years engaged in destructive raids deep into the western countries. They contributed to the collapse of the Moravian state, and their armies marched through Germany into France. Then in 955 Otto I of Germany defeated a large Hungarian army near Augsburg, and the raids came to an end. The Magyars settled down on their plain and began the slow process of building a state of their own. (The name Hungary derives from the name the western Europeans gave to the Magyars, Ugri or Ungri.)

Both the Byzantines and the western Europeans sent missionaries to Hungary and in 975, Geza (r. 972–96), the great-grandson of Arpad, the first known Hungarian chieftain, was baptized by western missionaries. Under his son Stephen (r. 996–1038) the country itself was converted to Christianity and, with the help of the papacy, established an organized church. In 1000, Stephen won from the pope the right to crown himself king, an act that made the kingdom a fief of the papacy and ensured Hungary's independence from its German and Slavic neighbors. Stephen was declared a saint in 1083.

The history of the Arpad dynasty (907–1301) is marked by constant strife between the rival claimants to the crown. In the twelfth century, following the practice of other eastern European rulers, the kings brought in peasants from the west to colonize their sparsely populated lands. Germans settled in northern and central Transylvania, and the Szekels, a people related to the Hungarians, settled in eastern Transylvania. These colonies were free communities governed by a provincial governor called a *voivode*.

In 1241, invading Mongols devastated the country and razed its cities. The population was reduced by an estimated 60 percent, and in some areas inhabitants of whole communities either fled or were massacred. After the Mongols retreated to Russia, King Bela IV (r. 1235–70), who had taken refuge in Dalmatia, returned and began to rebuild the kingdom. But the disruption had been so severe that it was beyond his powers to restore the kingdom to what it had been. Many of the local lords acted with utter independence while claiming that they were still loyal to the crown. After the death of Bela's son, Ladislav IV (r. 1272–90), the nobles had to search about for a male member of the Arpad dynasty and finally found Andrew III (r. 1290–1301) in Italy. Andrew proved to be a good king, but he died

The Court of Ivan the Terrible

In 1553 the Englishman Richard Chancellor visited Moscow. He had been seeking a northern passage to China and, failing, went to Moscow where he was received by Tsar Ivan. His description of the city and court follows.

The [city of] Moscow itself is great: I take the whole town to be greater than London with the suburbs: but it is very rude, and stands without all order. Their houses are all of timber, very dangerous for fire. There is a fair castle, the walls whereof are of brick, and very high: . . . the Emperor [Tsar] lies in the castle, wherein are nine fair Churches, and therein are religious men. Also there is a Metropolitan with diverse Bishops. . . .

The Emperor's or Duke's house neither in building nor in the outward show, nor yet within the house is so sumptuous as I have seen. It is very low built in eight squares, much like the old buildings of England, with small windows, and so in other points.

. . . I came into the Council chamber, where sat the Duke himself with his nobles, which were a fair company: they sat round about the chamber on high, yet so that he himself sat much higher than any of his nobles in a chair gilt, and in a long garment of beaten gold, with an imperial crown upon his head, and staff of crystal and gold in his right hand, and his other hand half leaning on his chair. . . .

From B. Dmytryshyn ed., Medieval Russia: A Source Book, 900–1700 *(New York: Holt, Rinehart and Winston, 1967), p. 188.*

without an heir and the nobles had to turn elsewhere for a successor.

The aspirants to the Hungarian throne were Charles Robert of Anjou, Wenceslas of Bohemia, and Otto of Bavaria. Wenceslas won out and managed to unite Bohemia, Poland, and Hungary under his rule. He was assassinated in 1306 and was succeeded by Charles Robert in 1308. Charles Robert (r. 1308–42), whose mother was an Arpad, was himself a scion of the royal house of Naples, which Charles of Anjou, the brother of Louis IX of France, had seized from the successors of Frederick II in 1266 (see p. 322). Still a boy when the Hungarian nobles elected him, Charles Robert grew up in Hungary.

Matthias I, the last native king of Hungary (from a seventeenth-century print).

The reigns of Charles Robert and his son Louis (r. 1342–82) were a time of prosperity for Hungary, Bohemia, and Poland. The Hungarians were working the gold mines in the Transylvanian Alps at full capacity, with about 40 percent of the production going to the king. Charles Robert and Louis patronized the arts, built grand buildings in the cities, and extended the kingdom. Louis, who was independently wealthy, was prodigal in granting rights and privileges to the nobility, and of course the nobility professed undying loyalty to him. In 1370, after the death of Kazimierz III, Louis was elected king of Poland and continued his liberal ways in dealing with the Polish nobles.

Louis left two daughters, Maria and Jadwiga, who inherited Hungary and Poland respectively. As we have seen, Jadwiga's marriage to Jagiello of Lithuania led to the founding of a new dynasty and to a lasting union with Lithuania. Maria was married to Sigismund of Luxembourg, who had himself crowned king of Hungary in 1387. From this time on, Hungary was a prize in the competition between the Luxembourgs and the Habsburgs of Austria, with the successors of Jagiello stepping in whenever they could. When Sigismund died, he left only a daughter. When she married Albrecht of Habsburg, Albrecht was accepted as king in Hungary. Then, when Albrecht died, in 1439, the nobles turned to Wladislaw Jagiello of Poland, who died fighting against the Ottomans in 1444.

He was succeeded by Albrecht's son Ladislav (r. 1444–57), but the real ruler of Hungary during Ladislav's reign was Janos Hunyadi, a great general. Hunyadi led the fight against the Ottomans until his death in 1456 and was then succeeded as general by his son Matthias Corvinus, who was elected king after Ladislav's death.

Matthias (r. 1457–90), the last Hungarian king of Hungary and a man of exceptional ability, held off the Ottomans and other enemies, rebuilt the cities, and assembled a huge collection of art, jewelry, and manuscripts. Using the wealth of the gold mines and whatever he could squeeze from the peasants, he brought

Silesia, Bohemia, and lower Austria under Hungarian control. But after his death, in 1490, those provinces fell away and the kingdom declined under a succession of weak kings. The Hungarian alliance with Poland remained in effect, but the Habsburgs proceeded to incorporate the rest of eastern Europe into their growing empire.

Suggestions for Further Reading

General

On the early Slavic migrations and culture, see F. Graus, "Slavs and Germans," in *Eastern and Western Europe in the Middle Ages,* ed. by G. Barraclough (1970). All the essays in this book are useful. In general, see F. Dvornik, *The Making of Central and Eastern Europe* (1949), and A. P. Vlasto, *The Entry of the Slavs into Christendom* (1970). Dvornik's *Byzantine Missions among the Slavs* (1970) is extremely useful for the settlement and conversion of the Croats and Serbs and for the mission of Constantine and Methodius. I. Boba, *Moravia's History Reconsidered* (1971), made the case that the Moravia of the mission was centered on Sirmium/Morava south of the Danube. On the history of the Bulgars, see R. E. Sullivan, "Khan Boris and the Conversion of Bulgaria. A Case Study of the Impact of Christianity on a Barbarian Society," *Studies in Medieval and Renaissance History* 3 (1966), and, from the Byzantine perspective, R. Browning, *Byzantium and Bulgaria* (1975).

Bohemia

Both Dvornik and Boba have much to say about the early medieval history of Bohemia. See also A. H. Hermann, *A History of the Czechs* (1975). Because of its close connection with Germany, comprehensive histories of medieval Germany have a good deal of information about Bohemia.

Poland

Norman Davies, *God's Playground: A History of Poland,* 2 vols. (1982), sets a new standard. *The Cambridge History of Poland,* 2 vols., ed. by W. Reddaway (1941, 1950) remains useful. For the late Piast period, see P. W. Knoll, *The Rise of the Polish Monarchy: Piast Poland in East Central Europe 1320–70* (1972). On Lithuania, see C. R. Jurgela, *History of the Lithuanian Nation* (1948), which historians consider flawed. O. Halecki, *The Borderlands of Western Civilization* (1952), is useful on Lithuania. See also J. R. Koncius, *Vlautas the Great, Grand Duke of Lithuania* (1964). *Baltic History,* eds. A. Ziedonis, W. L. Winter, and M. Valgemäe (1973), contains several articles of interest.

The Teutonic Knights

F. L. Carsten, *The Origin of Prussia* (1954), is the best work on the state created by the Teutonic Knights. For a general history of the order, see C. Krollmann, *The Teutonic Order in Prussia* (1938), and K. Gorski, "The Teutonic Order in Prussia," *Medievalia et Humanistica* 17 (1966). See also W. Urban, *The Baltic Crusade* (1975), which treats the Knights' conquest of Livonia and Estonia. For a broader view of the northern crusades, see E. Christiansen, *The Northern Crusades* (1980).

Russia

For a comprehensive survey of Russian history, see G. Vernadsky and M. Karpovich, *A History of Russia,* 5 vols. (1943–69). N. V. Riasanovsky, *A History of Russia,* 4th ed. (1984), and G. Vernadsky, *Russia at the Dawn of the Modern Age* (1959), are good one-volume surveys. See also F. Nowak, *Medieval Slavdom and the Rise of Russia* (1930). On the first entry of the Russians into Mediterranean history, see A. A. Vasiliev, *The Russian Attack on Constantinople in 860* (1946). On the Mongols in Russia, see G. Vernadsky, *The Mongols and Russia* (1953), and on the rise of Moscow, see J. Fennell, *Ivan the Great of Moscow* (1961). J. Blum, *Lord and Peasant in Russia from the Ninth to the Nineteenth Century* (1961), is an excellent study of social history. There is also a great deal of social history in D. H. Kaiser, *The Growth of Law in Medieval Russia* (1980). On the Khazars, see D. M. Dunlop, *The History of the Jewish Khazars* (1954).

Hungary

For a brief survey of the history of Hungary, see D. Sinor, *A Short History of Hungary* (1959), and C. A. Macartney, *Hungary: A Short History* (1962). On the early period of Magyar settlement, see C. A. Macartney, *The Magyars in the Ninth Century* (1930). On the Ottoman threat, see P. Coles, *The Ottoman Impact on Europe* (1968).

14

THE LATE MIDDLE AGES

*T*he fourteenth and fifteenth centuries were a time of chaos in western Europe. Decade after decade, Europeans were beset by drought, arctic winters, economic depression, war, rebellion, and plague. Neither ecclesiastical nor secular governments seemed capable of easing the distress, and at times the whole structure of European society seemed to be crumbling. Yet the social and political institutions that emerged from this troubled time turned out to be the most powerful in the world. The science and technology, the great navies and armies, the government institutions and the business structures that were to give Europe world supremacy for 400 years all took shape during the stretch of history marked by the Hundred Years' War, the Black Death, and the Great Schism.

THE TROUBLES OF THE FOURTEENTH CENTURY

Climate, Economic Depression, and Population Decline

From the eleventh century to the end of the thirteenth, the economy and population of Europe had been growing steadily. Peasant villages prospered and new lands were put under cultivation or reclaimed after centuries of neglect. The cities and their lords, looking to a bright future, undertook ambitious projects such as draining the Roman marshes and building dikes in the Netherlands. Though much of the land they brought into production was marginal, the projects seemed justified by the needs and opportunities of the time.

Then, around the middle of the thirteenth century, just as medieval civilization was reaching its height, a mini–ice

(OPPOSITE) FOURTEENTH-CENTURY IVORY SHOWING A JOUST AT A TOURNAMENT.

European Population[a]
A.D. 900–1300

A.D. 900

Iberian Peninsula	4,000,000
France	5,000,000
Italy	4,000,000
Germany/Scandinavia	4,000,000
British Isles	1,500,000
	18,500,000

A.D. 1100

Iberian Peninsula	7,000,000
France	6,200,000
Italy	6,000,000
Germany/Scandinavia	4,500,000
British Isles	2,000,000
	25,700,000

A.D. 1300

Iberian Peninsula	9,500,000
France	14,000,000
Italy	9,300,000
Germany/Scandinavia	11,500,000
British Isles	5,300,000
	49,600,000

[a]Figures exclude eastern Europe.

level. As the population declined, it grew weaker and more susceptible to disease.

The poor harvests triggered an economic depression that affected every region and every class. The cities had become dependent on the agricultural surplus, which had been reliable and substantial for many decades and had provided the main commodities for trade. The kings and barons relied for their income on the produce of the farmland or on land rents. And the large landholders, who had taken back their land from leaseholders to farm the lands themselves, suffered along with the peasants.

In the wake of the poor harvests, inflation set in, raising the prices of food and other farm products such as wool and flax. The higher prices in turn drove up the prices of manufactured goods. People on fixed incomes struggled to make ends meet, and a noticeable rise in government corruption occurred as officials came to depend on bribes and gifts as part of their income. People everywhere complained of the venality of the government and the church, and the moral authority of both declined.

The Bubonic Plague

Then, in 1348, bubonic plague swept across Europe. Bubonic plague is a bacterial disease spread by fleas that have bitten infected rats. It originated in southeast Asia and spread along the trade routes to the Middle East. From there it jumped to Constantinople, then to Italy, and then to all of Europe. In just two years, the plague killed about a third of the population; in some places the mortality rate was 80 percent. This first onslaught earned the name The Black Death, but the disease continued to appear here and there until around 1700.

The effect was enormous. Villages and farms were abandoned, and the labor force withered. Many of the peasants who survived migrated to the cities to replace workers who had died. The condition of the peasants who stayed in the countryside seems to have improved for a short time. They could now demand high wages

age set in. It was felt first in the far north, in Greenland, where communities established by Icelanders centuries before had to be abandoned. In 1258 the Icelanders officially declared that they would no longer try to ship goods to Greenland. In Europe, the change was felt later. Toward the end of the century, a series of bad harvests put an intolerable strain on the over-extended farmlands of Europe and brought widespread famine. By 1300, the population had ceased to grow and was even beginning to decline. Even worse famine struck in 1315–17 and had a devastating effect on the peasants, who had already lost their earlier prosperity and were living not far above the subsistence

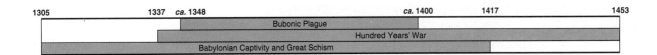

| 1305 | 1337 | ca. 1348 | ca. 1400 | 1417 | 1453 |

Bubonic Plague

Hundred Years' War

Babylonian Captivity and Great Schism

for their labor on the lords' demesnes enabling them to purchase the land of the peasants who had died, or to buy a release from their feudal obligations. For a few years everyone had more money, with incomes rising a bit faster than prices. But the prosperity was illusory, based on inflation rather than on an expanding market, and soon production fell to the level of demand.

In the cities, employers trying to reduce costs sought to roll wages back to the level of 1348. The kings supported them. England, for example, enacted the Statute of Laborers (1351) and other laws that required workers to accept customary wages (that is, the wages prevailing before the plague) and fixed the prices of food and other basic necessities at the 1348 level. Other kingdoms passed similar legislation.

Wages in the countryside continued to rise, however, and landholders tried to hold their peasants to the customary labor services they were obligated to supply, including plowing and harvesting, mending fences, and constructing buildings. In fact, lords now demanded that their peasants provide those services that in the past the peasants had usually managed to avoid. Some lords, finding labor costs too high to make farming cost-effective, leased their estates and let others worry about the problem.

In either case—whether the lord enforced customary services or converted the entire manor into rent-paying tenancies—the interests of the peasants and the landholder clashed. The peasants agitated for the commutation of the customary services into cash rents, because they would be better off either selling their crops or working as paid laborers. As time passed, the landholders tried to compensate for their declining income by enforcing their rights over the manorial commons, such as the meadows, fisheries, pastures, and woods, and by demanding the customary payments for the use of mills, ovens, and other "appurtenances." At last a demand arose for the abolition of all manorial obligations.

The lot of the workers in the towns and cities was no better than that of the peasants. Employers, craft guilds, and government officials all conspired to keep wages low and to protect local markets from outside competition. After the plague, artisans found it harder than ever to gain admittance into the craft guilds, and the gulf between masters and workers widened.

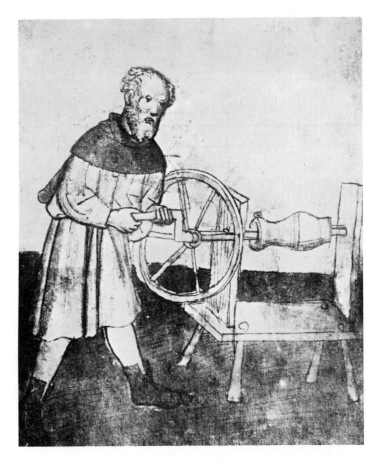

Miniature painting of a fourteenth-century pewterer turning a jug on a lathe, from the *Guild Book* of the Twelve Brothers' Foundation in Nuremburg.

The Black Death in England

Then that most grievous pestilence penetrated the coastal regions by way of Southampton and came to Bristol, and people died as if the whole strength of the city were seized by sudden death. For there were few who lay in their beds more than three days or two and a half days; then that savage death snatched them about the second day. In Leicester, in the little parish of St. Leonard, more than three hundred and eighty died; in the parish of the Holy Cross, more than four hundred, and in the parish of St. Margaret, more than seven hundred. . . .

And the price of everything was cheap, because of the fear of death, there were very few who took any care for their wealth, or for anything else. For a man could buy a horse for half a mark [about 7 shillings] which before was worth forty shillings, a large fat ox for four shillings, a cow for twelve pence, a heifer for sixpence, a large fat sheep for four pence. . . . And the sheep and cattle wandered about through the fields and among the crops, and there was no one to go after them or collect them. They perished in countless numbers everywhere, for lack of watching . . . since there was such a lack of serfs and servants, that no one knew what he should do. For there is no memory of a mortality so severe and so savage. . . . In the following autumn, one could not hire a reaper for less than eight pence [per day] with food, or a mower at less than twelve pence with food.

From Henry Knighton, Chronicle, *in* The Portable Medieval Reader, *ed by J. B. Ross and M. M. McLaublin (New York: Viking, 1949), pp. 218–19.*

The merchants and aristocrats responded to the disorder by behaving more harshly and more inflexibly than before. The medieval notion that everyone in the community had both rights and duties gradually gave way to the notion that the upper classes had all the rights and none of the duties.

As the turmoil and unrest intensified, people became susceptible to all sorts of fears and rumors. From the mid-fourteenth century on, several spiritual movements arose proclaiming that the end of the world was nigh. Even before the plague, in 1327, a rumor had spread in France that Jews and lepers were plotting to overthrow Christendom, and many people had lost their lives in the riots and trials that followed. In the latter part of the century, groups of flagellants wandered the countryside preaching the end of the world and scourging themselves with whips and ropes. Artists featured the figure of Death in their paintings, and villagers paraded through the streets in the "dance of death." Many preachers declared that God was punishing Christendom because the popes had withdrawn to Avignon.

Neither the workers nor the peasants had any legal means for improving their lot, and discontent grew. The Flemish towns experienced rebellions in 1255, 1267, 1275, 1280, and 1302, and everywhere in Europe the towns suffered riots and unrest throughout the fourteenth century. In Florence, the *popolo minuto*—the "little people"—rebelled against the government in 1378 in the so-called Ciompi rising.

In France, the peasants staged a rebellion in 1358, killing hundreds of nobles and their families and burning their manors. In the Peasants' Revolt of 1381 in England, rebellious mobs caused widespread damage and called for social reforms that would have transformed English society.

THE AVIGNON PAPACY AND THE GREAT SCHISM

Papal Government at Avignon

The city of Avignon, where Clement V (r. 1305–14), the former archbishop of Bordeaux, settled (see p. 326), was French in everything but political allegiance. It was an imperial city—with a charter from the emperor—situated in a county of Provence that belonged to the papacy. Clement V filled vacancies in the college of cardinals with Frenchmen, who in 1314 elected another French pope and stayed where they were. Until the end of the Avignon papacy, all the popes and most of the cardinals were French.

On the whole, the Avignon popes were able men, though not outstanding religious figures. Their talents lay in administration, law, and finance, and under them the centralization and bureau-cratization of the church, begun in the eleventh century, reached its culmination. For example, John XXII (r. 1316–34), who believed that the papacy had to have the financial resources to stand up against the secular powers, developed a financial system that funnelled a great deal of the money taken in by the church to the papal curia. The curia also strengthened its control over all church business. The resulting proliferation of offices and officials made the papal government the largest in Europe and helped consolidate its control over ecclesiastical offices throughout Christendom. From this time on, anyone who sought a post in a bishopric had to apply to the papacy; consequently, the bishops, who were themselves papal appointees, lost control over their own sees.

The papal government at Avignon was divided into four main branches: the chancery, the *camera apostolica* (the apostolic chamber), the Datary, and the judiciary. By the fourteenth century, the papal chancery, the first to develop, consisted of seven offices that prepared and dispatched routine administrative correspondence and documents. It also received petitions for papal action, reviewed the qualifications of candidates for ecclesiastical offices, and had official custody of the curial records.

The *camera apostolica* had emerged as a separate financial department during the thirteenth century, and under John XXII and his successors it expanded enormously. Its administrative head was the treasurer, and its policy-making head was the chamberlain. The title indicates that the chamberlain was once a household officer of the popes, and he was still chosen from the pope's personal entourage. At Avignon, the chamberlain became in effect the prime minister of the papacy. He handled most of the instructions sent to papal legates and ambassadors and nearly all the private and secret correspondence of the popes. He also controlled the papal mint, the tax collectors, and the papacy's extensive courier system. Moreover, he was responsible for the receipt and auditing of all papal revenues and

Manuscript illustration of the crucial point in the meeting of Richard II with the main body of the rebels during the Peasants' Revolt of 1381. Its leader, Wat Tyler, is being struck down by one of Richard's men.

supervised a court that heard disputes over papal finances.

The Datary was set up as a separate department in the first half of the fourteenth century to take over some of the chancery functions. It handled petitions that did not require judicial action. In cases that involved no dispute, the Datary disposed of appointments to benefices (income-producing properties), dispensations from provisions of the canon law (especially in routine cases of irregularities in marriages), and the granting of papal approval for the disposition of church property or offices.

The papal judiciary was an elaborate court system. The highest court in that system was the Consistory, which consisted of the pope and all the cardinals. The Consistory referred most cases that came before it to judges in the diocese or province from which they came—the judges-delegate—or to one of the lesser tribunals of the curia. Any number of cardinals could consitute a court to hear a particular case, but such courts tended to refer cases to trained auditors. Routine cases were handled by the *Rota*. A panel of auditors chosen from the judges who made up the *Rota* heard each case, and judgment was pronounced by all the judges after they had reviewed the evidence and the arguments. At any stage in

Death was a favorite subject for illustration in the late Middle Ages. Shown here is the Dance of Death from *ca.* 1400. Death, playing a trumpet decked with the papal banner of the keys of St. Peter, summons a pope.

the proceedings, a case could be referred to a special tribunal called the *Audientia* for a ruling on technical points and on the authenticity of the documentary evidence. Litigation in the papal courts was complicated and expensive and consequently was ideal for defendants who sought to delay the settlement of a case.

The pope and cardinals spent most of their time running the vast machinery of the papal government, and the cost of running the bureaucracy led them into what some critics denounced as rapacious practices. Disaffected by the wealth and worldliness of the Avignon papacy, many intellectuals withdrew their support. One of them was Petrarch (1304–74), the poet and scholar who coined the term "Babylonian Exile" (see p. 326). Saint Catherine of Siena (1347–80) bombarded the papacy with letters demanding that it return to Rome, and in a dispute with John XXII the emperor Ludwig IV of Bavaria (r. 1314–47) denounced the papacy as an institution subverted by political ambition and ill-gotten wealth.

As time went by, pressure intensified for the popes to return to Rome. Conditions in Rome, long subject to internecine conflict among the noble famiies and their supporters, improved during the reign of Pope Innocent VI (r. 1352–62), and in 1356 the treaty that ended the first phase of the Hundred Years' War (see below) led to the release of marauding bands of mercenaries who disrupted the peaceful atmosphere of Avignon. Urban V (r. 1362–70) returned the curia to Rome for a time, but after three years of vain attempts to reestablish papal authority in the Holy City, he went back to Avignon. Gregory XI (r. 1370–78) also returned to Rome, but he too failed and planned to retreat to Avignon. He died before he could do so, however, and left the cardinals in Rome threatened by a mob demanding election of an Italian pope. After electing the archbishop of Bari, many of the cardinals retreated to Avignon anyway. But the new pope, Urban VI (r. 1378–89), turned out to be a reformer determined to put an end to the corrupt practices of the curia. The Avignon contingent, seeking to preserve the system that had brought them wealth and

power, declared Urban's election invalid on the grounds that it had been held under the coercion of the mob. They then elected the Frenchman Robert of Geneva as Clement VII (r. 1378–94). Thus arose the Great Schism in the medieval papacy.

The Great Schism

With two popes, each claiming the authority to tax, the cost of running the papal government became doubly burdensome. To make matters worse, the popes hurled anathemas at each other, and the cry of scandal was added to other complaints. The secular rulers of Europe lined up on one side or the other depending on their own political interests. The French and their allies—Scotland, Navarre, Castile, Aragon, and various German dukes—supported Clement in Avignon. The enemies of France—England, Flanders, Portugal, the emperor Wenceslas, most of the German dukes, Bohemia, and Hungary—supported Urban in Rome. The Italian city-states were divided and regularly switched their allegiance from one pope to the other.

To resolve the schism, some churchmen proposed that both popes resign and that the combined colleges of cardinals elect a new pope. But the cardinals did not trust one another, and the popes themselves refused to take the first step toward this solution. Other churchmen, led by the members of the theology faculty at the University of Paris, suggested that a general council be called to decide the issue. This was an attractive idea, but it was not clear whether canon law permitted a council to depose a pope. For hundreds of years, at least since the reform movement of the eleventh century (see pp. 265–66), the church had emphasized the supremacy of the pope in ecclesiastical affairs. The pope was the supreme judge who "judges all and is judged by no one." He was the supreme legislator; no ecclesiastical law was valid without his approval. He was the one who summoned and presided over councils. As far back as the ninth century, when Leo III (r. 795–816) was charged with crimes, the bishops assembled by Charles the Great had declared that they could not judge the pope; only God could do so (see p. 229).

Twelfth-century canonists had already wrestled with the issues raised by this hierarchical view of the church. They had wondered what would happen if the pope, who was a man like other men, committed a crime or fell into theological error. How would the church deal with such a crisis? By the beginning of the thirteenth century, the canonists had worked out a theory that Jesus's promise in the statement "You are Peter . . . and the gates of Hell shall not prevail [against Peter and the church]" (Matt. 16.18)—that is, Peter or the church would never fall into sin— did not apply to the pope, Peter's successor, but to the church. If this interpretation was true, then a general council could be called to deal with an errant pope.

This idea was revived at the time of the Great Schism. The churchmen wanted to call a council to decide who was the true pope but were unsure of how to go about calling one. Some argued that the emperor could summon it, citing the example of Constantine I who had summoned the Council of Nicaea (see p. 118). Others thought that the college of cardinals could summon it. But many of them thought that only the pope had the authority to summon a council.

Given the failure of the churchmen to agree on how to summon a council, the schism dragged on. When Urban and Clement died, in 1389 and 1394 respectively, each college of cardinals elected its own pope, and both of them continued to claim the title.

In 1409, members of the so-called conciliar movement took the first step toward solving the problem by convincing the cardinals on both sides to cooperate in a council to be held at Pisa. Five hundred prelates came to the council and proceeded to depose both popes—Benedict XIII (r. 1394–1423) of Avignon, and Gregory XII (r. 1406–15) of Rome—as "schismatics and notorious heretics." Then they authorized the assembled cardinals to elect a new pope. The cardinals elected Alexander V (r. 1409–10). Benedict and Gregory promptly denounced both the council and the newly elected pope and,

The Great Schism   1378–1417

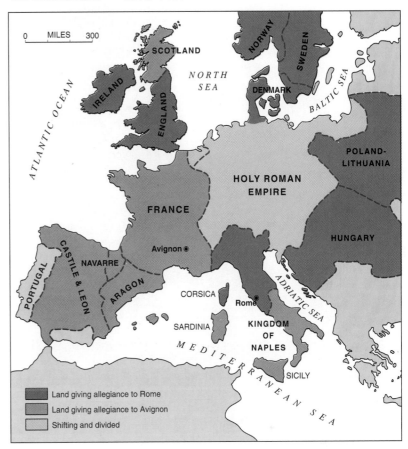

Land giving allegiance to Rome
Land giving allegiance to Avignon
Shifting and divided

with the support of their secular backers, continued as before. Alexander died while the council was still in session, and the cardinals immediately elected yet another pope, John XXIII (r. 1410–15). To the surprise of all, John asserted that as pope he had a higher authority and declared the council at an end. The churchmen left Pisa having accomplished nothing.

There were immediate calls for a new council, and finally, in 1414, John XXIII summoned a general council to meet at Constance. The council met and soon proceeded to depose all three popes. Gregory XII had anticipated the council's action and had sent out a call to the council himself, on the grounds that he was the true pope. He then abdicated (1415). John XXIII was forced to abdicate the

A manuscript illumination showing an antipope receiving his crown from the devil and in turn crowning an emperor as a pledge of mutual support against the true head of the church.

of the church, the council passed another decree requiring that a general council be held every five years.

As a cardinal, Martin V had supported the conciliar movement, but as pope he worked hard to reestablish papal supremacy over the councils. He and his successors succeeded in rendering the councils that met after Constance ineffective, but the Great Schism and the conciliar movement had in effect destroyed the medieval papacy. The popes no longer commanded the extraordinary prestige and power they had commanded since the eleventh century, and the papacy gradually declined to the status of an Italian principality.

ENGLAND IN THE LATER MIDDLE AGES

The expansionist policies of Edward I (see p. 314) had severely strained England's resources, and it was predictable that a reaction would set in after his death in 1307. The reaction was more acute than it might have been, however, because his son Edward II (r. 1307–27) proved a weak-willed, incompetent ruler. Instead of taking up the reins of government, he left them to civil servants and personal favorites. Finally, a group of barons, calling themselves the Lords Ordainers, obliged Edward to accept the Ordinances of 1311, which curtailed the authority of the royal household and required approval by Parliament of appointments to high government offices and of important policy decisions. The defeat of Edward's armies by the Scots at Bannockburn in 1314 further discredited him and left the barons in almost complete control of the government. But they too proved incompetent, and in 1322 a royalist party restored Edward to power. He immediately nullified the Ordinances but publicly acknowledged the validity of the idea that important legislation should be enacted in Parliament. Soon, however, Edward again succumbed to the influence of favorites. His farcical reign climaxed when his queen Isabelle ran off with her lover Mortimer, with whom she then led a successful rebellion against her husband. Edward was imprisoned and executed in 1327.

same year.* Benedict XIII, the Avignon pope, who was then 87 years old, refused to step down and retreated to his castle in Spain, where he died in 1423 still maintaining that he was the true pope. In 1417, the council elected a new pope, Martin V (r. 1417–31).

Seeking to confirm its place in the church's constitution, the council passed a decree that declared that a general council represented the whole church, held its power directly from Christ, and must be obeyed by all men including the pope in matters pertaining to the faith, the abolition of schism, and reform. Having established its legitimacy as a divine institution

* John, though he had called the council and had given it legitimacy, was not considered a true pope. So when in 1958 a new pope took the name John, he was designated the twenty-third of that name, John XXIII (r. 1958–63).

Edward III (r. 1327–77) was still a minor when he succeeded to the throne, and Isabelle and Mortimer ruled as regents. In 1330 the young king overthrew the regency in a *coup d'état* that cost Mortimer his life and Isabelle her freedom. Edward then took over the government and appeased the barons with minor concessions. In 1333 he defeated the Scots at Halidon Hill. Although the battle was of no great importance, it taught Edward that a war was a good way of distracting the barons from domestic grievances. He was soon to test that lesson in a war with France.

The Hundred Years' War: The First Phase

As we have seen, war between England and France had broken out under Edward

I and Philip the Fair and had led to the defeat of the papacy as arbiter of what kings could do in their own kingdoms (pp. 324–25). During the 1290s and the early 1300s neither Edward nor Philip had been in a position to mount a major campaign. Philip had been occupied with Flanders and with building up his power over the great feudal lords of his realm, and Edward had been intent on the conquest of Scotland, which had not gone well. Under Edward II, the war with France had petered out.

Edward III took it up again in 1340. There were many causes of conflict—competition over trade in Flanders (which depended on English wool), French support of Scotland, and the old English claim to Normandy and other French territory. But the immediate cause of the war was Edward's claim to the French crown

THE FRENCH AND ENGLISH SUCCESSIONS

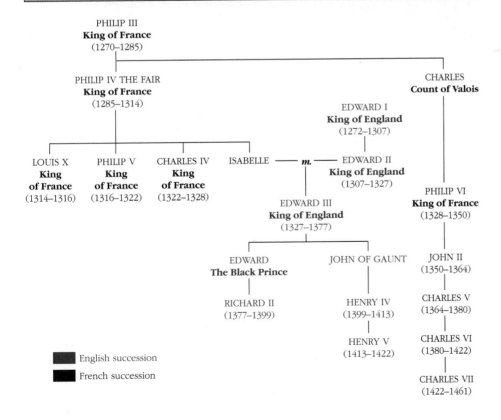

PHILIP III
King of France
(1270–1285)

PHILIP IV THE FAIR
King of France
(1285–1314)

CHARLES
Count of Valois

EDWARD I
King of England
(1272–1307)

LOUIS X
King of France
(1314–1316)

PHILIP V
King of France
(1316–1322)

CHARLES IV
King of France
(1322–1328)

ISABELLE —— *m.* —— EDWARD II
King of England
(1307–1327)

PHILIP VI
King of France
(1328–1350)

EDWARD III
King of England
(1327–1377)

EDWARD
The Black Prince

JOHN OF GAUNT

JOHN II
(1350–1364)

RICHARD II
(1377–1399)

HENRY IV
(1399–1413)

CHARLES V
(1364–1380)

HENRY V
(1413–1422)

CHARLES VI
(1380–1422)

CHARLES VII
(1422–1461)

English succession

French succession

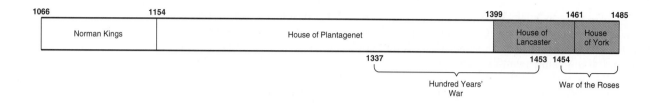

1066	1154		1399	1461	1485
Norman Kings	House of Plantagenet		House of Lancaster	House of York	

1337 — Hundred Years' War — 1453

1454 — War of the Roses

The Battle of Sluys in 1340 established English control of the Channel. This illustration from a copy of Froissart's *Chronicles*, which recount the first half of the Hundred Years' War, shows an English ship engaging a French vessel.

through his mother. The king of France at the time was Philip VI (r. 1328–50), descended from Philip III (r. 1270–85) through Charles of Anjou, Philip the Fair's brother. And Edward was Philip the Fair's grandson. No matter how the lawyers figured these relationships, Edward III was one degree closer to the French throne than Philip VI. But there were two problems: First, Edward's claim descended through a female, and the French lawyers argued that one who could not inherit the crown could not transmit it. Second, the French royal council would not accept Edward as king.

The war began with an amazing string of English victories. Edward won a naval battle at Sluys (1340), which gave him control of the English Channel. Then his army nearly annihilated the French army at Crécy (1346) and went on to capture Calais, which was to remain an English port for two centuries. Ten years later, his son Edward, called the Black Prince, defeated the French at Poitiers and captured King John of France. That battle ended the first phase of the war (1340–56). In the treaty that followed, the French agreed to pay a huge ransom for the release of their king and to cede about two-fifths of their country to the English. Edward III had reconquered most of the territories his ancestor King John had lost to the French in 1204.

Between the major battles of the war, the English conducted campaigns marked by systematic destruction. (A nineteenth-century historian published a list of substantial buildings destroyed that required two large volumes.) Moreover, in battle the English troops were armed with the highly effective longbow, a weapon developed during Edward I's reign. This weapon propelled an arrow with great power, had a long range, and could be reloaded rapidly. It could even penetrate chain mail. At Crécy, 15,000 English bowmen nearly wiped out 60,000 mounted French knights.

After the treaty of 1356, France fell into economic decline. The burden of the heavy ransom, together with the ravages of the Black Death, brought ruin to peasants and merchants alike and led to the great uprising of 1358, which was put down only after much bloodshed (see p. 354). The end of the war also led to the release of many mercenaries who turned to banditry and plagued cities and towns throughout the country, including Avignon.

England after Edward III

Edward, the Black Prince, predeceased his father, and Edward III was succeeded by his grandson Richard II (r. 1377–99). Richard was a boy when he became king, and the government was run by relatives and barons whose ineffectiveness prompted the peasant rebellion of 1381 (see p. 354). When Richard came of age in 1386, he set about restoring royal authority.

But Richard faced serious obstacles. Since the early days of the Hundred Years' War, most of the armed forces that England put into the field had been private companies paid by the king but recruited and commanded by the barons. That meant that any lord with a taste for war could maintain his own little army at government expense, a dangerous situation. Moreover, in trying to gain control of the government Richard had exiled the leading barons who opposed him and had confiscated their land. That action had united the barons who remained in England and had actually weakened Richard's position. In 1399 the barons rose in rebellion under Richard's cousin Henry of Lancaster, one of the barons Richard had deprived of his land and exiled a few years earlier. At a session of Parliament known as the Great Parliament, Henry had Richard deposed and then mounted the throne as Henry IV (r. 1399–1413). Richard died in prison.

The Hundred Years' War: The Second Phase

The Lancastrian kings, who ruled from 1399 to 1461, never quite lived down the violence by which Henry IV had seized the crown. Henry himself had to put down two dangerous rebellions, and his son Henry V (r. 1413–22) tried to rally the kingdom behind him by renewing the war with France. Henry V was a brilliant commander, and in 1415 at Agincourt in Normandy his small army of bowmen destroyed a French army of mounted knights. He was also the first to use siege artillery against walled cities (see p. 373).

After Agincourt, Henry entered into an alliance with the Duke of Burgundy—the most powerful lord in France after the king—and the French king Charles VI (r. 1380–1422) was obliged to accept a treaty. In 1421, according to that treaty, Charles disinherited his son, married his daughter to Henry V, and recognized that any son born of that union would inherit the French throne. When both Charles and Henry V died the next year, the two thrones were inherited by nine-month-old Henry VI.

The coronation led to a bitter struggle among the infant's uncles and cousins over who would govern in his name. Still, the English managed to deal with Charles VII, the disinherited son of Charles VI, when he renounced the treaty of 1421. They forced him to flee south of the Loire, and for a time it looked as if the English would be able to reinstate the terms of the treaty. Then the tide was turned by the appearance of a young woman, Joan of Arc.

Joan believed that she had been sent by God to rescue Charles VII and the French kingdom from the English. After overcoming the skepticism of the French court, she led a French force to victory at Patay near Orléans in 1429. Soon afterward, the English captured her and burned her as a witch. (The judgment was reversed and Joan was canonized as a saint in 1929.) At this point, the alliance between England and Burgundy broke down, and the French embarked on a war of attrition against the English. By 1453, only the port city of Calais remained in English hands, and the war came to an end.

The Hundred Years' War 1337–1453

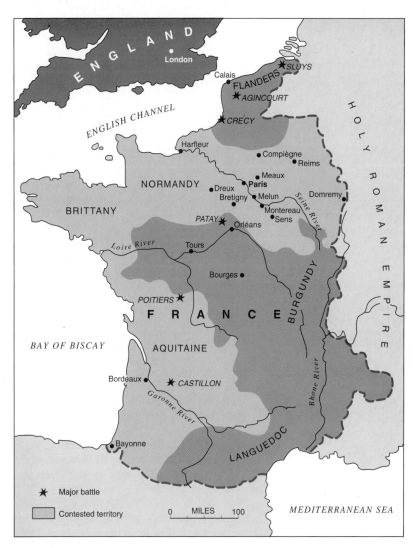

During the long war the old French aristocracy had been decimated by the English victories, and with the return of peace Charles VII named many members of the bourgeoisie as counselors and royal servants. His son Louis XI (r. 1461–83) continued that practice, and in his able hands France emerged as a strong bureaucratic state ruled by a king unfettered by the claims of baronial families.

In England, royal authority had been weakened by the competition over the regency during Henry VI's childhood, and the weakness was prolonged by Henry's mental instability. Throughout his adult life, he alternated between sanity and insanity and never succeeded in establishing a stable government. Moreover, the English setbacks during the closing years of the war created dissension among the men who might otherwise have made up for his shortcomings.

The War of the Roses

The main contestants for power in England were the House of Lancaster and the House of York, the oldest line of descent from Edward III. When Lancastrian Henry VI died in 1461, the Yorkists tried to install their leader, the Duke of York, as king. Civil war broke out over the succession. That war has long been known as the War of the Roses, because it was thought, mistakenly, that the symbol of the House of Lancaster was a red rose and that the symbol of the House of York was a white rose. The war, which went on until 1485, was the last attempt by the barons to take over the government. But it destroyed everyone who took part in it—the House of Lancaster, the House of York, and many of the great baronial families. So when Henry Tudor—an indirect, illegitimate, half-Welsh descendant of John of Gaunt (Edward III's son) seized the throne as Henry VII in 1485, he was in a position to build a new monarchy, relatively unchallenged by the baronial factions.

Henry VII (r. 1485–1509) was an excellent politician and administrator. He continued the policies of his predecessors, encouraging commerce and industry and running a frugal, effective government. Every king since Edward III had recognized that as long as England produced only raw materials—such as wool for the Flemish textile mills—it would never develop a strong industrial base. So they encouraged the migration of textile workers to England and protected the English textile industry as it grew. They also encouraged the expansion of English shipping. England was still far behind Flanders in textiles and behind Italy in shipping, but a good start had been made under Henry VII's policies. In the 24 years of his reign, Henry established the Tudor dynasty and prepared the way for a century of peace and prosperity in England.

The Development of Government Institutions

Three important institutional developments took place in England during the fourteenth and fifteenth centuries: the rise of the justices of the peace, the strengthening of Parliament, and the emergence of an independent judiciary.

Edward III had created the office of justice of the peace to help the sheriffs and feudal lords with the work of enforcing the law. The justices were usually well-to-do local landholders of the class that had long borne the responsibilities of local government. They were the knights of the shires who served as members of Parliament. Like sheriffs and tax collectors, the justices served without pay; their reward was status and the respect of the community. By the middle of the fifteenth century their power had grown to the point where they controlled local government. They arrested criminals and tried people accused of minor offenses. (Major cases were tried by circuit judges from the king's court.) They were responsible for enforcing the rules and regulations issued by the central government. They were expected to collect information for the King's Council and to report plots against the government. In practice, the justices of the peace often followed the orders of the most powerful baron in the district. Under the Tudors, however, the justices of the peace, with their wide knowledge of local affairs, became the chief agents of the crown in the counties.

Meanwhile, during the years of weak monarchs and wartime turmoil from Edward II to Henry VI, Parliament had emerged as an indispensable part of the government. Weak kings and usurpers alike sought its support. Moreover, Parliament was regarded as the most representative institution in the country. When Edward III and Henry IV asked Parliament to ratify the depositions of Edward II and Richard II respectively, it appeared that Parliament's assent was necessary even in matters concerning succession to the throne. Further evidence of the growing power of Parliament was that all laws having to do with taxation had to be submitted to it for approval.

The structure of Parliament also changed with the passing years. About 1340 the knights of the shires, who represented the counties, and the burgesses, who represented the towns, joined forces to form the House of Commons. Previously, the knights and the burgesses had acted separately in presenting petitions to the king and in approving taxes. Now Parliament consisted of two houses—the House of Lords and the House of Commons. And the House of Commons, unlike the assemblies of other countries, included nobles as well as commoners. The knights of the shires were landlords who sometimes married into the baronial families; some of them became barons themselves. Their presence in the House of Commons gave it far more influence than a mere assembly of burgesses like the French Third Estate (see p. 324). With the knights leading the House of Commons, the cooperation of the lords was usually forthcoming. So when both houses attacked a minister of the king, they could usually force him out of office.

By the fifteenth century, every important act of government had to be approved by Parliament. So well established had Parliament become that it survived even the period of strong kingship that began under the Tudors in 1485. But Parliament only gave legal validity to acts of government; it did not make policy, which was still the province of the king and his

An English court in the later Middle Ages. This miniature is from a law treatise of the reign of Henry IV (early fifteenth-century). At the top are the five judges of the Court of King's Bench; below them are the king's coroner and attorney. On the left is the jury, and in front, in the dock, is a prisoner in fetters, flanked by lawyers. In the foreground more prisoners in chains wait their turn. On the center table stand the ushers, one of whom seems to be swearing in the jury.

ministers. For example, Edward II and Richard II were not deposed by an act initiated by Parliament; Parliament merely ratified the actions of a few great barons. Not until the seventeenth century did Parliament begin to formulate policy.

Finally, as the result of a blunder committed by Edward III, the English judiciary achieved independence from the crown. In 1340, Edward became enraged when a shortage of funds temporarily halted his campaign in France; he returned home and fired all his ministers, including the royal judges. When Parliament, and the country at large, raised a cry of alarm, Edward was forced to restore the judges to their positions. It was clear that the English

Lawlessness in Fifteenth-Century England

John Paston was the son of a royal judge and well-to-do landowner in Norfolk. His father had bought the manor of Gresham, but in 1448 Lord Molyns claimed it, though he had no right to it. John Paston tried to settle the claim peacefully, but Molyns's men seized the manor house and Paston moved to another "mansion." While he was seeking help from his friends, Paston's wife was left to defend their home. She wrote her husband this letter late in 1448.

Right worshipful husband, I recommend me to you and pray you to get some cross-bows and windlasses to wind them with and arrows, for your house here is so low that no one could shoot out of it with a long-bow, even if we had great need. I suppose you could get these things from Sir John Falstaff [a friend of the Pastons]. And also I would like you to get two or three short pole-axes to guard the doors and as many jacks [padded leather jackets] as you can.

Partridge [leader of Molyns's men] and his fellows are sore afraid that you will attack them again, and they have made great preparations, as I am told. They have made bars to bar the doors crosswise, and they have made loop-holes on every side of the house to shoot out of both with bows and with hand-guns. The holes made for hand-guns are scarcely knee-high from the floor and no one can shoot out of them with a hand bow.

[Margaret Paston apparently took all this as a matter of course; she then turned to an ordinary shopping list.] I pray you to buy me a pound of almonds and a pound of sugar and some cloth to make clothes for your children and a yard of black broad-cloth for a hood for me.

The Trinity have you in His keeping and send you Godspeed in all your affairs.

Put into modern English from Norman Davis, ed., Paston Letters *(Oxford: Clarendon Press, 1958), pp. 9–10.*

King's Bench and the Court of Common Pleas. The King's Bench heard cases that directly pertained to the king and his interests, such as criminal cases and disputes over royal rights. (Crimes had come to be viewed as violations of the king's peace. They had formerly been regarded merely as injuries to a citizen to be avenged, preferably through law suit, by the injured party.) The Court of Common Pleas heard appeals of cases initiated by royal writs issued to litigants and that had been heard first in a shire or circuit court (see p. 309). In general, these were civil cases rather than criminal cases. All the judges of both the King's Bench and the Court of Common Pleas were appointed by the King.

Under Henry II and his successors, the royal courts were viewed as the means by which the king exercised judicial authority. That authority was limited, however, by the customary law dispensed by the age-old local courts. Englishmen continued to view the royal courts as belonging to the king (they still do) but they came to regard the law itself as a guarantee of specific rights. As far back as 1215, in the *Magna Carta*, the barons had asserted that all Englishmen had the right to a trial by a jury of their peers; the king could no longer ignore that right when it suited him, as King John had done. In 1328 Parliament had passed and Edward III had accepted the Statute of Northampton, which stated that no royal command should interfere with the course of the common law. In 1340, when Edward violated that statute by firing the royal judges, the reaction of the people made it clear that the judiciary was an arm of government and that it was not subject to the whims of the king.

Ironically, this turn of events tended to limit the role of the courts. In the thirteenth century, the royal judges, as officers of the king, had exercised wide discretion in dealing with the cases that came before them. In effect, they made law as they judged cases. Once the judiciary became independent of the king, however, judges refused to hear cases that lacked precedents. Their motive was to protect themselves from the charge that they were usurping political authority. They could claim that they were not making law and

regarded the judges not just as royal appointees, but as officers of the government responsible for dispensing justice. The event marked a fundamental shift in their view of the judicial system.

That system dated back to the royal court established by Henry II (r. 1154–89). During the thirteenth century, the royal court had split into two branches, the

987	1328	1589
House of Capet	House of Valois	

consequently were not engaging in policy decisions, which were properly the province of political agents such as the king and Parliament.

FRANCE IN THE LATE MIDDLE AGES

In France, as we have seen (p. 359), when the sons of Philip the Fair died, leaving only daughters to succeed them, Edward III had stepped forward to claim the French throne. The rule that the French invented to prevent succession by or through a woman was designed not only to bar Edward's claim but also to prevent any French baron from gaining the throne by marrying a reigning queen. In 1328, the barons put Philip of Valois, cousin of the last king and nephew of Philip the Fair, on the throne. Because Philip (r. 1328–50) owed his position to the barons, he had to spend most of his reign bestowing favors on his benefactors and keeping peace among warring factions. As a result, the loyalty to the crown that had emerged during the thirteenth century began to erode, and rebellions and acts of treason plagued the country. It was this state of affairs that contributed to the French defeats during the first phase of the Hundred Years' War.

Philip's son John (r. 1350–64) had no better fortune. The loss of territory and the heavy ransom levied after his capture by the English at Poitiers caused widespread dissatisfaction and in 1358 set off a bloody peasant rebellion called the *jacquerie*. (The nobles called all peasants jacques.) That same year, the Estates General, led by the Paris bourgeoisie, tried to take over the government. The attempt failed, because the Estates had had little experience in government and because their leaders received no support from the nobility. John's son Charles V (r. 1364–80) regained a good measure of royal au-

thority by suppressing his opponents at home and by inflicting a series of defeats on the English.

Charles VI (r. 1380–1422), who succeeded Charles V, was strong in neither mind nor character and after 1390 suffered intermittent spells of insanity. During his reign, government was conducted largely by princes of the royal family who quarreled bitterly over offices, pensions, and land grants. In 1419, when the duke of Burgundy, the king's cousin, was assassinated by followers of the duke of Orléans, the king's brother, the quarrels turned into civil war and the new duke of Burgundy allied himself with the English. In addition

Charles V, king of France.

The only known contemporary portrait of Joan of Arc.

to Burgundy, the duke had acquired Flanders and other provinces of the Low Countries, which made him the most powerful prince in France. His defection to the English proved disastrous. It was during this period of civil war that Henry V of England made his rapid conquests in France and forced Charles VI to disinherit his own son and to recognize any future son of Henry as heir to the French crown.

The Defeat of England

Charles VII (r. 1422–61) faced an almost hopeless situation when his father died. He had been disinherited, and the largest and richest part of France belonged to the English and their Burgundian allies. His army was weak, and he was not using it effectively. Then, in 1429 the peasant girl from the eastern frontier, Joan of Arc, appeared at court and announced that heavenly voices had ordered her to drive the English out of France (see p. 361).

Soon Charles had another stroke of good fortune. England under Henry VI was torn by factional strife, and in the competition for control of the royal government the leader of one of the factions offended the duke of Burgundy. The duke returned to the French cause in 1435. His defection weakened the English and facilitated Charles's recovery of northern France.

Road building in rural France (*ca.* 1448).

Joan of Arc had revitalized the ancient view that the French kingdom was holy and deserved the unswerving support of the people despite generations of misgovernment. Her belief that "to make war on the holy kingdom of France was to make war on the Lord Jesus" was shared by people of all classes. Despite civil war, treason, and treachery, a feeling of national pride began to stir among the French people. Throughout the chaos and confusion of the early fifteenth century the French clung to their faith in the French monarchy and in the Christian religion, foreshadowing the union of monarchy and religion on which the absolutist states of the early modern period were to be built.

The Restoration of Royal Power

All the battles of the Hundred Years' War had been fought on French soil, and whole areas of the country had been intentionally devastated by the English armies. Even during periods of peace, troops of unemployed mercenaries had terrorized and plundered the countryside. Perhaps because of the extent and the intensity of the suffering, royal power was restored more rapidly and more completely in France than it was in England. A king who showed any promise of putting an end to the disorder was accorded almost unlimited power to levy taxes. As soon as Charles VII had the English on the run, he began to levy taxes at will, without asking consent from the Estates General. His task was made easier by the fact that the Estates General was seldom called into session, and when it was called it had little authority. The real power lay with the provincial and regional assemblies, with the Estates of Normandy or of Languedoc rather than with the Estates General. And Charles was able to overcome the fragmented opposition of those local assemblies.

The same bemusement with provincial matters also deferred the French nobles from seeking to entrench themselves in the central government, which remained the preserve of the king and his bureaucrats. Thus the Hundred Years' War

The Reconquest of Spain

reinforced a tendency that had long been apparent in France—the tendency toward a strong king at the head of a bureaucratic state with all other political forces weak and divided. This French pattern would become the model for the rest of Europe during the early modern period.

SPAIN IN THE LATE MIDDLE AGES

Starting in the eleventh century, the kingdoms of Aragon, León, and Castile reclaimed the peninsula from the Moors, and the Moorish caliphate centered on Cordoba disintegrated into a collection of independent states. By the fifteenth century, Moorish holdings had been reduced to the little kingdom of Granada.

Like the rest of western Europe, Spain was wracked by civil wars in the late Middle Ages. The competition between the principal kingdoms, Castile and Aragon, was exacerbated by the lack of any fixed rule of succession in either kingdom. So whoever sat on either throne was almost sure to be challenged by a rival claimant. Moreover, because many kings of the period came to the throne as minors, frequent quarrels erupted over the regency and attempts by members of the royal family to displace the legitimate king with someone of their own choosing. Because peaceful reigns were rare, the Spanish kings had little opportunity to participate in European politics. At one point, the

kingdom of Castile became a pawn in the Hundred Years' War when the reigning king, Pedro I (r. 1350–69), was challenged by his illegitimate half-brother, Henry of Trastamara. The English supported Pedro, and the French supported Henry. The fate of the two claimants depended on the tide of war. In 1366, the French were in ascendancy and Henry mounted the throne. The next year the tide of war shifted in favor of the English and Pedro was back in power. He was killed in battle in 1369, and Henry ruled until his death in 1379. But throughout his reign Henry was constantly challenged by the kings of Aragon, Navarre, Portugal, and Granada.

The kingdom of Aragon had less trouble with successions, because it controlled a small empire from which it could provide for the younger sons of the royal house. They could be given the kingdom of Majorca (the Balearic Islands) or Sicily (and eventually Naples) in Italy.

Nevertheless, the disorder persisted in most parts of the peninsula until John II of Aragon married his son Ferdinand (r. 1479–1516) to Isabella, the heiress of Castile (r. 1474–1504). The union of the two crowns (1479) did not result in the actual merger of the two kingdoms, but it brought a large measure of security to the people of Spain.

On the whole, the Catholic Kings (as Ferdinand and Isabella were called) followed the French model; they allowed

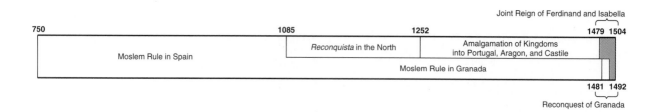

		Joint Reign of Ferdinand and Isabella

750 .... 1085 .... 1252 .... 1479 1504

Moslem Rule in Spain | *Reconquista* in the North | Amalgamation of Kingdoms into Portugal, Aragon, and Castile

Moslem Rule in Granada

1481 1492

Reconquest of Granada

A fifteenth-century Swiss halberd.

each province to keep its time-honored customs but appointed officials of the central government to do the governing. The Catholic Kings did not bear that title in vain; in a society of mixed ethnic population—Moors, Jews, and Christians—they made the Christian religion the test of loyalty. Jews and Moslems, even after they had converted, were suspected of secretly adhering to their old faiths, and some of them were driven into exile. The instrument of religious oppression was the Inquisition (see p. 282), which in Spain alone among the countries of Europe was a tool of the monarchy. The Spanish Inquisition was known for its harsh methods and penalties and for its use of the charge of heresy to achieve political ends. In 1492 Ferdinand and Isabella finally conquered Granada, which completed their conquest of the whole peninsula except Portugal, and forced the Moorish population to convert to Christianity. That same year they expelled the Jews from their kingdom.

The Jews and the Moors had accounted for a large part of Spain's skilled labor and they had dominated commerce, but the loss suffered by the country as a result of their suppression was not immediately apparent. By 1500, Spain was the strongest kingdom in Europe. It financed the exploration and conquest of the New World under the aegis of Isabella and the Castilians, and Ferdinand emerged as the arbiter of European politics. Even far-off England found it advisable to ally itself with Spain.

GERMANY IN THE LATE MIDDLE AGES

The history of the remainder of western Europe during the late Middle Ages paral-leled that of France and England. Everywhere there were rebellions, civil wars, and attempts to take over neighboring lands. But all this activity brought surprisingly little change. The political map of Europe in 1450 looked very much as it had in 1300, and most of the governments were pretty much the same.

In Germany, however, change was more evident. During the fourteenth century the peasants and townsmen of Switzerland gradually gained their independence from the Habsburg family, which had ruled this part of Germany, along with Austria, for many generations. The Swiss created an army of well-disciplined infantrymen armed with long pikes with which they could repel a charge by the elite cavalry troops of the German army. By the fifteenth century French kings and Italian princes, including the pope, were hiring whole companies of Swiss infantrymen.

The Swiss were also demonstrating the possibility of republican government to a Europe that had little confidence in democracy. Up to then, the only noteworthy republics had been the faction-ridden Italian cities, which at that very moment were losing their independence to tyrants, and the German towns that had tried and failed to form a permanent confederation and had remained weak and isolated.

But the Swiss Confederation, though loosely knit, endured. Each district, or canton, retained its own institutions, and no canton was ruled by a feudal lord. The towns were governed by wealthy burgesses, but the peasant cantons, where the movement for independence had begun, were almost pure democracies.

Change was also apparent in the Low Countries. During the fifteenth century the dukes of Burgundy gradually

Hapsburg and Luxembourg States

gained control over all the provinces of the Low Countries, roughly the area of modern Belgium and the Netherlands. Acquisition of the Low Countries, one of the richest and most urbanized sections of Europe, by the house of Burgundy removed their fate from that of the rest of Germany. As they gradually achieved a sense of national identity, however, their wealth made control of their country the object of a long series of wars that began in the fifteenth century and has continued into the twentieth.

Meanwhile a new power center was rising on the middle Danube as a product of the peculiar electoral habits of the German princes. By the fourteenth century

the number of princes taking part in imperial elections had been reduced to seven. Fearful of bestowing the title on any truly powerful prince, for some time they chose as emperors counts with small holdings. Though the title carried no real power, it bore enough social prestige to enable the emperors to marry heiresses of important thrones. It was by this route that the Habsburgs, petty princes in western Germany who had served briefly as emperors around 1300, managed to acquire the duchy of Austria and nearby counties. A little later, the count of Luxembourg, an equally obscure prince, was elected emperor and arranged a marriage through which his son acquired the kingdom of

Bohemia. Later Luxembourg emperors acquired Silesia and eventually Hungary. When the last male of the Luxembourg line died in 1438, his closest heir was the Habsburg duke of Austria. The union of the vast holdings of the Luxembourgs and the Habsburgs marked the beginning of the Habsburg empire, for five centuries one of the great powers of Europe (see pp. 336–37).

ART, LITERATURE, AND SCIENCE

During the late Middle Ages, art, literature, science, and technology all advanced, but advanced unevenly. We find a great many imitative and second-rate works alongside brilliant and historically important works. The most noteworthy advances were made in the arts and literature.

The Arts

After the thirteenth century, Gothic architecture had become imitative and overly ornate, and few churches of the fourteenth and fifteenth centuries are of commanding quality. One late medieval style is called

King's College Chapel, Cambridge: A fine example of the English perpendicular style of Gothic architecture.

the Flamboyant, for obvious reasons. In England, architects developed a Gothic style, called the Perpendicular, that emphasized height and soaring lines. The chapel of King's College, Cambridge, is an excellent example of the Perpendicular style.

Manuscript illumination reached new heights during the fifteenth century. The rich court of Burgundy supported talented artists who executed ambitious programs of illumination. Many of the manuscripts are so-called "books of hours," popular collections of readings from the service books of the church that were used as personal prayer books by the laity. In the wealthy households of the nobility, artists created superb works of calligraphy and illustration that have survived in whole or in part. The illustrators of these books introduced a realistic style that had a significant influence on future artists. Their detailed, realistic renderings of everyday life are an important source of information about the period.

It was during the fourteenth century that portrait painting first appeared in western Europe, along with the first attempts to treat landscapes with freshness and authenticity. Here again the most talented artists were those patronized by the dukes of Burgundy. The artists of the Flemish school of painting, which emerged in the late fourteenth and early fifteenth centuries, were the first artists to paint in oils and were worthy rivals of the Italian painters of the early Renaissance. The best-known Flemish painters—the van Eyck brothers, van der Weyden, and Memling—combined meticulous attention to detail with genuine religious feeling. Among the masterpieces of the period are Jan van Eyck's painting of Giovanni Arnolfini and his bride (1434) and his *Man in a Red Turban* (1433) which is a self-portrait.

Literature

In literature, the narrative poems derived from the romances of the twelfth century now emerged as fantastic stories (like those parodied by Cervantes in *Don Quixote;* see p. 471), and lyric poetry declined into society verse. Yet some authors demonstrated deeper psychological insights into human behavior, and there was notable improvement in the quality of prose writing. When Nicolas Oresme (*ca.* 1325–82), a scholarly French bishop, set about translating Aristotle's *Politics,* he had to invent or redefine a great many words, and in doing so he enriched the French language.

Geoffrey Chaucer (*ca.* 1340–1400), who began as a translator and adapter of French works, matured into one of England's most talented poets. His most famous work, the prologue to the *Canterbury Tales,* reveals his skill in describing individual characters and his wit in depicting human foibles. His characters include the "perfect, gentle Knight," the poor parson who taught Christ's lore "but first he followed it himself," the earthy Wife of Bath who had buried five husbands, and scoundrels such as the Miller and the Summoner. He may have met such characters while working in the royal customs service in the port of London, but it was through his genius that he translated such experiences into literary masterpieces like the *Canterbury Tales* and *Troilus and Criseyde.* Though Chaucer saw through pretense and sham, he had an affection for the world and its characters. His talents were recognized during his lifetime, and he rose quickly in society under the patronage of John of Gaunt, uncle of King Richard II.

The poet Francois Villon (1431–*ca.* 1463) was less fortunate. In his poetry he showed how close French society was to cracking under the strains of war during the first half of the fifteenth century. Though he cast his poems in the old forms, he depicted life in taverns and thieves' dens rather than courtly society. He confessed that he was a friend of the thieves and prostitutes of Paris and was himself convicted of crime. Villon expressed bitterness over his wasted life, however, and spoke of the hopes and fears of poor people and outcasts—the piety of an old woman, the last thoughts of men condemned to hang. The tendency toward realism, already evident in Chaucer, is even more apparent in Villon.

An example of the early Flemish style. These panels come from a triptych by Gerard David (*ca.* 1460–1523).

As church control over religious life declined, writers produced numerous devotional works for lay readers: meditations, visions, moral tracts, and the books of hours. Among the religious writings of the period was the *Imitation of Christ,* ascribed to Thomas à Kempis (1379/80–1471). It was a guide to the Christian life that emphasized the simple life and devotion to spiritual matters as the ideal. In the late Middle Ages it was the most-read religious work after the Bible.

The Vision of Piers Plowman by William Langland (*ca.* 1332–*ca.* 1400) is one of the first important works written in English after the Norman Conquest. Little is known of Langland, except that he lived during the fourteenth century and came from peasant stock. The language of *Piers Plowman* is archaic, but it is clearly English, not Anglo-Saxon. *Piers Plowman* is evidence of the widespread desire to transform religion into a strong social force. Langland's work criticized people of every class for their worldliness and selfishness; only by a return to the principles of the Gospel could the world be saved. There is nothing anti-church in the poem, but it clearly alludes to the failure of the ecclesiastical authorities to respond to the aspirations of ordinary people.

A fifteenth-century representation of Chaucer from the Ellesmere manuscript of the *Canterbury Tales.*

Science

We know little about what was being done in the sciences during the fourteenth and fifteenth centuries, and historians have usually disparaged what we do know as unoriginal and unimportant. Nonetheless, there were scientists of originality whose work had lasting value. Columbus based his ideas about geography on books written in the fourteenth and early fifteenth centuries. The reaction of some philosophers and theologians to Thomas Aquinas's views of the world freed scholars to some extent from their adherence to the Aristotelian ideas he had incorporated into his theological system. That freedom permitted wider speculation on scientific questions, particularly questions having to do with motion. Fourteenth-century scholars raised many of the issues that Galileo eventually used in revolutionizing the science of physics in the sixteenth century. For example, mathematicians at Oxford came extremely close to solving the problem of acceleration, and the French scholar Nicolas Oresme considered the possibility that the earth rotated.

From the twelfth century on, western scholars relied mainly on the work of the Greeks and the Moslems for knowledge of the world, but there were always some who were interested in science. That interest led eventually to the great discoveries of the early modern period. Copernicus and Galileo were trained in universities that used the methods and books of the late Middle Ages.

European civilization is an amalgam of Roman, Judeo-Christian, Celtic, Germanic, and countless other influences. As such, it has never had a single world view that could hinder the probing of the human mind. In China, a philosopher of Thomas Aquinas's stature might have become an unchallenged authority, but in the West he was subjected to searching critical appraisal. European society is comfortable with opposing points of view, as its literature and its politics show. In *Parzival* (*ca.* 1208), for example, Wolfram von Eschenbach contrasts the courtly with the divine, the Christian with the pagan, and deals fairly with non-Christian values even while showing the superiority of Christian values. In politics, the struggle between ecclesiastical authority and secular authority divided the European consciousness and enabled people to think of political order from the spiritual as well as the secular point of view.

Such attitudes are essential in scientific investigation, which relies on willingness to think about the world in new and unorthodox ways. Though comfortable with contradictions, Europeans worked hard to resolve them by focusing their attention on details. For example, they eventually resolved the problems of constitutional law that they encountered in struggling with the Great Schism by making small changes in the way they viewed the relationship between pope and council. Similarly, scientific thinkers concentrated on details, on observations and explanations of small things, confident that their studies would eventually produce results. And so they did, by revealing the inadequacy of currently accepted theories and by opening the way for Copernicus, Galileo, and Kepler to come up with new theories to explain the observations.

Technology

The Europeans of the Middle Ages were great innovators in technology. They

An early gun, lighter and more portable than the first cannon. The gun was placed on a forked stand and was braced against the ground by its long tail (illustration from a German manuscript, ca. 1405).

seized on inventions from the East, such as the stirrup, the horseshoe, and paper, and invented new implements of their own, such as the horse collar and the mechanical clock. The Chinese probably invented gunpowder, and they were using cannons about as early as the Europeans. But the Chinese were content with the primitive weapons they first created, and the Europeans carried on experiments in an effort to improve accuracy and reliability. The first European cannons often blew up in the face of the men who fired them, but by the end of the fifteenth century they had become fairly reliable.

The use of cannons meant that the castles of the nobility were no longer impregnable, and the military might of the nobility declined accordingly. Moreover, cannons were expensive, and only kings and great lords could afford to equip their troops with them. Thus the introduction of cannons tended to concentrate power in the hands of a few powerful men, especially the kings.

The use of cannons and the invention of smaller firearms stimulated advances in other branches of technology. Early gun barrels were extremely unreliable, but steel makers devised new metallurgical techniques and were soon producing higher-quality metal. To produce truly round barrels that could deliver the full effect of the charge, gunsmiths came up with better tools and more precise measuring instruments.

The increased demand for metals led to technological advances in mining and smelting as well. In the early Middle Ages, most ores had been drawn from easily accessible surface deposits. But by the late Middle Ages, miners in Germany, Bohemia, and Austria were sinking their shafts deeper and deeper and were pumping ground water out of their mines. Inventions like the cylinder pump, which drained the mines, prompted inventions in other industries. The principles employed in the invention of the cylinder pump, for example, led eventually to the invention of the steam engine.

The fifteenth-century invention of printing by means of movable type also owed much to advances in metallurgy. To

Early mechanical clockworks (*ca.* 1500). The first clocks had only one moveable hand.

cast usable type requires a metal that will take the exact shape of the mold into which it is poured. German metallurgists answered that need by creating an alloy that expands as it cools and fits the mold precisely. In 1453 Johannes Gutenberg produced the first European printed book, the Bible, using type cast with the new alloy.

Through patient experimentation and research, western Europeans also made great strides in navigation and seamanship. By the end of the thirteenth century they had ships that could tack against the wind and survive the violent storms of the Atlantic. Navigators could find their latitude, though not their longitude, by sightings of the stars and the sun; they knew that the earth was round and that the distance to the rich lands of the East was not impossibly great. French and

Spanish seamen reached the Canary Islands by the early fourteenth century at the latest, and by 1400 Portuguese sailors had made their way down the African coast, claiming Madeira and the Cape Verde Islands for their king.

Meanwhile, the Chinese were sending expeditions into the Indian Ocean, where they found rich countries and profitable trade; the Europeans had discovered only barren islands and disease-ridden coasts. The Chinese abandoned their efforts after a time, however, whereas the Europeans persisted. Still, it was almost two centuries before they reached the rich trading centers of the Orient and the treasures of the New World.

Almost as significant as the advances in navigation was the invention of the mechanical clock. The first clocks, which appeared in the fourteenth century, were not highly accurate. But clock design improved immensely with the discovery of the principle of escapement—the system by which the train of gears moves only a precise distance before it is checked and then released to move the same distance again. In the long run, the invention of reliable clocks had a profound effect on western Europeans. The precise measurement of time became a matter of great concern, a concern that for centuries differentiated European society from other societies. The insistence on precise measurement was a sign of the Europeans' uniquely rational attitude toward the world. The technological and scientific advances of the late Middle Ages stemmed from a desire to master nature rather than merely adjust to it, and the mechanization of the world picture, as one historian has called it, affected their approach to the workings of society and political institutions as well as to natural phenomena.

Suggestions for Further Reading

Economy and Society

On the economic depression of the fourteenth century, see the works cited in Chapters 10 and 12, particularly the *Cambridge Economic History*. See also M. M. Postan, *The Medieval Economy and Society* (1972), on the economic condition of peasants before the plague. On the bubonic plague, see P. Ziegler, *The Black Death* (1969), and R. S. Gottfried, *The Black Death* (1983). *The Black Death: A Chronicle of the Plague*, ed. J. Nohl, trans. C. H. Clarke (1924), contains a collection of contemporary sources. C. Cipolla, *Cristofano and the Plague* (1973), gives a graphic picture of a community's response to the plague, although he is studying a later epidemic. For a study of the effects of the plague, see *The Black Death: The Impact of the Fourteenth-century Plague* (1983), which contains the papers given at a conference at SUNY Binghamton; B. H. Putnam, *The Enforcement of the Statutes of Labourers during the First Decade after the Black Death 1349–1359* (1908); and on the effects in one locale, J. A. Raftis, "Changes in an English Village after the Black Death," *Mediaeval Studies* 29 (1967). For a sampling of the views on the effects of the plague, see W. Bowsky, ed., *The Black Death* (1971). For a general interpretation of the social unrest in the late Middle Ages, see R. H. Hilton, *Bondmen Made Free* (1973). *Social Unrest in the Late Middle Ages,* ed. F. X. Newman (1986), and *The English Rising of 1381,* ed. R. H. Hilton and T. H. Aston (1984), contain essays on the popular movements.

Avignon Papacy

See the work of A. C. Flick cited in Chapter 12. On the Avignon period, see G. Mollat, *The Avignon Papacy* (1963), and Y. Renouard, *The Avignon Papacy* (1970). On the Great Schism and the conciliar movement, see W. Ullmann, *Origins of the Great Schism* (1948); B. Tierney, *Foundations of the Conciliar Theory* (1955); and E. F. Jacob, *Essays in the Conciliar Epoch,* 3rd ed. (1963).

England

For late medieval England, see M. McKisack, *The Fourteenth Century* (1959), and E. F. Jacob, *The Fifteenth Century* (1961). S. Waugh, *England in the Reign of Edward III* (1991), is an excellent study of social and economic conditions. There are excellent histories of individual reigns: W. M. Ormrod, *The Reign of Edward III* (1990); B. Bevan, *Richard II* (1990); J. L.

Kirby, *Henry IV of England* (1970); R. A. Griffiths, *The Reign of Henry VI* (1981); and S. B. Chrimes, *Henry VII* (1972). On the history of Parliament, see P. Spufford, *Origins of the English Parliament* (1967), and R. G. Davies and J. H. Denton, eds., *The English Parliament in the Middle Ages* (1981). On justices of the peace, see B. H. Putnam, *Proceedings before Justices of the Peace* (1938).

France

On late medieval France, see P. S. Lewis, *Later Medieval France: The Polity* (1967). R. Vaughn, *Philip the Bold* (1962), *John the Fearless* (1966), *Philip the Good* (1970), and *Charles the Bold* (1973), give a history of the rise of Burgundian power. On Burgundy at its height, see J. F. Kirk, *Charles the Bold, Duke of Burgundy,* 3 vols. (1864–68), which treats the man in relation to his times. On the culture of the Burgundian court, see O. Cartellieri, *The Court of Burgundy* (1929), and P. Calmette, *The Golden Age of Burgundy* (1962).

The Hundred Years' War

E. Perroy, *The Hundred Years War* (1951), is the best short history. H. Lucas, *The Low Countries and the Hundred Years' War* (1929); K. Fowler, ed., *The Hundred Years War* (1971); H. J. Hewitt, *The Organization of War under Edward III* (1966); and J. B. Henneman, *Royal Taxation in Fourteenth Century France, 1322–1356* (1971). J. Keegan, *The Face of Battle* (1976), provides a brilliant description of the battle of Agincourt (1415). On Joan of Arc, see L. Fabre, *Joan of Arc,* trans. G. Hopkins (1954), a fine biography that presents a fascinating picture of France in the later period of the Hundred Years' War. See also the documents of the trial of Joan translated in *Jeanne d'Arc,* ed. T. D. Murray (1920). G. Pernoud, *Joan of Arc by Herself and Her Witnesses,* trans. E. Hyams (1966), presents a broad picture of Joan's mission and effect.

Spain and Germany

On late medieval Spain, see R. Altimira, *A History of Spain* (1949), and H. J. Chaytor, *A History of Aragon* (1933). R. I. Burns has studied the process of reconquest in *The Crusader Kingdom of Valencia: Reconstruction on a Thirteenth-Century Frontier* (1967), *Islam under the Crusaders: Colonial Survival in the Thirteenth-Century Kingdom of Valencia* (1973), and *Medieval Colonialism: Postcrusade Exploitation of Islamic Valencia* (1975).

On late medieval Germany, see G. Barraclough, *The Origins of Modern Germany* (1947); J. Leuschner, *Germany in the Later Middle Ages* (1980); and C. Bayley, *The Formation of the German College of Electors* (1949).

The Arts, Literature, and Science

On late medieval art, see J. Evans, *English Art 1307–1461* (1949); E. Panofsky, *Early Netherlandish Painting* (1953); L. Baldass, *Jan van Eyck* (1952); and M. Meiss, *French Painting in the time of Jean de Berry,* 2 vols. (1967–68), *Painting in Florence and Siena after the Black Death* (1951), and *The Limbourgs and their Contemporaries* (1974). J. Harthan, *The Book of Hours* (1977), is a history and commentary on the art of the books and contains many color plates. For a history of vernacular culture, see A. W. Ward and A. R. Waller, *The Cambridge History of English Literature,* Vol. 1 (1907). On Chaucer, see D. W. Robertson, *A Preface to Chaucer: Studies in Medieval Perspective* (1962). See also the works cited in Chapter 11. On late medieval science, see the works cited in Chapter 11. On the clock and other mechanical devices, see J. Gimpel, *The Medieval Machine* (1976). For the technology of firearms and sailing, see C. Cipolla, *Guns, Sails and Empires* (1965).

15

SOUTH AND EAST ASIA
CA. A.D. 600–1600

During the millennium considered in this chapter, the civilizations of South and East Asia continued to develop in their own distinctive ways. Even the two momentous events that transformed much of Eurasia during this period—the spread of Islam and the creation of the world's largest empire by the Mongols—affected India and China very differently. Meanwhile, the history of Southeast Asia continued to reflect—but not to mirror—that of India, while in Northeast Asia Japan fashioned its own culture and institutions under the stimulus of Chinese civilization.

INDIA

After the Guptas, India was divided into a number of states of varying duration and geographical extent. In studying this complex period, it is useful to distinguish North India from South India, even though some states for a time bridged this gap and even though major differences existed *within* each area.

In South India power tended to be focused in two major centers. One was the Western Deccan, where the rugged terrain of Maharashtra produced tough fighters. There the Chalyukas of Badani (their capital), beginning with Pulakeshin I (r. 535–66), developed an empire that reached its largest extent under Pulakeshin II (610–42). After this emperor was killed in battle, the Chalyukas were overthrown by the Rashatrakutas who seized Badani in 752. Their empire was even larger than that of the Chalyukas, but their most permanent monument is to be found at their capital of Ellora where they sponsored one of the world's greatest temples.

(OPPOSITE) MINIATURE MODEL HOMESTEAD (CLAY) FROM A MING DYNASTY TOMB (1368–1644).

Temple pavilion at Ellora, hewn
from natural rock (eighth
century).

The second southern power center
was in the Tamil-speaking area of the Co-
romandel Coast region. Here first the
Pallavas (roughly 250–910, with their
highpoint around 600) and then their
Chola successors (844–1279, highpoint
eleventh century) built their states. One
reason for taking special note of these two
states is that they played an influential role
in Southeast Asian history. The Tamil area
over which they ruled was a major source
for the diffusion of Indian culture to the
region. The Cholas, moreover, were able
to launch several naval expeditions to Sri
Lanka (Ceylon), and in 1020 they even
concluded a successful maritime campaign against the Sumatran-Malay state
of Shrivijaya.

The southern states, particularly that
of the Cholas, were among the most extensive and long lasting of the Indian states
during this period. Although they differed
in structure, they were all centered on the
sacred authority of the king, who was
identified with Indra and other deities.
Consecrated in solemn enthronement ceremonies, the king commanded the rever-
ent submission due to the protector of the
world. One Cholas institution that provided an important ritual and ideological
link between the center and outlying regions was that of special villages on the
plains governed by *brahman* assemblies
but also including residents of other
castes. The *brahman* priests were linked
to the center of authority by their religion
while at the same time they provided religious services to the peasant castes, with
whom they formed close ties.

This relationship between the *brahman* and the peasantry was facilitated by
the growth of devotionalism that had al-

ready appeared earlier in Hinduism. This movement, particularly in the South but by no means limited to that region, incorporated local deities into the Hindu pantheon and formed a religion basically congenial to settled cultivators. This faith inspired fervent hymns dedicated to Shiva and Vishnu performed in song and dance in Tamil temples. Their main themes were love for God and the personal inadequacy of the devotee. These hymns helped to fire the vitality of Hinduism and to undermine the appeal of Buddhism and other rival faiths.

Hinduism was also strengthened on the philosophical level, most notably by Shankara (*ca.* 788–820), India's most famous philosopher, whose basic teaching was an absolute monism. Although a southerner, Shankara wrote in Sanskrit and traveled widely in India, including the North, debating challengers, founding schools, and generally spreading his ideas.

Political fragmentation was characteristic of the North as well as the South. Here too, particularly from the eleventh century, a king exercised only a general overlordship over local warriors outside the area controlled directly by the throne. In a system somewhat similar to Western feudalism, the obligations of these warriors included financial payments, the use of the king's currency, military service, and attendance at the king's court as well as recognition of the king's sacred authority. A local warrior might also be obliged to offer his daughter to the king in marriage. Among the most notable northern rulers were the Rajputs ("Sons of Kings"), who were probably at least partly of central Asian descent but who were fiercely dedicated to the values associated with India's warrior (*kshatriya*) tradition. The Rajputs were able to stem the tide of Arab Islamic expansion in the eighth century. They and other Hindu rulers in North India maintained their independence until the establishment of the Delhi Sultanate.

The Moslem Invasions and the Delhi Sultanate

The first substantial and lasting Moslem presence in India came early in the eighth century when Arabs annexed Sind, the Indus delta region separated from the rest of India by desert. They incorporated their conquests into the Umayyad Empire and soon recognized Hindus as *dhimmis* (protected people, second-class subjects liable for special taxes, see p. 384). The Arabs were prevented from further expansion primarily by the Gujara-Pariharas (*ca.* 750–1027), who created an empire rivaling that of the Rashatrakutas in the South. However, Arab expansionism was only a minor episode in the broad sweep of Indian history. As ever, the main threat came from the northwest.

As we have seen, tough Hunna invaders from central Asia put an end to the Gupta Empire. Such incursions of warlike people from the northwest remained a major theme in Indian history, but with the coming of Islam a new element was added. Now the warrior peoples were imbued with a fierce sense of holy mission; they brought into India a world view that in many essential respects clashed with the native Hindu tradition. The Moslem faith in one God, one prophet, and one book contrasted with the complexity and tolerance of Hinduism, and a wide gulf

Nataraja Shiva as Lord of the Dance (Chola period, twelfth or thirteenth century).

The Rajput Code

A widow speaks to the page who witnessed her husband's death.

"Boy, tell me, ere I go, how bore himself my lord?"

"As a reaper of the harvest of battle. I followed his steps as a humble gleaner of his sword. On the bed of honor he spread a carpet of the slain, whereon, a barbarian his pillow, he sleeps ringed by his foes."

"Yet once again, boy, tell me how my lord bore himself?"

"Oh mother, who can tell his deeds? He left no foe to dread or to admire him."

She smiled farewell to the boy, and adding, "My lord will chide my delay," sprang into the flames.

As quoted in H. G. Rawlinson, India: A Short Cultural History *(New York: Appleton-Century, 1938), p. 202.*

existed between the hierarchical Hindu view of society and the Islamic belief that the ideal social order consisted of an essentially egalitarian community of believers. The interaction between Islam and Hinduism, often marred by misunderstandings, tension, and conflict, was to become a major theme in the history of the subcontinent.

By the eleventh century the region to India's northwest was under the control of warlike Turkic peoples who penetrated deep into India on raids from their base in modern Afghanistan. The most bloody and destructive of the raiding expeditions were those conducted by Mahmud of Ghazni (971–1030), who used the wealth looted from India to turn his own capital in eastern Afghanistan into a major center of Islamic culture.

For several centuries Turko-Afghan invaders were content to return to their home territory beyond the passes carrying their loot with them. But in the last quarter of the twelfth century a new group of Turko-Afghans appeared and in 1206 founded the Delhi Sultanate, which was to last for 320 years. The victory of Islam was accompanied by the wholesale de-

The Moslem Conquest of India
1192–1320

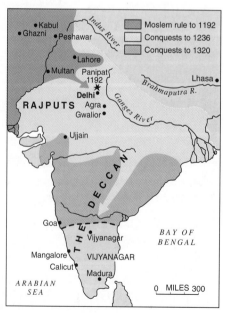

struction of Buddhist temples and centers of learning. Moslems had long resented Buddhism, which, like Islam, was a proselytizing religion. Buddhism had already suffered a serious blow in 751 when Islamic forces inflicted a severe defeat on a Chinese army on the Talas River near Samarkand, thereby hastening the end of the period when Buddhism flourished along the central Asia trade routes. Now the Turko-Afghans effectively destroyed a Buddhism already weakened by Hindu opposition and competition. The result was that the faith virtually disappeared in India until 1956 when a substantial number of Untouchables converted to Buddhism.

The Delhi Sultanate was founded by a Turkish slave-general, a Mamluk of the type prominent also in Egypt during this same period. The Mamluk dynasty (1206–90) was the first of five dynasties to rule in Delhi during the Sultanate. At this time, Turks, many of them slaves, and other foreigners filled key positions in the military and political establishments. In 1221, Chengis (Genghis) Khan, the great conqueror, led a Mongol expedition to the banks of the Indus but then withdrew from India. However, the Sultanate maintained a large army ready in case the Mongols returned. Military leaders were compensated for their service by grants of income from tax-exempt lands.

The Sultanate's decision to maintain a large army was only one of the ways the Mongols influenced the history of the subcontinent. Another was that, being cut off from central Asia, the rulers in Delhi necessarily concentrated their energies on India. Also, by destroying urban centers in central Asia and Iran, the Mongol conquests brought to India numerous refugee scholars, artists, and religious teachers who carried with them much of the high culture of their homelands. Notably, this included Persian as the prime literary language, which became the language of India's Moslem elite. But Persian influence was not confined to literature; it was apparent in architecture, textile design, and generally in court life and ceremony.

After the Mongol threat receded, the Sultanate's armies were occupied first in plundering expeditions and then in subduing much of the rest of India. The regime reached the height of its power under the second and third dynasties, the Khajli (1290–1320) and the Tughluq (1320–1414). It achieved its greatest territorial extent under the second Tughluq sultan, Muhammad (r. 1325–51), when most of India (except for Kashmir, the lower Indus Valley, and parts of the Rajput area) temporarily accepted Delhi's overlordship. However, the Sultanate had overextended itself and lacked the means to consolidate its conquests into a functioning empire. Nor did it have the power to compel the allegiance of distant tribute-paying vassals. Thus in 1336 the Hindu kingdom of Vijayanagar was founded, a state that remained the major southern power for two centuries and lasted for three. Like earlier Indian kings, the Vijayanagar rulers exercised a loose, ritualized overlordship over local chiefs and communities rather than presiding over a bureaucratic apparatus, as in China.

Elsewhere Moslem leaders also declared their independence. One of them proclaimed himself Sultan of the Deccan (South India) in 1347 and founded the Bahmini Dynasty, Vijayanagar's rival. It should be noted, however, that even though Vijayanagar appealed to Hinduism for its ideology, it regularly employed Moslems in its armies, just as Moslem states did not hesitate to employ Hindus.

A low point in the Sultanate's fortunes came in 1398 when Timur (Tamerlane) invaded India and sacked Delhi—the same Timur who checked the advance of the Ottoman Turks in the West. Under the fourth dynasty, the Sayyid (1414–51), Delhi remained weak, unable to prevent various regional rulers from establishing their own sultanates even in North India. The Sayyid dynasty was replaced by the Afghan Lodi (1451–1526), but it remained for a new group of foreign conquerors to match and surpass the earlier achievements of the Sultanate.

During the Sultanate period, Islam was firmly established in the Indian subcontinent, although the majority of Indians remained Hindus. The main agency for the spread of Islam was not

Moslem and Hindu in the Fourteenth Century

Ala-ud-Din [sultan of Delhi, 1296–1316] was a king who had no acquaintance with learning and never associated with the learned. He considered that policy and government were one thing and law another. "I am an unlettered man," he said, "but I have seen a great deal. Be assured that the Hindus will never become submissive and obedient until they are reduced to poverty. I have therefore given orders that just enough shall be left them of grain, milk, and curds from year to year, but that they must not accumulate hoards and property."

From the Moslem historian Barani, as quoted in H. G. Rawlinson, India: A Short Cultural History *(New York: Appleton-Century, 1938), p. 228.*

Tree of Life and Knowledge (southern India, Vijayanagar period, 1336–1546).

ca. 711	1206		1625	1857
Moslem Incursions and Indian Division	Delhi Sultanate		Mughal Empire	

the Sultanate and its military and civilian organs; nor was it the *ulama,* that is, "the class of state-supported judges, theologians, and preachers who were collectively responsible for upholding Islamic orthodoxy" in India as elsewhere in the Moslem world. Instead, the prime spreaders of Islam were Sufis, mystics not employed by the state. These men of religion belonged to various orders and varied widely in their methods and personalities: "Some of them wielded swords, others the pen, others a royal land grant, and still others a begging bowl. Some were introverted to the point of reclusive withdrawal, others extroverted to the point of militancy. Some were orthodox to the point of zealous puritanism, others unorthodox to the point of heresy."* This quotation, taken from a study of the Sufis in a single Indian state, suggests the adaptability and variety of Islam's holy men but also the dangers of overgeneralization.

*Richard M. Eaton, *Sufis of Bijapur 1300–1700* (Princeton: Princeton Univ. Press, 1978), p. 283.

A Portrait of Akbar by His Son

My father always associated with the learned of every creed and religion: especially the Pundits and the learned of India, and, although he was illiterate, so much became clear to him through constant intercourse with them, that no one knew him to be illiterate. . . . In his august personal appearance he was of middle height, but inclining to be tall; he was of the hue of wheat; his eyes and eyebrows were black and his complexion rather dark than fair; he was lion-bodied with a broad chest, and his hands and arms long. On the left side of his nose he had a fleshy mold, very agreeable in appearance, of the size of half a pea. . . . His august voice was very loud and in speaking and explaining had a peculiar richness.

Memoirs of Jahangir, trans. Rogers and Beveridge (London, 1909–14), pp. 33–34 as quoted in H. G. Rawlinson, India: A Short Cultural History (London: The Cresset Press, revised ed. 1952), pp. 317–18.

Many people came to Islam through peaceful conversion, not holy war; naturally many of the converts came from among those lowest in the Hindu social hierarchy. There was also a trend for Hindu devotionalism and Islamic mysticism to converge, as in the teachings of Kabir (1440–1518), a Moslem weaver, who asked, "If God be within the mosque, then to whom does this world belong?" He won many followers; his verses, written in the vernacular, drew on both Persian and Sanskrit to express themes derived from both traditions. Another syncretist was Nanak (1469–1538), the founder of Sikhism, who was born a Hindu but rejected caste and taught devotion to God. Under a succession of *gurus* (teachers) the Sikhs, spurred on by Mughal intolerance, later developed into a militant community in Nanak's home area, the Punjab (in the northern Indus Valley).

The Mughals

The Mughal empire was founded by Babur (1483–1530), but it was his grandson Akbar (1542–1605) who secured its future and constructed its institutional foundations. Babur and Akbar were Iranicized Turko-Mongols and as such continued certain policies of the Delhi Sultanate, including the furtherance of Persian culture. Akbar was unusual in marrying Rajput princesses—most of the Mughal emperors had Iranian consorts, including the lady buried in the world's most beautiful and perhaps most lavish mausoleum, the Taj Mahal. (Although designed by two Persian architects, this mid-seventeenth century building represents a blend of Persian and Indian elements.) Akbar's marriage policy was just one example of his general inclination toward religious tolerance and toward seeking to reconcile those he could not subdue by military force. The orthodoxy of his religious views has long been argued, but his sense of divine mission is apparent in his characterization of a king

The Mughal Empire   1605

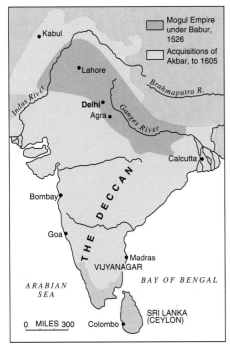

from turning into local power-holders, but it was hard on the people who actually worked the land because the holder of a *jagir* had no incentive to develop land he would soon lose. His interest was not in the well-being of the peasantry but in garnering the maximum revenue in the shortest possible time.

A substantial minority of townspeople were Moslem, but the great majority of peasants were Hindus as were the revenue collectors. Aside from paying their taxes, the villagers had little contact with

as "a light emanating from God, a ray from the world-illuminating sun." His good will toward Hindus was expressed not only in his own religious attitude but more concretely in his abolition of the tax levied on non-Moslems, and he further placated Hindus by forbidding the slaughter of cows.

Akbar divided the empire into provinces, and his government was conducted by *mansabdars.* These officials were holders of a *mansab,* a military rank defined in terms of the number of troops its hoider was obliged to supply. The *mansabdars* were supported by *jagirs,* assignments to collect revenue for the government as well as their salaries and expenses from designated lands. These lands were frequently scattered, subject to reassignment, and not hereditary. One reason for the Mughal success was that the emperors granted *jagirs* to, and thereby made allies of, a diverse elite including Rajputs and Afghans, Turkish and Iranian immigrants, South Indian Moslems, and prominent Hindus as well as Moslems from conquered regional states. The system was designed to prevent *mansabdars*

Akbar inspecting building operations of Fathpur Sikri (illumination from the Akbar-nama manuscript, *ca.* 1590).

the state; kinship and village groups remained dominant in their lives. Even in the cities, the state rarely interfered directly in people's lives, and various communities and groups enjoyed a substantial degree of autonomy. For example, when the Portuguese became the dominant seapower along India's western coast, the merchants of Gujarat in northwest India dealt with the Europeans quite independently of their sultan, who remained unconcerned as long as his own prerogatives were not involved. The land-oriented Mughal rulers were similarly indifferent.

The Mughal empire reached its greatest geographical extent under Aurangzeb (1657–1707), a controversial ruler known for his strict adherence to Islam. His reim-

position of the tax on nonbelievers was just one of the measures resented by Hindus. However, religious resentments were a less-serious problem than the developing crisis in the state's political economy. Most damaging was a growth in the number of *mansabdars* far in excess of the availability of *jagirs* with which to reward them. Pressures on the peasantry increased and there was rural unrest, but the discontent of the elite proved most dangerous to the regime. The succession after Aurangzeb of weak, uninspiring men to the throne and a general decline in administrative efficiency also placed strains on the loyalty of the empire's servants, undermining Mughal military power at a time when it was increasingly challenged

The Taj Mahal (seventeenth century).

by Marathas from India's west and by Afghans and Iranians from beyond the passes. In 1739 Nadir Shah (r. 1736–47), who ruled Iran, became the last foreign conqueror to enter India, devastate the North, and sack Delhi. Although after that a titular emperor remained in Delhi, actual power was in the hands of local potentates.

In 1765 one of these local rulers granted the British East Indian Company the right to collect revenue in his domains, and eventually the British became heirs to the Mughal empire. Up to this time, Europeans accepted and worked within the Mughal system. Although they had earlier gained control of the seas and thereby influenced India's trade and economy, and although individual Europeans helped to introduce new methods of warfare into India, they had remained largely peripheral to the mainstream of the subcontinent's history.

SOUTHEAST ASIA

Much of the diffusion of Indian culture described earlier (see Chapter 6) took place during the period discussed in this chapter. Other major events, such as the decline of Cambodia and changes affecting states of interior Java, were largely determined by internal developments. But Southeast Asia was also affected by Mongol expansionism and by the spread of Islam.

Although Mongol ambitions extended to Southeast Asia and Khublai Khan attempted to force Southeast Asian states into submission, the Mongols did not establish themselves in the area. The giant armada that Khublai sent against Java—where his troops landed in 1293—and the armies that he dispatched into what is modern Vietnam—where Hanoi was occupied three times—affected the local balance of power but did not drastically alter the course of history. Further west, the Mongols, after mastering the techniques of elephant warfare, defeated and conquered Pagan (1287). Yet, their efforts to control Burma failed, and old patterns of mutual dependence as well as conflict between the Burmese monarchs and the Buddhist monastic community continued to dominate Burmese history. The more immediate aftermath of the Mongol irruption was to leave Burma divided. This along with the collapse of Angkor, the other great mainland empire, opened the way for the creation of numerous small states and the emergence to new prominence of Thai rulers, although their states remained fragile because they were held together only by the personal relationship between king and elite.

In contrast to the fleeting impact of the Mongols, Islam became a permanent force in the Malay Peninsula and maritime Southeast Asia. The first Moslems in the area were doubtlessly traders, and Islam generally spread along the trade routes. Its fortunes were greatly increased by the growth of Malacca, whose ruler is said to have converted to Islam in 1414. Malacca, which commands the straits of the same name, became a great center of trade linking Sumatra, Java, and most of the other islands of modern Indonesia to far-off China, India, and ports of the Red Sea. The city participated in a giant international commercial network whose other major center was Gujarat, birthplace of many of the Moslem missionaries who came to Southeast Asia. Islam served as a link between Malacca and small states along the coasts of Sumatra and Java as well as ports in India and points west. Legends from Java, unlike those from Malaya, suggest a

Europeans Arrive in Malacca

After a while there came a ship of the Franks from Goa trading to Malaka; and the Franks perceived how prosperous and well populated the port was. The people of Malaka for their part came crowding to see what the Franks looked like; and they were all astonished and said, "These are white Bengalis!" Around each Frank there would be a crowd of Malays, some of them twisting his beard, some of them fingering his head, some taking off his hat, some grasping his hand. . . .

From Sejarah Melayu or Malay Annals, *trans. by C. C. Brown (New York: Oxford Univ. Press, 1970), p. 151.*

gradual process of conversion to Islam. Generally the diffusion of Islam was a gradual, uneven process that continued for many centuries and still continues.

In this connection, it is well to bear in mind the great vitality and powers of expansion exhibited by Islam during the fifteenth century, the era of the fall of Constantinople, at the other end of Asia, in 1453. Europe's rise to global supremacy came later, but the vanguard of European expansionism, the Portuguese, did arrive in Southeast Asia at the beginning of the sixteenth century. They seized Malacca in 1511 but were unable to maintain its commercial prominence. Instead, the trade was dispersed to the benefit of, among others, the sultanates of Johor at the tip of the Malay Peninsula and of Aceh on Sumatra. The first Dutch expedition reached the East Indies in 1596; a precursor to a much more ambitious effort than that of the Portuguese, it initiated a new age in the history of the islands that became modern Indonesia.

THE COSMOPOLITAN CIVILIZATION OF CHINA

The Tang Dynasty, 618–907

China was reunified in 589 by the Sui dynasty, which laid the foundations on which the Tang (T'ang) built one of China's most illustrious dynasties. Under the Tang, Chinese power once again extended to the Pamirs, and the influence of Chinese culture profoundly affected distant Japan. Within China, the south was more fully integrated into the society because the rich ricelands of the lower Yangzte River were now linked to the capital in the north by the Grand Canal built by the Sui.

The central government was organized into six ministries: Personnel, Revenue, Rites, War, Justice, and Public Works. These ministries reflected the range of government concerns and were to be retained by subsequent regimes into the twentieth century. Staffing the government were officials of aristocratic background. Most officials entered the civil

service through family connections even though the Sui initiated a government examination system, which the Tang continued. Indeed, the Tang was the last great age for the hereditary high aristocracy.

The magnificence of the Tang was well expressed in its capital, Changan (Ch'ang-an, modern Xian or Sian). Encompassing about thirty square miles, it was the largest planned city built anywhere in the world. Its roughly one million inhabitants also made it the most populous city in the world in its day; another million people lived in the area outside its walls. In accord with tradition, Changan was oriented so that both the city and the imperial palace faced south. Leading up to the palace and the government complex was an avenue 500 feet wide, well designed to impress envoys from lesser lands with the might and grandeur of the Chinese empire. The people of the city lived in rectangular wards, each a self-contained unit surrounded by walls, with entry provided through a gate that was closed each night.

Tang culture was doubly cosmopolitan: first, in that China was open to cultural influences from India and the distant west; second, in that China itself was the cultural model for the other settled societies of East Asia. Both aspects were reflected in the numerous foreigners in Changan. Some were students, including approximately 8,000 Koreans said to have been in Changan in 640. Other foreigners were engaged in commerce, coming from such distant lands as India, Iran, Syria, and Arabia. At Changan's West Market exotic foods and beverages were on sale, and one could watch performances of foreign acrobats, magicians, and actors. Stylish Tang ladies sported foreign coiffures, while painters and potters enjoyed rendering the outlandish features of the "barbarians" from distant lands. In keeping with the robust and cosmopolitan spirit of the age, a favorite pastime of its aristocratic ladies and gentlemen was polo, a game that originated in Persia. Women's participation in such athletic activities is worth emphasis in light of the very different ethos that prevailed later.

Changan was a religious as well as political center. Manichean, Nestorian,

Seated court lady, sculpture of the Tang period (618–906).

Stone relief of a horse and groom from the tomb of a Tang emperor.

Tang guardian lion of marble and polychrome (*ca.* 618–906).

and Zoroastrian temples testified to Tang tolerance, but their congregations were largely foreign. The opposite was true of the many Daoist and even more numerous Buddhist establishments. This was the golden age of Buddhism in China. Just as its pagodas dominated the capital's skyline, the Buddhist faith dominated the intellectual and spiritual horizon.

In the countryside, Buddhist temples performed important economic functions by operating mills and oil presses, maintaining vaults for self-deposits, and performing other banking services, including pawnbroking. The temples also held much land, and they profited from their connections with wealthy patrons who sought to evade taxation by registering land under a temple name. Some temples provided medical care; others entertainment. Architecture flourished, and Chinese Buddhist

sculpture reached a classical highpoint. At their best, Tang sculptures blend Indian delight in the corporality of mass with a Chinese sense of essentially linear rhythm.

The Tang was also the classic age of Chinese poetry, producing a number of excellent poets, including the two who came to be admired as China's best, Li Bo (Li Po, 701–63) and Du Fu (Tu Fu, 712–70). Li Bo was a free spirit who preferred to compose verse in a free style of his own rhythmic and verbal patterns. One of his favorite themes was wine, and there is even a story, most likely spurious, that on a nocturnal drinking expedition on a lake he fell into the water while trying to fish out the moon and drowned. Du Fu, in contrast, was particularly effective in a style of verse governed by elaborate rules of tone and rhythm as well as verbal parallelism. He wrote on many themes but is most admired for his social conscience and compassion. Some of his most moving poems describe the suffering and hardships of ordinary people. He could be severe in his political and social commentary:

> Inside the red gates wine and meat go
>   bad;
> On the roads are bones of men who
>   died of cold.*

*Quoted in A. R. Davis, *Tu Fu* (New York: Twain, 1971), p. 46.

An example of Chinese calligraphy. This stone rubbing was made from an inscription in the Regular Style by Ouyang Xun, a scholar and calligrapher of the Tang period.

安
風
無
欝
炎
之

體
有
金
蒸
景
至

涼
徐
淒
微
嶸
尤

渠
佳
動
氣
侍
流

These lines are from a long poem Du Fu wrote shortly before the dynasty was shaken and almost destroyed by the rebellion of An Lushan, a general stationed in the Northeast. The rebellion began in 755—only four years after defeat of a Tang army on the banks of the Talas River opened Central Asia to Islam—and it lasted until 763. Although the dynasty rallied after the defeat of An Lushan and made some important reforms, the general tendency was for regional military governors to assert their independence. Secular culture continued to flourish, but Emperor Wuzong (Wu-tsung 840–46), beset by financial problems, was unable to resist the temptation of the wealthy Buddhist establishment. In the resulting persecution, monastic lands and wealth were confiscated, monks and nuns returned to lay life, and Buddhist economic power was broken. The government did not concern itself with questions of belief, and the anti-Buddhist policy was promptly reversed by Wuzong's successor, but great damage had been done.

During its last fifty years the dynasty was beset by factionalism and growing eunuch power at court, mistrust between officials in the capital and those in the field, mismanagement, corruption, and incompetence. Bandit gangs, refuges for the desperately poor and dislocated, increased in number, size, and ambition. Forming themselves into confederations, they progressed from raiding to rebellion. Power, whether bandit or "legitimate," went to the strong and the ruthless. Even though the dynasty made occasional gains, each rally was followed by further decline. In the end, Changan was ruined. The city, which the first Han emperor had made his capital over a thousand years earlier, would never again be China's seat of power.

The Song Dynasty, 960–1279

China was reunited by the Song (Sung). This dynasty did not match the Tang in military power or geographic extent. Indeed, after 1127 North China was lost to the alien Jurchen Jin (Chin) state but continued in the south as the Southern Song.

581	618		906		1127	1234	1368		1644
Sui Dynasty	Tang Dynasty		Disunity	Song Dynasty	Jin Empire		Mongol Empire	Ming Dynasty	

960   1279

However, what makes the Song of crucial importance is the emergence of some of the basic features of late imperial China. Major developments included the formation of new elites in place of the old hereditary aristocracy, dramatic economic growth, and the creation of a new intellectual synthesis.

The turbulence that accompanied the decline and fall of the Tang destroyed the old aristocratic families and opened the way for new men who based their prestige on literary learning, their power and status on office holding, and their wealth on land ownership. Although these attributes did not necessarily overlap, when all three were present they reinforced each other: wealth enabled a family to educate one or more sons; education was the key to office; and office provided opportunities for the acquisition and retention of wealth.

After the loss of the North in the twelfth century, the tendency was for elite families to concentrate on strengthening their local roots by assuming leadership in local matters and forming marriage ties with similar families. To distinguish the new elite from the old aristocracy, scholars often refer to them as "the gentry." A further and vital distinction is between the office-holding upper gentry and the local gentry families, whose leaders served as intermediaries between their communities and the state.

The civil service examination system now came into its own as the preferred path to office. It linked the local and central elites, did much to validate the state's claim to meritocracy, and bestowed personal prestige on those able and fortunate enough to win a degree. The examinations were open to all men, excluding only a small minority such as the sons of criminals and the like, but, even though printing reduced the price of books, most candidates came from families of some

means or status. Structurally the system provided for an orderly progression through a series of written tests (three in the Song, more later). These began at the local level, included an examination in the capital, and culminated in a palace examination held under the emperor's personal auspices. The government went to great lengths to secure impartiality; papers were identified by number and copied by clerks before being submitted to the readers, who were thereby prevented from identifying the author of a paper through his calligraphy. For centuries, the battle of wits between would-be cheaters and the authorities was pursued with great ingenuity on both sides. Despite occasional scandals, the system enjoyed a reputation for honesty.

In the absence of the old aristocratic counterweight, the throne gained in power, but Song officials were by no means faceless bureaucrats. They had their own moral code and political views. Bureaucratic politics, however, tended toward factionalism. Factions could consist of men who agreed on policy matters, but

The Song and Jin Empires
TWELFTH CENTURY

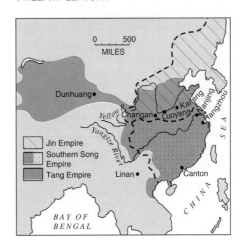

Detail from *Clearing Autumn Skies over Mountains and Valleys,* Song landscape scroll attributed to Guo Xi (Kuo Hsi, ca. 1020–90).

Detail of a handscroll showing scenes of daily life in the Southern Song dynasty (thirteenth century).

they were likely to form around personal relationships and temporary alliances. The ultimate power of decision rested with the emperors, who usually ruled by manipulating rather than intimidating their officials. The most outstanding political figure of the Song was not an emperor, but Wang Anshi (Wang An-shih, 1021–86), an official whose vision of integrating state and society remains controversial. Many of his measures dealt with fiscal and economic matters. He intended to help the small farmer, for instance, by establishing a program of state farm loans. Other reforms dealt with military and personnel problems. Some of his measures involved an increased use of money and thus represented a response to broader economic trends. However, his program ran into strong opposition, and Wang lost office seven years after he had initiated the reforms.

The increased use of money, including the first appearance of paper money, was but one aspect of impressive economic growth. This included progress in papermaking, book production, ceramics, tea processing, shipbuilding, and

a spectacular advance in the production of coal and iron. Coal and iron were mined in North China in an arc from southern Hebei (Hopei) to northern Jiangsu (Kiangsu). Iron was also carbonized to make steel for weapons, drilling bits for digging wells, and chains for supporting suspension bridges.

Because coal and iron were found in the north, production declined drastically when North China was lost to the Jin, but advances in agriculture benefited the South. Yields were increased by the use of improved tools, advances in water control, wider application of fertilizers, and introduction of new strains of rice, most notably an early-ripening variety native to central Vietnam. In the southeast it became common for a rice paddy to produce two crops a year, either two harvests of rice or one of rice followed by a crop of wheat or beans.

With increased production commerce flourished. Large ocean-going ships were built to carry several hundred passengers. They were navigated by compass, steered by an axial rudder, protected by watertight bulkheads, and armed with small rockets. After the loss of the North, the government derived considerable revenue from foreign trade, which it encouraged by maintaining harbors and canals, building

breakwaters, erecting beacons, operating warehouses, and even setting up hotels. The government encouraged ceramics export, and the discovery of Song shards not only throughout South and Southeast Asia but also in the Middle East and along the east coast of Africa attests to the wide popularity of the Song product.

Cities flourished; foremost among them was Hangzhou (Hangchow), the capital after the fall of the North. Its merchants, organized in guilds, offered their customers all kinds of products ranging from the staples of life to exotic perfumes and fine jewelry. Like the earlier Song capital in the North and unlike Changan of the Tang, Hangzhou grew haphazardly and featured all the attractions of a lively and thriving center of culture and entertainment, as well as the grimmer aspects of urban life—fire and crime. Hangzhou seems to have merited the praise it received from the cosmopolitan Venetian Marco Polo. Even though he saw the city late in the thirteenth century when it was no longer the capital, he described it as, "without doubt the finest and most splendid city in the world."

Song intellectual and artistic life was varied and lively. This was the classic age of landscape painting. Most influential was a revival of Confucianism that took

Porcelain winepot of the Song dynasty.

many forms. It inspired reformers like Wang Anshi, led to a revival of classical scholarship, and stimulated new achievements in historical studies and philosophical thought. The new Confucianism was at once a creed that gave meaning to the life of the individual, an ideology supporting state and society, and a philosophy that provided a convincing framework for

understanding the world. This constellation of values and ideas, often called Neo-Confucianism in the West, was an organic system in which each aspect reinforced the others. It is called Neo-Confucianism to distinguish it from earlier forms of Confucianism, but its formulators and practitioners thought of themselves simply as Confucians. More than that, they believed that they had retrieved the true meaning of the tradition, lost since Mencius. The most influential Neo-Confucian was Zhu Xi (Chu Hsi, 1130–1200) and his most influential writings were his commentaries on the *Four Books: The Analects, The Mencius,* plus *The Great Learning* and *The Doctrine of the Mean,* two chapters of the *Record of Rites* singled out by Zhu Xi.

Although influenced by Daoism and Buddhism, the Neo-Confucians rejected the two rival doctrines as fundamentally antisocial and immoral in advocating withdrawal from society and seeking purely personal (and therefore selfish) salvation. To Confucians social values were real and compelling, and the old concept of *ren* (*jen,* humaneness) received new emphasis.

Associated with Song Neo-Confucianism was an emphasis on moral seriousness and a moralism that made heavy demands on men and women. Moralists insisted that widows should not remarry and honored the woman who remained faithful to her betrothed even though he died before the marriage could take place. Yet, we must not exaggerate the influence of theorists on people's actual conduct. In practice, even among the elite (though not among royalty), most widows did remarry.

Also traceable to the Song is the beginning of foot-binding, a procedure that caused agonizing pain. Tiny feet were thought to enhance a young woman's attractiveness even as they deterred her from straying into mischief. To restrict foot growth, feet were wrapped tightly in bandages so that over time, the four toes of each foot were bent into the sole, and sole and heel were brought as close together as possible. Although foot-binding was later practiced widely, it was apparently uncommon during the Song and was never part of the Confucian social pro-

The Neo-Confucian Creed

Heaven is my father and Earth is my mother, and even such a small creature as I find an intimate place in their midst.

Therefore that which fills the universe I regard as my body and that which directs the universe I consider as my nature.

All people are my brothers and sisters, and all things are my companions.

Opening lines of "The Western Inscription" by Zhang Zsai (1020–77), from A Source Book in Chinese Philosophy, *trans. and compiled by Wing-tsit Chan (Princeton, N.J.: Princeton Univ. Press, 1963), p. 497.*

710	784		1185	1333	1573	1868
Nara Period	Heian Period		Kamakura Shogunate	Ashikaga Shogunate	Tokugawa Shogunate	

gram. The dynasty's leading female poet, Li Qingzhao (Li Ch'ing-chao, 1094–*ca.* 1152), never mentioned it.

The tone of Song civilization was profoundly civilian, but for many years it sustained itself against external threats by maintaining a large, well-equipped, if not always effective, army. The Song also entered into treaties with neighboring states that sometimes entailed payments and furthered its own interests by playing these states off against each other. After it lost the North, it survived in the South protected in part by its naval supremacy and by the difficulty northern cavalry had operating in the South with its paddies and waterways. Even after the Mongols conquered North China in 1234, the Song held out another 45 years before succumbing to those formidable world conquerors.

The Mongol Yuan Dynasty, 1279–1368

Even before Khubilai Khan (r. 1260–94) completed the conquest of China, he transferred his capital from Mongolia to Peking (Beijing), adopted the Chinese name "Yuan" for his state, and instituted Chinese court ceremonial. Thus he was careful to give at least an appearance of ruling in the Chinese manner. But his ambitions were not limited to China; we already noted his expeditions to Southeast Asia and to these must be added naval expeditions to Japan. To the west, he maintained control of Mongolia but was forced to give up an ambition to control central Asia. As a result, the Yuan was essentially a Mongol regime in China, not the Chinese part of a wider Mongol empire.

To prevent dependence on Chinese officials, the Mongols made a point of employing foreigners, mostly central Asians, though the most famous is Marco Polo. The Mongols accorded highest status to

Two Song ladies. Cave 165, Maijishan, Gansu.

Mongols. Next came Mongol allies, including central Asians and men from Southwest Asia, such as Turks, Persians, and Syrians. The third status group included inhabitants of North China, the native Chinese or descendants of other groups such as the Jurchen. At the bottom were the southerners who had resisted the Mongols longest and continued to be regarded with suspicion. This fourfold division of society affected recruitment and appointment of officials, conduct of legal cases, and taxation.

The Yuan generally accorded military officials preference over civilians, and the provinces had a great deal of autonomy. Because the Mongols were slow to reinstitute the examination system and to patronize scholarly learning, men who in other periods would have become scholars turned to other occupations such as medicine, fortune-telling, and the theater. It is no accident that this was the classic age of Chinese drama. Painting also flourished; the idea that a painting reveals the character of the man who created it existed in the Song, but it was prevalent

under the Yuan and inspired work in a great variety of styles. Even though China was once again open to foreign influences and hospitable to travelers from afar, this had no appreciable impact on the world of the scholar-painter, nor did the writings of Marco Polo and his successors show any awareness, let alone appreciation, of the art of the Chinese literati. Although there was a Catholic archbishop in Beijing and relations across the great Eurasian land mass were often cordial, these relations had a low priority on both sides of the world, for the distances were enormous and both Europe and China faced more immediate challenges and opportunities closer to home.

The Ming Dynasty, 1368–1644

The declining years of the Yuan saw the emergence of regional power centers and popular rebellion. One leader of rebellion, Zhu Yuanzhang (Chu Yuan-chang, r. 1368–98), emerged victorious and founded the Ming dynasty. He was a harsh and vigorous autocrat who personally decided all significant matters and even some not so significant. During the later days of the Ming, too, the effectiveness as well as the tone of government was to a large degree determined by the character of the emperors and their devotion to the work of government. Ming government thus ranged from the energetic efficiency of the first two emperors to the laxity of some of the Late Ming rulers, one of whom did not hold an audience for more than 25 years.

Meanwhile, the local gentry presided over local society that continued to move to its own rhythms. Prominent gentry lineages maintained cohesion by compiling lineage genealogies, maintaining ancestral halls and graveyards, conducting ceremonial sacrifices to lineage ancestors, and maintaining general guides for the conduct of lineage members as well as formal lineage rules. A penalty for severe infractions of these rules was expulsion.

The Ming was generally a period of economic growth and considerable prosperity. It was also capable of strong military assertiveness; from 1405 to 1433,

---

The Complaints of the Ming Founding Emperor

In the morning I punish a few; by evening others commit the same crimes. I punish these in the evening and by the next morning again there are violations. Although the corpses of the first have not been removed, already others follow in their path. The harsher the punishment, the more the violations. Day and night I cannot rest. This is a situation which cannot be helped. If I enact lenient punishments, these persons will engage in still more evil practices. Then how could the people outside the government lead peaceful lives?

What a difficult situation this is! If I punish these persons, I am regarded as a tyrant. If I am lenient toward them, the law becomes ineffective, order deteriorates, and people deem me an incapable ruler. All these opinions can be discerned in the various records and memorials. To be a ruler is indeed difficult.

Proclamation of the Hong Wu Emperor from Patricia B. Ebery, Chinese Civilization and Society: A Sourcebook *(New York: The Free Press, 1981), p. 125.*

The Ming Empire
Fourteenth to Seventeenth Centuries

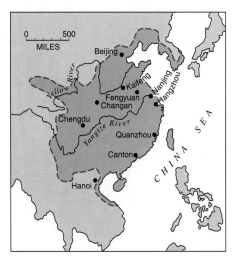

ished. Wang Yangming (1472–1529) stands second only to Zhu Xi in influence and importance. He insisted on the importance of inwardness and is also famed for his doctrine of the unity of knowledge and action. For Wang, knowing and acting were not only inseparable, they were two dimensions of a single process.

The Late Ming was an exciting time intellectually and artistically, but it was also a period of political decay that took a heavy toll in government efficiency and finally led to its collapse. It was ended by popular uprisings, but the real heirs of the dynasty were not Chinese rebels but Manchu leaders in the area northeast of

Porcelain jar of the Ming period showing ladies playing a game of *weiqi* (*go* in Japanese).

seven great maritime expeditions, commanded by a Moslem eunuch, were launched to Southeast Asia but also reached the Indian Ocean, Arabia, and the east coast of Africa. These expeditions illustrate Chinese strength in the fifteenth century, but, because they were an economic drain, they were discontinued, leaving the Europeans to take the lead in world navigation and discovery.

Printing, which had been invented in the Late Tang and spread during the Song, continued to expand in the Ming, along with literacy. Bookshops did a brisk business; among their best sellers were collections of model examination papers used by candidates to cram for their tests. But they also sold encyclopedias, colored prints, novels, and collections of short stories. There were also guides explaining the classics in simple language and books of moral instruction. Most prized by those who love Chinese literature are the Ming novels. Despite their literary excellence, they did not win respectability until the twentieth century. In traditional China, reading a novel was a surreptitious pleasure, something students did when their teacher was not looking—or vice versa.

This period also made notable contributions to drama, painting, and ceramics, and Neo-Confucian thought also flour-

China who were constructing a state in the Chinese manner. They established China's last dynasty, the Qing (Ch'ing, 1644–1911), which sought and won legitimization by ruling in a Chinese manner and continuing many Ming institutions while preserving special privileges for the Manchu elite.

Both the Ming and the Qing were much more concerned with China's Inner Asian frontiers, home of the Mongol and other nomadic invaders, than they were with European maritime expansionism. Indeed, under the Qing China reached its greatest territorial extent. As elsewhere, the first Europeans to arrive in Chinese waters were the Portuguese, whom the Chinese kept at arm's length because they could not drive them off. In 1557 they were allowed to use Macao in return for an annual payment. Of more interest to the Chinese court and officials were Jesuit missionaries who brought with them European science and technology as well as religion. By demonstrating the superiority of their astronomical predictions, they managed to displace Moslem and Chinese experts and established themselves in the Bureau of Astronomy, an important and prestigious office. The Jesuits even made some notable converts and were not seriously affected by the change of dynasties. However, they were there on Chinese terms, and the mission petered out in the middle of the eighteenth century when an impasse developed between the Qing emperor and the pope.

JAPAN

A major theme in Japanese history is the interplay between native and imported elements. In Japan's early history, culminating in the Nara Period (710–84), Chinese influence was enormous. Nara itself, Japan's first capital, was a miniature Changan; the court and political structure were modeled on those of China; writing, Buddhism, and Confucian moral values were among the Chinese imports. Yet, Japan never became just a smaller China. Here geography helped, for, while close

enough to the continent to receive its influences, Japan was far enough away not to be dominated by it. Other factors, too, made for the integrity of Japanese culture, including a language completely different from and unrelated to Chinese, a strong native animistic religion (Shinto), and a special aesthetic tradition. Furthermore, even during the Nara period, the Japanese state and society had their own character.

One difference between Japan and China was the role of the emperor. The Japanese emperor, unlike his Chinese counterpart, had an irrevocable sacred mandate based on divine descent. Thus, the Mencian idea that the mandate could be lost was disregarded. Political change in Japan took the form, not of deposing the emperor, but of controlling him; after the Nara period the emperor retained his religious aura and his powers of legitimization without any real political authority. In somewhat similar fashion, descent remained a major source of status in Japan.

The Nara period was followed by the Heian period (794–1185), when the capital was established in Kyoto and many Chinese imports were modified or discarded. Now, although Chinese remained the official written language, Japanese was written without depending solely on Chinese characters to render Japanese sounds. Instead, linguistic elements without Chinese equivalents were written in a syllabary *(kana)* with Chinese characters retained for nouns and the stems of verbs and adjectives to avoid confusion between homonyms. Art and architecture also departed from the international Tang style of the Nara period and became more Japanese in their concern with the texture of natural materials, especially wood, and a general penchant for asymmetry. The political system also contained a certain asymmetry as, behind the facade of imperial institutions, power came to rest in the hands of those (primarily the Fujiwara family) who held extensive rights in private, tax-exempt estates free from government interference.

This period was famed for its aristocratic culture when noble gentlemen and

The Silver Pavilion at Kyoto combines both Japanese and Chinese elements.

ladies devoted their lives to beauty and love. One product of this culture was the world's first major psychological novel, *The Tale of Genji,* written by Lady Murasaki. Prince Genji had perfect taste, wrote a beautiful hand, was exquisitely graceful, was ever sensitive to the beauty and sadness of nature's changing moods, and was responsive to the delicate emotions of his many ladies. What he lacked were the martial virtues of the warrior.

The Kamakura (1185–1333) and Ashikaga (1336–1573) Shogunates

During the Kamakura period the warrior class emerged and gradually occupied center stage. Although there had earlier been a provincial warrior aristocracy, these men had been willing to serve civilian masters until the Heian system broke down and warriors were called in to the capital to help settle a political dispute.

After some years of turmoil, a peculiarly Japanese institution emerged: the shogunate. The shogun derived his military power from the loyalty of vassals in an essentially feudal system but received his title and legitimacy from the emperor. For a time, the shogunate honored the economic rights of the old Kyoto establishment, but the balance of power now shifted to the military. In theory, the shogun was subordinate to the emperor but in practice the shogun had the upper hand.

The first shogunate got its name from Kamakura, a village in eastern Japan far away from the imperial court in Kyoto. The choice to keep warriors away from the charms of the imperial capital was a deliberate attempt to preserve the values of the warrior: valor, manly pride, vigor, and undying loyalty. Yet, such loyalty had to be rewarded. This was easily accomplished when the shogunate was fighting recalcitrant Japanese whose lands could be seized and reassigned. But there were no such spoils when the Mongols were defeated in 1271 and 1284. Worse still was the shogunate's inability to reward the forces it maintained for many years in anticipation of a third Mongol attack that never came.

An attempt at imperial restoration followed the collapse of the Kamakura shogunate, but its real successor was the shogunate established by the Ashikaga family in Kyoto. In many respects, particularly in culture, the ensuing period represented a fusion of the aristocratic culture of the capital and the traditions of the samurai (the Japanese term for *warrior*). A great cultural flowering occurred in this age of Nō drama, of tea masters and Zen aesthetics, of excellent pottery, of the classic Japanese garden, and of fine architecture drawing on Song as well as on native Japanese forms. However, politically the Ashikaga period degenerated into a century of warfare (1467–1573) followed by a shorter period (1573–1600) of unification and ended with the establishment of the last and strongest shogunate.

Interior of a house in Yoshiwara during the Tokugawa period (eighteenth-century woodcut print).

The Tokugawa Shogunate, 1600–1868

Under the Tokugawa the shogunate was once more separated from the imperial court in Kyoto. The shogun's capital was Edo, modern Tokyo. There, the shogunate's officials kept a close watch over regional lords who were burdened with new obligations—including an obligation to spend alternate years in Edo and leave wives and children behind as hostages when they did go back to their domains. Yet, within these domains the local lords were free to pursue their own administrative and economic policies.

A number of Tokugawa policies were meant to ensure a stable future. Thus a freezing of class lines drew a clear line between samurai and commoners. The most visible sign of samurai privilege was the exclusive right to wear a sword, yet in a time of peace his duties were largely civilian. Accordingly, the samurai were sent to school to attain at least a degree of Chinese learning, and the shogunate patronized Neo-Confucianism as a philosophy appropriate for the new age.

Intent on stability, the Tokugawa shogunate was not about to tolerate interference from abroad. At first, Portuguese ships and Jesuit missionaries had been warmly received in Japan, but this changed as Japanese leaders became aware not only of the dangers of European expansionism—as exemplified by the Spanish seizure of the Philippines—but also of the subversive potential of foreign influence. In 1606 Christianity was declared illegal, and in 1614 there was a serious campaign to expel missionaries. Many of the 300,000 Japanese Christians suffered grievously under Tokugawa persecution. In 1637–38 a rebellion in Shimabara, near Nagasaki, was fought under Christian slogans against a lord who combined merciless taxation with cruel religious suppression. Furthermore, trade as well as Christianity was seen as potentially subversive because it would benefit the coastal lords. Consequently, the Tokugawa prohibited not only the foreign religion but expelled all foreigners from the country and only allowed the Dutch to send an annual vessel to a tiny artificial island in Nagasaki harbor. Moreover, Japanese were prohibited from traveling abroad.

In the long run, of course, the Tokugawa shogunate did not achieve the stability envisioned by its architects. They, no more than anyone else, could stop change. Indeed, their very success in ensuring peace and tranquility led to unprecedented economic growth. Cities such as Edo and Osaka grew and developed their own distinct urban culture. An increased use of money and a new economy baffled the samurai and undermined the social and political order. By the middle of the nineteenth century, many felt that Japan was ripe for change.

However, in the seventeenth century it would have taken superhuman clairvoyance for a statesman in Japan, China, or India to realize that European civilization represented anything but a minor problem. In all three countries, leaders could look back on traditions that had withstood the test of time and contemplate the future with confidence. Little could they know that the future was to bring radically new challenges.

Suggestions for Further Reading

General

For a comparative perspective, see E. L. Farmer et al., *Comparative History of Civilizations in Asia,* 2 vols. (1977, 1986). Also see the general works suggested for Chapter 6.

India

The New Cambridge History of India promises to be a major resource. It begins with "The Mughals and Their Contemporaries" and will consist of eight volumes, two of which have been published to date: M. N. Pearson, *The Portuguese in India* (1987), and Burton Stein, *Vijayanagara* (1989). Also by Stein is *Peasant, State, and Society in Medieval South India* (1980), a major advanced analytical study. Two highly regarded books

deal with Islam in India: Aziz Ahmad, *Studies in Islamic Culture in the Indian Environment* (1964), and Sheikh Mohamad Ikram, *Muslim Civilization in India* (1964). A more specialized study is R. M. Eaton, *Sufis of Bijapur 1300–1700: Social Roles of Sufis in Medieval India* (1978). P. Spear, "The Mughul Mansabdari System," in E. Leach and S. N. Mukherjee, *Elites in South Asia* (1970), is a concise account of that complicated system.

Southeast Asia

D. G. E. Hall, *A History of South East Asia,* 4th ed. (1981), remains authoritative. Anthony Reid, *Southeast Asia in the Age of Commerce, 1450–1680.* Vol. I: *The Lands Below the Wind* (1988), treats the region as a single cultural zone. It conveys the texture of life and discusses the influence of Islam and Christianity. The first volume of *The Cambridge History of South East Asia* is scheduled for publication in 1993. C. Geertz, *Negara: The State in Nineteenth-Century Bali* (1980), is helpful in thinking about earlier Indianized states of Southeast Asia.

R. Winstead, *The Malays: A Cultural History* (1950), is a standard treatment. *Sejarah Melayu 'Malay Annals'* (1970), trans. C. C. Brown, is sometimes tedious but includes passages of great charm. D. K. Wyatt, *Thailand: A Short History* (1984), is definitive. M. Aung-Thwin, *Pagan: The Origins of Modern Burma* (1985), is "must" reading for the history of that country. Robert H. Taylor, *The State in Burma* (1987), devotes 65 pages to the precolonial state. M. C. Ricklefs, *A History of Modern Indonesia* c. *1300 to the Present (1980),* is a solid account.

China

Two volumes of *The Cambridge History of China* deal with the periods discussed in this chapter, Vol. 3, Part 1 (1979) on the Sui and Tang, and Vol. 7, Part 1 (1988) on the Ming. Also recommended are A. F. Wright, *The Sui Dynasty* (1978), and A. F. Wright and Denis Twitchett, *Perspectives on the T'ang* (1973). E. O. Reischauer, *Ennin's Travels in T'ang China* (1955), is an account by a Japanese monk. A Cooper, *Li Po and Tu Fu* (1973), is a fine introduction to these great poets.

Much scholarly attention has been paid to the Song in recent years. Among the good books on major facets of that period are J. W. Chaffee, *The Thorny Gates of Learning in Sung China* (1985); P. B. Ebrey, *Family and Property in Sung China: Yüan Ts'ai's Precepts for Social Life;* R. P. Hymes, *Statesmen and Gentlemen: The Elite of Fu-chou, Chiang-hsi in Southern Sung* (1986); and Paul J. Smith, *Taxing Heaven's Storehouse: Horses, Bureaucrats, & the Destruction of the Sichuan Tea Industry* (1991).

For the Yuan, see M. Rossabi, *Khubilai Khan: His Life and Times* (1987); J. W. Dardess, *Conquerors and Confucians:*

Aspects of Political Change in Late Yüan China (1973); and J. D. Langlois, ed., *China under Mongol Rule* (1981). C. O. Hucker, *The Traditional Chinese State in Ming Times* (1961), is succinct and definitive. Arthur Waldron, *The Great Wall of China: From History to Myth* (1990), is an authoritative account of the Ming dynasty's, and China's, most famous structure. It clarifies China's policy toward her nomadic neighbors and links past and present as well as history and myth.

For a fascinating account of a major Qing emperor, see J. Spence, *Self-Portrait of K'ang-Hsi* (1974). Philip A. Kuhn, *Soulstealers: The Chinese Sorcery Scare of 1768* (1990), provides insights into how the Qing government functioned as well as the mind-set of high and low. A number of books relate the social and economic history of the late imperial period to modern Chinese developments. An exceptionally useful and stimulating survey is Lloyd E. Eastman, *Family, Fields, and Ancestors: Constancy and Change in China's Social and Economic History 1550–1949* (1988).

Japan

The Cambridge History of Japan (1989–) is a good place to begin reading in depth. Also recommended is H. P. Varley, *Japanese Culture: A Short History,* 3rd ed. (1984). Tsunoda et al., *Sources of Japanese Tradition* (1958) is a valuable anthol-

ogy. The Kodansha *Encyclopedia of Japan* (1983) is a useful reference. For a recent compilation, see the "Suggested Readings" in Conrad Schirokauer, *A Brief History of Japanese Civilization* (1993).

Contacts with Europe

Recommended for China are Thomas H. C. Lee, ed., *China and Europe: Images and Influences in Sixteenth to Eighteenth Centuries* (1991) and J. Gernet, *China and the Christian Impact: A Conflict of Cultures* (1985). C. R. Boxer, *The Christian Century in Japan* (1951), is well written and informative. Also see G. Ellison, *Deus Destroyed: The Image of Christianity in Early Modern Japan* (1973), and Vol. 4 of *The Cambridge History of Japan.*

16

THE REVIVAL OF EUROPE

One of the most striking aspects of the late Middle Ages is that political leaders and scholars created so much that was new and exciting while society as a whole was suffering war, famine, and plague. Institutions that had stood for centuries gradually lost prestige and authority, but at the same time the seeds of a new era were being sown. In England, Parliament moved toward its modern status, and the idea that the judiciary should be independent of royal power won acceptance. Capitalism began to emerge as an economic system suitable for commerce and agriculture.

The writers and scholars of the fourteenth century were the first to recognize the vast distance between the culture of the classical world and the culture of their own time. Earlier scholars had thought of themselves as the continuers of ancient civilization; scholars of the new era thought of themselves as recoverers of that civilization. For them, ancient civilization had ended in the fifth century, when the Visigoths, Ostrogoths, and Franks overran western Europe. Scholars of the fifteenth and sixteenth centuries first referred to the thousand years dating from the end of the Roman Empire as the "middle ages."

With this new awareness came a new historical consciousness. Earlier historians, following the lead of Augustine (see p. 118), had divided history into epochs marked by crucial events in the relationship between man and God: History began with the Fall of Adam; the flood and Noah's rescue marked the beginning of a new epoch; Moses and the making of the covenant between God and the Jews marked a third epoch; the incarnation of God in Jesus inaugurated the current epoch; the Second Coming would bring all history to an end. Now, however, people

(OPPOSITE) SANDRO BOTTICELLI'S ALLEGORY OF SPRING SHOWS THE CLASSICAL INFLUENCE IN RENAISSANCE ART. BOTTICELLI WAS A MEMBER OF THE CIRCLE OF PLATONISTS GATHERED AT THE ACADEMY BY LORENZO DE MEDICI. THE IDEALIZATION OF THE HUMAN FIGURE IN ART IS "PAINTED PLATONISM."

were tracing the course of history according to intellectual and artistic milestones, not according to phases in the spiritual condition of humanity. At the moment, they were conscious of a revival of ancient civilization. Jakob Burckhardt, a Swiss historian of the nineteenth century, called that revival a renaissance.

Recently, however, historians have suggested that Burckhardt's term is somewhat inappropriate. True, there was a sharp break with medieval philosophy and a revival of classical learning, but in many other respects life in the fifteenth and sixteenth centuries was pretty much an extension of what life had been in the late Middle Ages. The economic and political changes that set in had little to do with the new ideas in scholarship and the arts. They were the consequences of a natural evolution from late-medieval society. The same is true of religious institutions, which went through profound changes in the sixteenth century. The next chapter is about those changes.

THE BACKGROUND OF THE RENAISSANCE

The new era opened against a background of economic depression, social unrest, and religious malaise. As we saw in Chapter 14, the droughts and famines that struck Europe toward the end of the thirteenth century had set off a decline in population that continued into the first half of the next century, and at midcentury the already weakened population was ravaged by the bubonic plague. During the next half-century the labor force continued its decline, a decline hastened by the breakdown of the manor and the guild. The structure of government and of society itself weakened, and the upper classes, led by the kings, tried desperately to preserve their privileges and fortunes by instituting drastic measures to keep prices and wages from rising. Europe was in woeful condition.

During the fifteenth century, institutions recovered their stability. The papacy regained much of its power with the defeat of the conciliar movement, even

though it no longer exercised the universal authority it had once wielded. The monarchies of England and Spain began to bring their kingdoms under central control, and by the end of the century the French monarchy was following their lead. The population began to grow again, and technological advances gave the economy new impetus. Europeans turned more adventurous and by the end of the century had rounded Africa to reach the East Indies and had found their way to the Americas.

The seeds of this recovery had taken root in Italy toward the end of the fourteenth century. During the two centuries between the death of Dante (1321) and the sack of Rome by mutinous imperial troops (1527), Italy's influence over the rest of Europe had grown enormously. Italians set the style in architecture, sculpture, and painting; they dictated the literary taste and the educational practices that Europeans would follow for centuries. Northern Europeans flocked to Italy to study engineering, art, politics, and business, and Italians frequented the courts of princes and kings throughout Europe—even in remote Moscow. Italian navigators ventured out on bold explorations of uncharted waters.

Several reasons explain why it was Italy that pioneered the way into the new era. In close contact with the advanced civilizations of the Byzantine Empire and Islam, the Italian cities had begun to flourish as early as the tenth century, when northern Europe was just completing its move into feudalism. Because its focus was essentially rural, feudalism provided little impetus for the growth of cities. In Italy, feudalism never became very strong, and by the early fourteenth century it existed there in name only.

Moreover, because of the conflict between the papacy and the German empire a unified monarchy never emerged in Italy. Consequently, many of the medieval institutions that dominated the northern kingdoms never gained a foothold there. In intellectual matters, Italy was never dominated by scholasticism, as were the universities of the north, and Gothic architecture and sculpture had little influence in Italy. Thus, because the Italians' intellectual and artistic proclivities were outside the paradigms of medieval civilization, Italians were more receptive than northerners were to new ideas and to new ways of viewing the world. Also, though they experienced the famines and plagues of the fourteenth century, the cities of Italy were large enough, rich enough, and strong enough to recover more quickly than the cities of northern Europe.

THE CITY-STATES OF NORTHERN ITALY

The main business of the northern Italian cities was international trade. A third of the population of Florence, for example, was engaged in importing wool, making finished cloth, and selling it in foreign markets. Nearly all the people in Venice and Genoa depended for their livelihood either directly or indirectly on trade with the Levant and with northern Europe. Not surprisingly, affairs in the northern Italian cities were largely in the hands of bankers, export merchants, and textile manufacturers.

The political power of the cities reached deep into the adjacent region, which meant that they could act in the manner of urban principalities—that is, as city-states. Feudal lords in the neighborhood soon joined the city elite. And as the small market towns and villages of the countryside (called the *contado*) were annexed, some city-states came to control domains of several hundred square miles.

By the late twelfth century, the population of the city-states was divided into classes defined partly by social and partly by economic criteria. The merchant bankers—called the *popolo grasso,* or "fat people"—constituted the ruling class. The craftsmen, shopkeepers, and other members of the lesser bourgeoisie—the *popolo minuto,* or "little people"—made up the largest class. The lowest class consisted of poor day laborers, who had little say in the political life of the cities. Well-to-do families and craft guilds supported hospitals and other service agencies to take care of this indigent class. To be associated

with these institutions brought a certain social cachet.

Unlike the class groups in the northern cities, the classes in the Italian cities rarely organized themselves into cohesive political entities. This was because in virtually every Italian city political parties supported either the emperor or the pope in their endless struggle for power, and the membership of those parties cut across class lines. These parties were descendants of the eleventh-century *patarini,* groups of townspeople who had fought the bishops for political control. Because most of the bishops were appointed by the emperor, the *patarini* had usually allied themselves with the papacy.

In the twelfth century, supporters of the Hohenstaufen emperors came to be known as Ghibellines, while supporters of the papacy were called Guelfs. Ghibelline was the Italian version of Waiblingen, the name of one of the Hohenstaufen castles; the Guelfs took their name from the Welfs, the family of the Bavarian dukes who were traditional rivals of the Hohenstaufens. Every city had its Ghibellines and Guelfs. By the thirteenth century, however, the parties, which continued to be known by their old names, no longer concerned themselves with the conflict between the pope and the emperor. They were only competitors for control of the cities, which had governments elected by all citizens who owned a certain amount of property.

Each party was led by one of the leading families of the city. The party that was out of power at the moment tried to win the support of the *popolo minuto* by blasting the incumbents and by promising to undertake a program of reform if elected. Occasionally, as in Florence in 1378, some reforms really were carried out after a transfer of power. Such reforms lasted only a short time, however, before they were scrapped in a new election or *coup d'état.*

The never-ending turmoil caused by the struggle between the Ghibellines and Guelfs drove many leading citizens from their cities. Whenever an able man won power and succeeded in restoring order by dictatorial means, he was hailed by the populace and accorded widespread

Equestrian statue of the condottieri Captain Bartolommeo Colleoni, who tried to create a state between Milan and Florence in the fifteenth century.

support. Such despots, as they were called, gained control of many Italian cities in the last fourteenth and fifteenth centuries and continued to command support even though they exiled, imprisoned, and executed their opponents. They managed to stay in the public's good graces by improving the city's public services, strengthening its defenses, imposing equitable tax systems, and seeing that the streets were safe. Many of them engaged architects and sculptors to build and adorn magnificent public buildings. They also wooed the public by waging wars with rival cities.

The despots had a hard time raising forces to fight a war, however, because the merchants and shopkeepers of the city, though eager to expand their markets, had no stomach for battle. Moreover, the despots suspected that they might be making trouble for themselves if they armed the townspeople. They hired mercenary troops called *condottieri,* who were well trained and fairly reliable so long as they were paid on time. In a showdown, however, the *condottieri* tended to be more loyal to their captain than to the man who was paying them, and some of the captains managed to seize power for themselves.

War and Diplomacy

In time, the city-states of northern Italy became so independent and so powerful that they were engaging almost constantly in wars and alliances with one another. By the early fifteenth century, they had begun to send ambassadors to the courts of Europe to report on potential allies and potential enemies. This was the beginning of modern diplomacy.

In the second half of the century, the five leading states—Venice, Milan, Florence, the Papal States, and the Kingdom of Naples—entered into a kind of "balance of power" with an unwritten understanding that no one of them would be allowed to become strong enough to threaten the others. Later, when France and Spain intervened in Italian affairs, they too began to engage in the practice of diplomacy and soon were working out a balance of power of their own. By the mid-sixteenth

century, resident ambassadors were common throughout western and central Europe, and France and Spain were maintaining a rough balance of power.

Milan, Venice, and Florence

Milan, the largest city in the Po Valley was the exemplar of the classic Italian city-state. At the end of the fourteenth century, Milan was ruled by Gian Galeazzo Visconti, a despot who made Milan into a leading manufacturing and trading city and who almost succeeded in uniting all of northern Italy under his power.

Venice, Italy's greatest commercial center, had risen to prominence in the ninth century as a Byzantine protectorate. Along with other interests in the eastern Mediterranean, it controlled the trade with Constantinople and Fatimid Egypt (see pp. 186–88). Built on a meager cluster of islands in the Adriatic Sea, Venice had never been touched by feudalism and was the first Italian city to hazard life under a republican constitution. Its government, the most stable in Italy, was conducted by a small council of merchants—the Council of Ten—led by a head of state called the doge. Every ounce of energy of the Venetian state and of the Venetian people was devoted to commerce. Venetian history included no revolutions but more than a few conspiracies. Venetians proclaimed their city, "the most serene republic." Until Venice began to acquire territory on the mainland during the fifteenth century, the city was relatively isolated from Italian politics.

Florence had outstripped its rivals Pisa and Siena as the leading city of Tuscany during the eleventh century. Florence, like Venice, was a republic. Its citizens took pride in their constitutional government and scorned their rivals for tolerating the rule of despots. They were particularly proud of having resisted Gian Galeazzo Visconti's attempt to take over their city.

Florentine society and politics were dominated by wealthy merchant bankers and textile manufacturers. Florentine bankers were regarded as the most astute on the Continent, and Florentine textiles

The Italian City-States   1454

The rise of the Medici: Cosimo de' Medici has the look of the wily businessman.

as the finest to be had. Unlike Venice, however, Florence was the scene of endless political intrigues and conspiracies, with the losers usually being forced into exile. (Dante suffered that fate.) The victors repeatedly tampered with the constitution in an effort to hold onto their position. Finally, in 1434, a party led by the banker Cosimo de' Medici (1389–1464) took control of the city. Cosimo was a political boss who preferred to work through others and used bribes and threats to ensure that his supporters won election to city offices. His son Piero (1416–69) and his grandson Lorenzo the Magnificent (1449–92) followed his ex-

ample, and Florence enjoyed sixty years of stability.

Although the Medici were not themselves despots, they behaved in the manner of despots by strengthening the defenses of the city and by patronizing the best artists and architects of the age. The first three Medici made Florence the center of the Italian Renaissance, and their descendants, who remained prominent in the city until the eighteenth century, were faithful patrons of the arts. They allied their family with the leading families of Europe, and two of the Medici became queens of France.

The palace of the Medici in Florence. Cosimo began construction of it in 1444.

ITALIAN URBAN CIVILIZATION

Baldassare Castiglione (1478–1529) in *The Courtier* defined the Renaissance man. The courtier combines the chivalric virtues—physical dexterity and strength, courage, skill in combat, courtesy—with the new virtues—knowledge of the classics, appreciation of art and literature, eloquence, and good taste. Above all, the courtier has grace; he excels effortlessly in everything he undertakes.

During the Middle Ages, courtliness had been associated with high birth. But the Renaissance courtier could be a self-made man, for talented and ambitious men were accorded considerable mobility. The *condottieri* captain Francesco Sforza (1401–66), for example, who overthrew the Visconti family to become Duke of Milan, founded a dynasty that ruled for a century. Leonardo da Vinci and the scholars Lorenzo Valla and Aeneas Silvius Piccolomini (who became Pope Pius II) were not highborn but were said to have *virtù*, a term that meant more than "virtue" in the modern sense; it also meant "virtuosity," that combination of genius and determination that made for greatness in statesmanship, art, and literature. Eventually, *virtù* came to mean the quality that makes for success.

Individualism

Above all else, the Italian Renaissance valued individualism. The Italians had never felt the full weight of feudal obligations, and their wealth came from commerce rather than from landed estates. That meant that their assets were readily available, making it possible for them to move from place to place whenever they found their situation oppressive or boring.

Mobility provided individuals with the opportunity to act independently and favored the man with the talent and courage to strike out on his own. Many merchants, craftsmen, scholars, and artists moved away from their hometowns, where they could find support from family and friends, to places where the market was good or patrons were ready to hire them, but where they would be on their

---

A Man of Virtù

Benvenuto Cellini, a Florentine goldsmith and sculptor, had struck medals and coins for Pope Clement VII (1523–34). He claimed that he had been insulted by a jeweler named Pompeo (who also worked for the pope), and after several quarrels, Cellini stabbed Pompeo to death in a street brawl. Clement VII had just died; Cardinal Farnese was elected pope on October 13, 1534, and took the name of Paul III.

After he had put affairs of greater consequence in order, the new Pope sent for me, saying that he did not wish any one else to strike his coins. To these words of his Holiness one of his gentlemen named Latino Juvinale [a Humanist] answered that I [Cellini] was in hiding for the murder of Pompeo of Milan, and set forth what could be argued for my justification in the most favorable terms. The Pope replied: "I know nothing of Pompeo's death but plenty of Benvenuto's provocation, so let a safe-conduct be at once made out for him." A great friend of Pompeo's was there; he was a Milanese called Ambrogio [Ambrogio Recalcati, a papal secretary]. This man said: "In the first days of your papacy it is not well to grant pardons of this kind." The Pope answered: "You know less about such matters than I do. Know then that men like Benvenuto, unique in their profession, stand above the law."

From Benvenuto Cellini, The Life of Benvenuto Cellini, *trans. by John Addington Symonds (New York: Scribner's, 1926), p. 144.*

own. Benvenuto Cellini (1500–71), a sculptor and goldsmith who described his violent and colorful career in his *Autobiography,* was an excellent case of the individualistic ethos occasioned by the mobility in Renaissance society. Cellini assumed that autobiography, which had been a rare literary genre in the Middle Ages, was a natural form of expression: "All men of whatsoever quality they be, who have done anything of excellence, . . . ought to describe their life with their own hand." He declared that ordinary laws of morality were meant for ordinary people, not for geniuses such as himself, and he claimed that the pope had once absolved him of murdering a man because the pope understood that he was above the law.

Secularism

The second characteristic of Renaissance society in Italy was its secular tone. People were endlessly interested in the things of this world—commerce, the design of houses, styles of dress, food and drink, and the enjoyment of leisure. In his *Decameron* (*ca.* 1350), Giovanni Boccaccio told one hundred stories featuring characters taken from contemporary society. The work provided a model for Italian prose writing but also presented personality types that reveal the interests and ideals of behavior of the period. Boccaccio's characters are not irreligious or anti-Christian, but they scorn the hypocrisy of priests and monks; they rejoice in the triumph of clever people over clerical busybodies; and they seem to say that paying attention to the affairs of this world is quite appropriate for the people who live in it. The secularism of the *Decameron* consisted of two components—a preoccupation with worldly affairs and a contempt for false spirituality and asceticism.

Humanism

Humanism derived from the study of classical literature; the humanist was a classical scholar. It was not the mere act of studying the classics that made the humanist but the implication that one who

---

Petrarch on the Classics and Christianity

You are well aware that from early boyhood of all the writers of all ages and races the one whom I most admire and love is Cicero. You agree with me in this respect as well as in so many others. I am not afraid of being considered a poor Christian by declaring myself so much a Ciceronian. [This is an allusion to a famous vision of St. Jerome in which God told him: "You are a Ciceronian and therefore not a Christian."] To my knowledge, Cicero never wrote one word that would conflict with the principles proclaimed by Christ. If, perchance, his works contained anything contrary to Christ's doctrine, that one fact would be sufficient to destroy my belief in Cicero and in Aristotle and in Plato. . . .

Christ is my God; Cicero is the prince of the language I use. I grant you that these ideas are widely separated, but I deny that they are in conflict with each other. Christ is the Word, and the Virtue and the Wisdom of God the Father. Cicero has written much on the speech of men, on the virtues of men, and on the wisdom of men—statements that are true and therefore surely acceptable to the God of Truth.

From a letter to Neri Morando, 1358, in Petrarch's Letters to Classical Authors, *trans. by M. E. Cosenza (Chicago: University of Chicago Press, 1910), pp. 18–19.*

---

did so was interested in the highest ideals of human behavior. Humanism was the study of man though the examples provided by classical literature and ancient history. As far back as the fourteenth century, the poet/scholar Petrarch (1304–74) had revived classical literary forms and had imitated the styles of the ancient writers. Later humanists followed his example, spurred on by Boccaccio's biography of Petrarch.

Led by Petrarch and Boccaccio, Renaissance Italians conceived a passion for everything relating to classical antiquity. Knowledge of classical literature was an indication of true gentility, and the humanists were held in high honor. Many humanists held positions as secretaries in the royal courts of Europe and as teachers of the children of noble families. Generally, they were self-made men who earned a living through their learning. Enthusiasm

Benvenuto Cellini did this bust of Bindo Altoviti about 1550.

Young student reading Cicero (detail from a painting by Vincenzo Foppa).

One humanist educator wrote, "We call those studies liberal which are worthy of a free man . . . that education which calls forth, trains, and develops those highest gifts of body and of mind which ennoble men." That is still the goal of liberal education.

Historical Consciousness

Petrarch and his fellow humanists were well aware that the Roman civilization they admired was quite different from their own and were careful to distinguish between the past and present. They could talk of the "fall of Rome" and of the "dark age" that separated the glorious time of Augustus, Vergil, and Cicero from their own. This was a new consciousness that enabled the humanists to see themselves and their society in historical context, which is a characteristic of the modern view of individuals and society.

FAMILY LIFE

The ideals of Renaissance family life were those of upper-class urban families—the families of bankers and merchants. The *populo minuto* imitated these ideals to the extent that their finances permitted.

Men got married rather late, usually to much younger women, and the husband was unchallenged head of the household. Because of the disparity of age, widows were almost as common as widowers. (Until modern times, men generally outlived their wife because of the frequency with which women died in childbirth.) A man was expected to have established himself as an upstanding member of the community before marrying, and his purpose in marrying was to have children who would carry on his family line and his profession. The role of the wife was to advance her husband's career by exhibiting her beauty, culture, and social grace. Consequently, it was important that women be faithful and virtuous, and a woman's virtue was a common theme in Renaissance literature. The need for a woman to remain faithful to her husband was so urgent that it even survived his

for the classics intensified after 1395, as scholars fled westward from Constantinople to escape the Ottoman Turks, who were advancing across Asia Minor. In Italy the Greeks found students eager to study the Greek language and Greek literature, and Lorenzo the Magnificent founded a Platonic Academy in Florence for the study and teaching of Greek philosophy. By the end of the fifteenth century a few Italians were studying Hebrew and Arabic in addition to Greek.

The humanists turned their attention to education as well. The secular schools of the Middle Ages had concentrated on preparing young men for a career in commerce. They taught reading, writing, and arithmetic, and little else. And the main purpose of the ecclesiastical schools had been to train clerics and monks; their intellectual standards were high, but of course all study focused on theology.

The humanists of the fifteenth century rediscovered the "liberal arts" that liberate the mind and the imagination through the study of great literature and philosophy. To that study they added training in behavior and athletic skill, thereby realizing the ancient goal of *mens sana in corpore sano* ("a sound mind in a sound body").

death. A man was advised to discourage his wife from remarrying after his death by arranging that his property would go to her only "if she remains a widow and lives with her children." Of course many widows did remarry, and families were often quite large.

A young woman married to an older man often had to cope with difficult circumstances. There might be little or no difference between her own age and the age of her husband's older children, and she might become embroiled in controversies between the various sibling groups. She might also be obliged to accept her husband's illegitimate children into the household and sometimes the children of his brothers or sisters as well. During prolonged absences of her husband, she was expected to manage the servants and their children, raise her children, run the household, and keep the family, the relatives, and the staff at peace.

Infants were normally put out for two years to a wet nurse—usually peasant women in the *contado*. When returned to the family household, they had to get to know their siblings and their parents and find a place for themselves in the family group. Many diaries from the period evidence the feelings of alienation and fear that often accompanied this entry into the home.

Between the ages of two and seven, children were almost exclusively under their mother's care. The father remained rather distant except in times of crisis, as when the child or the mother became seriously ill. The father entered the child's world when the child was ready to begin formal education, usually at the age of seven.

Boys were sent to a boarding school, where they spent three or four years learning to read and write both in Latin and the vernacular. They then spent another year or so studying accounting and business procedures and finally were placed as apprentices with a merchant or banker. Girls were educated at home in the household arts and in reading and writing.

Women were expected to come to their marriage with a dowry, and in Florence and many other cities parents could

How Children Should Be Raised

The Dominican Friar Giovanni Dominici (ca. 1356–ca. 1420) wrote a treatise on childrearing.

Children should be accustomed to eat coarse food, to wear cheap and common clothes. . . . They should also learn to wait on themselves, and to use as little as possible the services of maid and servant, setting and clearing the table, dressing and undressing themselves, putting on their own shoes and clothes and so forth.

After a boy reaches three years of age, he should know no distinction between male and female other than dress and hair. From then on let him be a stranger to being petted, embraced and kissed by you [the mother] until after the twenty-fifth year. Granted that there will not take place any thought or natural movement before the age of five . . . do not be less solicitous that he be chaste and modest always and, in every place, covered as modestly as if he were a girl.

Quoted by James Bruce Ross, "The Middle-Class Child in Urban Italy, Fourteenth to Early Sixteenth Century", The History of Childhood, ed. by L. deMause (New York: Psychoanalytic Press, 1974).

invest in dowry banks. They deposited a specified sum when their daughter was very young and let the fund grow through the accrual of interest until it was redeemed.

Women of the middle classes participated more directly in their husbands' affairs. From the little evidence we have, it appears that middle-class families emulated their betters by putting their children out to a wet nurse and providing them with a formal education. The men married late, and widowhood was common in this class. Some women found work in manufacturing—perhaps as weavers—and many women seem to have owned their own shops.

THE RENAISSANCE

Literature, Philosophy, and Scholarship

The early humanists tended to imitate the genres and styles of classical literature—letters, orations, moral essays, and poetry,

A seventeenth-century engraving showing a peasant father feeding his infant child.

Renaissance scholars created the discipline of critical scholarship, which calls for a careful linguistic and historical analysis of the literature of the past. Lorenzo Valla (*ca.* 1405–57) used linguistic analysis to prove that the Donation of Constantine (see p. 182), on which papal claims to temporal authority rested, was a crude forgery of the early Middle Ages. He also compared several Greek manuscripts of the New Testament with Jerome's vulgate translation (late fourth century) and uncovered many errors and distortions in the translation. His scholarly approach to literary texts influenced later scholars, including Erasmus (see p. 432), who produced the first critical edition of the Greek New Testament.

Social and Political Thought

Though most of the social and political thinkers of the Renaissance simply paraphrased the Greek and Roman classics, a few of them did original work. Leon Battista Alberti (1404–72), for example, in his *On the Family* analyzed the structure and interests of Florentine families. He reports that they prized prudence, thrift, foresight, and comfort; had strong family feeling and little interest in the affairs of society as a whole; and aspired to a house in the city and an estate in the country to produce the family's food. Alberti's account is one of the earliest treatments of what later came to be called the bourgeois virtues.

Baldassare Castiglione's *The Courtier* (written 1513–18, published 1528), as we have seen, dealt with the ideals of the noble class. Drawing on his experiences at the court of the duke of Urbino, Castiglione reformulated the ideal of "the gentleman." Though his work owed much to the chivalric tradition of the Middle Ages, it spoke of the goals of a liberal education and the idea that "nobility" derives from character rather than from the accident of birth.

Perhaps the greatest political theorist of the Renaissance was Niccolò Machiavelli (1469–1527), who combined wide reading in the classics, particularly history, with wide experience in politics. He served Florence as an ambassador to

for example. They also created new forms, however, such as the sonnet and the essay.

Renaissance philosophers drew heavily on the work of Plato, which had been introduced to the West by refugee Byzantine scholars in the 1390s. The leading members of the Platonic academy founded by the Medici were Marsilio Ficino (1433–99) and Pico della Mirandola (1463–94), who tried to reconcile Plato and Christianity much as Thomas Aquinas had tried to reconcile Aristotle and Christianity (see pp. 293–95).

France and as secretary of the state during a period when the Medici were out of power. When they returned to power in 1512, Machiavelli retired to his country estate. There he studied political history and reflected on what causes political breakdown, how political leaders obtain and hold power, and what can be learned from history.

In his long, rambling *Discourses on Livy* (Livy was a famous Roman historian) and in his brief essay, *The Prince,* Machiavelli sought to describe political life as he saw it, rather than as it should be. His analysis of the strengths and weaknesses of various types of constitutions shows that he favored the republican form of government, like that of Florence. In *The Prince,* however, he concentrated on the behavior of heads of state and their use of power. The book ends with a plea that Italians unify their country, throw out the foreign invaders, and recreate the glory of ancient Rome. *The Prince* became a grammar of political and diplomatic practice and was translated into many languages. Its realistic account of the world of politics and international relations earned Machiavelli a reputation as a proponent of dictatorship. Actually, although he believed that a strong, centralized state was desirable, he insisted that it must operate under a constitution suited to the character of the people. And the most educated populace would be best served by a republican constitution.

The Arts

Soon after the humanists rediscovered Roman literature, Renaissance architects turned their attention to Roman architecture. There were Roman buildings or their ruins everywhere, and architects set about analyzing the principles of design the Romans had followed. The greatest of the early Renaissance architects was Brunelleschi (*ca.* 1377–1446), who designed numerous churches with symmetrical design and stately facades. The most impressive example of Renaissance architecture was the church of St. Peter in Rome, which replaced a fourth-century basilica built by Emperor Constantine I. The largest church

A late sixteenth-century portrait of Niccolò Machiavelli by Santi di Tito. The artist has tried to suggest both the intellectual brilliance and the shrewdness of the man.

in Europe, St. Peter's was the work of several architects—including Bramante, Michelangelo, and Bernini—from 1506 to 1615.

Renaissance painting was strongly influenced by the techniques of Giotto (1276–1337), Dante's favorite painter, who introduced a sense of volume in his representations of figures and their surroundings, especially in a series of frescoes (paintings done on fresh plaster) in the church of St. Francis in Assisi. During the fourteenth century Italian painters had also become familiar with the realistic style favored by the Flemish painters of the Burgundian court. That style was raised to a new height by Masaccio (1401–*ca.* 1428), who suppressed irrelevant details and concentrated on the emotional aspects of the scenes he painted.

In the Middle Ages, painting and sculpture had usually been regarded as adjuncts to architecture. But during the Renaissance they emerged as independent forms of expression. Italian painters still painted frescoes on the walls of

Machiavelli on Cruelty and Clemency

Is it better to be loved than feared or feared than loved? It may be answered that one should wish to be both, but it is much safer to be feared than loved when one of the two must be chosen. Men on the whole are ungrateful, fickle, false, cowards, covetous. As long as you succeed, they are yours entirely. They will offer you their blood, property, life, and children when the need is distant, but when it approaches they turn against you. And a prince who, relying entirely on their promises, has neglected other precautions, is ruined. . . . Men have fewer scruples in offending one who is beloved than one who is feared, for love is preserved by the link of obligation which, owing to the baseness of men, is broken at every opportunity for their advantage, but fear preserves you by a dread of punishment which never fails.

Nevertheless, a prince should inspire fear in such a way that if he does not win love, he avoids hatred; because he can endure very well being feared while he is not hated, and this will be true as long as he abstains from taking the property of his subjects or their women. But when it is necessary for him to take the life of someone, he must do it with proper justification and for manifest cause, and above everything he must keep his hands off the property of others, because men more quickly forget the death of their father than the loss of their heritage.

From Niccolò Machiavelli, The Prince, trans. by W. K. Marriott (London: Dent, n.d.), pp. 134–35.

---

churches and monasteries, but they turned more and more to easel painting, creating pictures to be hung on the wall and enjoyed for their own sake. Though they still favored religious themes, they often drew on classical sources for their subjects, reflecting the influence of humanism.

Sculptors, too, turned to classical models for inspiration. Donatello (1368–1466), for example, was the first sculptor since Roman times to model a freestanding nude figure. His *David* opened the way to the creation of a succession of great sculptures that culminated in the masterpieces of Michelangelo (1475–1564). These works revived the Greco-Roman fascination with the beauty of the human body.

Many Renaissance artists achieved substantial public recognition and social prestige through their work. Although some patrons treated artists as common servants, many artists earned handsome commissions and lived as independent and honored members of society.

In their efforts to achieve realism, Renaissance painters studied the laws of perspective and human anatomy, and their notebooks and sketches contain countless studies of proportion and space and treatments of the human torso and limbs. They observed facial expressions and body posture so that they could reveal the exact emotional state of figures they portrayed. Leonardo da Vinci (1452–1519), for example, in his painting *The Last Supper,* departed from tradition by depicting, not the moment when Christ says to the apostles, "This is my body . . . ," but instead the dramatic moment when Christ announces, "One of you will betray me." By conveying the psychological state of each apostle, he achieves tremendous dramatic power.

Da Vinci's wide-ranging curiosity extended to the workings of mechanical devices as well as to the workings of the human body. He created designs for a helicopter and a self-propelled vehicle and made studies of perspective, light, and optics.

Michelangelo followed Da Vinci in searching for the psychologically charged moment. His painting of the Creation on the ceiling of the Sistine Chapel in the Vatican is focused on God's animation of Adam. And in his statue of Moses, Michelangelo portrays him at the moment when he catches sight of the Golden Calf, sitting tense, with a fierce expression, trying to control his rage over his people's idolatry.

Throughout these examples we find the Renaissance emphasis on human beings as they live here and now, in this world—troubled, striving, with unknown potential. Pico della Mirandola remarked in a famous *Oration* on man's dignity (1486) that God had given man something he had given to no other creature—freedom. All other creatures have their set patterns of behavior, but man's nature and destiny, Pico declared, are in his own hands. The people of the Renaissance had not lost their belief in God, but they gave new meaning to the Judeo-Christian idea that man was made in God's image: Like

God, man is a creator, a creator of his own character and his own destiny.

Along with artists and writers, the urban courts of Italy employed hundreds of musicians, craftsmen, mechanics, and engineers. Working together in a relatively small space, these specialists often cooperated and advanced one another's endeavors. Artists and physicians shared their knowledge of human anatomy. Painters worked out the principles of perspective and contributed to the study of mathematics. Physicians studied astronomy, because in medieval medicine the stars were thought to affect health. In fact, many of the instruments used to observe the stars were designed by physicians.

During the sixteenth century Italy was the center of European cultural life. Northern Europe had begun to recover from the famines and plagues of the late Middle Ages, but northerners with an interest in the arts and humanism traveled to Italy to study. No northern city approached Florence, Venice, or Rome as a center of artistic and intellectual life.

ECONOMIC GROWTH IN NORTHERN EUROPE

The wealth of Italy was based primarily on trade and industry, and from the thirteenth century to the sixteenth century, Italy was the banking center of Europe. The wealth of the nations of northern Europe was based primarily on agriculture and mineral deposits. To be sure, northerners engaged in commerce and industry, and many cities had substantial communities of merchants and manufacturers; Flanders, for example, produced excellent cloth for which there was a lively demand. But agriculture was the main source of wealth, for northern Europe is one of the richest agricultural regions on earth, and the extensive network of rivers made it possible to move the produce to the markets at low cost.

During the fifteenth century, a series of technological advances fueled a new burst of economic activity in the North. And the new industries such as cannon founding and printing required large initial investments in plant and machinery. From the start, these industries were organized as capitalistic enterprises—that is, enterprises in which wealth was used to create new wealth. This was a departure from medieval practice, when most wealth was used to buy "consumer" goods and was rarely accumulated to invest in improvements and increased production.

The managers of these capitalistic enterprises drew their workers from both town and countryside and created a large, mobile labor force that was subject to the vagaries of an economy that neither they nor their workers could control. Consequently, the workers were wealthier and at the same time less secure than medieval peasants and craftsmen had been.

Progressive landlords tried to introduce capitalism into agriculture by producing only the most profitable crops and animal products. Particularly in England—where wool production was well established—many landlords fenced in, or "enclosed," open fields that had formerly been reserved for the use of villagers, and some of them even enclosed cultivated land to accommodate huge flocks of sheep. At the beginning of the sixteenth

The Pitti Palace in Florence, now an art museum, was built by the early Renaissance architect Filippo Brunelleschi for the merchant Luca Pitti.

Donatello's *David* (*ca.* 1430–32). Compare this statue with the *David* by Michelangelo on the opposite page.

century, Thomas More, chancellor of England, complained that the enclosure movement was ruining the small farmers and was creating a class of "sturdy beggars" or "vagabonds" who posed a problem for town governments. Actually, the reason for the vagabonds was the growth in population. After two centuries of decline, population growth had resumed, and it outpaced the creation of jobs. Town governments built prisons and workhouses to house the tramps.

The wealth produced by the new industries tended to find its way to a few hands in a few places. For a brief time, the most powerful banking house in northern Europe was that of the Fuggers of Augsburg in southern Germany. Jakob Fugger (1459–1525), banker to the Habsburgs of Austria (see p. 370) and to the popes, could invest in Austrian mines and Spanish colonies and carry on dealings with every part of the continent. From about 1476 to 1576, however, the real center of banking was Antwerp (now in Belgium), with Lyons in second place. In the following century, Amsterdam took over the lead. By the later sixteenth century, financial power was shifting from Italy to the north.

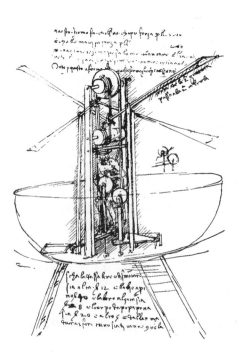

Leonardo da Vinci's design for a helicopter. The man uses a crank to flap the wings.

POLITICAL CONSOLIDATION AND CENTRALIZATION

Toward the end of the fifteenth century, the nations of northern Europe began to recover from the disastrous effects of war and plague. The War of the Roses (1455–85) produced a strong new dynasty in England (see p. 362), and after the end of the Hundred Years' War in 1453 the French kings were able to recover their power. In Germany, though the emperor remained weak, the marriage alliances contrived by the imperial family spread their influence across the Continent. And Spain too established a power base with the wealth extracted from its new colonies. In short, the kings of northern Europe were drawing close to achieving the absolute power that had eluded their medieval predecessors.

France

Although Charles VII (r. 1422–61) managed to drive the English from nearly all of their French territories, he was not a particularly effective ruler. He was, however, good at choosing able men to work for him (he was known as Charles "the Well-served") and getting them to strengthen the monarchy for him. In 1438, he asserted his authority over the French church by means of the Pragmatic Sanction of Bourges (see p. 428). In the 1440s, he solved his need for money by getting the Estates General to agree to a broadbased tax on land, which he continued to collect on his own authority thereafter. He organized a small but strong standing army (not more than 25,000 men). And he won the support of the merchant class, from which he recruited some of his best royal officials.

Charles's son Louis XI (r. 1461–83) was an able ruler who left the monarchy stronger than it had been since the early fourteenth century. He was a master of diplomacy—he was called "the Spider" because of his ability to trap his enemies in a web of intrigue—and won the admiration of Machiavelli. Louis's greatest enemy was Charles the Bold, duke of Burgundy (r. 1467–77), who outmaneuvered him while at the same time helping him to rid France of the last English troops. But Louis finally succeeded in stirring up Charles's eastern neighbors, and Charles died fighting a battle with Swiss pikemen.

The richest part of Charles the Bold's inheritance, the Netherlands, went to the Habsburg emperor Maximilian (r. 1493–1519) by way of his wife Mary, Charles's daughter. But the strategically located duchy of Burgundy went to Louis. Louis also married his son Charles VIII (r. 1483–98) to the heiress of Brittany, thus bringing the last feudal duchy under French control. Louis continued his father's policy of encouraging trade, maintaining the loyalty of the merchant class, and keeping firm control of the aristocracy and the church.

During the first years of his reign, however, Charles VIII spent most of his

Michelangelo's *David* (ca. 1501–04). Instead of representing David after his victory over Goliath, as Donatello had done, Michelangelo chose to represent him watching the approaching foe, with muscles tensed in gathering strength.

Michelangelo's statue of the horned Moses. The horns represent the rays of light that symbolize the divine inspiration of Moses as receiver of the Ten Commandments.

gon (r. 1479–1516) and Isabella of Castile (r. 1474–1504) enabled them to carry out a common foreign policy and helped them to transform their joint kingdoms into a European power. Another marriage at about that time further enhanced the position of Spain. The emperor Maximilian and his wife Mary of Burgundy had a son, Philip, who was heir to Austria through his Habsburg father and heir to the Netherlands through his mother. Philip married Joanna, the daughter of Ferdinand and Isabella, and their son, Charles, eventually became king of Spain (r. 1516–56) and ruler of the Netherlands, Austria, Milan, Naples, and the Spanish colonies in the New World. In 1519, the German princes elected him emperor as Charles V (see pp. 437, 457).

At the end of the fifteenth century, Spain was not yet wealthy or fully unified. The kingdoms of Aragon and Castile clung to their old institutions and to their own languages. The Spanish armies, however, were among the best in Europe. Then, with Columbus's discoveries in the New World, gold and silver streamed into the kingdom and transformed Spain into the leading power of sixteenth-century Europe (see pp. 453–58).

England

Henry Tudor (Henry VII, r. 1485–1509), who brought the War of the Roses to an end, succeeded in reestablishing peace and proved himself one of the ablest kings in English history. The ranks of the aristocracy had been thinned during the wars, and Henry filled them out with men loyal to his monarchy. He kept England out of foreign wars, encouraged trade, restored royal revenues, and eliminated all pretenders to the throne.

Henry's son, Henry VIII (r. 1509–47), inherited a full treasury, a united nation, and a relatively efficient administration. He introduced humanist learning to England and helped foster the English Renaissance. With the help and advice of his ruthless chief minister, Cardinal Wolsey, he issued numerous statutes to reform the Common Law and to correct abuses. His reign was one of the most innovative periods in the history of the English law.

An early printing press, as shown in an early sixteenth-century French print.

time consolidating his control of the country. Once that was done, he was ready to renew some of the ancient claims of the French monarchy. In 1494 he invaded Italy and asserted his claim to the kingdom of Naples as the heir of Charles of Anjou (see p. 322). The Spanish monarchy, which also had a claim to Italy, reacted quickly to the French invasion. For the next half-century, foreign armies ranging across Italy destroyed the prosperity and independence of the city-states. Eventually, Spain won out and made the kingdom of Naples a dependency of the Spanish crown. Though the French monarchy had suffered severe financial losses in the wars, it remained one of the most influential powers in Europe.

Spain

As we have seen, the momentous marriage (1469) between Ferdinand of Ara-

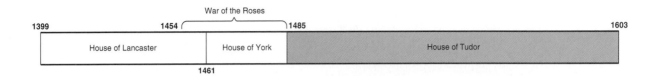

War of the Roses

1399	1454	1485	1603
House of Lancaster	House of York	House of Tudor	

1461

Henry married Catherine of Aragon, thereby joining England to the grand alliance of families associated with the royal house of Spain. But he and Catherine had only one daughter. Foreseeing a dynastic crisis, Henry sought to rid himself of his wife. When the pope refused to grant him a divorce, he proclaimed the Act of Supremacy in 1534, declaring himself the head of an English church free from the authority of the pope. Chancellor Thomas More, a humanist scholar and brilliant lawyer who succeeded Cardinal Wolsey in 1529, refused to accede to the king's assertion of authority and retired from his office in 1532. When he continued in his opposition to the king's remarriage and the Act of Supremacy, he was convicted of treason and was beheaded in 1535.

The Consolidation of Royal Power

During the sixteenth century, the European monarchs overcame the nobility, the representative assemblies, and the church in their determination to strengthen their power. They overcame the nobility either because it had been weakened by war, as in England, or because it could not afford the cost of the new military technology. Most of the kings compensated for the loss of the nobility by creating bureaucracies made up of educated, loyal men who strengthened royal finances by means of innovative taxes and sound financial management.

The representative assemblies—the Estates General in France, the Cortes in Spain, and Parliament in England—had achieved great power and influence during the fourteenth century, when the kings needed their help in dealing with the endless wars and the dire effects of the plague. In the fifteenth century, however, the power of the assemblies declined everywhere except in England. In most cases,

they themselves were to blame for their decline. Once the kings were no longer dependent on them for financial aid, the parochial interests of the delegates came

Jakob Fugger with his bookkeeper. The cabinet in the rear lists the names of cities where Fugger had branch offices—Innsbruck, Nuremburg, and Lisbon, among others (detail from a painting by Matthaus Schwartz, 1516).

Los Reyes don fernando y doña y sabel y la Re... almfata su hija doña   Juana.

Illumination of Ferdinand and Isabella of Spain—known as the "Catholic Kings"—with their daughter Joanna.

realm and for all sections of the country, it was hard to ignore. Moreover, it was an excellent source of support in time of need. When Henry VIII was trying to get the pope to grant him a divorce, for example, he summoned Parliament and asked for its support. By 1600, as a result of the frequent use Henry VIII and his successors made of it, Parliament had risen to a position of great influence in English government. By that time the representative assemblies on the Continent were hollow bodies under the control of absolute monarchs.

Finally, the monarchs overcame the church by preempting the appointment of prelates, by taxing the clergy without the permission of the pope, and by monitoring the appeal of cases to Rome. The kings of England and France had established the right to tax the clergy by 1300 (see p. 325), and the French king asserted the right to appoint prelates in 1438 in the Pragmatic Sanction of Bourges. In the Concordat of Bologna (1516) the pope granted Francis I (r. 1515–47) the right to nominate members of the higher clergy and to settle most ecclesiastical disputes that arose in France. The power to nominate amounted to the power to appoint. Even Ferdinand and Isabella, the Catholic Kings, asserted their right to appoint, to tax, and to reform the clergy within their kingdoms. In England, Henry VIII's Act of Supremacy (1534) gave him complete power over the church in one stroke.

The consolidation and centralization of power also proceeded in Norway and Sweden during the fifteenth and sixteenth centuries, and in Russia Ivan the Terrible (r. 1533–84) ruthlessly destroyed the power of the Russian nobility (see p. 346). But the process did not take place everywhere. Italy made no movement toward formation of a central government—to the dismay of Machiavelli—and in Germany the emperor was no more than a figurehead. When Charles V became emperor in 1519, his real strength lay in his position as duke of Austria, lord of the Netherlands, and king of Spain. In becoming emperor he gained some prestige, many responsibilities, but little power. Consequently, no one in Germany could resist the exactions

into play and destroyed the effectiveness of the assemblies. As the power of the kings rose during the fifteenth century, they manipulated the assemblies by playing the various factions off against one another, and the delegates began to avoid attending the meetings. The Estates General and Cortes met less and less frequently after the end of the fifteenth century.

In England, Henry VII used the Parliament to help establish his power. Once he was in control, however, he rarely called it into session. Nonetheless, because it spoke for all the privileged classes of the

Sir Thomas More, after Hans Holbein (1527).

of the papacy, which escalated steadily as the popes found themselves challenged elsewhere.

This lack of central authority in Germany was to be crucial in the sixteenth century. It contributed to the success of the Protestant Reformation, which became mixed up in the competition among the German princes. And it obliged the emperor to rely entirely on his hereditary domains in meeting the threat of the Ottoman Turks (see p. 189), who under Suleiman the Magnificent (r. 1520–66) captured Belgrade, took most of Hungary in the battle of Mohacs (1526), and almost seized Vienna in 1529.

Suggestions for Further Reading

General

The classic work on the Renaissance is J. Burckhardt, *The Civilization of the Renaissance in Italy* (1860). For a recent survey, see D. Hay, *The Italian Renaissance* (1977). W. K. Ferguson, *Europe in Transition: 1300–1520* (1963), emphasizes social and economic history. For a revolutionary view of the economic background of the Renaissance, see R. S. Lopez and H. A. Miskimin, "The Economic Depression of the Renaissance," *Economic History Review* 14 (1962), and the response by C. Cipolla, "Economic Depression of the Renaissance?" *Economic History Review* 16 (1963–64). For an overview, see A. Molho, *Social and Economic Foundations of the Italian Renaissance* (1969), and G. Huppert, *After the Black Death: A Social History of Early Modern Europe* (1986).

Italian Politics and Society

Recently, historians have written a series of works on individual Italian cities. See G. Brucker, *Renaissance Florence* (1969); D. Herlihy, *Pisa in the Early Renaissance* (1958); W. M. Bowsky, *The Finances of the Commune of Siena* (1970); D. S. Chambers, *The Imperial Age of Venice: 1380–1580* (1970); and C. M. Ady, *Milan under the Sforza* (1907). See also R. de Roover, *The Rise and Fall of the Medici Bank* (1963). For a general view, see D. Waley, *The Italian City Republics* (1969).

The classic work on the origins of modern diplomacy is G. Mattingly, *Renaissance Diplomacy* (1955). For background, see D. E. Queller, *The Office of Ambassador in the Middle Ages* (1967). On Renaissance warfare, see C. Oman, *History of the Art of War in the Sixteenth Century* (1937), and M. Mallett, *Mercenaries and their Masters* (1974).

On the Renaissance family, see L. deMause, ed., *The History of Childhood* (1974); J. Gage, *Life in Italy at the Time of the Medici* (1968); C. L. Lee, Jr., *Daily Life in Renaissance Italy* (1975); G. Brucker, *Giovanni and Lusanna: Love and Marriage in Renaissance Florence* (1986); and P. Aries, *Centuries of Childhood* (1962), a revolutionary work that uses art to show how views of children changed over time. *The Portable Renaissance Reader*, ed. by J. B. Ross and M. McLaughlin (1953), contains a selection from Alberti's *On the Family,* as well as other works. See J. Gadol, *Leon Battista Alberti: Universal Man of the Early Renaissance* (1969).

Humanism

On the origins of Renaissance humanism, see C. Trinkhaus, *The Poet as Philosopher: Petrarch and the Formation of the Renaissance Consciousness* (1979). On the humanist movement, see P. Kristeller, *Renaissance Thought,* 2 vols. (1961, 1965), and C. Trinkhaus, *The Scope of Renaissance Humanism* (1983). H. Baron, *The Crisis of the Early Italian Renaissance,* 2 vols. (1966), is an important treatment of the relationship between humanist thought and Florentine history in the early fifteenth century. On Renaissance political thought, see J. W. Allen, *Political Thought in the Sixteenth Century* (1928), and F. Chabod, *Machiavelli and the Renaissance* (1958). For an excellent biography of Machiavelli, see S. de Grazia, *Machiavelli in Hell* (1989).

Art and Architecture

There are many histories of Renaissance art and architecture. See P. and L. Murray, *The Art of the Renaissance* (1963); P. Murray, *Architecture of the Italian Renaissance* (1963); and E. H. Gombrich, *The Story of Art* (1953). See also Gombrich's article on the Medici as patrons of art in E. F. Jacob, ed., *Italian Renaissance Studies* (1960). For the early period, see R. Fremantle, *Florentine Gothic Painters from Giotto to Masaccio* (1975), and M. Meiss, *Painting in Florence and Siena after the Black Death* (1973). See also M. Baxendall, *Painting and Experience in Fifteenth Century Italy* (1972); J. R. Hale, *Italian Renaissance Painting from Masaccio to Titian* (1977); J. Pope-Hennessy, *An Introduction to Italian Sculpture,* 3rd ed., 3 vols. (1986); and R. Wittkower, *Architectural Principles in the Age of Humanism,* 4th ed. (1988).

Economic Growth

For a general history of the European economy, see the *Cambridge Economic History of Europe,* 3 vols. (1952–66). Volume 1 deals with agriculture; volume 2 with commerce and industry; and volume 3 with economic organization and policy. H. A. Miskimin, *The Economy of Early Renaissance Europe* (1969), is a good short survey. R. Ehrenberg, *Capital and Finance in* the Age of the Renaissance (1928), is the standard study of the Fuggers. See also E. Power and M. M. Postan, eds., *Studies in English Trade in the Fifteenth Century* (1953), and A. R. Bridbury, *Economic Growth: England in the Later Middle Ages* (1962). On the low countries; see H. Van Der Wee, *The Growth of the Antwerp Market and the European Economy* (1963). E. Eisenstein, *The Printing Press as an Agent of Change* (1979), is a good account of the invention and its effect.

France, England, and Spain

On late medieval France, see the works cited in Chapter 14. See also P. M. Kendall, *Louis the Eleventh* (1971); F. Pegues, *Lawyers of the Last Capetians* (1962); and J. H. Shennan, *The Parlement of Paris* (1968). On Spain, see the works cited in Chapter 14. On England, see the works cited in Chapter 14, and S. B. Chrimes, *Lancastrians, Yorkists, and Henry VII* (1964).

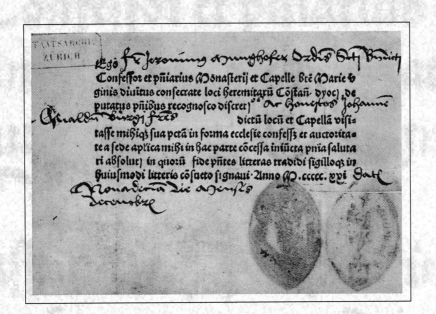

17

RELIGIOUS REFORM AND REVOLUTION IN WESTERN CHRISTENDOM

As we have seen, religious institutions were changing in the late Middle Ages. By the sixteenth century, the national churches of Europe were essentially under the control of the kings and the status of the pope had dwindled to that of an Italian despot. Many people had grown suspicious of the church and contemptuous of its leaders. So outraged had they become by the church's incessant demands for money that many had stopped attending church services altogether. This did not mean that their interest in religion had waned; it meant simply that they were looking elsewhere for religious guidance. Evangelical preachers abounded and attracted enthusiastic followings who applauded their charge that the church had grown worldly and corrupt. It did not help that the church was a demanding landlord to peasants and townspeople throughout Europe.

The new class of capitalistic merchants and industrialists also was at odds with the church, which had never managed to incorporate business ethics into its system of values. The church still shared the view of the ancient Romans that business was inevitably corrupting and morally suspect, and it still imposed the Judaic injunction against usury (charging interest on loans). Throughout the Middle Ages, merchants had often borrowed money to finance their business and had resorted to ruses to escape the charge of usury. With the rise of capitalism, the tension between the commercial classes and the church intensified, because capitalism was based on the idea that money invested in an enterprise ought to produce a return. Moreover, businessmen were angered by the church's failure to practice what it preached, pointing out that many church officials were themselves greedy and unscrupulous.

One of the questions put to students in debating practice was, "Can an archdeacon be saved?" (The archdeacon was the principal administrative officer of a bishopric.)

EFFORTS TO REFORM THE CHURCH

Late Medieval Reform Movements

The state of the church during the papal stay in Avignon and the Great Schism (see pp. 354–58) seemed so dismal that many laymen began to seek salvation on their own. They did not break openly with the church; they simply ceased to rely on it. They came together in groups, small at first, such as the Brethren of the Common Life in the Low Countries and the Rhineland, to encourage one another to lead a devout Christian life and to seek direct contact with God through mystical experiences. The Brethren produced some impressive works of devotion, like the *Theologica Germanica* (the "German Theology"), that influenced later reformers. They also founded schools that contributed to the educational revival of the fifteenth and sixteenth centuries; Erasmus (see p. 432), for example, was educated in a Brethren school. Conservative churchmen looked on these reformers with suspicion, but most of the groups managed to remain within the bounds of orthodoxy.

A more radical element wanted to mount a thoroughgoing reform of the church, preferably directed by laymen. As early as 1324 Marsilius of Padua, in his *Defensor pacis,* had argued that the state should control the church just as it controlled other organizations, like guilds. If the state could regulate physicians, he reasoned, it could also regulate priests. The church condemned Marsilius's book, but reformers continued to be inspired by his ideas.

Another critic of the church was the Oxford professor John Wycliffe (*ca.* 1320–84). At first concerned with questions having to do with the ownership of private property, Wycliffe became convinced that the church was being corrupted by wealth and that the state should take over its property holdings. The secular rulers applauded this suggestion, of course, and protected Wycliffe from the wrath of the clergy. Wycliffe went on to question the orthodox doctrine that the bread and wine in the communion service are transformed into the body and blood of Christ. He ended up by attacking the whole administrative structure of the church as corrupt and unauthorized by the Bible. He also encouraged his followers to translate the Bible so ordinary people could understand its message without the mediation of the clergy.

Though Wycliffe had no intention of launching a popular movement, his ideas spread rapidly beyond the scholarly circles for which he wrote. Preachers carrying the Wycliffite English Bible traveled about the country telling people about his radical proposals. Many of those preachers became social reformers as well and gained an impressive following among the lower and middle classes in England. Their preaching contributed to the radicalism that triggered the great Peasants' Rebellion of 1381 (see p. 354). When the king and nobles put down the rebellion, they took care to suppress the radicals as well. But the suppression was not wholly successful. The radicals—called Lollards (from the Dutch word *lollaert,* meaning mumbler, which was used to describe religious radicals on the Continent)—went underground and continued to foment unrest until the English Reformation of the sixteenth century.

Such reform movements drew much of their strength from the decline of the church after the Great Schism. In 1395 the French became so exasperated with their pope, Benedict XIII of Avignon, that the French clergy, under pressure from the government, withdrew their obedience from him for five years. This was the first instance of a strategy that was to have a fateful future: the rejection of papal authority by the clergy of a large nation under pressure from the secular government.

John Huss

Even after Wycliffe's death, his ideas continued to exercise great influence on the

Continent as well as in England. The English king Richard II (r. 1377–99) married Anne of Bohemia, and Czech students began to come to England to study. When they returned home, they carried Wycliffe's teachings with them. In time, those teachings found a home at the University of Prague (founded 1348).

In 1402, John Huss (*ca.* 1369–1415), a brilliant young professor at the university, emerged as a leader of the Czech reformers. In his preaching he drew on the teachings of Wycliffe: Faith must be based on the Bible, which is the only source of authority; Christ, not the pope, is the true head of the church; salvation comes from God through Christ, not through ritual ceremonies and a corrupt priesthood. In 1414 Huss was excommunicated by the pope. But he remained at liberty, and his ideas were accepted by a majority of the Czech people.

In that same year, Huss was invited to defend his ideas at the Council of Constance (called to resolve the Great Schism; see p. 357). He eagerly accepted and traveled to Constance under the emperor Sigismund's guarantee of safe conduct. On his arrival he was charged with heresy and was imprisoned, the emperor's guarantee notwithstanding. In fact, Sigismund withdrew his protection as soon as the charge of heresy was leveled. The leaders of the council ordered Huss to recant his views in public, but he stood firm. In the dramatic trial that followed, the issue was whether the Bible and the individual's conscience were the source of religious authority, as Huss argued, or the Catholic church was, as the council insisted. Not surprisingly, the council fathers condemned Huss to death and ordered that he be burned at the stake. He was executed outside the walls of Constance in May 1415.

The following year, the council condemned a follower of Huss, Jerome, to be burnt at the stake, and before the council disbanded in 1418 civil war had broken out in Bohemia. Not until 1436 were some of the more conservative Hussites and the church able to reach an agreement. The agreement recognized a Bohemian church with control over its own ecclesiastical appointments and with its own liturgical practices, notably the right to offer the cup as well as the bread to communicants. For the first time, the Roman church had entered into an agreement with condemned heretics after excommunicating them and preaching a crusade against them.

A pair of woodcuts by Lucas Cranach the Elder contrasting Jesus and the pope. On the left, Jesus is driving the moneychangers from the temple; on the right, the pope is taking money for indulgences.

THE PAPACY'S TRIUMPH OVER THE CONCILIAR MOVEMENT

Though the Council of Constance succeeded in ending the Great Schism, it was unable to institute any meaningful reform, which had been one of its principal goals. The English and German delegates tried in vain to get the council to consider reform before turning to the election of a new pope; the other delegates were more interested in healing the schism first. Once Martin V (r. 1417–31) had been elected, the council leaders waved aside the mild report of a committee they had set up to study church abuses and declared the council ended without ever taking up the question of reform. So the fifteenth-century church continued to countenance corruption under the leadership of a pope who set a standard of worldliness.

The leaders of the council at Constance had decreed that the church must summon a general council every five years. But Martin V saw to it that the decree

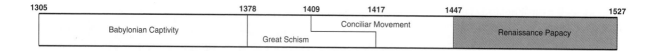

1305		1378	1409	1417	1447	1527

Babylonian Captivity

Great Schism

Conciliar Movement

Renaissance Papacy

was ignored. At a time when most European kings were humbling their parliaments and their nobles, the popes chose to abolish regular councils and to humble the princes of the church, the cardinals. By the time Nicholas V (r. 1447–55) became pope, the possibility that the church might evolve into a limited monarchy had vanished. Since that time, every general council has been under the control of the pope.

That victory left the papacy stronger in some respects, weaker in others. No one within the church could any longer challenge the power of the pope, but the pope was now isolated from leaders of opinion—both clerical and lay—particularly in northern Europe. The period of the concordats followed (see p. 420). In France, Charles VII in effect created a national, or "Gallican," church, restricting the pope's power to appoint and tax the clergy. In England and Spain, the kings followed suit, but in Germany, which lacked a central government strong enough to stand up to the pope, the papacy retained its rights of appointment, taxation, and jurisdiction.

The period between the accession of Nicholas V to the papacy (1447) and the sack of Rome by imperial Spanish troops (1527) is often called the age of the Renaissance papacy. During that period, many of the popes were well-educated patrons of humanists and artists, while others were despots; some were both. Nicholas V founded the Vatican library, one of the world's great repositories of books and manuscripts. Pius II (r. 1458–64), before his election as pope, had been a celebrated Sienese humanist, Aeneas Sylvius Piccolomini. Julius II (r. 1503–13) initiated the rebuilding of St. Peter's. Sixtus IV (r. 1471–84) was said to have died in a fit of rage at the conclusion of a peace settlement; and Julius II was known as "the Warrior Pope." Alexander VI (r. 1492–1503) tried to carve a principality out of the Papal States for his illegitimate son, Cesare Borgia.

The papacy had often been embroiled in politics during the Middle Ages, but in those days politics meant international politics, with grand principles of political authority at stake. The Renaissance popes, by contrast, were embroiled mainly in Italian politics, with only dynastic interests at stake. In time, the papacy became thoroughly Italianized. (In fact, since the end of the Great Schism in 1417, only two non-Italians have ever been elected pope, in 1522 and 1979).

Julius II (r. 1503–13), the warrior pope, painted by Raphael.

THE PROBLEMS OF THE RENAISSANCE CHURCH

The Renaissance church had problems elsewhere besides in the papal curia where venality and nepotism reigned. Most of the bishops and archbishops of the church were of noble birth, and many of them had been appointed to their office by a king or a pope as a reward for their loyal service rather than for their piety or administrative ability. Typically, the newly appointed bishop paid a substantial part of his first year's income to whoever it was who had appointed him. Not only was this contrary to canon law, it gave the bishop a strong incentive to siphon off as much money as he could from his diocese. Moreover, many bishops and archbishops held more than one office—which also was contrary to canon law. In a diocese with an absentee bishop, the bishop's income was drained from the local economy, and the diocese was left to the mercy of the greedy priests and secular lords. One bishop is said to have visited his bishopric only once, to be buried.

Even conscientious bishops found that they had little power to appoint competent clergy or to reform abuses within their dioceses. Much of the power that had formerly belonged to the bishops had either fallen into the hands of local laymen or the pope. Consequently the parish priests tended to be ignorant and immoral. Moreover, because the priests had to raise money to pay taxes to their bishop and to local laymen, they became almost as rapacious as their superiors. Normally the income of a church consisted of tithes (that is, a tenth of the income of parishioners), first fruits (a small share of the early harvest), and oblations (gifts from parishioners). By the sixteenth century priests were augmenting that income by charging a fee for baptisms, marriages, and burials.

Monastic orders had also lost prestige. Many monasteries in the cities performed as parish churches because the population had grown too large for the parish priests to handle. This activity involved the monasteries in the affairs of the world, and they followed the example of the priests in squeezing their congregations for money.

By the late fifteenth century, the monastic orders were no longer attracting pious novices but men who wanted to serve parishes and to rise to positions of power and wealth in society. The monks acquired a reputation for living rich and secular lives.

The most common complaint leveled against the church was that it sold spiritual benefits for money. The church was land rich, but cash poor, and it had to find ways to support itself. But the methods it used to raise money and the purposes to which the money was allegedly put—wars, rich living, and the like—outraged many of the faithful. Clergy at all levels were criticized, but the papacy was considered the worst offender.

The sale of indulgences was the practice that aroused the most heated criticism, although it was far from the most important source of papal income. An indulgence was a remission of the temporal penalty for sin imposed by a priest in the sacrament of penance. Christians were required to confess their sins and receive penance (a penalty) at least once a year. Penances ranged from saying prayers to going on a crusade or a pilgrimage; the severity of the penance depended on the seriousness of the sin and the condition of the sinner.

During the Middle Ages, the practice of commuting a penance with a money payment had become common, and in the fourteenth century the popes devised a doctrine that held Christ and the saints had accumulated a "treasury of merits" from which Christ's vicars—the popes—could dispense benefits to the faithful through indulgences. In the fifteenth century, Sixtus IV (r. 1471–84) expanded this doctrine by claiming that the pope had the power to release the souls of the dead from the penances they were undergoing in purgatory—the state in which the soul purged its sins before being admitted to paradise. Sixtus's pronouncement transformed the traffic in indulgences into a booming business and a real moneymaker. It was hard for people to resist an opportunity to ease the suffering of the soul of a dead parent or spouse. Yet when it became clear that the money from the sale of indulgences was going not to pious purposes but to war and ostentatious living, many laymen concluded that the church was selling salvation for profit.

RESPONSES TO CORRUPTION

Criticism and Reform of the Church in the Fifteenth Century

Many church leaders of the late fifteenth century were of course conscientious, pious men who found it difficult to answer the criticism leveled at the church. Not only were the abuses undeniable; the status of churchmen in general had declined. The Europe of 1500 was more secular in its outlook than the Europe of 1400. Imbued with the ideas of the Renaissance, many people now considered a career in business, politics, or the arts to be as attractive as a career in the church and no less likely to lead to salvation.

Moreover, during the fifteenth century the lower and middle classes had come to embrace a popular piety accompanied by religious practices that verged on superstition and idolatry—the cults of the saints, for example, and the veneration of relics. In what one historian has called the "supersaturated" religious atmosphere of the fifteenth century, perceptive church leaders came to realize that the church was vulnerable to troublesome questions: What is the essence of Christianity? Is it the ritual and the elaborate hierarchy? Is it the veneration of relics or participation in a pilgrimage? Or is it loving one's neighbor and living simply, as Christ lived?

Church leaders were well aware of the new power of secular rulers to appoint bishops, tax the clergy, and limit papal control over the churches in their realms. And they knew that the kings could initiate religious reform of their own, often for political purposes. In fact, reform by royal command was sometimes well motivated and effective: In Spain, Cardinal Jiménez de Cisneros (1436–1517), backed by Ferdinand and Isabella, carried out many church reforms early in the sixteenth century. But always the danger remained that reform by a secular ruler, no matter how well motivated, might result in state control of the church and its property.

Several reform movements were launched within the church, none of them effective. The Brethren of the Common Life, as we have seen, pursued its quiet way of life and founded schools to educate a new Christian elite, but it had little effect on the church. In Florence between 1494 and 1498, one of the most remarkable preachers of the age, the Dominican Savonarola, tried to reform the inhabitants of one of the richest and most secular cities in Europe. He preached repentance and piety and attacked both secular and church leaders. Savonarola held to the medieval view that the church itself was divinely constituted and could never be in need of reform, but that when the individuals who served it grew corrupt they should and must be reformed.

That idea of reform had already begun to disappear. The intention of the leaders of the councils of Constance (1414–18) and Basel (1431–37) had been to reform the church by assigning substantial power to councils and by making the pope a limited monarch. Even more radical, John Huss preached the reform both of individual Christians and of the church as an institution. But the church demonstrated its unreadiness for such reform: it ignored the conciliar movement and had both Huss and Savonarola burned as heretics.

Christian Humanism

Humanism, which, as we have seen, extolled the eloquence and power of the ancient authors, spread from Italy to northern Europe during the fifteenth century and was well established there by the early sixteenth century. Northern Europeans came to Italy to study with humanists, books and translations were shipped north from Italy (some of the most important printing presses were in northern Italy), and Italian humanists kept up a lively correspondence with their northern counterparts.

The humanism that took root in northern Europe is often called Christian humanism to distinguish it from the

Italian variety, but the name is somewhat misleading. Even though the Italian humanists were primarily interested in pre-Christian authors, they were themselves Christians and never denied their Christian faith. The fact that the northern humanists were more interested in the early Christian authors and writings suggests that in some sense they were more "Christian" than the Italians, though at base their interests were the same.

In their studies of the New Testament, the Christian humanists sought to explore the faith of the apostles as revealed in the language of the biblical account. They concentrated especially on the letters of St. Paul, which constitute a substantial body of material. They also studied the works of the church fathers—Greek writers such as Origen and Gregory of Nazianzus and Latin writers such as Augustine and Jerome. There they found straightforward, detailed explanations of the Christian faith free of the abstruse theological accretions of medieval commentators and scholastic theologians. They held St. Jerome in the highest esteem, because his Latin was closest to that of Cicero and because he was the most accomplished literary scholar of the western church fathers.

The main goal of the Christian humanists was to retrieve the original texts of Christianity. During the Middle Ages, intellectuals read the Bible only with the aid of learned commentaries, just as they used a technical gloss when they read legal, medical, or philosophical texts. All the major works were accompanied by a standard commentary, called a *glossa ordinaria,* that became in effect part of the works themselves. The humanists scorned those commentaries, which were often ungrammatical, dense, and rich in jargon. They sought instead the eloquence of the early church writers, who spoke in the original voice of Christianity.

The Christian humanists first set out to produce accurate texts of the Bible and the early Christian writings. In Spain, Cardinal Jiménez set scholars to producing a monumental edition of the Bible in which the original Hebrew and Greek texts appeared in parallel columns with the Latin. In Germany, Johann Reuchlin (1455–1522) promoted the study of Hebrew as a means of understanding the Old Testament, while a group of German Dominicans—who saw such study as a threat to the authority of the church—sought to destroy all books written in Hebrew.

The Christian humanists were in a sense conservative in their attempt to get back to the original texts, but they were radical in their conviction that the individual human being had a unique spiritual capacity. They called for translations of the Bible into the vernacular so that ordinary people could participate in the Christian experience and understand the need for reform. In France, Jacques Lefèvre d'Etaples (1455–1536) translated the New Testament into French (1523). In England, Thomas More (1477–1535)—the royal chancellor who was executed in 1535 for his loyalty to the Roman church

A Catholic, Sir Thomas More, on the Church

The true Church of Christ is the common known church of all Christian people not gone out nor cast out. This whole body both of good and bad is the Catholic Church of Christ, which is in this world very sickly, and hath many sore members, as hath sometime the natural body of a man. . . . The Church was gathered, and the faith believed, before any part of the New Testament was put in writing. And which was or is the true scripture, neither Luther nor Tyndale [translator of the New Testament into English] knoweth but by the credence that they give to the Church. . . . The Church was before the gospel was written; and the faith was taught, and men were baptized and masses said, and the other sacraments ministered among Christian people, before any part of the New Testament was put in writing. . . . As the sea shall never surround and overwhelm the land, and yet it hath eaten many places in, and swallowed whole countries up, and made places now sea that sometime were well-inhabited lands, and hath lost part of his own possession in other parts again; so though the faith of Christ shall never be overflown with heresies, nor the gates of hell prevail against Christ's Church, yet in some places it winneth in a new people, so may there in some places by negligence be lost the old.

From The Workes of Sir Thomas More *(London: Scholar Press, 1978), pp. 527, 852, 853, 921.*

(see p. 419)—detailed in his book *Utopia* the ironies and hypocrisies of society and called for the spread of true Christianity through education.

Erasmus

The acknowledged leader of the Christian humanists was Erasmus of Rotterdam (*ca.* 1469–1536), who in his youth had attended a school run by the Brethren of the Common Life. He was committed to the study of early Christian writers and had absorbed the ideals—though not the secular interests—of the Italian humanists. Erasmus devoted his life to scholarship, in the conviction that knowledge would help save the church.

Erasmus, by Holbein.

After making an exhaustive comparison of ancient manuscripts, Erasmus produced the first critical edition of the Greek text of the New Testament (1516). In his preface, he urged that his work be used as the basis for new translations of the Scriptures into the vernacular languages. He summarized the goal of Christian humanism with this statement: "I utterly dissent from those who are unwilling that the sacred Scriptures should be read by the unlearned translated into their vulgar tongue, as though Christ had taught such subtleties that they can scarcely be understood even by a few theologians, or, as though the strength of the Christian religion consisted in men's ignorance of it." In countless letters and books Erasmus proclaimed a "philosophy of Christ"—the love of God and neighbor that to him was the essence of Christianity.

Erasmus, through his intellect, learning, literary skills, and lively sense of humor, had an enormous influence on his contemporaries. He acknowledged the Renaissance commitment to life in this world by insisting that the love of God and neighbor be expressed through a life of good works. He ridiculed monks and priests who insisted that withdrawal from the world was the ideal form of the Christian life. He also rejected ceremonies and fasts as routes to heaven by imagining what Christ might have said: "I promised [to Christians] the inheritance of my Father, not to cowls, prayers, or fasts, but to works of charity."

Although Christian humanism demonstrated the power of education to bring about reform, it was far too intellectual to arouse the interest of the general population.

LUTHER'S REVOLT

On October 31, 1517, an Augustinian friar named Martin Luther (1483–1546), who was professor of Bible in the little University of Wittenberg in Saxony, submitted 95 theses—or propositions—to his colleagues to serve as the material for a debate on the subject of indulgences. Luther had become outraged by the efforts of a Dominican friar named Tetzel to hawk indulgences to the residents of Magdeburg with the following sales pitch: "So soon as coin in coffer rings, the soul from Purgatory springs." Though the proceeds were supposed to go toward the building of the new church of St. Peter in Rome, half actually ended up with the archbishop of Mainz and the Fugger banking firm of Augsburg (see p. 416).

Luther's theses, which were immediately printed and debated throughout Germany, caused a sensation. They touched on a note of resentment that was ready to be sounded:

> *There is no divine authority for preaching that the soul flies out of purgatory immediately the money clinks in the bottom of the chest. . . . It is certainly possible that when the money clinks in the bottom of the chest, avarice and greed increase. . . . All those who believe themselves certain of their own salvation by means of letters of indulgence will be eternally damned, together with their teachers. . . . Any*

Erasmus's Preface to His Edition of the New Testament

I utterly dissent from those who are unwilling that the sacred Scriptures should be read by the unlearned translated into their vulgar tongue, as though Christ had taught such subtleties that they can scarcely be understood even by a few theologians, or, as though the strength of the Christian religion consisted in men's ignorance of it. The mysteries of kings it may be safer to conceal, but Christ wished his mysteries to be published as openly as possible. I wish that even the weakest woman should read the Gospel—should read the epistles of Paul. And I wish these were translated into all languages, so that they might be read and understood, not only by Scots and Irishmen, but also by Turks and Saracens. To make them understood is surely the first step. It may be that they might be ridiculed by many, but some would take them to heart. I long that the husbandman should sing portions of them to himself as he follows the plough, that the weaver should hum them to the tune of his shuttle, that the traveller should beguile with their stories the tedium of his journey.

From Erasmus, "Paraclesis," Novum Instrumentum, *trans. by Frederic Seebohm, in* The Oxford Reformers *(New York: Dutton, 1914), p. 203.*

Contemporary caricature of Johann Tetzel hawking indulgences. The last line of the jingle is: "So soon as coin in coffer rings, the soul into heaven springs."

Christian whatsoever, who is truly repentant, enjoys plenary remission from penalty and guilt, and this is given him without letters of indulgence.

At this time, Luther was 34 years old, the brilliant son of a prosperous peasant turned miner who had been able to afford a university education for his son. As a young man, Luther had experienced several emotional crises and had eventually decided on the life of a friar. Though it was the age of humanism and the new learning, he chose to live a religious life and to pursue scholastic learning, which still dominated the university curriculum.

Luther found no spiritual solace in the prayers, confessions, and penances of the monastic community, however. He sought forgiveness of his sins but found no assurance of God's forgiveness in the ceremonial acts of worship. Instead, he became increasingly guilt-ridden and doubtful about his ability to save himself.

Suddenly he came to an understanding of what St. Paul had meant when he said that a man is saved not by obeying the Jewish law but by his faith in Christ alone. He realized that he had been trying to satisfy God by scrupulously observing church ritual, which was no less demanding and no more effective than the Jewish law against which Paul had preached. He found it unthinkable that human beings, corrupted by sin, could win God's favor by performing some good deed or sacramental act. He came to believe that God alone can save people's souls and that all the sinner can do is to have faith in the possibility of God's forgiveness.

In working out the revolutionary implications of his new understanding, Luther slowly came to the view that ceremonies and sacraments, pilgrimages and indulgences—everything the medieval church called "good works"—were irrelevant at best and dangerous at worst. His first act was to deny the efficacy of indulgences, causing sales of indulgences in Germany to drop off sharply. When the Dominicans, the chief dealers in indulgences, persuaded Pope Leo X (r. 1513–21) to condemn Luther's theses, he was gradually driven into denying the authority of the pope. He also came to believe that John Huss had been right on certain points, despite his being condemned by the Council of Constance, and this belief led him to deny the authority of councils as well.

At last Luther was summoned to appear before the emperor Charles V at an imperial diet (council) held at Worms in April 1521 to defend his theses. Like John Huss a century earlier, he was given a guarantee of safe conduct on his journey to Worms. There he declared to the emperor and assembled dignitaries that he was bound by the authority of the Scriptures and by his own conscience rather than by the authority of the pope or council. He could not recant his theses, he said, because his conscience was "captive of the Word of God" and because it was "neither safe nor right to go against conscience."

The emperor permitted Luther to return to the protection of Frederick, the Elector of Saxony, and until his death in 1546, Luther remained in Wittenberg

Luther on Justification by Faith

For the word of God cannot be received and honored by any works, but by faith alone. Hence it is clear that, as the soul needs the word alone for life and justification, so it is justified by faith alone and not by any works. For if it could be justified by any other means, it would have no need of the word, nor consequently of faith. . . .

It is evident that by no outward work or labor can the inward man be at all justified, made free and saved, and that no works whatever have any relation to him. And so, on the other hand, it is solely by impiety and incredulity of heart that he becomes guilty and a slave of sin, deserving condemnation; not by any outward sin or work.

Therefore the first care of every Christian ought to be to lay aside all reliance on works, and strengthen his faith alone more and more, and by it grow in the knowledge, not of works, but of Christ Jesus, who has suffered and risen again for him.

From Martin Luther, On Christian Liberty, *trans. by H. Wace and C. A. Buchheim, in* First Principles of the Reformation *(London: Murray, 1883), pp. 107–08.*

teaching, preaching, and writing. In his new view of Christianity, the active life of a merchant or a housewife was as spiritually rewarding as the life of a monk or a nun, and he himself married a former nun, with whom he had six children. Meanwhile, the revolt against the papacy that he had initiated gathered momentum and spread across northern Europe. By the late sixteenth century, the unity of western Christendom had been shattered.

Luther's Work

Luther's religious thought contained three main, closely related principles: salvation through faith rather than through good works, the ultimate authority of the Bible, and the priesthood of all believers. Luther wrote hundreds of letters and tracts defending his ideas, but his greatest literary accomplishment was his German translation of the Bible (completed in 1534). He wanted to put the Bible into the hands of every German, for he was convinced that there was no essential difference between a priest and a layman. A dedicated layman reverently reading the Scripture was closer to the divine truth than a worldly pope proclaiming the dogma of the church. Thus a pious layman could serve God as well as a priest or a monk. The literary quality of Luther's translation was so impressive that the work is considered to have been the foundation for the modern language known as High German.

Luther's original protest had been purely religious in nature, but by 1520 he was appealing to German nationalism. "What has brought us Germans to such a pass that we have to suffer this robbery and this destruction of our property by the Pope?" he asked. That question drew a quick response from princes eager to confiscate church property, from businessmen unhappy over papal taxation and over ecclesiastical rules governing business practices, and from devout laymen and priests shocked by the corruption of the church. Though the purpose of his revolt was to enable people to reconcile an honest life with the highest spiritual aspirations, some people seized on it for their own selfish purposes.

IV. D. Pl. I.

I. Buys, inv. et delin.   Reint Vinkeles sculp. 1782.

Luther burns papal bulls, symbolizing his rejection of papal authority.

Luther had no intention of setting up an independent church to compete with the church of Rome. But at last he became convinced that the church founded by Christ had strayed from its true path after the conversion of Constantine, when the church became entangled in worldly affairs, and that the bishop of Rome was not

Title page of the first German translation of the Bible, by Martin Luther, printed in 1534 with the approval of the Elector of Saxony.

the true vicar of Christ but the Antichrist. He wanted the church to return to the pure faith and the simple religion of the apostles. In the purified church there would be only two sacraments—baptism and communion—rather than the seven sacraments of the Catholic church. There would be a simplified ritual in German rather than in Latin, and there would be more emphasis on the congregation's participation in the service. Luther wrote many hymns in which he incorporated these ideas, and those hymns are still sung today.

The split between the "Lutheran" and "Catholic" churches occurred gradually and without Luther's explicit approval. The conflict over the nature of the true church continued unresolved until at last each church embraced its own beliefs and rejected the beliefs of the other.

THE SPREAD OF LUTHERANISM

Unlike the failed reforms of the fifteenth century, Lutheranism—one of the most radical movements in Christian history— spread quickly across northern Europe. One reason for its rapid acceptance was the availability of the printing press, which Gutenberg had invented in the middle of the fifteenth century (see p. 373). Luther and his followers wrote hundreds of tracts and had them printed for widespread distribution. The nineteenth-century historian Leopold von Ranke calculated that in 1523 Luther and his supporters published nearly 400 books and pamphlets.

Another reason for the rapid acceptance of Lutheranism was the early support of the humanists. The humanists were themselves reformers, and they saw in Luther's program many of the principles they were espousing. Like them, Luther rejected the commentaries of the medieval theologians and sought to return to the unadorned text of the Bible. And like them, Luther respected the church fathers and attacked the financial abuses of the church. But while the humanists criticized the medieval commentators for obscuring the text of the Bible with their graceless prose, Luther criticized them for their

faulty theological opinions. And while the humanists valued the church fathers for what they said about the faith of the early Christians, Luther valued them for their simple, direct explications of the meaning of the biblical text. For Luther, the sole source of authority was the Bible, particularly the New Testament.

Further, the humanists wanted to reform only the practices of the church, while Luther and his followers came to view the church itself as illegitimate. Erasmus and Cardinal Jiménez, for example, concentrated on freeing the biblical text from the clutter of the medieval commentaries, whereas the Protestants (as Lutherans were called after 1529, when they presented a "protest" at an imperial diet) claimed that the Scripture was the sole basis for faith and for an understanding of Christ.

The difference is further illustrated by a comparison between a reform document that the cardinals, inspired by the humanists, presented to Pope Paul III (r. 1534–49) in 1538 and Luther's *Address to the Nobility of the German Nation* (1520). After affirming the authority of the church, the cardinals urged the reform of the parish churches, the elimination of nonresident bishops, a restriction on the sale of indulgences to one sale a year, and a reform of the judicial system. Luther complained about the same abuses, and in much harsher language, but he sought to eliminate their root causes. For example, the cardinals urged strict enforcement of the rule of celibacy to ensure the chastity of clerics; Luther argued that clerics should be permitted to marry.

Despite the differences between the humanist cardinals and Luther, many leading humanists, including Erasmus and Thomas More, supported him at first. More broke with him in 1523, in his *Letter against Luther,* and Erasmus broke with him in 1524.

Luther also received early support from many priests and monks, especially in the German cities. The cities had many grievances against the church: it controlled their prime real estate, and it insisted that the clergy be exempted from local taxes. Moreover, the church's tax levies fell most heavily on the urban populations. In city after city, conservative members of the clergy were quietly replaced by followers of Luther. Because so many of the cities held imperial charters, the reformed churches were in effect state churches, and in another decade or so Lutheranism would be established as the state religion by some of the German princes.

The peasants too responded to Luther's message at first, but they lost interest after the Peasants' Rebellion of 1524–25. Although the aims of the rebellion had to do with social reform—the abolition of serfdom and the burdens of the manorial system—the rebels interpreted Luther's pronouncements as support for their program: "Therefore do we find in the Scripture that we are free," they argued, "and we will be free." In a bitter condemnation of the rebels, Luther replied that the freedom he was speaking about was spiritual not social, and the rebels felt he had betrayed them. As time passed, Luther and his supporters found themselves caught between the reactionary Roman Catholic church and the radical lower classes.

Finally, Germany's lack of centralized government prevented its resistance to the spread of Lutheranism. Although the emperor Charles V (r. 1519–56) never wavered in his orthodoxy, he was preoccupied with trying to hold his vast dominions together and with repelling military threats on every side. From 1522 to 1559, Charles and his son Philip were fighting a series of wars with France, while Charles and his brother Ferdinand, Duke of Austria, were trying to stem the advance of the Turks up the Danube Valley.

Not until 1547—the year after Luther's death—did Charles turn his attention to Lutheranism, which by then had been accepted by about half the German principalities. He launched a confused religious war against the princes who supported Luther that dragged on until 1555, when he permitted his brother Ferdinand to conclude the Religious Peace of Augsburg. That peace allowed the free cities and principalities of the empire to choose between Lutheranism and Catholicism and bound them to respect each other's

Contemporary engraving depicting a noble lady and her son kneeling before peasant rebels to plead for their lives during the Peasants' Rebellion (1524–25).

choice. Essentially, the agreement made religion the prerogative of the ruler of each principality; anyone who disagreed with his ruler could migrate to another principality.

The Peace of Augsburg constituted the first official recognition that western Christendom was in a state of disunity and would remain so. In the end, northern Germany became mostly Protestant; southern Germany remained Catholic. Outside Germany, Lutheranism took root only in Scandinavia, where Denmark, Norway, and Sweden became Lutheran by midcentury. The German provenance of Lutheranism limited its appeal abroad, where another form of Protestantism, that of John Calvin, won acceptance.

OTHER PROTESTANT MOVEMENTS

In addition to Wittenberg, other important centers of reform were Zürich, Basel, Strasbourg, and especially Geneva. In each of these cities a form of Protestantism emerged that was significantly different from Lutheranism. The so-called "reformed" churches that resulted had a more highly developed system of theology and church organization and put greater stress on the moral conduct and political action of their members than did the Lutheran churches.

Bucer and Zwingli

Among the early leaders of these Protestant movements were the humanists Martin Bucer of Strasbourg (1491–1551) and the Swiss scholar Ulrich Zwingli (1484–1531). As a Dominican friar, Bucer had been influenced by the humanism of Erasmus. Once he became familiar with Luther's views, however, he left the Dominican order and married a nun. He was excommunicated in 1523, and from 1524 to 1548 he led the reform movement in Strasbourg, where he introduced various liturgical changes. Throughout the years he participated in colloquies held in Worms, Regensburg, and Hagenau aimed at reconciling Catholicism and Protestantism and also was active in trying to reconcile Lutheranism with other Protestant movements, particularly the one led by Zwingli.

Zwingli, who was born in a rural village in the Swiss Alps, studied classics in Basel. He too fell under Erasmus's influence and was especially attracted to the idea of a renascent Christianity based on the Scriptures. Zwingli became a priest, beginning as a village parson in 1506, and rose to become the "people's priest" in Zürich (1518). In this prestigious position, which enabled him to stay abreast of the ideas of the day, he became familiar with the activity of Martin Luther. Historians still debate the extent of the influence of Luther's ideas on Zwingli. Zwingli himself claimed that he had arrived at Luther's basic ideas on his own before reading Luther's works.

As in many other cities, the reform movement in Zürich proceeded by stages. In 1522, some of the citizens violated the church's dietary laws during the Lenten season, and the city council appointed a commission to investigate. The bishop of Constance, who had jurisdiction over Zürich, protested that he had the exclusive right to judge matters of religious discipline, but the commission, of which Zwingli was a member, proceeded anyway. The commission's report was equivocal, but Zwingli soon published a sermon in which he argued that, because Christians were free from the law, as St. Paul said,

they did not have to obey dietary rules imposed by the church. A person's faith, he argued, had to do with his or her beliefs and motivations, not with the observance of actions prescribed by the church. Luther, of course, had reached the same conclusion.

In 1523, the city council of Zürich, in an effort to dispel public confusion and unrest, announced a debate on questions of religion. Zwingli prepared for the debate by drawing up a list of 67 conclusions on matters of doctrine, morals, and church discipline. His main ideas reflected that the Scriptures alone were the basis of true Christianity, and they carried the day. After this, Protestantism was widely accepted in Zürich. The question now became whether the paintings, stained-glass windows, and sculptures should be removed from the city's churches. Zwingli's position was that once the church members had become true Christians they would no longer need such outward signs of faith, and he suggested that the images be removed gradually. The people were less patient, however, and in 1524 they stripped the interiors of the churches—whitewashing the walls, pulling down the crucifixes, and destroying the windows and sculptures. Finally, in 1525, the reformers, with Zwingli in the lead this time, replaced the Mass with a simple service in commemoration of the Last Supper. The city council supported their action by issuing a law that did away with the Mass altogether.

Calvinism

John Calvin (1509–64) was born in Noyon, France, and as a young man was sent to the University of Paris to study law. He was more interested in humanism than in law, however, and soon dropped his legal studies to concentrate on Greek and Latin. In 1532, he published a commentary on Seneca's treatise *Concerning Clemency.* Around this time he had what he later called a conversion to Protestantism, and in 1534 he moved to Basel, where there were many Protestants. In Basel, he wrote a theological treatise, called the *Institutes of the Christian Religion,* which he intended to be a comprehensive treatment of the Protestant religion. The first edition of this work, only six chapters long, was published in 1536. Calvin then revised and enlarged the work until the fourth edition, with eighty chapters, was published in 1559. The *Institutes* was the first systematic presentation of Protestant theology.

Calvin visited Geneva in 1536. He had no intention of staying until Guillaume Farel (1489–1565), a leading Protestant who had introduced Protestantism to the city two months before, persuaded him to become his assistant. Together, Farel and Calvin undertook a vigorous program of reform that aroused opposition because of their impatience and the strictness of their approach. In 1538, a majority of Catholics were elected to the city council, and Farel and Calvin were driven from the city. Farel went to Neuchâtel, where he remained the rest of his life. Calvin went to Strasbourg, where he came under the influence of the moderate reformer Martin Bucer.

Apparently, Protestantism had taken root in Geneva, however, because in 1541 the city council invited Calvin to return. Although he seems to have done so reluctantly, he remained there until his death in 1564. During those years, he worked diligently for reform in the church of Geneva and gradually asserted his power over the city council itself. By the late 1550s, Geneva had become a virtual theocracy—a city-state governed by the clergy.

Building on Luther's doctrine of salvation by faith alone, Calvin constructed a system that emphasized the sovereignty of God and the depravity of man. At the center of that system was the doctrine of predestination: God, through his inscrutable will, destined some men to be saved and others to be damned. Consequently, the idea that one can win salvation by performing "good works" is absurd. Calvin also held that a true and fervent faith in Christ and the Scriptures was a sign that one was among the elect of God and that the performance of good works was evidence of that faith.

In 1559, Calvin established an academy in Geneva comprising schools of arts, law, medicine, and theology. Perhaps because of his own fame, he was able to attract an excellent faculty, and within a few years the academy was flourishing, with more than 1,500 students from all over Europe. Geneva itself became a model for Presbyterian or Reformed churches in France, England, Scotland, the Netherlands, the Rhineland, Bohemia, and Hungary, and later for churches in North America and Dutch South Africa.

Calvin advocated that each local church should have a ruling body composed of ministers and elders (or presbyters) who were to meet regularly in councils (called synods) with the officials of the other churches in the district. Because Calvinism was particularly resistant to secular control, it never became "nationalized," as Lutheranism had. Moreover, because it possessed a systematic theology, it could be adopted by reformers everywhere.

Sketch of John Calvin drawn by a student, perhaps during a lecture.

Calvin on Predestination

Predestination we call the eternal decree of God, by which he has determined in himself, what he would have to become of every individual of mankind. For they are not all created with a similar destiny; but eternal life is foreordained for some, and eternal damnation for others. . . .

In conformity, therefore, to the clear doctrine of the Scripture, we assert, that by an eternal and immutable counsel, God has once for all determined, both whom he would admit to salvation, and whom he would condemn to destruction. We affirm that this counsel, as far as concerns the elect, is founded on his gratuitous mercy, totally irrespective of human merit; but that to those whom he devotes to condemnation, the gate of life is closed by a just and irreprehensible, but incomprehensible, judgment. . . .

How exceedingly presumptuous it is only to inquire into the causes of the Divine will; which is in fact, and is justly entitled to be, the cause of everything that exists. . . . For the will of God is the highest rule of justice; so that what he wills must be considered just, for this very reason, because he wills it.

From John Calvin, Institutes of the Christian Religion, *trans. by John Allen (Philadelphia: Westminster Press, 1930), Book III, Ch. 21, pars. 5, 7; Ch. 23, par. 2.*

By the 1550s Calvinists were in many parts of Europe, but they constituted a majority only in Geneva and Scotland. Elsewhere, they formed a well-organized minority that left its mark on society. Calvinism gave rise to Puritanism in England, to the Huguenots in France, and to the Dutch Reformed church. It served as the militant wing of Protestantism.

THE RADICALS

Other reformers had more radical agendas linked to the social unrest of the period. In Germany particularly—where capitalism was making rapid progress—workers and peasants hard hit by economic change turned to old ideas of social and religious reform. During the 1520s in Switzerland and in the upper Rhine Valley, little groups of people came together and proclaimed that the only true church was a voluntary association of believers, not an official institution like the churches of the Lutherans or the Catholics. Holding that baptism was a sign of belief, many of these groups in-sisted that only adults could be baptized—an idea that dated back to certain heretical groups of the twelfth century. Their opponents called them Anabaptists, or re-baptizers. The Anabaptists had a simple liturgy and generally interpreted the Bible literally. Most of them refused to take an oath—in court or elsewhere—or to accept public office or serve in the army. Some of the groups practiced the sort of communism described in the second chapter of Acts (2:44–47).

The Anabaptists were persecuted by Catholics and Protestants alike. After being driven from southern Germany, many of them found their way to the Netherlands, Bohemia, Poland, and England. It was during the seventeenth century in England and in the English colonies in America that the ideas of the Anabaptists were fully realized. Modern Baptists (who practice only adult baptism), Congregationalists (who recognize the autonomy of local congregations), and Quakers (who rely on an "inner light") all trace their origins to the sixteenth-century Anabaptists.

The more rigid Protestants objected to all religious paintings and sculpture as leading to idolatry. In this engraving of 1579, Calvinists are pulling down statues of saints and destroying stained-glass windows.

ANGLICANISM

Although several kings took over their national churches during the late Middle Ages, they were not motivated by a desire for reform. In England, though the breach with Rome signaled by the Act of Supremacy in 1534 was followed by change, Henry VIII did not intend to depart from orthodox Catholic belief and practice. He made it clear that he would continue to suppress heresy, whether Lutheran or Anabaptist. Still, he found that he could not seal England off from Protestantism or maintain his break from Rome without the support of Protestant sympathizers. To evidence his willingness to compromise he approved the distribution of an English translation of the Bible.

By the time of Henry's death in 1547, a Protestant clergy had emerged within the English church under the leadership of Thomas Cranmer, archbishop of Canterbury (r. 1533–53). Under Henry's son, Edward IV (r. 1547–53), Cranmer set about transforming the English church into a Protestant church. He assembled the best parts of the Catholic liturgy and translated them into English to form the majestic Book of Common Prayer (1549). In his first version of his collection he tried to accommodate both Catholics and Protestants, but he satisfied neither. So he issued a fully Protestant version in 1552. This prayer book eventually became a literary symbol of Anglicanism, as Luther's Bible and Calvin's *Institutes* had come to symbolize Lutheranism and Calvinism.

The advance of Protestantism in England was further accelerated by Henry VIII's dissolution of the monasteries. Because the monasteries belonged to international orders, they were incompatible with the new national church headed by the king. Furthermore, monasticism had lost much of its appeal, and many of the houses were no longer abiding by the rules of their orders. Beginning in 1536, Henry confiscated the properties of the monastic communities and incorporated them into the crown lands. By 1539, the dissolution of the monasteries was complete. Although the confiscations virtually doubled the royal income, it was still not

Radical Protestantism: The Teaching of Menno Simons

Menno Simons (1496–1561) was one of the ablest leaders of the radical wing of the Reformation. Simons's followers formed the Mennonite church, which still exists. His ideas also contributed to the development of the Baptist church. He never summed up his doctrine in a single document; it has to be put together from scattered pamphlets.

We do not find in Scripture a single word by which Christ has ordained the baptism of infants, or that his apostles taught and practiced it. We say that infant baptism is but a human invention. . . . To baptize before that which is required for baptism, namely faith, is to place the cart before the horse.

Never should any commandment be observed which is not contained in God's holy Word, either in letter or in spirit.

The regenerated do not go to war nor fight. . . . How can a Christian, according to Scripture, consistently retaliate, rebel, make war, murder, slay, torture, steal, rob, and burn cities and conquer countries?

Where have you read in the Scriptures, that Christ or the Apostles called upon the power of the magistracy against those who would not hear their doctrine or obey their words? . . . Faith is a gift of God, therefore it cannot be forced on anyone by worldly authorities or by the sword.

We must be born from above, must be changed and renewed in our hearts and thus be transplanted from the unrighteous and evil nature of Adam into the righteous and good nature of Christ, or we cannot be helped in eternity by any means, divine or human.

From "Selections from the Writings of Menno Simons," in The Medieval World and Its Transformations, *ed. by G. M. Straka (New York: McGraw-Hill, 1967), Vol. II, pp. 463, 466, 467, 468, 470.*

enough to support the monarchy's costly wars. Consequently, Henry and his successors gradually sold the old monastic properties to aristocratic families, who thereby acquired an economic interest in preserving the breach with Rome.

The Protestant reformation in England came to a halt in 1553, when Henry's oldest child, Mary, daughter of Catherine of Aragon, came to the throne. To vindicate her mother, Mary tried to reunite

Title page of Daniel Featley's *Description* of 1645, known also as "The Dippers Dipt," a satirical view of the Anabaptists.

she was an educated, intelligent woman, and she knew that she would have to be patient. She had the Book of Common Prayer revised once again, to make it acceptable to Catholics and Protestants alike. She refused "to make windows into men's souls," as she put it—that is, she would persecute only those who openly and persistently opposed her. Even after the pope excommunicated her in 1570, she tolerated Catholics so long as they refrained from political activity. But she treated as a traitor anyone who challenged her right to the throne.

Elizabeth's moderate policies did not please all her subjects. Radical Protestants continued to demand that the English church be purified of all traces of Catholicism. These "Puritans" were strong in Parliament, and the queen occasionally had to deal harshly with them, but they helped to establish the idea that patriotism required independence from Rome.

The Anglican church viewed Presbyterianism—which was dominant in Scotland and had made some headway in England—with suspicion and was contemptuous of the Baptists. During the seventeenth century, the Anglican church became progressively more conservative, and today many Anglicans insist that their church is not "Protestant" at all. Rather, they argue, it was the Catholic church that strayed from the true path and Henry VIII and Cranmer who preserved the church of Christ.

the English church with Rome. She canceled all antipapal legislation, deposed Cranmer, purged the church of his supporters, and had Cranmer and about 300 other Protestants burned as heretics. Mary's reign of terror (she was known as Bloody Mary) and her marriage to Philip II of Spain offended her English subjects as inhumane and as an affront to their patriotism. As a result, Protestantism came to be identified with patriotism in the public mind.

Mary died in 1558, and Elizabeth, the daughter of Henry VIII and his second wife, Anne Boleyn, succeeded to the throne as Elizabeth I (r. 1558–1603). Elizabeth understood that her legitimacy as queen depended on the validity of Henry's divorce and on his Act of Supremacy. But

THE CATHOLIC REFORMATION AND THE COUNTER REFORMATION

The leaders of Protestantism thought of themselves as reformers, and the movement they set in motion is still known as the Protestant Reformation. Catholics, of course, viewed them as rebels and their reformation as a revolt. For them, true reformation could take place only within the church. Churchmen and pious laymen had been calling for reform ever since the fourteenth century, but the Protestant challenge heightened the pressure and helped to precipitate a great new reform movement in the middle of the sixteenth century. Historians call that movement the Catholic Reformation, or the Counter-Reformation. Actually, these were two different movements. The Catholic Reformation was a reform of the church, while the Counter-Reformation was a Catholic response to the Protestants. That response was vigorous; the church used torture and imprisonment as well as gentler means of persuasion to bring wayward Catholics back to orthodoxy.

The pressure for the reform of the Catholic church had produced some action even before Luther sounded his pro-

test. In the late fifteenth century, the Oratory of Divine Love was founded in Genoa as a lay brotherhood similar to the Brethren of the Common Life in the north. The Oratory sought to encourage a simple Christian life among laymen and to reform the clergy, who were gradually admitted to it as members. The movement spread to other Italian cities, and by the second quarter of the sixteenth century it had become the main source of ideas for reform within the church.

The impetus toward internal reform coincided with a decline in the political

Europe after the Reformations

Engraving showing the third session of the Council of Trent (1562–63). An amphitheater was set up in the church of St. Maria Maggiore.

peror Charles V, Clement entered into an alliance with Francis I of France. But with the sack of Rome in 1527 by undisciplined imperial troops, Italy came under imperial control and the political aspirations of the papacy vanished. Clement's successor, Paul III (r. 1534–49) turned his attention to reform and named cardinals who themselves were eager for reform. Eventually he summoned a great council to the city of Trent—which was under German control—to work out a reform program.

The Council of Trent met in three sessions—1545–48, 1551–52, and 1562–63. Toward the end of the first session, Emperor Charles V urged the council to open direct negotiations with the Protestants. To thwart that proposal, the pope moved the meeting to Bologna, knowing that no Protestant would appear in a city under papal control. For its second and third sessions, the council returned to Trent. In the third session, it issued a series of reform decrees.

Among those decrees was a declaration that salvation was indeed granted by God alone and that salvation resulted from faith, but that good works were a demonstration of faith and a confirmation of the working of God's mercy in the doer. The council also asserted that ultimate religious authority resided *both* in the Bible *and* in tradition, as interpreted by the Roman Catholic church. It urged that seminaries be established to train priests, and those seminaries did in fact foster a gradual reform of the priesthood. Finally, it ruled that clerics could not hold multiple offices and reaffirmed the absolute supremacy of the pope over the clerical hierarchy.

power of the papacy. The last of the politician popes of the Renaissance was Clement VII (r. 1523–34), who rejected calls for reform and acted like a traditional Italian despot. To counter the power of the em-

The second and third sessions of the council were dominated by Philip II of Spain (r. 1556–98), who was determined that Spain would resist the Protestant threat. He emerged as the leader of the Counter-Reformation, promoting the revival of a militant church throughout Europe. The spearhead of the Counter-Reformation was a new order founded by Ignatius of Loyola (1491–1556), a Spaniard of Basque descent. While serving as a soldier in the wars between the Habsburgs

Ignatius of Loyola, founder of the Jesuit Order, holds a book with the text "to the greater glory of God."

and the French, Ignatius had suffered a severe wound and had spent months recuperating. During his convalescence, he had read several books on the lives of the saints, the only reading material at hand, and had decided to become a Christian knight in the service of the Virgin Mary. As he found his way into his new life, he worked through a series of "spiritual exercises," which he later recommended to his followers. The exercises called for intense concentration on the most vivid details of hell and of the life and death of Christ as a means of strengthening one's will toward salvation. While Ignatius was studying at the University of Paris (John Calvin was a fellow student), he enlisted nine of his friends to become the nucleus of a new order called the Society of Jesus. Pope Paul III approved the order in 1540, and its members became known as Jesuits.

The Jesuits wore no distinctive habit; they dressed as their work required. They swore an oath of allegiance to the pope and underwent rigorous training for hazardous assignments. They carried out secret missions in Protestant regions, where they would be executed if caught. Through their clandestine operations, they strengthened the pope's control over the church; they ran the best schools in Europe; and they reclaimed most of Bohemia, Poland, Hungary, and southern Germany from Protestantism.

The inquisition was revived as an instrument of church reform when Ferdinand and Isabella instituted a royal inquisition in Spain in 1480. Their lead was followed by the Habsburgs in the Netherlands in 1523 and by Spanish powers in Italy in 1542. In 1559, the papacy instituted a system of censorship known as the Index. This was a list of printed books that Catholics were forbidden to read. The Index was approved, with some modifications, by the Council of Trent in 1563.

The Catholic Reformation brought new vitality to the church and enabled it to close ranks against the Protestants. By the second half of the sixteenth century a strong church, reorganized and backed by Spanish power, faced an array of Protes-

tant organizations that had already begun to compete with one another for followers.

Luther tweaks the beard of Calvin as both of them pull the hair of the pope. This satirical engraving presents a Catholic view of the Reformation controversy.

The Results of the Reformation

Some of the results of the Protestant Reformation are clear: It split Christendom into several competing churches. It halted the trend toward secularism that had been evident in the late Middle Ages. After Luther, all issues were religious issues and for the next century the most serious conflicts in Europe were religious conflicts.

Modern historians have debated the political, economic, and cultural effects of the Protestant Reformation. Did it foster capitalism by recognizing the possibility of serving God in one's secular calling and by extolling the bourgeois virtues of thrift and self-discipline? Did it help kings create absolute monarchies by supporting the idea that royal power came directly from God? Did it deflect the course of art history by cleansing the medieval churches and refusing to decorate the new churches? The historical record does not furnish answers to these questions, but the effort to answer them has produced some influential historical works.

Suggestions for Further Reading

Background of the Reformation

Several works put the Reformation in a historical context. See S. Ozmont, *The Reformation in Medieval Perspective* (1971); G. Strauss, *Pre-Reformation Germany* (1972); and J. Bossy, *Christianity in the West, 1400–1750* (1985). On the background of Protestantism, see H. Oberman, *The Harvest of Medieval Theology* (1963), and A. McGrath, *The Intellectual Origins of the European Reformation* (1987). J. Huizinga's *The Waning of the Middle Ages* (1924) is the classic work on the cultural changes during the fourteenth and fifteenth centuries.

The Religious Upheaval

On the Hussite movement, see M. Spinka, *John Huss and the Czech Revolution* (1941); F. G. Heymann, *John Zizka and the Hussite Revolution* (1955); and H. Kaminsky, *A History of the Hussite Revolution* (1967). On the spread of humanism, see P. O. Kristeller, "The European Diffusion of Italian Humanism," *Renaissance Thought II* (1965), and L. Spitz, *The Religious Renaissance of the German Humanists* (1963). On Erasmus, see J. Huizinga, *Erasmus* (1952), and R. H. Bainton, *Erasmus of Christendom* (1969). For a specialized study of Erasmus's reform views, see J. B. Payne, *Erasmus: His Theology of the Sacraments* (1970). Erasmus's writings are widely available; see, for example, J. P. Dolan, ed., *The Essential Erasmus* (1964).

There are many histories of the Protestant Reformation. H. Holborn, *A History of Modern Germany: The Reformation* (1959), is excellent on Germany. See also B. Moeller, *Imperial Cities and the Reformation* (1972), and G. Strauss, *Luther's House of Learning* (1978). L. W. Spitz, *The Renaissance and Reformation Movements,* Vol. 2 (1971), is an excellent brief history. J. Lortz, *The Reformation in Germany,* 2 vols. (1969), gives a fair statement of the Catholic view. A. G. Dickens, *The German Nation and Martin Luther* (1972), emphasizes the urban nature of the Reformation. H. J. Hillerbrand, *The Protestant Reformation: A Narrative History* (1964), contains a good anthology of contemporary writings.

On the spread of Protestantism, see S. Ozment, *The Reformation of the Cities* (1975). On Zwingli, see W. P. Stephens, *The Theology of Huldrych Zwingli* (1986). On the iconoclasm of the Protestant movement, see C. M. N. Eire, *War Against the Idols* (1986), and C. Christensen, *Art and the Reformation in Germany* (1980). W. Bouwsma, *John Calvin* (1988), is a fine biography and introduction. F. Wendel, *Calvin, The Origin and Development of his Religious Thought* (1963), is an excellent introduction. On the radicals, see G. H. Williams, *The Radical Reformation* (1962); F. H. Littell, *The Free Church* (1958); R. H. Bainton, *The Travail of Religious Liberty* (1951); and C. L. Clausen, *Anabaptism: A Social History* (1972). The best work on England is A. G. Dickens, *The English Reformation* (1964). J. J. Scarisbrick, *Henry VIII* (1968), is a brilliant work. For the Puritans, see P. Collinson, *The Elizabethan Puritan Movement* (1967).

An excellent discussion of the Catholic Reformation is H. Daniel-Rops, *The Catholic Reformation,* 2 vols. (1961). See also A. G. Dickens, *The Counter Reformation* (1969). For the Council of Trent, the definitive work is H. Jedin, *History of the Council of Trent,* of which the first two volumes appeared in English translation in 1957.

Results of the Reformation

On the economic, political, and cultural consequences of the Reformation there are wide differences of opinion. The starting point of modern debate was an "essay" by M. Weber, *The Protestant Ethic and the Spirit of Capitalism* (1905). *Protestantism and Capitalism: The Weber Thesis and Its Critics,* ed. by R. W. Green (1973), is a convenient collection of selections from the literature. See also L. W. Spitz, *The Reformation: Basic Interpretations* (1972), and R. Kingdon and R. Linder, *Calvin and Calvinism: Sources of Democracy* (1972). For a readable and perceptive survey of the period, see A. G. Dickens, *Reformation and Society in Sixteenth-Century Europe* (1966).

18

THE AGE OF DISCOVERY

In the early Middle Ages, Europeans knew of the world beyond the horizon only from the works of the ancient geographers. Then they learned something more through their contacts with the Arabs, Moors, Vikings, Magyars, and Mongols. But they had only the vaguest notions of East Asia, except that it was the source of the spices and curiosities that the Arabs brought to market. And they knew nothing at all of the southern hemisphere or the vast American continents.

Consequently, the explorations of the late fifteenth century had a revolutionary effect on their consciousness of the world and their place in it. For the first time in history they had direct experience of all the inhabited continents of the world and of the people who lived on them. By the middle of the sixteenth century, European intellectuals were pondering the question of how to deal with people who had built impressive civilizations without the benefit of divine revelation or Christian sanction.

THE EMERGENCE OF OCEANIC TRADE

The Early Voyages

In 1400, Europeans knew scarcely more about the world than the Romans had, for only a few of them had ever ventured beyond the Mediterranean Basin. The crusades had enlarged the vision of western Europeans somewhat, but not beyond the limits of the ancient world.

Only the Scandinavians had caught a glimpse of far horizons. Their sagas tell of voyages of Leif Ericson and other bold Viking seamen to North America. During

(*OPPOSITE*) ASTROLABE—USED IN ANCIENT TIMES TO CALCULATE THE POSITION AND ANGLE OF THE STARS. IN THE MIDDLE AGES IT BEGAN TO BE USED FOR NAVIGATION.

the eleventh century, the Icelanders established settlements on Greenland and around Hudson Bay and apparently coasted down the eastern shores of North America. The Hudson Bay settlements seem to have been abandoned after a short time, but the Greenland settlements survived until the middle of the thirteenth century, when a cooling trend in the earth's climate made them uninhabitable. The last official contact between Iceland and the Greenland settlements took place

(Top) Mediterranean war galley with lateen sail (*ca.* twelfth century); *(middle)* lateen-rigged vessel, much like Columbus's *Niña* (early fifteenth-century); *(bottom)* Spanish galleon of sixteenth century, the typical long-distance ship for Spanish commerce.

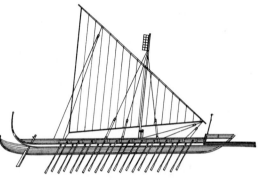

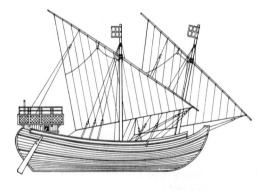

in 1258, though there is archaeological evidence that English sailors were still visiting them at the end of the century.

Meanwhile the Italians were opening up an overland trade route to China. The Polo family of Venice, and Franciscan friars as well, demonstrated that China could be reached by land across the vast steppes of central Asia. Marco Polo (*ca.* 1254–1324) traveled to China with his father and uncle in 1271 and remained at the court of the Mongol emperor for more than fifteen years. On his return in 1295, he wrote an account of the journey that was widely read in Europe and contributed greatly to the Europeans' knowledge of the East and stimulated their interest in Chinese civilization. But after the collapse of the Mongol empire in the fourteenth century, the overland route to China was no longer safe, and the demand for eastern wares was satisfied by Arab sailors operating in the Indian Ocean who brought spices and textiles to Alexandria and Beirut to be distributed by the Venetians to European markets.

By the end of the sixteenth century, these uncertain contacts with the East had been replaced by a regular trade of worldwide proportions. The ocean had become a busy highway on which Europeans controlled all the traffic, and it was becoming clear that the empires of the future would be built on mastery of the seas. When the first ship to circumnavigate the globe sailed into its home port in 1522, Europeans had already begun to build a network of trade around the earth that would bring all the civilizations of the world under their influence in the centuries ahead.

The Preconditions for Exploration

The age of exploration could not have occurred before revolutionary advances had been made in the design of ships and in the tools of navigation. The Vikings had made short voyages across the North Atlantic—Greenland was only a twelve-day sail from Norway—but in their small, open boats, even those trips were daring. What made the western explorations possible was a rare climatic condition that occasionally gave Scandinavian sailors a hazy glimpse of land beyond the horizon. From the western coast of Iceland they could "see" Greenland: In the winter, when the water is colder than the air, land far beyond the horizon—over the curvature of the earth—is sometimes reflected in the sky, giving would-be explorers confidence that they will reach land just beyond the range of sight.

But the Scandinavians' boats were too small and too unseaworthy to permit regular contact with the settlements in Greenland and North America. Before Europeans could push out across the Atlantic and plant colonies linked to the mother country, they needed more seaworthy ships and more reliable navigational aids.

It was a long time before oceangoing ships became available, however. The oar-propelled galleys of the Mediterranean served well enough in coastal waters, but sailors rarely struck out into the open sea—and then only to cross such narrow stretches as the passage between Sicily and North Africa. By the thirteenth century, Genoese and Venetian galleys were venturing out into the Atlantic to Morocco and Flanders, but they still hugged the coastline going and coming. To sail the open sea, mariners needed ships with sails rather than oars, and with broad, round hulls rather than the long, narrow hulls of the oar-propelled galleys. The fifty or more rowers who manned a galley burned up an enormous number of calories each day and consequently required vast amounts of food—far more than a galley could carry. Only sailing ships with small crews could make voyages across the Atlantic that lasted for months.

By the fifteenth century the Portuguese had designed such a vessel. The squat, three-masted caravel had two masts with the square sails favored by the Europeans and one mast with the triangular lateen sail favored by the Moslems. The square rigs were best for running before the wind, while the lateen rig was better suited to sailing close to the wind. The caravel was slower and less maneuverable than the galley, but it had more space for cargo and provisions for long voyages.

Mariners had had means of determining their direction of sail and their po-

sition for centuries. The astrolabe (already in use in the eleventh century and perhaps as early as the third century B.C.) enabled them to determine latitude by measuring the elevation of the sun and stars. The compass (used in Europe by the thirteenth century) gave them their direction in cloudy weather when the sun and stars were obscured. (No way to determine longitude precisely developed until the eighteenth century, when Edmund Halley—for whom the comet is named—devised a reasonably accurate method.)

The exploration of the oceans required substantial financial resources to construct and man the oceangoing vessels. City-states—from the Phoenicians to the Italians—were the original providers of shipping, but transoceanic voyages required resources far beyond the capacities of city-states. Only after the European monarchs had consolidated their power and unified their countries did there exist powers with enough wealth to man and equip fleets of oceangoing vessels. Thus, after 1400 the kingdoms gradually replaced the cities as the major supporters of shipping.

The Motivations for Exploration

The motivations of individual European ship captains varied, but it is clear that they had both religious and worldly motives. Christians believed that the longed-for end of the world would not take place until all were converted to Christianity. The desire to convert all the peoples of the world was always part of the motivation of explorers and their patrons.

One motivation for exploration was the desire to find new trade routes to East Asia. The spices used to preserve meats and make them palatable—pepper from India, cinnamon from Sri Lanka (Ceylon), ginger from China, nutmeg and cloves from the East Indies—were absolute necessities in an age without refrigeration. The Arabs controlled the trade between Alexandria and East Asia. The Venetians controlled it between Alexandria and Europe. And these monopolies made those necessities extremely expensive. The monarchs of western Europe were

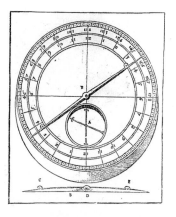

Drawing of an early compass, designed by Agricola (Georg Bauer, 1494–1555), the father of mineralogy.

Toynbee on the Age of Discovery

Since A.D. 1500 the map of the civilized world has indeed been transformed out of all recognition. Down to that date it was composed of a belt of civilizations girdling the Old World from the Japanese Isles on the north-east to the British Isles on the north-west. . . . The main line of communication was provided by the chain of steppes and deserts that cut across the belt of civilizations from the Sahara to Mongolia. For human purposes, the Steppe was an inland sea. . . . This waterless sea had its dry-shod ships and its quayless ports. The steppe-galleons were camels, the steppe-galleys horses, and the steppe-ports "caravan cities." . . . The great revolution was a technological revolution by which the West made its fortune, got the better of all the other living civilizations, and forcibly united them into a single society of literally world-wide range. The revolutionary Western invention was the substitution of the Ocean for the Steppe as the principal medium of world-communication. This use of the Ocean, first by sailing ships and then by steamships, enabled the West to unify the whole inhabited and habitable world.

From Arnold J. Toynbee, Civilization on Trial *(New York: Oxford University Press, 1948), pp. 67–70.*

most of it wrong—to make success seem likely. They took as fact Ptolemy's estimate that the circumference of the earth was about 8,000 miles. That meant that Japan and China lay only a few thousand miles west of Europe. And because they believed that Africa was much smaller than it is, they thought they could sail around it and soon arrive in Asia. In short, they reckoned that they could sail either east or west and reach their destination in a reasonable amount of time.

Portuguese Exploration

Prince Henry the Navigator (1394–1460), the young son of King John I of Portugal (r. 1385–1433) contributed a great deal to the scientific and seafaring knowledge of the day through his work at a remarkable observatory at Sagres on Cape St. Vincent, at the tip of Portugal. He devoted his life to organizing, equipping, and sending out fleets to explore the coast of Africa, and he had a notion that he could outflank the Moslems and discover lands they knew nothing about. But his main goal was to find gold—a goal he realized when his fleets reached the Gold Coast of Africa in the 1450s.

After Henry's death, the Portuguese lost interest in exploration for a time. They did discover and settle clusters of small islands in the Atlantic—the Madeiras and the Azores. Although the islands did not prove very profitable, the discovery showed that there was land to be found eight hundred miles out in the Atlantic and encouraged further exploration.

Henry's interest in voyages of discovery was taken up again by his grandnephew, King John II (r. 1481–95), who encouraged Portuguese explorers to find an all-water route to India. By 1488 Bartholomeu Dias had discovered the Cape of Good Hope, and in 1497 Vasco da Gama rounded the Cape with four ships. He reached Calicut on the Malabar Coast of India in 1498 and was back in Lisbon with two of his ships in 1499. In 1500 Pedro Álvares Cabral led a large fleet to Brazil and then sailed on to India, where he established the first Portuguese trading stations. At first the Portuguese met with a

eager to find a way to lower the cost of importing them.

Another motivation was the need to find new sources of precious metals. The only way Europeans could pay for imports from Asia was with gold or silver bullion. Asians had no interest in accepting lumber or foodstuff in payment, and in any case such products were too bulky or perishable to be used in long-distance trade. By 1400 the gold and silver mines of Europe, which had never been especially productive, were nearly exhausted. To support the steady flow of gold and silver to Asia, European monarchs were eager to locate new sources of supply.

THE FIRST EXPLORATIONS

By the late fifteenth century many bold mariners along Europe's Atlantic coast were eager to set sail. They had the motivation, the ships, and the instruments they needed to venture out onto the unknown sea. They also had enough information—

hostile reception from the Hindus and the Moslems of India. Da Gama was not impressed by Indian civilization and apparently said as much. Several of Cabral's men were killed by Moslems. But within a few years the Portuguese had built a commercial empire in India under the bold leadership of Afonso de Albuquerque (1453–1515), who served as governor of Portuguese India from 1509 to 1515.

Albuquerque had already been active in the area before he became governor. He had conquered Goa, a coastal region in western India, which he later made his capital, and had established strategic fortresses in East Africa to disrupt the Arabs' trade with India. (The Arabs had established themselves along the East African coast in the Middle Ages and used the ports as staging posts for their trade in the Indian Ocean.) As governor, he seized Malacca to control the trade between the Spice Islands and the Indian Ocean, and took over Ormuz, an island in the Persian Gulf from which he could disrupt Arab shipping. He tried but failed to take Aden, which would have given him control of the Red Sea, through which the Arab-Venetian trade passed. By the time Albuquerque died, Portugal had taken control of much of the spice trade and had established strategic bases all the way from Africa to the East Indies.

That success was short-lived, however. Although Portugal drew large profits from these early ventures, it lacked the resources to maintain permanent colonies in India and to support the navy required to protect its trade. Italian, German, and Flemish bankers soon took over the Portuguese trade, and even the spices that still arrived at Lisbon were sent on to Antwerp for distribution. The burden of empire had grown heavy by the time Portugal fell under Spanish control in 1580.

Columbus and Spanish Exploration

In 1484, before the Portuguese had reached the Cape of Good Hope, a Genoese sailor named Christopher Columbus (1451–1506) had tried in vain to persuade the Portuguese king, John II, to back him

Vasco da Gama.

The Portuguese as others saw them: African bronze sculpture of a Portuguese man.

in a voyage of exploration to the west. Relying on the accounts of Portuguese sailors and on Ptolemy's estimate of the size of the earth, Columbus was convinced that he could reach Japan (then called Cipangu) by sailing due west. But he could find no one to back him with ships and money. The Portuguese were content to follow up the explorations of Henry the Navigator along the coast of Africa, and Ferdinand and Isabella were busy with the conquest of the kingdom of Granada, the last Moorish stronghold on the Iberian peninsula.

In January 1492, Granada fell to Spain, and Ferdinand and Isabella turned to other matters. After much hesitation, and against the advice of her counselors, Isabella agreed to back Columbus. With one brilliant voyage the Spanish reached the New World.

Columbus landed in the Bahamas on October 12, 1492, thinking he had come

The World of the Voyager

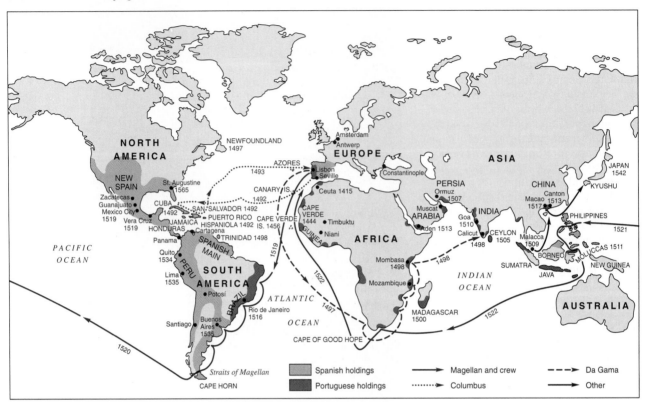

Map legend:
- Spanish holdings
- Portuguese holdings
- Magellan and crew
- Columbus
- Da Gama
- Other

Christopher Columbus, the Genoese sailor who sailed west in search of Japan and found the New World. This portrait of Columbus is thought to be the closest existing likeness of him. It is a copy, made in about 1525, of an earlier painting that has been lost.

upon some islands in the Japanese archipelago. Throughout four voyages, until his death in 1506, he remained convinced, even after reaching the mainland, that he had reached Japan and China and gave the name "Indians"—at that time a general term for East Asians—to the people he found.

It was a fellow Italian, Amerigo Vespucci (1454–1512), head of a branch of the Medici bank in Seville, who recognized what Columbus had discovered. After voyages in 1499 and 1501, Vespucci described what he saw in letters that were published and read throughout Europe. In one he referred to the great southern continent in the west as *Mundus novus*, a New World. Later mapmakers labeled both the northern continent and the southern continent "America," after Amerigo.

Incidently, it was Vespucci's letters that inspired Thomas More to write his *Utopia* (see pp. 431–32).

The Treaty of Tordesillas, 1494

Spain and Portugal competed for possession of the western continents from the very beginning. (Portugal's claim rested on the voyage of Cabral in 1500.) To avoid going to war, they turned to the pope, Alexander VI, to settle their claims. Alexander, who was himself a Spaniard, drew a line of demarcation 100 leagues (about 300 miles) west of the Cape Verde Islands (off the coast of West Africa), which clearly favored Spain. Dissatisfied, the Portuguese persuaded the Spanish to negotiate the Treaty of Tordesillas (1494), which drew a line of demarcation from pole to pole 370 leagues west of the Cape Verde Islands.

The Portuguese assumed that the line applied only to the western hemisphere (it gave them Brazil, though they did not know it at the time), while the Spanish assumed that it went clear around the earth. According to their interpretation, the Spanish could claim the Moluccas, the heart of the Spice Islands, and part of what is now Indonesia. Given the progress the Portuguese were making in the East Indies, the conflicting interpretations of the treaty might have led to war after all. But Spain became so occupied with its new possessions in the Americas that in 1527 it sold its claims in the eastern hemisphere to Portugal.

The Spanish remained determined to find a westward route to the Orient, however. When the Spanish explorer Vasco Núñez de Balboa sighted the Pacific Ocean from the Isthmus of Darien in Central America, the Spanish thought that somewhere they might find a passage across the New World. In 1519, the Portuguese navigator Ferdinand Magellan—with Spanish backing—negotiated the treacherous straits off the southern tip of South America and sailed across the Pacific only to be killed by natives in the Philippines. His navigator, Sebastian del Cano, brought one of Magellan's five ships back to Lisbon in 1522 by way of the Cape

of Good Hope. This was the first ship to circumnavigate the world.

THE SPANISH EMPIRE IN THE AMERICAS

While Magellan was on his historic voyage, Spanish conquistadors discovered and overcame wealthy civilizations in Mexico and Peru. The most notable of the conquistadors were Hernando Cortés and Francisco Pizarro. In 1519–21 Cortés conquered the formidable Aztec Empire in Mexico with 600 men, sixteen horses, and a few cannon, and in 1533–34 Pizarro, with an even smaller force, conquered the Incan Empire in the Andes Mountains of Peru.

The Aztecs and the Incans were wealthy, sophisticated peoples, but they were no match for the Spaniards. The Spanish troops were small, but well disciplined and daring, and their leaders took advantage of every opportunity. Moreover, both the Aztec and the Incan empires were highly centralized, and once

Cortés accepting the surrender of Quauhtemoc, last king of the Aztecs. The artist was a Spanish-trained native from Tlaxcala, who chronicled Cortés's conquest for Mexico. Notice the mixture of European and Indian styles.

the rulers had been disposed of there were no local leaders to take over. Even more destructive than the military superiority of the Spaniards were the diseases (especially smallpox) they brought with them. The native populations had no natural defenses against those diseases, and soon they were so reduced in numbers that resistance was impossible.

Though it is difficult to estimate the size of the population of Mexico before the conquest, it appears to have been at least 25 million. It had dropped to about 6 million by 1540, to 4 million by 1563, and to 2.5 million by 1600. By about 1650, it had reached 1.5 million. Thereafter, it climbed gradually and reached a little more than 3.5 million in 1793. By contrast, the population of goats, sheep, and cattle that the Spanish introduced into Mexico rose dramatically in the second half of the sixteenth century. From 1550 to 1620, the number of goats and sheep rose from about half a million to 8 million, while the number of cattle rose from about 10,000 to 100,000. The small plots once tended by the native farmers had been taken over by great herds of range animals that destroyed the vegetation and reduced the land to a desert.

Spain's new empire overseas created conflict between groups with different interests and different goals. The settlers who went out to the New World wanted to build a manorial system based on the old European model, using the forced labor of the native population. They were unwilling to take orders from the Spanish government or to serve its interests. The government in turn wanted to exercise absolute power over the colonies and to exploit the rich sources of precious metals it knew to be there. The friars wanted to convert the native population to Christianity.

The fact that the native population was civilized but non-Christian raised serious theological and moral questions. Spanish scholars turned for answers to the works of medieval thinkers who had speculated about whether the biblical texts that specify that rulers receive their authority from God (such as 1 Samuel 9–31 and Romans 13) applied to rulers who did not

accept or did not know the Bible. Questions also arose regarding marriages of the natives. The church considered marriage to be a sacrament in which God joins husband and wife. Were the marriages of heathens valid? Medieval theologians and lawyers had declared that marriages of non-Christians were valid but not licit. In other words, the union was created by God but the marriages were not recognized by the church. The distinction they were making was between acts performed in accordance with natural law (which stems directly from God) and acts performed in accordance with human law (which stems only indirectly from God, through the medium of human institutions). The sixteenth-century Spaniards made much of this distinction. They concluded that the Indians lived by natural law alone but that they were God's people even without the benefit of the church. The leading proponent of this theory was a Spanish Dominican, Bartolomé de Las Casas (1474–1566).

Las Casas had gone to the New World in 1502 to convert the heathens and had soon become engaged in a struggle to win them better treatment. He and his fellow missionaries wanted the converts to be treated as fellow Christians, and he made several trips to Spain to win support for that goal. In the early 1520s, he took part in a program to found free cities for Christianized Indians. But when the project failed, he returned to Spain and retired to a Dominican house. In retirement, he wrote many learned works promoting his scheme as well as a long *History of the Indians.*

In the end, a compromise was worked out among the conflicting interests of the settlers, the government, and the friars. The settlers were permitted to use the forced labor of the Indians, but under the regulation of the government. The friars were given freedom to evangelize and Europeanize the native population. By contemporary standards, these policies were quite humane, and the Spanish came close to achieving what the Portuguese had failed to accomplish in the East and what the English never attempted in North America: the Christianization and

Europeanization of a whole native population.

Nonetheless, the main goal of the Spanish Empire was economic exploitation. With the discovery of rich silver mines in Mexico in 1545, the Empire gave itself over to the extraction and shipment of silver. After 1564, a silver fleet of twenty to sixty ships would gather every spring in Havana harbor to be convoyed by warships to Seville. And every spring the government officials would wait anxiously until the bullion was safely landed; silver was the key to Spain's power.

Despite their obsession with silver production, the Spanish were also aware of the agricultural potential of their holdings. The wet lowlands of the Caribbean were well suited to sugar cane cultivation, and sugar became an important commodity. When it turned out that the Indian workers were highly vulnerable to disease, however, the Spaniards began to import black slaves from Africa. Eventually, many Spaniards and Indians intermarried, and the mestizos—offspring of mixed marriages—outnumbered the purebred of either race. The Africans, however, remained enslaved outside society.

IMPERIAL SPAIN: THE REIGN OF PHILIP II

With the wealth from its colonies in the New World, Spain became the most powerful nation in Europe. And with the succession of the Habsburg emperor Charles V (r. 1516–56) to the Spanish throne through his mother Joanna, the daughter of Ferdinand and Isabella, Spain acquired a new role in European affairs. Charles, who had inherited Austria through his father, Maximilian, and the Netherlands through his mother, Mary of Burgundy, was elected emperor in 1519. He used Spanish money and Spanish troops to counter the Protestant heretics, to protect Austria from the Turks, and to extend the Spanish conquest of the New World. Although these ambitious enterprises taxed Spain's resources, under Charles and his son King Philip II (r. 1556–98), the nation proved almost equal to the

Las Casas on the American Indians in the Sixteenth Century

It has been written that these peoples of the Indies, lacking human governance and ordered nations, did not have the power of reason to govern themselves—which was inferred only from their having been found to be gentle, patient and humble. It has been implied that God became careless in creating so immense a number of rational souls and let human nature, which He so largely determined and provided for, go astray in the almost infinitesimal part of the human lineage which they comprise. From this it follows that they have all proven themselves unsocial and therefore monstrous, contrary to the natural bent of all peoples of the world.

. . . Not only have [the Indians] shown themselves to be very wise peoples and possessed of lively and marked understanding, prudently governing and providing for their nations (as much as they can be nations, without faith in or knowledge of the true God) and making them prosper in justice; but they have equalled many diverse nations of the world, past and present, that have been praised for their governance, politics and customs, and exceed by no small measure the wisest of all these, such as the Greeks and Romans, in adherence to the rules of natural reason.

From Bartolomé de las Casas, Apologética historia de las Indias, *in* Introduction to Contemporary Civilization in the West, *3rd ed. (New York: Columbia University Press, 1960), Vol. 1, p. 539.*

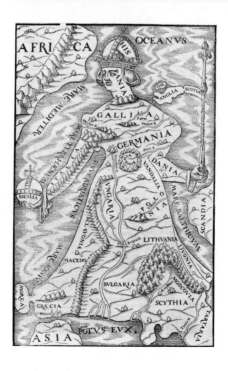

Contemporary map showing Spain as the head and crown of sixteenth-century Europe.

task. The sixteenth and early seventeenth centuries were the golden age of Spain.

In 1555–56 Charles V divided the Habsburg holdings between his brother Ferdinand and his son Philip. To Ferdinand went the Habsburg possessions in Austria, Bohemia, and Hungary, along with the imperial crown (still elective in theory, but by now always bestowed on a Habsburg). To Philip went the crowns of Castile and Aragon—still technically separate, but united since the death of Isabella (1504) and Ferdinand (1516). With Spain went its possessions in the New World, the kingdom of Naples, and the duchy of Milan (in effect control of all Italy), and the Netherlands. For a century and a half the "Austrian Habsburgs" and the "Spanish Habsburgs," were separate ruling houses that cooperated closely in matters of dynastic policy. Even though Philip's realm included the Netherlands, it was more tightly knit and centralized than that of his uncle.

Although Philip was the scion of a central European family, he was thoroughly Spanish in speech, thought, and character. After 1559, when the Habsburgs concluded peace with France, he spent all his remaining years in Spain. Though conscientious, he was distrustful of his advisers, unable to delegate authority even in minor matters, and rigorously Catholic in religion. His goal was to restore the unity of Christendom with the Spanish king as its temporal head.

Europe about 1560

Economic Policy

After the discovery of the Mexican mines, the value of the annual shipments of silver rose dramatically. In the early years it amounted to something less than $300,000; by about 1550 it had risen to more than $4,000,000; and by 1600 it was about $12,000,000. Then a steady decline set in, and by about 1660 the average value was down to $1,200,000. The crown's share was about one-quarter of the total.

As a result of the influx of bullion into Spain, prices rose steeply after centuries of relative stability. By the middle of the sixteenth century, inflation was rampant and had spread to the rest of Europe. It has been estimated that prices in Spain quadrupled in the course of the century.

The rise in prices outstripped the rise in tax revenues, and Philip II was forced to repudiate his government's debts three times—in 1557, 1575, and 1596. These repudiations, which were tantamount to declarations of bankruptcy because Philip was announcing that he could not and would not repay his debts, sent shockwaves through the financial institutions of Europe. Besides damaging Spain's credit, the inflation ruined its infant industries, which had appeared robust early in the century. Because inflation developed first and rose fastest in Spain, its industrialists were at a disadvantage in the international market, and Spain suffered a regular trade imbalance. Spanish industry languished, and bullion flowed out of the country. When the silver mines in America began to peter out in the mid-seventeenth century, the Spanish economy had already been ruined, and the nation quickly declined into a second-rate power.

Religious Policy

Philip II's religious views were the most intolerant of his time. He once said that he would rather be king of a desert than of a land of heretics. His grandparents, Ferdinand and Isabella, had already forced the Moors to convert to Christianity, had expelled the Jews from their kingdoms (1492), and had delegated to the Spanish Inquisition responsibility for see-

On Philip II of Spain

The pallor of his complexion was remarked on by all observers, and most of them drew the proper conclusion, namely, that it indicated a weak stomach and lack of exercise. Reddened eyes were a penalty of his excessive devotion to the written word both day and night. . . . Reading and writing occupied the major portion of Philip's day. . . . He had taken deeply to heart his father's injunction to direct everything himself, and never to give his full confidence even to the most faithful of his ministers, and the natural result was that his time was completely occupied with receiving and answering reports and letters. . . . Reports, reports, and even more reports; Philip was literally submerged with them in his later years, and moreover he did not stop at reading them; he annotated them, as he went along, with comments on matters as absurdly trifling as the spelling and style of the men who had written them—all in that strange, sprawling hand of his, one of the most illegible hands of an age more than usually replete with chirographical difficulties.

From R. B. Merriman, The Rise of the Spanish Empire in the Old World and in the New (New York: Macmillan, 1934), Vol. IV, pp. 21–24.

ing that the converts remained Christian. Nonetheless, it was widely believed that the Moriscos (Moslems who had converted to Christianity) continued to practice Islam in private. In 1566, Philip ordered them to stop using the Arabic language, to give up their traditional dress, and to stop taking hot baths, as was their custom. Three years later, when the Moriscos rebelled in protest against this suppression of their cultural heritage, Philip savagely put down the rebellion and drove them out of Andalusia, where most of them lived. Many of them left Spain for North Africa, depriving Spain of their contributions as leaders of Spanish agriculture and industry.

Philip's actions were part of a comprehensive anti-Moslem policy. Philip led the struggle to control the Turks in the eastern Mediterranean, though with only limited success. In 1570 the Turks took Cyprus from the Venetians, and in 1571 a combined Spanish and Venetian fleet defeated the Turks at Lepanto in the Gulf of Corinth. Though the victory was hailed

The baptism of Moslem women, from a Spanish relief (1520).

throughout Europe, the Christian forces failed to follow it up.

For a short time after Lepanto, Philip was at the height of his power and prestige. But the moment was brief. During the last quarter of the sixteenth century, his dream of a revived Catholic Europe under his authority was shattered by the revolt of the Netherlands, the rise of English seapower, and the accession of a former Protestant to the throne of France.

THE REVOLT OF THE NETHERLANDS

In the sixteenth century, the 3 million people in the seventeen provinces of the Netherlands constituted one of the most prosperous populations in Europe. The comfortable houses of Bruges, Ghent, Antwerp, and Amsterdam had been built with the profits of a flourishing textile industry and a far-flung commercial net-

ca. 1400		1519	1581	1648
Low Countries United under Dukes of Burgundy		Spanish Rule	Dutch Wars of Independence	

work. Though the provinces had been united under the personal authority of the dukes of Burgundy during the preceding century, there was little sense of nationalism until Charles V became duke. Charles was the closest thing to a native ruler the united Netherlands had ever had, but once he became emperor he sacrificed the interests of the Dutch and Flemish cities to his imperial aims and prompted the first stirrings of nationalism in the provinces.

Under Philip II, religious tension added to the Netherlanders' alienation from Habsburg rule. The Netherlands were a crossroads of ideas as well as of commerce, and the teachings of Luther and Calvin had early taken root there. By the 1550s, well-organized Calvinist minorities existed in most of the cities.

Philip's intransigent religious policies were bound to alienate many of his Dutch and Flemish subjects. Their urban-commercial culture had for centuries been out of tune with the church's restrictive attitude toward business practices, and they had adopted an attitude of moderation in religious matters. That attitude had enabled them to countenance the rise and survival of such groups as the Brethren of the Common Life (see p. 426) and it was totally at odds with the king's religious fanaticism. To make matters worse, Philip violated the traditional limits of his authority as duke of the provinces by interfering in the internal affairs of the cities. In 1566 Calvinist mobs went on a rampage, breaking images of the saints and smashing stained-glass windows in Catholic churches throughout the Netherlands.

Philip sent the duke of Alva with about 10,000 Spanish regulars to suppress the iconoclasts, and Alva set up a regime that came to be known as the "Council of Blood." He boasted (with some exaggeration) that during his six years in the Netherlands (1567–73), he executed 18,000 people. His government also confiscated enormous tracts of land and imposed a 10 percent sales tax that seriously injured commerce.

Alva's measures served only to solidify resistance, and by 1572 the Dutch had found a leader in William the Silent, prince of Orange, the wealthiest landowner in the provinces. Although William lost almost every battle he fought against the Spanish, he had political wisdom, integrity, and patience. He also had a deep hatred of religious fanaticism. Dutch nationalism grew stronger under his leadership, helped by the actions of the Spanish themselves. In 1576, the Spanish responded to Calvinist excesses by staging a frightful sack of Antwerp, known as the "Spanish Fury." Frightened, the seventeen provinces rushed into an agreement to form a united front against Philip—the so-called Pacification of Ghent (1576).

The united front was led by moderate Calvinists and Catholics, but soon religious fanatics on both sides seized control. In the savage civil war that ensued, the Calvinists—who were better organized than the Catholics—gained the upper hand. The Catholics fled south to the ten Walloon provinces that were under the protection of the Spanish troops, while the Calvinists moved north to the Dutch provinces. In 1579 those provinces formed the Union of Utrecht, which ultimately evolved into the United Provinces, or the Dutch Netherlands, and declared their independence from Philip II in 1581. The

Example of propaganda badge worn by Dutch "Sea Beggars." The insurgents' hatred of Catholicism is expressed in the inscription: "Better the Turks than the pope."

The Division of the Netherlands   1581

southern provinces remained under Habsburg rule until 1830, when they became the kingdom of Belgium.

The Rise of the Dutch Netherlands

After declaring their independence, the Dutch Provinces struggled for two generations before achieving real independence. William the Silent was assassinated in 1584, and his successors carried on his able, disinterested leadership. Although the "United Provinces" was never more than a loose confederation, the Dutch fought with a fierce stubbornness whenever the need arose.

In 1578, Philip II, angered by the Pacification of Ghent, sent the duke of Parma—one of the age's best military leaders—to remedy the situation. But the Dutch privateers—"Sea Beggars"—joined with the English to control the English Channel and prevent Parma from resupplying the Spanish troops. This meant that Parma and Philip were in conflict with England—where Philip had once been Queen Mary's royal consort. This struggle led to the Spanish decision to send a great flotilla to clear the English Channel (see p. 464). The defeat of that armada ended any chance Spain might have had to reconquer the Dutch provinces. Not until 1648, however, did Spain formally recognize Dutch independence.

Dutch Prosperity

The Dutch emerged from the conflict with Spain as the most powerful commercial nation in Europe. By the early seventeenth century they were building more ships—and better ships—than all other nations combined. It was said that they built 2,000 per year, and they were taking over more and more of the carrying trade of Europe and of the world. During the war with Spain, the Dutch had closed off Antwerp—which was under Spanish control—by damming its harbor, and Amsterdam had become the commercial and financial capital of Europe.

The Dutch handled much of the grain trade of the Baltic and a large part of the carrying trade of England, France, Italy, and Portugal. When Philip II closed Lisbon to the Dutch—after seizing the Portuguese crown in 1580—the Dutch went directly to the source of spices in the Moluccas. In 1602 the Dutch East India Company was formed and was soon operating out of headquarters at Batavia on the island of Java. By the middle of the seventeenth century the Dutch had taken over Portugal's richest holdings in the East, and in 1652 they set up a colony at the Cape of Good Hope to serve as a way station on the route to Asia. A few decades earlier, they had almost ousted the Portuguese from Brazil and had founded the colony of New Amsterdam on Manhattan Island in the Hudson River (1624), which became the center for a large Dutch carrying trade in the New World. When the French and English began to develop their own overseas empires in the seventeenth century, they found the Dutch ahead of them wherever they went.

ELIZABETHAN ENGLAND

Elizabeth I (r. 1558–1603) was the last of the direct descendants of Henry VII Tudor

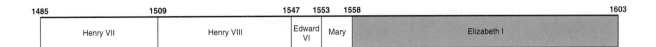

1485	1509	1547	1553	1558	1603
Henry VII	Henry VIII	Edward VI	Mary	Elizabeth I	

(r. 1485–1509; see p. 418). She was a cautious, reflective ruler whose instinct was to temporize and compromise. Although she could never submit to papal authority—the pope had declared the marriage of her mother, Anne Boleyn, to Henry VIII invalid—she followed a moderate religious policy and was conservative in matters of theology and liturgy.

Elizabeth temporized and compromised in foreign policy too. She tried to avoid committing herself, kept a dozen intrigues afoot to give herself an avenue of escape, and seems to have aimed at avoiding war at any cost. The chief foreign danger to the realm was the French influence over Scotland. Elizabeth's cousin, Mary Stuart, Queen of Scots, had married the heir to the French crown in 1558, and the alliance between the French and Scots promised to be troublesome.

But when the Scotsman John Knox returned from Geneva and began preaching Calvinism in 1559, he undermined the influence of Catholicism and the French. This time Elizabeth made a quick decision and allied herself with the Calvinist party in Scotland. By 1560, the Kirk (the Scottish church), the pro-English party, and Knox were in control, and the French had lost their foothold in Scotland.

In 1561, Mary Stuart returned to Scotland after the death of her husband, hoping to reestablish Catholicism along with her own authority. But she faced unbending opposition from Knox and the Kirk, and after a second marriage that turned out badly she was forced to abdicate in 1567. A year later Mary fled to England, where Elizabeth received her coolly but permitted her to stay. Mary soon became the center of French and Spanish plots against Elizabeth who kept a watch on her but refused to imprison or execute her. Then in 1587, when Elizabeth's ministers presented her with incontrovertible evidence of Mary's complicity in an assassination plot, Elizabeth reluctantly consented to Mary's execution.

The Conflict with Spain

Although there were many reasons for conflict between Spain and England—particularly English support of the Dutch—Philip II and Elizabeth I remained on good terms for more than twenty years. That stretch of tranquillity gave English industry and commerce a chance to expand and grow strong. When the inflationary spiral ruined Spanish industry, the English were ready to supply the Spanish colonies with manufactured goods. In 1562, an aggressive merchant named Sir John Hawkins was the first Englishman to carry goods from England and slaves from Africa directly to the Spanish settlements in the New World. The Spanish sought to prevent such direct traffic, which drew profit from their colonies and brought nothing to the mother country, and in 1569 Sir John and his cousin Sir Francis Drake were almost sunk by a Spanish fleet. In revenge, Drake seized that year's silver shipment from Peru to Spain. Then, from 1577 to 1580, he duplicated Magellan's voyage around the world, demonstrating the vulnerability of the Spanish Empire. Meanwhile, other English mariners probed the coasts of North America in search of a Northwest Passage that would outflank the Portuguese route to the East Indies.

It was the revolt of the Netherlands that finally broke the peace between Spain and England. For centuries, the English had had close commercial ties with the Low Countries; Flanders, for example, had long been the best customer for English wool and other goods. Moreover, Englishmen sympathized with their fellow Protestants in the United Provinces, and English privateers—the Sea Dogs—cooperated with the Sea Beggars, their Dutch counterparts, in disrupting Spanish shipping and communications. For their part, Philip II's ambassadors in England were deeply involved in plots against Elizabeth's life, one of which, as we have seen, led to the execution of Mary Stuart.

Elizabeth I of England, and her signature. The silver medal commemorates the defeat of the Spanish Armada.

The Armada

When the Spanish Armada challenged the ancient lords of the English on their own grounds, the impending conflict took on the aspect of a judicial duel in which as was expected in such duels, God would defend the right. . . . So when the two fleets approached their appointed battleground, all Europe watched. For the spectators of both parties, the outcome, reinforced, as everyone believed, by an extraordinary tempest, was indeed decisive. The Protestants of France and the Netherlands, Germany and Scandinavia saw with relief that God was, in truth, as they had always supposed, on their side. The Catholics of France and Italy and Germany saw with almost equal relief that Spain was not, after all, God's chosen champion. From that time forward, though Spain's preponderance was to last for more than another generation, the peak of her prestige had passed. . . . So, in spite of the long, indecisive war which followed, the defeat of the Spanish Armada really was decisive. It decided that religious unity was not to be reimposed by force on the heirs of medieval Christendom, and if, in doing so, it only validated what was already by far the most probable outcome, why, perhaps that is all that any of the battles we call decisive has ever done.

From Garrett Mattingly, The Spanish Armada *(Boston: Houghton Mifflin, 1959), pp. 400–01.*

Then in 1588 Philip decided to make a bold attempt on England itself. He assembled an enormous fleet, the so-called Invincible Armada, and sent it north to clear the English Channel and prepare the way for an invasion of England by the duke of Parma, who was engaged in operations against the Dutch. The English met the Armada with smaller, faster ships that could fire at longer range than the Spanish ships, and when the Armada anchored off Calais to await Parma, English fire ships caused panic among the Spaniards. The Armada fled north, and the English attacked again off Gravelines, scattering the Spanish ships. North Sea storms completed what the English had started, and fewer than half of the Armada's ships struggled home by sailing north and west around the British Isles.

The victory lifted the morale of Englishmen and Protestants everywhere. It ended the threat of a Spanish conquest of England and made it impossible for the Spanish to reconquer the United Provinces. When a peace was finally signed in 1604, the English and the Dutch met the Spaniards as near equals.

THE FRENCH WARS OF RELIGION

The rise of Spain and the relatively peaceful reign of Elizabeth I in England relied in part on the weakness of France, the largest and most populous nation in Europe. From 1562 to 1593 the French were embroiled in civil and religious strife that the monarchy was powerless to control.

Although France was the largest nation in Europe under a single monarch, it

The British fleet attack the Spanish Armada.

1328		Civil Wars 1562 1593	1793
	House of Valois		House of Bourbon

1589

was less unified than either England or Spain. The aristocracy was still powerful, and the provinces still held on to their local customs and privileges. The divisiveness grew even more severe with the spread of Calvinism into France.

The French Calvinists—nicknamed the Huguenots (the origin of the name is unknown)—had about 2,500 churches. Huguenot congregations formed a small but well-organized and aggressive minority supported by people at the highest levels of French society. Arrayed against the Huguenots were the Catholic aristocracy, the University of Paris, and the Parlement (high court) of Paris. The monarchy itself was opposed to the spread of Calvinism, because it could not control the Protestant churches as it did the Catholic church under the Concordat of Bologna (1516).

After the death of King Henry II, husband of Mary Stuart of Scotland, in 1559, royal authority fell into the hands of the Queen Mother, Catherine de' Medici, who controlled the French government during the reigns of Henry's two weak brothers—Francis II (r. 1559–60) and Charles IX (r. 1560–74)—and during the reign of Henry's son Henry III (r. 1574–89). Catherine was an astute ruler, but she lacked formal authority and was powerless to prevent the religious fanatics—both Calvinist and Catholic—from making war on one another. Discontented nobles and the provinces sided with the Calvinists. The monarchy and most of the nobility sided with the Catholics. Both sides appealed for foreign support—the Huguenots to the English and Dutch, the Catholics to Spain. England and Spain actually sent troops, mostly at the beginning and the end of the wars.

The fighting was savage, and large areas of France were devastated. Though the Catholics won most of the battles, they could not destroy the Huguenots. In 1572 Catholic fanatics convinced Catherine that

they could put an end to the strife with one decisive blow. At two o'clock in the morning of St. Bartholomew's Day (August 23), armed bands of Catholics attacked and killed several Huguenot leaders who were in Paris for the wedding of the Huguenot Prince Henry of Navarre and the king's sister. The St. Bartholomew's Day Massacre touched off an explosion of violence that soon spread to other cities. Between late August and October, more than 10,000 Huguenots—3,000 in Paris alone—were murdered. The events intensified religious hatred in France and across Europe. Pope Gregory XIII and Philip II of Spain hailed the massacre as a milestone in the fight against

Religion and Patriotism

A Spanish ambassador reporting the words of a French Catholic in 1565:

Nowadays Catholic princes must not proceed as they once did. At one time friends and enemies were distinguished by the frontiers of provinces and kingdoms, and were called Italians, Germans, Frenchmen, Spaniards, Englishmen, and the like. Now we must say Catholics and heretics, and a Catholic prince must consider all Catholics of all countries as his friends, just as the heretics consider all heretics as friends and subjects whether they are their own vassals or not.

An English Protestant writing in 1589:

All dutiful subjects in this land desire with all their hearts the continuance of God's religion; the preservation of Queen Elizabeth; and the good success of the English navy. These particulars, I grant, are not expressed in flat in the Lord's Prayer; but they are contained within the compass of, and may be deduced from the petitions of that excellent prayer. Whosoever doubteth of this is void of learning.

As quoted in Erich Marks, Die Zusammenkunft von Bayonne *(Strassburg: K. J. Trübner, 1889), p. 14; as quoted in Benjamin Hanbury,* Historical Memorials Relating to the Independents *(London: Congregational Union of England and Wales, 1839–44), Vol. I, p. 71.*

Protestantism, but Protestants throughout Europe were horrified.

The wars dragged on for twenty years, growing more and more confused and purposeless, until the Huguenot Henry of Navarre came to the throne as Henry IV (r. 1589–1610). Although Henry was the nearest male heir to the crown, his relationship to Henry III was quite distant, and he had trouble making his claim stick. The Catholics took over Paris, and Spanish troops from the Netherlands moved into France led by the duke of Parma. After four years of fighting and maneuvering, Henry decided to renounce his Protestantism and become a Catholic, which he did in 1593. He did not, however, turn against his former co-religionists. Five years later he issued the Edict of Nantes, which granted the Huguenots freedom of conscience, freedom of worship, equal civil rights, and control of approximately 200 fortified towns. The Edict constituted the first official recognition that two religions could coexist within one nation.

The Effects of the Wars of Religion

In the world of Philip II and Elizabeth I, religion had a strong influence on political and social conflicts. The conflicts themselves grew out of economic changes that predated the Protestant Reformation, but religious convictions embittered every issue and made moderation impossible. Some monarchies that had been moving toward the consolidation of power— for example France and Germany— were weakened by the religious strife. Others— such as Spain and England— were strengthened. In Spain, Charles V and Philip II championed the cause of embattled Catholicism. In England, after Mary tried to reverse the reformation that grew out of the Act of Supremacy, Protestantism became associated with patriotism.

Just as the Great Schism in the Roman church (1378–1417) had motivated thinkers to devise a new constitutional theory of the church—conciliarism—so the wars of religion inspired new political theories. French theorists, for example, created a doctrine of political obligation that justified rebellion against constituted authority under certain conditions. And Protestants in Germany, the Netherlands, and France cited that doctrine to justify their rebellion against monarchs whom they accused of seeking to subject them to a false religion. After a generation of religious war, the French writer Jean Bodin (1530–96) developed a new, secular theory of political sovereignty that justified obedience to properly constituted authority without appeal to religious doctrine. That theory had a powerful influence on later political thought.

A less benign result of the religious paroxysm was a terrifying witch-craze in Europe that began in the mid-sixteenth century and lasted nearly a century. During the craze, thousands of people— mostly women—were burned at the stake or hanged as witches. The horror seems to have begun when the religious passions set off by the Protestant and Catholic Reformations got mixed up with ancient, pre-Christian superstitious beliefs and practices. Almost every community had its wizard and cunning woman to whom neighbors turned when the ministrations of priest or physician did not avail. From time to time during the Middle Ages, such women had been convicted of malevolent

Massacre of St. Bartholomew's Day, 1572 (detail from a painting by an eyewitness, François Dubois).

witchcraft—that is, of attempting to use occult means to inflict death or disease on others.

During the sixteenth century, the number of people accused of witchcraft increased dramatically. The accused were tortured into confessing the most fantastic acts—participating in obscene "witches' sabbaths" and creating diabolical schemes to harm their neighbors. Because they were also forced to name their accomplices in their pacts with the Devil, one arrest led to others. Often dozens, even hundreds, in a single community were burned at the stake.

By 1660 the craze was subsiding, and by 1700 it had all but disappeared as religious passions cooled and as toleration became the norm. Moreover, the rise of modern science led educated people to suspend belief in miracles, invisible spirits, and occult forces. The century-long witch-craze was one of the most tragic episodes in the history of Europe.

THE EUROPEAN WORLD IN THE LATE SIXTEENTH CENTURY

The Condition of the Peasants

Although we have been concentrating on urban life in the last two chapters, the vast majority of Europeans lived in the country during these years. By the end of the sixteenth century, significant changes had occurred in the economic and social condition of the peasants. In France and western Germany, the peasants' lot had improved. In Spain, eastern Germany, and other eastern European countries, it had deteriorated.

In most of western Europe, the disastrous plagues of the fourteenth century had undermined the old feudal system whereby peasants were obliged to perform services for their lords. As a result, life in the villages and regular cultivation of the fields broke down. When conditions began to improve in the fifteenth century, landholders granted favorable terms to the peasants to induce them to return to the fields. Some of the landholders had been ruined by the plagues and

Illumination from a Book of Hours (Flemish, *ca.* 1500) shows peasants harvesting grain.

had sold their land to their own peasants. By the late sixteenth century about 5 percent of the peasants in France and western Germany owned their own land, and another 5 percent remained bound in serfdom. The rest of them leased the land they worked. Increasingly, however, the law permitted them to sell or grant their rights in the properties they leased.

In 1480, the king of Castile released all peasants from serfdom and gave them proprietary rights in their land. But within a couple of generations the royal government was encouraging the importation of cheap grain, and the Castilian peasants derived little benefit from their emancipation. The peasants of Aragon, who had not been released from serfdom, also suffered under the government's policy. By the late sixteenth century, peasants throughout Spain were caught up in a serious economic depression.

When the condition of the peasants in Europe finally began to improve, the condition of the eastern peasants continued to sink lower and lower. In northeastern Germany, for example, a region of large estates with access to rivers to carry crops to market, the landholders imposed full-fledged serfdom on their peasants in the late sixteenth century. In Russia, Tsar Ivan the Terrible (r. 1533–84) rewarded his noblemen for service to the state by granting them large estates with the right to force the peasants into serfdom (see p. 345).

Urban Life in the Sixteenth Century

As far back as the twelfth century, the towns and cities of Europe had begun to achieve virtual independence through charters granted by kings and emperors. The charters freed them from the control of the feudal lords and gave them the right to govern themselves. By the sixteenth century, the cities had become independent in both political and economic matters, and their influence was felt throughout Europe.

One historian has compared citizenship in the early modern city to membership in a club. Every aspect of life was regulated by special associations under the control of the city council. Craft guilds and religious fraternities governed the lives of their members and provided social security.

Pieter Bruegel's *Children's Games.*

A young man could expect to be elected to a lower office in his guild about six years after becoming a master and to a higher office after another eight years. The principal officers of the major guilds were almost assured of an important position in the city government.

Most cities had religious confraternities or brotherhoods that cut across membership in the various guilds. These organizations were responsible for staging city-wide festivals in cooperation with the guilds, and the fact that men from all walks of life participated in these events helped reduce the potential for conflict among the guilds. Officeholders in a brotherhood often moved to positions in the city government.

Cities were usually divided into wards to facilitate the conduct of government. Each ward was responsible for ensuring security within its boundaries and for providing a certain number of men for the city militia. The wards also furnished men to stand night watch on the city walls and at the gates. Although some wards were dominated by one of the guilds (for example, butchers and tanners usually settled along a river), in most neighborhoods the population was quite mixed, with the rich living alongside the poor. About a fifth of the urban population, more in large cities, consisted of day laborers and other poor people who were not members of any guild. They did, however, have acknowledged status in their ward.

Usually the city gates were opened at 4 A.M. and closed at 8 P.M., about an hour after the workday ended. During the night a curfew was imposed on the city to discourage crime and keep the peace. Saturday was payday, when workers got off early, and Sunday was a day of rest. *Children's Games*, painted by the Flemish artist Pieter Bruegel the Elder (*ca.* 1525–69), suggests what a typical Sunday may have been like in a sixteenth-century city.

Because men did not marry until they had set themselves up as substantial citizens, there were usually many young men about town. Rape, including group rape, was common, and the authorities were always on the watch for such offenses. The larger cities usually had a public brothel in which the women were licensed. Even prostitutes who worked the streets were licensed and wore badges to prove it. The public bathhouse was another place where young upper-class men could find prostitutes.

In many cities young men's associations patterned themselves on the religious brotherhoods, though their purpose was anything but religious. The members amused themselves at the expense of the "establishment," and their officers bore such titles as Prince of Youth and Abbot of Fools.

Women played an important role in the sixteenth-century city not only as wives but as craftspeople and merchants. Their principal role was as wife and mother, but a craftsman could not function—indeed, some guilds would not permit him to function—without a wife. She raised the apprentices and often ran the shop where the master's products were sold. Although the guilds guarded their craft secrets jealously, members were permitted to share them with their wives.

Many women also participated in the commercial life of the cities. They engaged in silk weaving, retailing, and brewing and often functioned as agents for foreign merchants. They were accorded no role in city government, however, or in other public business.

ART, LITERATURE, AND SCIENCE

Art

Renaissance art reached its zenith in the first two decades of the century with the memorable accomplishments of Leonardo da Vinci (1452–1519), Raphael (1483–1520), Albrecht Dürer (1471–1528), and Michelangelo (1475–1564). In the last years of his life, Dürer, influenced by Luther's view that the style and subject matter of the Renaissance were too pagan, simplified his work and concentrated on biblical scenes. In the next generation, the German painter Hans Holbein the Younger (1497–1543) was a talented portraitist who traveled to Switzerland and England to execute commissions. He settled in En-gland as a court painter and created portraits of Henry VIII, Thomas More, and other prominent figures.

Michelangelo also abandoned the high Renaissance style after 1520 and developed a new style that departed from the serenity of his early work. For example, his ceiling frescos in the Sistine Chapel, painted around 1510, are organized in carefully planned panels with figures reminiscent of the classical sculpture that inspired the Renaissance, and the Genesis story is represented in a series of static images. By contrast, his wall fresco of the Last Judgment in the same chapel, painted during the 1530s, is a crowded scene of twisted bodies in which the action of condemnation and salvation of souls is captured in dynamic fashion. In sculpture, too, Michelangelo proceeded from observance of the classical ideals of the Renaissance, through a rebellion against proportion and graceful lines, to the creation of tortured shapes of great emotional power.

Some artists, like the Venetian painter Titian (*ca.* 1477–1576), continued to work in the Renaissance style. Others favored a new style known as Mannerism, because they painted in the manner of (the late) Michelangelo. Two of the most notable Mannerists were Tintoretto (1518–94) and El Greco (*ca.* 1548–1614). Tintoretto was a Venetian who tried to combine the style of Titian with the late style of Michelangelo. He painted scenes of saints and miracles and executed some large wall paintings. His works convey a sense of movement and action, similar to that of Michelangelo's Last Judgment. El Greco (Domenicos Theotocopoulos, born on the island of Crete) studied in Venice and Rome and eventually settled in Spain, where he hoped to become a court painter. But Philip II favored the work of second-rate Spanish Mannerists, and El Greco (as the Spaniards nicknamed him) never found favor in Madrid, Philip's new capital. El Greco was a highly original artist who paintings exude a strong mystical aura and whole sparse, elongated figures project great tension and strength.

The Flemish artist Hieronymus Bosch (*ca.* 1450–1516) painted dark, foreboding

Virgin with Sts. Ines and Tecla, by El Greco.

showing agricultural labors appropriate to each month of the year. In his few religious paintings, such as the "Slaughter of the Innocents," he depicts the moment before the crucial scene occurs, so that the viewer is caught up in suspense. His son Pieter also painted scenes of peasant life, along with works depicting hell, and Jan favored landscapes and still lifes. Members of the Bruegel family were still painting well into the eighteenth century.

Literature

In literature, the sixteenth century was the great age of drama. Medieval drama evolved from the religious festivals at which the guilds staged plays dealing with the lives and miracles of the saints. University students too had been putting on plays since the thirteenth century. At first their plays were based on the stories of biblical figures, such as Daniel and Herod. But during the fifteenth and early sixteenth centuries the students turned to secular dramas fashioned on Roman models and intended for educated audiences. The great age of theater began in the 1570s when actors and playwrights in England and Spain formed professional companies that played to the general public.

In London, several companies were founded in the 1570s, and two playwrights attracted an enthusiastic following Thomas Kyd (1558–94) and Christopher Marlowe (1564–93). Kyd's *Spanish Tragedy* and Marlowe's *Tamburlaine* were the first popular successes of the English stage. Kyd's play, about a father who exacts revenge for his son's death, established revenge as a favorite theme of English tragedy. Marlowe's plays are dominated by powerful, romantic figures who control the action. He was the first playwright to use blank verse in dramatic writing.

It was Marlowe's contemporary, William Shakespeare (1564–1616), who emerged as the greatest English poet and dramatist. Shakespeare wrote his plays for a company of twenty or so actors, the Lord Chamberlain's Company (later called the King's Company), that continued to perform for more than two decades. Theater

works on religious themes that exaggerate the physicality of human life. Modern scholars have discovered in them a complex, visual language that reflects Bosch's mystical view of the world. The Bruegels—Pieter the Elder (*ca.* 1525–69), Pieter the Younger (1564–1637), and Jan (1568–1625)—preferred to paint scenes from everyday life. Pieter the Elder favored rural scenes, including a series companies were expected to present a play six afternoons a week throughout the year and consequently had to keep about fifty plays in their repertory. Shakespeare must have written many plays that were never published, because he considered them the property of his company. Eighteen of them, however, were published in illegal editions during his lifetime. After his death, his friends published his surviving manuscripts in a folio volume in 1623. The first edition of Shakespeare's work contained 36 plays; since then scholars have added another, *Pericles*, on the likelihood that some of the scenes in it were written by Shakespeare. The plays consist of tragedies (*Hamlet* and *King Lear*), comedies (*Taming of the Shrew* and *As You Like It*), and histories (*Richard III* and *Henry V*). Shakespeare took his themes from classical and English history and from Italian works, which had become popular in England early in the sixteenth century.

The typical theater of Shakespeare's London was a large, round building without a roof that could hold as many as 3,000 people. In Shakespeare's Globe Theatre, the audience stood in the pit below the stage or in the boxes along the walls. Admission to the pit cost only a penny or two, which meant that watching a play was one of the most inexpensive pastimes in the city. Admission to the boxes cost much more.

There were smaller theaters as well, such as Blackfriars, where Shakespeare's company also performed. These were rectangular buildings that could hold only a few hundred people. Admission to these theaters was more expensive than admission to open theaters, and the plays written for them appealed to a more sophisticated audience. It is estimated that English playwrights wrote more than 6,000 plays between 1580 and 1640, about 2,000 of which have survived.

In Spain, the theater became popular soon after the middle of the century and, as in England, experienced a great increase in popularity during the 1570s. Spanish plays combined dramatic scenes with interludes of dance and musical entertainment. Unlike the English companies, the Spanish companies employed women as entertainers and actresses. The Spanish playwright Lope de Vega (1562–1632) wrote about 1,500 *comedias*, of which 500 have survived. In writing this stupendous number of plays he used only a few plot lines, but he achieved spectacular fame and great success.

By contrast, the greatest literary figure of sixteenth-century Spain, Miguel de Cervantes (1547–1616), led a life of hardship and penury. He began writing plays in the early 1560s, but after getting into trouble with the law he ran off to Rome. There he enlisted in the navy that Philip II was forming to fight the Turks, and he distinguished himself at the Battle of Lepanto (1571; see p. 459). In 1575, while on his way back to Spain to seek an officer's commission, he was captured and enslaved by the Turks of Algiers, and for the next five years he repeatedly tried to escape while his family tried to raise a ransom. Finally freed, he returned to Spain and took a job in the royal bureaucracy in Seville. Accounting was not his strong suit, however, and he was constantly in trouble with his superiors. He left the royal service in 1600.

While still working at his job in Seville, Cervantes began to write again and won first prize for poetry in a contest held in Zaragoza in 1595. After leaving government service, he spent three years writing a great satire on the chivalric romances that had become phenomenally popular in Spain. This work, *Don Quixote*, which recounts adventures of a knight and his squire, became immediately popular. Philip III (r. 1598–1621), observing a young man convulsed with laughter over a book, is said to have remarked that the young man was either crazy or was reading *Don Quixote*. The work was first translated into English in 1612 and has been translated into more languages than any other book except the Bible. Toward the end of his life, Cervantes published the first short stories to be written in Spanish, in a work titled *Twelve Exemplary Novelas* (1613).

Although theater did not become popular in France until the seventeenth century, French writers of the sixteenth century contributed to the foundations

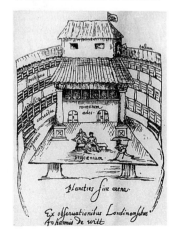

A contemporary drawing (1596) of the Swan Theatre in London.

of modern literature. Michel Montaigne (1533–92), a French nobleman educated as a humanist, created the genre of the essay after retiring from the royal court in disgust over the fanaticism engendered by the wars between the Huguenots and the Catholics. In his *Essays,* Montaigne explored human nature in a manner both witty and wise.

Science

During the sixteenth century Nicholas Copernicus (1473–1543), Tycho Brahe (1546–1601), Johannes Kepler (1571–1630), and Galileo Galilei (1564–1642) combined theory with experimentation and observation to transform the medieval world view. Copernicus, who was educated at the universities of Padua and Cracow, spent most of his adult life in a monastery in Prussia trying to resolve the discrepancy between the observed movement of the planets and the Ptolemaic view that the planets and the sun orbit the earth. Eventually, in a work published the year of his death, he proposed that the earth and the other planets circle the sun.

Copernicus's heliocentric theory did not gain wide acceptance until late in the century. In fact, the Danish astronomer Tycho Brahe made careful observations of the movement of the planets in an effort to demonstrate the validity of the Ptolemaic view. Instead, they led him to the conclusion that Copernicus was right and that the discrepancy between the observed movements and the Ptolemaic theory was even greater than Copernicus had thought.

Copernicus had still subscribed to the ancient view that the planets move in circular orbits. Brahe's observations were not entirely consistent with that view, however, and his assistant, Johannes Kepler, eventually demonstrated that the planets follow elliptical orbits and provided a mathematical explanation for their movement.

Galileo, a professor at the University of Padua, confirmed Copernicus's theory by using a telescope he built after hearing about a spyglass that had been invented in Holland. The telescope, which magnified objects thirty times, enabled him to make many revolutionary discoveries. He was the first to observe the mountains on the moon, the rings of Saturn, and the components of the Milky Way. He also provided mathematical explanations of the movement of physical objects and described the behavior of the pendulum in clocks. In his most famous experiment he dropped objects of different weights from the leaning tower of Pisa to show that all objects fall with the same rate of acceleration and then devised a mathematical formula for the universal rate of acceleration of falling objects. Galileo once remarked, "The book of nature . . . is written in mathematical characters."

In Chapter 21, we will deal with the scientific revolution of the sixteenth century in greater detail.

Suggestions for Further Reading

Geographical Discovery

For a detailed account of the geographical discoveries of the fifteenth and sixteenth centuries, see J. H. Parry, *The Age of Reconnaisance* (1963). For the technological basis of the explorations, see C. Cipolla, *Guns and Sails in the Early Phase of the European Expansion* (1966). For the Mediterranean background of oceanic navigation, see M. E. Mallet, *Florentine Galleys of the Fifteenth Century* (1967), and F. C. Lane, *Venetian Ships and Shipbuilders of the Renaissance* (1934).

Effects on Europe

On the effect of the discoveries on Europe, see J. H. Elliott, *The Old World and the New* (1970). H. H. Hart, *The Road to the Indies* (1950), describes the Portuguese expeditions; J. B. Brebner, *The Explorers of North America, 1492–1806* (1933), and A. P. Newton, *The European Nations in the West Indies, 1493–1688* (1933), treat exploration in particular areas. The best account of Columbus is S. E. Morrison, *Admiral of the Ocean Sea,* 2 vols. (1942). For an overall view, see Morrison's

The European Discovery of America (1971). For good histories of the early Spanish colonies, see C. H. Haring, *The Spanish Empire in America* (1947); L. Hanke, *The Spanish Struggle for Justice in the Conquest of America* (1949); and R. Cameron, *Viceroyalties of the West* (1968).

Spain

On Spain in the sixteenth century, J. H. Elliott, *Imperial Spain, 1469–1716* (1964), is excellent. R. T. Davies, *The Golden Century of Spain, 1501–1621* (1937) and *Spain in Decline, 1621–1700* (1956), are sometimes controversial but good accounts. For the effect of imperialism on Spanish government, see J. H. Parry, *The Spanish Theory of Empire in the Sixteenth Century* (1940). E. J. Hamilton, *American Treasure and the Price Revolution, 1501–1650* (1934), is the starting point for studies of the economic effects of empire. See also C. Cipolla, *Money, Prices and Civilization in the Mediterranean World* (1967). The classic work on the Armada is G. Mattingly, *The Spanish Armada* (1959). F. Braudel, *The Mediterranean and the Mediterranean World in the Age of Philip II*, 2 vols. (1972–73), is a masterpiece.

The Netherlands

The best history of the Dutch rebellion is P. Geyl, *The Revolt of the Netherlands, 1555–1609* (1932) and *The Netherlands Divided, 1609–1648* (1936). For a well-written biography of William the Silent, see C. V. Wedgewood, *William the Silent* (1944), and on the English involvement in the rebellion, see C. Wilson, *Queen Elizabeth and the Revolt of the Netherlands* (1970).

Elizabethan England

There is a wealth of good scholarly books on Elizabethan England. See J. Neale, *Queen Elizabeth I* (1952). C. Read's thorough biographies, *Mr. Secretary Walsingham*, 3 vols. (1925), and *Mr. Secretary Cecil* (Lord Burghley), 2 vols. (1955, 1960), provide detailed information about the politics of the period. For a social history, see A. L. Rowse, *The England of Elizabeth* (1950) and *The Expansion of Elizabethan England* (1955). On the English explorations, see J. A. Williamson, *The Age of Drake*, 3rd ed. (1952).

France

There is not much work in English on sixteenth-century France. J. W. Salmon, *Society in Crisis: France in the Sixteenth Century* (1975), is the best general treatment. J. E. Neale, *The Age of Catherine de' Medici* (1943), and H. Pearson, *Henry of Navarre* (1963), are useful. On the government, see N. M. Sutherland, *The French Secretaries of State in the Age of Catherine de Medici* (1962). J. W. Thompson, *The Wars of Religion in France, 1559–1576* (1909), is still useful. For brief scholarly accounts, see F. C. Palm, *Calvinism and the Religious Wars* (1932), and A. J. Grant, *The Huguenots* (1934). On the development of French political thought during the civil wars, see W. F. Church, *Constitutional Thought in Sixteenth Century France* (1941).

Social History

On rural life in the sixteenth century, see E. Le Roy Ladurie, *The Peasants of Languedoc* (1974), and M. R. Weisser, *The Peasants of the Montes* (1976). N. Z. Davis covers various aspects of French social history in a series of essays in *Society and Culture in Early Modern France* (1975). See also L. Febvre, *Life in Renaissance France* (1979). G. Huppert, *After the Black Death: A Social History of Early Modern Europe* (1986), concentrates on urban society. There are several excellent studies of individual cities. See G. Strauss, *Nuremburg in the Sixteenth Century* (1976); C. R. Friedrichs, *Urban Society in an Age of War: Nördlingen, 1580–1720* (1979); and C. Pythian-Adams, *Desolation of a City* (1979), concerning Coventry, England. On urban women, see M. C. Howell, *Women, Production, and Patriarchy in Late Medieval Cities* (1986).

Art and Literature

On the art of the sixteenth century, see W. Friedländer, *Mannerism and Anti-Mannerism in Italian Painting* (1957). The works of Marlowe, Shakespeare, Lope de Vega, Cervantes, and Montaigne are available in numerous modern editions.

19

POLITICAL AND ECONOMIC CRISES: THE SEVENTEENTH CENTURY

The seventeenth century was the century in which modern European civilization took on recognizable form. Political, social, and economic upheavals almost as dangerous as those that had shaken medieval civilization in the fourteenth century convulsed Europe. In the 1640s, great rebellions weakened England, France, and Spain, the three most powerful European monarchies. The last wars of religion merged with wars to expand commerce or to overthrow or preserve the balance of power. Weather, famine, and plague compounded the ravages of war. In Germany and Spain, the Thirty Years' War (1618–48) and plague epidemics actually forced the population downward. Prolonged economic depression marked the middle decades of the century. Harvests repeatedly failed. Starvation and disease followed. The flow of silver from the New World that had stimulated the European economy dropped off sharply. After 1670, growth turned upward again, but only gradually. Poverty sharpened social unrest and inadequate revenues limited state power.

That unpromising environment nevertheless gave birth to a new Europe that was richer, controlled more of the world's commerce, and had more effective government in 1700 than in 1600. The troubles of the fourteenth century and the religious conflicts of the sixteenth century had slowed the process of building the sovereign territorial state begun in the thirteenth century. But it now proceeded rapidly. In the realm of theory, state-building required defining the concept of sovereignty. In the realm of practice, it meant concentrating supreme power in some organ of the state. And Europe simultaneously underwent an intellectual revolution, a sharp change in conceptions about humanity and the universe far deeper and broader in its consequences than the Italian Renaissance (see pp. 408–11).

FRANCE'S SEARCH FOR ORDER AND AUTHORITY, 1598–1661

The anarchy and religious violence that lasted from 1562 to the Edict of Nantes in 1598 deeply marked seventeenth-century France. Three feeble kings had allowed the unruly great nobles to challenge the monarchy. Civil wars had torn the fabric of trade that linked the merchants and manufacturers of the towns. The wanderings of ragged, undisciplined armies had savaged the peasantry. The population longed for security despite a continuing suspicion of any authority that might attack local privileges or increase taxes.

The lawyer Jean Bodin (*ca.* 1530–96), the most penetrating political thinker of the tragic years of the Wars of Religion, offered a theory that spoke to the universal yearning for order. Bodin's *The Republic*

(1576) argued that a well-ordered state must give supreme power—sovereignty—to some organ of the state, preferably the monarchy. Bodin defined sovereignty as the essential characteristic of the state: the power of "giving laws to the people as a whole without their consent."

The laws of God and nature still bound Bodin's sovereign. But Bodin insisted that no human agency must limit the sovereign. Power must be "absolute," not divided, to be effective. Neither *parlements* (the highest French law courts) nor the Estates General should veto or modify decisions of the sovereign.

Bodin defined sovereignty far more clearly than previous theorists. He persuasively presented it as the only alternative to insecurity and civil war. The French absolute monarchy of the seventeenth century appeared to fulfill Bodin's prescription and became the model and envy of many of Europe's rulers.

Henry IV and Sully: Order Restored

Henry IV (r. 1589–1610), ex-Huguenot and victorious founder of the Bourbon dynasty, began the process of restoring royal power and French prosperity. He was a popular king—courageous, vigorous, humorous, tolerant, and sound in his judgment of subordinates. But he spent much time in pursuit of game and women and happily left the routine business of government to his chief minister, Maximilien de Sully, an austere ex-Huguenot artillery officer. Sully restored the monarchy's solvency by canceling some debts, avoiding expensive foreign wars, and patching up the inefficient, corrupt, and inequitable tax system.

The monarchy, like most early modern governments, "farmed" its taxes—that is, it granted the right to collect taxes to private contractors who paid the government a fixed sum and then extracted all they could from the population. The tax burden fell most heavily on the peasants, because nobles and the upper classes in the towns were exempt from major taxes. The nobility opposed attempts to redistribute the tax burden and helped to bring

---

Roots of the Modern State: Jean Bodin on Sovereignty

Political thinkers had recognized the fact *of sovereignty for some time, but Bodin was the first to express the* idea *in clear and uncompromising terms.*

Sovereignty is supreme power over citizens and subjects unrestrained by laws. . . . A prince is bound by no law of his predecessor, and much less by his own laws. . . . He may repeal, modify, or replace a law made by himself and without the consent of his subjects. . . . The opinion of those who have written that the king is bound by the popular will must be disregarded; such doctrine furnishes seditious men with material for revolutionary plots. No reasonable ground can be found to claim that subjects should control princes or that power should be attributed to popular assemblies. . . . The highest privilege of sovereignty consists in giving laws to the people as a whole without their consent. . . . Under this supreme power of making and repealing laws it is clear that all other functions of sovereignty are included.

From Jean Bodin, Six Books Concerning the Republic, *from the Latin version of 1586, trans. by F. W. Coker, in* Readings in Political Philosophy *(New York: Macmillan, 1938), pp. 374–77, 380.*

Triumphal Entry of Henry IV into Paris, a large sketch by the great Peter Paul Rubens (*ca.* 1630).

down the French monarchy in 1788–89 over that very issue (see pp. 584–85). Sully nevertheless did improve the system he inherited by attacking the crooked and inefficient tax farmers who as a rule pocketed as much as half the taxes collected before they reached the treasury. The reestablishment of internal order allowed agriculture and commerce to recover and increased the government's revenues, especially from customs duties. By the time a Catholic fanatic assassinated Henry IV in 1610, France's treasury contained a sizable surplus.

Richelieu and the Consolidation of the Monarchy, 1610–42

A few years of weakness at the center reduced the work of Henry IV and Sully to ruins. The regency of Henry's widow, Marie de' Medici, allowed rapacious courtiers the run of the treasury and permitted Spain to intervene once more in French affairs, sometimes in bizarre alliance with the Huguenots. Incompetence

soon dissipated the financial surplus Sully had left and led in 1614 to a summoning of the Estates General of France to one of its rare meetings. But the deliberations of the Estates General soon produced deadlock over taxation and religious issues between the First and Second Estates (the clergy and the nobility) and the Third Estate (the middle classes of the towns, represented largely by provincial royal officers). The Estates General dissolved inconclusively, and did not meet again until 1789, on the eve of the French Revolution.

Fortunately for the monarchy, a minister far more powerful than Sully soon emerged. Henry IV's son, Louis XIII (r. 1614–43), assumed the throne and in 1624 appointed a brilliant young cardinal, Armand Jean du Plessis de Richelieu (1585–1642), as chief of the king's council. From then until his death Richelieu was the real ruler of France. The great Cardinal, rather than any member of the Bourbon dynasty, founded the French absolute monarchy.

The great cardinal: Richelieu, founder of the modern French state, painted by Philippe de Champaigne.

Richelieu had the clearest and most penetrating mind of any statesman of his generation as well as a largely deserved reputation for diabolical cleverness. He sought to establish beyond challenge the power and prestige of the French monarchy. He came to his task with a startling grasp of political and diplomatic possibilities, an infallible memory, and an inflexible will unconstrained by moral scruple. Richelieu admired Machiavelli (see pp. 412–14), and the heart of the Cardinal's political creed was *raison d'état,* "reason of state": the good of the state was the supreme good. That good justified the use of any means whatsoever—a stern creed that Richelieu nearly reconciled with his own religious conscience. He deemed it "essential to banish pity" when judging "crimes against the state," for mercy in the present only led to greater bloodshed in the future. He coolly sent innocent men to their death to terrify troublemakers. When Louis XIII expressed moral qualms, Richelieu beat the king's objections down with brutal frankness: "Man is immortal; his salvation is hereafter; the state has no immortality, its salvation is now or never."

Richelieu pursued four objectives: he sought to destroy the power of the Huguenots, crush the great nobles, exclude the Habsburgs from French internal politics, and decide in France's favor the Bourbon–Habsburg rivalry abroad that dated from the sixteenth century. The Edict of Nantes, the compromise of 1598 that ended the religious civil wars, had allowed the Huguenots to garrison about 200 towns. Richelieu persuaded Louis XIII that he would never be master in his own house until he had wiped out this "state within a state." A monopoly of force within its borders, then as now, was the essential characteristic of statehood.

Rumors that the government had de-

cided to attack them provoked the Huguenots to rebel. Richelieu besieged and captured their chief stronghold at La Rochelle on the Atlantic coast. Despite his contempt for what he described as the "pretended Reformed religion," he nevertheless allowed the Huguenots to worship as they pleased once he had destroyed their political and military autonomy. He sought to conciliate Protestants abroad who might help him in war with Spain and Austria, and he hoped to make dependable citizens of the Huguenots. In that he was successful. The Huguenots served the crown in the war of 1635–59 against the Habsburgs and remained loyal in the great domestic crisis of the Fronde (see next section) that followed Richelieu's death.

Richelieu's attack on the nobility was less successful. Noble plotting threatened him until the end of his career. In response, he developed networks of spies, created a special tribunal to try noble lawbreakers, and sternly forbade duelling, a privilege that symbolized the nobility's freedom from ordinary restraints. The great nobles who had governed provinces almost by hereditary right gradually lost their powers to appointees of the crown called *intendants.* These temporary appointees came not from the old "nobility of the sword" but from the commons or the *noblesse de robe,* who were ennobled judicial officeholders of middle-class ancestry who had bought their offices from the crown. The economic and social privileges of the nobility survived Richelieu, but he curtailed its political power.

Richelieu was no financier and was no more interested in bettering the condition of the common people than were the rulers of other early modern states. He spent large sums to rebuild the armed forces and even more in wars against the Spanish and Austrian Habsburgs, Bourbon France's chief rivals for the leadership of Europe. He left the state's finances and the peasantry that supported those finances in worse condition than he had found them. But his subtle diplomacy and well-timed intervention in the Thirty Years' War (see pp. 489–91) made France instead of Spain the leading European power.

At his death in 1642, Richelieu left behind him the most powerful state in Europe. His success in establishing relative peace within France's own borders made economic growth possible, and France's steadily increasing power made Richelieu's creation the model for royal absolutism throughout the continent.

Mazarin, the Fronde, and the Coming of Louis XIV

Richelieu's death and that of Louis XIII in 1643 put the great Cardinal's work to a severe test. Louis XIV was a child of five when his father died, and his mother, Anne of Austria, became regent. She left the business of government to the man whom Richelieu had trained as his successor, the Italian Cardinal Giulio Mazzarini (1602–61), known in France as Mazarin.

Mazarin lacked his former master's relentless will and self-confidence. He sought to continue the war against Spain until the defeat of the Habsburgs, and to maintain the prestige of the monarchy that Richelieu had restored. But the nobility despised Mazarin as a foreign upstart, and the urban middle classes hated him for the high taxes that war demanded. The result was a movement known as the Fronde, the most serious rebellion against the monarchy before the Revolution of 1789.

The word *fronde* referred to a game of the unruly children of Paris, who threw dirt at passing coaches. The rebellion coincided with a period of severe harvest failures and lasted from 1648 to 1652. Like the children's game, it was annoying, but it ultimately failed to deflect the monarchy from its path. The Fronde's leaders were the judges of the *parlements,* or high courts; the chief financial officers who owned their offices and were thus heredi-

tary bureaucrats; and the nobility under the guidance of princes of the royal family. Each group hoped merely to increase its own influence, not destroy the French monarchy or upset the established social order.

They also failed to agree on a joint program beyond the purely negative policy of exiling Mazarin. The *parlements,* which began the struggle, stood for the privileges of the bureaucrats who controlled the courts and the ramshackle tax machinery. They wanted the king to rule with their advice rather than through councilors whom he could make or break at his pleasure. They insisted especially that he impose no tax without their consent. The nobles, who joined the rebellion later, had no intention of letting the *parlements* become dominant. They instead sought to abolish the upstart *intendants* and regain their old powers as provincial governors.

The result might have been different had any group dared to mobilize fully the deep-seated resentment of the lower classes—a resentment expressed throughout the century in urban riots and peasant rebellions against taxes and government. A few theorists, especially Huguenots, had argued that subjects possessed a "right of resistance" to unjust authority. But unlike the contemporary English rebellion, which asserted that right by defeating the king, the groups that led the Fronde were unwilling to unleash forces from below that might prove uncontrollable. Their conservatism, combined with the disunity of the rebels, eventually led to the Fronde's collapse.

Mazarin fled the country in 1651 and again in 1652–53 but returned to the saddle without difficulty, thanks to the support of Anne of Austria. By 1659, he had achieved victory over Spain. France gained two counties in the Pyrenees and the daughter of Philip IV of Spain as a bride for the young Louis XIV. That outcome symbolized the humiliation of Spain and the triumph of France as the leading power in Europe. The young king profited both from widespread revulsion against the disorders of the Fronde and from the prestige of foreign victories.

Cardinal Mazarin.

Fighting in Paris during the
Fronde, 1648.

The morning after Mazarin's death in March 1661, Louis XIV announced to his ministers that he would henceforth be his own first minister. Richelieu had triumphed at last. The French monarchy had outlasted Huguenots and Fronde at home and Habsburgs abroad. Louis XIV henceforth ruled as an absolute monarch, endowed with a fuller sovereignty than any yet seen in the western Europe.

ENGLAND: IN SEARCH OF CIVIL AND RELIGIOUS LIBERTY, 1603–60

While Richelieu and Mazarin laid the foundations of absolute monarchy by divine right in France, England was slowly developing a constitutional, parliamentary system. The English groped toward a conception of sovereignty rooted in law and lodged in the hands of an assembly that represented the community—or at least its more wealthy and influential members. England was not alone in its resistance to absolute monarchy, but the result elsewhere tended to be anarchy and confusion as in Poland, or the victory of the crown as in France. In the end, the English example prevailed over absolutism. The "mother of parliaments" in London ultimately inspired parliamentary government in England's colonies and across modern Europe. But the road to constitutional monarchy in England was hard. It led through civil war and the execution of a king.

The Tudors: Crown and Parliament

England had always been peculiar. The strong monarchy of the Tudors (1485–1603) was part of a general European trend, but the survival and strengthening of Parliament under such a monarchy had no parallel elsewhere. While rulers on the Continent sought to abolish representative assemblies, the Tudors grudgingly used Parliament to legitimate laws and taxes. In the delicate area of religion, the Tudors found Parliament indispensable. Henry VIII had aspired to rule as an autocrat but had needed Parliament to break with Rome. Mary had asked Parliament to restore England to the Roman Church by statute. Elizabeth I had by statute once more broken with the Pope.

Elizabeth quarreled with her Parliaments, but the threat from Spain and the political good sense of both the queen and the parliamentary leaders had prevented a break. Both parties tacitly recognized that only Parliament could make a law or impose a tax. Parliament in turn recognized that making policy, especially foreign policy, lay within the sphere of "royal prerogative." Elizabeth's Parliaments tried more than once to reform the Anglican Church in a Puritan direction and to nudge the queen on foreign policy—presumptuous acts for which Elizabeth scolded them sharply. But she was too popular for Parliament to challenge her directly and too astute to demand a clear definition of her prerogative.

Under the Tudors, Parliament acquired a corporate feeling and a sense of being an integral part of government. The absence of provincial estates or privileges like those in France further increased its power. By the sixteenth century the lower house, called the House of Commons (see p. 363), represented both the landed gentry of the countryside and the richer merchants of the towns. The gentry also governed England at the local level as justices of the peace, for the English monarchy had failed to develop paid bureaucrats like the French *intendants*.

England was peculiar socially as well as politically. It lacked the Continent's rigid legal boundaries between social "orders." The gentry—baronets, knights, esquires, and simple "gentlemen"—were all commoners in the eyes of the law. Unlike its French counterpart, England's titled nobility was minuscule in numbers, a mere 121 English peers in 1641. The gentry included the younger sons of the nobility, who received neither land nor title thanks to the system of primogeniture that preserved noble estates by passing them in their entirety to the eldest son. Noble younger sons thus linked nobility and gentry; many pursued middle-class careers in the law or even commerce. At the same time, English merchants continually moved upward into the gentry by buying land. English society was hierarchical, but less so than continental societies. The comparative unity of England's gentry and nobility made the Parliament that represented them uniquely self-confident. That self-confidence was one source of the fateful clash between Crown and Parliament.

James I: Crown against Parliament

The Tudors had long ago put a stop to private wars waged by the high nobility. Under Elizabeth I, foreign and domestic

A formal meeting of Parliament in 1625. The Lords are seated; the Commons stand outside the bar.

1485		1603	1642	1660		1714
House of Tudor		House of Stuart	Civil War and Republican Experiments		House of Stuart	

peril had rallied the Commons to the monarchy. But peace with Spain in 1604 and Europe's growing absorption in the Thirty Years' War after 1618 (see below) eliminated the danger of foreign invasion. The absence of threats inevitably lessened the authority of the Stuart family that succeeded Elizabeth, who was childless, in 1603.

James I (King of Scotland and of England, r. 1603–25) was the son of Mary, Queen of Scots. Well-meaning but pedantic, he failed to understand the political realities of the kingdom he had inherited from Elizabeth. The regents who ran Scotland after his mother's exile had raised him as a Protestant, but he had not relished that grim Presbyterian upbringing. His aims were entirely reasonable; he sought peace with Spain, toleration of England's Catholic minority, the union of England and Scotland, and a strong but benevolent monarchy.

But James, afflicted with a tendency to drool, preferred hunting, banqueting, and dalliance with male favorites to the sustained effort needed to govern. He failed to inspire confidence. And unlike Elizabeth, who often concealed her imperious will in ambiguous language, James made things dangerously clear. In a famous speech to the House of Commons in 1610, he proclaimed that "The state of monarchy is the supremist thing on earth; for kings are not only God's lieutenants upon earth, and sit upon God's throne, but even by God himself they are called gods." That lack of tact, his disorderly style of life, and the conspicuous financial corruption and bumbling foreign policy of the chief royal favorite, the Duke of Buckingham, offended many of the groups represented in Parliament.

The House of Commons began to attack the royal prerogative with arguments based on innovative readings of England's common law. The king in return denounced the parliamentary opposition.

The "country"—the nobility and gentry who ruled England at the local level and represented it in Parliament—attacked the "court party" of the increasingly friendless king. "Country" spokesmen denounced the court as secretly Catholic, influenced culturally by Spain and France, and financially and morally corrupt. The delicate Tudor balance collapsed.

Crown and Parliament clashed over three related issues: religion, money, and foreign policy. The Puritans and their sympathizers in the House of Commons wished to "purify" the Anglican Church of everything that still savored of Catholicism, from "Popish" ritual to the authority of bishops. James for his part knew from his youth in Scotland the Presbyterian system of church government that the Puritans sought. He was convinced that it would remove the church from royal control and threaten the monarchy itself. "No bishop, no king," he shouted in a moment of frustration.

Parliament continued to denounce the extravagance of the court and soon denied James the money needed to meet Elizabeth I's war debts and the rising cost of government in an age of inflation. James then raised money without parliamentary approval by increasing customs duties. Parliament contested his right to do so, but the courts ruled in the king's favor. The seeming subservience of the courts to the royal will further annoyed Parliament.

James I's foreign policy likewise exasperated his critics. He was too friendly with Catholic Spain for Puritan tastes, he did little to defend Protestants abroad against militant Catholicism, and he tried in vain to marry his son Charles to the daughter of the king of Spain. When James chided the House of Commons in 1621 for even discussing his foreign policy, the House bristled. It passed a unanimous Protestation defending its right to discuss "the arduous and urgent affairs concern-

The indolent James I.

ing the King, State, and defence of the realm, and of the Church of England." That was revolutionary talk. James tore the resolution from the Commons' *Journal* with his own hand, but he could not undo what the Commons had done. An aggressive and influential element among his subjects demanded rights and powers that he was unwilling to grant.

Charles I and the English Revolution, 1642–49

This crisis rapidly worsened after Charles I (r. 1625–49), second of the Stuarts, came to the throne. Charles tried to placate Parliament by attacking Catholic states. But Buckingham, the foppish favorite inherited from his father, failed to capture Cadiz in Spain or to save the French Huguenots besieged at La Rochelle. Parliament had urged war but had failed to grant sufficient taxes. Charles therefore levied a forced loan and imprisoned those who objected. In 1628 Parliament drew up a formal protest, the "Petition of Right," and compelled Charles to approve it. The Petition established that the king should henceforth levy neither taxes nor loans "without common consent by Act of Parliament" and that the government should imprison no one without showing cause. The king's subjects had begun to claim ever-broader rights against the state.

In 1629 Charles again roused the House of Commons to fury by asserting his full control of church and state. The Commons in reply declared that whoever introduced practices savoring of Catholicism into the Anglican Church was "a capital enemy to this kingdom and commonwealth," and that anyone who advised or submitted to taxation without parliamentary consent was "a betrayer of the liberties of England." The Commons thus raised the issue of the power to make law. Where did that power lie—in the king or in Parliament? The old answer, that it lay in the "king-in-Parliament," was no longer convincing. James I and Charles I between them had brought into the open the conflict between royal prerogative and the traditional "liberties of England" that descended ultimately from the *Magna Carta* of the barons (see pp. 311–12).

Charles, more stubborn than his father, ruled without Parliament from 1629 to 1640. In an attempt to duplicate Richelieu's absolutism, he chose advisers whose slogan was "thorough," such as Thomas Wentworth, Earl of Strafford, for political matters, and William Laud, Archbishop of Canterbury, for church affairs. Charles and his advisers devised new methods of taxation that did not require Parliament's approval and provided money enough to run the government so long as it stayed out of war. Laud challenged the Calvinist doctrine of predestination and sought to reestablish the authority of the bishops and reintroduce ritual into the Anglican service. The Puritans denounced him as a disguised Catholic. Up to 20,000 religious dissenters emigrated to the Netherlands or to bleak and distant Massachusetts. And Charles was unable to raise enough money to create the twin pillars of French-style absolutism—a royal administrative machine and a royal standing army.

Charles nevertheless prevailed until 1637–38. Then Laud tried to force the Anglican Book of Common Prayer on fiercely Presbyterian Scotland while Charles, with amazingly poor timing, alienated the Scottish nobility by seeking to reclaim from them the church lands they had acquired under Henry VIII. A fierce Scottish army was soon encamped in northern England. Charles and Strafford, unable to raise an army willing to fight, had to summon Parliament to vote money to buy the Scots off. The "Long Parliament" met in November 1640 and remained in session until 1653. It became a workshop of revolution. It sent Strafford and eventually Laud to the execution block. It dictated that the king must summon Parliament at least every three years. It outlawed all nonparliamentary taxation. It abolished the special royal law courts that had been the chief instruments of Charles's "Eleven Years' Tyranny." In less than a year (1640–41) Parliament destroyed absolute monarchy in England.

Charles secretly vowed revenge but acquiesced. He had no choice, for his government had alienated virtually all of the traditionally loyal groups whose cooperation he needed to rule England. Then the Catholics of Ireland decisively altered the

The autocratic Charles I.

situation by imitating the Scottish revolt and slaughtering Protestant settlers whom Elizabeth I and James I had planted in Ireland. Suppressing the Irish required raising an army once more—and Parliament distrusted the vengeful king too much to allow him to control that army. Simultaneously, the radical Puritans in Parliament abolished bishops in the Anglican Church. The inescapable issue of whether king or Parliament was to control army and church thereupon split England's upper classes. The growing political and religious radicalism of the House of Commons gave Charles what he had until then lacked—a royalist party that would fight to reassert his prerogatives. He attempted to arrest his parliamentary opponents in January 1642. By summer England was at war.

What was at first a confused struggle between factions of nobility and gentry soon turned into the English Revolution. Both Parliamentarians and Royalists claimed to support traditional English political and religious freedoms. London,

The English Revolution   1642–49

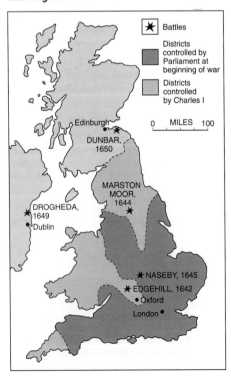

most towns, the middle classes, and the economically advanced southeast of England generally supported Parliament, although much of the population sought to remain neutral. Many rural areas and the backward northwest supported Charles. But the divisions between the parties did not correspond closely to England's economic, social, or regional divisions. Nobility, gentry, and artisans from all over England fought on both sides. The fierce religious and ideological issues at stake split many families, both noble and gentry.

Unlike the Fronde, in which narrow interest groups failed to proclaim programs with broad appeal, the English Civil War and Revolution offered dramatic alternatives to the established order—parliamentary monarchy instead of royal absolutism, and a Presbyterian Church with elected "presbyters," or elders, instead of an Anglican Church under crown-appointed bishops. Unlike the Fronde, the English Revolution produced radical movements that sought to abolish the monarchy, the established Church, and the landlords. "Levellers," "Diggers," and millenarian sects such as the "Fifth Monarchy Men" sought to inaugurate a new age of radical equality, or rule by "saints."

Parliament based itself in London, Europe's largest city, and proved more successful than the king at raising money and armies. Oliver Cromwell, a brilliant and ruthless cavalry officer, helped create a "New Model Army" drawn largely from his fellow Independents, strict Bible-reading Puritans who believed in democratically organized independent congregations with little or no church structure.

Cromwell and Parliament's numerically superior and ideologically motivated army ("Truly, I think he that prays best will fight best") defeated the king's forces decisively in June–July 1645. The king surrendered a year later. Then the army broke with the Presbyterians, who had dominated Parliament since the Anglicans had withdrawn in 1642 to join Charles I. Groups in Parliament and army with views ranging from social and religious moderation to extreme radicalism quarreled over the constitutional and religious settlement. The king sought to exploit the divisions among his opponents by devious negotiations. In November 1647 he escaped from custody to launch a brief second round of civil war.

The Independents in the army were now determined to root out all opposition. They purged Parliament of their Presbyterian rivals, defeated the king, and called the untrustworthy "Charles Stuart, that man of blood, to an account for the blood that he had shed." Cromwell, after initial hesitation, had Charles I executed in 1649, abolished the monarchy and the House of Lords, and set up a republic or "Commonwealth" with the "rump" of the Long Parliament as its government and with himself as its unchallenged leader. Parliament had tried a king ordained by divine right for treason against his own subjects, had cut off his head, and had abolished the very institution of kingship. England had set an example that was long remembered.

Cromwell's Dictatorship

Unlike later continental figures who seized command of a state through revolution, England's new dictator was a deeply religious man who did not initially seek supreme power. Yet power, and inevitable opposition to his will, brought out Cromwell's ruthlessness. He suppressed with fire and massacre the Irish rebellion that in 1641–42 had helped trigger the Civil War. He drubbed the Scots in two great battles when they intervened in favor of the son of Charles I. He presided over a naval war with the Dutch from 1652 to 1654. He wrathfully dissolved the rump of the Long Parliament in 1653, saying "You are no Parliament, I say you are no Parliament; I will put an end to your sitting." But he failed in his efforts to guarantee religious toleration to all Protestants except determined Anglicans and to find a satisfactory constitutional basis for government.

Cromwell attempted to rule with the consent of Parliament and through a written constitution, the "Instrument of Government"—the first such document in the history of a major state. He took the title of Lord Protector instead of king, but quar-

---

Democratic Radicalism in the English Revolution

With victory assured, Cromwell's army turned to politics. In 1647 a Council of the Army debated constitutional issues at Putney, outside London. Radicals and representatives of the common soldiers, influenced by the Levellers, pressed for political rights for all men. Gentry figures such as General Ireton, Cromwell's forceful son-in-law, countered with the claim that only ownership of land conferred the right to representation.

MAJOR RAINBOROUGH: I think that the poorest he that is in England hath a life to live, as the greatest he, and therefore truly, sir, I think it's clear, that every man that is to live under a government ought first by his own consent to put himself under that government, and I do think that the poorest man in England is not at all bound in a strict sense to that government that he hath not had a voice to put himself under.

GENERAL IRETON: Government is to preserve property. . . . The objection does not lie in the making of the representation more equal but in the introducing of men . . . in this government who have no property in this kingdom. . . .

SEXBY [a representative of the troops]: I see that though liberty were our end, there is a degeneration from it. We have ventured our lives to recover our birthrights and privileges as Englishmen, and by the arguments urged there is none. There are many thousands of us soldiers that have ventured our lives; we have had little property . . . yet we have had a birthright. But it seems now, except a man hath a fixed estate in this kingdom, he hath no right in this kingdom. I wonder we were so much deceived.

From Puritanism and Liberty, *ed. by A. S. P. Woodhouse (Chicago: University of Chicago Press, 1951), pp. 53, 62, 69.*

---

reled with Parliament as bitterly as had the Stuarts. In 1655 he installed an open military dictatorship to keep Parliament from disbanding his army and persecuting his coreligionists. Most Englishmen still rejected religious toleration, especially toleration of the religious and political radicals who made up a large part of Cromwell's army. And it became increasingly evident that England—like other states in the following centuries—could not break with history and set up a new regime simply by drafting a constitution. An unwritten "constitution" already existed, deeply ingrained in English political traditions.

Oliver Cromwell, by Samuel Cooper.

Cromwell's death in 1658 made General George Monck, his most important military subordinate, the most powerful figure in England. Monck recognized that Parliament was the only alternative to military dictatorship and that restoring Parliament also required recreating the monarchy. In 1660, a "Convention Parliament" under his protection invited the son of Charles I to return from France and take up the crown.

The Legacy of the English Revolution

The Civil War had made clear that England would not tolerate an absolute monarchy. Strafford and Laud had tried to do for Charles I what Richelieu and Mazarin had done for Louis XIV. But whereas the Frenchmen had died in their beds, the Englishmen had lost their heads to the executioner. The new Parliament confirmed many of the severe limits to royal power that the Long Parliament had set before the outbreak of the Civil War. The turmoil of the first half of the century left most Englishmen with half-expressed convictions that had lasting effects—a fear of too great a concentration of power, a deepened respect for government by law rather than by royal command, a reverence for Parliament as the defender of individual rights against royal despotism, and a fervent distaste for standing armies.

The restoration of King Charles II: the coronation in Westminster Abbey (from a contemporary print).

The early seventeenth century was a brilliant age in the history of English literature and thought. It included Shakespeare's mature work and the early years of the great poet John Milton. In 1611 the Authorized, or King James, Version of the Bible first emerged from the presses. Its sonorous cadences have influenced the writing of English to the present day. Statesmen and pamphleteers arguing for royalist, parliamentary, or radical principles likewise made this a formative period of modern political thought.

Thomas Hobbes's *Leviathan* (1651) distilled the political insights of the years of civil war. Under the influence of Thucydides' great history of the Peloponnesian War (see pp. 52–53), of which Hobbes wrote the first English translation, Hobbes saw in humanity "a perpetual and restless desire of power after power." Without some authority to enforce law, society would disintegrate into "a war of every man against every man." Life without government was "solitary, poor, nasty, brutish, and short." Hobbes, following Huguenot thinkers seeking to justify revolt against France's Catholic monarchy, postulated that humans set up sovereign powers through agreements or contracts.

But Hobbes drew from this "contract theory" of government conclusions opposite to those of the Huguenots, and of Cromwell and his army, who had declared "the king is king by contract" and had severed Charles I's head for violating that contract. For Hobbes, society agreed to obey the sovereign because the sovereign alone could maintain order. To ensure the maintenance of order, the sovereign's powers had to be absolute and unquestioned. Hobbes's contract therefore bound only the subjects, not the ruler. "There can happen no breach of the Covenant on the part of the Sovereign; and consequently none of his Subjects . . . can be freed from his subjection."

Hobbes thus took contract theory and transformed it into a justification of unfettered and arbitrary power. English political theorists during the remainder of the seventeenth century devoted much effort to finding some way to refute Hobbes—to subject political power to the restraint

of law and to the consent of the governed. But they, too, remained fearful of the ever-present threat of violence and chaos against which Hobbes had created his absolute sovereign.

GERMANY: DISINTEGRATION AND DISASTER, 1618–48

The consequences of the absence of sovereign power and the "war of every man against every man" were nowhere so visible as across the North Sea in Germany. While France built the mightiest monarchy

The title page of Thomas Hobbes's *Leviathan*, one of the fundamental works of Western political theory. Hobbes described the sovereign power of the state as "that great Leviathan, or rather (to speak more reverently) that mortal God, to which we owe under the Immortal God, our peace and defence."

in Europe and England underwent a crisis from which it emerged with new strength, the German-speaking peoples suffered the Thirty Years' War. It was in reality four successive wars that began in 1618 in Bohemia, spread to the rest of the Holy Roman Empire, and before its end in 1648 involved most major continental powers. It was a savage and demoralizing conflict that left central Europe poorer and weaker than the states to its west for the next 150 years.

The Causes of the Thirty Years' War

The war sprang from a complicated mixture of religious and political quarrels. The Peace of Augsburg (1555) had ended the previous round of religious war in central Europe (see p. 437) by dividing the German states between Catholic and Lutheran rulers. Each prince had received the right to determine the religion of his subjects. But in the following decades most Catholic bishoprics in north Germany had fallen into Lutheran or secular hands. The spread of Calvinism introduced a further source of friction, for the Peace of Augsburg had not recognized Calvinism nor assigned it any territories. Protestant successes caused increasing discontent in the Catholic camp.

In 1608, the foremost leader of the Catholics, Duke Maximilian of Bavaria, roughly disciplined the Protestant town of Donauwörth. That action led Frederick V, the Calvinist ruler of the Palatinate, a small state on the middle Rhine, to form a Protestant Union of German princes and cities. In reply, Maximilian organized a Catholic League with the support of German Catholic princes and the Jesuits. By 1609 the Holy Roman Empire had fractured once again into two hostile religious and military alliances. Protestant Union and Catholic League faced each other with hatred and suspicion, each determined to bar the other from further gains.

1. Revolt in Bohemia, 1618–20

These signs of anarchy and religious division within the Holy Roman Empire prompted the Habsburgs, who held the imperial title, to try to rebuild their authority. They began by seeking to consolidate their hold over their long-time family domains of Austria, Bohemia, and Hungary. The aging emperor Matthias secured the election of his heir-apparent, Ferdinand of Styria, as king of Bohemia in 1617.

Bohemia was a flourishing territory in which two chief nationalities (Germans and Czechs) and a variety of religions (Catholicism, Lutheranism, Calvinism, and remnants of the Hussite movement of the fifteenth century) lived in relative peace under Habsburg promises of toleration. But Ferdinand was a zealous Counter-Reformation Catholic. He had ruthlessly recatholicized Styria, and the Protestant majority in the Bohemian Estates rightly feared that he planned the same for Bohemia. In May 1618 the Bohemians therefore threw their imperial governors from the windows of Prague castle (an incident thereafter known as the "defenestration of Prague"). The Estates raised an army, declared Ferdinand deposed, and offered the crown of Bohemia to Frederick V of the Palatinate. Frederick's unwise acceptance extended the war from Bohemia to the Empire as a whole. His Protestant Union took the side of the Bohemian Estates, while Maximilian of Bavaria swung the Catholic League behind Ferdinand, who had been elected emperor.

The Bohemian phase of the war ended swiftly. In November 1620 the Imperial forces crushed the Bohemian rebels at the battle of the White Mountain near Prague. Frederick V fled, and Emperor Ferdinand proceeded to make Bohemia over at the cost of wrecking its economy and society. War and plague cut the population almost in half. The Czech nobility lost everything. Half the land in Bohemia changed hands through confiscation, and Ferdinand created a new nobility of adventurers from as far away as Ireland. The Jesuits, with Ferdinand's full backing, set out to reconvert the country to Catholicism by force. Within ten years they had stamped Protestantism out or driven it underground. The Czechs became a people without a ruling class and without a claim to an independent existence for two centuries. The Habsburgs and their Catholic allies had decisively won the first round of the great war.

2. Danish Intervention and Catholic Triumph, 1625–29

The fall of Bohemia terrified the German Protestants and elated the Catholics. The Spanish Habsburgs had also intervened against the Protestant states of north Germany, and the armies of the Catholic League were everywhere triumphant. But common danger failed to unite the Protestants. The Lutherans feared a Calvinist victory in Bohemia more than an Imperial triumph. The Lutheran kingdom of Saxony had actually helped Ferdinand put the Czechs down. And although Frederick V was the son-in-law of James I, Protestant England gave no help; James I and his successor Charles I were locked in their struggle with Parliament.

The king of Denmark joined his fellow Protestants in 1625, but his principal motive was greed for territory in north Germany. Within a year, the Catholics had beaten him back. Albrecht von Wallenstein, a brilliant military entrepreneur who had offered the emperor his services, crushed the Danes with an expert mercenary army that at its height numbered 125,000 men. Wallenstein's long-term aim was probably to secure central Europe for himself. His immediate goal was to build an Imperial Habsburg military machine that could eliminate the Protestants without the help of the Catholic League. By 1628 Wallenstein and the League were as much at odds on the Catholic side as Calvinists and Lutherans were on the Protestant. Religion slowly receded in significance as the war became a struggle between armies and states alone, a struggle for mastery in Europe.

The Habsburg and Catholic cause reached its high-water mark in 1629. Denmark withdrew, leaving Wallenstein's army supreme. The Catholic League and Jesuit advisers persuaded Ferdinand to issue an Edict of Restitution that restored to Catholic hands all church lands lost to Protestantism since 1552. Carrying out the edict meant yet more bloodshed to restore the dispossessed Catholic bishops of Protestant north Germany. That would also destroy both the rough religious balance between Catholicism and Protestantism in Germany and the power balance between the north German states on the one hand and Austria and Bavaria on the other. That threat finally roused Lutherans inside and outside Germany to action.

3. The "Lion of the North": Gustavus Adolphus, 1630–32

In 1630 Sweden, a country until now on the periphery of the European state system, intervened to check the Habsburgs. Its masterful king, Gustavus Adolphus, was the ablest ruler of his generation. Sweden had a population of roughly 1.25 million people, perhaps a fifteenth of the population of France. But Gustavus had cultivated rich copper and timber exports, a sophisticated iron and armament industry, and the most advanced army of the day. That army was not large, but it was the first in Europe recruited by universal conscription, and it possessed a high morale born of fierce patriotism. It also had the first uniforms, the first artillery light enough for battlefield maneuver, improved muskets, regular pay, and discipline, a rarity indeed in the Thirty Years' War. Its victories over Russia, Denmark, and Poland between 1611 and 1629 made the Baltic almost a Swedish lake.

Gustavus stepped into the great war in Germany to defend Sweden's Baltic interests, which Wallenstein appeared to threaten. But as the war continued, Gustavus began to toy with a broader aim— the creation of a federation of German Protestant states under Swedish leadership. He arrived too late to save the great city of Magdeburg from sack, massacre, and destruction by the Imperial forces in May 1631, an event that for generations symbolized the all-devouring brutality of this war. But in the fall of 1631 Gustavus shattered the Imperial armies at Breitenfeld in Saxony, and marched triumphantly to the Rhine.

That emergency compelled the Emperor to recall Wallenstein, whom he had dismissed at the insistence of the Catholic

League. Gustavus defeated Wallenstein decisively at Lützen in 1632, but paid for victory with his own life. Without Gustavus's leadership the outnumbered Swedes could not maintain their dominance in Germany. Swedish weakness in turn freed the Emperor from dependence on his over-mighty subject, Wallenstein, who perished by assassination at Ferdinand's orders. In the fall of 1634 the Imperial armies checked the Swedes at the battle of Nördlingen. Gustavus Adolphus had saved German Protestantism but had failed to decide the war.

4. France Intervenes, 1635–48

The most powerful state of all now acted, opening the fourth and final phase of the war. Since his appointment as chief minister in 1624, Richelieu had followed the war closely through his ever-present ambassadors and agents. His aim was to crush both Austrian and Spanish Habsburgs and to end Habsburg encirclement of France. Under his leadership, Catholic France accepted as allies all opponents of the Habsburgs regardless of religion. His first allies were the Protestant Dutch, who in 1621 had again gone to war with their ancestral enemy, Spain. Then Richelieu subsidized Sweden. But the Imperial defeat of the Swedes in 1634 forced him to choose between direct French intervention and Habsburg domination of Europe. In May 1635 he chose intervention; France declared war on Spain and allied itself with Sweden and Germany.

The Thirty Years' War had by then lasted for seventeen years. It continued drearily for a further thirteen years, for neither side had the strength to force a decision. French, Swedish, and Dutch armies slogged across central Europe pursuing or pursued by the Habsburg forces. The rebellions of Portugal and of the rich province of Catalonia in 1640 weakened Spain. In 1643, on the battlefield of Rocroi

The siege of Magdeburg in 1631 by Habsburg and Catholic forces, which ended with one of the bloodiest massacres of the war.

in the Netherlands, the French finally crushed the Spanish army and its legend of invincibility. Habsburg allies soon deserted the Empire, and the Swedes besieged Prague and menaced Vienna. The Habsburg attempt to roll back the Reformation in Germany and establish mastery over central Europe had failed.

Peace of Exhaustion: Westphalia, 1648

Habsburg defeat opened the way to the peace negotiated between 1644 and 1648 at the Congress of Westphalia. The gathering was Europe's first great peace conference and the first interstate meeting of importance since the Council of Constance of 1414–18 (see p. 427). But unlike Constance, the atmosphere and the business of the Congress that met at Münster in western Germany were entirely secular. The Congress was a meeting of sovereign states that recognized no earthly superior and only the most shadowy common interests. The unity of medieval "Christendom" had dissolved.

The Congress confirmed the importance of the sovereign state and set a framework for central European politics that lasted until 1801–06. In recognizing the right of the German principalities to make alliances and to declare war, the Congress accepted the disintegration of the Empire into more than 300 separate sovereignties. Switzerland and the Dutch Netherlands finally achieved recognition as independent states. France acquired ambiguous rights to Alsace, and Sweden gained strips of German territory along the Baltic and the North seas. The two German states of Brandenburg and Bavaria increased their territory and prestige.

As for religion, the Congress reaffirmed the principle of partition according to the religion of the ruler established in the Peace of Augsburg of 1555, and at last added Calvinism to Catholicism and Lutheranism as one of the recognized faiths. To prevent further dispute, the Congress froze the ownership of church lands as of 1624. North Germany remained Protestant and south Germany Catholic. Only France and Spain failed to reach

---

The Sack of Magdeburg   1631

For a generation after the destruction of this German city, the phrase "Magdeburg quarter" meant "no quarter."

Then was there naught but beating and burning, plundering, torture, and murder. Most especially was every one of the enemy bent on securing much booty. When a marauding party entered a house, if its master had anything to give he might thereby purchase respite and protection for himself and his family till the next man, who also wanted something, should come along. It was only when everything had been brought forth and there was nothing left to give that the real trouble commenced. Then, what with blows and threats of shooting, stabbing, and hanging, the poor people were so terrified that if they had had anything left they would have brought it forth if it had been buried in the earth or hidden away in a thousand castles. In this frenzied rage, the great and splendid city that had stood like a fair princess in the land was now, in its hour of direst need and unutterable distress and woe, given over to the flames, and thousands of innocent men, women, and children, in the midst of a horrible din of heartrending shrieks and cries, were tortured and put to death in so cruel and shameful a manner that no words would suffice to describe, nor no tears to bewail it.

From Otto von Guericke, in Readings in European History, *ed. by James Harvey Robinson (Boston: Ginn, 1906), Vol. II, pp. 211–12.*

---

agreement. Their war continued until Mazarin secured, in the Peace of the Pyrenees of 1659, the victory that Richelieu had sought.

The Consequences of the Thirty Years' War

The Thirty Years' War had been a terrifying demonstration of the anarchy that Europe's state-builders sought to avoid. It was one of the most destructive wars in recorded history. In Europe no later conflict matched it in ruthless devastation until the new "thirty years' war" of 1914–45. Armies pillaged, raped, and murdered their way across central Europe. The soldiery wiped towns off the map and reduced cities to a small fraction of their original populations. Cultivated land reverted to waste. Destruction of livestock even more than of crops crippled a primitive and mostly agrarian economy, for

Europe in 1648

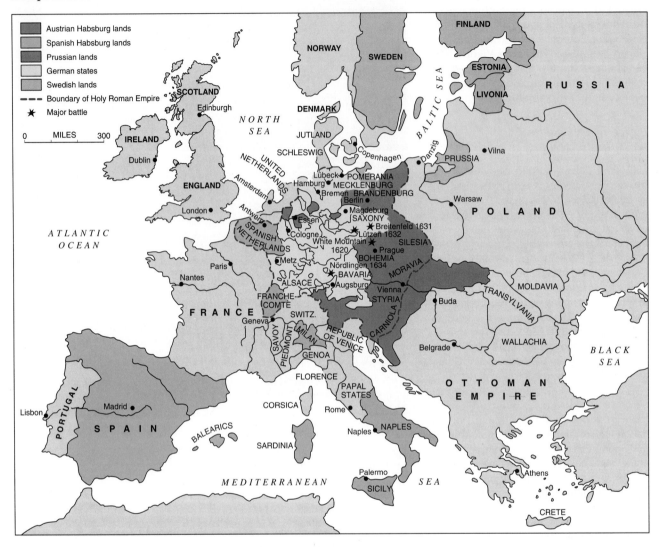

plough and dairy animals were difficult to replace. Starvation and the massive plague epidemics that marched with the lice-ridden armies killed more than the sword.

The Holy Roman Empire (including Bohemia) lost an estimated 4 million out of roughly 21 million inhabitants. A few areas lost up to 80 percent of their population. The war also had deep psychological, social, political, and economic effects. The peoples of central Europe were soon happy to acknowledge any authority, however brutal, that promised peace. The fragmentation of the Holy Roman Empire

into small states quirkily divided by customs barriers hampered economic recovery. The war helped delay until the nineteenth century the emergence of a state called "Germany," and helped make its emergence an event that shook Europe and the world.

DUTCH UNREST AND SPANISH DECLINE

The political upheavals of the early seventeenth century touched many areas of

Europe other than France, England, and central Europe. Even distant Russia underwent an anarchic "Time of Troubles" before settling down uneasily under the rule of the first Romanov tsar in 1613. In the west, violent convulsions shook the Netherlands and Spain.

By 1609 the northern areas of the Netherlands had achieved effective independence from Spain and enormous economic success. An aggressively Calvinist party nevertheless pressed for renewed war against Spain in the southern Netherlands. Its leader was Maurice of Nassau, son of William the Silent, chief of the House of Orange and commander of the highly competent Dutch army. A second party, that of the merchant class, enjoyed the support of the religiously tolerant Arminians (those unwilling to accept Calvin's stern doctrine of predestination). It hoped to reestablish trade with Spain.

In 1619 Maurice of Nassau overthrew this "peace party" and had its leader executed after a political trial. The war with Spain resumed in 1621 and continued inconclusively until the Peace of Westphalia. Tensions between the House of Orange and the mercantile "regent class" continued throughout the century. For two decades after 1650 the "regents" dominated Dutch affairs. But when invasion— from France rather than Spain—came again in 1672, the old conflicts reopened. A mob in The Hague tore the leading regent, Johan de Witt, limb from limb and publicly sold his remains. The Dutch summoned the head of the House of Orange, the young Prince William, to lead them victoriously against overwhelming odds.

In Spain, religious-ethnic persecution marked the beginning of irreversible decline. In 1609 the monarchy and the Inquisition launched a campaign similar to the expulsion of Spain's 150,000 Jews after 1492 (see p. 459). In fanatical pursuit of religious uniformity and "purity of blood" *(limpieza de sangre),* the authorities deported to north Africa in 1609–14 as many as 275,000 Moriscos, the insufficiently converted descendants of the Moors who had given the Iberian peninsula much of its civilization. That savage persecution

deprived Spain of a creative minority that it sorely needed. Plague and economic collapse reduced the population dramatically, from perhaps 8.5 million in 1600 to 7.5 million in 1650.

War, both foreign and domestic, also contributed to Spain's decline. The leading minister from 1621 to 1643, the proud Count-Duke of Olivares, committed Spain to war in Germany in 1620 and against the Netherlands in 1621. War with France as well in 1635 placed unbearable tax burdens on the Spanish monarchy's patchwork of provinces jealous of their traditional rights and liberties. Olivares struggled gloomily to establish a centralized administration with an effective system of tax collection. But as so often happened in early modern Europe, centralization—the creation of a modern state machine—provoked bitter revolt. In 1640 Portugal, forcibly united with Spain since 1580, made good its independence by force. The rich province of Catalonia attracted French support and defied the monarchy until 1652. Spain's Italian possessions also revolted.

Spain thus had to yield to France the position of leading power in Europe in 1659. Spain's political and military decline was in part a consequence of the overambitious policies of Olivares. But its deeper causes were economic and internal. Of all the powers, Spain suffered most from the crises of the European and world economy of the seventeenth century.

EUROPE'S POPULATION AND ECONOMY IN CRISIS

A suddenly hostile climate and a drastic fall in prices intensified the ravages that never-ending war inflicted on the societies of seventeenth-century Europe. Despite the slowly gathering force of commerce and industry, agriculture still dominated Europe's economy. The tyranny of the seasons in turn dominated agriculture. And during what historians have termed the "little ice age," the cold century and a half between the 1590s and the 1740s, that tyranny was harsh indeed. Usually ice-free rivers repeatedly froze over in winter. Springs and summers turned rainy and cold.

Even in the relatively warm fifteenth and sixteenth centuries, England had suffered one poor harvest in four, and one disastrous harvest in six. Between 1594 and 1597 rain and cold wrecked four harvests in succession from Ireland to east central Europe; the result was widespread famine. The harvests from 1647 to 1652–53 were similarly catastrophic, especially in France and Spain. The 1690s were the coldest decade in 700 years; in 1696–97 about a quarter of the population of Finland perished by famine. The "great cold" of 1709–10 produced a general crop failure in France. Beggars froze to death in the streets of Paris.

Human and animal epidemics inevitably accompanied famine, for malnutrition reduces resistance to disease. Spain lost perhaps a half-million dead from bubonic plague in 1647–52, and outbreaks were widespread until the early eighteenth century. The population of Europe dipped slightly (see Figure 19-1). Only after 1750 did a mellower climate, croprotation techniques pioneered in the Low Countries, New World crops such as the potato and maize, and dramatic improve-

ments in transport allow a new and sustained increase in Europe's population.

A second force intensified the effects of the seventeenth-century climate on Europe's fragile economy and population—the movement of prices. In the sixteenth century two trends had united to produce a "price revolution": the sudden and massive influx of New World silver and gold, and the rapidly increasing sophistication of Europe's merchants and bankers, who had multiplied the effective volume of money by speeding its circulation and by using credit far more extensively than in the past. In consequence, by 1600 prices had reached levels four to five times above those of 1500. That inflation, although modest by twentieth-century standards, had deeply unsettling effects on societies that still adhered to the medieval myth of a "just" price. The penetration of money ever deeper into the countryside brought with it price fluctuations that intensified the distress of the peasantry and ruined aristocrats who failed to adapt to the hard new age of profit and loss.

After about 1620 the influx of New World silver slowed as production in the mines of Mexico and Peru peaked. Loss of revenue helped cripple the policies of Olivares. Throughout Europe price inflation gave way to deflation, and hectic growth to stagnation. The wars and troubles after 1620, from the Thirty Years' War to the English Revolution and the Fronde, further intensified the economic depression. Only after 1670 did some northern areas of Europe, most notably England and the Dutch United Provinces, once more begin to enjoy a steady prosperity. In Spain, the pressure of taxes to finance Olivares' wars and the dead hand of his bureaucracy crushed what little independence and enterprise the middle classes of Castile had possessed. In the countryside, as in the Spanish New World, sheep replaced peasants. In France, the pressure of the monarchy's taxation, further intensified in the wars of Louis XIV after 1667 (see pp. 510–12), caused repeated revolts.

Yet Europe survived and grew—despite the "little ice age," deflation, and war—thanks above all to economic innovation. In industry—the production of

FIGURE 19-1   **The Population of Europe, 1000–1700 (including Russia west of the Ural Mountains)**

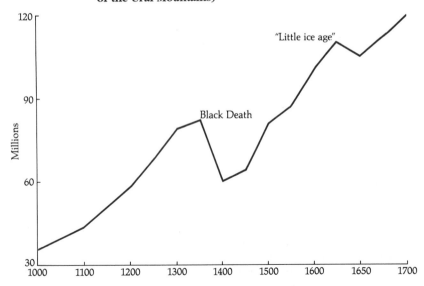

goods for market using specialized labor and machines—new techniques rapidly gained ground. In the 1580s, the Dutch introduced power saws worked by windmills. Water-driven power hammers for forging became common. Coal, at least in England, became the cheapest source of energy. Coal fueled London's growth from 200,000 inhabitants in 1600 to more than 550,000—Europe's largest city—by 1700. Coal made the English glass industry the most modern in Europe, and supplied London's shops with glass windowpanes at which visitors marveled.

All over Europe, commerce and industry began to break out from the medieval framework of town and guild monopolies. A new form of craft organization that bypassed the guilds, the "putting-out system," spread from the Low Countries. Traveling merchants supplied rural home workers with raw materials, then returned to collect the finished product. "Putting-out" was particularly effective in the greatest industry of early modern Europe, textiles. It was also well suited to an age in which techniques were simple and hand or animal power drove most industrial equipment. To the peasant family, it provided income that in years of crop failure might mean the difference between life and death. Putting-out slowly eroded guild restrictions, channeled money into the countryside, and dissolved the old peasant barter economy. It was a major source of Europe's economic growth.

In trade and finance, the century was one of continued rapid change. An ever-widening banking network spread across Europe, from Seville facing the New World to the grain and timber ports of the Baltic. A new institution apparently invented in Italy, the joint-stock company, made possible a far more widespread mobilization of capital than traditional family firms or partnerships. Individuals who were not necessarily traders could buy "shares" in great commercial enterprises such as the Muscovy Company (1553), the English East India Company (1600), and the Dutch East India Company (1602). The company directors then used the shareholders' money for their operations. Soon a vast market developed in the "shares" themselves, the ancestor of the modern stock exchange.

A further source of change was geographic. By the middle of the seventeenth century the westward and northward shift in Europe's economic center of gravity that had begun even before 1492 was complete. The Mediterranean and central Europe became backwaters. Venice, although victorious over the Turks at sea, suffered disastrous shrinkage both in its industries and in its trade with the eastern Mediterranean. The westward shift of trade to the New World and around the Cape of Good Hope helped destroy German banking dynasties such as the Fuggers of Augsburg. Then the Thirty Years' War completed Germany's economic ruin.

But even economies open to the ocean failed. Spain, thanks to religious persecution, rigid government controls, and high taxes, soon yielded much of its New World trade to Genoese and Dutch merchants. Antwerp, the great trading and banking center of northern Europe until the mid-sixteenth century, failed to assert its political independence from Spain. It lost its economic position as well to its Dutch neighbors to the north. The founding of the Bank of Amsterdam in 1609—the same year as the truce by which Spain recognized Dutch independence—symbolized the supremacy of the Dutch Republic as the center of Europe's economy, a supremacy that lasted throughout the seventeenth century. But the republic, with a tiny territory and a population that reached 2 million in 1650 but then remained essentially unchanged until 1800, was little more than a glorified city-state.

The future belonged to those powerful engines of growth, the modern "national markets" within the large territorial states, France and England. France seemed by far the richest, for it possessed the largest territory of any state west of Russia and a population greater than any other. But its agriculture suffered badly in the "little ice age." France's sheer size, the absence of good roads or navigable waterways, and the numerous customs barriers between provinces, and between towns and countryside likewise stunted growth. France's centralized war-making state crushed the peasants under a taxation that, along with dues to landlords and Church, deprived them of roughly half their income.

Nor did the efforts of France's government to promote economic growth help. The great finance minister of Louis XIV, Jean-Baptiste Colbert (see p. 506) made an almost despairing attempt to promote the development of industry and commerce in the face of the economic depression that lasted through the 1680s. In the 1670s he founded many enterprises, including cannon foundries and textile mills staffed with Dutch experts. He strengthened the guilds as a means of ensuring the quality and uniformity needed to promote exports. He attempted to crush the Dutch with tariffs and with Louis's wars. Colbert was the most consistent adherent of a series of loosely linked notions, characteristic of a world of warring states, usually known as "mercantilism"—state intervention to promote industry and maximize

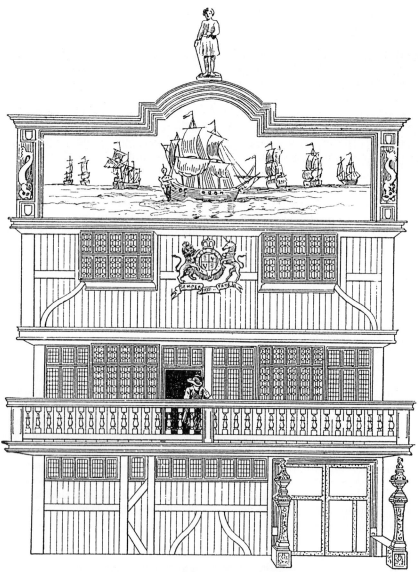

Ships bearing precious merchandise from the far side of the world: the front of the earliest headquarters of the English East India Company. Photo courtesy of the Granger Collection.

FRONT OF THE OLD EAST INDIA HOUSE.

The world's first stock exchange, at Amsterdam, in the mid-seventeenth century.

exports, protective tariffs to prevent imports, and strenuous attempts to create a trade surplus that would suck in gold and silver from competitors. Such methods long outlived the seventeenth century, but they did not help France. Most of Colbert's industries proved ruinously unprofitable, and his reinforcement of the guilds was a disaster for French industry. His tariffs damaged France more than the Dutch. France's commercial economy developed, but largely despite Colbert.

England was different. It too employed "mercantilist" practices, such as the Navigation Acts that after 1651 restricted all trade with England and its colonies to English ships, and channeled colonial products through English ports. England, too, fought wars with the Dutch over commerce in 1652–54, 1665–67, and 1672–74. But internally, England was already a large unified market; its guilds were decayed relics; its textile, coal, and iron industries were gradually expanding. By 1700 its economy, the least "mercantilist" and state-controlled in Europe, owed a third of its national product to commerce and industry, while the proportion in France was a fifth or less. In the long term, England's economy could not fail to have an impact on the wider world opened up in the age of discovery.

THE EUROPEAN EMPIRES

Europe's overseas expansion slowed briefly in the seventeenth century. Spain needed time to digest the conquered Aztec and Inca empires. In India, China, and Japan the Europeans faced ancient civilizations that still had the power to hold them at arm's length. Developing the North American wilderness required settlers in numbers unavailable until Europe's population growth resumed. And the extension to the outside world of the warlike competition between European states slowed Europe's economic penetration of the non-European world.

Trade and plunder had lured the Europeans overseas. Portugal persisted in that pattern, and its "colonies," with the exception of its early settlements on Madeira and its great land empire in Brazil, remained fortified trading posts that dealt in spices or slaves through native middlemen. The Dutch sought to follow the Portuguese example after 1600, when they seized control from Portugal of the Indian Ocean and China Sea. But in their Spice Islands south of the Philippines the Dutch soon found that maintaining exports required more than trading posts. As the Spaniards discovered during their feverish search for gold and silver in the Americas, trade and plunder led to rule and settlement.

The new model colonies of the seventeenth century were thus settlement colonies. The pattern dated from Portugal's settlement in the 1420s of the uninhabited Atlantic island of Madeira, and Spain had followed it in the Americas after the 1520s. The function of the settlement colonies was to produce raw materials essential to the mother country. That purpose required the export of European institutions, technology, plants, and animals to set up overseas societies on the European model. In Africa, malaria and yellow fever killed the vast majority of Europeans who attempted to penetrate inland, and Europe's military technology did not yet provide superiority over the natives on their own ground. Native middlemen and rulers continued to provide apparently inexhaustible supplies of slaves; the trading-post system persisted.

But in the New World, settlement was possible. And settlement meant production of the commodity most prized after gold and silver—sugar. Cultivating that addictive substance, first brought to Europe by the Crusaders, required backbreaking labor. As the Portuguese had demonstrated on Madeira, enslaved natives from the Canary Islands or from Africa most conveniently supplied that labor. Tobacco, coffee, and in East Asia tea and spices created similar patterns of cultivation and settlement. The riches that these products generated proved an irresistible source of conflict.

The Struggle for Mastery in the East

East of Africa and south of China the Portuguese soon lost the trading empire they had established after the voyages of Vasco de Gama. Dutch, English, and French interlopers appeared. Portugal was too economically and demographically weak and too technologically backward to hold empires both in the New World and in the East simultaneously, and its subordination to Spain from 1580 to 1640 exposed it to attack by Spain's enemy, the Dutch. Portugal's rivals founded powerful East India Companies: the English in 1600, the Dutch in 1602, the French in 1664. The Dutch proved the most ruthless, well-organized, and successful. Their seizure of the Cape of Good Hope in 1652 created the largest white community in Africa as a way-station for their shipping. Their massacre of English merchants on Amboina in 1623 and their control of Batavia on Java from 1619 and of the strategic Malacca strait after 1641 persuaded the English to concentrate on India. There England and France set up trading posts on the Portuguese model at Bombay, Madras, and Calcutta for England, and at Pondicherry for France. The Mughal empire that dominated South Asia barred the way inland. Only its collapse after 1707 opened the road by which Britain ultimately established its hegemony in the Mughals' place (see Chapters 22 and 27).

Sugar and Slavery in the Caribbean

In the Caribbean, the Dutch, English, and French competed for crumbs from Spain's overfilled table. After war between the Dutch and Spain resumed in 1621, the Dutch sought to damage Spain by seizing sugar-rich Brazil from Spain's dependency, Portugal. The Dutch failed, but they did take the Caribbean island of Curaçao as a base for raids on Spanish commerce. England settled Barbados in 1624 and gained Jamaica in 1655, while the French took Guadeloupe and Martinique. They had come for plunder like the Dutch, but they stayed to grow sugar. And sugar plantations required a ready supply of labor—

A tropical Amsterdam, complete with canals: the great Dutch port of Batavia, on Java (1682).

unfree labor. The Caribbean Indians were becoming extinct, thanks to smallpox, massacres, and slave labor exacted by Spain. The interloping powers therefore brought their own labor with them. On Barbados, white small farmers who cultivated tobacco gave way in the 1640s and 1650s to large, efficient plantations grouped around great sugar mills. At first white contract labor worked the plantations. These "indentured servants" worked off the price of their passage to the New World by years of servitude. But white labor could not compete with black slaves from Africa. Slaves were virtually unlimited in supply and cost less than whites—slavery was for life, not three, five, or seven years.

African rulers, Arabs, and Portuguese had pioneered the slave trade long before the discovery of the New World. The Portuguese had experimented with slave cultivation of sugar on Madeira. Extending that savage system to the New World required the transportation across the Atlantic of almost a million Africans in the course of the seventeenth century. Death rates ran as high as 20 percent during transport inside Africa and another 20 percent on the Atlantic crossing. Disease and ill-treatment prevented the slave populations in the New World from reproducing enough to increase their numbers. Expanding the sugar economy thus required the import of ever-greater numbers of slaves. A triangular trade pattern developed—Europeans took goods such as weapons, rum, or tobacco to Africa, bartered them for slaves whom the kings of west Africa had seized from neighboring tribes and kingdoms, and exchanged the slaves in the West Indies for tropical goods that included molasses from which to make more rum. As the Portuguese slowly lost control of the west coast of Africa, the Dutch, English, and French stepped in to supply slaves to their own sugar islands and—through smuggling—to the plantations of Spain. Slavery, whether in the European colonies, the Islamic world, or Africa itself, had as yet attracted little attention as an institution of peculiar cruelty.

North America: The Dutch, the French, and the English

North of the sugar islands lay an immense waste of swamp and woodland: North America. Its only known resources were the codfish off Newfoundland and the furs and timber of its great forests. But three powers nevertheless attempted settlements there in the hope of breaking Spain's near-monopoly of the New World. The failure of Sir Walter Raleigh to found a colony in Virginia during the 1580s revealed some of the difficulties. Cold winters and poor soil made the creation of a tropical plantation economy difficult. Hostile natives were still relatively strong. Planting a permanent colony in North America required the transport of a large labor force and its support over

The inhabitants of the New World, as seen in the 1580s by John White, one of the leaders of Raleigh's failed attempt to establish a colony on Roanoke Island, Virginia.

many years until the settlement achieved self-sufficiency. That demanded capital, numerous emigrants, and unshakable determination.

The Dutch and French failed both demographically and economically. The Dutch explored the Hudson River in 1609 and had settled New Amsterdam on Manhattan Island by 1624. But their colony of "New Netherland" never became more than a center for trade and fur exports. The English seized it in 1664, immediately before the second of their wars with the Dutch (see p. 514).

The French excelled in the backwoods. Jacques Cartier discovered the St. Lawrence River in 1535 and Robert de La Salle coursed the Mississippi in 1682. France's explorers and fur-trading *coureurs de bois* ("wood runners") were more adventurous and France's Jesuit missionaries more determined than the New World representatives of any other European state except perhaps the Portuguese of Brazil. By 1605 French settlers had planted villages in Acadia, and in 1608 Samuel de Champlain founded Québec. By 1640 perhaps 3,000 French inhabited Canada, but the population had reached only 10,000 by 1700.

Growth was slow because the French government succeeded too well in imposing French absolutism and social patterns on its colonies. It regulated and stultified economic life while granting land in large blocks to a few proprietors under semifeudal conditions. Except under Colbert in the 1660s and 1670s, it gave French peasants little inducement to emigrate. For religious reasons it strictly barred from Canada all Huguenots, who took their economic talents to the English colonies instead. A cluster of French settlements spread across the St. Lawrence Valley, but the English settlers to the south far outnumbered the "New France" of lords and peasants.

England's constitutional and religious struggles spurred emigration. English governments, whether Stuart or Cromwell, encouraged colonizing projects but left great latitude to individuals or joint-stock companies in founding colonies. Above all, English governments allowed religious minorities to settle in English colonies. That speeded mightily the growth of an enterprising, independent, and rapidly multiplying population.

The Virginia Company planted England's first successful colony at Jamestown in 1607. It almost failed, but then the settlers discovered the rage in Europe for a native weed, tobacco. That cash crop paid for the manufactured goods they needed from England—and ultimately for African slaves to cultivate the tobacco. The small band of religious dissenters who landed at Plymouth in 1620 lost half their number during the first winter. But the Massachusetts Bay Company, which founded Boston, was able to profit by the Pilgrims' experience. In 1630 it transported 900 settlers across the ocean in a large and well-planned operation. Thanks in part to Laud's persecution of dissenters, the population of Massachusetts had swelled within ten years to about 14,000. By 1650 the population of "New England" was about 20,000. The settlers were soon shipping fur, fish, and timber to England.

By 1700 the English colonies held almost 200,000 settlers and dominated the continent. Twelve colonies existed, offshoots of the original settlements or created by royal grants. Georgia, the thirteenth, was founded in 1732. And unlike New France, which suffered under a royal central administration of Québec, the English colonies were in effect self-governing. Each colony acquired an elected representative assembly that passed its laws and controlled taxation. A royal governor appointed by London was in theory not responsible to the assembly. But because the governor generally depended on the assembly for his salary, his executive power and London's reach were in practice limited. In the 1660s Parliament did its best to impose mercantilist practices by requiring the export of some colonial goods exclusively to England in English or colonial ships. Those restrictions caused much complaint and smuggling. After the Glorious Revolution of 1688 (see p. 515) London gradually became less insistent on asserting its authority. The colonists accepted regulation of their trade so long as enforcement was lenient.

Unlike the colonial subjects of all other powers, the inhabitants of British North America thus became increasingly accustomed to self-government. Without conscious design, England had fashioned a new kind of empire. Armed trade had been the foundation of the Portuguese and Dutch empires. The empire of Spain placed a ruling class of soldiers, planters, and missionaries in command of large native populations. But the Protestant English felt none of the responsibility for the Indians that weighed upon the missionaries of Spain, nor could the English exploit the labor of the thinly settled Indian populations of North America. Instead, the English settlers and the Dutch of New Holland simply displaced the natives. England transferred an entire European population to a new environment and allowed it to blend institutions brought from home with innovations that new surroundings demanded. The result was a unique, unplanned experiment in economic, political, and religious freedom.

Russia Reaches the Pacific

While France and Britain were pushing westward across North America, the Muscovite state was pressing eastward from the Ural Mountains across Siberia toward the Pacific. Muscovy reached the Pacific first; no ocean separated its new dominions from the center of its power around Moscow. In 1581 groups of Cossacks—the "pioneers" or "frontiersmen" who had earlier pushed back Tartars and Turks and had settled the lower valleys of the Dnieper, Don, and Volga rivers—struck eastward from the Urals. Their fierce leader, Yermak, enjoyed the patronage of Tsar Ivan IV, the Terrible. Like the French in Canada, the Cossacks sought furs, particularly the incomparable sable. They therefore followed the pine forests and the northern tundra rather than the open plains to the south. The innumerable rivers and lakes of Siberia allowed the Cossacks, like the French *coureurs de bois,* to flow swiftly eastward, occasionally halting to found fortified outposts.

The Cossacks reached the Pacific in the early 1640s, three generations and

3,000 miles after their eastward movement began. Unlike America, no great mountain chains barred the way. Resistance from the small Tartar states and the numerically weak tribal peoples of Siberia was slight. The advanced civilization of China ultimately checked Muscovite expansion in the Amur River valley. In 1689, Russia and China concluded their first treaty at Nerchinsk, and Russia withdrew from the Amur basin for almost 200 years.

Like the English, the Cossacks sought freedom as well as furs. Their early communities in Siberia were as wild and lawless as the later towns of the American West. But like the French administration in North America, the despotism of the tsars soon reached out across vast distances to clamp its administration and taxes on the lucrative fur trade. By 1700 several hundred thousand Russians had settled Siberia. By the end of the century, Russian traders had ventured across the Bering Strait to Alaska and down the North American coastline in search of seals. Long before the English in America reached the Pacific, the Russians had through individuals daring and government backing staked a claim to the northern half of Asia and had reached out toward the Western Hemisphere.

The first half of the seventeenth century was thus a period of fierce turmoil both within Europe and in Europe's relations with the wider world. The French monarchy consolidated itself but remained vulnerable to its turbulent nobles. The English monarchy for a time collapsed. From 1618 to 1648 the states of central Europe—and outside powers from France to Sweden—fought the last and bloodiest of the wars of religion. European economic and population growth faltered under the battering of wars, epidemics, and the "little ice age." Yet Europe's expansion into the outer world continued ceaselessly, if less swiftly than in the sixteenth century. The rise of Europe's new territorial states continued; new theories and methods of statecraft and new economic techniques made them bastions of order and relative prosperity in a violent and anarchic world. Yet after 1600, one state rose so high that it threatened to overthrow the balance of power on which Europe's state system rested.

Suggestions for Further Reading

General

D. Ogg, *Europe in the Seventeenth Century* (1925, 1960), and G. N. Clark, *The Seventeenth Century* (1931), offer useful surveys. G. Parker, *Europe in Crisis* (1979), reflects recent work in the field. For a model comparative analysis of the upheavals that convulsed most early modern states, see P. Zagorin, *Rebels and Rulers, 1500–1660* (1982). M. S. Anderson, *War and Society in Europe of the Old Regime, 1619–1789* (1988), surveys one powerful force for change.

The Great Powers

For events in France, see the detailed survey of R. R. Treasure, *Seventeenth Century France* (1966). C. V. Wedgwood, *Richelieu and the French Monarchy* (1962), and C. J. Burckhardt, *Richelieu: His Rise to Power* (1964), are informative. P. Goubert, *The Ancien Regime: French Society, 1600–1750* (1973), is excellent on French social structure. On England, see especially C. Hill, *The Century of Revolution, 1603–1714* (1961); L. Stone, *The Causes of the English Revolution, 1529–1642* (1972); and C. V. Wedgwood, *The King's Peace, 1637–1641* (1955), and *The King's War 1641–1647* (1958). M. Ashley, *The Greatness of Oliver Cromwell* (1966), and C. Hill, *God's Englishman* (1970), deal in lively fashion with a central figure. P. Laslett, *The World We Have Lost,* 2nd ed. (1971), gives an enthusiastic introduction to England's seventeenth-century social history. S. Schama, *The Embarrassment of Riches* (1988), is entertaining on the culture and politics of the Dutch Republic. On events in central Europe, see especially R. W. J. Evans, *The Making of the Habsburg Monarchy* (1979); C. V. Wedgwood, *The Thirty Years' War* (1938); and G. Parker et al., *The Thirty Years' War* (1974).

The European and World Economies

On Europe's economic crisis, see especially C. M. Cipolla, *Before the Industrial Revolution* (1976); F. Braudel, *Civilization and Capitalism, 15th–18th Centuries* (1982); and *The Cambridge Economic History of Europe,* Vol. 4 (1967). C. McEvedy and F. Jones, *Atlas of World Population History* (1978), provides the best set of—admittedly speculative—population figures.

For relations between Europe and the world, see particularly J. H. Parry, *The Age of Reconnaissance* (1964), and J. H. Elliott, *The Old World and the New* (1970). A. W. Crosby, *The Columbian Exchange* (1972), and *Biological Imperialism: The Biological Expansion of Europe, 900–1900* (1986), provide elegant treatments of neglected but decisively important events.

20

ABSOLUTISM AND CONSTITUTIONALISM 1660–1715

The last half of the seventeenth century was the age of France. Its population of roughly 18 million in 1650 dwarfed the 7.5 million of Spain and the roughly 5 million of England. Its economy and its bureaucratic-military machine were the largest in Europe. Much of Europe imitated its culture, a subject treated more fully in the following chapter.

But French power had limits. Internally, high taxation, government regulation of the economy, religious persecution, and oppressive censorship stunted economic growth. Externally, Louis XIV's attempts to dominate Europe created a series of coalitions against France. In the two great worldwide conflicts of 1689–97 and 1701–15, England, the Dutch Republic, and Habsburg Austria compelled even the "Sun King" of France to recognize the law of relations between states: the law of the balance of power.

Other powers declined with giddying speed, or stagnated. Sweden, outclassed militarily thanks to its small population, ceased to be a great power. The Ottoman Turks mounted their last great threat to western Europe, and then began the decline that soon made their empire the "sick man" of the state system. The internal anarchy and external decline of Poland that led to its disappearance from the map between 1772 and 1795 became visible. Spain sank further. The Dutch settled down to enjoy their riches.

Winners emerged as well. Austria defeated the Turks and consolidated the Habsburg hereditary possessions into a state more centralized than anything before it in south-central Europe. England took command of the outer seas from the Dutch, as the Dutch had taken it from Portugal. Russia, until now a backward power outside the European system, suffered the first of the barbaric "revolutions

(OPPOSITE) ABSOLUTISM: THE YOUNG LOUIS XIV, READY FOR THE PURSUIT OF GLORY, BY GIOVANNI LORENZO BERNINI, 1665.

The Sun King's emblem.

from above" that transformed it into a military giant. And the uncouth electorate of Brandenburg, an obscure state on the eastern fringes of Germany, began its fateful rise to great power status.

THE FRANCE OF LOUIS XIV

Louis XIV, the "Sun King" (r. 1643–1715), was the living symbol of French military,

political, and cultural domination. He was born in 1638 and took power decisively into his own hands the day after Mazarin's death in 1661. He died at the age of 77 and left the throne to his great-grandson. By temperament and training he incarnated divine-right monarchy—the notion that hereditary kingship was the only divinely approved form of government, that kings answered to God alone for their conduct, and that subjects owed absolute obedience to their king as the direct representative of God on earth. His education was sketchy, and he had little imagination and no sense of humor. But he had the qualities needed to rule—a willingness to work relentlessly, a commanding presence, and an imperious will.

Louis may not have spoken the famous words ascribed to him—"I am the state." But he practiced them. He sought to personify the concept of sovereignty. He took a deep interest in the elaborate etiquette and ceremonies of his court, for they dramatized his supremacy over the nobility. He also conducted the business of the state in person, as his own "first minister," from Mazarin's death in 1661 to his own in 1715, a dedication uncommon in monarchs. He set his preferred pastimes of hunting and womanizing aside when the state demanded it. "If you let yourself be carried away by your passions," he once remarked, "don't do it in business hours."

The administrative machine that served Louis XIV culminated in a three to five member "High Council" of great ministers that met with him almost daily. Professional "secretaries" at the head of bureaucracies then executed the decisions taken in council. In the provinces, the *intendants,* the royal administrative officers that Richelieu had created, received ever more power to enforce the king's will.

Three great ministers of middle-class origin—Jean-Baptiste Colbert, Michel Le Tellier, and his son, the Marquis de Louvois—directed the administration under the king's close supervision. Colbert, cold, gloomy, and fanatically precise, served as Controller General of Finance. He cut waste, streamlined the tax system, and gave France its first serious attempt at

---

Bishop Bossuet on Absolutism

Jacques Bénigne Bossuet was tutor to Louis XIV's son in the 1670s, and the most zealous and prominent theorist of the king's absolutism.

The royal power is absolute. With the aim of making this truth hateful and insufferable, many writers have tried to confound absolute government and arbitrary government. But no two things could be more unlike. . . . The Prince need render an account of his acts to no one. . . . Without this absolute authority the king could neither do good nor repress evil. . . . God is infinite, God is all. The prince, as prince, is not regarded as a private person: he is a public personage, all the state is in him; the will of all the people is included in his. As all perfection and all strength are united in God, so all the power of individuals is united in the person of the prince. What grandeur that a single man should embody so much! . . .

From Jacques Bénigne Bossuet, "Politics Drawn from the Very Words of Scripture," in Readings in European History, *ed. by James Harvey Robinson (Boston: Ginn, 1906), Vol. II, pp. 275–76.*

1589	1610	1616	1643		1715		1774	1793

an annual budget. He sought to force France's economic growth by punitive tariffs against the Dutch, state-supported industrial projects, and colonial enterprises. He doubled the king's net income between 1661 and 1671. Le Tellier and Louvois, the ministers of war, then spent the proceeds.

The old French monarchy had imposed its authority through its law courts, the *parlements*. It had also frequently consulted provincial assemblies or the Estates General of France. The new monarchy that Richelieu had founded and Louis XIV perfected imposed its authority and its taxes by decree. Louis XIV checked the pretensions of the *parlements* and deliberately neglected to summon the Estates General. The new army paid for by Louis XIV's taxes mobilized French manpower and militarized French society to an unprecedented extent. It also provided the force to crush—often with mass hangings—the many attempts at tax rebellion in the provinces. Above all, the king completed Richelieu's work of destroying the political power of the French nobility.

The Domestication of the Nobility

The Fronde had forced Louis XIV to flee Paris three times, and had left him fiercely determined to break the turbulent nobility. His principal weapons were three: First, he denied the nobility its traditional share in the power of the state and sharply curtailed its independent power in the provinces. He chose his ministers almost exclusively from commoners, rotated *intendants* to prevent collusion with the local nobility, and treated *parlements* and provincial assemblies with contempt. Second, he cheapened the status of the nobility by increasing its numbers; the title of marquis soon became almost a joke. Finally, he required the high nobility to serve him at court.

That service was bound up with Louis XIV's deliberate display of himself as the symbol of the state. In 1683 he moved court and government from the Louvre palace in central Paris to Versailles, fifteen miles away. There he made his home in the formal gardens and ornate chateau that he had built on marshland, at great cost in lives and treasure.

Louis XIV on the Duties of a King

In the 1660s and 1670s, Louis XIV and his staff prepared notes to instruct his son in the art of ruling.

I have often wondered how it could be that love for work being a quality so necessary to sovereigns should yet be one that is so rarely found in them. Most princes, because they have a great many servants and subjects, do not feel obligated to go to any trouble and do not consider that if they have an infinite number of people working under their orders, there are infinitely more who rely on their conduct and that it takes a great deal of watching and a great deal of work merely to insure that those who act do only what they should and that those who rely tolerate only what they must. The deference and the respect that we receive from our subjects are not a free gift from them but payment for the justice and the protection that they expect to receive from us. Just as they must honor us, we must protect and defend them, and our debts toward them are even more binding than theirs to us, for indeed, if one of them lacks the skill or the willingness to execute our orders, a thousand others come in a crowd to fill his post, whereas the position of a sovereign can be properly filled only by the sovereign himself.

. . . of all the functions of sovereignty, the one that a prince must guard most jealously is the handling of finances. It is the most delicate of all because it is the one that is most capable of seducing the one who performs it, and which makes it easiest for him to spread corruption. The prince alone should have sovereign direction over it because he alone has no fortune to establish but that of the state.

From Louis XIV, Memoirs for the Instruction of the Dauphin, *ed. by Paul Sonnino (New York: Free Press, 1970), pp. 63–64.*

The medal on the left (1661) celebrates the young Louis's purported accessibility to his subjects. The one on the right (1685) extols the new discipline and professionalism of his armies.

The palace of Versailles (1686), with the king arriving by carriage.

Louis moved with impassive dignity through the innumerable court gatherings in the mirrored halls of Versailles. Years of self-conscious practice in kingship had given him a public façade—cool, courteous, impersonal, imperturbable—that fitted perfectly the artificiality of the small world of the court, as far removed from reality as Versailles itself was physically removed from the bustle of Paris. In that atmosphere, a ball seemed as important as a battle, and holding the basin for the king's morning ablutions became a task as coveted as the command of armies. Instead of competing in the provinces for political power against the monarchy, nobles squandered their fortunes in jock-

eying for prestige under the king's vigilant eye.

He left the nobility one other outlet—war. Military service harnessed the nobility's inborn aggressiveness to the purposes of the state. But that outlet also had a political cost. It created a noble "war party" at court that encouraged the king's own megalomania.

The Destruction of the Huguenots

The only potential challenges to Louis's absolutism besides the nobility were religious forces and groups. The king clashed with several popes who disputed his "Gallican" claim to control the Church in France. But those quarrels never led to a break with Rome, for in doctrine Louis XIV was strictly orthodox. And after 1680 he became increasingly concerned about the fate of his own soul. When his queen, Maria Theresa, died in 1683, he gave up all mistresses except the pious Madame de Maintenon, whom he secretly married. The king's growing piety naturally expressed itself politically. The wars of religion were over, but in the late seventeenth century religion and affairs of state remained tightly intertwined.

Louis XIV enthusiastically persecuted the Jansenists, an austere group of Catholic "puritans" who emphasized the teachings of St. Augustine on original sin, human depravity, and the need for divine grace. Louis, whose confessors were Jesuits, thought the Jansenists impertinent in their disapproval of his numerous mistresses, and subversive as well, for the pope had condemned them. In 1710–12 Louis razed their principal monastic center to the ground.

But it was the Huguenots, one of the most loyal and industrious groups in France, who felt the full force of Louis XIV's religious enthusiasm. Two religions under one prince was indeed, by seventeenth-century standards, an anomaly. And the French clergy had long insisted that the continued existence of Protestantism in France was an insult to the king's dignity and authority. After 1679 Louis apparently embraced the idea of atoning for his own numerous sins of the

flesh—and his negotiations with the Ottoman Turks, enemies of Catholic Habsburg
Austria—by crushing heresy in France.

He began by gradually tightening his
interpretation of the Edict of Nantes, by
which Henry IV had granted toleration to
the Huguenots and ended France's religious civil wars in 1598. He forced Protestants to convert, destroyed their chapels,
and quartered royal troops on their families. In 1685 he took the final step. At the
urging of his Jesuit advisers, he announced that since all heretics had recon-
verted to Catholicism, the Edict of Nantes
no longer served any purpose and was
therefore revoked. The state closed all remaining Protestant churches and schools,
and the Church baptized all Protestant
children as Catholics. Louis enforced the
revocation with imprisonment, torture,
and condemnation to the galleys. Many
Huguenots continued to practice their
faith in secret. Perhaps 200,000, more than
a fifth of the Protestant population of
France, fled to England, the Dutch Netherlands, Brandenburg, and the New World.
Their industry and skill contributed mightily to the rapid economic growth of their
new homes.

The revocation of the Edict of Nantes
was an act of religious intolerance that
rivaled the Spanish expulsion of the Moriscos in 1609–14, the Habsburg ravaging
of Bohemia after the battle of the White
Mountain in 1620, or the systematic im-
poverishment and degradation of the
Catholics of Ireland by English conquerors
from Elizabeth I to Cromwell and his successors. But in those cases, unlike that of
France, ethnic hatred had compounded
religious savagery. The revocation of the
Edict of Nantes was unique in the seventeenth century—a major act of barbarism
that was *purely* religious in intention. It
was the last such act in western Europe
until Germany's attempt to exterminate
the European Jews between 1941 and
1944.

Literature and Fashion: The Primacy of France

To dramatize his conception of kingship,
Louis chose as his emblem the sun god,
Apollo. The symbol of the sun, on whose
rays all earthly life depends, became the
theme of the architecture and sculpture
of the new palace at Versailles. The "Sun
King" patronized and presided over an
"Augustan Age" of French culture. As befitted such a patron, the prevailing taste
was classical. It emphasized form, order,
balance, and proportion—the presumed
ideals of reasonable individuals throughout history.

In 1636, Pierre Corneille (1606–84),
the father of French classical tragedy,
wrote *Le Cid,* the first of a series of powerful dramas that glorified willpower and
the quest for perfection. Corneille was still
active when Louis began his personal rule,
but the dramatist's brilliant younger contemporary, Jean Racine (1639–99), soon
eclipsed him. Racine wrote more realistically than Corneille about human beings
in the grip of violent and sometimes
coarse passions. He brought French tragedy to its highest perfection between 1667
and 1677. Then he underwent a religious
conversion that caused him to renounce
drama as immoral.

Some of the admirers of the tragedies
of Corneille and Racine had little respect
for the comic playwright Molière (1622–
73), but his biting satirical drama became
a model for future dramatists. From 1659
to his death he was the idol of aristocratic
audiences at Versailles. All three playwrights concentrated on portraying types,
not individuals—the hero, the man of
honor violently in love, the miser, the hyp-
ocrite—embodiments of human passions
and foibles that belonged to all times and
places. Partly as a result, French classical
drama of the age of Louis XIV was easily
exportable. French literary standards
influenced cultivated Europeans everywhere, although French literary creativity
flagged in the later years of Louis XIV's
reign, as religious persecution, political
censorship, and economic exhaustion intensified.

In the other arts, and in social conven-
tions, France likewise swayed the rest of
Europe, although Louis XIV's growing
religious intolerance and military aggressiveness prompted resistance to French
culture, especially in Protestant republics

Engraving of a performance of Molière's last play, *Le Malade imaginaire* (1673). Molière died on stage on the fourth night of the performance.

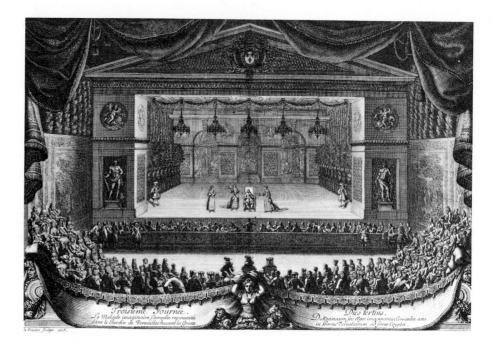

such as the Dutch United Provinces, where middle-class art and manners flourished. French fashions in dress nevertheless spread across Spain, Italy, and much of Germany. The heavy French Baroque style, exemplified by Louis's palace at Versailles, broke the supremacy in architecture that Italy had enjoyed since the Renaissance. French became the language of diplomacy and polite conversation, and the court of the "Sun King" set the tone for countless smaller courts throughout Catholic Europe. As Florence had been the center of the Italian Renaissance, and Spain of the Counter-Reformation, so France in the late seventeenth century was the center of European politics, diplomacy, and culture.

France's Bid for the Domination of Europe

Richelieu and Mazarin had begun the process of creating a large, dependable standing army to replace the disorderly semi-mercenary, semi-feudal military system of the preceding century. Louis and his formidable ministers of war, Le Tellier and Louvois, completed the task. The ministers subordinated the aristocratic officer

corps and the provincial private armies to royal authority, developed an efficient supply system, standardized the organization of infantry and artillery, and followed the example of Gustavus Adolphus by having the troops wear uniforms. The Seigneur de Vauban, the father of modern military engineering, invented the first effective bayonet and perfected the science of building—and smashing—fortifications in the age of gunpowder. Above all, Le Tellier and Louvois provided Louis with numbers. By the 1660s he possessed by far the largest and best-equipped army in Europe: 100,000 men in peace and up to 400,000 in war, numbers not seen in the West since the fall of Rome.

This unprecedented power inevitably brought the temptation to use it. War aroused the enthusiasm of the nobility and kept it occupied in ways that did not threaten the state. War exercised and justified the enormous and costly standing army. Above all, successful war enhanced the glory of the monarch, a glory that was Louis XIV's constant concern. Perhaps war would make him the arbiter not only of France but of Europe as well.

Louis XIV's first two wars (1667–68, 1672–79) were relatively limited in aim.

The decline of Spain and the collapse of the Holy Roman Empire left a power vacuum on France's eastern borders; Louis therefore sought to annex the Spanish Netherlands (later Belgium), Franche-Comté, and parts of western Germany and to reduce the Dutch to vassalage. In each of the two wars, alliances that at different times included the United Provinces, Sweden, and the Habsburg monarchy checked him after initial French victories. The Dutch held off his first onslaught in 1672 by opening their dikes and flooding the countryside. England simultaneously attacked the Dutch by sea but withdrew from the war in 1674. By 1678 Louis had gained only Franche-Comté and a few border fortresses in Flanders.

Thereafter, Louis briefly chose legal chicanery over musketry. He established French courts called Chambers of Reunion to "reunite" to France all lands on France's borders that had in the past been dependencies of French territories. That gave him control of the independent Protestant republic of Strasbourg in 1681, much to the indignation of the inhabitants and of Protestants throughout Europe. The revocation of the Edict of Nantes in 1685 provided further evidence of his arrogance.

In 1686 the Habsburg emperor, along with Spain, Sweden, and several German states, formed the defensive League of Augsburg. Habsburg victories in Hungary over the Turks, who were allied with Louis, shifted the balance in the West against Bourbon France. Louis replied with the most senseless atrocity since the Thirty Years' War—his armies systematically devastated the Palatinate, a rich region of western Germany, in 1688 simply to cow his enemies. That act instead helped weld them together. And French distraction in Germany allowed William of Orange, ruler of the Dutch Netherlands and Louis XIV's most implacable enemy, to claim the English throne in 1688–89. England and the Dutch, the two greatest economic and sea powers of the age, then joined the League of Augsburg and closed the circle around over-mighty France.

The participants' worldwide interests made this war the first *world* war, waged in India, the Caribbean, and North Amer-

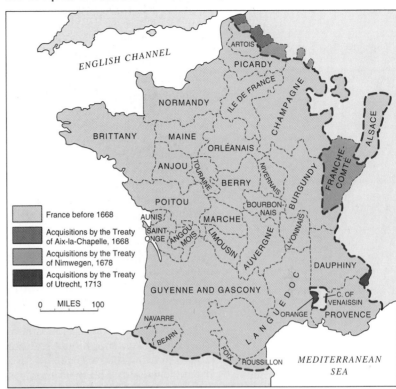

The Conquest of Louis XIV   1661–1715

- France before 1668
- Acquisitions by the Treaty of Aix-la-Chapelle, 1668
- Acquisitions by the Treaty of Nimwegen, 1678
- Acquisitions by the Treaty of Utrecht, 1713

0   MILES   100

ica as well as in Europe. After ten years of fighting, France agreed to the Peace of Ryswick in 1697. Louis retained the gains made before 1678 but had to renounce nearly all conquests after that date except Strasbourg. England emerged from the war stronger than it had been in 1689, and France weaker.

The War of the Spanish Succession, 1701–14

The Peace of Ryswick lasted only four years. Louis had made peace in the hope of gaining a greater prize than any for which he had yet contended—the Spanish Empire. Charles II of Spain, bizarre end-product of generations of syphilitic degeneration and Habsburg inbreeding, and last of the Spanish Habsburg line that had ruled since 1516, was losing a 30-year struggle against numerous diseases. By 1697 he was close to death and had no direct heir. That raised an issue of vital

Officer and musketeer of the French Guard (late seventeenth century).

importance to all Europe: would the Spanish Empire fall to Emperor Leopold I of the Austrian Habsburg line, would it pass to the French Bourbon dynasty (for Louis XIV was both the son and the widower of Spanish Habsburg princesses), or would it be dismembered by its rivals?

England and the Dutch had obvious economic and strategic interests in preventing France from grasping Spain's colonial trade or the Spanish Netherlands. Louis seemed willing to compromise and twice concluded secret treaties that partitioned the Spanish dominions with the English and Dutch. But when news of the second treaty reached Madrid, the dying Charles II refused to see parts of his Catholic empire pass to Protestant powers. Instead, he made a will that left all his dominions to a grandson of Louis XIV. After the death of Charles II in 1699, Spain proclaimed that grandson King Philip V of Spain.

Louis XIV tore up the secret partition treaties, recognized the will of Charles II, and sent French troops to claim the Spanish Netherlands. In 1701 William of Orange formed yet another coalition against France. England, Holland, and Emperor Leopold I of Austria bound themselves to fight until they had ended the threat of Bourbon control of Spain and of the Spanish colonies. Louis had made his last and most far-reaching bid for the domination of Europe. But this time his enemies were as unyielding and powerful as he was.

Warfare had by now become thoroughly professional. In the long wars since 1618, innovators such as Gustavus Adolphus, Maurice of Orange, Le Tellier, and Louvois had replaced noble amateurs and independent military contractors with professional officers corps that bore the "king's commission." Ragged bands of freebooters yielded to disciplined ranks rigidly drilled in the new fire tactics. The combination of musket and bayonet united fire and shock in one weapon and drove out the clumsy combinations of pikemen and musketeers that had ruled the battlefield since the Spanish victory at Pavia in 1525. Commanders learned to coordinate infantry, the new mobile artillery, and cavalry. Sieges, thanks to Vauban, became scientific exercises.

In the new world war of 1701–14, the French soon found themselves outdone. Two commanders of genius led the Allied armies—England's John Churchill, first Duke of Marlborough, and the great Habsburg general and scourge of the Turks, Prince Eugene of Savoy. Marlborough's diplomacy held the ramshackle coalition together. His generalship smashed the great armies of Louis XIV in four battles of unprecedented slaughter that cost France up to 80,000 casualties—Blenheim (1704), Ramillies (1706), Oudenarde (1708), and Malplaquet (1709). England trounced the French at sea and seized Gibraltar, from which it thereafter dominated the western Mediterranean. An allied army even invaded Spain and several times took Madrid.

Louis XIV, with France exhausted militarily and in the grip of famine, sued for peace in 1709–10 on almost any terms. The Allies thereupon demanded that he send French troops to help expel his own grandson from Madrid. That was too great a humiliation. Louis XIV refused, and appealed with success to his subjects. Famine and economic crisis filled the French armies with new recruits, who preferred the risks of the battlefield to the certainty of starvation. An anti-foreign reaction in Spain helped drive the English and Austrian invaders out. In 1710 the English war party, the Whigs, gave way to the Tories, and a war-weary England recalled Marlborough. In 1712 the French severed Prince Eugene of Savoy's communications and forced him to retreat. It was the Allies' turn to seek peace.

The Peace of Utrecht, 1713–14

In theory, the Peace of Utrecht of 1713 and other treaties of 1714 that ended the war of the Spanish Succession gave France the prize that Louis had sought since 1701. Louis's grandson remained on the throne of Spain—but only on condition that no subsequent Bourbon should unite the crowns of Spain and France. And Louis gave up all conquests east of the Rhine and his bid for the Spanish Netherlands and Spain's colonial trade. France survived as the greatest single power. But the war had drained it of money and blood, and had made Louis XIV's government bankrupt and hated. When the great king died at last in 1715, France's common people reputedly "openly returned thanks to God."

England was the chief victor. It emerged from the war with the dominance of the seas that it held until the twentieth century. From France it took Newfoundland, Acadia (modern New Brunswick and Nova Scotia), and the Hudson's Bay Territory. It kept Gibraltar and Minorca, seized from Spain, and received the *Asiento*—the profitable privilege of supplying African slaves to the Spanish colonies.

The Austrian Habsburgs gained the Spanish Netherlands (which now became the Austrian Netherlands) and replaced Spain as the dominant power in Italy through the acquisition of Milan, Naples, and Sicily. Two new smaller powers, Brandenburg-Prussia and the Duchy of Savoy, increased their territories and prestige; they had chosen the winning side. The Dutch achieved their minimum war aim—they kept the Scheldt River closed, thus blocking the trade of Antwerp, the chief port of the Austrian Netherlands. But the long strain of fighting France for almost half a century had demoralized them. They could no longer compete at sea with England and soon slipped from the ranks of the great powers.

The Peace of Utrecht ended the first bid for European hegemony since the days of Philip II of Spain. Louis XIV's attempt to gain for France the domination of western Europe and the wider world had summoned up, through the workings of the balance of power, the coalition that had checked France. War had prevented the universal domination of one power. The European state system had survived a challenge to its very existence.

ENGLAND: THE EMERGENCE OF PARLIAMENTARY MONARCHY

While Louis XIV consolidated absolute monarchy in France, the English created a constitutional monarchy controlled by Parliament. The restoration of king, Parliament, and Anglican Church in 1660 had established a balance between Crown and Parliament. But that balance had remained unstable. Who was to exercise sovereignty—the king, or the gentry and merchants of Parliament? What would the religious settlement be, and who would make it? Who would control foreign policy? These questions had dominated the preceding forty years of turmoil and civil war. They still awaited answers.

Charles II and the "Cavalier Parliament"

Charles II (r. 1660–85), unlike his too stubborn father, was witty, attractive, worldly, a king of hearty sexual appetites and shrewd political sense. He had lived long in exile in France and took his cousin Louis XIV as his model. Charles was resolved not to risk exile or execution in the manner of his father. He instead hoped to restore England to Catholicism and to establish a French-style absolute monarchy through stealth, manipulation, and compromise. That ambition Charles II pursued through 25 years of court intrigue, party politics, and secret diplomacy that kept both Parliament and ministers guessing about his intentions.

The "Cavalier Parliament" of 1661–79 held a commanding position at the beginning of the reign. It was the preserve of the gentry, and of the aristocracy, now partly restored to its ancient influence in both local and national government. Both groups were for the moment strongly royalist and determined to stamp out all remaining political and religious radicalism. But they also had no intention of allowing the Crown to be financially independent of Parliament.

In place of the old idea that "the king should live of his own," Parliament now granted Charles a regular income from customs and excise duties. But it was not enough to meet even the ordinary expenses of government, let alone the expenses of Charles's wild doings at court or of his numerous mistresses and illegitimate children. And foreign war was unthinkable unless Parliament voted money. Charles therefore allowed Parliament, under the leadership of his father's adviser, Edward Hyde, Earl of Clarendon, to have its way for a time.

The House of Commons, on the Great Seal of England (1651).

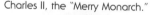

Charles II, the "Merry Monarch."

Parliament thus dictated the religious settlement. The Cavalier Parliament was as strongly pro-Anglican as it was pro-royalist. Between 1661 and 1665 it passed statutes known inaccurately as the "Clarendon Code"—Clarendon himself favored toleration—that excluded from local government Puritans who "dissented" from the established Church and purged Puritan ministers from the Anglican clergy. Later legislation barred dissenters from Parliament, from service in the army or navy, and from the universities at Oxford or Cambridge.

Puritanism and social radicalism appeared to be intertwined. The Cavalier Parliament was therefore determined to stamp out the first and discourage the second. But while the Clarendon Code lowered the social status of dissenters and narrowed their opportunities, it did not greatly decrease their number. Presbyterians, Congregationalists, Baptists, and Quakers formed persistent religious minorities that bitterly opposed both Anglicanism and Catholicism. Charles himself sought toleration as a first step to restoring Catholicism. In 1672 he issued a "Declaration of Indulgence" that suspended the operation of the Code against both Puritans and Catholics and appeared to assert—in the manner of Charles I—that royal prerogative could thwart acts of Parliament. Parliament forced him to withdraw the Declaration and imposed on him a Test Act that excluded non-Anglicans from civil and military office. To the Anglican gentry of Parliament, Puritans remained radicals and Catholics traitors.

Foreign Policy: The French Alliance

Two natural calamities, a fierce outbreak of bubonic plague that killed 60,000 of the 450,000 inhabitants of London in 1665 and a fire that destroyed much of the city in 1666, contributed to widespread unrest. Public opinion blamed the fire on an imaginary Catholic plot. Uneasiness increased as king and Parliament drifted apart over foreign policy. In 1665 Parliament forced Charles into a war with the Dutch over trade, but denied him the money needed to win. When swift victories did not follow, Parliament unfairly held Clarendon responsible and exiled him.

After Louis XIV began his attack on the Spanish Netherlands in 1667, English opinion began to see the military power of Catholic France as more threatening than the commercial rivalry of the Protestant Dutch. But Charles held to his connection with Louis, and in 1670 Charles allied England with France against the Dutch through the notorious secret Treaty of Dover. In the Treaty, Louis XIV offered money and French troops if Charles were to declare himself a Catholic and reconvert England to Catholicism.

Charles was probably unsure of how far down that road he meant to travel. He did acquire both a pro-French foreign policy and a French mistress who reported secretly to Louis XIV's ambassador. English forces also attacked the Dutch along with the French in 1672. Between 1675 and 1681 Charles concluded with Louis four additional secret agreements in which he undertook to thwart Parliament's anti-French moves in return for more French money. The existence of this close understanding with Louis inevitably leaked out and created fear of French domination and a return to Catholicism. The landed classes represented in Parliament were increasingly suspicious of Charles II and prone to panic.

London's catastrophic great fire of 1666.

Whigs and Tories: The Origins of Modern Party Politics

In 1678 these accumulated fears exploded in the lurid "Popish Plot." A disreputable former Anglican clergyman named Titus Oates concocted a story about a Jesuit plot to kill the king, to place his Catholic brother James, Duke of York, on the throne with French help, and to massacre England's Protestants. Parliament described it as "a damnable and hellish plot, for assassinating and murdering the king and rooting out and destroying the Protestant religion." A new civil war seemed about to break out.

The Earl of Shaftesbury, a great land-owner who had fought for Parliament in the Civil War, rallied a "Country Party" that campaigned fiercely to exclude James from the succession to the throne. In response, an Anglican and royalist "Court Party" assembled, although at first without much enthusiasm, to support Charles II and his brother. The Court Party denigrated the Shaftesbury group as "Whigs," a name hitherto applied to Scottish Presbyterian rebels. The Whigs in turn baptized their antagonists "Tories," a kind of Irish Catholic brigand.

The Whigs controlled the three brief Parliaments that followed the dissolution of the Cavalier Parliament in 1679. Shaftesbury and his associates merrily pressed the execution of some 35 Catholics for alleged complicity in the imaginary Popish Plot. But the Whig leaders overplayed their hand. Opinion swung back toward the king, and it was soon the turn of the Whigs to suffer. By 1681 Shaftesbury had fled abroad, the inventors of the Popish Plot were disgraced or executed, and Charles II was stronger than any monarch since the early days of James I. Until his death in 1685 Charles ruled without Parliament, with his brother James by his side and with the subsidies of Louis XIV filling his coffers.

These difficult years were nevertheless momentous for the West's tradition of political liberty. This struggle between the king and factions of the gentry in Parliament created the ancestors of modern political parties—groups organized for the purpose of electioneering and of controlling government through a representative assembly. Whigs and Tories were in part the descendants of the Parliamentarians and Royalists of the 1640s. But the great crisis of the 1680s produced, instead of civil war, the system of Parliamentary rule that England later passed on to its colonies and indirectly to the West as a whole.

The "Glorious Revolution" of 1688

James, Duke of York, succeeded his brother Charles II in 1685 as James II (r. 1685–88). He was a bigoted convert to Catholicism who lacked Charles's shrewdness and flexibility. Within three years he had infuriated almost every political and religious group of importance in England, and had provoked the revolution that Charles II had succeeded in avoiding.

Early successes made him overconfident. He introduced Catholics into the high command of both army and navy, and camped a standing army a few miles from London. He surrounded himself with Catholic advisers and attacked Anglican control of the universities. He claimed the power to suspend or dispense with acts of Parliament. In a vain attempt to win the support of Puritans as well as Catholics, he issued a Declaration of Indulgence along the lines of his brother's—thus further alienating the Anglican establishment. By revoking borough charters and browbeating sheriffs, he tried to ensure the election of a Parliament favorable to his policies. These measures, along with the example of Louis XIV's revocation of the Edict of Nantes in 1685, terrified England's Protestants.

The event that triggered James II's downfall was a happy one—the unexpected birth in June 1688 of a son to his Catholic queen. Until then, Protestants had consoled themselves with the thought that James II's two elder daughters by another marriage, Mary and Anne, were Protestants, and would succeed James. Now the existence of a Catholic male heir prolonged the Catholic absolutist threat indefinitely into the future. But unlike the events of 1641, the king had no "king's party." He had alienated Anglicans and

James II, who swiftly alienated even traditional supporters of the monarchy (engraved after a painting by Sir Godfrey Kneller, 1688).

dissenters, Tories and Whigs, aristocracy and commoners. The result was a bloodless "revolution," a rapid and fundamental political change that established the limited or parliamentary monarchy that has persisted to the present.

The agent of James II's downfall was William of Orange, *stadholder* and hero of the Dutch Republic, the man who had opened the dikes to halt the French invasion in 1672. In 1677, in pursuit of allies against France, he had married James II's eldest daughter, Mary, and had thus acquired a claim to the English throne. In June 1688 a group of prominent Englishmen, both Whigs and Tories, invited William to cross the English Channel and save the Protestant cause in England. That November William landed a Dutch army on the southern coast and marched slowly toward London. The countryside rose against James II, and William tactfully allowed the friendless king to flee to France. An improvised Parliament declared that James had abdicated the throne by flight and invited William and Mary to become joint sovereigns on condition that they ac-

cept a "Bill of Rights" that severely limited royal power.

This bloodless "Glorious Revolution" established at last the sovereignty of Parliament, which had made a king. William was strong-willed, but his priorities were continental and Dutch—the forging of an ever more powerful coalition against Louis XIV. He therefore grudgingly accepted Parliament's conditions. The "Jacobite" supporters of James II and his son invaded Ireland in 1690 and staged two bloody rebellions in the Scottish Highlands in 1715 and 1745, but all attempts at a second Restoration failed. Parliament had won. England had decisively rejected the French absolutist model of Louis XIV.

The Bill of Rights emphatically barred the king from suspending acts of Parliament or interfering with the courts. It furnished a base for the steady expansion of civil liberties in the generation after 1688. Parliament established religious toleration and freedom from arbitrary arrest. Censorship of the press quietly withered. The king had to summon Parliament annually, for he could neither pay nor control his

The speaker of the House of Lords offers William and Mary the English crown (from a contemporary engraving).

armed forces without parliamentary consent. Regular meetings of Parliament in turn strengthened the political parties and made the king dependent on their support. The monarch vetoed a parliamentary bill for the last time in 1707.

Hobbes Answered: John Locke and the Theory of Limited Government

The English Civil War and Glorious Revolution followed the Dutch revolt against Spain as the second of the Western revolutions that ended absolute monarchy and ultimately led to democratic representative government. Tradition demanded that English leaders in 1641–49 and 1688–89 deny that their acts were revolutionary. Parliament chopped off the head of one king and replaced another in the name of the *traditional* "liberties of England." But that half-fiction was unsatisfactory.

John Locke (1632–1704), a friend of the Earl of Shaftesbury who had founded the Whig party, provided a theoretical foundation for what Parliament had done and for the subsequent evolution of representative government. Locke probably wrote most of his *Of Civil Government: Two Treatises* while in political exile in Holland in 1683–89, but it emerged from the presses in 1690 as a belated rationale for the acts of Parliament during the Glorious Revolution. In it he at last answered Thomas Hobbes's justification of absolute sovereignty with a convincing theory of limited government.

Locke attacked the divine-right theory of monarchy and challenged Hobbes's claim that the only alternative to anarchy was absolute authority. Locke's first principle was that all individuals possess a natural right to "life, liberty, and property." That notion was revolutionary in an age of entrenched privilege. It remains revolutionary in our own, in which dictatorships or narrow oligarchies rule much of humanity. Locke derived the rest of his system from this premise of "natural rights," and from a more optimistic view of human nature than that of Hobbes. Like Hobbes and many predecessors and contemporaries, Locke argued that government was a contract in which humanity exchanged the anarchy of the "state of nature" for the security that government provided. But Locke's insistence that human rights were "natural" and prior to all government allowed him—unlike Hobbes—to limit the authority of government. The source of sovereignty, thanks to the natural rights of the governed, was the governed themselves: "The people alone can appoint the form of the commonwealth." It therefore followed, for Locke, that a government that acted without the consent of the governed dissolved the contract and gave the subjects a right to resistance or to revolution.

Locke also provided a principle for organizing government. Fearing concentration of power, he proposed a strict separation of powers that would allow the elected representatives of the people to check a tyrannical executive. Above all, he relentlessly emphasized property as the foundation of all freedom and the purpose of government itself: "The great and chief end. . . . of men's uniting into commonwealths and putting themselves under

John Locke (1632–1704), champion of "natural rights" and government by consent.

Locke on Government by Consent   1690

Compare with "Bishop Bossuet on Absolutism," page XXX.

Men being, as has been said, by nature all free, equal, and independent, no one can be put out of this estate and subjected to the political power of another without his own consent, which is done by agreeing with other men, to join and unite into a community for their comfortable, safe, and peaceful living, one amongst another, in a secure enjoyment of their properties, and a greater security against any that are not of it. . . . When any number of men have so consented to make one community or government, they are thereby presently incorporated, and make one body politic, wherein the majority have the right to act and conclude the rest. . . . Absolute, arbitrary power, or governing without settled standing laws, can neither of them consist with the ends of society and government, which men would not quit the freedom of the state of Nature for, and tie themselves up under, were it not to preserve their lives, liberties, and fortunes, and by stated rules of right and property to secure their peace and quiet.

From John Locke, Of Civil Government: Two Treatises *(New York: Everyman's Library, 1924), pp. 164–65, 186.*

government is the preservation of their property." Some twentieth-century commentators have denigrated what they describe as Locke's doctrine of "possessive individualism," his equation of property and liberty—but have failed to offer examples of societies that enjoy liberty without property.

In the eighteenth century, Locke's ideas were a powerful rationale for a society based on wealth rather than on inherited privilege and for a new kind of government, limited in its powers. Inalienable natural rights, government by consent, the right of revolution, and the sanctity of property seemed increasingly "self-evident" to Englishmen after 1688, and ultimately to the American colonists in 1776.

The Emergence of the Cabinet System

At the level of practice rather than theory, factional struggles in Parliament replaced struggles between king and Parliament after 1688. The Glorious Revolution made gentry and merchants the real masters of both central and local government in England. Generally speaking, aristocratic landowners, bankers, merchants, and most dissenters were Whigs, while the smaller gentry, the Anglican parish clergy, and some great lords were Tories. But parties were still loosely organized, and small cliques often held the balance of power.

Given the fluidity of parliamentary alignments and the monarchy's residual powers, it took more than a century for a smoothly operating system of constitutional government to emerge through the slow accretion of precedent. The ultimate answer was the "cabinet system."

Under Charles II, a "cabinet council," or inner circle of important ministers had taken shape. Gradually the members of this "cabinet" discovered that settling major issues among themselves and then presenting a united front to the king was the most efficient way to conduct business. A leader—the "prime minister"—inevitably emerged within the cabinet.

During the reigns of William and Mary (1689–1702) and of Mary's sister, Queen

Anne (1702–14), monarchs still considered their ministers responsible to the crown rather than to Parliament. But to gain Parliament's support in war or peace both William and Anne found it advisable to choose their ministers from the majority party in Parliament. By Queen Anne's death in 1714, real power in England was slowly falling into the hands of a cabinet of ministers who controlled a parliamentary majority, often by bribery, and who felt themselves ultimately responsible to the political interests of the landed and moneyed classes represented in Parliament. By almost imperceptible stages, the world's first—and most influential—representative parliamentary government was evolving.

The Religious Settlement

The Glorious Revolution also produced an unprecedented measure of religious toleration. The fanaticism unleashed in the Civil War had given religious intolerance a bad name, and both Anglicans and Puritans were now more afraid of Catholic France than of one another. In addition, King William, thanks to the Dutch Republic's unique tradition of toleration, insisted on a religious truce. The result was the "Toleration Act" of 1689, which allowed dissenters to worship as they pleased and to educate their clergy and laity in schools of their own. Most of the existing anti-Catholic statutes, along with the acts excluding dissenters from civil and military offices remained in effect, but after 1689 their enforcement lacked vigor.

The Act of Settlement of 1701 provided that the sovereign should always be an Anglican Protestant. That finally quieted fear that a Catholic might succeed to the throne. The act also settled the succession, in case James II's two daughters should die without children, on the descendants of the daughter of James I who had married the ill-fated Frederick V of the Palatinate before the Thirty Years' War. That provision brought the Elector of Hanover to the throne in 1714, when Queen Anne died without direct heirs and ended the Stuart dynasty.

Medal of Queen Anne (1702–14).

Ireland and Scotland: Coercion and Union

Civil War and Glorious Revolution also indirectly furthered the unification of the British Isles. England, Ireland, and Scotland had all had the same king from the time of James I's succession in 1603, but union went no further than the common crown. The two smaller kingdoms, especially Ireland, suffered greatly during the seventeenth century from involvement in England's religious and political struggles.

The native Irish were Catholic; Protestant England therefore despised them and feared them as potential allies of Catholic Spain and France. To cope with that strategic threat, James I had settled Protestant colonists in the northeastern province of Ulster. But the Ulster Protestants were Presbyterians and soon became anti-Stuart, while the Catholic Irish were generally loyal to the Stuart dynasty. In 1641 the Catholics revolted. Cromwell crushed them with fire and terror in 1649, and massacred the Catholic garrisons at Drogheda and Wexford ("... being in the heat of action, I forbade them to spare any that were in arms in the town."). In 1690, James II landed in Ireland with French troops and Catholic support, but William of Orange routed him at the Battle of the Boyne. The much-celebrated anniversary of that Protestant victory remains to the present day an occasion for religious bloodshed in Ulster. After the Boyne, English and Irish Protestant landlords systematically persecuted the Catholic Irish and their religion, while reserving both economic and political power for themselves.

The Scots, who had given England a king in 1603, had somewhat better fortune. Scotland had only a sixth of England's population, but its Protestantism, its long tradition of parliamentarism, its military power, and its poverty—which made it unrewarding as prey—enabled it to make a satisfactory bargain. Scottish resistance to the imposition of Anglicanism had triggered the crisis that ultimately led to Civil War in 1642. Nevertheless, much of Scotland, especially the Highlands inhabited by the turbulent and ruthless Catholic clansmen, remained strongly attached to the native Stuart dynasty. From 1650 to 1745, the clans provided a base for risings in support of the Stuarts. The Scots parliament accepted the Revolution of 1688 but refused the Act of Settlement of 1701. It threatened to choose a king of its own— possibly the exiled pretender James II— if James II's last daughter, Anne, died without producing an heir.

That threat frightened England into serious negotiation. In 1707 the Whig government and the Scots agreed to an Act of Union that eliminated the risk that Scotland might choose a separate monarch and created the kingdom of "Great Britain." Scotland retained its own laws and its Presbyterian state religion but surrendered its separate parliament in return for representation in London and full participation in the dynamic English economy. The loss of political independence and the coming of a money economy even to the wild Highlands caused disgruntlement, especially among the clans. But the Act of Union was successful, unlike England's difficult relationships with Ireland or with the colonies in America. Scottish merchants and administrators helped build the British empire. Scottish philosophers, economists, and historians contributed mightily to the widening of human knowledge in the eighteenth century known as the Enlightenment (see pp. 543–48).

The Growth of British Power

A final consequence of the Glorious Revolution, after parliamentary government, religious toleration, and the settlement with Scotland, was to unite crown and Parliament on foreign policy and to turn the energies of the next generations from domestic conflict to foreign war. Given England's fear of Catholicism, William of Orange had no difficulty bringing his new kingdom into the Grand Alliance against Louis XIV, who had given refuge to James II. Parliamentary monarchy soon demonstrated that it was more deadly to its enemies than Stuart absolutism. The government of William and his successors was able to raise money, the sinew of war, in ways that only the Dutch could match.

Anti-Catholic woodcuts showing the "prodigious cruelties" of religious warfare in Ireland (1689).

In 1694 William's Whig ministers created a Bank of England to mobilize England's growing commercial and financial power against France. Within a few days of its founding, the Bank had raised over a million pounds of investors' money, and it promptly lent the money to the government at 8 percent interest. The resulting permanent national debt was a revolutionary instrument. It financed the defeat of Louis XIV and provided the foundation for the subsequent commercial and maritime supremacy of Britain. Throughout the next century British wealth, transmuted into ships of the line, gave the island kingdom a striking power out of all proportion to its size and population. The Peace of Utrecht of 1713 gave British sea power a position without serious rivals. Britain's victory heralded the elimination of France as a colonial competitor and Britain's domination of the world outside Europe.

CENTRAL AND EASTERN EUROPE, 1648–1721

An imaginary line running north from the Adriatic Sea to the Elbe River that flows into the North Sea divided the economy

The Economic and Social Division of Europe

of early modern Europe into two sharply defined halves. West of that line, the towns and their trade were increasingly dominant. The majority of the population still lived on the land, but most peasants were free workers and many of them small landowners. Most serfs had become agricultural wage laborers in and after the crisis of the Black Death. Most nobles had become landlords who hired labor for wages, or simply lived on rents from tenants. Though still a minority, the urban middle classes were growing in influence.

East of the line, in Hungary, Bohemia, Poland, Prussia, and Russia, lay a land of lord and peasant. Towns were small, poor, and weak. Noble estates were larger and the landed nobility far more powerful politically than in western Europe. And in the sixteenth and seventeenth centuries, noble power was still growing. Grain prices rose with the price revolution of the sixteenth century, and the growth of the trading networks centered on Antwerp and Amsterdam offered export markets. That situation provided an economic rationale for the imposition of a "second serfdom" in eastern Europe. The nobles sought to lower labor costs by binding their peasants to the land and imposing on them two to five days a week of compulsory labor. The profits they earned on exports in turn further increased the nobles' power. And in politics, the states of eastern Europe encouraged and promoted noble domination. Either the state *was* the nobility, as in Hungary or Poland, or it made a tacit bargain that delivered the peasants to the nobility in return for noble service to the state, as in Brandenburg-Prussia and Russia.

As in western Europe, states were machines for power. They had to be, for the flat plains of central and eastern Europe offered no "natural frontiers" to check the invader. A state could remain a state only if it had an army. But the gunpowder revolution of the fifteenth century had so raised the costs of armies that only strongly centralized states with relentless tax systems could afford them. Few such states existed in central and eastern Europe in the seventeenth century. Most eastern rulers faced the same obstacles to centralized government that western rulers had faced two centuries or more before—a powerful landed nobility, a church that owned large portions of the land, a middle class too small to bear the weight of heavy taxation, desperately poor agriculture, limited commerce, infant industries, and a peasantry tied to the land and thus incapable of meeting the need of new industries for labor.

The Holy Roman Empire

The one large political organization that bridged eastern and western Europe was the Holy Roman Empire. But the Thirty Years' War had left it a political fiction. A Habsburg remained emperor and a Diet or deliberative assembly met "perpetually" at Regensburg after 1663. But the Empire had no common army, administration, taxes, laws, calendar, or tariffs. It included perhaps 1,800 political units and petty rulers, including free cities, free imperial knights, Church principalities, and the kingdom of Bohemia. The Peace of Westphalia had recognized the full sovereignty of the 300 or so larger units within the Empire and had accorded France and Sweden the right to take part in the Diet's deliberations. This Empire, as Voltaire (see p. 545) remarked in the mid-eighteenth century, was "neither Holy, nor Roman, nor an Empire."

The ruling families of a few large states—Bavaria, Saxony, Hanover, Brandenburg, and Austria—sought to expand their territories and prestige by war or marriage. Augustus the Strong of Saxony, in addition to fathering, according to legend, more than 300 children, secured election in 1696 as king of Poland. In 1701 the Elector of Brandenberg obtained the emperor's consent to style himself "king in Prussia." And in 1714 the Elector of Hanover became king of Britain. But only two great powers emerged from the wreck of the Holy Roman Empire—Austria and Brandenburg-Prussia.

The Habsburgs: Europe and Austria Defended

The attempt of Emperor Ferdinand II (r. 1619–37) to revive and strengthen the

Empire under Habsburg control collapsed in the Thirty Years' War. The Habsburgs of Vienna thereafter turned to a policy that Ferdinand had also fostered. They sought to consolidate and expand their hereditary lands in Austria and the Danube Valley into a centralized monarchy that could hold its own against the states of western Europe. The chief architect of that policy was Emperor Leopold I (r. 1658–1705), with the help and occasional prodding of capable civil servants and a remarkable general, Prince Eugene of Savoy.

Achieving the Habsburg objective required the reduction of Austria, Bohemia, and Hungary to obedience. In the Duchy of Austria and neighboring Tyrol, Leopold's lawyers established his ascendancy over the nobility. Bohemia was even less of an impediment. The Emperor Ferdinand II had smashed its native Czech nobility after the Battle of the White Mountain in 1620, and in 1627 had made the previously elective crown of Bohemia a hereditary possession of the Habsburg family. Hungary, on the fiercely contested border between the West and Islam, was different. Although the Habsburgs had usually been the elected monarchs there since early in the sixteenth century, the Ottoman Turks directly or indirectly ruled almost two-thirds of the kingdom. The Hungarian Protestants were numerous and inclined to fear the Turks less than they feared the Catholic Habsburgs.

But the Ottoman Empire was no longer the power that had taken Constantinople in 1453, smashed the Hungarians at Mohács in 1526, and sought Mediterranean mastery at Lepanto in 1571. The Ottomans failed to keep pace with the West in technology, above all in the technology of war. Their metal-working, their cannon and handguns, remained those of the sixteenth century. Ottoman logistics and tactics likewise failed to match the growing professionalization that overtook war in the West during and after the Thirty Years' War. But Ottoman troops nevertheless remained fearsome in the attack and tenacious in defense. And after 1656, the Ottoman central government briefly revived under a vigorous line of grand viziers (first ministers to the Sultan), the

The crown of the Holy Roman Empire of the German Nation, used from 961 to 1792.

Prince Eugene of Savoy, who ended the Ottoman Turk threat to central Europe.

Köprülü family. In the 1660s the Ottomans began a new thrust up the Danube Valley against their Habsburg antagonists.

But Austria prevailed in the end. From July to September 1683 a Turkish army of more than 100,000 besieged Vienna after laying waste to everything in its path. Volunteers rushed to Austria's aid from all across the Continent. The greatest pope of the century, Innocent XI, proclaimed Europe's last crusade against Islam. A coalition army under the leadership of King John Sobieski of Poland descended from the heights outside Vienna upon the Turks and routed them. For the next sixteen years, Austria and its allies fought their way laboriously back down the Danube Valley. In 1697, Prince Eugene of Savoy at last broke the Turkish army at the battle of Zenta, near the present Serbian-Hungarian border. Turkey ceased to be a threat, and soon became a victim.

The resulting Peace of Carlowitz in 1699 gave the Habsburgs all of Hungary. The Emperor crushed the Hungarian Protestants and executed many of them for treason. The Hungarian nobility retained its serfs and privileges in return for recognizing the ultimate sovereignty of Vienna. But the Habsburgs imprudently left local administration to the nobility and failed to create a uniform, centralized system of administration for all their possessions. Eugene's victories nevertheless established a strong state in the Danube Valley where none had existed before. The Treaties of Ryswick in 1697 and Carlowitz in 1699 thus marked the emergence of the two new great powers that had risen to check the overbearing ambition of Louis XIV—Britain and Austria. And two further contenders for great power status had also begun their ascent—Brandenburg-Prussia and Russia.

The Curious Rise of Brandenburg-Prussia, 1614–1701

Prussia, the power that emerged from the obscure Electorate of Brandenburg, was the most improbable of all seventeenth- and eighteenth-century claimants to great-power status. The Habsburgs

and even the primitive Grand Duchy of Muscovy had extensive territories. The Hohenzollern dynasty that created Prussia had been mere margraves—counts of a "mark," or frontier province—in Brandenburg since 1417. The one distinction of the small, sandy, barren principality around Berlin was that after about 1230 it was one of the seven "electorates" of the Holy Roman Empire, states whose rulers—at least in theory—voted to elect the emperor.

In the early seventeenth century, by the accidents of dynastic inheritance, the Hohenzollern family acquired two further territories of importance—the Duchy of Cleves and some neighboring lands on the Rhine in 1614, and the Duchy of Prussia on the Baltic coast to the northeast in 1618. The total population of all Hohenzollern possessions was perhaps 1.5 million. The provinces lacked defensible boundaries, standing military forces, and a central administration other than the household of the Elector. Each of the provincial estates jealously guarded its inherited privileges. Nothing suggested that these territories had the makings of a powerful state, especially after the Thirty Years' War had devastated Brandenburg. Berlin had lost more than half its population, and the Hohenzollern dominions as a whole had probably lost almost one-third of their people, a loss that took forty years to make up.

One man changed this situation. Frederick William of Hohenzollern, the Great Elector (r. 1640–88), was the first of the line of remarkable rulers that made Prussia. Born in 1620, he succeeded to power in 1640 after an education in Holland that had emphasized the latest in statecraft and technology. A devout Calvinist, he had learned toleration from the Dutch. In an age of fanaticism he respected the Lutheranism of his subjects. Above all, he learned from the helplessness of Brandenburg. "A ruler is treated with no consideration if he does not have troops and means of his own," he advised his son in 1667. "It is these, Thank God! which have made me considerable since the time that I began to have them."

Frederick William, the Great Elector, painted by his contemporary, Mathias Czwiczeic.

He inherited in 1640 a poorly equipped and mutinous army of 2,500 men. Before the end of the Thirty Years' War in 1648 his ceaseless efforts had increased it to 8,000 disciplined troops; by his death in 1688 he had a peacetime force of 30,000 that could expand to 40,000 in time of war. In the 48 years of his reign, the Great Elector built upon Brandenburg-Prussia's meager population the strongest military power in Germany, except for Austria.

That achievement rested on administrative centralization and the crushing of the provincial estates that largely controlled taxation. In Brandenburg he struck a bargain with the Estates in 1653 that provided a lump sum with which he raised further troops. The force in turn allowed him to collect taxes without further votes by the Estates, which—like Louis XIV—he never summoned again. In Prussia, far to the east, the townsmen were more stubborn than in Brandenburg, and the hard-bitten nobility, the *Junkers* (from *Jungherr,* "young lord"), proved unruly. The provincial opposition turned to Poland for support, but Frederick eventually crushed its resistance and executed its leaders. After campaigns against both Poland and Sweden, he also secured clear title to Prussia, which he had originally held as a fief from the king of Poland.

Despite some setbacks, Frederick nevertheless set up a tax system under civil servants of his own choosing that extended to all his territories. He deprived the nobility of the power it had exercised through the Estates and pressed it into state service as officers in the new standing army. In return, he confirmed and strengthened Junker control over the serfs. Power, not the betterment of the lowly, was the Great Elector's objective.

But against the background of the Thirty Years' War, the creation of the standing army and the order it brought was nevertheless a contribution to the welfare of the population. Devastation by foreign armies was even worse than Junker oppression. Moreover, Frederick William helped revive and improve agriculture after 1648 and encouraged industry and commerce. He made Brandenburg a haven for religious refugees—Lutherans, Calvinists, and large numbers of Huguenots after Louis XIV revoked the Edict of Nantes in 1685. These immigrants, together with Dutch, Swiss, and other newcomers, brought new skills in agriculture and industry, helped increase the population, and added considerably to the strength of the state. He welcomed even the more radical Protestant sects and the Jews but drew the line at the Jesuits, whom he considered too intolerant.

Frederick William's foreign policy was cautious. He sold his support to a succession of temporary allies in return for subsidies that helped pay for his army, while avoiding heavy fighting. The Swedes came close to Berlin in 1675, but he drove them off at the battle of Fehrbellin, a sign of Brandenburg-Prussia's rise and of Sweden's decline.

The recognition in 1701 of the Great Elector's son as Frederick I, "King in Prussia" (that is, in the province of Prussia, outside the boundary of the Empire), symbolized the appearance of a new power in Europe. In 1720, at the end of the Great Northern War that paralleled in eastern Europe the War of the Spanish Succession, the Hohenzollerns gained Pomerania and the vital port of Stettin from Sweden.

Prussia, as the Hohenzollern lands became known, had in eighty years transformed itself from a chance collection of feeble provinces into a state on the threshold of great power status. The weakness of its neighbors, rivals, or overlords—Sweden, Poland, Russia, and the Empire—gave it the opportunity. But this "Sparta of the North" rose primarily through its own efforts, through its army. All states in the fiercely competitive European system were machines for war, but Prussia devoted to its military relatively more of its population, resources, and energies than any other state. The army was the first institution common to all the Great Elector's lands, and its supporting bureaucracy was the model for Prussia's later organs of civil government. The nobility served the state in the army and bureaucracy and came to identify itself with state and army to an extent without parallel elsewhere.

That army, the army that conquered true great-power status for Prussia in the coming wars of the mid-eighteenth century, *was* the Prussian state.

Russia: Peter the Great's Revolution from Above

To the east of Prussia, Sweden, Poland, and the Ottoman Empire, no great power existed in the seventeenth century. The only contender was Muscovy, a state closer in constitution to the Ottoman Empire than to anything in Europe. As in the Ottoman Empire, India, and China, the Muscovite tsar "owned" his territory and his subjects, who enjoyed no rights against the state. That was no accident. Muscovy acquired its statecraft from Byzantium, and above all from the Mongols, its overlords from around 1240 until 1480 (see pp. 344–45).

The rulers of Muscovy were fully conscious of their uniqueness. They ridiculed the "limited" monarchs to the west as "men under contract" to their subjects and representative assemblies. In a letter addressed to Queen Elizabeth I of England in 1570, Tsar Ivan the Terrible had mocked her as no true sovereign but as one who had "men who rule beside you, and not only men, but trading boors." In Russia, even nobles lacked rights—even property rights—against the state; Ivan broke the hereditary nobility, or *boyars,* by torture, massacre, and wholesale confiscation of land in the 1560s and 1570s. He largely replaced them with a new "service nobility" that owed abject obedience to the autocrat. Scorn and hatred of foreigners characterized Muscovy's external relations. The alternation of despotism and anarchy marked its internal politics.

The unlamented death of Ivan the Terrible in 1584 indeed led to anarchy: a "Time of Troubles" that lasted until the coming in 1613 of the Romanov dynasty, which ruled Russia until 1917. Thereafter, religious strife compounded the weakness of the state. A reforming leader of the Orthodox Church, Patriarch Nikon, provoked a devastating schism in the 1660s by revising ritual and liturgy to bring them closer to the original Greek text of the Bible. That exasperated the traditionalist masses, to whom the Old Slavonic texts were sacrosanct. The Church split into a shallowly based state church and fiercely independent sects of "Old Believers" who braved execution and exile for their faith. As many as 20,000 may have burned themselves to death in the belief that the end of the world was at hand.

Abroad, Russia suffered defeats against Swedes, Poles, and Turks, and remained cut off from the Baltic and the Black Sea. English merchants made contact with Moscow in the 1550s by the icy route around Norway to the bleak port of Archangel on the White Sea. German merchants were also active in the capital. But Russia's chief import, then and later, was the West's technology, especially its military technology. Western culture—the Renaissance and Reformation—reached only as far as Catholic Poland.

In 1689, a new monarch, Peter I (r. 1682–1725), seized power at the age of seventeen in a palace coup. He was nearly seven feet tall, with inexhaustible energy and appetites, and a ferocious will. His insatiable curiosity led him to spend much time with the Dutch and Germans who lived in the "German Quarter" of Moscow. There he probably conceived the ambition of making Russia a great power by rapidly adopting Western technology, civil and military institutions, and customs. The partial realization of that ambition ultimately earned for him the title of Peter the Great.

Peter at first allowed others to rule for him. But in 1695 he ventured a first campaign against the Turkish fortress of Azov, where the Don River enters the Black Sea. The attack failed, but in 1696, with the help of Swiss, Dutch, and Habsburg experts, he built a fleet on the Don River, cut the fortress off from supplies and reinforcements, and stormed it. The lesson Peter I drew was that he needed additional Western experts to create a navy and to modernize his outmoded army.

In 1696–97, thinly disguised as a private citizen, Peter visited Holland, England, Germany, and Austria. There he learned how societies centuries ahead of

1462	1613		1917
Grand Dukes of Moscow and First Tsars of Russia	House of Romanov		

Peter I — 1689 / 1725
Catherine II — 1762 / 1796

Russia built ships, made munitions, and conducted government and diplomacy. He worked in the shipyards, eagerly questioned everyone he met about Western naval and military technology, and drank steadily through the night with his Russian companions. When he returned to Russia, he brought with him more than a thousand Western experts—seamen, gunners, shipwrights, engineers, mathematicians, surgeons.

An outburst of xenophobia at home cut short his European tour. The *strel'tsy,* a barbarous and undisciplined palace guard that he had thwarted in his seizure of power in 1689, remained a threat. In 1696, in league with the "Old Believers" and distrustful of Peter's increasingly obvious intention of introducing Western innovations, the *strel'tsy* marched on the Kremlin. Peter hastened back to Moscow to find that trusted aides had suppressed the revolt. He then made an example of the rebels that long haunted even the memories of his countrymen, accustomed to indiscriminate bloodshed. He executed a thousand *strel'tsy* to the accompaniment of torture on a scale not seen since Ivan the Terrible.

Peter also determined to use his autocratic sovereign power to "westernize" his subjects externally, by force if need be. In 1699–1700 he forbade the traditional long robes and the beards that his subjects wore in the belief that God was bearded and that man was made in his image. The tsar himself took a hand in the shaving of his courtiers. He fought the resulting antiforeign and Orthodox reaction with brutal repression. He also ended the seclusion of women and instituted Western-style social gatherings of both sexes at which polite conversation and ballroom dancing rather than strong drink were the chief entertainments. In his will to transform Russia, he brooked no opposition; when his son and heir Alexis showed himself a slothful dev-

otee of tradition, Peter I had him arrested, tortured, and put to death in 1618.

But Peter I's priorities were above all military. He sought first to imitate Western power, not Western civilization. Beginning in 1699, he set up a new army using German and other foreign experts as officers. An overwhelming defeat by the Swedes at Narva in 1700 only spurred him on; Russia either had to modernize its army or perish. The tsar encouraged the vital iron industry of the Urals, set up cannon foundries, and created schools for gunnery, navigation, engineering, and officer training. By 1709, the year of his great victory over Charles XII of Sweden at Poltava, Russia had a modern army of more than 100,000 troops. By the end of Peter's reign in 1725, that army had swelled to 210,000 regulars and 100,000 auxiliaries that included the dreaded Cossack cavalry. The navy had grown from nothing to 24 ships of the line. Those were powerful forces indeed for a state with a population of only 8 million.

The army, the largest in eastern Europe, had the chance to achieve results, for Russia was at peace only one year in all of Peter's long reign. In the south, Peter failed to hold Azov and had to leave the Turks to his successors. But in the Great Northern War, the tsar seized from Sweden the vital coastline on the Gulf of Finland. That gave him the "window on the sea," the direct contact with western Europe through the ice-free southern Baltic that was his primary geopolitical goal.

Peter's subjects, who bore the weight of his gigantic social engineering project, paid dearly for these military successes. The effect of Peter's sometimes haphazard social and fiscal legislation was to divide a relatively complex society with a variety of subtle status gradations into two great classes—the "service nobility," and the more or less enserfed peasantry. A century after Peter I, a Russian intellectual could

Contemporary cartoon of Peter cutting the beard of a Russian noble. Those who kept their beards had to pay a tax and carry a license (below).

still quip bitterly that Russian society consisted of "slaves of the sovereign [the nobles], and slaves of the landlord [the serfs]; the former are called free only with regard to the latter."

Peter systematized the service nobility system he had inherited. All landowners owed service, and he decreed in 1714 the hated innovation of primogeniture, which forced noble younger sons off the land and into the army or navy. By instituting a fourteen-step "Table of Ranks" in 1722, Peter defined nobility in terms of one criterion alone, service. He made explicit what Louis XIV and the Great Elector could only practice—that service to the state, not birth, determined rank. In Russia, a lieutenant's commission now automatically brought noble status. That provided a career leading to ennoblement for the ambitious sons of commoners and helped divert them into state service and away from commerce and industry.

The peasantry, not the nobility, paid most heavily for Peter's innovations. In return for its service, the nobility gained a freer hand than ever before in dealing with serfs. A new tax census classified as a serf anyone whose position was doubtful. And the state demanded from the peasantry forced labor, military service, and taxes on an unprecedented scale. Supporting the new army required conscription, on the model of Sweden. After 1705 each twenty households had to furnish one recruit every year. The state provided the new military industries with serfs and convicts as labor, while a new head tax ("soul tax") tripled both state income and the tax burden. Forced labor and taxation, by one estimate, extorted from each household the equivalent of 125 to 187 days of labor each year. The ultimate result was depopulation, as peasants died of their privations or fled to the Don Cossacks to the southeast.

After 1709 Peter moved the seat of government from Moscow to a new city built on conquered territory on the Gulf of Finland: St. Petersburg, named for his patron saint. That change was the symbol of his aim to rival the West. The new city faced west, and its nearby naval base, Kronstadt ("royal city" *in German*),

The bronze horseman: Peter the Great decrees the founding of St. Petersburg, Russia's window on the West.

claimed mastery of the Baltic. The methods that created the new capital, and its price, were also characteristic both of Peter's work and of that of later autocrats who sought to imitate him in Russia and in other backward states. St. Petersburg rose in an unhealthy marshland at the mouth of the Neva River and was a deliberate break with the Moscow-centered past. Peter compelled nobles and merchants to settle and build there. Construction proceeded rapidly through annual forced labor drafts of 20,000 peasants, many of whom perished from disease and exposure.

This new capital, founded on the bones of dead peasants, became the center of a new bureaucratic structure that Peter erected haphazardly over the primitive central administration he had inherited. The Western conception of "the state," as distinct from the private staff of the sovereign, now made its entry into Russian history. Peter set up provincial administrations, supervisory boards to coordinate the bureaucracy, and a "senate," or central administrative body to interpret his orders. He also created an organ, the *Preobrazhenskii Prikaz,* to ferret out "political crime," from tax evasion, to criticism of the tsar, to coup attempts. The deliberate vagueness of its charter, its sweeping authority, and its ruthless suppression of individuals for their political opinions rather than for their deeds made it the ancestor of the modern police state.

The new Russian state thus dominated its society in a way unknown even in Brandenburg-Prussia, much less in western Europe. The state mastered the Orthodox Church, already weakened by the great schism. After 1700 Peter neglected to appoint a patriarch and made the Church a mere department of his bureaucracy. The state defined the nobility by its service, and by demanding residence at St. Petersburg reinforced an already existing pattern of absentee landlordism that weakened the grip of the nobility on rural society. The state stunted the towns and ensured that the small and fearful middle classes that eventually emerged would be dependent on state employment and state contracts.

The state then ordered its subjects to develop a consciousness, a public opinion. Peter was the first Russian sovereign to speak of "the common good." He founded Russia's first newspaper. He recognized that rivaling the West ultimately required voluntary collaboration from his subjects and the development of economic and intellectual initiative *from below.* But as his successors discovered, initiative from below was a deadly threat to the autocracy's own power. That tension, the result of grafting Western technology and military institutions onto non-Western social and political structures, was a pattern often seen later. Its consequence was a cycle of repression, "thaw," and further repression that has continued to the present.

But that ultimate consequence of Peter's work was far in the future when he died in 1725. What he left was a Russian great power, a military giant, irrevocably part of the European state system. And his example created a tradition of dynamic autocracy, of brutal revolutions from above carried through by pitiless force, that later Russian rulers sought to imitate or surpass.

The Losers: Sweden and Poland

While Prussia grew and Russia transformed itself, their Swedish and Polish neighbors declined. Sweden had burst on Europe as a military power of the first rank when Gustavus Adolphus swept into Germany in 1630–31. The Baltic virtually became a Swedish lake, with Swedish outposts that stretched from the Gulf of Finland to the North Sea. Copper, iron, and agriculture were Sweden's chief resources; superior cannon and muskets its chief military advantage. But Swedish power rested on shaky foundations. The country had a population of less than 2 million—not much larger than Brandenberg-Prussia or the Dutch Republic. The empire that Gustavus Adolphus had acquired was overextended; its enemies, from Russia and Poland to Prussia and Denmark, were hungry for revenge.

When young Charles XII (r. 1697–1718) came to the Swedish throne, a coali-

---

Peter the Great: The Bronze Horseman

The first and greatest modern Russian poet, Aleksandr Sergeyevich Pushkin (1799–1837), summed up Peter's place in Russian history in "The Bronze Horseman" (1833), named for the tsar's statue at St. Petersburg.

That square, the lions, and him—the one
Who, bronzen countenance upslanted
Into the dusk aloft, sat still,
The one by whose portentous will
The city by the sea was planted . . .
How awesome in the gloom he rides!
What thought upon his brow resides!
His charger with what fiery mettle,
His form with what dark strength endowed!
Where will you gallop, charger proud,
Where next your plunging hoofbeats settle?
Oh, Destiny's great potentate!
Was it not thus, a towering idol
Hard by the chasm, with iron bridle
You reared up Russia to her fate?

From Alexander Pushkin, Collected Narrative and Lyrical Poetry, *trans. by Walter Arndt (Ann Arbor: Ardis Publishers, 1984), p. 437.*

---

tion of Russia, Poland, and Denmark pounced on his Baltic territories. But Charles proved a greater commander even than Gustavus Adolphus. He crushed the coalition's forces in a series of lightning campaigns. Then success intoxicated him. In 1708–09 he launched Sweden into a foolhardy attempt to smash Russia and met devastating defeat at Poltava in the Ukraine. He subsequently escaped to Turkey, spent some years at the Ottoman court seeking allies, and died in the siege of an obscure Norwegian fortress in 1718. His meteoric career exhausted Sweden. In the peace settlements of 1719 to 1721 that ended this "Great Northern War," Hanover, Denmark, Prussia, and Russia divided up Sweden's Baltic empire. Sweden retired for good into the ranks of second-class powers.

Poland, an elective monarchy originally formed in 1386 through the union of the crowns of Poland and Lithuania (see p. 342), suffered a similar fate. Polish prosperity and culture had reached their peak

The Baltic: A Swedish Lake   1621–1721

in the sixteenth century. Roman Catholicism had linked Poland to western Europe and had conveyed the influence of the Renaissance, the Protestant revolt, and the Counter-Reformation. But by the beginning of the seventeenth century Poland's economic and political decline had begun.

In France, Prussia, and Russia the state tamed the nobility. In Poland the nobility gradually became the state, thanks to the elective character of the monarchy. Until the 1570s the Polish nobility had usually elected the legal heirs of their monarchs. But thereafter they chose candidates who appeared to favor their own interests. By 1700 the nobility had deprived the monarchy of most of its powers.

Noble power had consequences. It sank the peasants as deeply in serfdom as anywhere else in Europe. It checked the small, weak towns, prevented the rise of urban middle classes, and froze the Polish economy in rural backwardness. Above all, it concentrated political power in the Polish Diet, which now represented only the nobility, since representatives of the towns no longer dared attend.

The Diet's procedure, tailor-made to preserve noble domination, was notorious—one negative vote, the "*liberum veto,*" could block any action. Moreover, the *liberum veto* allowed any member to "explode" a Diet session—to dissolve it and wipe out all legislation it had passed up to that moment. Of 57 Diets held in the century after 1652, all but nine "exploded." In one case a member cast a veto simply to see what would happen. And if by some accident legislation did emerge from the Diet, no machinery existed to enforce it against the provincial assemblies of lesser nobles or the private estate jurisdictions of the landed magnates. John Sobieski (1674–96), a native Pole of high integrity, was the last great king. He saved Vienna from the Turks but failed to save Poland from its nobility. After him, Poland declined into incoherence and eventual extinction at the hands of Austria, Russia, and Prussia between 1772 and 1795.

ABSOLUTISM, CONSTITUTIONALISM, AND THE BALANCE OF POWER

The half-century from 1660 to 1715 was thus a period of dramatic change. Internally, absolute divine-right monarchy reached its height in the France of Louis XIV. Powers from Madrid to St. Petersburg attempted to imitate the French model. Nevertheless, a few smaller peoples such as the Swiss had rejected monarchy in favor of republican government. The Dutch "Sea Beggars" had even shown that a republic could compete in the great-power arena. But it took England's Glorious Revolution and Marlborough's victories to demonstrate to Europe that even the greatest powers could choose alternatives to absolute monarchy.

Externally, relations between states and the workings of the balance of power almost completely superseded the religious-ideological conflicts that had rent Europe before 1648. France's bid for mastery after 1672 provoked the rise of England and Austria as great powers. Two great empires of the sixteenth century, Spain and the Ottoman Turks, continued their decline. Two peoples of limited resources and numbers, the Dutch and the Swedes, briefly claimed great-power status in the mid-seventeenth century but lacked staying power. Two new powers appeared in eastern Europe to join the balance—military Prussia and semibarbaric Russia. The rivalries of these states—Britain against France, France against Austria, Austria against Prussia, Austria and Russia against the Ottoman Empire—were the forces that moved European war and diplomacy after 1715.

Medals celebrating an abortive "Treaty of Eternal Peace" between Russia and Poland (1686). (*Above*) King John Sobieski, Poland's last great king. (*Below*) Personification of Poland and Russia.

Suggestions for Further Reading

Western Europe

J. Stoye, *Europe Unfolding, 1648–88* (1969), and J. B. Wolf, *The Emergence of the Great Powers, 1685–1715* (1951), provide useful introductions, but see also W. Doyle, *The Old European Order, 1660–1800* (1978). C. J. Friedrich and C. Blitzer, *The Age of Power* (1957), covers the general theme of this chapter. R. Hatton, *Europe in the Age of Louis XIV* (1969), is excellent on social history. P. Goubert, *Louis XIV and Twenty Million Frenchmen* (1970), wittily relates the career of the king to the social history of France. See also J. B. Wolf, *Louis XIV* (1968), and W. H. Lewis, *The Splendid Century* (1954), an elegant account of the reign. On England, see especially C. Hill, *The Century of Revolution, 1603–1714* (1961). G. N. Clark, *The Later Stuarts, 1660–1714* (1934), is a fine synthesis. C. H. Wilson, *England's Apprenticeship, 1603–1763* (1965), covers England's emergence as a great power.

Eastern Europe

For the lands east of the Elbe, see especially S. H. Cross, *Slavic Civilization Through the Ages* (1948), and O. Halecki, *Borderlands of Western Civilization* (1952). On Germany, see H. Holborn, *A History of Modern Germany, 1648–1840* (1964). R. W. J. Evans, *The Making of the Habsburg Monarchy* (1979), and H. G. Koenigsberger, *The Habsburgs and Europe* (1971), are useful surveys. On Prussia, S. B. Fay and K. Epstein, *The Rise of Brandenburg-Prussia to 1786* (1937, 1964), is concise. See also F. Carsten, *The Origins of Prussia* (1954). B. H. Sumner, *Peter the Great and the Emergence of Russia* (1950), is a useful short account. For analysis, see especially R. Pipes, *Russia under the Old Regime* (1974), and J. Blum, *Lord and Peasant in Russia from the Ninth to the Nineteenth Century* (1961).

21

THE SCIENTIFIC REVOLUTION AND THE ENLIGHTENMENT

ntil the seventeenth century the growth of knowledge about nature had been slow, fumbling, and frequently interrupted. Scholars had observed events in nature, had in many cases recorded them, and had sometimes derived useful generalizations from them. But "experiments" in the modern sense had been largely absent, and scientific inquiry was scarcely distinguishable from theological speculation.

That changed. By the eighteenth century, during the age of rapidly broadening and deepening knowledge that became known as the Enlightenment, the West had accumulated a large body of principles verifiable by experiment. Those principles in turn allowed the prediction and manipulation of nature. That type of knowledge has continued to accumulate, with revolutionary effect. The ever-accelerating understanding of and mastery over nature, for good or ill, was the achievement of the West, the first civilization in history to make a clear distinction between science on the one hand and religion or magic on the other.

THE SCIENTIFIC REVOLUTION

A new method of inquiry, later called the "scientific method," emerged from the universities of Western Europe in the late thirteenth and fourteenth centuries. After 1600 it achieved wide currency in western Europe. The new method was a combination of careful observation and controlled experiment with rational interpretation of the results, preferably using mathematics. That was the origin of modern science, an enterprise that a great twentieth-century mathematician-philosopher described as

(OPPOSITE) TWO OF GALILEO'S TELESCOPES.

the "vehement and passionate interest in the relation of general principles to irreducible and stubborn facts."

The Medieval Universe

Precisely *why* the West took the lead in scientific speculation over the other great civilizations, China, Islam, and India, remains unclear. Even in the West, deep-rooted traditional assumptions about the nature of the universe dominated thought for centuries. Medieval learning dictated that the universe was a finite sphere with the earth at the center. Between the center and the outermost limit, nine transparent spheres supposedly carried stars, planets, sun, and moon in their daily revolutions about a motionless earth. The earth was the realm of change, decay, and original sin. The heavens were the realm of perfection and changelessness. Sun, moon, and heavenly bodies were perfectly spherical and moved in spherical tracks to the accompaniment of an ethereal "music of the spheres." The assumed dichotomy between heavenly perfection and earthly corruption demanded a sharp separation

The observatory of the Danish astronomer Tycho Brahe was the finest of the sixteenth century. Note the domes protecting the instruments.

between the laws of heavenly and of earthly physics.

Even in the Middle Ages, not all scholars found this picture of the universe convincing. By the thirteenth and fourteenth centuries a small but increasing number had begun to question it, including Franciscan monks, perhaps inspired by their founder's sensitive feeling for nature. The study of the Greco-Arabic scientific texts that had reached the West stimulated a group of scholars at Oxford and Paris to apply mathematical reasoning to problems of physics and astronomy, such as motion and acceleration. Professors at the University of Padua continued these speculations in the fifteenth and sixteenth centuries. At Padua, a center of medical training for three centuries, scholars vigorously debated the proper method of studying nature in the course of arguments about Aristotle. The medieval universities kept interest in science alive and nurtured the first faint beginnings of the scientific revolution.

Most Europeans of 1500, however, did not question the Greek authorities, who had decreed that the normal state of everything in the universe was a state of rest. Aristotle had said that bodies moved only if a mover pushed or pulled them. Galen of Pergamum, in the second century A.D., had described the anatomy of the human body so convincingly that doctors still saw it through his eyes. In that same century, the Greco-Egyptian astronomer Ptolemy had compiled mathematical descriptions of the observed movements of the planets so ingenious that European authorities saw no need to discard them until after 1500. Ptolemy assumed that all motion in the heavens was circular and proceeded at a constant rate. But because the observed pattern of actual planetary motion in the heavens was not precisely circular, Ptolemy had invented the "epicycle," an additional small circle in which the planet moved while traveling around the circumference of its larger "sphere" around the earth. He and his successors needed eighty epicycles to force the observed motion of the planets to fit the theory, but in the end Ptolemy's system explained what astronomers saw. Even more important, it permitted the prediction of lunar and planetary motion with some precision. At the close of the Middle Ages, few scholars saw much need to improve upon the observations and theories of the ancients.

The Background of Change

Nevertheless, forces in European society in the fourteenth, fifteenth, and sixteenth centuries prepared the way for a challenge to this orthodoxy. Artisans and craftsmen gradually adopted techniques more advanced than those of their medieval predecessors. Ever-smaller and more precise pocket watches took their place alongside the massive mechanical clocks of the medieval cathedrals. The development of the glass industry and the invention of the lens at some point before 1300, to take but one example, gave the promise of vastly extending humanity's ability to observe natural processes. Breakthroughs in shipbuilding and navigation (see p. 451) permitted the voyages of discovery, which in turn stimulated interest in nature generally.

The Renaissance, with its emphasis on literature and art and its veneration for the wisdom of the ancients, was in some respects hostile to the new science. But the Humanists were interested in Greek scientific texts as well as in Greek literature, and Renaissance patrons of artists were also patrons of inventors and technicians. Humanistic study revealed that ancient scientific authorities had differed among themselves on key issues, just at the moment when the authority of Galen and Ptolemy was becoming shaky for other reasons. Anatomical studies by the great Renaissance artists and the increasing practice of dissection suggested that Galen had made mistakes. Growing skill in mathematics exposed the clumsiness of Ptolemy's calculations. By the opening years of the sixteenth century, conditions were ripe for a dramatic shift in the West's underlying assumptions about the universe.

Vesalius and Copernicus: Observation and Calculation

In 1543 two notable scientific works heralded the end of medieval science. Andreas Vesalius, a Flemish anatomist at the University of Padua, published *On the Structure of the Human Body,* a marvelously careful description of human anatomy based on direct observation during dissection, and illustrated with accurate plates. Vesalius did not free himself completely from the authority of Galen, nor did his book offer much theoretical insight. But it was an influential example of the power of observation.

Even more powerful in its ultimate effect was the work of a Polish scholar, Mikolaj Kopérnik, better known as Copernicus. *On the Revolutions of the Heavenly Bodies* was a brilliant mathematical treatise that showed how to reduce Ptolemy's 80 epicycles to 34 by assuming that the earth turned on its axis once a day and moved around the sun once a year. Unlike Vesalius, Copernicus was not primarily an observer. During study at Padua in the early years of the century he had learned that some ancient authorities had held that the earth moved. That assumption made the motions of the moon and planets far simpler to explain mathematically than the medieval earth-centered theory. Copernicus, following the equally medieval notion that "nature always acts in the simplest ways," eventually discarded Ptolemy on grounds of logic, rather than from observation. His ideas gradually spread.

In 1600, the Inquisition tried a former monk named Giordano Bruno as a heretic and burned him at the stake in Rome. He had published works arguing that the universe was not a closed sphere but infinite in extent, that numberless suns and planets like our own filled it, and that God was equally present in every planet or atom in the cosmos. He also maintained that the existence of the infinite made it impossible to arrive at absolute truth, or find limits to the extent of knowledge. Copernicus had inspired him, although Copernicus himself believed in the finite

The Copernican revolution: the
new sun-centered solar system.

sphere of the fixed stars and the uniqueness of the earth. Despite the fires of the
Inquisition, Bruno's intuition of the infin-
ity of the universe ultimately prevailed. It
was the beginning of modern cosmology.

The Purposes and Method of Science: Bacon and Descartes

Two major prophets of the early Scientific Revolution, Francis Bacon (1561–
1626) and René Descartes (1596–1650),
followed Copernicus. Bacon, an English
lawyer, statesman, and essayist, waged a
vigorous scholarly battle against the de-
ductive method of medieval scholasticism,
which began with premises usually taken
on authority and deduced from them their
logical consequences. That might help to
organize truths already known, argued
Bacon, but it could never discover new
truths. Only inductive reasoning, starting
from direct observation of phenomena

and developing principles that explained
them, could produce new truths.

Bacon set a practical goal for science,
the "domination" of humanity over nature.
He pictured an imaginary future society
of scientists whose end was to benefit
mankind by conducting hundreds of experiments that discovered useful facts.
Bacon failed to appreciate the importance
of mathematical models, and he found
Copernicus unconvincing. Although he
praised experimentation, he performed almost no experiments and collected his
evidence in the traditional way, from
books. His writings nevertheless dramatized the importance of empirical research. The founding in 1662 of the Royal
Society of London, the first scientific society in England, owed much to Bacon's
inspiration. He was the remote ancestor of
the great laboratories and team-research
projects of the twentieth century. His goal,
the mastery of nature through rational

analysis, has distinguished the West from the other historic civilizations.

Descartes, a French mathematician and philosopher, was an even more important figure than Bacon, but he lacked Bacon's intuitive understanding of the need for observation. To Descartes, the excitement of science lay in mathematical analysis and theory. In a famous autobiographical account, he told how the literature and philosophy that he had studied as a youth had left him unsatisfied because he reached no *certain* conclusions. By contrast, the precision and certainty of mathematics aroused his enthusiasm. He set out to discover a mathematical "method of rightly conducting the reason and discovering truth in the sciences."

In November 1619, in a moment of intuition, he saw the exact correspondence between geometry and algebra—the truth that equations and curves on graphs were interchangeable. That intoxicating vision suggested to him a new way of grasping ultimate truth. If humanity systematically doubted all notions based on authority or custom and started with clear and precise ideas known to be true, it might deduce systematically the entire universe from a few simple principles, just as he had derived curves from equations.

Descartes was one of the first to believe that science could save humanity. His enthusiasm was infectious and outran the knowledge available in the seventeenth century. He reduced the universe, including the human body, to a mathematically intelligible machine. Only the human intellect. he believed, resisted mathematical description. He therefore defined it as being outside the world of matter: The mind comprehended the world but did not exist in it. His generalizations in astronomy, physics, and anatomy were often premature, and his passion for system building went far beyond his capacity to confirm generalizations by experiment. He did important work in optics, but that in no way confirmed his far-ranging theories.

Nevertheless, Descartes' enthusiasm for scientific "method," his belief that mathematics could describe all phenom-

ena, and his insistence on systematic doubt of all earlier theorizing left a profound mark on the scientific thinking of the three centuries that followed. Descartes made it easier for his successors to reject old ideas, and they gradually came to accept his belief that mathematics must be the language of science.

Experiment and Mathematics

Bacon and Descartes were too optimistic. Bacon thought that a generation of determined experimentation would establish a solid structure of knowledge about the universe. Descartes expected that a few basic mathematical axioms would soon lead, by deduction, to a universal science. He also believed in a universe far simpler than it now appears. One of Descartes' pupils even described the world as a gigantic piece of clockwork.

Meanwhile, experimentation and mathematics were developing steadily in the hands of a growing host of scientists. William Gilbert (1544–1603), court physician to Elizabeth I, coined the word "electricity" and deduced that the earth itself was a huge magnet. His *De magnete* (1600) remained the foremost work on magnetism until the early nineteenth century. William Harvey (1578–1627), who had studied at Padua, argued in a work published in 1628 that the blood must circulate from arteries to veins to heart, then on to the lungs, back to the heart and back once more to the arteries. He did this by estimating the amount of blood the heart pumped in a minute and arguing that it must go somewhere. Later in the century the new microscope revealed the tiny capillaries that actually connect arteries to veins.

Evangelista Torricelli (1608–47), Blaise Pascal, and others investigated the ancient proposition, long believed by most scholars, that "nature abhors a vacuum." They created vacuums in test tubes, invented the barometer, and discovered that the pressure of the atmosphere varies between sea level and mountain top. They proved inherited wisdom false, and their work showed a growing precision in observation and an increasing skill in

Scientific revolutionaries of the seventeenth century: Francis Bacon *(above)* and René Descartes *(below)*.

Harvey Discovers the Circulation of the Blood

Since calculations and visual demonstrations have confirmed all my suppositions, to wit, that the blood is passed through the lungs and the heart by the pulsation of the ventricles, is forcibly ejected to all parts of the body, therein steals into the veins . . . flows back everywhere . . . from small veins into larger ones, and thence comes at last into the vena cava and to the auricle of the heart; all this too in such amounts that it cannot be supplied from the ingesta [food] and is also in greater bulk than would suffice for nutrition.

I am obliged to conclude that in all animals the blood is driven around a circuit with an unceasing, circular sort of motion, that this is an activity of the heart which it carries out by virtue of its pulsation, and that in sum it constitutes the sole cause for the heart's pulsatile movement.

From C. C. Gillispie, The Edge of Objectivity *(Princeton, N.J.: Princeton University Press, 1960), p. 71.*

controlling experiments and in quantifying their results.

Mathematics likewise rapidly advanced. The invention of decimals and of logarithms early in the century made calculation easier. Pascal inaugurated the study of probability. At the end of the century Sir Isaac Newton and Baron Gottfried Wilhelm von Leibniz (1646–1716) crowned the work of many others by simultaneously but separately inventing the calculus, which provided the first mathematical method for describing accelerating or decelerating motion.

Kepler: The Foundations of Celestial Mechanics

Observational techniques and mathematical methods first united in astronomy and physics—producing results of a beauty and explanatory power that shattered for good all traditional notions of the place of science in human knowledge and of humanity in the universe.

The German astronomer Johannes Kepler (1571–1630) believed Copernicus's theory, but found discrepancies in it troubling. He worked from the observations of

his master, the Danish astronomer Tycho Brahe (1546–1601), which were far more accurate than those available to Copernicus. Brahe's data ultimately caused Kepler to discard reluctantly the universal belief, which Copernicus had not challenged, that heavenly bodies moved in circles.

Kepler concluded that the ellipse, whose properties scholars had studied since the time of the Greeks, fitted Brahe's observations of Mars, the planet whose motion most contradicted the Ptolemaic and Copernican systems. The orbits of the planets, Kepler suggested, were elliptical, with the sun at one of the two foci of the ellipse. Further, he demonstrated that a line from the sun to a planet swept out equal areas of the ellipse in equal times and that the cube of the distance of each planet from the sun was proportional to the square of the time of its revolution. That was astounding proof of the intuition of Descartes and others that nature was in some mysterious sense mathematical. A geometrical figure, studied for centuries as an abstract form, "fit" the facts of nature. By implication, nature was perhaps itself a machine, intelligible to the careful observer equipped with mathematics.

The New Universe: Galileo

Kepler's work describing many of his findings appeared in 1609. During that same year a professor at Padua and Pisa, Galileo Galilei (1564–1642), turned on the heavens a newly invented instrument, the telescope. He soon published an account of what he saw. The changeless perfection and perfect sphericity of the heavenly bodies had dissolved before his gaze. He saw that the moon had craters and mountains, that spots moved on the sun, that rings encircled Saturn, and that Jupiter had four moons of its own. A bright new star— a supernova—had already appeared in 1572, and Brahe had noted it. In 1577 a new comet had cut a path through what should have been unchanging crystalline spheres. Now Galileo's telescope shattered forever the unchanging, finite, spherical universe of the Middle Ages. Thoughtful scholars suspected that Bruno had been right. Humanity was looking out into infinite space, at a sparse population of stars like the sun that might themselves have solar systems.

The medieval distinction between earthly and celestial physics was apparently dissolving. The moon and sun were not perfect globes and the stars were not changeless. Nor was the earth any longer the motionless center of the universe. The earth, like Mars and Jupiter, was a planet circling the sun against a backdrop of silent, infinite space. Perhaps the same forces and laws operated both on earth and in the heavens.

Such views soon attracted the wrath of the Church of the Counter-Reformation, which had denounced the Copernican theory in 1616. The Roman Inquisition condemned Galileo himself in 1632, threatened him with torture, and forced him to retract his theories. The legend soon arose that after repudiating his "heretical" view that the earth moved around the sun, he nevertheless muttered stubbornly under his breath "*Eppur si muove*"—"It *does* move." Nor could the Inquisition suppress Galileo's brilliantly written dialogues, which contributed mightily to the overthrow not only of Ptolemy in favor of Copernicus, but also of Aristotle in favor of a new physics.

The speculations of the fourteenth-century Franciscan monks inspired Galileo's physics, but he was far more thorough and accurate than they in developing mathematical formulas to describe motion. He worked out by experiment the law of falling bodies—the distance fallen increases as the square of the time. He saw that projectiles followed parabolic paths that were the resultant of the two forces acting upon the projectile—the initial impetus that launched it and the downward pull of the earth. That insight was the beginning of modern ballistics, the scientific foundation of the new warfare.

Galileo also came close to formulating the key concept of modern mechanics, the law of inertia: that bodies tend to remain at rest or to continue in motion in straight lines unless outside forces act upon them. That deceptively simple proposition—fundamentally opposed to Aristotle's concept of motion as the result of

some mover's action—was the source of the law of gravitation. Galileo prepared the way, but it was a man born in the year Galileo died who made that decisive breakthrough.

The Synthesis of Celestial and Terrestrial Mechanics: Newton

Sir Isaac Newton (1642–1727), the greatest figure of the Scientific Revolution, was the man who married Kepler's astronomy to Galileo's mechanics, broke down all distinctions between celestial and terrestrial physics, and accomplished at least part of Descartes' dream of establishing a "universal science." A fundamental intuition came to Newton while he was still a student in his twenties at Cambridge University: the force that bends the moon into its orbit about the earth must be the same force that pulls an apple from its branch to the ground. A reciprocal force of attraction between every body in the universe must exist, and that force—although as yet unexplained—must be calculable.

Newton's earliest calculations came close enough to mathematical proof to persuade him that the same force indeed operated on the moon and on the apple, and that this force varied "directly as the product of the masses" involved and "inversely as the square of the distance" separating those masses. For some time after formulating this "law" of gravitation in 1664–66 he seems to have lost interest. But twenty years later a friend, the astronomer Edmund Halley (who calculated the orbit of the famous comet), persuaded Newton to publish. Newton developed the necessary mathematics—the calculus—to prove his theory to his own satisfaction. He published his conclusions in 1687 in his *Philosophiae naturalis principia mathematica,* the "mathematical principles of natural philosophy." It was one of the most influential books in the history of human thought.

Newton's law of gravitation provided a simple and elegant explanation of a growing mass of data in astronomy and physics and laid the foundations of future research in both sciences. Newton also

The greatest scientific revolutionary of all: Sir Isaac Newton, painted by Kneller.

improved on Bacon and Descartes by giving the scientific method its classic formulation in his fourth "Rule of Reasoning":

In experimental philosophy [science] we are to look upon propositions collected by general induction from phenomena as accurately or very nearly true, notwithstanding any contrary hypotheses [theories] that may be imagined, till such time as other phenomena occur, by which they may either be made more accurate or liable to exceptions.

Newton's support of the experimental or inductive approach was aimed against the premature generalizing, the theoretical "system[s] . . . little better than a Romance," of Descartes and his followers. But Newton, unlike Bacon, was fully convinced of the necessity of mathematical theory. Newton combined at last both celestial and terrestrial physics on the one hand, and empirical observation and mathematical interpretation on the other.

Newton's Universe

News of Newton's work spread rapidly among laymen, thanks to popular scientific works that soon began pouring from the presses of London and Amsterdam. The new universe that Newton disclosed was far different from the cozy finite universe of the Middle Ages. Bodies moved through infinite space in response to predictable, universally operating forces. Mass, force, and motion were the key concepts, and mathematics made them intelligible.

The question "Why?" had obsessed the scholars of the Middle Ages, who had felt they understood a natural phenomenon once they had discovered its purpose. Seventeenth-century scientists limited themselves to asking "How?" The discovery of regular patterns in natural processes satisfied most of them. The world of Kepler, Galileo, and Newton was a vast machine, working according to laws expressible in mathematics, laws understandable by anyone who followed the proper experimental and mathematical

Newton invented and built this first reflecting telescope.

methods. The telescope continued to reveal an ever-larger portion of an apparently infinite universe. The new astronomy, after displacing the earth as the center of the universe, displaced the sun as well. The microscope, after the 1660s, began to reveal the wonders of the infinitely small foundations of life—bacteria, spermatozoa, cells, capillaries.

The question "Why?" nevertheless remained unanswered. What was the place of God and of humanity in this universe? That question did not become acute until the eighteenth century. No prominent seventeenth-century scientist thought that he was reading God out of the universe. Descartes considered himself a good Catholic and apparently did not see the theological dangers inherent in his sharp separation of the world of matter from the world of mind. Newton spent many of his later years absorbed in theological speculation and alchemy. The border between science and religion or magic was still fluid, and possible contradictions between faith and science were not clearly evident to most seventeenth-century scientists, or to their audience.

The French philosopher-scientist Blaise Pascal (1623–62), inventor of probability theory and of the first calculating machine, and contributor to fields as diverse as the calculus and the dynamics of gases and fluids, indeed attempted a synthesis between faith and the new sciences. For Pascal, "the whole visible world [was] only an imperceptible atom in the ample bosom of nature," and the universe "an infinite sphere, the center of which is everywhere, the circumference nowhere." "The eternal silence of these infinite spaces frightens me," he confessed. Yet to examine a mite, "with its minute body and parts incomparably more minute, limbs with their joints, veins in the limbs, blood in the veins, humors in the blood, drops in the humors, vapors in the drops," was equally astonishing. "What is man in nature? A Nothing in comparison with the Infinite, an All in comparison with the Nothing, a mean between nothing and everything." Pascal related the new universe explicitly to Christianity, to Christ's sacrifice on the cross, which made humanity, despite its apparent insignificance, the greatest presence in the universe beside God. Others soon saw less need to invoke Christianity.

By the later seventeenth century the hold of religious orthodoxy on Europe's intellectual elite was beginning to weaken. Religious authorities could no longer simply forbid scientific speculation or experiment. The burning or torture of "heretics" like Giordano Bruno slowly went out of fashion, except in Spain. And scientists themselves began to demarcate their activities sharply from questions of faith. The charters of the many scientific societies and academies that sprang up throughout Europe during the century usually contained clauses forbidding purely theological or political discussion and establishing that the group would not investigate "ultimate" or "final" causes.

The earliest history of the Royal Society of London, published in 1667, suggests that scientific discussions offered a peculiar attraction to thoughtful individuals during and after a fanatically bitter religious and civil war such as the English Revolution. Science, which by definition dealt with the empirically verifiable, might thereby become politically and theologically neutral and benefit humanity in practical ways. Scientific truth gradually emerged as an alternative to theological truth. It was not entirely accidental that modern science arose as religious warfare went out of fashion, amid general revulsion at the devastation that fanaticism had wrought.

Nevertheless, Newton's new "world picture" did not explicitly contradict religious feeling. Some indeed found in the mechanistic universe a source of religious awe. Baruch or Benedict Spinoza (1632–77), an Amsterdam lens grinder and philosopher descended from the Jewish communities that Spain had expelled, concluded that the new universe of mass, force, and motion, operating in strict obedience to inexorable laws, *was* God. Spinoza saw no need to consider God as above, behind, or beyond nature, as a "free cause" apart from natural law. God was not "Creator" or "Redeemer," but a "God *or* Nature" that included all being

and incarnated natural law: "God never can decree, nor ever would have decreed, anything but what is; God did not exist before his decrees, and would not exist without them." Humanity, like all else, was part of the natural order and thus of God, and wisdom consisted of contemplating that order with serenity and delight.

Both Jewish and Christian contemporaries considered Spinoza a dangerous atheistic radical, although he was the mildest, kindliest, and most optimistic of men. Most of his works emerged in print only after his death. Contemporaries pointed out that to claim that humanity was part of God made it difficult to explain evil. Later critics discerned in "Whatever is, is in God" a dangerous fatalism. But Spinoza's notion of religion was destined to have great influence in the eighteenth century.

THE CULTURE OF THE BAROQUE

The age of the scientific revolution was also, especially in the Catholic areas of the Continent, the age of the "baroque" style in the visual arts. The baroque sprang up in the later sixteenth century, reached its climax about the middle of the seventeenth, and came to its end around the middle of the eighteenth. Eighteenth-century critics invented the term *baroque* (French for "odd" or "irregular"), after tastes had again changed, to stigmatize seventeenth-century art as a grotesque corruption of Renaissance styles. But by the late nineteenth century critics had come to consider the baroque a great achievement. More than most styles, it is difficult to define because it reflected the contrasts and contradictions of seventeenth-century culture as a whole—religious ecstasy and worldly sensuality, credulity and rationalism, violence and respect for order.

Baroque painters and sculptors portrayed voluptuous women in repose, heroes in battle, and saints in ecstasy with equal skill and zest. In general, the dominant notes of the baroque were tension, conflict, the grandiose, and the dramatic. Renaissance painters and writers had been interested in humanity itself. Baroque artists depicted the conflicts of humanity against the universe, of man against man, and of man within himself on a tragic and heroic scale.

Instructive parallels exist between the thought-worlds of the baroque artists and those of the seventeenth-century scientists. Galileo and Newton studied bodies or masses moving through space under the influence of conflicting forces such as gravitation and centrifugal force. To the great French dramatists of the age—Corneille, Racine, and Molière—the objects of study were typical human beings torn between conflicting forces such as love and duty. Space intrigued baroque painters. The Dutch master Jan Vermeer (1632–75) portrayed figures in a space bathed in and suffused with light. The greatest of Dutch painters, Rembrandt van Rijn (1606–69), spotlighted figures in the midst of darkened space, while others pictured them floating through apparently infinite voids. To baroque artists the supernatural was natural. The scientists' concern with mass, force, and motion paralleled the painters' and poets' concern with individuals caught in the tension between elemental forces. The typical hero of baroque literature, critics have suggested, is Satan in John Milton's *Paradise Lost* (1667), the

only great epic poem in English. Swayed by colossal passions, Satan moves through vast three-dimensional spaces and bends the forces of the universe to serve his implacable will to domination: "To reign is worth ambition though in hell:/Better to reign in hell than serve in heav'n." But God frustrates Satan's designs in the end.

The most typical, although not usually the most beautiful products of baroque architecture were the great palaces: Versailles and the remodeled Louvre in France, Schönbrunn in Austria, or Blenheim, the regal residence in England that Marlborough received for his victories. The style of these buildings was fundamentally Renaissance-classical, but grander, more ornate, and above all larger, often to the point of excess. As with the many descendants of Versailles, the neoclassical official buildings of later centuries, excess served a political purpose. Sheer mass emphasized the power of the state. In this, as in much else, Louis XIV led the way. Even some baroque religious architecture, such as the massive elliptical colonnades that the great Giovanni Lorenzo Bernini (1598–1680) erected to frame St. Peter's in Rome, conveyed the majesty of God rather than his mercy.

The most original creation of the baroque were the operas that originated in Italy early in the seventeenth century. Drama set to music had existed in the West since the twelfth century. But the music had been essentially choral and polyphonic until around 1600, when a group of Florentine composers devised a "*dramma per musica*" (drama through music) in which the characters sang their parts as simple melodies without choral accompaniment. Opera immediately became, and has remained, a vast popular success. The grandiose and palatial stage settings, the dramatic conflicts of the action, and the emotional power of the music exactly suited the taste of the period. Italian composers led the way until the end of the seventeenth century—Claudio Monteverdi (1567–1643), Girolamo Frescobaldi (1583–1643), Alessandro Scarlatti (1660–1725), and the greatest master of Italian Baroque music, Antonio Vivaldi (1675–1741). But it was an Englishman, Henry

The glories of the baroque: altarpiece in St. Peter's, Rome, by the Italian master Giovanni Lorenzo Bernini (1598–1680).

Purcell (*ca.* 1658–95), who wrote the most moving opera of the century, *Dido and Aeneas* (1687).

ORIGINS OF THE ENLIGHTENMENT: SEVENTEENTH-CENTURY THOUGHT ABOUT HUMANITY

While the vast majority of the population of western Europe remained medieval in outlook, the most adventurous minds of the seventeenth century fashioned notions about humanity that rested on Renaissance ideas but pressed far beyond them. The rediscovery of the ancient world, the great overseas voyages, and the scientific revolution led seventeenth-century thinkers into new territory. Their efforts ultimately inspired the greatest break in the history of European thought since the collapse of the Roman Empire, the eighteenth-century flowering of modern conceptions of humanity known as the Enlightenment. The new ideas of the seventeenth century fall conveniently into three categories: individualism, relativism, and a rationalism tempered with empiricism.

Individualism

Radical thinkers of the seventeenth century were increasingly inclined to celebrate the individual. The most intense Christian piety of the period—whether it was the Catholic devotion preached by St. François de Sales, the stern conscience of the Puritans and Jansenists, or the warm inner conviction of the German Pietists—was highly individualistic. That trend was equally evident in political theory. The fashion was to start with the individual and then seek explanations of and justifications for the existence of societies and states.

Supporters of the divine-right theory of kingship remained numerous, but by the middle of the seventeenth century the notion of an explicit or implicit "contract" between people and ruler was widespread. Hobbes and a few others, including Spinoza, argued that this contract, once made, was irrevocable and that it

Opera singers of the baroque: detail from an opera setting drawn by Ludovico Burnacinia, Vienna (1674).

bound the ruled but not the ruler. Others, like the Parliamentarians in the English Civil War and John Locke in political philosophy, argued for a right of rebellion against rulers who broke the terms of the contract by acting against the general welfare.

The idea of a "social contract" soon took its place alongside the notion of the "political contract." Society, according to social-contract theorists, was itself the result of a voluntary agreement among individuals who had been absolutely independent in their original "state of nature." The two ideas mixed, somewhat confusedly, in the works of Locke and of later political philosophers. In both contracts, the individual with his rights and his "natural" independence logically came first; then came society or the state. The more radical thinkers of the seventeenth century thus came to think of society as an artificial organization of independent individuals that rested on their consent. That was a radical break with the medieval conception of society as an organism or a "body" of which individuals were mere "members," each with an assigned place.

Relativism

The greatest thinkers of the Middle Ages were confident that the peoples of Christendom were chosen by God, and that divine revelation gave humanity all necessary truths. But that self-assurance weakened during the sixteenth and seventeenth centuries, thanks to Humanism, to the voyages of discovery, and to the development of science.

Humanism had begun to reveal Greco-Roman civilization in some detail. Ancient literature, art, and historical writing brought alive a long-dead society that offered numerous alternatives to the medieval Christian system of belief. The Renaissance had first created the modern disciplines of history, archaeology, and philology. Seventeenth-century scholars broadened and deepened them. Thoughtful Europeans thus learned that other societies had existed in other times with values, beliefs, and institutions quite different from their own. That recognition was the origin of the concept of historical relativism, of the notion that value systems—including those of Christian Europe—were historical phenomena subject to change.

The age of discovery added to historical relativism a geographical counterpart. The discovery in America and Asia of other societies shattered European provincialism. The tribal hunter-gatherers of America and Africa, the urban civilizations of Aztecs and Incas, and the great empires of Asia with their advanced arts and amenities inspired study and reflection. Perhaps the "noble savages" of the New World were happier than the more cultured but "corrupted" Christians of Europe. Perhaps Persian sages and Chinese philosophers had something to teach Christians. Each society had different standards—was any value system grounded on anything more solid than custom? Doubts on these points affected increasing numbers of European thinkers in the seventeenth and eighteenth centuries. And scientific discovery likewise widened their vision of humanity's place in nature. European Christianity was not alone in time and space, and humanity itself might not be alone in the universe.

The work of Pierre Bayle (1647–1706), the great scholarly skeptic of the later seventeenth century, exemplifies the results of historical study, geographical exploration, and scientific discovery. Bayle was born a Huguenot, briefly converted to Catholicism, and then renounced all orthodox belief when his brother died in a French dungeon during an attempt at forced conversion. Bayle took up residence in the relatively tolerant Dutch Netherlands and devoted the latter part of his life to a crusade against superstition, religious intolerance, and dogma of all kinds. In 1697 he published a huge rambling book, the *Historical and Critical Dictionary,* which had enormous influence on Enlightenment thought. Into the book he poured a relativism and skepticism acquired through extensive historical study, an amateur knowledge of science, and experience.

He defied convention by insisting that religion and political stability were not identical—atheists could be good citizens. He denounced religious conversions by force. He ridiculed astrology, a form of superstition even more current then than now. He derided tales of miracles. He distrusted all historical authorities, including the writers of the Old Testament, unless their account of events was inherently credible. An admirer of Descartes, his test of truth was "reason," and many scriptural accounts failed that test. Bayle was the most destructive critic of his generation. His war against traditional religion replaced, and in part derived from, the scarcely ended wars of religion.

Rationalism and Empiricism

The leading thinkers of the seventeenth century began a process that reached completion only in the eighteenth century: the replacement of the lost certainties of religious belief with a new object of worship—reason. It was the faculty that in theory distinguished humanity from the animal world. It was trustworthy; the triumphs of seventeenth-century science had proved that. An increasingly optimistic age concluded that reason gave humanity the *certain knowledge* of the world that religion no longer appeared to offer.

Reason also provided a law, "natural law," to replace the foundation that religious belief now failed to provide for human knowledge. The idea of a law of nature that served as a standard of behavior for all humans at all times was not new.

Greek philosophers such as Aristotle had enunciated a version of it, the Stoics had pressed it further, and Cicero had given the idea classic formulation:

> There is in fact a true law—namely, right reason—which is in accordance with nature, applies to all men, and is unchangeable and eternal. By its commands this law summons men to the performance of their duties; by its prohibitions it restrains them from doing wrong.

St. Augustine had then Christianized that law by identifying it with the law of God. The medieval scholastics had enthusiastically proclaimed that law to be the basis of earthly law and morality. During the Renaissance and the Reformation, the rediscovery of texts of the ancient Stoics and the work of Protestant scholars such as the father of modern international law, the Dutch jurist and diplomat Hugo Grotius (1583–1645), had secularized natural law once more, as a "law" inherent in the nature of humanity. Grotius, in *On the Law of War and Peace* (1625), attempted to find in natural law some basis for a "law of nations" that would transcend and moderate the religious fanaticisms of the Thirty Years' War. And the discovery of scientific "laws of nature," such as Kepler's laws of planetary motion, further reinforced the belief that natural laws of human behavior must also exist. Success in proving mathematical and scientific laws inspired faith that reason could discern "natural law" in human affairs.

The most influential example of that faith was John Locke's claim that every individual in the "state of nature," before the existence of organized societies, possessed certain "natural rights," most notably life, liberty, and property. From that premise it followed, as proof followed axiom, that humanity had formed societies and set up governments mainly to preserve those rights. Whereas Descartes had hoped to deduce the universe from a few central mathematical principles, Locke in his *Second Treatise of Government* (1690) assumed that he could deduce society and government from a few simple axioms about humanity and natural law.

An undercurrent of empiricism, of respect for the evidence of the senses, nevertheless qualified that enthusiastic rationalism. Here too, Locke led the way in his *Essay Concerning Human Understanding* (1690), which many readers hailed as the counterpart in the study of humanity to Newton's work on the forces of nature. Locke argued that all human ideas came from the experience of the senses. The mind at birth was a *tabula rasa,* a clean slate, on which experience gained through the senses gradually imprinted conceptions. No "innate ideas" existed, and contrary to Descartes, no axioms were self-evident. Outside forces acting upon the mind explained all human ideas.

That was the purest empiricism. Locke hoped that it would provide a weapon for destroying the superstitions and prejudices of the past. It proved destructive of much else, including some of Locke's own doctrines. Locke's theory of the mind did away with original sin, for experience might mold the *tabula rasa* of the mind to do good rather than evil. It did away equally with the revelation on which Christianity rested and with mathematical axioms, for neither derived from the senses. Above all, it undermined Locke's own conception of "natural rights" that were innate and not based on experience.

The rationalism of Locke's natural-law theory of society clashed both with the empiricism of his theory of the mind and with the relativism in time and space that the Humanists and the great navigators had disclosed. The Enlightenment inherited this agonizing contradiction between rationalist faith in natural law and empiricist trust in sense-experience and in the evidence of comparative history.

THE EIGHTEENTH CENTURY: THE ENLIGHTENMENT

The task that the leading thinkers of the eighteenth century set themselves was to popularize the methods and principles of seventeenth-century natural science and to apply those methods and principles to God, humanity, and society. Scientific discovery continued, but the most brilliant writers of the age concentrated their effort on applying the new scientific method to long-festering human ills—economic, social, political, and ecclesiastical. Their concern was less to discover new truth about nature than to apply the methods of natural science to the transformation of society.

The eighteenth century's own name for this movement was "the Enlightenment"—*les lumières* in French. The term suggested the dawn of a new age of reason and knowledge after a long dark night of ignorance, superstition, intolerance, and despotism of kings and priests. That new light was the light of science, as the great English poet Alexander Pope (1688–1744) elegantly proclaimed:

Nature and nature's law lay hid in night;
God said, "Let Newton be," and all was light.

Correspondence, exchange of publications, and travel linked together a cultural movement that transcended state and religious boundaries. "Enlightened" writers and readers spanned Europe, from Russia to Spain, from Edinburgh to Naples, from the Philadelphia of Benjamin Franklin to the Virginia of Thomas Jefferson. But the center of the movement was indisputably Paris.

That was no accident. Most other countries were either too small or too backward to become major centers of Enlightenment thought and agitation. The major exception, England, had already fought its battles for religious toleration and political freedom. It had established after 1688 a freedom of thought and publication unprecedented elsewhere, even in the Dutch Netherlands. It had already had an Enlightenment, or "pre-Enlightenment," through Hobbes, Locke, and many others. By 1715, the England of gentry and merchants was too successful, both internally and externally, to provide much

nourishment for intellectual movements that fed on dissatisfaction with the existing order. Only the Scots, who delighted in stirring up their richer and duller neighbors to the south, were an exception. The philosopher and historian David Hume (1711–76) and the economist Adam Smith (1723–90) were major Enlightenment figures, and Edinburgh, the capital of Scotland, was one of the great centers of eighteenth-century European thought.

Three tendencies in French society united to make France the center of the Enlightenment. First, French government after the death of Louis XIV in 1715 became steadily more inept and ineffectual, both internally and in its wars and diplomacy (see pp. 563–64). Weakness at home and defeat abroad sapped the prestige of the existing order and of the Church that upheld it. Second, the aristocracy began to take its revenge on the monarchy that had reduced it to the role of courtly lapdog. In the realm of ideas, that revenge consisted of the articulation and eager propagation of potentially subversive ideas. Finally, the gradually increasing wealth that commerce and industry produced gave the growing urban middle classes an increasing consciousness of their own worth and importance. That consciousness led to rising social tension between the privileged and the less privileged. And that tension helped encourage an increasing body of literature that attacked the existing order at its weakest points: the obscurantism of the Church, the ineptitude of the noble-dominated royal administration, and the foolishness and arrogance of the nobility itself.

The weapons of the French Enlightenment writers were clarity, wit, and a deliberate ambiguity designed to ward off the wrath of officialdom. Government censors were often too slow-witted to catch hidden barbs aimed at Church or state, and after mid-century they often secretly agreed with the critics. Censorship stopped only the most blatantly subversive or obviously blasphemous attacks on the existing order. After the 1750s censorship was almost powerless against the flood of social criticism and satire that poured from the presses. The source of that flood was Paris, the center of the intellectual life of continental Europe. There the greatest intellectual figures of the age met and conversed in the *salons* or weekly gatherings that intellectual women of the aristocracy had begun to organize. The inhabitants of this world of ideas, whether commoner or noble, shared a common feeling that they were leading a revolution of ideas without precedent in European history, a crusade to end the absurdities and barbarities of the old order.

The "Philosophes": Voltaire, Montesquieu, Diderot

At first, London helped inspire Paris. The conventional date for the beginning of the Enlightenment as a movement was the visit to England in 1726–29 of a certain François Marie Arouet (1694–1778), better known by his pen-name, Voltaire. The French government had twice imprisoned Voltaire in the Bastille fortress in Paris for alleged or actual witticisms made at the expense of royal or noble personages. On the second occasion he had only achieved freedom by promising to leave for London. The man who came to personify the Enlightenment thus had good reason to hate the old regime.

In England, Voltaire read Newton and Locke, and relished the relative freedom of English society in comparison with his own. After returning to France he published *Philosophical Letters on the English* (1733), which passed on to his readers Newton's main principles and popularized Locke's theories of human nature and limited government. Voltaire skillfully contrasted the rationality of Newton's method and the tolerant reasonableness of the English way of life with the arbitrary and capricious realities of Church, state, and society in France.

Voltaire's English letters set the tone of Enlightenment propaganda in France for the next half-century. They were "philosophical" in the broad sense, because they reflected on the facts of human existence and attempted to discover their meaning, and because they searched for general principles useful to humanity as a whole. But the *philosophes*, as Voltaire

---

---

and kindred spirits became known, had little use for metaphysical speculation. They were less philosophers than popularizers, crusaders for the application of the best intellectual tools of the century to social problems. Voltaire was the greatest of them—the most prolific, the wittiest, the most readable, and perhaps the angriest. His preferred targets were bigotry, superstition, and despotism.

"*Écrasez l' infâme,*" cried Voltaire in his innumerable letters, pamphlets, stories, and satires: crush that "infamous thing," the Church. In the famous entry on "Religion" in his *Philosophical Dictionary* (1764), he described a vision he claimed to have had of a desert filled with piles of bones of "Christians with their throats slit by one another in theological disputes." He went on to report a philosophical conversation with the shades of Socrates and Jesus, who both deplored the spectacle he had just seen. And he attacked the religious intolerance of contemporary France as vigorously as the barbarism of the past. When he died in 1778, Voltaire was the most widely read author in Europe, the first writer to have made a fortune from the sale of his own writings. Paris buried him with a ceremony worthy of a king.

Voltaire, almost as skeptical as in life, by the master-sculptor Jean-Antoine Houdon (1781).

A second leading Enlightenment figure was the Baron Charles Louis de Secondat de Montesquieu (1689–1755), sometime president of the *Parlement* of Bordeaux. Montesquieu tried to create a "social science" by applying the methods of the natural sciences to the study of society. In his most famous work, *The Spirit of the Laws* (1748), he suggested that climate and other environmental factors helped determine forms of government, and he tried to discover what form of government best fitted a given set of environmental conditions. *The Spirit of the Laws* was not "scientific" by later standards, but it was the first serious attempt since the Greeks at tracing relationships between systems of government and the environment. In his popular *History of Civilization* (1756),

Voltaire took over and elaborated Montesquieu's concepts.

Montesquieu, like Voltaire, found Locke's theory of limited government persuasive. As a French noble he wished to limit the perceived excesses of royal absolutism. He followed Locke in concluding that the ideal political form called for the separation and balancing of powers within government. That conclusion later had great influence on the authors of the American Constitution (see p. 695).

A third major figure of the French Enlightenment was Denis Diderot (1713–84), co-editor of the famous *Encyclopédie,* an immense encyclopedia designed to sum up the totality of human knowledge. Despite Jesuit protests and cuts by timid printers, it appeared in 35 volumes between 1752 and 1780. Diderot was an enthusiast for science and saw the relationship between science and technology more clearly than most *philosophes.* The most remarkable feature of the *Encyclopédie* was the plates that show machinery and industrial processes. But Diderot was no mere compiler; he was a confident prophet of the Enlightenment's this-worldly religion of humanity. The entries and content of the *Encyclopédie* reflected the interests and enthusiasms of Diderot and his fellow *philosophes* and contained many of their most trenchant writings. The work was an immense success and became the bible of the "enlightened" everywhere. Through it ran faith in humanity's reason, pride in its accomplishments, and sublime confidence in its future.

Historical Relativism in Montesquieu: The Effects of Climate and Geography

In Asia they have always had great empires; in Europe these could never exist. Asia has larger plains; it is cut out into much larger divisions by mountains and seas . . . and the rivers being not so large form more contrasted boundaries. Power in Asia, then, should be always despotic; for if their subjugation be not severe they would soon make a division inconsistent with the nature of the country.

In Europe natural divisions form many nations of moderate extent, in which ruling by laws is not incompatible with the maintenance of the state: on the contrary, it is so favorable to it that without this the state would fall into decay. It is this that has formed a genius for liberty that renders each part extremely difficult to be subdued and subjected to a foreign power. . . . Africa is in a climate like that of the south of Asia and is in the same servitude. . . .

Monarchy is more frequently found in fertile countries and a republican government in those which are not so, and this is sometimes a sufficient compensation for the inconveniences they suffer by the sterility of the land. Thus the barrenness of the soil of Attica established a democracy there.

From Charles de Secondat de Montesquieu, The Spirit of the Laws *(Bohn Standard Library edition), Vol. I, Book XVII, Chs. 6, 7; Book XVIII, Ch. 1, pp. 289–91.*

The Enlightenment Faith

No intellectual movement is successful unless it has followers as well as leaders. The Enlightenment, like the Renaissance, produced its full quota of earnest hacks and disreputable scribblers. It also enjoyed a public, vast by previous standards, of silent supporters. Twentieth-century scholarship has shown that the *Encyclopédie* enjoyed astonishing sales in tiny provincial towns. Periodicals, libraries, book societies, and literary and scientific discussion groups spread knowledge, social criticism, and scandalous gossip. The main ideas of the Enlightenment took root all over Europe, and a new generation absorbed from them entirely new conceptions of human nature, society, and religion. Five words, each of which bore a heavy freight of meaning in the eighteenth century, sum up these ruling ideas: *reason, nature, happiness, progress,* and *liberty.*

The eighteenth century believed as passionately in reason as the seventeenth, but with a difference. The "reason" of Voltaire relied more upon experience and less on mathematics than that of Descartes. It was a weapon of skeptical inquiry based on observed facts—or on what Voltaire thought were facts—rather than a method of deduction from axioms. To the thinkers of the Enlightenment, reason was the alternative to superstition and prejudice. It was the only sure guide to the principles that governed humanity and nature. Reason could discover the fundamental rationality of the universe, and it could also make human societies more rational. The *philosophes* were less interested in "pure" science than in applied science, less concerned with intellectual system-building than with specific reforms. They regarded reason as a down-to-earth tool, applicable equally to agriculture, government, social relations, astronomy, and physics.

Nature was a second favorite word of the Enlightenment. The precise meaning the *philosophes* attached to "nature" was not always clear, but to nearly all of them "nature" or "the natural" was the proper standard for measuring God and humanity. A thing "according to nature" was reasonable and therefore good. Voltaire and his contemporaries brought the idea of natural law to the peak of its prestige. One of them devised the following definition of natural law:

The regular and constant order of facts by which God rules the universe; the order which his wisdom presents to the sense and reason of men, to serve them as an equal and common rule of conduct, and to guide them, without distinction of race or sect, towards perfection and happiness.

Order and law, then, ruled throughout the universe of the *philosophes*—laws of economics, of politics, and of morality as well as of physics and astronomy. Reason permitted the discovery of those laws. Humans might ignore or defy them but did so at their peril. To the "enlightened," the road to happiness lay in conforming to nature and nature's laws. The enlightened elite of the eighteenth century looked on those who "broke" nature's laws in the same spirit as the clergy of the Middle Ages had looked on heretics who broke God's laws: they were rebels against the order of the universe.

Happiness in this world, not salvation and eternal rejoicing in the next, was the end the *philosophes* had in view. The Enlightenment, like the Scientific Revolution, was a secular movement. When Thomas Jefferson (see p. 579) cited "the pursuit of happiness" along with life and liberty as inalienable human rights, he was expressing a general sentiment of the age. Medieval Christianity's toleration of misery in this life in the expectation of rewards in the next angered the *philosophes*. They demanded the realization of Christian ideals here and now. They abominated cruelty, judicial torture, slavery, and the callous treatment of the insane. An enlightened Italian civil servant of the Habsburgs, Cesare Beccaria (1738–94), was the first to suggest that savage penalties do not necessarily prevent crime and to propose a theory of penology. The *philosophes* were also cosmopolitan and even pacifist in temper. Voltaire penned some of the bitterest passages ever written about the "insanity" of war and the absurdity of blind patriotism.

Progress was an even more central constituent of the Enlightenment faith than happiness. The *philosophes* took the Christian idea of the spiritual progression of humanity from the Creation through the Incarnation to the Last Judgment, and secularized it. The progress of civilization, they believed, was now out of God's hands and in those of humanity, thanks to the discovery and use of nature's laws in government, economics, and technology. The *philosophes* were in general confident that both humanity and society were perfectible through human effort.

This was a major revolution in Western thought. The Middle Ages could not have conceived of progress that was unrelated to God. Renaissance thinkers still felt themselves inferior to the heroic Greeks and Romans. But even before a symbolic literary battle between "ancients" and "moderns" that began in 1687, some thinkers had suggested that the "moderns" were as good as, and probably better than, the "ancients." By 1750 a French *philosophe,* economist, and civil servant, Anne-Robert-Jacques Turgot, could suggest that the essential element in history was humanity's slow struggle upward toward the discovery of the scientific method.

In 1794 the Marquis de Condorcet, a mathematician and aristocratic reformer under sentence of death during the French Revolution, wrote a *Sketch for a Historical Picture of the Progress of the Human Mind* that summed up all the optimism of his century. He saw "the strongest reasons for believing that nature has set no limit to the realization of our hopes" and foresaw "the abolition of inequality between nations, the progress of equality within nations, and the true perfection of humanity."

Progress, Condorcet concluded, was now "independent of any power that might wish to halt it" and "will never be reversed." The scientific method was irrevocably fixed in the human mind, and scientific knowledge of natural laws would continue to accumulate. Progress was thus accelerating, irreversible, and infinite. The coming "perfection of mankind" was an intoxicating vision, a vision the majority of the enlightened shared despite the abundance of historical evidence suggesting that civilizations declined as well as rose. How Condorcet reconciled his vision of progress with his own status as fugitive from the executioners of the Revolution of "Liberty, Equality, Fraternity" is unclear.

Liberty, indeed, was yet another favorite word of the *philosophes.* They were acutely aware of the prevalence in France of arbitrary arrest and restrictions on speech, religion, trade, and employment. Looking at England through lightly rose-tinted glasses, they envied Englishmen their economic, political, and religious liberties. Their concern for liberty was potentially the most explosive tenet of their faith, but few considered that violence was necessary to secure it. Liberty, for the *philosophes,* was inseparable from reason. Reason would soon reveal the true natural laws governing all things, from trade, to government, to religion. The artificiality and corruption of the present would become evident to all. A "benevolent despotism," an enlightened philosopher-king, would lead humanity into a new golden age—or so Voltaire and many other *Encyclopédie* authors hoped. But what if despotism was by its very nature not benevolent?

The Enlightenment and Religion

The new ideas inevitably had religious consequences. To the enlightened, religious fervor savored of the fanaticism of the wars of religion. The Enlightenment only prized enthusiasm for its new religion of reason, progress, and the "perfection of humanity." The fashionable form of belief common among the eighteenth century's educated elite came to be Deism, the belief in a God who is Creator but not Redeemer. The God of the Deists was a celestial watchmaker who had made the universe, wound it up, and then stepped aside to let it run according to natural law that he had laid down. God did not concern himself with humanity or act in or through human history.

The essence of religion, for the Deist, was thus awe and reverence before the rationality and perfection of the universe—a feeling reflected in the beautiful hymns of Isaac Watts still heard in many Protestant churches. To a Deist such as Voltaire, talk of revelation, miracles, or the special intervention of God in the natural order was false. Dogma and ritual were "superstition," for humanity needed only reason to see God. The heart of natural religion was a morality common to all mankind. "Light is uniform for the star

Sirius," Voltaire wrote, "and for us moral philosophy must be uniform."

Deism obviously tended to undermine orthodox Christianity and to substitute for it a rationalist belief in God as First Cause and in "natural law" as humanity's moral guide. A few *philosophes* such as Diderot went further and dared the censors by pushing beyond Deism to atheism. For Baron Paul Henri d'Holbach (1723–89), the universe contained nothing but matter, humanity itself was a conglomeration of atoms, and natural law determined all events. Holbach was the complete "materialist," an ancestor of much nineteenth-century thought.

Economics, Society, and Politics

The *philosophes* were interested in social and political issues, but they were reformers, not revolutionaries. Their formula for reform was simply to discover by reason and experience the natural laws that should operate in any given situation and to clear away all supposedly artificial obstacles to their operation. The result, "reason" indicated, would be "progress" toward happiness and freedom.

That outlook encouraged the beginnings of the modern discipline of economics. In 1758 François Quesnay published his *Economic Survey,* which proclaimed the existence of natural economic "laws" and urged an end to all restrictions, such as government control of grain supplies and prices, that prevented those laws from operating. But Quesnay and French economists of his school were too much the products of France's predominantly agricultural society. They saw agriculture as the source of all wealth and damned industry as "sterile" and commerce as parasitic. Adam Smith of Edinburgh saw more clearly. In *An Inquiry into the Nature and Causes of the Wealth of Nations* (1776), the first classic of modern economics, Smith extended the concept of "natural liberty" to commerce and industry.

He denounced all "mercantilist" practices, although he admitted that an age of warring states might make measures such as the Navigation Acts necessary for a time. In general, however, Smith maintained that state interference with the workings of the natural law of supply and demand decreased rather than increased national wealth. The "invisible hand" of natural law, Smith argued, was a self-regulating mechanism that automatically maximized the wealth and freedom of any society that respected it. To tamper with it was both dangerous and self-defeating.

In political theory, similar lines of reasoning led to three distinct schools of thought. The first rested on the notion of "enlightened absolutism." The *philosophes,* children of their age, were no democrats. Voltaire thought government should be for the people, but by kings: "The people, stupid and barbarous, needs a yoke, a cattle prod, and hay." Most *philosophes* hoped for a mellowing of divine-right monarchy into a benevolent "enlightened" philosopher-kingship that would govern—perhaps with well-rewarded *philosophe* advice—according to natural law rather than royal caprice. A second, smaller school believed that "reason" pointed in the direction of an English-style constitutional monarchy based on natural rights and on a contract that bound the sovereign to respect his subjects' liberties. And a very few advanced a third theory, still too radical to be of much immediate influence: the theory of democratic government. That school's foremost prophet was the eccentric Jean-Jacques Rousseau (1712–78), author of *The Social Contract* (1762).

Rousseau: Prophet of Democracy and Despotism

Rousseau, a native of Geneva, appeared in Paris in 1742 after a wandering youth. He came to know Diderot and other *philosophes* and for a time attempted to join them. But he was never easy in their company. He trusted reason but relied even more on emotion. He trusted nature, but to him nature was the unspoiled simplicity of the noble savage, of humanity before the coming of civilization. After a sudden vision experienced in 1749, he became convinced that humanity had lost more than it had gained by cultivating the arts and sciences. He lost all faith in progress.

An idealized view of Rousseau, misfit and social critic, from an eighteenth-century playing card.

The seeming artificiality of Paris society increasingly irritated him, and he broke with his former friends. Voltaire thought him insane, and in his miserable later years Rousseau indeed suffered from delusions of persecution.

Rousseau was the greatest social critic of the Enlightenment. By temperament he was a shy and sensitive misfit who desperately wanted to belong. He knew himself to be "good," on the model of the "noble savage." He therefore blamed his unhappiness, his failure to fit in, on the alleged artificiality of existing society. That society of kings, aristocrats, and priests—he felt—had "corrupted" and humiliated him. Consequently he imagined an alternative, not as a program for revolution—although many readers took it as one—but as a critique of existing societies.

Rousseau's utopia, described in *The Social Contract,* was a "direct democracy," a small and tightly knit community of free male citizens (like most men of the Enlightenment, Rousseau considered it part of "the order of nature that woman obeys man"). Government consisted of the citizens meeting face-to-face. From their de-

liberations, Rousseau was confident, a "general will" would inevitably emerge. For humanity's essential goodness, in Rousseau's view, meant that a society that governed itself was immune from dissent and conflict. And by agreeing to form a community, Rousseau's citizens had in any case willingly sacrificed all individual rights to the group. Once the "general will" became known, all owed it absolute obedience.

Perhaps Rousseau had in mind an idealized image of Geneva as he wrote *The Social Contract.* In that city-state, citizens knew and trusted one another, and the minority normally accepted the majority's view with good grace, out of loyalty to the community. But it was Sparta, that least individualist and most austerely military of the Greek city-states, that recurred frequently in Rousseau's pages. It was his favorite model.

Perhaps Rousseau's knowledge of Sparta—of its relentless regimentation, its murderous *krypteia* or secret police, its ruthless enslavement of all surrounding cities—was imperfect. Perhaps, as some modern scholars assert, his proposals for a "progressive" education that would bring out the child's "natural" goodness and intellectual curiosity make Rousseau a prophet of individual freedom rather than Spartan uniformity. Perhaps his hostility to kings and aristocrats, indeed his aversion to all forms of authority, absolve him of responsibility for excesses committed after 1789 in the name of the "general will." But his theory of democracy was nevertheless a stunning illustration of the consequences—even the unintended consequences—of ideas.

Locke and Montesquieu had argued that the guarantee of political liberty was the separation of executive and legislative powers. Concentration of power threatened freedom. Their theory derived from an essential pessimism about human behavior, a long experience of human ambition and fallibility gained in the world of politics. Their theory of liberty was "negative"—liberty arose when institutional and legal checks limited the powers of government. That negative theory of liberty, of individual rights *against* government, was the foundation of modern representa-

Rousseau: The Despotism of the General Will

The problem is to find a form of association . . . in which each, while uniting himself with all, may still obey himself alone, and remain as free as before. This is the fundamental problem of which the Social Contract provides the solution: . . . the total alienation of each associate, together with all his rights, to the whole community. . . . Each man, in giving himself to all, gives himself to nobody. . . . Each of us puts his person and all his power in common under the supreme direction of the general will, and, in our corporate capacity, we receive each member as an indivisible part of the whole. . . . In order that the social compact may not be an empty formula, it tacitly includes the undertaking, which alone can give force to the rest, that whoever refuses to obey the general will shall be compelled to do so by the whole body. This means nothing less than that he will be forced to be free.

From Jean-Jacques Rousseau, The Social Contract *(New York and London: Everyman's Library, 1913), Book I, Chs. 6 and 7, pp. 14–18.*

tive democracies such as Britain and the United States.

Rousseau, an intellectual without worldly experience, took an entirely different view. For him humanity was "good" with the goodness of the noble savage. That goodness would express itself naturally in politics once the artificial restraints and corrupting influences of the old society fell away. Checks and balances, the separation of powers, the protection of specific rights would serve no purpose if "the people" governed itself. The "general will," by definition, could not will harm to itself! Rousseau's theory of liberty was "positive"—his liberty was the willing obedience to laws and decisions that the individual himself had helped to make. Rousseau's theory of liberty thus set no limit at all on what government could do if it expressed—*or claimed to express*— the general will. In a justly famous passage in *The Social Contract,* Rousseau even asserted that the community could force individuals to be free. That hard phrase was the precursor of an even harder reality after 1789.

Utopian visions like those of Rousseau, it later became clear, often originated among and appealed to intellectuals alienated from their societies. Utopianism flourished best under autocracies—like that of the successors of Louis XIV—that pursued policies sufficiently repressive to generate dissent, but not repressive enough to crush it. And the utopian search for a society without conflict, of which Rousseau was the greatest forerunner and prophet, could even lead to an attack on representative democracies whose "negative freedoms" appeared to foster doubt, unhappiness, and disunity. Rousseau died in 1778, but only chronology bound him to the Enlightenment. His true home was the post-1789 world of revolution, nationalism, and Romanticism that he helped to shape.

ARTS AND LETTERS IN THE EIGHTEENTH CENTURY

The art and literature of the later seventeenth and early eighteenth centuries reflected the belief of Enlightenment scientists and philosophers in the rationality, intelligibility, and order of the universe. Rationalism blended easily with classicism. The regularity and harmony of Newton's universe seemed to accord both with the balance, proportion, rationality, and restraint for which classical Greek architecture and Greek and Roman writers had striven. The dictators of literary and artistic taste at the close of the seventeenth century were classicists. When *philosophes* like Voltaire wrote dramas, they accepted classical standards as unquestioningly as had Corneille and Racine. The architects of the Georgian buildings of England and the beautifully proportioned Place de la Concorde in Paris accepted classical rules of balance and unity with equal zeal. Enthusiasm for classical antiquity reached its post-Renaissance climax after 1748, when Europe discovered the remains of the Roman city of Pompeii in startlingly well-preserved condition under the ashes and cinders from Mt. Vesuvius that had covered it in A.D. 79.

An Age of Prose

The "age of reason" was an age of prose. Essays, satirical tales, novels, letters, and histories were the characteristic literary forms of the eighteenth century. Authors bent their energies to description and narrative rather than to suggestion and imagination. The essays of Joseph Addison and Richard Steele, which began to appear in 1709, sketched a delightful picture of English rural society. Jonathan Swift's *Gulliver's Travels* (1726) and Voltaire's *Candide* (1759) offered biting social and philosophical commentary. As the century progressed, the novel emerged as the favorite form of literary expression; the most enjoyable example was perhaps Henry Fielding's *Tom Jones* (1749). Philosophy, economics, and history prospered alongside fiction. The eighteenth century's greatest monument of historical scholarship was Edward Gibbon's history of *The Decline and Fall of the Roman Empire* (1776–88), which in a luminous style that will forever delight its readers, sardonically described the "triumph of barbarism and religion" over the greatest empire of the ancient world.

Painting, especially fashionable portraits, well disclosed the elegant aristocratic flavor of eighteenth-century society. The delicate-featured and exquisitely groomed women who look coolly down on the observer, and the worldly, sometimes arrogant, faces of their husbands under their powdered wigs suggest the artificiality of aristocratic society, and sometimes the hardness of character of those who inhabited it. Opulent furniture and tableware, and the great town and country houses of nobles and wealthy merchants, reflect the same aristocratic elegance.

But not all books and art served the enjoyment of the aristocracy. The first newspapers written for a wide audience of educated readers emerged in the eighteenth century. William Hogarth (1697–1764) made engravings of his satirical sketches of English society and sold them by the thousands. Above all, novelists, dramatists, and musicians in London and Paris began to appeal to a middle-class audience. The Paris stage, with productions such as *The Barber of Seville* (1775) and *The Marriage of Figaro* (1784), by Pierre de Beaumarchais, turned a keen satirical edge against the aristocracy. The heroes and heroines of novels tended increasingly to imitate the middle-class origins of their audiences.

An Age of Music

But the greatest cultural achievement of the age was its music—above all, German music. Two great Germans dominated the musical world of the early eighteenth century: Johann Sebastian Bach (1685–1750) and George Frederick Handel (1685–1759). Handel in his oratorios for chorus and instruments and Bach in his richly varied works for keyboard instruments, chamber groups, orchestras, and choruses, realized all the dramatic and emotional possibilities of the baroque style. As the century drew on, the orchestra, which had originated in the seventeenth century, expanded and took in new instruments, the piano replaced the harpsichord, and music began to move from the aristocratic salon into the public hall.

Franz Joseph Haydn (1732–1809), who wrote both for chamber groups and for orchestras, developed the musical forms known as sonatas and symphonies. The other outstanding musical personality of the latter half of the century was Wolfgang Amadeus Mozart (1756–91), probably the most brilliant musician in history. Born at Salzburg in Austria, he began his career as a child prodigy, lived only 35 years, and died in poverty. But witnin that short span he produced over 600 compositions that included unequalled mas-

terpieces of invention and form—string quartets, sonatas, concertos, masses, symphonies, and operas such as *Le Nozze di Figaro* (The Marriage of Figaro, 1786), *Don Giovanni*(1787), and *Die Zauberflöte* (The Magic Flute, 1791).

THE LIMITS OF THE ENLIGHTENMENT: RELIGION, PHILOSOPHY, AND LITERATURE

The Enlightenment was the creation of a small elite, although many of its ideas circulated widely and penetrated far down the social scale. It was largely confined to western Europe and the English-speaking world. And countercurrents soon arose to challenge the supremacy of reason in philosophy and of rational structure and classical balance in art.

Contrary to the expectations of many Enlightenment figures, religion did not give way to Deism or wither away. Many Protestants found a compromise between Christian faith and the Enlightenment's rationalism, humanitarianism, and tolerance. The result was the nineteenth-century development of a liberal Protestantism. Others took the road of more intense piety. The cold rationality of Deism held no appeal for emotional natures, and only the educated could understand it. Hence the wide popularity of two warmly emotional Protestant movements, Pietism in Germany and Methodism in England and America. Both emphasized the importance of the inner religious experience of individual "conversion." Pietism was a second and milder Protestant Reformation that challenged not the pope, but the twin extremes of dogmatic orthodoxy and Deism that verged on unbelief. Individualist, tolerant, and indifferent to ceremonies, Pietism attracted followers among both Catholics and Protestants.

John Wesley (1703–91) was the leader of a somewhat parallel revival of a warm and personal Christian piety in England in the years following his conversion in 1738. When the Anglican clergy resisted his efforts, he took his message directly to the people. He addressed huge outdoor congregations and prayer meetings in remote chapels, taught his followers to sing their

Wolfgang Amadeus Mozart: the culmination of eighteenth-century music.

way to heaven with the hymns of his brother Charles, and deluged his congregations with streams of pamphlets from his printing presses. In the end, Anglican opposition forced Wesley to leave the established church and create a new denomination, Methodism, which took its name from the "methodical" piety of Wesley's followers that the orthodox had originally mocked. Methodism touched many thousands of Englishmen and women at home and in the colonies who found the dry intellectualism of much eighteenth-century Anglicanism repellent. Methodism's wide following, its emphasis on otherworldly concerns, and its conspicuous loyalty to existing political authority in this world made it a more effective buttress of the social order than Anglicanism.

Even philosophers saw reason's limits. David Hume, who along with Adam Smith was one of the greatest figures of the Scottish Enlightenment, started from a close study of the great French skeptic Bayle. Hume ended by denying the possibility of certainty. Only the experience of the senses, unverifiable by any independent means, kept the mind informed about external reality. And for Hume, sense-experience was a sequence of disjointed impressions, upon which the

John Wesley preaching.

mind—and the mind alone—imposed regularities, patterns, connections.

Hume's position, which has remained logically unassailable, cut at the root of the Enlightenment faith in the capacity of reason to discover laws in nature and human behavior. Hume did not doubt the validity of Newton's laws as a rule of thumb. What he denied was that anyone would ever be in a position to claim with certainty that Newton's laws applied to *all* times and in *all* places throughout the universe. Even observations that seemed to confirm those laws might not do so, for the evidence of the senses might be a snare. The sun *might* rise tomorrow; but then again it might not.

Hume was happy to concede that some kinds of knowledge were more certain than others. But he was the first philosopher to see the full depths of the

predicament into which the collapse of the medieval religious certainties had plunged humanity. In the philosopher's study, if not in practical affairs, certainty was unattainable. That was "the whimsical condition of mankind." The observer's point of view helped determine what the observer saw. Knowledge, like the human value-systems that varied through historical time and geographic space, was relative.

Hume's skepticism did not yet shake an optimistic age that sought to replace God with Newton's clockwork universe. But a few farseeing figures nevertheless understood what he had done. The greatest philosopher of the century, Immanuel Kant (1724–1804), took up Hume's challenge, although Kant never traveled more than a few miles from his native city of Königsberg in East Prussia. In his *Critique of Pure Reason* (1781), the most demanding of all the great works of Western thought, Kant saved scientific reason, at least in his own judgment, by limiting its domain to appearances, to the data of sense-experience.

The mechanical world of physics, Kant argued, *was* knowable with certainty, although only knowable to an observer equipped with concepts built into the mind, such as space and time, What was not knowable with certainty, for Kant, were the *true* natures of the "things-in-themselves" that humans perceived through their senses. Nor could reason deal with the domain of metaphysics and religion, the realm of things that transcended experience. To many thinkers, Kant's refutation of Hume merely confirmed the Scot's skepticism. Others reacted by taking Kant, who himself argued for the necessity of belief in God as one foundation of morality, as a point of departure for a renewed leap into faith in religion.

In literature, the slowly gathering revolt against the Enlightenment took the form of a celebration of emotion that defied classical notions of rationality and balance. French and English novelists cultivated extremes of sentimentality. Heroines suffered heartrending misfortune and mistreatment, while the author sought at every turn to arouse the reader's anger, pity, love, or terror. The most influential example was Samuel Richardson's 2,000-page tear-jerker, *Clarissa* (1748), which influenced Rousseau's *Nouvelle Héloise* (1761). The bizarre, grotesque, and fantastic returned to fashion. In both architecture and literature, critics began to revive the Gothic style, despised since the Renaissance.

In Germany, which had never fallen totally under the sway of the French Enlightenment, a "Storm and Stress" (*Sturm und Drang*) movement in literature emphasized the great elemental emotions and denied the supremacy of reason. Johann Gottfried von Herder (1744–1803) conceived a philosophy of history that emphasized the uniqueness of each nation or race, the individuality of its genius, and the falsity of any view that denied that uniqueness in the name of universal reason. Johann Wolfgang von Goethe (1749–1832) published at the start of his long literary career *The Sorrows of Young Werther* (1774), a morbidly sentimental tale ending in suicide. The "Age of Reason" thus summoned up its opposite and successor—the age of Romanticism. The new age prized fierce emotion over harmony and equilibrium, and celebrated individual and national peculiarity over the Enlightenment's universal reason.

The Scientific Revolution and the Enlightenment were the most decisive break in the history of Western thought. The world picture of fifth-century Greece and of the Old and New Testaments, preserved through the Middle Ages and Renaissance, now gave way to a distinctively "modern" cast of mind. The world of Luther and Loyola, of Charles V and Philip II, was still organically related to the Middle Ages. The world of Newton and Locke, of Voltaire and Rousseau, was unmistakably our own.

Suggestions for Further Reading

The Scientific Revolution

M. Ashley, *The Golden Century* (1968), offers a fine survey of seventeenth-century social and cultural history. A. R. Hall, *The Scientific Revolution 1500–1800* (1966), is the best recent account. H. Butterfield, *The Origins of Modern Science 1300–1800* (1949), is highly readable, but C. Brinton, *The Shaping of the Modern Mind* (1953), covers a longer period. T. S. Kuhn, *The Copernican Revolution* (1957), describes the transformation of astronomical thought and offers an influential interpretation of how science advances. On the social background of scientific development, see D. Stimson, *Scientists and Amateurs: A History of the Royal Society* (1948). G. de Santillana, *The Crime of Galileo* (1955), elucidates the most famous case in the history of freedom of thought.

The Enlightenment

P. Hazard, *The European Mind: The Critical Years, 1680–1715* (1935, 1952), offers a still-useful study of the transition from Scientific Revolution to Enlightenment. The most searching interpretation of the Enlightenment as a whole is E. Cassirer, *The Philosophy of the Enlightenment* (1932, 1951). C. Becker, *The Heavenly City of the Eighteenth-Century Philosophers* (1932), attacks the *Philosophes* as doctrinaires, while P. Gay, *The Enlightenment: An Interpretation,* 2 vols. (1966–69), defends them. N. Hampson, *A Cultural History of the Enlightenment* (1969), is a useful introduction. C. R. Cragg, *Reason and Authority in the Eighteenth Century* (1964), and D. Mornet, *French Thought in the Eighteenth Century* (1929), deal with England and France respectively. R. S. Westfall, *Never at Rest: A Biography of Isaac Newton* (1981), discusses some of the leading intellectuals of the period, but see also T. Bestermann, *Voltaire* (1969), and J. N. Shklar, *Men and Citizens: A Study of Rousseau's Social Theory* (1969). L. Krieger, *Kings and Philosophers, 1689–1789* (1970), relates thought to politics. On specific topics, see M. F. Bukofzer, *Music in the Baroque Era* (1947); A. Boime, *A Social History of Modern Art*, vol. 1, *Art in an Age of Revolution, 1750–1800* (1987); B. Semmel, *The Methodist Revolution* (1973); G. R. Craig, *The Church in the Age of Reason* (1961); and E. Fox-Genovese, "Women and the Enlightenment," in R. Bridenthal et al., *Becoming Visible: Women in European History* (1987).

ILLUSTRATION CREDITS

INDEX